THE JEWISH PEOPLE

HISTORY • RELIGION • LITERATURE

THE JEWISH PEOPLE

HISTORY • RELIGION • LITERATURE

Advisory Editor
Jacob B. Agus

Editorial Board
Louis Jacob
Jacob Petuchowski
Seymour Siegel

The New Testament and Rabbinic Judaism

By

DAVID DAUBE

ARNO PRESS

A New York Times Company

NEW YORK • 1973

Reprint Edition 1973 by Arno Press Inc.

Copyright © , 1956, By David Daube
Reprinted by permission of David Daube

Reprinted from a copy in
The Princeton Theological Seminary Library

THE JEWISH PEOPLE: History, Religion, Literature
ISBN for complete set: 0-405-05250-2
See last pages of this volume for titles.

Manufactured in the United States of America

———◆———

Library of Congress Cataloging in Publication Data

Daube, David.
    The New Testament and rabbinic Judaism.

    (The Jewish people: history, religion, literature)
    Reprint of the ed. published by University of London,
Athlone Press, London, which was issued as no. 2 of
Jordan lectures in comparative religion.
    Includes bibliographical references.
    1. Bible. N. T.--Criticism, interpretation, etc.
2. Rabbinical literature--Relation to the New Testament.
I. Title. II. Series. III. Series: Jordan lectures
in comparative religion, 2.
BM535.D34 1973   225.6'6   73-2191
ISBN 0-405-05257-X

SCHOOL OF ORIENTAL AND AFRICAN STUDIES

UNIVERSITY OF LONDON

Jordan Lectures in Comparative Religion

II

The Louis H. Jordan Bequest

The will of the Rev. Louis H. Jordan provided that the greater part of his estate should be paid over to the School of Oriental and African Studies to be employed for the furtherance of studies in Comparative Religion, to which his life had been devoted. Part of the funds which thus became available was to be used for the endowment of a Louis H. Jordan Lectureship in Comparative Religion. The lecturer is required to deliver a course of six or eight lectures for subsequent publication. The first series of lectures was delivered in 1951.

JORDAN LECTURES 1952

The New Testament and Rabbinic Judaism

By

DAVID DAUBE

Regius Professor of Civil Law
in the University of Oxford,
Fellow of All Souls College

UNIVERSITY OF LONDON
THE ATHLONE PRESS
1956

Published by
THE ATHLONE PRESS
UNIVERSITY OF LONDON
at 2 Gower Street, London, W.C.I

Distributed by Constable & Co. Ltd.
12 *Orange Street, London,* W.C.2

U.S.A.
John de Graff Inc.
64 West 23rd Street,
New York, 10

Printed in Great Britain by
WESTERN PRINTING SERVICES LTD.
BRISTOL

To

HERTA BABETTE

'*I am an Hebrew and I fear the Lord*'
(JONAH 1.9)

'*I call heaven and earth to witness that whether it be Gentile or Israelite, man or woman, slave or handmaid, according to the deeds which he does, so will the Holy Spirit rest on him*'
(TANNA DE-BE ELIYYAHU, p. 48)

PREFACE

This volume contains the second series of Jordan Bequest Lectures, delivered at the School of Oriental and African Studies in 1952. Much of what is contained in them was read to Professor C. H. Dodd's Seminar at Cambridge though not published, for example, Part I, Chapter VI, Paragraph B, The Feeding of the Multitude, and Part III, Chapter VII, Violence to the Kingdom.

The following sections are based on publications:

Part I, Chapter II, Paragraph A, A Supernatural Birth, on 'Two Notes on the Passover Haggadah', *Journal of Theological Studies (JTS)* 50, 1949, 53ff.

Part II, Chapter II, Principle and Cases, on 'Three Questions of Form', *JTS* 45, 1944, 21ff.; Chapter III, Paragraph B, Divorce, on 'Reconstruction of the "Aramaic Gospels"', *Bulletin of the John Rylands Library (BJRL)* 29, 1945, 11ff. (on Mark 10.6); Chapter IV, Participles of the Correct Practice, on 'Forms of Old Testament Legislation', *Proceedings of the Oxford Society of Historical Theology*, 1944/5, 36ff., and 'Appended Note' to E. G. Selwyn, *The First Epistle of St. Peter*, 1946, 2nd ed. 1947, 467ff.; Chapter V, A Baptismal Catechism, on 'The History of Proselyting', *Chayenu* 8, no. 10, 1945, 10f.; Chapter VI, Public Retort and Private Explanation, on 'Public Pronouncement and Private Explanation', *Expository Times (ET)* 57, 1946, 175ff.; Chapter VII, Socratic Interrogation, on 'A Rhetorical Principle in the Gospels', *ET* 54, 1943, 305f.; Chapter VIII, Four Types of Question, on 'Four Types of Question', *JTS*, N.S. 2, 1951, 45ff.; Chapter X, The Last Beatitude, on 'Three Questions of Form', *JTS* 45, 1944, 21ff.

Part III, Chapter I, Rabbinic Authority, on '*Exousia* in Mark 1. 22 and 27', *JTS* 39, 1938, 45ff.; Chapter IV, Eye for Eye, on 'Matthew 5. 38f.', *JTS* 45, 1944, 177f., and *Studies in Biblical Law*, 1947, 102ff. (on Lex Talionis); Chapter VI, Redemption, on *Studies in Biblical Law*, 1947, 39ff. (on Law in the Narratives), and 'Concerning Methods of Bible-Criticism', *Symbolae Frederico Hrozný Dedicatae*, pt. 1 (*Archiv Orientální* 17), 1948, 88f.; Chapter VIII, Paragraphs C, D, E and F,

The Crucifixion, Jesus's Grave, Jesus's Burial Clothes and The Anointing at Bethany, on 'The Anointing at Bethany', *Anglican Theological Review* 32, 1950, 186ff.; Chapter IX, The 'I Am' of the Messianic Presence, on 'Two Notes on the Passover Haggadah', *JTS* 50, 1949, 53ff.; Chapter XI, Missionary Maxims in Paul, on 'Missionary Maxims', *Studia Theologica* 1, 1947, 158ff.; Chapter XII, A Missionary Term, on '*Kerdaino* as a Missionary Term', *Harvard Theological Review* 40, 1947, 109ff.; Chapter XIII, Terms for Divorce, on 'New Testament Terms for Divorce', *Theology* 47, 1944, 65ff., and Paragraph B, 'And if a woman shall put away her husband', on 'Reconstruction of the "Aramaic Gospels"', *BJRL* 29, 1945, 17ff. (on Mark 10. 12); Chapter XIV, Samaritan Women, on 'Jesus and the Samaritan Woman', *Journal of Biblical Literature* 69, 1950, 137ff.; Chapter XV, Two Aramaisms, on 'Reconstruction of the "Aramaic Gospels"', *BJRL* 29, 1945, 3ff. (on Torrey's Translation), and Paragraph A, 'Multitude' and 'Width', on '*Ochlos* in Mark 2. 4', *ET* 50, 1938, 138f.; Chapter XVI, Amen, on 'Three Questions of Form', *JTS* 45, 1944, 21ff.; Chapter XVIII, Paragraph A, A Symbol of Ezekiel in Revelation, on 'Ueber die Umbildung biblischen Rechtsgutes', *Symbolae Friburgenses in honorem Ottonis Lenel,* 1933, 245ff., and Paragraph B, *Arepo* in the Sator Square, on '*Arepo* in the Sator Square', *ET* 62, 1951, 316; Chapter XIX, Chronology, on 'Two Haggadic Principles in the Gospels', *JTS* 44, 1943, 149ff., and 'Two Notes on Paradise Regained', *Review of English Studies* 19, 1943, 205ff.; Chapter XX, Paragraph A, A Construction *ad sensum*, on 'Reconstruction of the "Aramaic Gospels"', *BJRL* 29, 1945, 22ff. (on Matthew 26. 64); Chapter XXXI, The Interpretation of a Generic Singular, on 'Interpretation of a Generic Singular in Galatians', *Jewish Quarterly Review* 35, 1945, 227ff.

I have cut down, or added to, the evidence for my views, or even modified the latter, without indicating the change. I have not found it possible to consider more recent literature, and only the flimsiest notice is taken of the first reports about the Dead Sea Scrolls. My impression, however, is that modern research tends to support my approach. For instance, more and more writers come to the conclusion that the early Church's real conflict with the Synagogue was not about secondary matters such as the Golden Rule or the relation of intention and deed or even the nature of Messianic activity, but about the affirmation by the Church and denial by the Synagogue of Jesus's Messiahship and divinity. Again, it is becoming ever clearer that Palestinian Judaism of the first century was far more varied and flexible than preoccupation with the particular line which ultimately prevailed would lead one to assume. A notion like that of virgin birth, however incompatible with orthodox tenets, may not at the time have been universally so considered. The effect on one another of the numerous sects, major and minor, is not to be underrated. Finally, the sharp distinction between a Hellenistic and a Rabbinic Judaism in the New Testament period is being abandoned as it is found that many Hellenistic ideas had crept into, or been consciously taken over by, Rabbinism long before, and that the process, though slowed down, was not halted. Some Jewish scholars take offence at the suggestion of foreign influence. Yet the exclusion of Hellenistic ideas would not prove the Rabbis free from such influence; only they might have adopted the narrow, chauvinistic attitude of some of the surrounding nations, or perhaps have practised *imitation par opposition*. Surely, the greatest were those who, without sacrificing the essentials of their religion, made use of human achievement regardless of its origin.

I have had helpful discussions with the Reverend C. K. Barrett of Durham University, Professor W. D. Davies of Princeton University, Dr. Cecil Roth of Oxford University and Mr. R. Yaron of Jerusalem University; and I received constant encouragement from the late Professor F. S. Marsh of Cambridge University. My gratitude is due to the Director and the Academic Board of the School of Oriental and African Studies for inviting me to deliver these lectures and for undertaking their publication. I am also indebted to Mr. J. R. Bracken, Secretary to the Publications Committee of the School, for his kindness in making the business arrangements and to the officers of the Athlone Press.

D.D.

CONTENTS

PART III: CONCEPTS AND CONVENTIONS

ABBREVIATIONS

1. BIBLE, OLD TESTAMENT

Apoc. Bar.	Apocalypse of Baruch	Isa.	Isaiah
Cant.	Canticles	Jer.	Jeremiah
Chron.	Chronicles	Lam.	Lamentations
Dan.	Daniel	Lev.	Leviticus
Deut.	Deuteronomy	Macc.	Maccabees
Eccles.	Ecclesiastes	Mal.	Malachi
Ecclus.	Ecclesiasticus	Neh.	Nehemiah
Est.	Esther	Num.	Numbers
Exod.	Exodus	Prov.	Proverbs
Ezek.	Ezekiel	Ps.	Psalms
Gen.	Genesis	Sam.	Samuel
Hab.	Habakkuk	Test.	Testament
Hos.	Hosea	Zech.	Zecharaiah

2. BIBLE, NEW TESTAMENT

Col.	Colossians	Pet.	Peter
Cor.	Corinthians	Philip.	Philippians
Eph.	Ephesians	Rev.	Revelation
Gal.	Galatians	Rom.	Romans
Heb.	Hebrews	Thess.	Thessalonians
Jas.	James	Tim.	Timothy
Matt.	Matthew	Tit.	Titus

3. RABBINIC SOURCES

Ab.	Aboth	Ed.	Eduyoth
Ab. de-R.N.	Aboth de-Rabbi Nathan	Er.	Erubin.
		Git.	Gittin
Ar.	Arakhin	Hag.	Hagigah
A.Z.	Abodah Zarah	Hal.	Hallah
Bab.	Babylonian	Hor.	Horayoth
B.B.	Baba Bathra	Hul.	Hullin
Ber.	Berakoth	Jerus.	Jerusalemite
Bet.	Betzah	Kel.	Kelim
Bik.	Bikkurim	Ker.	Kerithoth
B.M.	Baba Metzia	Ket.	Ketuboth
B.Q.	Baba Qamma	Mak.	Makkoth
D.E.	Derekh Eretz	Meg.	Megillah

Mekh.	Mekhilta	San.	Sanhedrin
Men.	Menahoth	Sem.	Semahoth
Mid.	Midrash	Shab.	Shabbath
Mish.	Mishnah	Sheb.	Shebiith
M.Q.	Moed Qatan	Sheq.	Sheqalim
M.S.	Maaser Sheni	Siph.	Siphra or Siphre
Ned.	Nedarim	So.	Sotah
Neg.	Negaim	S.O.	Seder Olam Rabba
Nid.	Niddah	Suk.	Sukkah
Onk.	Onkelos	Ta.	Taanith
Oho.	Oholoth	Tam.	Tamid
Pal.	Palestinian	Tanh.	Tanhuma
P. de-R. El.	Pirqe de-Rabbi Eliezer	Targ.	Targum
P. de-R.K.	Pesiqta de-Rab	T. de-Be El.	Tanna de-Be
	Kahana		Eliyyahu
P.R.	Pesiqta Rabbathi	Tos.	Tosephta
Pes.	Pesahim	Yad.	Yadaim
Qid.	Qiddushin	Yal.	Yalqut
R.	Rabbi	Yeb.	Yebamoth
R.H.	Rosh Hashanah	Zeb.	Zebahim

4. OTHER SOURCES

A.N.	Attic Nights	Mor.	Moralia
Anal. Pr.	Prior Analytics	Nic.E.	Nicomachean
Ant.	Jewish Antiquities		Ethics
Apol.	Apologia	O.M.	De Opificio Mundi
Bell.	Jewish War	Or.	De Oratore
Bell. Jug.	Bellum	Part. Or.	De Partitione
	Jugurthinum		Oratoria
C. Ap.	Against Apion	P.O.	De Pythiae Oraculis
Clem. Rec.	Clementine	Poet.	Poetics
	Recognitions	Prel. St.	Preliminary Studies
Coniug. Praec.	Coniugalia	Q.D.I.S.	Quod Deus
	Praecepta		Immutabilis Sit
Cyrop.	Cyropaedia	Q.H.S.S.	Quomodo Historia
Decal.	Decalogue		Scribenda Sit
Deipn.	Deipnosophists	Rhet.	Rhetoric
Dial.	Dialogue	R.R.	De Re Rustica
Ep.	Epistle or Epistles	Sat.	Satires
Hist.	Histories	Sept.	De Septenario
Il.	Iliad	Strat.	Stratagems
Inv.	De Inventione	Symp.	Symposium
I.O.	Institutio Oratoria	Thuc.	De Thucydide
Leg. Spec.	Special Laws	Top.	Topica
Mem.	Memorabilia	V.S.	De Verborum
			Significatione

PART I

MESSIANIC TYPES

I

Joseph

THE events recorded in the New Testament, and the manner in which they are recorded, naturally reflect the Messianic speculations current among the Jews of the period. Thus certain features and actions of Jesus recall those of Isaac, Moses, David, Elijah, the Suffering Servant and so on, persons whose lives were popularly looked upon as prefigurations of that of the Saviour, or who were expected actually to play a part in the last days. It is indeed clear that all references to such Messianic types have not yet been noticed. A few examples of this kind may here be given, some admittedly doubtful, others as plain as anything can be in this field.

That the disciple who betrayed Jesus bears the same name as that brother of Joseph at whose suggestion he was sold is probably a mere coincidence. Still, it is interesting that, whereas according to the Biblical account, Judah's intention in recommending a sale was to prevent murder, the Rabbis hold that he ought to have adopted Reuben's attitude and taken Joseph home to his father. In other words, for the Rabbis, by bringing about the sale of Joseph, Judah committed a grievous sin.

Chapter 37 of Genesis ends with the sale of Joseph. Chapter 39 begins by saying that he was brought down to Egypt and goes on to recount what befell him there. Between these two chapters, there is 38, the story of Judah and Tamar, introduced by the words: 'And it came to pass at that time that Judah went down from his brethren.' The Rabbis are exercised by the position of this story and try to establish a connection with the preceding events. They conclude that Judah's 'going down from his brethren' means his being lowered in dignity, or even his being deposed and expelled.[1] One is reminded of John's notice—not to be found in the Synoptics—that Judas, once Satan had entered into him,

[1] Gen. Rabba on 38.1, Exod. Rabba on 32.7.

left the company.[1] However, even this is hardly more than coincidence. The detail in John can be fully explained without assuming any outside influence.

The figure of Joseph, then, does not seem to have been drawn upon by the New Testament writers.

---

[1] 13.30.

II

Moses

THERE are, on the other hand, numerous unmistakable references to Moses—for example, the command to Joseph, after the death of Herod, to 'go into the land of Israel, for they are dead which sought the young child's life', which echoes the command to Moses in Midian to 'return into Egypt, for all the men are dead which sought thy life'.[1] No purpose would be served by enumerating the well-known parallels. It may suffice to draw attention to three points.

A. A SUPERNATURAL BIRTH

The first, though not capable of proof, may deserve consideration even as a possibility: there seems to be a trace of a Jewish legend of a conception without a human father, and the child in question may well be Moses. This would not be a virgin birth—both Miriam and Aaron were older than Moses. But it would be close enough to be of interest.

Long before the time of the New Testament it had become usual to recall on Passover eve the mighty deeds of God for Israel; and the Midrashic exposition of a certain portion of Deuteronomy[2] preserved in the Haggadah, the service for Passover eve, forms the nucleus of the recital.[3] That portion is a brief Credo, originally for use by a person offering the first-fruits in the temple; it is a solemn proclamation stating that the nation was enslaved in Egypt, that God delivered it with signs and wonders, and that he has now brought it into the promised land. The Hebrew word employed in this pericope for 'to proclaim' is *higgidh*.[4] The very term by which the recital of Passover eve is designated, 'Haggadah', is taken from it.

The Midrash, in the typically Rabbinic manner, attributes a very specific meaning to every detail in these verses, and, wherever possible,

[1] Matt. 2.20, Exod. 4.19.   [2] 26.5 ff.   [3] See Mish. Pes. 10.4.   [4] Deut. 26.3.

attempts to prove it by reference to other Scriptural passages. Thus one verse in Deuteronomy[1] reads: 'And he saw our affliction, and our distress, and our oppression.' Of 'our distress' the Midrash remarks: 'This means the sons, as it is written (in Exodus[2]), Every son that is born ye shall cast into the river.' This, in its way, is a reasonable exegesis. In the eyes of the Rabbis, of all causes for distress that the Israelites had in Egypt, the destruction of the male children was the most terrible, and Josephus, for example, thinks the same.[3] Yet that order of Pharaoh was followed by the miraculous rescue of Moses. Accordingly (the Rabbis argue) the meaning of 'he saw our distress' is to be inferred from 'Every son that is born ye shall cast into the river.'

Similarly, 'our oppression' is explained by the Midrash as follows: 'This means the coercion—the cruel tasks laid upon them—as it is written (in Exodus again[4]), And I have also seen the oppression wherewith the Egyptians oppress them.' Here the connection is quite obvious, in sense and in wording: 'oppression' is common to the verse from Deuteronomy and that from Exodus.

Difficulties arise, however, when we come to the comment on 'our affliction'. The Midrash declares: 'This means the abstention from sexual intercourse, as it is written (in Exodus[5]), And God saw the children of Israel, and God knew.'

The view that at some stage in Egypt marital union did not take place appears in several Rabbinic sources.[6] Some Rabbis contemplate enforced abstention, decreed by Pharaoh, some voluntary abstention for the purpose of atonement, and some voluntary abstention undertaken because of the threat to any male offspring. The last-mentioned idea is probably the oldest: it would naturally occur to ancient Jewish interpreters of the Biblical narrative. Now it is indeed quite intelligible why 'our affliction' was associated by the Rabbis with this episode. The verb 'to afflict' occurs in those statutes which enjoin fasting and—at least in Rabbinic interpretation—abstention from sexual intercourse: 'Ye shall afflict your souls.'[7] But it is far from clear how they came to regard the notice 'And God saw the children of Israel, and God knew' as supporting this exegesis.

The only satisfactory explanation seems to be that the author of the

---

[1] 26.7, second half.   [2] 1.22.   [3] Ant. 2.9.2.208.   [4] 3.9.   [5] 2.25.
[6] Exod. Rabba on 1.15 and 2.25 at the end, Bab. Yoma 74b, Bab. So. 11b f. Cp. Bab. B.B. 60b at the end.   [7] Lev. 16.29, 31, 23.27, 32.

Midrash took 'to know' in the sexual sense. The Israelites abstained from marital relations. God saw their affliction, and he 'knew'. In other words, it may well be that, for the author of this Midrash, as natural propagation was impossible, the women—or perhaps only the mother of Moses[1]—conceived from God himself. After all, once the Rabbis had formed the opinion that in consequence of Pharaoh's decision to kill any newborn sons the Israelites refrained from intercourse, they had to find some answer to the question how Moses nevertheless came to be born in that period.

One or two orthodox solutions are still extant. For example, when Pharaoh promulgated his decree and Amram, because of this threat to any male offspring, divorced Jochebed, she was already in the third month of pregnancy. But the relative lateness of this explanation is obvious. First, the narrative of the separation of Amram and Jochebed is preserved in two sources; yet only one of these contains the notice that she was already with child.[2] Secondly, if she was already with child, how could her husband hope to thwart Pharaoh's plan by divorcing her? Clearly, in the original version of the narrative she was not pregnant.

It is worth recalling that according to the Rabbis the death of Moses was caused, not by the angel of death, but by a kiss of God. Later the legend was extended to include his brother Aaron, later still to include his sister Miriam as well, and in the end to include all pious men.[3] But when the idea was first propounded, with reference to Moses alone, it was hardly less bold than, and may have corresponded to, the idea of a direct intervention of God at Moses's birth.

Again, that the verb 'to know' in the verse concerned should have

[1] This possibility is by no means ruled out by the position of Exod. 2.25 ('and God knew') after the narrative of Moses's birth and flight to Midian, 2.1 ff. The Rabbis were quite capable of regrouping the texts when it suited them and, in fact, formulated a principle—'There is no before and after in the Torah'—allowing much freedom in matters not affecting the *halakha*, the law. See below, in Part III, under Chronology.

[2] Only Exod. Rabba on 1.15 and 2.2, not Bab. So. 12a.

[3] Jerus. Targ. ascribes this end only to Moses; it translates Deut. 34.5, 'Moses died according to the word (*pe*, mouth) of the Lord', by 'through the kiss of the Lord'. Of Aaron, Num. 33.38 tells us that 'he went up into the mount according to the word of the Lord, and died there'. Though in strictness the clause 'according to the mouth of the Lord' qualifies the going up and not the dying, Bab. B. B. 17a shows that as early as in the Tannaitic era it was regarded as indicating that Aaron died in the same manner as Moses. The further extension to Miriam had also taken place by the time of Bab. B. B. 17a. But it obviously created difficulties, there being no Scriptural passage on which to rest it. It was only R. Eleazar (second half of 3rd cent.) who discovered a way in which even Miriam's supernatural death might be derived from the Bible; see also Bab. M.Q. 28a. In Cant. Rabba on 1.2, 'Let him kiss me with the kisses of his mouth' is treated as evidence that all pious men die as Moses did.

given rise to speculations is not surprising. It has no object, either express or implied, and this is highly unusual. Modern critics have long suspected that the object may have dropped out.[1] The LXX has καὶ ἐγνώσθη αὐτοῖς, 'and he became known to them', be it in order to avoid the bare 'and God knew' or be it in order to combat the interpretation of the words as alluding to a virgin birth.[2]

Anyhow, on the basis outlined, the verse 'And God saw the children of Israel, and God knew' would indeed fit very well where it comes in the recital of Passover eve.

The question of date arises. Certainly, even if the legend came into existence after the New Testament, it would not be without relevance: it would still show that the notion of a supernatural or virgin birth was not absolutely alien to the Jewish mind. There can be little doubt, however, that, if there was such a legend, it is older than the New Testament. For one thing, as already pointed out, the section of the Haggadah in which it is contained is among the earliest. For another, when once the Christian heresy had sprung up, the tendency must have been to suppress rather than to work out ideas of this nature.

This brings us to a final point. There do exist indications that the Midrash under notice was disliked, and this would of course speak in favour of the suggestion advanced. We have already seen that, possibly, the rendering of the LXX—'he became known to them' instead of 'God knew'—was directed against a dangerous interpretation. Onkelos radically alters the whole verse. He translates: 'And the servitude of the children of Israel was revealed before the Lord, and the Lord said he would deliver them.' This is very striking and does look like another illustration of Onkelos's aversion from any anthropomorphisms. The connection of the verse with sexual abstention is definitely rejected, and the verb 'to know' is avoided. He must have had a strong reason for such thorough rewriting. The Jerusalemite Targum also introduces enough changes to eliminate any conceivable allusion to a virgin birth: 'And the Lord saw the trouble of the servitude of the children of Israel, and the repentance which they practised in secret was revealed before the Lord, for they did not know of one another (i.e. of one another's repentance).' No mention is made of sexual abstention. The cryptic

---

[1] Dillmann, *Die Bücher Exodus und Leviticus*, 2nd ed., 1890, 21. In Exod. 3.7 there is an object: 'I know their sorrows'.
[2] The rendering presupposes only a small change in the vowels of the Hebrew: *wayyiwwadha' 'alehem* instead of *wayyedha' 'elohim*.

phrase 'and God knew' is interpreted as expressing the commonplace idea that God takes note of a sinner's change of heart even if no one else does. And, significantly, as in Onkelos, the verb 'to know' is not used of God: the conduct of the Israelites 'was revealed before him'. The verb is indeed retained, but it refers to the Israelites and has its usual meaning: 'they did not know of one another's repentance'.

No less suggestive than these translations is the attitude of Midrash Rabba to the verse in question. With one exception, none of the comments preserved makes use of the notion of sexual abstention. (As is to be expected, one interpretation is similar to that we find in Onkelos, and one to that in the Jerusalemite Targum.) The exception runs as follows: 'And God saw—this means, he saw their abstention; and God knew—this means, he knew that the time had come which he had fixed to Abraham (for the redemption of his descendants).' Here the verse is associated with the episode of the abstention just as in the Haggadah. Only the 'knowing' has nothing to do with it, and is given an innocent meaning. The result is that the reader is left wondering what may be the justification for connecting the verse with that episode. Why should his observation of the conduct of the Israelites have reminded God that the date foretold to Abraham had arrived?

Perhaps we may here add that, in the Gospel according to the Hebrews, Mary is not a human woman. She is Michael or a power or the Holy Ghost.

It was, then, only in the Haggadah that the objectionable legend survived without being explained away; we do not meet with it anywhere else, though we do meet with what seem to be signs of suppression. The Haggadah is a piece of liturgy, and it is more difficult to expurgate liturgy than almost any other kind of literature.

If the foregoing argument is tenable, it furnishes support for the view —which appears to be increasingly favoured by modern scholars on other grounds—that the narrative of Jesus's birth originated in a properly Jewish rather than Hellenized milieu.

B. A Prophet without Honour in his Country

The complaint that 'a prophet is not without honour save in his country'[1] occurs in several ancient works. No wonder, seeing that it

---

[1] Matt. 13.57, Mark 6.4, Luke 4.24, John 4.44.

refers to a genuine experience of deplorable frequency. If the New
Testament pericopes in which it is to be found are influenced by a
Rabbinic anecdote about Moses, they are influenced only as far as the
mode of exposition is concerned. The substance is entirely independent.

According to Hama bar Hanina, Moses was removed from his
father's house at the age of twelve in order that later, when God sent
him to the oppressed Hebrews, they would believe him.[1] Had he
grown up at home and then proclaimed to them the name of the God
at whose bidding he acted, they would have said that he had simply
been informed by Amram, who was in possession of a tradition which
Joseph had handed on to Levi and Levi to Kohath—Amram's father.[2]
As, however, he had early been removed from his father's house, 'the
people believed'.[3]

The differences between this story and that concerning Jesus's rejection in his native city are numerous and considerable. To name only
one: in the case of Moses, the danger of a prophet being rejected in his
country was foreseen and averted.

Nevertheless, in Matthew and Mark at least, there are two features,
apart from the general idea of the incident, curiously reminiscent of the
Rabbinic tale. First, the lengthy enumeration of Jesus's relations—'Is
not this the carpenter's son? is not his mother called Mary? and his
brethren James and Joses?'—may correspond to the detailed account of
how Moses might have got to know about the name of God—'his
father has handed it on to him, for Joseph handed it on to Levi, Levi to
Kohath and Kohath to Amram'. Secondly, the New Testament episode
ends by a reference to the people's unbelief, just as the Rabbinic one
ends by a reference to their belief.

Hama bar Hanina lived about the middle of the 3rd cent. A.D. If he
invented the anecdote about Moses, it is, of course, of little importance to an understanding of Matthew and Mark. But he may well be
transmitting, and refashioning, a story that was already current in New
Testament times. Perhaps his interest in it was due to what appears to
have happened to his father: to go by a somewhat doubtful reading,[4]
R. Judah the Prince (about A.D. 200) had refrained from ordaining

---

[1] Exod. Rabba on 4.18 (following a quotation of 4.27).
[2] For this tradition, cp. Exod. Rabba on 3.16 towards the end.
[3] Exod. 4.31.
[4] Pal. Ta. 68a. Bacher, *Die Agada der Palästinensischen Amoräer*, vol. 1, 1892, p. 1, n. 2,
prefers the version of Eccles. Rabba on 7.7.

Hanina because 'they cried out against him at Sepphoris as an inhabitant of Sepphoris'; that is to say, he was despised by his fellow-citizens.

C. INTERCESSION

The third point concerns Moses's mediation between God and Israel. The Bible tells us that when the Israelites had worshipped the Golden Calf, Moses insisted on sharing their fate. According to the Rabbis, he offered to die, or even did die, in order that they might live.

Admittedly, by the time of the New Testament, the idea of a just man giving his life as *kopher*, λύτρον, 'ransom' or 'expiation', for the community or the sinners was common in Judaism. It is prominent in the Fourth Book of Maccabees, and Paul would have preferred to be 'accursed from Christ for his kinsmen according to the flesh'.[1] None the less it is probable that for early Christian writers the example of Moses was of particular significance.

Let us remember that he was considered 'the first redeemer' just as the Messiah would be 'the last'. The antithesis is not extant in utterances prior to the 3rd cent. A.D.,[2] but that may be accidental. Again, the Bible, where it describes his death, calls him 'the servant of the Lord'.[3] True, it does the same with Joshua.[4] But the passage about Moses interested the Jewish theologians more. It is widely held that those Talmudic texts which identify Moses with the suffering Servant of the Lord in Isaiah are inspired by Christian teaching.[5] They may be, but it is difficult to see why they must be. Further, while the Rabbis contend that each patriarch and prophet 'gave his life for Israel' in the sense that he offered it,[6] it is apparently only Moses whose offer was accepted. He could have entered the promised land on condition of cancelling his previous wish that the Israelites should be forgiven the worship of the Golden Calf. But he exclaimed: 'Let Moses and a hundred like him die rather than a nail of one of the people be harmed.'[7] Joshua ben Levi,

---

[1] Strack-Billerbeck, *Kommentar zum Neuen Testament aus Talmud und Midrasch* (thereafter quoted as Strack-B.), vol. 2, 1924, pp. 274 ff., vol. 3, 1926, pp. 260 ff.

[2] E.g. Num. Rabba on 6.22.

[3] Deut. 34.5. Dante speaks of *Mosè ubbidiente*. My brother Benjamin Daube wondered whether he chose the epithet because its sound suggests *ebed* or *obed* ('ebhedh, 'obhedh), 'servant'.

[4] Joshua 24.29.

[5] J. Z. Lauterbach, *Jewish Encyclopedia*, 9, 1905, p. 51, *s.v.* Moses.

[6] Mekh. on Exod. 12.1.   [7] Deut. Rabba on 29.4.

the author of this anecdote, belongs to the first half of the 3rd cent A.D. The main idea, however, may be far older.

Finally, there is a Midrash dealing with the breaking of the Tables.[1] Moses realized that, under the strict law, the worship of the Golden Calf would mean the end of the nation, since it is laid down that he who sacrifices to idols 'shall be utterly destroyed', 'shall be *ḥerem*'.[2] Therefore, the Midrash continues, 'he joined, united (*ḥibber*) his life, self ('*eth naphsho*) with them' and committed the sin of breaking the Tables; whereupon he asked God[3] either to pardon all or to reject him as well— there was now no difference. A legend like this may well have contributed to the notions of all sinners being gathered and saved in Jesus, and of Jesus, sinless, being made sin or curse for others.

It might perhaps be argued that it is the legend which is indebted to Christianity. This, however, is unlikely. The legend is comparatively simple, whereas the Christian notions are very intricate. Moreover, the latter refer so specifically to Jesus that one cannot very well imagine their being watered down and transferred to Moses.

---

[1] Exod. Rabba on 34.1.   [2] Exod. 22.19 (20).   [3] Exod. 32.32.

III

Samuel

SAMUEL is no Messianic figure. But in Talmudic literature he is called
'the *Rabban*, the foremost master, teacher, of all prophets';[1] and his
prominence among the prophets is recognized in Acts and the Epistle
to the Hebrews.[2] Moreover, as God allowed Hannah to conceive him
in answer to her prayers, he represents for the Rabbis the righteous
child granted to parents who come together 'in holiness' (*biqedhusha*).[3]

That the narrative of Samuel's birth influenced the Lukan stories of
the birth of the Baptist and the birth of Jesus is well known. The Magni-
ficat, for example, closely follows the song of Hannah. The presentation
of the infant Jesus at the Temple probably contains a reminiscence of
the presentation of the boy Samuel at the sanctuary of Shiloh.[4] Jesus's
parents make a yearly pilgrimage to Jerusalem comparable to that of
Samuel's parents to Shiloh. Luke concludes his account of the childhood
of Jesus by saying that he 'increased in wisdom and age and in favour
with God and man'; just so 'the child Samuel grew on and was in
favour both with the Lord and also with men'.[5]

In view of these acknowledged parallels, it may be justifiable to call
attention to a story about the young Samuel teaching at the sanctuary
although it is transmitted by a Rabbi who flourished as late as the
middle of the 3rd cent. A.D. We shall come back to this problem of
date. The story is[6] that Samuel, when brought to Shiloh by his parents,
observed that the priests misinterpreted one of the sacrificial regulations.
He remarked on it and was summoned before Eli, where he established
his point by a convincing exegesis of a precept from Leviticus.[7] Eli paid
tribute to his fine argument. But he also reminded him that anyone

---

[1] Pal. Hag. 77a, where Judah the Prince uses the appellation.
[2] Acts 3.24, Heb. 11.32.
[3] Tanh. on Num. 5.13.
[4] Creed, *The Gospel according to St. Luke*, 1930, 39.
[5] Luke 2.52, I Sam. 2.26.   [6] Bab. Ber. 31b.   [7] 1.5.

teaching a *halakha*, a legal regulation, in the presence of his superior—
in this case Eli himself—deserved to be put to death. It was only
Hannah's intercession which saved her son. His prophetic qualities,
however, were henceforth undoubted.

It is no doubt conceivable that Eleazar ben Pedath, of the 3rd cent.,
invented this legend in order to give an ampler meaning to three
verses in I Samuel.[1] 'And they slew a bullock'—*scil.* the priests
slaughtered it incorrectly; 'and they brought the child to Eli'—*scil.*
because he had questioned the procedure; 'and she said, I am the woman
that stood by thee here praying unto the Lord'—*scil.* she said so to Eli
after he had pronounced the learned boy guilty of a capital offence; 'for
this child I prayed'—*scil.* though Eli assured her that even if Samuel had
to die for laying down a *halakha* in the presence of his superior, God
would give her other sons instead, she insisted that it was Samuel, 'this
child', she wanted to have. If we assume that the legend dates from the
3rd cent., it has of course no bearing on Luke's story.

We cannot, however, rule out the possibility of its being much
earlier. Eleazar ben Pedath may well have done no more than connect
it with, 'prove it' by reference to, certain verses in I Samuel. On this
hypothesis, Luke—or his precursors—may have regarded the Rabbinic
gifts of the boy prophet Samuel as foreshadowing those of the boy
prophet Jesus. We are not concerned with the historicity of the incident
reported by Luke. All that is here suggested is that the Jewish model, if
it existed in his time, may have contributed to his selection of this scene
and to his manner of depicting it.

According to the Gospel of Thomas,[2] which also contains the
episode of Jesus teaching in the Temple, Jesus reduces the doctors to
silence and himself expounds the Law. Creed holds[3] that 'in Luke the
boy is a genuine learner'. There is a great deal of truth in this. But, for
one thing, we do not know whether the Gospel of Thomas is entirely
dependent on Luke, so that any deviations must be secondary; it may
preserve parts of a version of the incident no less old than Luke,
though, admittedly, this is far from likely. For another thing, even in
Luke, we ought perhaps not to press too much the reference to Jesus
'hearing' the doctors and 'asking them questions'. In the very next sentence we are told how all were astonished 'at his understanding and
answers'. In the Talmudic anecdote concerning Samuel, the boy also

---

[1] 1.25–7.   [2] 19.   [3] *Op. cit.*, 45.

begins by asking the priests why they do so and so, and only then goes on to point out their error.

Needless to say, there remain enormous differences between the story about Samuel and that about Jesus. Let us, however, in conclusion, note three remarkable points of correspondence.

First, as his mother rebukes him, Jesus replies: 'Wist ye not that I must be in my Father's service' or 'in my Father's House?' Samuel's parents left him at the sanctuary from his earliest childhood.

Secondly, the mother of Jesus plays a more prominent part in the episode than his father, and her anxious love for him is touchingly depicted. The same is true of Samuel's mother in the Talmudic parallel.

Thirdly, Jesus 'was subject unto his parents' and he 'increased in wisdom and age and favour with God and man'. Now this sequence of ideas—subjecting oneself and finding favour—is interesting. (We omit the clause which, in Luke, separates them, namely, that Mary kept these things in her heart.) It is to be met with in early Christian catechetical material. Paul in Romans 13 enjoins subordination to the state and other social duties. In the following chapter he deals with vegetarianism and urges that, though no food is unclean, one should have some consideration for the prejudices of a fellow-Christian: 'for he that in these things serveth Christ is acceptable to God and approved of men'.[1] Similarly, I Peter[2] demands subjection to the authorities because 'so is the will of God, that with well doing ye may put to silence the ignorance of foolish men'. In Luke, to be sure, Jesus gives in not to the state or the prejudices of a fellow-being, but to his parents. This is not, however, a vital difference. He is represented as setting an example of Christian morality, and I Peter contains an injunction almost directly applicable to this case:[3] 'Ye younger, submit yourselves unto the elder; yea, all be subject one to another and be clothed with humility; for God giveth favour to the humble.'

Yet here, too, the evangelist may have had in mind the figure of Samuel. For one thing, let us note that the association of self-abasement with acceptability to God and men goes back to Jewish teaching. According to the Letter of Aristeas[4] 'it is a principle that God accepts the humble and the human race loves those willing to be in subjection to them'. Several hundreds of years later (first third of the 4th cent.

[1] 14.18.   [2] 2.13 ff.   [3] 5.5; cp. also Col. 3.20.   [4] 257.

A.D.) a favourite saying of Abaye was that a Jew should be yielding to
both his co-religionists and gentiles, in order to be agreeable to God and
man.[1] For another thing, apart from the fact that the Rabbis generally
ascribe particular humility to Samuel,[2] the Old Testament itself
records that whereas Eli's sons were wicked and 'hearkened not unto
the voice of their father',[3] Samuel 'ministered unto the Lord before Eli
the priest';[4] and we have already seen that when Luke wrote of Jesus
that 'he increased in wisdom and age and in favour with God and man',
he was drawing on the Old Testament notice that 'the child Samuel
grew and was in favour both with the Lord and also with men'.

To sum up, considering the late appearance of the Rabbinic legend of
Samuel, it would be rash to assert that the Lukan pericope must have
been inspired by it. A dogmatic denial of any influence, however,
would be equally wrong. The question must remain an open one.

[1] Bab. Ber. 17a.   [2] E.g. Tanh. on Num. 21.7.   [3] I Sam. 2.25.   [4] I Sam. 2.11, 18.

IV

Saul

A. GENERAL

THE case for Saul is worth consideration. Patai, in a recent article,[1] points out analogies between Old and New Testament symbols of royalty. He notes: (1) Samuel recognizes Saul one day after God announced his coming. The Baptist recognizes Jesus one day after announcing his coming.[2] (2) As Samuel sees Saul, God says: 'Behold the man I spake to thee of, this same shall reign over my people.' As the Baptist sees Jesus, he says: 'Behold the Lamb of God which taketh away the sin of the world. This is he of whom I said, After me cometh a man which is preferred before me' etc.[3] (3) Saul's public proclamation follows his choice by means of the oracle. Jesus's public proclamation follows his choice by means of the descent of the dove.[4] (4) When Saul is anointed, the Spirit enters into him, so that he turns into another man.[5] In other ancient installation rites, the person elected dies and is reborn as a god. That this idea was current also among the Hebrews is suggested by passages like this from Psalms:[6] 'Yet have I set my king upon the holy hill of Zion. I will declare: the Lord hath said unto me, Thou art my son, this day have I born thee.'[7] Possibly Patai might have added two verses referring to Saul himself, namely, those which say[8] that, when he had been fetched from his hiding-place to be acclaimed, 'he was higher than any of the people' and there was 'none like him among all the people'. When Jesus is baptized, the Spirit of God descends upon him, and he is proclaimed to be the son of God.[9] (5) Jair, one of the Judges, 'had thirty sons that rode on thirty ass colts,

[1] *Hebrew Union College Annual* 20, 1947, pp. 154 f., 170, 176.
[2] I Sam. 9.15 f., John 1.19 ff.　　　　　　　　　　　　[3] I Sam. 9.17, John 1.29 f.
[4] I Sam. 10.20 ff., Matt. 3.16 f., Mark 1.10 f., Luke 3.22, John 1.32 ff.
[5] I Sam. 10.6, 9. Cf. 16.13, of David.　　　　　　　　　　　　[6] 2.6 f.
[7] Or II Sam. 7.14, I Chron. 17.13, Ps. 89.27 f.
[8] I Sam. 10.23 f.　　　　[9] Matt. 3.16 f., Mark 1.10 f., Luke 3.21 f., John 1.32 ff.

and they had thirty cities';[1] another, Abdon, 'had forty sons and thirty nephews, that rode on three score and ten ass colts';[2] Solomon, when crowned, was made to ride on 'king David's mule' or 'the king's mule';[3] and Zechariah's prophecy about the king, 'lowly and riding upon an ass', is well known.[4] Jesus also rides on an ass.

B. JOHN

Not all these parallels are equally striking. Perhaps we should distinguish between the Synoptics and the Fourth Gospel. This has all analogies occurring in the Synoptics—the proclamation after a sign from heaven, the descent of the Spirit and the riding on an ass—plus two besides, the recognition one day after the announcement and the presentation opening with 'Behold'. The value of the first of these two may be diminished by the fact that, in John 1, it is several times that one event succeeds another on the following day.[5] On the other hand, it is just conceivable that the awkward duplication of verses 29-34, 'The next day, John seeth Jesus coming and saith, Behold the Lamb of God', by 35-37, 'Again the next day after John, looking upon Jesus, saith, Behold the Lamb of God', has something to do with the two days of Saul with Samuel.[6] At any rate, whereas those installation rites which the Fourth Gospel has in common with the Synoptics—proclamation after a sign, descent of the Spirit and riding on an ass—appear to come from a general stock of notions concerning installation rather than from the particular narrative of Saul, those peculiar to the Fourth Gospel— recognition one day after the announcement and presentation by 'Behold' and so on—are more specifically reminiscent of the latter.

After all, Saul was the first king of Israel and is mentioned as such— not merely as of the tribe of Benjamin—even in Paul's brief historical survey.[7] Moreover, there is a school of Rabbis which explains away any discreditable actions he committed and makes of him an ideal king. Paul was not influenced by it—for him, God 'removed' Saul[8]—but John may have been. Once we think of Saul as an ideal king, the whole relationship between the Baptist and Jesus in the Fourth Gospel becomes comparable to that between Samuel and Saul.

---

[1] Judges 10.4.　　　[2] 12.14.　　　[3] I Kings 2.38, 44.　　　[4] 9.9.
[5] 1.29, 33, 43. Maybe 2.1 also ought to be understood as one day after 1.43, 'the third day' signifying the third day after 1.29.
[6] I Sam. 9.19 ff.　　　[7] Acts 13.21.　　　[8] Acts 13.22.

C. Jesus's Flight from Kingship

One detail not listed by Patai deserves attention. John tells us that Jesus, when the people 'would come and take him by force that they might make him king, departed again into the mountain himself alone'.[1] Saul, about to be acclaimed as king, hid and had to be fetched.[2]

In Saul's case, the hiding had been a formal act belonging to the established pattern of coronation.[3] This original significance, however, was no longer understood in New Testament times—though, curiously, the idea of the Messiah hiding until his appearance is common. Of Saul's hiding, the Rabbis invariably say—even those who do not generally idealize him—that it was due to his humility. The incident is one of the great proofs that 'he who flies from rulership, rulership will pursue him'.[4] Josephus has four paragraphs about it, taking the same line.[5] Whether the Jewish interpretation was influenced by Greek philosophy—Plato held that the man best fitted to govern would not covet the office—may be left undecided.

If the Fourth Gospel alludes to Saul, it must be in the Rabbinic sense. It may not be superfluous to add that this would not affect the question of historicity; there is no reason why John should not depict a true occurrence in language connecting it with an earlier one which, in his view, throws light upon it.

The Sinaiticus is interesting. It reads 'the people would take him by force and proclaim him king', καὶ ἀναδεικνύναι, instead of 'the people would take him by force in order that they might make him king', ἵνα ποιήσωσιν, thus more closely approaching the formal language of coronation. It also reads (this time with some support from versions) 'Jesus flees', φεύγει, instead of 'Jesus departed', ἀνεχώρησεν, thus more directly expressing the idea of flying from rulership.

The upshot seems to be that, while Saul does not figure as a Messianic type in the Synoptics, there is some evidence, however inconclusive, that he does in John.

[1] 6.15. [2] I Sam. 10.21 ff. [3] Patai, *op. cit.*, 178 f.
[4] Tanh. on Lev. 1.1. This attitude was far from universally shared. An old Midrash represents Alexander as asking the Elders of the South how a man might become liked by his fellows. They reply: 'Let him hate kingship and dominion.' But he retorts: 'Let him love kingship and dominion and do good to the creatures' (Bab. Tam. 32a).
[5] Ant. 6.4.5.62 ff.

V

Elijah

OF Elijah we do know that speculations concerning him were present in the minds of those who witnessed or wrote about the events described in the New Testament. They may account for two incidents not so far associated with him: the way in which Jesus is acclaimed on entering Jerusalem, and the rending of the veil of the temple.

A. 'BLESSED IS HE THAT COMETH IN THE NAME OF THE LORD'

As Jesus is about to enter Jerusalem, the multitude, according to Mark, greets him by a quotation from Psalm 118: 'Hosanna; Blessed is he that cometh in the name of the Lord.' They also shout: 'Blessed is the kingdom of our father David' and so on, but this is clearly Mark's, or his source's, interpretation of the greeting. Matthew understands it in the same way, putting 'Hosanna to the son of David; Blessed is he that cometh', etc. Luke refers not to David but to the king in general; and he omits 'Hosanna'. The multitude cries: 'Blessed is the king that cometh in the name of the Lord.' John, finally, introduces 'the king of Israel': 'Blessed is the king of Israel that cometh in the name of the Lord.'[1] The question is whether the evangelists are justified in ascribing a Messianic meaning to the greeting, and if so, whether they have given it the right kind of Messianic meaning.

It has long been seen that, in the view of some Rabbis, the verse 'Blessed is he' and so on, together with a few that precede it and a few that follow it in the Psalm, was composed when David became king,[2] and will be recited again when the Messiah appears.[3] Unfortunately,

[1] Ps. 118.26, Mark 11.9 f., Matt. 21.9, Luke 19.38, John 12.13.
[2] Targ. Ps. 118.22 ff., Bab. Pes. 119a; see Strack-B., vol. I, 1922, pp. 876, 849 f.
[3] Mid. Ps. on 118.24; Strack-B., vol. I, p. 850.

though this exegesis definitely existed by the first half of the 3rd cent., we cannot say whether it goes back to the 1st. One point, however, is suggestive. The Rabbis put several lines, not only 'Blessed is he' etc., into the mouth of the public welcoming David or the Messiah. For example, when the Messiah appears, the people inside Jerusalem will say, 'O Lord, save, I beseech thee' ('O Lord, Hosanna'), those outside, 'O Lord, send prosperity', those inside, 'Blessed is he that cometh in the name of the Lord', those outside, 'We bless you of the house of the Lord', and so they will complete the Psalm.[1] The crowd welcoming Jesus also combines 'Save, I beseech thee' and 'Blessed is he', two verses at least. Luke, it is true, omits 'Hosanna'. But its genuineness cannot be doubted. Very likely he considered that it would be unintelligible to Greek readers.

Let us look at another piece of evidence, from the service at the circumcision of a Jewish boy. All over the world, it begins by the boy being brought into a room where the participants in the service are already assembled, and the latter exclaiming: 'Blessed is he that cometh', *barukh habba'*. The child is then placed on a chair called 'the throne of Elijah'. From this moment, variations occur. In some rites, he is circumcised on this chair, in others he is taken to another, ordinary chair for the circumcision.

The usual explanation of 'the throne of Elijah' is that, for the Rabbis, Elijah is the 'messenger of the covenant' mentioned in Malachi,[2] and as such invisibly supervises every circumcision, every initiation into the covenant of Abraham; therefore a seat must be provided for him. It is, however, possible that, at its inception, the custom symbolized the hope that the child himself would prove to be Elijah: so he must be enthroned, just in case. Rab (of the first half of the 3rd cent. A.D.) interpreted the Psalmist's warning 'Touch not mine anointed' as directed against unkindness to school-children.[3] The 'cup of Elijah' which Jews put on the table on Passover eve may be compared, though, admittedly, it seems to be very much later than 'the throne'. Some Passover eve, Elijah will arrive. Hence it is necessary every year to have a cup ready for his use.

The differences in rites as to the place of the child during the actual circumcision may reflect a change in interpretation. That rite according

[1] Ps. 118. 25 ff., Mid. Ps. on 118.24.
[2] 3.1.　　　　　　[3] Bab. Shab. 119 b; see Ps. 105.15.

to which the boy remains on 'the throne of Elijah' may be the older, dating from the period when he was thought of as, conceivably, Elijah. The other rite, according to which he is circumcised on an ordinary chair, may have grown up when this identification of a child with Elijah fell into disfavour—anti-Christian motives would account for this—and when the original idea was replaced by that of Elijah watching the ceremony as an invisible angel.

If, in the New Testament age, some Messianic symbolism was applied to any male child—whether or not it took just this form of 'the throne of Elijah'—it becomes far easier to fit the narratives of the adoration of the Magi or the shepherds into a Jewish milieu. The same is true of the miracle which Luke says happened at the circumcision of the Baptist, whom the gospel, in its present form at least, does clearly assimilate to Elijah.

Be this as it may, certain it is that, at the opening of a service at circumcision, Elijah is greeted by 'Blessed is he that cometh'. The words may be addressed to the angel Elijah accompanying the boy or to the boy *qua* Elijah: in either case are they addressed to Elijah. Once again, however, the question of date is complicated. We cannot trace the greeting beyond medieval collections of Jewish observances.[1] This does not, of course, rule out its existence long before. The authors of those collections tell us that they made them because otherwise ancient traditions would be forgotten. As Malachi announces of the messenger of the covenant that 'Behold, he shall come, saith the Lord of hosts', it must have been natural for the Rabbis to connect with him—i.e. with Elijah, the same person in their eyes—the verse 'Blessed is he that cometh in the name of the Lord'. In other words, quite apart from the service at circumcision, this was as appropriate a greeting for Elijah as for the Messiah himself or other figures that were 'to come'. Elijah, it will be recalled, is introduced as 'the coming one' in several synoptic pericopes.[2]

[1] Ibn Yarhi, the Tanya, Abudarham. Possibly P. de-R. El. may be added. In this work (29 at the end), Mal. 3.1, 'Behold, he shall come', is associated with 'the throne of Elijah': an indication, perhaps, that at any rate by this time the greeting 'Blessed is he that cometh' was usual in the service at circumcision.

[2] Matt. 11.14, 17.10 ff., Mark 9.11 ff., maybe also Matt. 27.49, Mark 15.36. As a rule, modern editors and commentators quote only Mal. 3.23 as Old Testament basis. But 3.1, which alone uses the verb 'to come', is absolutely necessary as well. The Elijah who 'shall first come and restore all things' derives from the messenger who 'shall prepare the way before me, behold he shall come'.

On balance, the evidence favours the assumption that the greeting of Jesus by the multitude was of a Messianic character. There is agreement on this point between all evangelists. It is underlined by the prediction Jesus utters according to Matthew and Luke,[1] 'Ye shall not see me till ye shall say, Blessed is he that cometh in the name of the Lord'—'Hosanna' is here not included. And several lines of Rabbinic testimony converge to support this interpretation. Exactly which Messianic figure, however, the crowd had in mind is far more dubious. It may have been the son of David, the king or the king of Israel: we need not go into the relation between these. But it may also have been Elijah.

B. The Veil of the Temple

Mark tells us that, on Jesus's death, 'the veil of the temple was rent in twain from the top to the bottom'.[2] Codex Bezae and the Itala are even more explicit: 'it was rent in two parts', not just 'in twain'.

Matthew and Luke both put the miracle together with others said to have occurred, the former with an earthquake and opening of graves, the latter with an eclipse of the sun.[3] This, however, throws little light on the specific meaning of the event. As Luke pairs it off with the eclipse, the result is that, in his account, the rending of the veil precedes Jesus's death. But in looking for the original significance, we must start from Matthew and Mark, where it follows it. In modern literature, a good many interpretations are to be found, none of them satisfactory. The latest writer holds that the notice expresses an early *theologoumenon* of the Church, concerning the removal through Jesus's death of obstacles in the way to God.[4]

Most probably, we ought to proceed from the action of Elisha when Elijah ascended into heaven: 'And Elisha saw it and he cried, My father, my father, the chariot of Israel and the horsemen thereof. And he took hold of his clothes and rent them in two pieces.'[5] In Rabbinic times, there were prescribed occasions on which a man had to rend his garment. In this connection, the incident quoted acquired particular importance. The Rabbis noted the emphatic 'he rent his clothes in two pieces' instead of a plain 'he rent his clothes'; and, in their usual manner, based on it the teaching that, in certain cases, the two parts into which you

---

[1] Matt. 23.39, Luke 13.35.   [2] 15.38.   [3] Matt. 27.51 ff., Luke 23.44 f.
[4] Lindeskog, *Coniectanea Neotestamentica* 11, 1948, pp. 132 ff.   [5] II Kings 2.12.

have rent your garment may never be sewn together again. The cases are the death of your father, your mother, your teacher of Torah, the Patriarch (Nasi) or the Father of the Court (Abh-beth-din), the receipt of terrible news, the utterance of a blasphemy by someone in your presence, the burning of a Scroll of Law and, finally, the destruction of Judaean cities, the temple or Jerusalem.[1]

When we consider the stress laid in the New Testament on the complete splitting of the curtain into two—or, according to some readings, two parts—from top to bottom, it is safe to find here an allusion to the rite practised as a sign of deepest sorrow. We need not decide whether the death of Jesus is likened to that of a teacher of Torah or to the destruction of the temple. Either or both comparisons may play some part, as also the idea that those responsible for the crucifixion are the real blasphemers, and not Jesus at whose words the High Priest had rent his clothes.[2] It may be noted that Luke, who places the rending of the veil before Jesus's death, thus completely obscuring its original import, omits this gesture by the High Priest.[3] Presumably, he did not think his readers would understand the rite.

The question whether the miracle did in fact happen is not here relevant. We are concerned only with the manner of its representation, which connects it with a mourning rite—and, indeed, with the prototype, in Rabbinic eyes, of this rite, the action of Elisha on Elijah's ascension. It is difficult not to believe that this episode was in the mind of the author of the notice about the veil of the temple.

Support is furnished by the passages concerning the assumption of Jesus at the close of the gospels of Mark and Luke and at the beginning of Acts.[4] True, the authors may no longer be conscious of a connection with the end of Elijah. But at some stage of the tradition such a connection no doubt existed. We need only compare the Lukan 'he was parted from them and carried up into heaven' with the description in the Old Testament, 'they parted them both asunder and Elijah went up into heaven'. The incident of the veil may be regarded as, in a way, adumbrating these references to the assumption.

Among the various explanations in early Christian literature, there is one—to be found in a work of Jewish-Christian provenance[5]—which

---

[1] Bab. M.Q. 25b f., Mish. San. 7.5 (on blasphemy in particular).
[2] Matt. 26.64 f., Mark 14.62 f.   [3] 22.67 ff.   [4] Mark 16.19, Luke 24.51, Acts 1.2.
[5] Clem. Rec. 1.41: 'lamentans excidium loco imminens'.

at least sees in the miracle a sign of mourning, though not for Jesus's death but for the approaching end of the temple. Another point worth a mention is that the word *pargodh*, which in the Targum stands for the curtain separating the holy of holies from the outer chamber, may also denote a tunic. If the story originated in Aramaic-speaking circles, the extension of the custom of rending one's garment to the veil of the temple—the tunic of the temple—must have been particularly easy.

So far we are on safe ground. May we go further? It is tempting to suggest that, in Matthew and Mark, the notice concerning the veil together with some verses preceding and following it forms a much more closely knit pericope than has hitherto been realized.[1] As Jesus cries out, 'Eli, Eli, lama sabachthani', some bystanders think he is summoning Elijah[2] and mockingly remark, 'Let us see whether Elijah will come to save him.' After this, the rending in two of the veil of the temple, reminiscent as it is of what Elisha did when his master was translated, may well be intended as an answer to the mockery: here is Elijah himself, or one that is greater.

Even the centurion's confession[3] may correspond to Elisha's cry, 'My father, my father, the chariot of Israel and the horsemen thereof.' In the Targum, 'my father' is changed into 'my Rabbi', no doubt in deference to the view, recurring in Matthew, that, as a title, 'my father' is not ordinarily suitable for human beings.[4] The rest is paraphrased by 'who was better for Israel by his prayer than chariots and horsemen'.[5]

That the distinction was transferable to other prophets and teachers may be seen from the way king Joash addresses Elisha himself on his last sick bed,[6] 'O my father, my father, the chariot of Israel and the horsemen thereof'; and, for Rabbinic times, from the Aramaic version of Chronicles,[7] which speaks of 'Moses, the teacher of Israel, whose merit was better for them than horsemen and chariots', and from the

---

[1] Matt. 27.46–54, Mark 15.34–9.
[2] The misunderstanding was possible because in New Testament times *'eli* was not the only form for 'my God': the ancient form *'eliya* had not yet died out and was apparently used by Jesus. See Guillaume, 'Matthew XXVII, 46 in the Light of the Dead Sea Scroll of Isaiah', *Palestine Exploration Quarterly*, 1951, pp. 78 ff.
[3] Matt. 27.54, Mark 15.39, Luke 23.47.
[4] Matt. 23.9; see Strack-B., vol. 1, 1922, p. 919.
[5] Cp. Xenophanes, as reported by Athenaeus (Deipn. 10.414a f.): 'My wisdom is better (for the city) than the strength of men and horses.'
[6] II Kings 13.14.
[7] I Chron. 2.55.

story of the last moments of Eliezer ben Hyrcanus (beginning of the 2nd cent. A.D.), on whose death his old antagonist Joshua ben Hananiah quoted the words of Elisha.[1] The centurion's confession is rather different in substance, but its position at least may owe something to the old precedent.

[1] Pal. Shab. 5b ('my Rabbi'), Bab. San. 68a ('my father').

VI

Ruth and Boaz

We now go on to Ruth and Boaz. Their influence has not so far been recognized at all. Yet it would be surprising if a couple so prominent among the ancestry of the Messiah, and possessing so many features capable of a Messianic interpretation, had been absolutely neglected by the authors of the New Testament. As a matter of fact, allusions can be shown to occur in two pericopes at least: the Lukan narrative of the annunciation, and the narrative of the feeding of the multitude preserved in all four gospels.

A. The Annunciation

In the narrative of the annunciation, Mary is made to resemble Ruth.

1. 'To overshadow'

To substantiate this proposition, it is necessary to find out about the antecedents of the puzzling term ἐπισκιάζω, 'to overshadow'. It is used on three occasions: once, in Acts,[1] where the sick hope for a cure if 'the shadow of Peter overshadows them', another time, by all three Synoptics, in the narrative of the transfiguration, of a cloud which 'overshadows' some disciples and out of which a voice proclaims Jesus 'my beloved son',[2] and finally, by Luke, in the narrative of the annunciation, of the power of the Highest that is to 'overshadow' Mary so that she will bear a son, Jesus.[3]

It is an exact equivalent of Hebrew ṣalal or Aramaic ṭallel, which, while literally denoting 'to overshadow', is very often applied to the descent on a person or object of the divine presence, the Shekhinah. The Hebrew noun ṣel or the Aramaic ṭelal signifies 'shadow' both in the literal sense and in the figurative of 'shelter'. In addition, the verb can

[1] 5.15. [2] Matt. 17.5, Mark 9.7, Luke 9.34. [3] 1.35.

mean 'to cover', and the noun 'a cover', 'a roof', 'a tabernacle' or 'a booth'. Other Aramaic nouns of the same root, *meṭalela'* and *meṭalalta'*, are indeed exclusively used as designating 'a cover' or 'a booth'.

In the Old Testament, *ṣalal* occurs only in two obscure passages; the LXX omits it in the one,[1] and renders it by καθίστημι, 'to become quiet', in the other.[2] However, the LXX seems to assume the verb in two further texts, translating it by σκιάζω, 'to shade';[3] and Theodotion manifestly assumes it in yet another, of some theological significance, and translates it by ἐπισκιάζω, 'to overshadow'—we shall have to come back to this one.[4] Symmachus employs the verb ἐπισκιάζω in a passage where the Hebrew has the noun *ṣel*, 'shade'.[5] As for this noun *ṣel*, the LXX normally translates it by σκιά where the notion of 'shadow' predominates, and by σκέπη where that of 'shelter' predominates.

So much for the Hebrew *ṣalal*. The Aramaic *ṭallel* is very common in the Aramaic versions of the Old Testament, the Targumim, and we shall give a number of typical illustrations presently. In the original text it is to be met with twice. Shallun built a gate and 'covered it', 'made a roof over it', LXX στεγάζω;[6] and under the tree of which Nebuchadnezzar dreamt, the beasts 'sought shadow' (the verb here is in the Aphel, *'aṭlel*), LXX σκιάζω, Theodotion κατασκηνόω.[7]

As we propose to show, the use of ἐπισκιάζω in the New Testament can be appreciated only if we proceed from the Semitic equivalent, *ṣalal* or *ṭallel*. Why has this never been done? Two other explanations have stood in the way.

Some scholars hold that the idea in the narrative of the annunciation is the same as in a discourse by Philo,[8] where he gives an allegorical comment on the verse from Genesis:[9] 'After that, the sons of God came in unto the daughters of men, and they bare children to them.' This means, Philo says, the fellows of darkness, i.e. lies, mating with man's inferior passions and begetting vices; which can only happen 'after that', i.e. after the pure rays of reason have ceased to shine and the light of understanding is 'overshadowed'. However, any connection with Luke

---

[1] Ezek. 31.3 (Hiphil).   [2] Neh. 13.19.
[3] II Sam. 20.6, Hebrew *wehiṣṣil*, of *naṣal*, 'and he will escape', a variant of LXX καὶ σκιάσει, 'and he will shade'; Jonah 4.6, Hebrew *lehaṣṣil lo*, again of *naṣal*, 'to deliver him', LXX τοῦ σκιάζειν αὐτῷ, 'to shade him'.
[4] Num. 11.25, *wayya'ṣel*, really 'and he put aside', of *'aṣal*, but looking little different from a Hiphil of *ṣalal*.   [5] Hos. 4.13.
[6] Neh. 3.15.   [7] Dan. 4.9.   [8] Q.D.I.S. 1.3.   [9] 6.4.

is out of the question. No conceivable bridge leads from this application of the verb, in the sense of 'to obscure', 'to darken', 'to keep from light', to the message 'the power of the Highest shall overshadow thee'.

A second group of scholars argues in this way. In the LXX, ἐπισκιάζω three times represents sakhakh, 'to cover',[1] and once shakhan, 'to dwell'.[2] The latter text, referring to the cloud which 'abode' on the tabernacle, is clearly relevant to both the transfiguration and the annunciation. Hence (they argue) ἐπισκιάζω in these narratives equals shakhan.

But this is a palpable non sequitur. The fact that the LXX in one case renders 'to dwell' by 'to overshadow' does not entitle us generally to identify 'to overshadow' with 'to dwell'. The verb 'to dwell', shakhan, occurs more than a hundred times and is nowhere else translated by 'to overshadow'. Of the three texts where 'to overshadow' stands for 'to cover', sakhakh, two are just as relevant as that where it stands for 'to dwell', namely: 'The Lord shall cover thee with his feathers', and 'O Lord, thou hast covered my head in the day of battle.'[3] So, obviously, is the passage where Theodotion puts ἐπισκιάζω for what he takes to be ṣalal: 'The Lord overshadowed them (the elders of the people) with his (Moses's) spirit.'[4]

We shall try to indicate the special reasons why the LXX in the instances referred to deems 'to overshadow' a suitable rendering of 'to dwell' or 'to cover'. For the moment, it may suffice to remark that the range of ṣalal or ṭallel is more than wide enough to account for these applications. At any rate, in searching for the Hebrew and Aramaic background of ἐπισκιάζω in the New Testament, the proper course surely is to start from the centre, i.e. from the verbs for 'to overshadow', and not from peripheral uses, i.e. from a verb primarily denoting something quite different. As far as Luke is concerned, it is all the more dangerous to rob ἐπισκιάζω of its etymological meaning as in Acts, in the notice about the healings performed by Peter, it is undeniably employed in the most literal sense.

[1] Ps. 91.4 (Hiphil), 140.8, Prov. 18.11 (Hiphil). The case of Prov. 18.11 is very doubtful. If ἐπισκιάζω is intended as a rendering of maśkith, the LXX makes a mistake: this Hebrew noun really derives, not from sakhakh, but from śakha, and it signifies 'imagination'. It may, however, be δόξα by which the LXX means to render maśkith. If so, ἐπισκιάζω is intended as a rendering of ḥoma, 'wall', laxly taken in the sense of 'protective cover'.

[2] Exod. 40.35.

[3] Ps. 91.4, 140.8.

[4] Num. 11.25.

2. The transfiguration

We need not enlarge on this passage from Acts, except to repeat that when we are told of 'Peter's shadow overshadowing the sick', it is impossible to assume any other meaning than that of *ṣalal* or *ṭallel*.[1]

In the narrative of the transfiguration, Peter proposes to build three booths, one for Jesus, one for Moses and one for Elijah. Probably he is thinking of the role of the booth on the Feast of Booths, namely, as symbolizing God's immediate guidance and protection. In any case, it is in reply to his proposal that a cloud 'overshadows' them.

To illustrate the connotations of the term in this context, it may be observed that the Aramaic for 'Feast of Booths' is 'Feast of *meṭalayya*' ' 'Feast of Covers'—of the root *ṭallel*, 'to overshadow'.[2] The Aramaic version of the Biblical section in which this Feast is instituted shows how closely associated are the ideas of the festal booth and the divine presence in a cloud. The injunction 'Ye shall dwell in booths seven days' is translated by 'Ye shall dwell in *meṭalayya*' seven days',[3] but in the next verse, for 'that your generations may know that I made the children of Israel to dwell in booths when I brought them out of Egypt', the Targum puts 'to dwell in the *meṭalletha*' of clouds',[4] or even 'to dwell in the *meṭalletha*' of clouds of glory'.[5]

Similarly, where the Bible says 'And they took their journey from Succoth', R. Akiba regards 'Succoth' not as a place-name but as standing for 'booths' in the sense of 'clouds of glory'.[6] Several times the Hebrew *sukka*, 'booth', is rendered by *ṭelal*, 'shadow' or 'booth'; as in the verse from Job,[7] 'Can any understand the spreadings of the clouds or the noise of his tabernacle', or that from Psalms,[8] 'In time of trouble he shall hide me in his pavilion.' Isaiah's prophecy,[9] 'And the Lord will create upon Zion a cloud of smoke, and there shall be a booth, *sukka*, for a shadow, *ṣel*, in daytime', in the Targum appears as 'And the Lord will create upon Zion a cloud of glory which will overshadow it, *'aṭṭel*, and over Jerusalem there will be a booth, *meṭalletha*', of clouds to overshadow it, *'aṭlel*.' It is noteworthy that, under Rabbinic law, in a

---

[1] A suggestion regarding this mode of healing will be made below, in Part III, under The Laying on of Hands.
[2] Targ. Lev. 23.34 Onk. and Jerus., Gen. 35.14 Jerus., Num. 29.12, 17, 20 f. Jerus., Zech. 14.16 ff.
[3] Lev. 23.42 Onk.; *meṭalalta*' Jerus.   [4] Onk.   [5] Jerus.
[6] Mekh. on Exod. 13.20.   [7] 36.29   [8] 27.5.   [9] 4.5 f.

booth which was to serve on the Feast of Booths, the shaded part had to be larger than the unshaded.[1]

However, quite a few texts are of interest though there is no mention of a booth. During their wanderings in the desert, the Lord's cloud, we learn, 'standeth over the people'; according to the Targum, it 'overshadows them', *attel*.[2] 'The cloud of the Lord was upon the tabernacle by day'; according to the Targum, 'the cloud of the glory of the Lord overshadowed it', *atlel*.[3] 'The cherubim were covering the mercy seat with their wings'; according to the Targum, 'they were overshadowing it', *tallel*.[4] 'The Lord is thy shade', Hebrew *ṣel*, in the Targum becomes 'The Lord overshadows thee', *tallel*.[5] 'Hide me under the shadow of thy wings', *ṣel*, becomes 'under the shadow of thy Shekhinah', *telal*.[6] 'He shall abide under the shadow of the Almighty', *ṣel*, becomes 'in the shadow of clouds of glory', *telal*.[7] 'He shall cover thee, *sakhakh*, with his feathers, *'ebhra*, and under his wings, *kanaph*, shalt thou trust', becomes 'He shall overshadow thee, *tallel*, with the shadow, *telal*, of his Shekhinah and under the shadow, *telal*, of his glory shalt thou trust.'[8] 'Ye, the wings of a dove' becomes 'Ye, the congregation of Israel, which resembles a dove, overshadowed by clouds of glory', *'ittallel*.[9]

Two more uses are remarkable. First, the Aramaic equivalent of the Hebrew phrase 'to come under the wings of the Shekhinah', which signifies 'to be converted to Judaism', is 'to come under the *telal*— cover, shadow—of the Shekhinah'.[10] Secondly, we come across in the Targum the expression 'to be overshadowed, *'ittallel*, by the spirit of prophecy'.[11] We have already adverted to a parallel in Theodotion, who uses ἐπισκιάζω of God's 'overshadowing' the elders with the spirit of Moses.[12]

Against the background of these quotations, the employment of 'to overshadow' in the narrative of the transfiguration appears perfectly natural. Moreover, we can now understand why, in the LXX, ἐπισκιάζω occasionally does service for a Hebrew word the literal meaning of which is by no means the same. Where the Shekhinah was

---

[1] Mish. Suk. 1.1, Lev. 23.42 in Jerus.
[2] Num. 14.14 Onk.; it 'is a shadow over them', *matlul*, Jerus., unless the reading *matlel* is correct, in which case the meaning is the same as in Onk.
[3] Exod. 40.38 Jerus.   [4] Exod. 25.20, 37.9 Jerus.; *'atlel* Onk.
[5] Ps. 121.5.   [6] Ps. 17.8.   [7] Ps. 91.1.   [8] Ps. 91.4.   [9] Ps. 68.14.
[10] Ruth 2.12, Deut. 23.16 Jerus.
[11] I Chron. 2.55, connecting *śukhathim* with *sakhakh*, 'to cover'.   [12] Num. 11.25.

concerned, the verb 'to overshadow' was evidently highly popular. That was so not only because it evoked the idea of 'the cloud of the Lord', but also because it was respectful and less crudely physical than other terms.

In one text,[1] ἐπισκιάζω replaces *shakhan*, 'to dwell'. So, in the Targum, we have seen, *ṭallel* may replace '*amadh*, 'to stand',[2] or be inserted where the Hebrew is without any verb, simply speaking of 'the cloud on the tabernacle'.[3] In three texts, ἐπισκιάζω is put instead of *sakhakh*, 'to cover'. Two of them are concerned with the coming down of the Shekhinah to help: 'The Lord shall cover thee with his feathers', and 'O Lord, thou hast covered my head in the day of battle.' In both, the Targum also uses *ṭallel*, 'to overshadow',[4] as it does in another passage where the Hebrew has *sakhakh*: 'The cherubim were covering the mercy seat with their wings.'[5] It should be remembered that *sukka*, 'booth', is connected with *sakhakh*. The third case of ἐπισκιάζω for *sakhakh* is of a different sort: 'The rich man's wealth is his strong city, and his opinion of it greatly overshadows.'[6] Here ἐπισκιάζω means 'to cover', 'to form a protective roof'. We have already adduced an original Old Testament text where *ṭallel* has this sense.[7] In the Targum, this application of the verb is frequent;[8] and we may again recall the noun *ṭelal*, or others of the same root, in the sense of 'booth', *sukka*. Comparable Hebrew phrases are 'the shadow, *ṣel*, of my roof', LXX σκέπη,[9] and—quite near the rich man's wealth the opinion of which 'overshadows'—'in the cover, *ṣel*, of wisdom, and in the cover, *ṣel*, of money', LXX σκιά.[10]

3. *The annunciation*

Let us proceed to the annunciation. A fair number of the passages already cited are here pertinent too: all those referring to a descent of the Shekhinah in a general sense, and more particularly, that containing the notion of 'being overshadowed by the spirit of prophecy'. Gabriel says to Mary: 'The Holy Spirit shall come upon thee and the power of

---

[1] Exod. 40.35.   [2] Num. 14.14.
[3] Exod. 40.38. I Chron. 2.55 also belongs here: the Targum derives *śukhathim* from *sakhakh* and puts '*iṭṭallel*, 'to be overshadowed by the spirit of prophecy'.
[4] Ps. 91.4, 140.8.   [5] Exod. 25.20, 37.9.
[6] Prov. 18.11. Our argument needs little modification if ἐπισκιάζω is intended as representing, not *maśkith*, but *ḥoma*.
[7] Neh. 3.15, LXX στεγάζω.
[8] E.g. Exod. 36.19 Jerus., I Kings 6.9.   [9] Gen. 19.8.   [10] Eccles. 7.12.

the Highest shall overshadow thee.' The Spirit and the Shekhinah are here descending at the same time.

There is, however, one text which seems to be specifically responsible for the terminology in question, Ruth's request to Boaz:[1] 'I am Ruth thine handmaid; spread therefore thy wing over thine handmaid, for thou art a redeemer.'

In Rabbinic literature, Ruth is celebrated both as representative of the true proselyte and as an ancestress of David and the Messiah. Her life is often interpreted as prefiguring Messianic events, and where this is done, Boaz sometimes stands for God himself, or at least speaks and acts as God himself would. Thus his words, 'Hearest thou not, my daughter, go not to glean in another field, neither go from hence, but abide here by my maidens',[2] are declared to mean: 'Hearest thou not, thou shalt have no other gods before me,[3] this is my God and I will praise him,[4] abide here by my righteous ones.'[5]

Further examples will be adduced in discussing the narrative of the feeding of the multitude. At this point, we may be content with observing that an allusion in the narrative of the annunciation to the scene between Ruth and Boaz ought to cause no surprise.

If we turn to the Rabbinic exegesis of Ruth's request, it must be borne in mind that, at this moment, she is not yet married to Boaz. For a man like Goethe, this was only in keeping with the natural, rustic character of the Book of Ruth, in his judgment the sweetest idyll composed in antiquity. But the Rabbis could not see it in this light. They took it for granted that the situation, however awkward it might look at first sight, was reconcilable with the most refined notions of morality. This aspect is indeed accentuated in the case of Mary, who was a virgin. There was an even wider discrepancy between appearances and the truth, and we should only expect one or the other of those who narrated the story to have been conscious of the Old Testament parallel.

Now the Rabbis solve the problem by proving that Ruth's conduct, far from being immodest, is ideal; and, significantly, it is the phrase, 'Spread thy wings over thine handmaid', LXX $\pi\epsilon\rho\iota\beta\alpha\lambda\epsilon\hat{\iota}s$ $\tau\grave{o}$ $\pi\tau\epsilon\rho\acute{v}\gamma\iota\acute{o}\nu$ $\sigma o\upsilon$ $\epsilon\pi\grave{\iota}$ $\tau\grave{\eta}\nu$ $\delta o\acute{v}\lambda\eta\nu$ $\sigma o\upsilon$, on which they dwell in this connection. It is considered to reveal exceptional chastity. Samuel ben Nahman, of the 3rd cent. A.D., contrasts it with Potiphar's shameless

---

[1] 3.9.   [2] 2.8.   [3] Exod. 20.3.   [4] Exod. 15.2.

[5] That 'maidens' equals 'righteous ones' is deduced from Job. 40.29; see Ruth Rabba on 2.8.

D

'Lie with me'.[1] An anonymous Midrash goes as far as to conclude from it that Ruth was the purest of all women. When we add to this the opportunity presented to Rabbinic typologists by the end of the sentence, 'for thou art a redeemer', it is obvious that here was a most suitable expression for the New Testament narrative.

Perhaps we should here also draw attention to the Rabbinic legend,[2] transmitted by Resh Lakish, 3rd cent., and resting on the circumstantial report 'So Boaz took Ruth, and she was his wife' instead of either 'So Boaz took Ruth' or 'So she was his wife', that when Ruth married, she —like Sarah and Rebekkah—had no womb, and that God specially prepared her so that she could have a child. No doubt this legend is only a remnant of a vast amount of speculation about the phrase in question and others in its immediate neighbourhood, such as 'the seed which the Lord shall give thee (Boaz) of this young woman'[3] or 'the Lord gave her (Ruth) conception'. The latter expression is certainly peculiar. Yet the Midrash Rabba, in its present form, contains not a single observation on it. Considering the profusion of Rabbinic comments on phrases far less unusual, this can only mean that such observations as existed were deemed unsuitable by the time the Midrash Rabba was redacted. They had become unsuitable owing to the use Christianity had made of these ideas.

But how, it may be asked, did 'to spread one's wing over a person' become 'to overshadow'? One factor may have been that the cloak worn by pious or scholarly men, and distinguished by 'wings', borders, specially made in accordance with the law concerning the showfringes,[4] was called *tallith*, from the root *telal*, 'shadow'. Now the expression 'to spread the *tallith* over a woman' is used in Rabbinic literature[5] as a refined alternative for 'to cohabit with a woman'. We may safely assume that it was coined under the influence of two Old Testament passages: one from Ezekiel,[6] where God reminds Jerusalem how 'Thy time was the time of love, and I spread my wing over thee', and the other Ruth's request 'Spread thy wing'. It follows that some Rabbis must have paraphrased this request by 'Spread thy *tallith*'— which comes very near 'Overshadow'.

[1] Gen. Rabba on 39.7. In Ruth Rabba on 3.9, the idea is attributed to R. Berechiah. Clearly, Berechiah had it from Helbo, who was Samuel b. Nahman's pupil.
[2] Ruth Rabba on 4.13.   [3] This may at one time have been brought together with Seth, 'another seed instead of Abel', as the Messiah's ancestor; see Gen. Rabba on 4.25, and below, Part III, A Generic Singular.   [4] Num. 15.37 ff.
[5] Bab. Qid. 18b; cf. Mekh. on Exod. 21.8.   [6] 16.8.

Another point, however, seems even more important. In the verse
where Boaz addresses Ruth as having come 'under the wings of God',[1]
the Aramaic version translates 'under the *ṭelal*—cover, shadow—of the
Shekhinah of his glory'. Even the Hebrew comments of the Rabbis
paraphrase 'under the shadow—*ṣel*—of God'; and R. Abin, of the early
4th cent., compares a line from Psalms, 'The children of men put their
trust under the shadow—*ṣel*—of thy wings.'[2]

No doubt there were Aramaic versions translating 'Spread thy wing'
by 'Spread the shadow of thy wing' or simply 'Overshadow'. Several
of the texts quoted earlier on may be compared, for instance: Hebrew,
'He shall cover thee with his feathers, and under his wings shalt thou
trust', Targum, 'He shall overshadow thee with the shadow of his
Shekhinah, and under the shadow of his glory shalt thou trust.'[3] But
even if there were no such versions, the rendering 'Spread the shadow
of thy wing' or 'Overshadow' was the appropriate one as soon as the
scene was transferred to a higher sphere, of the kind to be found in
Luke. Quite possibly, the mention of 'the power' of God, the δύναμις,
is also connected with this elevation to a higher sphere. The Rabbis,
where they wish to avoid bluntness, resort to euphemisms like 'to lay
one's power (*reshuth*) over a woman.'[4]

To be sure, the Targum as we have it before us contains a different
rendering. But the way it deals with the text speaks in favour of rather
than against our thesis. It avoids not only the elevated 'Spread the
shadow of thy wing', but also the literal 'Spread thy wing'. What it
puts is 'Mayst thou take me to wife'. For this astonishing introduction
of homely—though certainly not shameless—speech there must be a
reason. It is in conflict both with the original Hebrew and with all those
Rabbinic references to the particular dignity of Ruth's mode of expression.[5]

The explanation is that the version before us is designed to counter
some dangerous interpretation of the text, an old one, older than the
Targum—the overshadowing by God. It does not matter whether it is
directed against a Jewish school or—more likely—against the Lukan
narrative itself. In either case it supports the view that the language of

[1] 2.12.   [2] Ps. 36.7; see Ruth Rabba on 2.12.
[3] Ps. 91.4.   [4] Jerus. Targ. Deut. 21.14.
[5] True, the full translation of the Targum is 'May thy name be called over thine handmaid and mayst thou take me to wife.' But even the first half of this exclamation, based as
it is on Isa. 4.1, cannot be considered exceptionally refined.

the latter is influenced by this passage from Ruth. For if it is directed against a Jewish school, that is the one which has left traces in Luke; and if it is directed against the narrative itself, it is evidence that the public had no difficulty in detecting the allusion to Ruth.

If the original author of the narrative was familiar with Hebrew, he may, indeed, when using 'to overshadow', have found an additional attraction in a possible pun: one created in the shadow, *beṣel*, of God might be declared to be created in the image, *beṣelem*, of God.[1] It is not, however, very likely that this pun plays a part, since there is nothing else in the annunciation that would suggest the idea of Jesus as the Second Adam; and the passage from the Book of Ruth is quite sufficient to explain the choice of verb.

It only remains to add that Mary's words, 'Behold the handmaid of the Lord',[2] are still from the same source. 'I am Ruth thine handmaid; spread therefore thy wing over thine handmaid', says Ruth to Boaz. This designation of Mary, which has inspired so many wonderful prayers and poems of the Middle Ages, has its ultimate origin in the Book of Ruth.

B. The Feeding of the Multitude

In the narrative of the feeding of the multitude,[3] it is the Messianic, Christian community itself which experiences a miracle foreshadowed in the life of Ruth, while the role of Boaz is now taken over by Jesus. The motif, however, is treated very differently by the Synoptics and John; and it may be best to begin by a general comparison of their versions of the narrative. It will emerge that John has profoundly altered both the form and the substance of the feeding of the multitude as it appears in the Synoptics.

1. *Form*

First, for the question of form. Like them, he starts by putting a transition, 'Jesus went over the sea' etc.;[4] the situation, 'He saw a great company' etc.;[5] a dialogue introducing the need, the resources and a command of Jesus, 'Whence shall we buy bread?' etc., and 'Make the

---

[1] Cp. Gen. 1.27.   [2] 1.38.
[3] Matt. 14.13 ff., 15.32 ff., Mark 6.31 ff., 8.1 ff., Luke 9.10 ff., John 6.1 ff.
[4] John 6.1-4. No proper transition in Matt. 15.32 ff., Mark 8.1 ff.   [5] John 6.5.

men sit down';[1] and the execution of the command, 'So the men sat down'.[2] But from this point onwards, he goes his own way.

In all the Synoptics, there follow (1) blessing and distribution, and (2) the miracle, namely—leaving out of account variations not here relevant—'They did all eat and were filled and took up of the fragments that remained twelve baskets full.'[3] There would be little justification, from the formal point of view, for a threefold division, (1) blessing and distribution, (2) reception of the food, (3) the miracle of the remains. To make such a division would be succumbing to the spell of John, where, as we shall see, it does apply.

In the Synoptics, formally, 'They did eat and were filled and took up' constitutes one unit, the miracle. That is to say, we have before us a simple miracle story, telling us how a multitude was feasted—and opulently feasted—with little. It is a necessary feature of a pre-rationing feast that one need not care about every morsel—'ut reliquiarum sit potius aliquid quam te hinc patiar non satiatum discedere', in Cicero's words[4]—and in Rabbinic discussion it is taken for granted that a banqueting-hall is strewn with fragments, small and big.[5] We must also remember that, in those times, pieces of bread served for spoons and forks: in the course of a good meal, many must have been discarded. The same argument, of course, holds good if we think of the fragments not as bits thrown away or dropped, but as a proper part of the meal with which the diners could not cope. Where a meal takes place in the open air, the distinction between food dropped and food not finished up would in any case be fluid.

No doubt even in the Synoptics, this feature of the remains is strongly emphasized, and expressed at greater length than the eating and being filled. We shall come back to this. For the moment, it ought to be realized that a clause does not become a separate item in a narrative pattern by mere emphasis or length. If we had to recount what happened to the poor widow saved by Elisha,[6] it would be: 'She sold the oil and paid her debt and she and her children lived of the rest.' Surely, that is one unit, though the last member is longer than the rest. It would

---

[1] John 6.5–10.
[2] John 6.10. No special mention of this in Matt. 14.19, 15.35, Mark 8.6.
[3] Matt. 14.19–21, 15.36–8, Mark 6.41–4, 8.6–9, Luke 9.16 f.
[4] Top. 5.25. Cp. also Athenaeus, Deipn. 1.13a: 'In Homer the feasters do not carry home what is left over but, being sated, leave it behind where the feast took place.'
[5] Bab. Ber. 52b.   [6] II Kings 4.7.

remain one unit even if we said: 'She sold the oil and paid her debt and she and her children lived of the rest until the day when they were gathered unto their people.' There is a line in the Song of Moses: 'I will pursue, I will overtake, I will divide the spoil.'[1] The treatment of this by Handel in *Israel in Egypt* is illuminating. The singer has repeatedly to sing only 'I will pursue, I will overtake, I will divide', omitting 'the spoil'. Then he has to end by an emphatic 'I will divide the spoil.' Yet the whole clause of three members forms one musical unit throughout.

The Synoptic 'They did eat and were filled and took up of the fragments twelve baskets' is no different from either of these cases. However, whether this is admitted or not, one thing seems indisputable: there is in the Synoptics a straightforward, unbroken sequence from eating and being filled to leaving a good deal lying about.

In John, item (1) also is blessing and distribution.[2] But the distribution itself constitutes a preliminary miracle, and thus a preliminary conclusion of the story. Each was given 'as much as they would'. The supernatural wealth of the host is revealed already at this stage. This is in none of the Synoptics. John's story could perfectly well end here, say, with a remark: 'And the people believed in him.'

The supreme miracle, however, is yet to come; and it consists, not in a miraculous feast, not in eating and being filled, but exclusively in bread remaining—or probably, if we may anticipate one of our conclusions, in all the bread remaining. The eating and being filled are indeed mentioned, but only incidentally, in subordinate clauses: 'when they were filled', and 'the fragments which remained unto them that had eaten'.[3] It is the least notable details of a story which we are used to seeing dismissed in this fashion: 'when they were filled', 'unto them that had eaten'. In contradistinction to the Synoptics, the gathering of the remains alone is reported in a main clause: 'They filled twelve baskets with the fragments which remained.'

Moreover, it is brought about by a fresh command of Jesus, to be met with in none of the Synoptics: 'He said, Gather up' etc. This command, it may be noted, again contains the key-word 'to remain': 'Gather up the fragments that remain.' The word is not absolutely indispensable here. Further, it is this miracle of the remains which is recognized by the people as the sign of the prophet 'that should come into the world'.[4] There is no equivalent in the Synoptics.

[1] Exod. 15.9.   [2] John 6.11.   [3] John 6.12 f.   [4] John 6.14.

If we give due weight to the formal position, we shall arrive at this contrast. In the Synoptics, we find (1) blessing and distribution, (2) the miracle, a feasting of many with little, one feature of the feast, the leaving over of ample fragments, being accorded some prominence. In John, we find (1) blessing and preliminary miracle, the plentiful distribution, 'as much as they would', (2) a fresh situation, 'when they were filled', (3) a fresh command of Jesus, 'Gather up', (4) the execution of the command resulting in the culminating miracle, the remains: 'Therefore they gathered up, and filled twelve baskets', and (5) recognition of the miracle and inference: 'The men, having seen the miracle, said, This is that prophet that should come.'

That John is secondary is shown, apart from other considerations some of which will be mentioned later on, by the very form. For one thing, his pattern is highly elaborate compared with the Synoptic. For another, it would have been impossible to refer to the eating and being filled in subordinate clauses, in passing only, had the matter never figured in main clauses, so that it was gradually taken for granted.

When the story was first told, they must have put it: 'And they did all eat, and were filled.' They could not then have put it: 'And when they were filled', as if it were the most natural thing in the world.[1] The statement that 'the Israelites went out of Egypt'[2] must have preceded the hymns depicting the wonders that were done 'when Israel went out of Egypt'.[3] It is John who deviates from the original form.

Why? What is the purpose of this change? There are two factors.

In the first place, as already remarked, the Synoptics, though keeping the eating, being filled and leaving over in one sequence, do stress the leaving over. Probably they did it because that was the visible, undeniable part of the miracle. There is a vulgar Jewish joke about a Jew who, pressed by a missionary, undertakes to accept half of each Christian tenet; for example, he will believe that Jesus fed a multitude on five loaves, but not that they got enough. Though the joke is modern, the attitude it expresses is as old as miracles. It would be met by 'pushing' the objective fact of the copious remains.

John goes a step further. He has only two objective facts as miracles, the plentiful distribution and the remains; and he reduces the subjective

---

[1] *The Virgin and the Gipsy* by D. H. Lawrence opens: 'When the vicar's wife went off with a young and penniless man . . .' But this is a rather sophisticated device, one purpose of which may well be to *épater le bourgeois*.

[2] E.g. Exod. 12.41.   [3] Ps. 114.1.

elements, the eating and being filled, to the rank of accompanying circumstances. In other words, he is pursuing to its extreme conclusion the course indicated by the Synoptics.

However, this is not the whole explanation. There is something else behind it.

In the second place, then, John has turned a simple miracle story into a parable. For the Synoptics, though there was little food, the multitude ate, were satisfied and left the place full of morsels or victuals unfinished. For John, though there was little food, each was given as much as he liked—a proof of inexhaustible wealth; and when the meal was over, plenty remained, in fact, as we shall suggest, he probably implies that there was as much bread as before if not more—a proof that here was imperishable bread. The exact meaning of this we need not here work out. No doubt the bread he has in mind is not only the true doctrine and life in general, but also, and maybe chiefly, the Eucharist.

In such a parable, the eating and being filled, the very miracle of the simple feasting story, can only be the occasion for the miracle of the remains. Moreover, on this basis, we can explain not only his negative alteration, the cutting down of the eating and being filled, but also his positive ones, the insertion of (a) a special command of Jesus to gather up the remains, and (b) the declaration of the people that this is the expected prophet. The demonstration of the imperishable bread deserves a full-dress introduction and statement of effect on the public.

2. Substance

So far we have argued mainly from form. But the two principal results are borne out by the contents and a comparison with other pericopes.

The one conclusion we reached was that John represents as miraculous only the visible facts of the plentiful distribution and the remains. This is supported by the following details.

The men who recognize Jesus as the prophet do so 'having seen' the miracle. That this is no accidental wording is clear from its subsequent repetition in a rebuke Jesus administers to the same people: 'Ye saw the miracles.'[1] The plural 'miracles' here includes Cana. The phrase 'to see the miracle', it should be observed, is frequent in John,[2] and a remark

---

[1] John 6.26.
[2] See, in addition to the verses quoted, 2.23, 4.48, 6.2, 6.30.

like 'this beginning of miracles did Jesus in Cana, and manifested forth, ἐφανέρωσεν, his glory'[1] also belongs here.

John's constant use of σημεῖον, 'sign', for 'miracle', now appears more purposeful. In the Synoptics, the term is employed only in depicting the attitude of the unbelieving who want visible evidence. To this, the passage about Herod who 'hoped to have seen some sign done by Jesus'[2] is not, as Bauer thinks,[3] an exception; we are here told about Herod's state of mind, the word 'sign' is put from his, not from Luke's point of view.

John, on the other hand, by using the word as the legitimate description of Jesus's deeds, impresses on his readers that visible proof was offered to any who had eyes to see. It follows that, when he concentrates on the objective facts in the narrative of the feeding of the multitude, he is not merely working out a line adumbrated in the Synoptic version before him—even the Synoptics, we saw, stressed the leaving over as the undeniable part of the miracle. He is also giving expression to a general, anti-Synoptic idea of his own, a different evaluation of 'signs'.

The other conclusion which we have to test is that John makes the miracle consist in the plentiful distribution, a proof of inexhaustible wealth, and above all, in the remains, a proof that here was imperishable bread.

Before enumerating some confirmatory points, however, one reservation may be stated. John nowhere says in so many words that he assigns a new meaning to the remains; and that they are not, as in the Synoptics, just a quantity of food left lying as it dropped or which could not be finished, but all the original bread again or even more. He nowhere says this expressly, he only gives strong hints. This is consistent with his manner on other occasions. But it is the reason why we do not put forward this matter as more than highly probable. What does appear certain is that, whether all the bread or only some of it is restored, John intends to convey the idea of incorruptibility.

Now for a list of points in support.

The earliest comment on the question is certainly the passage in the apocryphal Acts of John:[4] 'Our loaves were preserved entire', ὁλόκληροι ἐφυλάσσοντο. This is exactly the interpretation we are advocating.

---

[1] 2.11.   [2] Luke 23.8.   [3] *Das Johannesevangelium*, 2nd ed., 1925, p. 42.   [4] 93.

John alone gives us to understand that only bread remained, but no fish: 'They filled twelve baskets with the fragments of the loaves.' In the Synoptics, the fragments are indeterminate, anything that fell down or was too much to be eaten up; they are just the traces of a huge feast. In one version, we are actually informed that they included fish.[1] In John, the miracle concerns only the bread broken by Jesus, the heavenly food or Eucharist.

John alone mentions the exact number of the loaves a second time in describing the culminating miracle: 'They filled twelve baskets with the fragments of five barley loaves.' If twelve baskets can be filled with the remains of five loaves, then it is right to infer that the loaves are unconsumed if not more numerous than before the meal.

John alone uses $\sigma\upsilon\nu\acute{\alpha}\gamma\omega$ for 'to gather up the fragments'; it occurs both in the command and execution. This verb, however, may also mean 'to join together'. The Synoptics all use $\alpha\ddot{\iota}\rho\omega$, 'to take up'. When we consider that it is $\alpha\ddot{\iota}\rho\omega$ which corresponds to the Hebrew word common in such connections, natal,[2] John's choice of $\sigma\upsilon\nu\acute{\alpha}\gamma\omega$ does suggest an ulterior motive. The verb is used in several important sections, for example: 'And he that reapeth gathereth fruit unto life eternal.'[3] An additional reason of a rather different nature he may have had for putting $\sigma\upsilon\nu\acute{\alpha}\gamma\omega$ we shall mention when discussing the Rabbinic background of his version.

John alone states the purpose of the gathering up of the fragments 'that nothing be lost'. The notion is Rabbinic. A man had prepared a banquet for distinguished guests; when they did not turn up, he invited the poor, 'that it might not be lost'.[4] No doubt one of the objects the Rabbis pursued when insisting on the duty to collect the fragments of a meal from the floor was 'that they be not lost'. The Shammaites urged that the taking up must precede the cleaning of one's hands, since otherwise, as a result of water pouring down, 'one would lose' the victuals on the floor.[5] The prohibition of destroying a fruit-bearing tree in Deuteronomy was interpreted very widely. Some held that if a person lived on finer, rarer bread, refusing the ordinary, plentiful sort, he was transgressing that law.[6] However, John, in his usual, subtle fashion, makes the phrase far more significant. 'That

---

[1] Mark 6.43.   [2] Bab. Ber. 52b.   [3] John 4.36.
[4] Pal. San. 23c; see Strack-B., vol. 2, 1924, p. 479.
[5] Bab. Ber. 52b. Superstition may also have played a part: see Bab. Hul. 105b and, for pagan circles, Athenaeus, Deipn. 4.149c.   [6] Deut. 20.19, Pal. Shab. 140b.

nothing be lost', with him, means 'that all the bread be there again'. It is noteworthy that the order is, not 'Gather the fragments that they be not lost', but 'Gather the fragments that nothing be lost.'

In John alone it is the disciples, not the people at large, who gather up. The difference, long recognized, can now be explained. In the Synoptics, the action is merely a characteristic part of the successful feast, on a level with eating and being filled. In John, it is the very sign shown to the people. It must be done by the disciples.

John assigns a conspicuous role to the word 'to remain'. In the Synoptics, it is not emphasized. We hear of 'the taking up of the fragments that remained'; and one version—the same which expressly includes fish among the fragments—simply speaks of 'the fragments', without adding 'that remained'.[1] John has it in the order to the disciples, which, as we saw, is not known to the Synoptics: 'Gather the fragments that remain, that nothing be lost.' The word is here not only superfluous but also somewhat unnatural—unless a deeper sense is connected with it. He also has it in the verse saying that the fragments were gathered. But instead of the Synoptic 'fragments that remained', he puts: 'fragments which remained unto them that had eaten'. In the Synoptics, 'that remained' adds little to the sense; the Johannine 'which remained unto them that had eaten' is too heavy, too full, to be overlooked. The verb περισσεύω means 'to remain' in the sense of 'to remain over after use of the rest'. On this occasion, John suggests, the people received incorruptible bread, with the paradoxical result that the remains equalled or maybe exceeded the whole. Nothing was found lost, that is, after the disciples had gathered 'what remained over unto them that had eaten', i.e. 'what remained over unto them despite, or even because of, their eating'.[2]

The subsequent censure of the crowd by Jesus[3] also is now fully intelligible. Jesus reproaches the people for coming, not because of the signs, i.e. Cana and the remains, but because of the eating and being filled. Had John been a form critic, he might have put it thus: 'Ye seek me not because of the main clauses, but because of the subordinate clauses.' In John's version of the narrative of the feeding, the handing out of the food 'as much as they would' and the gathering of the frag-

---

[1] Mark 6.43.
[2] According to Julius Paulus (quoted by Gellius, A.N. 1.22.9), περισσόν might signify either *quod supervacuum esset ac non necessarium* or *quod abundans nimis et affluens et exuberans.*
[3] John 6.26.

ments are described in main clauses, while the actual meal appears only in 'unto them that had eaten' and 'when they were filled'. At any rate, no sharper distinction than we find in this rebuke could be drawn between the eating and being filled, as inessential, and the remains, as the real sign. It sounds almost like an open attack on the Synoptics.

The following verse[1] greatly gains in significance: 'Labour not for the meat which perisheth, but for that which endureth', ἐργάζεσθε μὴ τὴν βρῶσιν τὴν ἀπολλυμένην ἀλλὰ τὴν βρῶσιν τὴν μένουσαν. This manifestly alludes to the gathering up of the fragments by the disciples ἵνα μήτι ἀπόληται, 'that nothing perish'. By that action they had demonstrated the incorruptibility of the Eucharist, and of the divine food in general.

The different verbs for 'to eat' and 'to be filled' which John uses in the narrative and Jesus's rebuke also suit the thesis we are submitting. In fact, they are another illustration of his extreme care and subtlety in verbal questions.

In the narrative,[2] he tells us about the miracle as he wishes it to be understood. So the Synoptic χορτάξω is replaced by πίμπλημι. The former, 'to make absolutely full', would stress the wrong, worldly aspect.[3] Similarly, φαγεῖν is replaced by βιβρώσκω. Both mean 'to eat'. But the latter, though not essentially more refined, is associated with βρῶσις, 'the true meat', in the same chapter[4] as well as similar contexts. On the other hand, both χορτάξω and φαγεῖν are kept in Jesus's censure, only a little further on:[5] 'Ye seek me because ye did eat, ἐφάγετε, of the loaves, and were filled, ἐχορτάσθητε.' Here where the attitude of the vulgar is depicted, the primitive Synoptic terminology is resumed. This, incidentally, is another conclusive piece of evidence that John knew the Synoptic version, and that his own is a development from it.

Of particular interest is the fact that John has treated the marriage at Cana in exactly the same manner as the feeding of the multitude.[6]

It is safe to assume that, though this incident is not represented in the Synoptics, some version of it was current prior to John: his artificial pattern clearly presupposes a simpler one, we might say one of a Synoptic character. Now what must have been the climax of the original story, the turning of water into wine and perhaps the resulting

---

[1] John 6.27. [2] John 6.12 f.
[3] Cp. Athenaeus, Deipn. 3.99e, where the refined word to use instead of χορτάξω is said to be κορέννυμι. [4] John 6.27. [5] John 6.26. [6] John 2.1 ff.

carousal of the party, hardly appear at all. We hear nothing of a carousal, and of the turning of water into wine only in a subordinate clause, in the verse telling how the butler tasted the water 'that was made wine';[1] as if it went without saying, as if such a thing happened every day. The point of John's miracle is no longer the providing a large company with wine though there had seemed to be only water, but the providing of superior wine. This alone occupies a main clause: 'When the ruler of the feast had tasted the water that was made wine, he saith, Thou hast kept the good wine until now.'[2]

Surely, the original story culminated in a sentence like: 'And the water was made wine and they bare it to the guests and they found it very good.' John concentrates exclusively on the quality, just as in the feeding of the multitude. That is the sign.

It may be added that the sign of the true wine, like that of the imperishable bread, is preceded by a second command and a note that this was performed. The first command was that the pots should be filled.[3] This corresponds to the order that the multitude should sit down. It is at this point that the original version must have put the ending: 'And the water was made wine' etc. John, however, inserts a fresh command, 'Draw out now and bear unto the ruler of the feast',[4] corresponding to 'Gather up' etc. There follows the remark 'And they bare', which corresponds to 'Therefore they gathered up'.

Further, as in the Johannine feeding of the multitude, the sign shown at Cana is followed by recognition and inference. 'This beginning of miracles did Jesus and manifested forth his glory, and his disciples believed on him' is an appendix very similar to 'The men, having seen the miracle that Jesus did, said, This is that prophet.'

But even the preliminary miracle is to be met with again. In the feeding of the multitude, inexhaustible wealth is suggested by each obtaining 'as much as they would'. At Cana, the servants filled those tremendous pots with water 'up to the brim'.[5]

There is yet another argument for our view: in several respects, the way John has turned the feeding of the multitude from a simple miracle story into a parable is paralleled, or maybe foreshadowed, by an episode preserved in Matthew and Mark, where Jesus reminds the disciples of the feeding.[6]

[1] John 2.9. [2] John 2.9. [3] John 2.7.
[4] John 2.8. [5] John 2.7. [6] Matt. 16.5 ff., Mark 8.14 ff.

The miracle is here too treated as a parable, and though there are important disagreements with John, four similarities at least are worth observing. In the first place, no mention whatever is made of eating and being filled. The miracle consists in the remains alone—no matter precisely what significance may be attached to them in these passages. In the second place, it is definitely only bread which remains. The fish is entirely suppressed. In the third place, it is the disciples who are supposed to have taken up the fragments, not the people at large. And in the fourth place, the remains are thought of as a σημεῖον, a visible sign. This we may infer both from the position of the episode, which directly follows a demand by the Pharisees of concrete evidence, of a σημεῖον,[1] and from the fact that the disciples themselves are represented as of little faith. That, in John, visible proof is designed not only for those of little faith but for any who can see, we had occasion to point out before; here we have before us an example of a disagreement.

3. Old Testament and Rabbinic roots

It is time to advert to a few neglected points concerning the Jewish roots of the story.

The Synoptic pattern, as is well known, is highly reminiscent of the feeding of a multitude by Elisha;[2] and so is a good deal of the substance. But the actual miracle is worded in a different way. The men fed by Elisha 'did eat and left thereof'; the clause has two members. The Synoptics write: 'They did all eat and were filled and took up the fragments that remained.' This clause has three members; the reference to being filled is not to be found in the Old Testament narrative. It is surprising that the Old Testament model for the Synoptic version has never been discovered. It is a verse from Ruth:[3] 'And Boaz reached her parched corn, and she did eat and was filled and left thereof.'

Three things ought to be remembered. In the first place, for the Rabbis, Ruth was one of the outstanding converts. A special law authorizing the reception into Judaism of Moabite women had been enacted for her sake—at least, so the Rabbis taught.[4] What is more, in the very section which ends in her being given to eat by Boaz, he invokes on her the blessing of God, 'under whose wings thou art come to trust'.[5] This blessing is the Biblical basis for all the Rabbinic expressions

---

[1] Matt. 16.1 ff., Mark 8.11 ff.   [2] II Kings 4.42 ff.
[3] 2.14.   [4] Pal. Yeb. 9c.   [5] 2.12.

representing conversion as a coming under the wings of the Shekhinah or the like.

In the second place, Ruth was an ancestress of David and thus of the Messiah.

In the third place, the particular passage in question was interpreted by the Rabbis in a way that must have rendered it a most apt Old Testament testimonial.

For example, 'She did eat—in this world, and was filled—for the days of the Messiah, and left thereof—for the Age to Come.'[1] Or the three blessed periods are three glorious reigns of descendants:[2] 'She did eat—in the days of David, and was filled—in the days of Solomon, and left thereof—in the days of Hezekiah'; or again, 'She did eat—in the days of David and Solomon, and was filled—in the days of Hezekiah, and left thereof—in the days of Rabbi Judah.' Rabbi Judah the Prince belonged to the house of David. No doubt the third king in such schemes would often be the Messiah.

Occasionally, Ruth is taken as directly standing for one or the other of her descendants, and Boaz for God.[3] Thus where she stands for David, we find this exegesis: 'And Boaz said unto her, At mealtime come thou hither—this refers to God calling David to the kingdom; and eat of the bread—this refers to the bread of the kingdom; and dip thy morsel in the vinegar—this refers to the sufferings, *yissurin*, of David; and she sat beside the reapers—this refers to David's temporary loss of the kingdom through Absalom's revolt; and he reached her parched corn—this refers to the kingdom being given him again; and she did eat and was filled and left thereof—this means David eating in this world, his eating for the days of the Messiah and his eating for the Age to Come.' Needless to say, all these equations are supported by proof-texts, in the usual Rabbinic fashion.

Ruth may even represent her last descendant, the Messiah, Boaz again standing for God: 'And Boaz said unto her, At mealtime come thou hither—this means, Approach to the kingdom—and eat of the bread—this means the bread of the kingdom—and dip thy morsel in the vinegar—this means the sufferings, *yissurin*, as it is said,[4] But he was wounded for our transgressions—and she sat beside the reapers—this means, his kingdom will be turned aside from him for a while, as it is

[1] Bab. Shab. 113b.
[3] Ruth Rabba on 2.14, Yal. *ad loc.*
[2] Bab. Shab. 113b.
[4] Isa. 53.5.

said,[1] For I will gather all nations against Jerusalem to battle and the city shall be taken—and he reached her parched corn—this means, the kingdom will return to him, as it is said,[2] And he shall smite the earth with the rod of his mouth.' Presumably in the eyes of the author who makes Ruth stand for the Messiah, 'she did eat' etc., would just indicate the rich Messianic feast.

However much or little weight we may attach to any one of these Rabbinic utterances, there is no doubt that the text figures prominently in Messianic speculation. As for the date, one of the interpretations quoted is definitely Tannaitic, of the period prior to A.D. 200.[3] Moreover, R. Johanan or Jonathan of the 3rd cent.,[4] when lecturing on the verse under notice, was able to enumerate ten different allegorical interpretations of the kind adduced. Since we must allow a considerable time for the growth of such a number, we are brought fairly near the New Testament era.

One more interpretation taking a different line deserves attention.[5] The feeding of Ruth was declared miraculous because, it was held, she received little and yet it turned out more than enough. The Hebrew for 'parched corn', qali, was explained as qalil, 'slight'; and the passage 'he reached her parched corn' was understood in the sense 'he reached her little only'. The conclusion was drawn that, since she 'did eat and was filled and left thereof', a special blessing must either have attached to his hand or have been at work within her, and it was decided that the latter was the case. The date of this statement is about A.D. 300, but in all probability there were earlier, similar ones.

In the narrative of the feeding of the multitude, then, a meal prepared for Ruth by her redeemer, Boaz, is conceived as an adumbration of one prepared for the Messianic community by Jesus. Once this relation is recognized, several features of the Johannine version take on an increased significance.

John alone specifies the nature of the bread as barley bread; in fact he does so twice.[6] This may well be due, not only to the influence of the story of Elisha, who fed a hundred men with twenty loaves of barley,[7] but also to that of the Book of Ruth, where barley is mentioned quite

---

[1] Zech. 14.2.   [2] Isa. 11.4.
[3] Bab. Shab. 113b: 'She did eat for this world, and was filled for the days of the Messiah, and left thereof for the Age to Come.'
[4] Johanan figures in Ruth Rabba, Jonathan in Yalqut.
[5] Ruth Rabba on 2.14.   [6] 6.9, 13.   [7] II Kings 4.42.

frequently—from the moment that Ruth and her mother-in-law 'came to Beth-lehem in the beginning of barley harvest'.[1] After all, the barley in Ruth occasionally becomes a Messianic symbol in Rabbinic interpretation. When Ruth left Boaz after her nocturnal visit, he gave her six measures of barley.[2] The Midrash considers it the marriage price. But as it looks a somewhat poor one, it is taken as alluding to six descendants, namely: David, Hezekiah, Josiah, Hananiah, Mishael, Azariah, Daniel and the Messiah. (Note that these are eight, not six. But there is no need to worry. The three friends of Daniel count as one: they are given only one proof-text together.)

The re-interpretation by John of the remains as equalling or exceeding the original amount may also be based on an artificial exegesis of a phrase common to both the story of Elisha and that of Ruth. In both, as in the Synoptics, there is an abundant meal, and some food is left over. Incidentally, in these Old Testament narratives, the remains are clearly not pieces dropped or thrown on the ground, but that part of the meal which cannot be finished. John's idea that, though a feast has taken place, the entire bread is again in existence may derive from an over-literal reading of the texts: the men fed by Elisha 'did eat and left',[3] and Ruth 'did eat and was filled and left'.

The meaning is, of course, 'and left thereof'; and the current English version in one case at least[4] adds 'thereof' in italics. But John may have felt justified in interpreting more strictly, 'and they did eat, *scil.* the food, and left, *scil.* the food', or 'and she did eat, *scil.* the food, and was filled, *scil.* with the food, and left, *scil.* the food'—all the food, not only some. From the strict grammatical point of view, it was possible to supply as object the entire bread; and it was possible whether he proceeded from the Hebrew, *wayyo'khelu wayyothiru, watto'khal wattiśba' wattothar*, or from the Greek καὶ ἔφαγον καὶ κατέλιπον, καὶ ἔφαγε καὶ ἐνεπλήσθη καὶ κατέλιπε.

We have already referred to John's substitution of συνάγω, 'to gather the fragments', for the Synoptic αἴρω, 'to take them up'. But to the reason we have given, another may now be added. In Ruth, the clause 'and she did eat and was filled and left' is followed by a verse beginning 'and she rose to glean'.[5] The Hebrew verb 'to glean' is often represented by συνάγω in the LXX; and though the LXX in this passage has

---

[1] 1.22.
[2] 3.15.
[3] II Kings 4.44, Ruth 2.14.
[4] II Kings 4.44.
[5] 2.15.

E

συλλέγω, it has συνάγω elsewhere in the Book of Ruth.[1] John may have read 'and she did eat and was filled and left and rose to gather' —'to gather' in the sense of 'to gather the fragments of the meal'. And he introduced this term into the feeding of the multitude. There is unexpected support for this assumption. In the Hebrew Bible, though 'she left' is marked by a Silluq, as the last word of the verse, it is pointed, not with a Qameṣ, but with a Pataḥ. This strongly suggests that, for one school of Rabbis, the verse did not end here but included the words 'and she rose to glean'. The next verse began by: 'And Boaz commanded his young men'. Presumably John started from this tradition, according to which 'and she did eat and was filled and left and rose to glean' belonged together.

A borrowing from Ruth may account for the strange use of ἐργάζομαι in: 'Labour, ἐργάζεσθε, for that meat which endureth. Then said they unto him, What shall we do that we might work the works of God, ἵνα ἐργαζώμεθα τὰ ἔργα τοῦ θεοῦ. Jesus answered, This is the work, τὸ ἔργον, of God, that ye believe on him whom he hath sent.'[2]

In the same section where the feeding of Ruth is described, we are told of the blessing Boaz pronounces on her:[3] 'The Lord recompense thy work, and a full reward be given thee of the Lord God of Israel, under whose wings thou art come to trust.' The verse, we saw, furnished the Rabbis with the technical term for 'conversion'. The point here to be made is that the Rabbis emphasize[4] that Ruth's 'work' consisted in seeking refuge under the wings of God. The LXX has ἐργασία for this 'work'. John's application of the word sounds like an echo.

This is not to deny that he may be thinking also of the consecration of the Levites,[5] 'that they may execute the service of the Lord', ὥστε ἐργάζεσθαι τὰ ἔργα κυρίου. Many of John's references to the Old Testament are 'multivalent', deliberately suggestive of several passages.[6]

However, these are matters of detail. What is of greater interest is that with Ruth as the starting-point, the evolution of the pattern of the narrative becomes quite clear. It is, in fact, a strikingly consistent evolution.

In Ruth, we find the plain 'and she did eat and was filled and left

---

[1] 2.2, 7.   [2] John 6.27 ff.   [3] Ruth 2.12.   [4] Ruth Rabba on 2.12.
[5] Num. 8.11. Perhaps even of Joshua 22.27, though the LXX as we know it has here λατρεύειν λατρείαν κυρίου.
[6] For the background of this feature, see C. K. Barrett, 'The Old Testament in the Fourth Gospel', *Journal of Theological Studies*, 48, 1947, pp. 155 ff.

thereof'. Even here, there is a slight emphasis on the leaving over, for the line is obviously ascending: eating—being filled—leaving over. The narrative itself confirms the importance of the latter: a few verses further on[1] we hear that she took the remains home for her mother-in-law.

Just so, in the chapter about a miraculous feast provided by Elisha, we may paraphrase:[2] 'and they not only ate but even left thereof'. God does not stint his guests. In the narrative of Elisha and the widow's oil cruet too the sufficiency of the divine gift for more than the immediate need is accentuated:[3] 'Sell the oil and pay thy debt and live thou and thy children of the rest.'

In the Rabbinic comments, the position is unchanged. In form, the three members remain equal, though, in thought, there is always a rise from the first to the third; for example, this world—the days of the Messiah—the Age to Come.

The Synoptics, while still preserving an unbroken sequence, have lengthened the third member and rendered it more colourful, more concrete and detailed: 'and they did eat and were filled and took up of the fragments that remained twelve baskets full'. We are well on the way to a fundamental change in form. The limit is reached within which a unit can be kept intact when one of its parts acquires excessive weight.

John takes the final step. He breaks off the third member and makes of it a separate unit, provided with its own introduction, i.e. fresh situation and command, and its own conclusion, i.e. recognition of the miracle.

In conclusion, the question may be raised whether there was a stage when the feeding of the multitude was not associated with that of Ruth. Possibly there was, and it is represented by that version—in Mark—which, on the one hand, expressly includes fish among the fragments and, on the other, does not introduce the notion 'to remain', περισσεύω.[4] This notion may have been taken over from Ruth after the narrative as a whole was already established.

True, the LXX in Ruth uses καταλείπω. But, first, the LXX frequently translates the Hebrew verb by some form of περισσεύω or a derivative. Secondly, there are cases where one MS. employs the former root and another the latter.[5] Thirdly, how close the two are may also be seen from phrases like τὸ περισσὸν τὸ καταλειφθέν.[6]

---

[1] 2.18.   [2] II Kings 4.44.   [3] II Kings 4.7.   [4] Mark 6.42 f.
[5] Judges 21.16, τοῖς ἐπιλοίποις and τοῖς περισσοῖς.
[6] II Kings 25.11; cp. Judges 21.7.

PART II

LEGISLATIVE AND NARRATIVE FORMS

I

'Ye Have Heard—But I Say Unto You'

IN inspecting a few Rabbinic legal and narrative forms in the New Testament, we may perhaps first take a form of law which, in the course of its transfer to the different setting, underwent a considerable change. Yet for a true understanding of the New Testament section containing it, it is essential to take account of its original use and significance.

In Matthew, in the sermon on the mount, we find a series of injunctions intended to illustrate the position of Jesus as upholder, not destroyer, of the Law.[1] They all more or less follow this pattern: 'Ye have heard that it was said by them of old time, Thou shalt not kill. But I say unto you, That whosoever is angry with his brother shall be in danger of the judgment.'

This form falls into two parts. The first gives a Scriptural rule narrowly interpreted, the second a wider demand made by Jesus. The first, in Hebrew, would open: *shema'tem ma shenne'emar*. The translation 'Ye have heard' is not technical enough. In Rabbinic discussion, *shome'a 'ani*, 'I hear', 'I understand', or rather, 'I might understand', introduces an interpretation of Scripture which, though conceivable, yet must be rejected. For example, an old Midrashic exposition of the fifth commandment begins thus:[2] 'Honour thy father and thy mother. I might understand, *shome'a 'ani*, Honour them with words only.' The Midrash goes on to refute this proposition and to show that the commandment refers not only to respectful speech but also to the duty of maintaining your parents. Quite often, as in this instance, the interpretation introduced by 'I hear', 'I might understand', is primitive, narrow, literal, compared with that accepted in its stead.

In fact, how closely the root 'to hear', 'to understand', is associated with literal interpretation may be seen from the two early technical

[1] 5.21 ff.   [2] Mekh. on Exod. 20.12.

terms for 'literal meaning': *shamu'a* and *mishma'*, 'that which is heard'. Furthermore, *hashshome'a*, 'he who hears', is used in the sense of 'he who sticks to the superficial, literal meaning of Scripture' in the hermeneutic rule[1] according to which 'a general summary (like the notice concerning man's creation in the first chapter of Genesis) may be followed by detailed facts (the story of man's creation in the second chapter) which are merely a repetition giving more particulars; he who hears—i.e. he who takes Scripture literally—will form the erroneous belief that the second account refers to different facts, but in reality it is merely a repetition with more particulars'.

There is good reason, then, for translating the first part of the Matthean form by: 'Ye have literally understood', or 'Ye might understand literally'. 'Ye have literally understood what was said by them of old time, Thou shalt not kill.'

It may be observed that, on this basis, an old puzzle can at once be solved. Twice in the sermon on the mount the words, 'Ye have heard' lead up to a quotation not really to be found in the Old Testament: 'Ye have heard, Thou shalt not kill, and (only) he who shall kill shall be in danger of the judgment', and 'Ye have heard, Thou shalt love thy neighbour and hate thine enemy.'[2] The clauses 'and only he who kills shall be in danger of the judgment', and 'thou shalt hate thine enemy', do not occur in the Pentateuch at all. However, as soon as we proceed from the translation 'Ye have literally understood', the additions cease to be troublesome. 'To understand' does not necessarily introduce a strict quotation; the quotation may be provided with a comment. The Rabbis remark on the fifth commandment: 'I hear, I might understand, Honour with words only.' Just so, Matthew writes: 'Ye have literally understood, Thou shalt not kill and only he who kills shall be in danger of the judgment.' There is here neither error nor falsification. In modern writing, we should mark off the comment by a phrase like *scilicet*. That was not necessary where the force of 'to hear' was properly appreciated.

As for the second part, 'But I say unto you', what is its nearest Rabbinic equivalent? The question may be put in a different way: what is the form employed by the Rabbis when they repudiate those interpretations introduced by 'I might understand'? Those interpretations are always refuted by some recognized argument. Mostly this is

---

[1] The 13th of Eliezer ben Jose Ha-gelili's 32.
[2] 5.21, referring to Exod. 21.13, Deut. 5.17, and 5.43, referring to Lev. 19.18.

another text from Scripture. Thus the primitive interpretation of the fifth commandment is disproved by a passage from Proverbs:[1] 'Honour thy father and thy mother. I might understand, Honour them with words only. But there is a teaching in what another verse says (Proverbs), Honour the Lord with thy substance. So honouring means honouring with food, drink and clean garments.' There need not, however, be recourse to another text. The argument against the objectionable, narrow interpretation may consist in a logical deduction—an inference *a minori ad maius* or the like—and, significantly, the usual Hebrew verb for establishing such a deduction is *'amar*, 'to say'.

Here is an illustration, a comment by R. Judah the Prince on the notice: 'And the Lord came down upon mount Sinai.'[2] He explains: 'I might hear this as it is heard, I might understand this according to its literal meaning, *shome'a 'ani kishemu'o*. But thou must say, *'amarta*: If the sun, one of the many servants of God, may remain in its place and nevertheless be effective beyond it, how much more He by whose word the world came into being.'

Evidently, there is a Rabbinic form expressing a contrast between the 'hearing', the 'literal understanding', of a rule and what we must 'say' it actually signifies. Here lies the source of Matthew's pattern.

At this point, however, the real problem for form criticism only begins. There are striking differences between the Rabbinic form and the Matthean. If our method is correct, they must reflect the differences in setting; or in other words, any deviations in Matthew from the Rabbinic model must be explicable by his changed premises and objects. This is indeed the case. Matthew has adapted an academic form to his peculiar legislative purposes.

In the Rabbinic form, it is the cautious, scholarly, devout interpreter of holy writ who speaks and is spoken to. 'I might understand literally' —'I', namely, the scholar investigating the text. 'But thou must say'— 'thou', namely, again, a scholar investigating, a fellow-scholar addressed in an imaginary debate. To put it differently, the expounder begins by considering a possibility ('I might understand God's descent on mount Sinai literally') and goes on to refute it as if it had been submitted to him by a colleague in the course of discussion ('But thou must say, there are grounds for not taking it in this way').

The setting in life is academic, dialectic exegesis, and this comes out

[1] 3.9.   [2] Mekh. on Exod. 19.20.

in a further suggestive feature. The refutation, opening by 'But thou must say', does not simply contradict the original proposition; it reasons, it shows why another must be substituted. Judah the Prince, when rejecting the literal interpretation of 'And the Lord came down on mount Sinai', does not simply declare: 'I might understand this literally. But thou must say, the Lord did not come down and his activity reached mount Sinai though he remained in his place.' He gives an argument: 'But thou must say, If the sun, a servant of the Lord, can remain in its place and yet produce effects elsewhere, how much more the Lord himself.'

In the Matthean form, little remains of this atmosphere of self-contained, orderly exposition. Instead of 'I might understand literally', we find 'Ye have understood literally' or 'Ye might understand literally'. The interpretation to be discarded is not a possibility turned over in his mind by an exact scholar. It is put into the mouth of a public as yet blind or even antagonistic. Then, the reply also is far from academic in tone. 'But I say unto you' replaces the Rabbinic 'But thou must say'. Note not only the first person, 'I say', but also the 'unto you', not present in the Rabbinic form. The tone is not academic but final, prophetic, maybe somewhat defiant. Nor is there any reasoning. The correct attitude is simply stated: 'But I say unto you, That whosoever is angry with his brother shall be in danger of the judgment', with no argument *a minori ad maius* or the like.

The point is that, in Matthew, we have before us, not a scholarly working out by some Rabbis of a progressive interpretation as against a conceivable narrow one, but a laying down by Jesus, supreme authority, of the proper demand as against a view, be it held by friends or enemies, which would still take the exact words of the Scriptural precept as a standard of conduct. Jesus, supreme authority, lays down the proper demand: this accounts for 'But I say unto you, That whosoever is angry' etc. The demand is opposed to a view held among those addressed which would still take the exact words of a precept as basis: this accounts for 'Ye have understood literally what was said' etc. The setting in life of the Rabbinic form is dialectic exposition of the Law; that of the Matthean is proclamation of the true Law. All differences are intelligible once we are clear as to these settings.

But, it might be asked, is it not more likely, despite all this, or because of it, that Matthew's pattern does not come direct from the other? Is not the gulf between mere exposition and authoritative legislation too great to allow us to assume an intimate connection? And may it not be that Matthew created his pattern independently, though indeed using Rabbinic terms?

The answer is that the gulf is very much smaller than we have so far made it to appear. On the one hand, the Rabbinic form is considerably less detached, less academic, than one might think at first sight. The first part, 'I might understand literally', in many if not most cases puts an interpretation which is not only theoretically conceivable, but which is actually maintained somewhere, be it by an older school or a contemporary, rival school or—occasionally—a heretical sect. We have repeatedly quoted Judah the Prince's comment on 'And the Lord came down on Sinai', which opens: 'I might understand this literally'. The paragraph immediately preceding this in the Midrash shows that R. Akiba did adhere to a rather literal explanation. Judah the Prince was combating Akiba's view. The phrase 'I might understand literally', therefore, is not quite so speculative and peaceful as it sounds. It is not, in other words, quite so far removed from 'Ye have understood literally'.

This is confirmed by the second part of the Rabbinic form, 'But thou must say' and so on. Here an imaginary fellow-scholar is addressed and instructed. The interpretation to be excluded, that is, is represented as favoured by an opponent—a scholarly, friendly opponent, it is true, but still a 'thou' in need of guidance.

Moreover, this second part, 'But thou must say' and so on, though it advances a recognized logical justification for replacing the literal meaning by a freer, yet in effect does substitute a new, freer meaning. Nor were the religious leaders of the time unaware that exegesis might be tantamount to legislation. That was precisely the reason why Samaritans and Sadducees refused to accept the results produced in this way as binding. We may also recall the parable, preserved in the Talmud itself,[1] of Moses unable to follow a discussion in R. Akiba's academy—so remote is the Law as expounded by Akiba and his disciples from the Law Moses thought he was giving. Clearly, 'But thou must say' contains a strong element of discretionary power. The seed is there which, given certain conditions, might develop into the absolute 'But I say unto you'.

[1] Bab. Men. 29b.

On the other hand, the Matthean form is far milder, less revolutionary, than one might incline to believe. As we mentioned at the beginning, these declarations, 'Ye have heard—But I say unto you', are intended to prove Jesus the Law's upholder, not destroyer. The relationship between the two members of the form is not one of pure contrast; the demand that you must not be angry with your brother is not thought of as utterly irreconcilable with the prohibition of killing. On the contrary, wider and deeper though it may be, it is thought of as, in a sense, resulting from and certainly including the old rule, it is the revelation of a fuller meaning for a new age. The second member unfolds rather than sweeps away the first. That authoritative 'But I say unto you' has in it a good deal of the reasoning 'But thou must say'.

Indeed, it is only when this factor is properly realized that a familiar, serious difficulty disappears. The injunctions under notice, we are expressly informed, are designed as illustrations of 'Think not that I am come to destroy' and so on. Yet, on a superficial reading, they appear to illustrate the very opposite: 'Ye have heard the Law saying this— But I say something different.' It is only by bearing in mind the descent of this pattern from the Rabbinic one outlined that we can solve the problem and understand Matthew's meaning. There is no conflict. Tertullian is right in describing the new Law as *plenius, perfectius, eruditius, instructius* than the old; but he does not describe it as opposed to old.[1] Matthew's is a Rabbinic gospel.

Three points may be added in support of our thesis. First, Paul, in Romans, also emphasizes that his doctrine means not destroying but upholding the Law.[2] And he also at once proceeds to demonstrate this by a typically Rabbinic use of some texts from Scripture. He does not, indeed, employ the antithesis 'I might understand literally—But thou must say', but still he argues in a good, technical, Rabbinic manner. The affinity with Matthew is striking.

Secondly, in the announcement 'I am not come to destroy the Law but to fulfil it', the Hebrew behind 'to fulfil' is *qiyyem*, 'to uphold'.[3] It would lead too far afield here to substantiate this proposition, but let us take it as established. One nuance of *qiyyem* which seems to play a part in this passage is 'to uphold Scripture' in the technical sense of 'to show that the text is in agreement with your teaching'. This is a frequent

---

[1] Apol. 45.3.   [2] 3 and 4; see above all 3.31 ff.
[3] See Guillaume, 'The Midrash in the Gospels', *Expository Times*, 37, 1926, 394 ff.

application of the verb, based on the idea that the test of any teaching you propound is whether, proceeding from it, you can give full effect to, 'uphold', every word of the Law. For instance, R. Pappias asserted that God, when remarking 'The man is become as one of us', likened man to the angels.[1] Akiba vehemently rejected this interpretation: 'That is enough, Pappias.' Pappias retorted: 'But how then doest thou uphold, *qiyyem*, this verse?' Whereupon Akiba explained that it meant 'The man has gone one of the two ways, the evil one, of his own choice.' The Hebrew *mimmennu* may signify 'of us' or 'of himself', and Akiba prefers the latter sense: 'The man is become as one (*scil.* of the two ways) of himself (*scil.* of his own choice).' This is a typical example of one disputant—in this case Pappias—defying another—Akiba—to prove that, with his view, he can 'uphold' Scripture. Sometimes a Rabbi will not wait for the challenge but call on himself in this way. That is to say, having advanced a doctrine, he will immediately himself put the question, 'But how do I uphold this or that text?' and conclude by smoothing away the difficulty.[2] Often the 'upholding' is done by showing that, though at first blush one might 'hear', 'understand', a text in a certain manner, in reality its import is different.[3] Surely, structures like these constitute the background of the Matthean pattern taken together with the heading 'I am not come to destroy the Law but to uphold it.' This heading takes up a challenge—no matter from what side we assume that it came—and what follows is legislation, yet defence and argument as well.

Thirdly, when we consider the arrangement of this section of Matthew as a whole, we find a general principle put at the head, 'I am not come to destroy, Your righteousness shall exceed that of the Pharisees', and the rest consists of illustrations, all of one pattern, 'Ye have heard' and so forth. This sequence of principle and cases is very common in Rabbinic literature. We shall presently say a few words about it.

Before doing so, however, we must still add a note concerning the date of the antithesis 'I might hear, understand—but thou must say.' There can be no doubt that it goes back to the New Testament period. True, we have no direct evidence before R. Ishmael, in the first half of

---

[1] Gen. 3.22; see Mekh. on Exod. 14.29.
[2] E.g. Mekh. on Exod. 12.5, 6, 11, 34, 20.25.
[3] E.g. where Akiba 'upholds' Ps. 106.20; see Mekh. on Exod. 14.29.

the 2nd cent. But it is so well established by this time that it must be considerably older. This is not to deny that Matthew may have been familiar with an earlier and slightly different variant.

One point is worth mentioning. Ishmael and his school never say 'I might hear what is said by them of old time' or 'I might hear what is said', but merely 'I might hear'. When Schechter tentatively suggested a connection between Matthew's 'Ye have heard' and the Rabbinic 'I might hear',[1] it was the additional words in Matthew which caused Bacher to dismiss the idea.[2] But the probability is that, originally, the Rabbis also used a fuller version. The alternation in Matthew of 'what is said by them of old time' and 'what is said' is suggestive: when he wrote, there already was a shorter as well as a longer form. By Ishmael's time, the Rabbis had made a further abbreviation, saying simply 'I might hear'—no wonder, considering how very frequently they availed themselves of the phrase in their expositions.

[1] *Jewish Quarterly Review*, 10, 1898, p. 11, n. 3.
[2] *Älteste Terminologie der Jüdischen Schriftauslegung*, 1899, p. 190, n. 3.

II

Principle and Cases

LET us now turn to the arrangement of the section as a whole: the proclamation of a general principle, 'I am not come to destroy, Your righteousness shall exceed that of the scribes and Pharisees', followed by a series of illustrations, 'Ye have heard, thou shalt not kill, but I say unto you, that whosoever is angry with his brother shall be in danger of the judgment; Ye have heard, thou shalt not commit adultery, but I say unto you' and so on. It has been maintained that this form must be Greek. But there is no justification for this view.

In its simpler applications, the form is to be found even in the Old Testament. Nor is this surprising. The form presupposes a certain degree of systematization, but not an exceptionally high one. Once this stage is reached, lawgivers all over the world will find the arrangement convenient. The fifth of Alfred's Laws begins with a general proposition that every church has a right of sanctuary, and then follow details as to the meaning and limits of this.[1] No. 5 of the Laws of Canute runs in Robertson's rendering:[2] 'Concerning heathen practices, We earnestly forbid all heathen practices', and then follow details of such practices. Similarly, in Ecclesiastes,[3] there comes first the general principle: 'To every thing there is a season and a time to every purpose.' After this come the illustrations: 'A time to be born, and a time to die; a time to plant' and so on.

Or take a slightly less primitive example from Leviticus.[4] A general introduction, stating that you must not do as the Egyptians and Canaanites do, is followed by the detailed prohibitions of adultery, incest and the like. Admittedly, the introduction is later than the details. But this does not alter the fact that the author who, at some date, prefixed it intended the structure: general principle—particular cases.

---

[1] Attenborough, *The Laws of the Earliest English Kings,* 1922, pp. 66 f.
[2] *Laws of the Kings of England from Edmund,* 1925, p. 177.   [3] 3.1 ff.   [4] 18.1 ff.

Actually, had he repeated the idea governing his introduction in the code itself—and it may be assumed that though he did not repeat it expressly, it was in his mind all the time—we should get something not unlike the Matthean scheme: 'Do not as the Egyptians and Canaanites do. They commit adultery—you should not. They marry their sisters— you should not', etc.

In Rabbinic literature, we come across far more intricate applications of this form; moreover, it is clear that it is employed quite consciously. One chapter of the Mishnah begins:[1] 'If a man wounds another, he is liable on five counts, for injury, for pain, for healing, for loss of time, and for the indignity inflicted.' The text goes on to deal with each of these five points in detail. Another passage[2] opens with the general principle that 'If aught that conveys uncleanness by overshadowing is divided and brought into a house, R. Dosa ben Harkinas declares it clean while the Sages declare it unclean.' This principle is illustrated by a number of examples: 'If a man touches two pieces of carrion, each a half-olive's bulk', and so on. In all these cases, according to the principle prefixed, R. Dosa declares the person in question clean, the Sages declare him unclean. Again, the Mishnah enunciates the rule[3] that if a court (a Beth-din) gives a decision inconsistent with a minor, secondary precept only—say, with a mere detail concerning the observance of the Sabbath—it may be presumed to have acted from an innocent error. The implication is that a decision subverting a main institution of the Law—say, one denying any need to observe the Sabbath—must have sprung from wilful defiance. The rule is illustrated by a few decisions which, though they would be wrong, would not be regarded as deliberately wrong. And these examples are all framed in the same way: 'The Sabbath as such is regulated in the Law, but it is allowed to carry a burden on the Sabbath. Idolatry as such is regulated in the Law, but it is allowed to bow down before an idol' and so on.

The following case may be of special interest. One section of the Mishnah[4] begins thus: 'In these things the School of Hillel changed their opinion and taught according to the opinion of the School of Shammai.' To be sure, this is just a heading, not a principle. But this hardly makes any difference in the present connection. At any rate, the general heading is followed by some particular instances, which are just as lengthy as the particular illustrations in Matthew. In all cases the

[1] B.Q. 8.1.   [2] Ed. 3.1.   [3] Hor. 1.3b.   [4] Ed. 1.12.

original opinion of the School of Hillel is given, then the argument by which the Shammaites convinced their opponents, and the conclusion is always in the same words: 'The School of Hillel changed their opinion and taught according to the opinion of the School of Shammai.' That is, we get a veritable refrain. This structure reminds one very much of the sermon on the mount, with its general principle and elaborate yet systematically arranged illustrations.

Perhaps a brief consideration of Tannaitic terminology shows better than any amount of examples how conscious the Rabbis were of the distinction between principle and detail or illustration. It may suffice to adduce four terms.

The word *'abh*, literally 'father', 'ancestor', is used, in technical language, to denote a comprehensive notion; *toladha*, literally 'descendant', signifies a narrower notion falling under it. For instance, 'the pit' counts as one of the *'abhoth neziqin*, of the principles of causation of damage—the historical reason being that the opening of a pit into which a beast might fall is mentioned in a legal section of the Pentateuch.[1] Now if you leave broken glass lying about, thus causing damage, this would be a *toladha* of 'the pit', a particular instance falling under the principle.[2]

Again, the noun *guph*, literally 'body', is employed as meaning a fundamental principle of the Torah. The commandment to keep the Sabbath, for example, is considered a *guph*, as opposed to any detailed precept concerning the Sabbath, such as the prohibition of carrying a burden.[3] We have seen that a court giving an incorrect decision regarding a detail is presumed to have done so by mistake, whereas the abolition of a *guph*, according to the Mishnah, inevitably betrays a spirit of godlessness.

Of particular relevance is the term *kelal*, literally 'the universal', signifying a basic commandment of the Torah and opposed to *peraṭ*, 'the individual', which means a detailed rule. It is worth noting that, according to R. Ishmael, who taught in the first half of the 2nd cent., 'the basic commandments were made known to Moses at Sinai, but the details in the tabernacle'. (For Philo,[4] the Ten Commandments, given by God's own mouth, were the principles of all law, κεφάλαια νόμων, summarizing the special provisions, ἐν μέρει διατάγματα, which latter were given through Moses.) This view was combated by Akiba, for

[1] Exod. 21.33 f.   [2] Mish. B.Q. 1.1, 3.1.   [3] Hor. 1.3.   [4] Decal. 18 f., Leg. Spec. 1.1.1.

F

whom all rules, general or detailed, went back to Sinai.[1] The importance of Ishmael's utterance, for our purposes, lies in the fact that, in his eyes at any rate, the form here discussed—first general principle, then particular rules—was good enough to have been the form chosen by God when he gave Moses the Law. God, in Ishmael's opinion, proclaimed the fundamental principles first, at mount Sinai, and only later the detailed provisions.

A similar distinction between *kelal* and *peraṭ*, incidentally, was applied by the Rabbis to the narrative portions of the Bible. The two accounts of man's creation in Genesis, for example, were explained by means of a hermeneutic rule, already mentioned:[2] Scripture sometimes 'starts by giving a general summary of an event—*kelal*, the first, brief account of man's creation—and then goes on to relate facts—the second, longer account—which are merely a detailed description—*peraṭ*—of the same thing'.

Finally, the interrogative adverb *keṣadh*, 'how?' ought to be mentioned. It is frequently to be met with as introducing the illustrations of a general principle. In three of the examples we have adduced, this adverb is inserted between the principle and its illustrations.[3] For instance, there is the principle that if a court gives a decision contrary to a specific provision only, it need not be regarded as having wilfully defied the Law. At this point the question *keṣadh* comes: 'How?', 'What exactly does this mean?' Whereupon the illustrations follow to which we have already referred—the decision that you may carry a burden on the Sabbath, that you may bow down before an idol, or the like. To give an idea of the way in which this adverb is employed, we may perhaps say that in Matthew, if it were translated into the language of Mishnic discussion, we might well put *keṣadh* between the heading and the rest: 'Your righteousness shall exceed that of the scribes. How?, *keṣadh*? Ye have heard', and so on.

The upshot seems to be that it is quite unnecessary to look for a Greek background to the Matthean arrangement. The evidence strongly suggests that it goes back to a thoroughly Jewish milieu.

[1] Bab. Hag. 6a.
[2] Above, in discussing 'Ye have heard—but I say unto you'.
[3] B.Q. 8.1, Ed. 3.1, Hor. 1.3b.

III

Precept and Example

THE Rabbis marked off *halakha*, matters of law, from *haggadha*, matters which, though of religious importance, do not affect the law. The exegesis of a Scriptural passage would proceed on different lines according as it was undertaken with a view to the former or the latter. This division has left many marks on the New Testament. One interesting aspect is its relation to the question whether precept or example should be a man's guide. Let us look at a few pericopes from this angle.

A. THE SABBATH

The first dispute about the Sabbath is caused by the disciples of Jesus plucking corn. According to Mark and Luke,[1] Jesus in defence refers to David and his band who, as they felt hungry, ate the showbread reserved for the priests. According to Matthew,[2] Jesus, in addition to this argument, mentions the priests breaking the Sabbath for the sake of the temple service—for instance, by slaughtering animals for sacrifice or by burning the sheaf of firstfruits—and remarks that something greater than the temple is now concerned. (The Pharisees held that the sheaf must be offered on the second day of Passover even if it falls on a Sabbath. The reaping in this case involves additional ceremony: the person about to cut it asks three times whether he may do the act 'on this Sabbath' and is told three times that he may.[3] Matthew's readers, then, knew of at least one occasion on which the plucking of corn on a Sabbath was permissible and even enjoined.)

It is agreed on all hands that the argument given by Matthew alone, and not by Mark and Luke, is an addition. We may leave open the question whether or not the addition is authentic in the sense that it was at one time introduced by Jesus himself. Nor, for that matter, need we

---

[1] Mark 2.23 ff., Luke 6.1 ff.   [2] 12.1 ff.   [3] Mish. Men. 10.3, 9.

decide whether or not the original argument, to be found in all three Synoptics, actually goes back to him. There appears to be no reason why it should not. But, for the present purpose, it suffices to distinguish between two stages of the dispute, an earlier—represented by Mark and Luke—where the defence invokes the action of David, and a later—represented by Matthew—where it invokes the action of David plus the rules concerning the temple service. What is the meaning of this development?

The original argument—from David's conduct—was of a spontaneous, popular kind, but it was anything but conclusive from the scholarly, legal point of view. For one thing, in the case of David, it had not been a question of the Sabbath at all. David, when hungry, had eaten of the showbread; which was no proof, technically, that you might, in a similar situation, break the Sabbath. But an even more serious objection was that what Jesus adduced was the conduct of a historical figure, instead of a law. He quoted a narrative saying that David had acted in a certain way, but not a provision allowing you to act in this way. It was not so much that David might conceivably have been wrong: the Rabbis no less than Jesus assumed that, for one reason or another, his action had been justified.[1] The flaw in the argumentation was more fundamental than that.

It was of the essence of the Rabbinic system that any detailed rule, any *halakha*, must rest, directly or indirectly, on an actual precept promulgated in Scripture. It must rest on it directly or indirectly: that is to say, there was no need for a *halakha* to be laid down in so many words, so long as it could be derived from some precept by means of the recognized norms of hermeneutics. One of these norms, for example, was the inference *a fortiori*, or as the Rabbis termed it, *qal waḥomer*, 'the light and weighty'. If a man knowingly kept a dangerous animal and it killed a person, Scripture allowed the guilty owner to escape the death penalty on payment of a fine: 'then he shall give for the ransom of his life whatsoever is laid upon him'.[2] The Rabbis concluded that, *a fortiori*, the place of 'eye for eye, tooth for tooth' etc., lesser penalties than death, should be taken by monetary damages.[3] However, even here, be it noted, the *halakha* was ultimately based on a real precept, an express permission, 'then he may give for a ransom whatsoever is laid upon him', not on a mere historical datum. Historical data

[1] E.g. Bab. Men. 95b.   [2] Exod. 21.30.   [3] Mekh. on Exod. 21.24.

belonged to the province of *haggadha*. They might serve to inculcate moral lessons, general religious truths, wisdom; they might also serve to illustrate and corroborate a *halakha*. But they could not form its primary source.

To be sure, the principle in question was the result of a long and slow evolution. But by the middle of the 1st cent. A.D., notwithstanding certain vestiges of a less rigorous attitude, it was, if not firmly established, at least rapidly gaining ground. On the whole, what a patriarch or a pious king—or, as we shall see, even God—had done on a particular occasion was considered all-important as far as *derekh 'ereṣ*, the good life in general, was concerned; the Rabbis constantly reminded people of Abraham's hospitality to strangers or the meekness of Moses. Given certain conditions, it was also regarded as helpful to a more accurate understanding of a *halakha*, a detailed law. But it was not by itself an adequate basis for a *halakha*. Laws must be ordained, their character as commands, prohibitions or concessions must be clearly recognizable.

It may be worth remarking on the technical expressions 'thou findest' and 'we have found' which are frequent in Tannaitic literature. They refer *inter alia* to historical occurrences,[1] and particularly to such as might seem to invite imitation. But it is significant that the moral drawn is nearly always *haggadhic*: he who maligns a fellow-man may deserve heavier punishment than he who commits a straightforward assault, or the patriarchs and prophets were willing to lay down their lives for Israel.[2] Where 'thou findest' or 'we have found' occurs in the domain of *halakha*, normally, the argument merely supports a conclusion arrived at on the ground of a precept,[3] or it survives in connection with a problem of a highly theoretical nature: the problem, for instance, whether, though in general none may marry the widow of a king, a king may do so.[4]

Another technical phrase is illuminating. A Rabbi advocating a doctrine may say of a Biblical passage that 'though it supplies no proof (*ra'aya*), yet it does supply a suggestion (*zekher*)'. This phrase is not uncommonly used by Tannaites when they can rest a *halakha* only on a

---

[1] We are not here concerned with the entirely different case where an expression of this kind introduces an established *halakhic* doctrine, in order that further conclusions may be drawn; as e.g. in Mish. Men. 12.5, 'We find that wine may be offered in a certain way, therefore oil may be offered in that way.'

[2] Mish. Ar. 3.5, Mekh. on Exod. 12.1.

[3] Mekh. on Exod. 12.22—though the rule to begin and end a journey in daytime is really *haggadhic* rather than *halakhic*.   [4] Mish. San. 2.1.

historical example but not on an actual precept. We are told that if a couple are married for ten years without having children, the husband should take another wife (not a strict *halakha*, it is true); and, it is added, 'though there is no proof, yet there is a suggestion' in Abraham's taking Hagar.[1] The author fully realizes that a precedent like this has not the force of a commandment.[2]

Again, the arguments introduced by the phrase *minnayin*, 'Whence?', 'From what Scriptural passage do we know?', are of interest. The passage supplied in the answer does not always contain a precept; it sometimes contains an example. Occasionally this may be due to the survival of laxer methods of proof—where example was as good as precept. Moreover, the question often concerns *haggadha*; for instance, 'Whence do we know that the Israelites in the desert refrained from unchastity and tale-bearing?'[3] In such a case, of course, no reference to a precept is needed. But even where the question concerns *halakha*, it may be about a detail or definition rather than the actual rule. There is a rule that a circumcised child may be bathed even if this involves a breaking of the Sabbath. How long does this rule apply? It is certainly valid, the Rabbis hold,[4] as long as three days. 'Whence do we know that the child may be bathed on the third? Because it is written,[5] *And on the third day when they were sore.*' The Biblical example merely serves to render the *halakha* clearer or more precise.

As a technical argument, then, the mention of the temple service on a Sabbath to be found in Matthew is far superior to that of David's appropriation of the showbread to be found in Mark and Luke as well. Not only does the temple service provide a correct parallel to the action of the disciples, in that it really has to do with the Sabbath—or, more precisely, with the problem under what circumstances its observance must give way to other considerations. What is of almost greater importance is that the argument from the temple service on a Sabbath rests on a definite precept. That offerings should be brought even on a Sabbath, in other words, that in this sense the temple service should take precedence over the observance of the Sabbath, is expressly laid down in Scripture:[6] 'And on the sabbath day two lambs of the first

---

[1] Tos. Yeb. 8.4, referring to Gen. 16.3.
[2] Which does not mean that a precedent constantly used to support a *halakha* may not gradually acquire the status of a true proof. Abraham's action is treated as such by Simeon ben Lakish in the 3rd cent. A.D.; see Pal. Yeb. 7c.   [3] Mekh. on Exod. 12.6.
[4] Mish. Shab. 9.3; cf. 19.3, which represents Eleazar ben Azariah (about A.D. 100) as making use of the passage from Genesis.   [5] Gen. 34.25.   [6] Num. 28.9 f.

year without spot, the burnt offering of every sabbath, beside the continual burnt offering.'

Possibly the fact that this second argument is introduced by 'Or have ye not read in the law' is significant. The words 'in the law' are not used in introducing the first argument, from David's conduct. They may be intended to draw attention to the distinctive nature of the addition. At any rate, the scholarly, strictly Rabbinic character of the addition is underlined by the employment of a hermeneutic norm to which we have already adverted, the inference *a fortiori*, the *qal wahomer*. Scripture—thus the argument in Matthew runs—ordains that the observance of the Sabbath must yield to the temple service; *a fortiori* it must yield in the present case, where something greater than the temple demands consideration. There is nothing *haggadhic* about this. The argument is of a kind which no student of *halakha* could lightly dismiss.

B. DIVORCE

There is one other pericope in the gospels, about divorce,[1] where two different Old Testament texts are cited in support of the same decision, and the development seems to have been similar—from proof by reference to an example to proof by reference to a precept. This time, however, the addition must definitely have been made at a fairly early date. Mark as well as Matthew gives both the texts. The second one must, therefore, have been added either prior to Mark or, at the latest, by Mark himself. As Matthew's version of this pericope differs in important respects from Mark's, we shall begin by analysing the latter. It will emerge from our discussion that, where Matthew differs, he has changed the Markan account.

1. *Mark*

Let us, then, inquire into Mark. As the first argument in support of Jesus's attitude to divorce, we are told what God did on the sixth day: 'From the beginning of the creation, male and female created he them.' The words 'male and female created he them' are a quotation from Genesis.[2] At one stage, as we propose to demonstrate presently, this argument stood alone. The other quotation, 'For this cause shall a man leave his father and mother' etc.,[3] had not yet been added.

---

[1] Matt. 19.3 ff., Mark 10.2 ff.   [2] 1.27, 5.2.   [3] Gen. 2.24.

The question arises—and we may point out that it would arise even if there had been the two quotations from the outset: What is the precise force of this argument, 'male and female created he them'? At first sight it looks quite irrelevant, speaking neither in favour nor against divorce; or perhaps rather in favour, seeing that God created two independent beings. Modern commentaries incline to slur over the difficulty. The true explanation lies in the fact that, for the Rabbis, this verse contained the doctrine—familiar to readers of Plato[1]—of the ideal, androgynous man, the doctrine that when God first created man, he created him as both man and woman in one.[2]

The reasons why the Rabbis connected the doctrine with just this verse are two. For one thing, they had to harmonize this verse, 'male and female created he them', with the narrative[3] according to which Adam came first and Eve was only subsequently formed from one of his ribs. A plausible solution was to maintain that the original Adam was a composite being, and that this was the meaning of the verse in question. For another thing, the Hebrew text wavers between singular and plural. It starts by using the singular 'man'—'God created man in his image'—and then goes on to put the plural 'them'—'male and female created he them'. What sort of being might it be, the Rabbis asked themselves, of whom one could equally well speak in the singular or plural? Again the answer was that the verse must refer to the androgynous man.

That this interpretation of the verse goes back to New Testament times is certain. Philo has it.[4] It occurs in many different Rabbinic sources. Moreover, the Rabbis inform us that the authors of the LXX, for the enlightenment of their gentile public, slightly altered the verse 'male and female created he them': they translated 'a male with his female parts created he them', or 'male and female created he him'— 'him' in the singular. Now admittedly, the LXX in the form it has come down to us does not contain these modifications. But there is every reason to believe that the Rabbis did find them in some Greek versions. We shall presently point out a similar modification of another verse,[5] still preserved in the LXX as we have it. Even if the Rabbis did not find those variants, such a tradition concerning the authors of the LXX could never have grown up had the teaching to which it refers,

[1] Symp. 189 C ff.
[2] Gen. Rabba on Gen. 1.26 f., Mekh. on Exod. 12.40.
[3] Gen. 2.18 ff.
[4] O.M. 24.76.
[5] Gen. 2.24.

i.e. of the androgynous Adam, not been of very considerable age. Exactly how the myth reached the Rabbis we need not here decide. Probably it came to them from Plato, though we must bear in mind that Plato himself no doubt had it from the Orient. It does not give the impression of a native Greek product; and, quite possibly, by putting it into the mouth of Aristophanes, Plato means to suggest that he does not want it taken too seriously.

Obviously, understood in this sense, the statement that 'from the beginning male and female created he them' was a powerful argument against divorce. God had made the ideal man androgynous, man and woman forming one inseparable being. That was an example of even greater authority than, say, the conduct of a figure like David: it was an example set by God himself in creating the world. The exhortation 'What therefore God hath joined together, let not man put asunder' now becomes intelligible. In the present text, it follows the second quotation, 'For this cause shall a man leave his father and mother', with which it has no logical connection. But, originally, it came directly after 'From the beginning, male and female created he them.' God made man and woman in one. That example should be heeded: man is not entitled to break up a unity which God, by proceeding as he did in creating the world, showed to be the perfect state of things.

The exhortation confirms not only our explanation of the whole discussion by reference to the teaching of the androgynous Adam—the words 'what therefore God hath joined together' and so on will make sense on no other basis—but also our thesis that at one stage, the argument rested solely on the first quotation from the Old Testament, 'From the beginning' and so on. The second quotation, 'For this cause' and so on, separates the first from the conclusion drawn from it, it comes abruptly between 'From the beginning male and female created he them' and 'What therefore God hath joined together let not man put asunder.' The second quotation, that is, bears every sign of being an insertion—be it Mark's work or earlier than Mark.

A linguistic detail respecting the verbs συνζευγνύειν, 'to join together', and χωρίζειν, 'to put asunder', may be noticed. Their choice in this context was almost certainly favoured by the fact that they are reminiscent of ζεύγνυσθαι, in the sense of 'to marry', and χωρίζεσθαι, in the sense of 'to leave one's husband or wife'. In other words, while the usual translation 'What therefore God hath joined together, let not man put asunder' is perfectly correct, as a secondary meaning at least something more specific seems to have been intended: 'What therefore God hath married into one'—the prefix συν may well express the idea 'into one', and in the Matthean parallel Codex Bezae and Itala actually add εἰς ἕν—'let not man divorce'. In support, we may recall the Rabbinic *ziwwegh* or *zawwegh*, a verb going back to the Greek ζεῦγος. It may denote 'to join things together' in any way, but it is often used of God's 'joining together husband and wife' and, in the form *hizdawwegh* or *'izdawwagh*, signifies 'to be married'. According to the Jerusalemite Targum,[1] for example, 'God taught us to marry (here *barzegh* is employed, the second part of which also derives from ζεῦγος) bridegrooms and brides by his marrying—*zawwegh*, from ζεῦγος—Eve to Adam.'

Pursuing our inquiry, we may observe that the pronouncement 'From the beginning male and female created he them', alluding as it did to the androgynous Adam, would simply puzzle the unlearned, and even the learned might not immediately see the deeper implications. In other words, it was a pronouncement deliberately obscure, hinting at the truth, but not stating it in plain language.

It cannot be accidental that Philo, in commenting on the verse from Genesis, should remark that the androgynous nature of the original man may be perceived 'by those who have the faculty of keen vision'; or that Paul, whom also we shall find making use of the myth, should add on one occasion[2] that 'this is a great mystery'. It is true that Paul may be describing as a mystery less the teaching of the androgynous Adam as such than its application to the relation between Christ and the church. Evidently, however, that teaching counted as esoteric, a secret the full understanding of which was reserved for the initiated. Moreover, we shall see, when we discuss the form which may be characterized as public retort and private explanation, that this Markan pericope is not the only instance in the gospels where Jesus is represented as answering his opponents by a saying difficult to grasp, which he later expounds to his disciples.

About the explanation given to the disciples in the present case, a few words must here be said: it provides yet further evidence that the entire pericope must be understood against the background of the myth of the androgynous man. Jesus declares that it is adultery for a man or

---

[1] Deut. 34.6.   [2] Eph. 5.32.

woman to re-marry after divorce.[1] Now as far as the woman is concerned, this might be regarded as merely a consequence of the rejection of divorce. That is to say, if marriage is indissoluble, if divorce makes no difference, then a wife remains married to her husband even after divorce, and clearly commits adultery by cohabiting with another man. The same, however, is not true of a man who re-marries after divorce. Certainly, he also, if divorce is not recognized, is still married to his first wife. But, so long as the law allows polygamy, it cannot be adultery if he takes a second one—be it before or after separation from the first. Yet Jesus does here speak of adultery even where it is the husband who re-marries.

The point is that the doctrine on which his decision is based involves the rejection, not only of divorce, but also of polygamy. It does so because it sees in marriage an imitation of the ideal, androgynous state of man. Once marriage is conceived of in this fashion, it becomes just as criminal for a husband to take a second wife while the first lives as for a wife to take a second husband while the first lives. The ideal state is disrupted in the former no less than in the latter case.

It is significant that the pronouncement declaring the husband's re-marriage adultery recurs only in two other passages of the New Testament: in the parallel chapter of Matthew to which we shall come back, and in Luke.[2] Luke, we shall submit in a different chapter (on Violence to the Kingdom in Part III), seems to show traces of a context where the androgynous man played a part; in any case this evangelist came from a society which had long ceased to countenance polygamy. Paul probably also looks upon a husband's re-marriage during his wife's lifetime as in principle adulterous. He writes[3] that only if an unbelieving wife or husband dissolves the union, the believing 'brother or sister is not under bondage'. Surely the implication is that, except for this case, re-marriage would be illicit—and no less so for a brother than for a sister.

By contrast, in the sermon on the mount, Matthew appears deliberately to avoid the notion of adultery by the husband.[4] There is no reflection on polygamy in the proposition that 'whosoever shall put away his wife causeth her to commit adultery'. It means that, since

---

[1] The prevalent reading of Mark 10.12 refers to 'a wife putting away her husband', another to 'a wife departing from her husband'. The problem will be discussed below, in Part III, under Terms for Divorce; it has no bearing on the thesis here submitted.
[2] 16.18.   [3] I Cor. 7.15.   [4] 5.32.

marriage is indissoluble, a woman who re-marries after divorce is an adulteress; but the husband who divorced her, thus encouraging her to feel free, bears the moral responsibility. We must remember that the essential words in a bill of divorce were: 'Lo, thou art permitted to any man.'[1] If there was a stage at which the saying did not contain the proviso 'saving for the cause of fornication', the original import may conceivably have been similar to that of a saying by Simeon ben Azzai (first half of the 2nd cent. A.D.). He compares a husband who hates his wife to a murderer, for such a man will institute proceedings even against an innocent woman and not rest till she is sentenced to death.[2] He will, that is, represent her as having committed misconduct—which in Greek might be expressed by $\pi οιεῖ\ αὐτήν\ μοιχευθῆναι$.

One thing is clear: nothing is said or implied in this verse about a second marriage by a husband after divorce—or, for that matter, before. Again, it is generally admitted that I Timothy[3] and Titus[4] take polygamy for granted.

It follows, then, that there is in the New Testament no opposition to polygamy but that based on the teaching of the androgynous Adam. Moreover, there was a tendency among Jewish New Testament authors—i.e. a tendency not shared by Luke—to suppress this opposition as they forgot about, or came to disapprove of, its basis.

However, we must return to the argument from 'male and female created he them'. Profound as it was, it again suffered from a major flaw if it was to be used in serious, scholarly controversy with the Rabbis: like the argument from David's conduct, it invoked an example instead of a precept, it adduced what God had done on a particular occasion instead of what God had said should or should not be done.

Certainly, no example from history could have more weight than one set by God. What is more, of the examples set by God, none could have more weight than those he set in creating the world. To approach the original, ideal creation as God had planned it was a great aim in the eyes of the Rabbis. Nevertheless, even an example set by God in ordering the world essentially belonged to the domain of *haggadha*, and supplied no adequate foundation for a specific *halakha* such as the prohibition and non-recognition of divorce. The Rabbis would appeal to

---

[1] Mish. Git. 9.3. As we shall see under Terms for Divorce, Josephus in Ant. 15.7.10.259, speaks of a man divorcing his wife as 'conceding', 'permitting', her, $ἐφιέναι$.

[2] D.E. 11.   [3] 3.2.   [4] 1.6.

God's example in enunciating general rules of religious, moral or prudent conduct, *derekh 'ereṣ*; they would also appeal to it in elucidating a *halakha* already established on other, proper grounds. But further they would not go.

To illustrate this. The Rabbis, we said, would appeal to God's example in enunciating rules of religious, moral or prudent conduct. Thus in the Testament of Zebulun, the nation is warned against putting up two rival leaders—the reference probably is to the terrible conflict between Hyrcanus II and Aristobulus II:[1] 'Be not ye, therefore, divided into two heads, for everything which the Lord made hath but one head.' Manifestly we are in the realm of *haggadha*, in this case political advice. Again, Job, we learn from R. Judah ben Bathyra, of the first third of the 2nd cent. A.D., decided never to have more than one wife at a time, because he considered that 'if it had been fitting for Adam to have ten wives, God would have given him ten, but he gave him only one'.[2] Such a consideration would be quite in order from the Rabbinic point of view. It would lead, not to a *halakha* which you must follow, but to a recommendation, far from binding, of the course most fitting for man, i.e. most in accordance with *derekh 'ereṣ*. It is significant that the Rabbi simply refers to God giving Adam one wife, without specifying a particular verse. There is no need to be so exact in a matter of *haggadha*.

It is not, indeed, unlikely that Judah ben Bathyra consciously mitigated an earlier doctrine. In other words, he—or his source—may have been acquainted with a decision of the kind to be met with in the New Testament, a decision put forward by some circles as a binding *halakha* in favour of monogamy and rested by them on the interpretation of certain verses from Genesis as speaking of the androgynous being. But, while recognizing monogamy as the more desirable practice, he did not agree that it was the law; so he advocated it in a vaguer manner, as forming part of the code of *derekh 'ereṣ*. If this is the history behind his comment, it becomes all the more evident what enormous importance the Rabbis attached to the distinction between *halakha* and *haggadha*.

The Rabbis would also appeal to God's example in elucidating a *halakha* already established on other, proper grounds. Here we may mention that the verse 'male and female created he them' played a part

---

[1] 9.4.   [2] Ab. de-R.N. 2.5a; the Biblical basis for this Midrash is Job 31.1.

in the discussion[1] as to how many children a man ought to have and whether or not he had done his duty if they were all of one sex. But two things should be noted. First, the primary *halakha* laying down the duty of procreation was based by the Rabbis on an actual precept—or rather, on what they considered an actual precept since, grammatically, it was an imperative—namely, the words:[2] 'Be fruitful and multiply.' The verse 'male and female created he them' was introduced only as a help to a more exact understanding of this *halakha*. Secondly, it is very doubtful whether, in the Talmudic period, the duty of procreation was a *halakha* in the strict sense at all. It may well have been nearer a moral duty, a duty falling under *derekh 'ereṣ*, the behaviour expected of a good man. Ben Azzai, in the first third of the 2nd cent., openly admitted that he preferred to remain unmarried in order to devote all his time to the study of the Torah. He could hardly have dismissed in this manner, say, the duty to eat unleavened bread and bitter herbs in the first night of Passover.

Apparently, as time went on, the argument from example was found less and less satisfactory. So an argument from precept was added, just as in the case of the dispute about the Sabbath: 'For this cause shall a man leave his father and mother, and they twain shall be one flesh; so then they are no more twain, but one flesh.'

It is important to realize that the motif of the androgynous Adam is here still present. We accept, of course, the shorter variant, which quotes only part of the Old Testament verse. The longer variant, which completes the quotation by adding 'and he shall cleave to his wife', is a palpable assimilation to Matthew—but Matthew we shall consider later. For the moment, we proceed from Mark's 'For this cause shall a man leave his father and mother, and they twain shall be one flesh.'

Whoever inserted this verse interpreted it as meaning that, in marriage, the two separated halves of the original composite being meet again and, having done so, should stay re-united. It is only if it is taken in this way that the verse, though deprived of the clause 'and he shall cleave to his wife', yet decrees the indissolubility of marriage. In fact, that clause is cut out precisely in order to retain the esoteric character of the reply. If the words 'and he shall cleave to his wife' were included, there would be an open injunction in plain language declaring marriage indissoluble. Without these words, what remains is 'they

---

[1] Mish. Yeb. 6.6, Tos. Yeb. 8.4, Bab. Yeb. 62a.   [2] Gen. 1.28.

twain shall be one flesh'—a commandment fully intelligible only to those who have the key.

At this stage of the controversy, Jesus is still made to ward off his antagonists by a mysterious saying, an allusion to the ideal being that is man and woman in one. The only real difference between the original argument, from 'male and female created he them', and the additional one, from 'they twain shall be one flesh', is that the former appeals to an example—God created the ideal man androgynous—while the latter appeals to a precept—it is one of God's commandments that the two divided halves should join again for good.

2. Confirmatory evidence

Eight points may be mentioned as corroborating our conclusions. First, the quotation from the Old Testament, 'For this cause shall a man leave his father and mother and they twain shall be one flesh', is followed by a brief comment: 'so that they are no more twain, but one flesh'. The similarity to Plato, where he introduces the theory of love as the craving for one another of the two separated halves of a composite being, is striking:[1] 'If such is your desire', the god says to two lovers, 'I propose to fuse and weld you into a single piece, so that from being two you may become one.'

Secondly, Philo, we saw, adopts the myth of the androgynous Adam. He also adopts the notion of love we have just outlined, and, significantly, he seems to associate it with the verse 'For this cause' etc.[2] According to the Bible, God brought all animals before Adam to name them; then he created Eve, whom Adam acknowledged as a true companion; it is at this point that we find the verse 'For this cause shall a man leave his father and mother and they twain shall be one flesh.' According to Philo, God brought the animals before Adam to name them; then he created Eve, a true companion; then 'love supervenes, and brings together and fits into one the divided halves, as it were, of one being'. Surely this is a paraphrase of 'and they twain shall be one flesh'.

Thirdly, Paul twice adduces the verse from Genesis, and both times he is influenced by its interpretation as meaning that, through sexual intercourse, a man and woman actually become one being. In I

---

[1] Symp. 192E. If there are traces of an analogous theory in Plutarch, Coniug. Praec. 33, in Mor. 142E, they are very faint indeed.

Corinthians[1] he quotes only the words 'and they twain shall be one flesh'; and he uses them to support his argument that if a Christian, whose body is a member of Christ, associates with a harlot, he is making a member of Christ into a member of a harlot since he and the harlot become one body, ἐν σῶμα. In Ephesians[2] he quotes the words 'For this cause shall a man leave his father and mother and they twain shall be one flesh.' In all probability, like Mark, he deliberately suppresses 'and he shall cleave to his wife', in order to concentrate on the mysterious, esoteric teaching contained in the ending of the verse, 'and they twain shall be one flesh'. The quotation, it will be remembered, is followed by the remark: 'This is a great mystery.' Admittedly, most codices do include the part 'and he shall cleave to his wife'. But Origen affirms in so many words that it is not to be found in Paul; in fact he cites this passage from Ephesians as an example of the freedom with which New Testament writers modify Old Testament texts. The conclusion, therefore, seems justified that the clause, omitted by Paul, was inserted at an early date, by way of assimilation to Matthew and the full Old Testament text. Be this as it may, the verse, for Paul, provides a Scriptural basis for a husband's duty to love his wife 'as his own body' or 'as his own flesh'. Their union approaches the state of the original, androgynous Adam. And it corresponds to the union between Christ and his church.

Fourthly, in the Gospel according to the Egyptians, we are told that Jesus, asked by Salome when his kingdom would finally arrive, replied: 'When ye have trampled on the garment of shame, and when the two become one and the male with the female is neither male nor female.' 'The two become one' may well be a reference to the verse from Genesis; and it is clearly taken to signify the coming into existence of the ideal, androgynous being and the disappearance of the distinction between the sexes—and of their passions. II Clement[3] quotes the fragment under notice—with slight modifications—and comments on it. But it considerably rationalizes its source when it explains that the words 'the male with the female is neither male nor female' mean: 'A brother, when he sees a sister, does not think of the woman in her, nor she of the man in him.' It is worth noting that, according to Paul,[4] once people are baptized into Christ, 'there is neither Jew nor Greek, neither bond nor free, neither male nor female'.

[1] 6.16.   [2] 5.31.   [3] 12.2.   [4] Gal. 3.28.

Fifthly, the quotation in Mark follows the LXX. So does the Matthean parallel, and so does Paul both in I Corinthians and Ephesians. The Hebrew text—supported by the Targum and the Book of Jubilees[1] —has not 'and they twain shall be one flesh', but 'and they shall be one flesh'. It looks as if the LXX (supported, it is true, by the Samaritan Pentateuch) had inserted 'twain' in order to enjoin monogamy, considered as the more civilized practice by the Greeks; and as if this verse had been deemed the appropriate place for such an injunction because commentators already read into it the meeting in marriage of the two halves of the androgynous being. We have already noted Rabbinic reports to the effect that the LXX introduced the androgynous Adam into another verse.[2] Even if it should be held, however, that the LXX preserves the original reading and that the word 'twain' has been eliminated from the Massoretic Hebrew,[3] the difference remains important. The word must have been eliminated for some reason, which can only have been that some circles interpreted 'twain' as ordaining monogamy. The interpretation, if we take this line, would have to go back to a time prior to the Book of Jubilees, since this work, in agreement with the Hebrew text, omits 'twain'.

The next few points are particularly interesting—the Rabbinic treatment of the verse. Sixthly, then, the Rabbis recognized both divorce and polygamy. Consequently, they were driven to an entirely different exegesis. The prevalent view among them was[4] that the injunction was addressed not only to the Jews but also to the gentiles; it was a 'Noachian commandment', valid for all mankind, and forbidding unnatural intercourse. More precisely, the first clause, 'a man shall leave his father', in the opinion of the Rabbis, was directed against marrying one's father's widow even if she was not one's mother; the next, 'a man shall leave his mother', was directed against marrying one's mother; 'he shall cleave to his wife' was directed against homosexuality and adultery, both the noun 'wife' and the possessive pronoun 'his' being emphasized; finally, 'and they shall be one flesh' was directed against intercourse with beasts. Now the remarkable thing is that this interpretation of 'and they shall be one flesh', however unlike Mark's, Philo's or Paul's in its result, does also presuppose the concept of

---

[1] 3.7. [2] Gen. 1.27, 5.2.
[3] This view is taken by R. Kittel, *Biblia Hebraica*, 2nd ed., 1912; but he seems to have overlooked Jubilees. [4] Bab. San. 58a.

G

marriage as the re-union of the divided halves of an original whole. R. Akiba—of the first third of the 2nd cent.—tells us how the Rabbis come to understand the words in that peculiar way, as a prohibition of intercourse with beasts. He explains that, by putting 'and they shall be one flesh', Scripture means to restrict a man to such intercourse as really makes him and his partner into one—which is not the case where he comes together with a beast. It emerges that if the verse in Mark has reference to the fusion of man and woman into the perfect composite being, this is quite consistent with the ideas current in the Rabbinic circles of the time. That they persisted in subsequent centuries may be seen from a remark by R. Asi, of about A.D. 300.[1]

Seventhly, there are even traces in Rabbinic literature of a doctrine which made 'and they shall be one flesh' into the basis for, if not a prohibition, at least a disapprobation of divorce. The admonition in Isaiah,[2] 'Hide not thyself from thy flesh', is occasionally interpreted as enjoining kindness to one's divorced wife.[3] Clearly, she is still part of him who was her husband.

Lastly, of one Rabbi at least, Simeon ben Johai, about the middle of the 2nd cent. A.D., we know that, though he could not declare divorce illegal, he strongly disapproved of it; and his disapproval seems to have been linked with, on the one hand, the notion of husband and wife approaching the ideal, androgynous being and, on the other, the notion of Solomon's Song allegorically depicting God's relation with Israel. Simeon[4] commented on the fact that the Old Testament provisions concerning divorce open with the clause 'When a man hath taken a wife'[5] instead of with 'When a wife hath caused herself to be taken to a man.' His explanation was that, in marrying, it is the man who seeks what he has lost—the rib. That the Rabbi should have read an allusion to restoration of the androgynous state by marriage precisely into the Biblical permission of divorce must be regarded as a very bold expression of his feelings on the matter. To this we have to

---

[1] Gen. Rabba on 2.24 at the end.   [2] 58.7.   [3] Lev. Rabba on 25.39.

[4] Bab. Qid. 2b. In Bab. Nid. 31b the interpretation is ascribed to Dosethai ben Jannai, of the end of the 2nd cent. No doubt Dosethai took over Simeon's teaching.

[5] Deut. 24.1. It is universally held (see e.g. the standard edition of the Babylonian Talmud and W. Bacher, *Die Agada der Tannaiten*, vol. 2, 1890, p. 104) that the Rabbi refers to Deut. 22.13, where the same clause occurs. But, obviously, this is to deprive his remarks of their very point. Maybe the transfer of his interpretation from 24.1 to 22.13 was deliberately undertaken by medieval authorities, who recognized its dangerous implications in its original setting.

add the famous story[1] of the couple who had remained childless for ten years and came to Simeon to be divorced. He advised them to separate with a banquet just as they had married with a banquet. After the feast the husband said to his wife that, when she returned to her father's house, she should take with her whatever she liked best. While he was asleep, she had him carried to her father's house, since there was nothing she liked better than him. The Rabbi then prayed for them and they did get a child. The anecdote ends with the moral that, if a wife who prizes her husband more than anything else will be blessed, how much more will Israel be blessed for prizing God above anything else and exclaiming—in the words of Solomon's Song—'We will be glad and rejoice in thee.'[2] In some indirect way, the idea that a marital union ought never to be dissolved is brought into connection with the bond between God and Israel.

3. Matthew

When we turn to Matthew, we find that he—or one of his sources—completes the second quotation from the Old Testament, adding 'and he shall cleave to his wife'. Presumably he no longer connects the verse with the teaching that marriage means a re-union. So the words 'and they twain shall be one flesh' are not, for him, of sufficient force; he needs the clause which may be interpreted as a direct, open rejection of divorce—'and he shall cleave to his wife'. In other words, according to Matthew, Jesus's argument against divorce is not veiled but intended to be intelligible to all.

As a corollary, whereas in Mark the ultimate consequences of the decision—namely, 'Whosoever shall put away his wife and marry another committeth adultery' and so on—are entrusted to the disciples only, in Matthew they are explained to the Pharisees as well. There is no mystery about divorce. The subsequent private discussion between Jesus and his disciples, in Matthew, does not concern divorce or polygamy at all, but the question whether marriage as such is a good thing.

In Matthew, the androgynous Adam is abandoned. The quotation 'male and female created he them' has become almost devoid of meaning. All emphasis is now on the precept, 'For this cause shall a man' etc.

[1] Cant. Rabba on 1.4.   [2] Cant. 1.4.

It might be asked why, though giving up the teaching concerning the androgynous man, Matthew nevertheless retains one of its implications: namely, the rejection of polygamy, or more particularly, the view that even the husband who re-marries after divorce is guilty of adultery. As we saw, this would not follow from a mere prohibition of divorce; it follows only where divorce is prohibited because marriage is looked upon as a re-union of the composite being—here a husband re-marrying breaks up the ideal unity no less than a wife re-marrying. Matthew, who no longer accepts the premise, should logically have dropped the inference. He does not do so in this pericope.

Probably, the explanation is quite simple: we cannot expect perfect logical consistency. Very likely, the wording of the pronouncement in this context was too firmly established to be changed. As we had occasion to observe before, Matthew does modify it in the sermon on the mount. There it is taken out of the discussion with the Pharisees and placed into a different series of sayings. Hence the evangelist is less reluctant to adjust it to a polygamous milieu.

However, though Matthew himself is presumably no longer influenced by the notion of an androgynous being, there is reason to believe that it played a part in that source from which he took the private reflections of Jesus and his disciples concerning marriage as such: 'It is not good to marry, There be eunuchs for the kingdom's sake.' More precisely, that source may well have argued on these lines: by marrying a woman, a man unites with her so that they become one body; instead of exclusively belonging to Christ, he makes himself part of another human being; marriage therefore is not worthy of the perfect Christian.

Paul, in I Corinthians,[1] argues thus: a Christian's body is a member of Christ; he must not, therefore, associate with a harlot, for by doing so his body and hers would become one—according to the verse 'they twain shall be one flesh'—and thus a member of Christ would be defiled; in fact, it is best not to touch any woman whatever—*scil.* but to belong entirely to Christ; however, a decent marriage is far preferable to fornication; and once concluded, marriage is indissoluble. That Paul's teaching rests on the myth of the androgynous being is beyond question. And his teaching is just of the type we are postulating for Matthew's source: since a man's marriage means his merging in a com-

[1] 6.15 ff.

posite being, it also means his withdrawing his body from exclusive union with Christ—hence he had better remain single.

The term αἰτία in the clause 'If the case of the man be so with his wife, it is not good to marry' is an old crux. Its normal meanings are 'imputation' and 'cause', neither of which is really suitable. With all due reservation—for such points can rarely be more than conjectural—let us note that, in Hebrew and Aramaic, the words '*illa*', 'pretext' or 'cause', and '*il'a*', 'rib', are so near in sound that occasionally, it seems, one is spelt—or misspelt—like the other.[1] The latter is used by the Targum in the story of Eve's creation. Conceivably, at an Aramaic stage of the tradition, the clause under discussion contained a direct reference to Genesis.

It should be added that in Matthew the argument from the example of God or the natural world governed by him is by no means uncommon.[2] But it is used to support general rules of nobility and piety—goodness to enemies, trust in God, in short, *haggadha*.

4. *The Zadokite Fragments*

It is instructive to compare with the New Testament development the not dissimilar one to be found in the Zadokite Fragments.[3] In this work, there is a paragraph directed against polygamy, and probably also against divorce.

Three Biblical texts are quoted. The first is 'male and female created he them'; this is called 'a fundamental principle of the creation'. No doubt when this text was first adduced, it was interpreted as referring to the ideal, original creation of the androgynous Adam.

The second text is that which tells us that the animals 'went in two by two'.[4] This may be a later addition, made at a time when the myth concerning the androgynous man had ceased to play a part in this context. On the other hand, it may be as old as the first quotation. Whichever it is—with its emphatic 'two and two', it was not too bad a proof of the universal validity of the 'fundamental principle of the creation': the latter applied even to animals.

The third text is the law enjoining that the king 'shall not multiply wives to himself'.[5] This is almost certainly an addition. In a way, it was not a good text at all. It had nothing to do with any 'principle of the creation'. It clearly referred to the ruler only, but not to ordinary per-

[1] See the dictionaries. [2] 5.45 ff., 6.26 ff. [3] 7.1 ff. [4] Gen. 7.9. [5] Deut. 17.17.

sons. It was of a far less inclusive scope than the first two texts. But it was added because it was superior to them in containing a precept and not merely an example.

In strictness, neither the way God created the first man nor the way he dealt with the animals when he ordered the world a second time, in the ark, furnished a sufficient basis for a *halakha*, a detailed rule binding on people. To establish a *halakha*, an actual commandment was required; and one confined to the king was better than none. One could always argue that everybody should live up to the highest standard, or that all good Jews were equal to kings. In the course of expounding a verse from Amos, 'I will raise up the tabernacle of David',[1] the Zadokite Fragments claim[2] that 'the king' means 'the congregation'; and Simeon ben Johai, of the middle of the 2nd cent. A.D., in a *halakhic* discussion opines that all Israelites are to be considered 'kings' children'.[3]

C. THE HELLENISTIC BACKGROUND

We have now presented two controversies between Jesus and the Pharisees—a dispute about the Sabbath and the dispute about divorce—as well as a paragraph about divorce from the Zadokite Fragments where an argument invoking an example from history was supplemented by one invoking a precept. It is safe to assume that, in all three cases, the addition was undertaken with a view to satisfying the Rabbinic requirements of a proper *halakha*, as distinct from *haggadha*. Before leaving this topic, we may point out that, if we wish fully to appreciate the Rabbinic attitude in this matter, it is not enough to study the Jewish sources in isolation. To be sure, the principal factors contributing to the Rabbinic system were of native origin. But it looks as if, in the detailed and minute elaboration of the system, the Rabbis had drawn on ideas which, while ultimately going back to Greece, were in Hellenistic times taught by the rhetorical schools throughout the Mediterranean world.

Here we can only indicate some of the speculations that seem to have influenced their thought. As is well known, Aristotle holds that philosophical theories are powerless to stimulate the mass to moral nobility; the mass needs legal precepts imposing penalties on the

---

[1] 9.11.   [2] 9.7.   [3] Mish. Shab. 14.4.

disobedient.[1] Philo[2] praises Moses for combining the two methods. In Seneca and Quintilian, however, the antithesis is not between philosophical theories and legal precepts, but between philosophical theories and examples.[3]

This was, of course, the more popular view. We must remember, however, that it inspired not only writers of anecdotes and fables— Phaedrus says: 'exemplis discimus'[4]—but also serious historians like Thucydides. That the good historian's work must be a κτῆμα εἰς ἀεί, or, conversely, that people should turn to it for guidance, was a commonplace demand, as may be seen from Aristotle, Cicero, Lucian and many others.[5]

Again, that particular kind of example, the model conduct and pronouncements of a sage whose company you are enjoying, was cultivated by high and low, by the disciples of Socrates, Zeno, R. Johanan ben Zaccai or Jesus[6] no less than by those of many a worthless charlatan. Indeed, taking the wise man's conduct and pronouncements as an example, one may within this example again distinguish between his conduct, which supplies examples in the narrower sense, and his pronouncements, which supply philosophical theories. Thus we are told how Socrates educated his disciples 'by word and his own practice':[7] and for Philo[8] he who attains virtue by being taught fixes his attention on what is said by a wise person (hence Abraham 'hearkened to the voice of Sarah', not simply 'to Sarah'[9]), while he who attains virtue by practice fixes his attention on what a wise person does (hence Jacob 'hearkened to his father and mother', not 'to their voice'[10]).

When we are told in the Letter of Aristeas[11] that it is safer 'to hear' about the provisions of the Torah from a wise man than 'to read' them, this is a deliberate combination of two elements: full recognition of the Scriptural precepts on the one hand, and praise of the living example of the sage as the only true way towards the goal on the other.

[1] Nic. E. 10.9.3 ff. [2] O.M. 1.1 ff. [3] Seneca, Ep. 6.5, Quintilian, I.O. 12.2.29 ff.
[4] 2.2.2. Cf. Frontinus, Strat. 1 pr.: 'ita enim consilii quoque et providentiae exemplis succincti duces erunt unde illis excogitandi generandique similia facultas nutriatur'.
[5] Thucydides 1.22.4, Aristotle, Rhet. 2.20.8, Cicero, Or. 2.9.36, Lucian, Q.H.S.S. 42, 53—also Frontinus, in the passage quoted in the preceding footnote.
[6] E.g. Xenophon, Mem. 4.1.1, Cyrop. 8.1.21 ff., Seneca, Ep. 6.5 f., also Digest 40.2.5.
[7] Xenophon, Mem. 4.3.18, 4.4.25 (λέγων τε καὶ αὐτὸς ποιῶν, λέγων τε καὶ πράττων); cp. also 1.2.17 and Cyrop. 1.2.8. In the introductory letter to Rhet. to Alexander it is said that the king's subjects will take as example his 'life and reason'—his practice and principles. By contrast, self-governing states will follow the law as example. (The law itself can be called example since, in the view of the author, it is reason defined by common agreement.) [8] Prel. St. 69 f. [9] Gen. 16.2. [10] Gen. 28.7. [11] 127.

In the same work there is a further relevant passage:[1] 'Our lawgiver first of all laid down the principles of piety and righteousness and inculcated them point by point, not only by prohibitions but also by the use of examples, demonstrating the injurious effects of sin.' This is a statement characteristic of the more enlightened Rabbinic schools. The ultimate aims of religion are piety and righteousness; the detailed prohibitions to be found in Scripture keep man from wandering from these aims; and the narrative portions of Scripture are designed to illustrate the soundness of the prohibitions. As far as the relation between detailed prohibitions and narrative portions is concerned, the former are definitely assigned primacy: the precepts are binding as leading to the end, the examples merely help you to see their purpose.

Philo, on the other hand, inclines to accord primacy to the narrative portions. He describes the holy men of the Bible as 'unwritten laws' of which the enacted laws are copies.[2] At the same time, we also find him expressing the view which occurs in the Letter of Aristeas—that the stories of those men are recounted in order to prove the compatibility of the enacted laws with nature.[3]

Josephus[4] says that young Jews must learn to read the holy books, in order to become familiar with the laws and never to transgress them even from ignorance, and with the deeds of their forefathers, which they should imitate. But, significantly, the duty of thus following both precept and example is represented by him as resting on a commandment of the lawgiver, in Deuteronomy.[5] Precept is the ultimate guide.

However, good Rabbinic doctrine as all this is, it is hardly accidental that the rhetoricians conceive of the respective roles of precept and example in a similar way. Certain of Aristotle's remarks on deductive and inductive reasoning are in point.[6] He opposes proof consisting in an enthymeme to proof consisting in examples. The former, he holds, is objectively far preferable, since it proceeds from universals. But the latter makes a stronger appeal to an audience, since the ordinary man feels more at home with particulars than with universals. Therefore, what a really good orator ought to do is to furnish proof consisting in

---

[1] 131.   [2] Abraham 1.3 f., Moses 1.162.
[3] Abraham 1.5. But even here he concludes that, properly, the enacted laws are nothing but memorials of the lives of the virtuous men.
[4] C.Ap. 2.25.204.   [5] 6.7, 11.19.
[6] Rhet. 1.2.8 ff., 2.20.1 ff., 3.17.5, Problems 18.3, Anal. Pr. 2.24.

an enthymeme, and then add an example by way of confirmatory evidence.

In Quintilian, we come across a less philosophical and narrower variation of the theme;[1] but its bearing on the question of the authentic basis of *halakha* is all the clearer. He points out that if you advocate a certain decision of a dispute, you may refer to the example of another court which on a previous occasion dealt with a similar problem, or even with exactly the same problem. (In the latter case, Quintilian would assume an example only in a loose sense,[2] but we need not here pursue the distinction.) Your argument from such a decision will then be open to several counter-arguments, among them, that circumstances have changed since the previous occasion so that the present dispute must be judged differently, or that quite generally it is wrong to adhere to precedent instead of dealing with each dispute according to its merits. However—Quintilian goes on—if you invoke, not just the decision of an ordinary court, but that of the senate or emperor, these counter-arguments will not be possible. Decisions by the senate or emperor have the force of law, they are not mere precedents, mere examples, but precepts, binding for good. With this kind of problem ventilated in the rhetorical schools, it is easy to imagine that the Rabbis found there much to interest and help them.

This is not the place to examine the relation of precept and example to another proof invariably listed by the rhetoricians, namely, authority, i.e. the opinion of a nation, a great man or a god.[3] Nor can we inquire how far the recognition of example influenced, and was influenced by, such concepts as tradition, *mos maiorum* and so on. The special position of the example set by a god or by God, the special position again of the ideal creation as it first came from his hands— these and allied problems would lead us too far afield. But it may not be amiss to repeat that an investigation of the wider background of Talmudic teaching, that is to say, of the more important Hellenistic views about precept and example, would throw much light on the Rabbinic treatment of the Torah—as also on the efforts of those who had to erect and defend a fresh, rival system.

---

[1] I.O. 5.2.1 ff.; cp. 5.11.1 ff.
[2] Cp. 5.2.1 with 5.11.36.
[3] Aristotle, Rhet. 2.23.12, Cicero, Top. 2.8, 4.24, Quintilian 5.11.36; 'the authority of examples' is mentioned, e.g., in Cicero, Inv. 1.30.49, Quintilian 5.11.1.

IV

Haustafeln

A. Participles of the Correct Practice

THERE is a post-Biblical form of legislation where the action enjoined, allowed or prohibited is expressed by a participle. The Mishnah[1] lays down that 'On the first days of the months—which are half-festivals— women may sing dirges for the dead, but they may not wail; after the corpse has been buried, they may not even sing dirges.' In the original, the directions are all in the participle: 'On the first days of the months, women are singing dirges for the dead but they are not wailing; after the burial, they are not singing dirges.' Or quite literally: 'On the first days of the months, women singing dirges for the dead but not wailing; after the burial, not singing dirges.' Another rule ordains:[2] 'The prose- lyte may bring the first-fruits, but he may not make the Avowal,[3] I profess that I am come unto the country which the Lord sware unto our Fathers for to give us.' Literally, this runs: 'The proselyte (is) bringing the first-fruits, but (he is) not making the Avowal.' Or again:[4] 'When the month of Ab comes in—in which the temple was destroyed —one has to reduce gladness.' Literally: 'When Ab comes in, (they are) reducing gladness.'

What are we to make of this form? It occurs not a single time in the Old Testament. Nor, apparently, is it to be found in any of the non- Jewish Semitic systems. Yet in the earlier part of Talmudic literature, in Mishnah, Tosephta and Baraitha, it is more frequent than any other form: a counting might well show four-fifths of the Tannaitic law, religious or secular, to be given in this form. It is used in permissions, positive precepts, prohibitions. 'On the first days of the months, women are singing dirges but they are not wailing'—here we have a permission and a prohibition; 'When the month of Ab comes in, they

---

[1] M.Q. 3.9.   [2] Mish. Bik. 1.4.   [3] Deut. 26.3.   [4] Mish. Ta. 4.6.

are reducing gladness'—here we have a positive precept. It is used where there is one addressee—'The proselyte is bringing the first-fruits'—and where there are more—'Women are singing dirges'. It is used in precepts specifying the addressees—'Women are singing dirges'—and in precepts speaking quite generally—'In the month of Ab they, that is to say, everybody, are reducing gladness.'

To repeat, this form, to be met with neither in the Old Testament nor in other Semitic systems, dominates the earlier post-Biblical codifications. Here is a nice test for form criticism. If the principles of form criticism are right, these participles must be rooted in a specific experience and need affecting the Jewish people in the first few centuries after the completion of the canon. We submit that this is in fact the case.

The distinctive feature of the situation in that period was that, according to Rabbinic doctrine, the age of authoritative revelation was closed and that all further legislation bore the character of interpretation and stabilization of custom. Certainly, there were circles still prepared to acknowledge prophecy: the group responsible for the Zadokite Fragments, for example, or the followers of John the Baptist and Jesus, even, apparently, some of the more popular shades of Phariseism. (In the story of Susannah, Daniel, who advocates a Pharisaic innovation, does so as a messenger of God.[1] It may have been this element rather than minor points which caused the Rabbis to reject the work.) But as for the main stream of Rabbinic Judaism, the position was as just described: direct revelation no longer took place. It is this setting in life which accounts for the form under notice, the participles as a means of injunction, permission or prohibition. More precisely, the form reflects the Rabbinic view of the secondary, derivative, less absolute nature of post-Biblical rules.

To substantiate this explanation, let us examine the form as such, apart from the literary data mentioned. As we said, in this form of legislation the action enjoined, allowed or prohibited is expressed by a participle. The Hebrew participle, as is well known, often stands for our present tense: it is, in fact, the nearest equivalent possible. In particular, however, it stands for our present tense as referring to a habitual event, action or omission. Where the English version has 'One

---

[1] See the writer's remarks in *Revue Internationale des Droits de l'Antiquité*, vol. 2, 1949, p. 201.

generation passeth away and another cometh',[1] the original has 'One
generation (is) passing away and another (is) coming.'

Now in many languages that mood of the verb which denotes a
habitual action or omission can also be used, more specifically, to
denote a habit that is desirable, required by custom. The English
phrase 'It is not done' signifies 'It is not, by general consent, regarded as
desirable, it ought not to be done'; and I might tell my child that 'A
boy gets up in a bus when a grown-up looks for a seat', meaning, 'A
boy should get up, is expected to get up.' In France, notices like 'On ne
fume pas dans cette allée' are more usual than straightforward prohibitions like 'Smoking prohibited'; and even in Germany, where
authoritative commands are not entirely unknown, you might find
'Hier wird nicht geraucht'.

It is in this function, as an expression of the course to be taken in
accordance with proper interpretation and custom, that the participle
became the typically Rabbinic form of legislation. If we want to give it
a name, we should call it, not imperatival participle or participial
imperative, but rather advisory, didactic participle or perhaps best,
participle stating the correct practice. There was a wide gulf between
the Bible, the direct word of God, and Rabbinic elaboration and
systematization; and the Rabbis, conscious of it, evolved their own
form, significantly different from the forceful imperatives and imper-
fects of the Old Testament. It is the interpreter, the learned student of
the holy text, who speaks in a rule like 'The proselyte is bringing the
first-fruits, but he is not making the Avowal, I profess that I am come
unto the country which the Lord has promised unto our Fathers.' It is
the guardian of custom, the codifier of ritual in every sphere of life, who
speaks in a rule like 'On the first days of the months, women are singing
dirges but they are not wailing', or 'When the month of Ab comes in,
one is reducing gladness.'

We shall have to emphasize when we proceed to the discussion of
Rabbinic Authority (in Part III) that the further back we go in Rabbinic history, the freer we find the Rabbis in their decisions. Uniformity
came relatively late. In the three centuries preceding the destruction of
the Second Temple, different classes, schools and individuals held
different views even on important questions. But those warring parties
never considered one another as outside Judaism. They all based them-

[1] Eccles. 1.4.

selves on the Pentateuch: that made them belong to one religion. The task now was to establish the right meaning of Biblical law and to collect and fix the manifold traditions governing the practice of the people.

In the earlier phase of this process at least, it would have been quite out of place to dictate. A Rabbi would state his decision, or rather opinion, not as on a level with the supreme and absolute revelation of the Bible, not as an unavoidable, fundamental principle, but in this pedestrian, scholarly, didactic participle-form, corresponding to our 'One does this or that'. Even a regulation like that of the High Priest John Hyrcanus (of the second half of the 2nd cent. B.C.), concerning Tithes, seems to have employed this form—if indeed we may rely on the version preserved in the Gemara.[1] That ruling attempted a solution of the problem of Tithes at once satisfying the scrupulous and not imposing too heavy a burden: 'He who buys produce from an *Am-Haaretz*, an Uninstructed, is separating from it the Heave-offering of the first Tithe' and so on. Though a decree of the High Priest, it was a matter, not of divine command, but of working out the correct thing to do.

In a way, the transition from the powerful imperative commandments of the Pentateuch to the participle of the correct practice represents the same development in the field of legislation as does the transition from Psalm to Benediction in the field of liturgy. The Psalm is a form typical of the prophetic age; it is characterized by a bold immediacy of vision. The Benediction, *berakha*, is typical of early Tannaitic piety; it blesses God for qualities and deeds attributed to him in Scripture. The Rabbis, while making use of Biblical Psalms in temple and synagogue, refrained from composing new ones. (Here also, we find exceptions in one or two of the extremer sects.) The form they created and cultivated was the Benediction, more theological and less spontaneous than the Psalm. Just so, in the field of legislation, they preferred the sober, pious participle of the correct practice.

At this point, however, the question arises wherein lies the obligatory element of this form? There is no direct command, 'Do' or 'You shall do'. There is not even any express reference to a requirement such as 'It is needful to do so'. (Precepts introduced by 'It is needful' may occasionally be found in Tannaitic works.[2] In medieval codifications—

[1] Bab. So. 48a.   [2] E.g. Mish. Shab. 2.7.

Maimonides and so on—they are no less frequent than the participles.) The correct practice is simply represented as a fact, 'Women are singing dirges but are not wailing'; or in English, 'It is not done', 'A boy gets up'. How can a statement of fact impose a duty or grant a privilege?

The answer is that the teacher or lawgiver employing this form addresses an élite among whom the right thing, provided only it is known, is done—or at least is supposed to be done—as a matter of course. There is no need of exhortation or warning. He appeals to the self-respect of his public. In English, 'It is not done' more often than not implies 'In a decent society like ours, it is not done', and 'A boy gets up when an elderly person looks for a seat' means something like 'One belonging to that fine class of beings, namely, boys, gets up.' These precepts formulated as objective descriptions of customs have a flavour of exclusiveness which other forms, 'Do', 'You shall do', 'It is needful', have not.

I remember a scene in a French park, when a man, who thought himself particularly subtle, smoked despite the notice 'On ne fume pas dans cette allée', and, on being reprimanded by the attendant, replied: 'Mais vous voyez que l'on fume.' The attendant did not know how to counter this argument. In point of fact, however, the smoker, by advancing it, had excluded himself from the civilized public for whom the notice was intended. That public would require no prohibition; it would require only information as to the recognized practice of the place.

This form appeals to the self-respect of a superior group: it must be found suitable, for example, for the constitution of a body like the boy scouts—'A boy scout helps anyone in need.' Clearly, it would accord with the attitude of the early Pharisees: they were the *perushim*, 'those who kept apart'.[1] With some exaggeration, we might paraphrase the provisions quoted: 'In our exemplary community, as opposed to lesser ones, women are singing dirges but are not wailing, the proselyte is bringing the first-fruits' and so on.

No doubt the form gradually became stereotyped and more and more similar in import to other forms of legislation. The author of the particular precept 'Women are singing dirges but are not wailing', for

---

[1] This is not to say that T. W. Manson must be wrong in asserting ('Sadducee and Pharisee', *Bulletin of the John Rylands Library* 22, 1938, pp. 12 ff.) that the name originally signified 'those holding Persian beliefs'.

instance, may no longer have had in mind anything else than 'Women may sing dirges but they must not wail.' Nevertheless it is safe to conclude that, in its 'ideal', original application, the participle was designed to guide a superior type of person anxious to follow the right path. On this basis we can also understand why post-Tannaitic authors show far less predilection for the participle: Pharisaism was now the orthodox doctrine, it had ceased to be the affair of an élite among Jewry.

It is demonstrable that several Rabbinic rules which in course of time became generally accepted at first were not even intended to be binding on the whole people, but represented the convention of a special select group only. An example is furnished precisely by the law respecting Tithes, the regulation of which by John Hyrcanus we have just mentioned. There was the sect of the *Habherim*, the Associates, who undertook to observe the minutiae of Tithes and levitical cleanness. We possess what appears to have been part of their constitution in the time of the Second Temple. One paragraph says:[1] 'An Associate is not selling produce to an Uninstructed, and is not visiting an Uninstructed and is not receiving an Uninstructed in his own raiment.' Manifestly this code embodied the practice of a select community, not a law universally valid.

In such provisions the participle ought definitely not to be taken in its fully developed legislative sense: 'An Associate may not receive an Uninstructed.' It is almost used in the ordinary fashion, for making a detached observation, 'An Associate does not receive, is not accustomed to receive, an Uninstructed'—except that there is that implicit appeal to pride of which we have spoken. Indeed, we are not yet here very far from the Biblical 'A wise man is departing from evil, but the fool is raging':[2] the proper conduct is set down, even set down in a manner leaving no doubt as to the desirability of adopting it, extolled, depicted with all its advantages, but it is not actually enjoined. In tracing the rise of the participle-form in Tannaitic legislation, this background of conventions of special groups must not be overlooked.

Once the setting in life, the original function, of the participle in Rabbinic codifications is appreciated, some curious details become intelligible. On the one hand, in countless Rabbinic provisions, the participle certainly has the value of an imperative or imperfect. 'On the first days of the months women are not wailing' does closely approach

[1] Mish. Demai 2.3.   [2] Prov. 14.16.

'They must not wail.' It is worth noting that imperative and imperfect, coming down from the Biblical period, live on in Tannaitic law, though occupying a modest place only in comparison with the participle; and that sometimes the participle and one of the older forms are used side by side in the same paragraph of a code—obviously equivalent in that context. To quote such a precept:[1] 'The schoolmaster is supervising (participle) the reading of the children on Friday evening, but he himself may not read (imperfect) lest he forget about the commencement of the Sabbath.'

On the other hand, there are at least three points showing that the participle never acquired full imperative force in all connections, that it always retained something of its character as an expression of the customary, the agreed, the proper, as distinct from the authoritative, the revealed, the absolute. First, the participle never occurs in a specific demand on a specific occasion. It never stands for an imperative or imperfect of the kind 'Leave this room' or 'Today is the first of the month of Nissan, so these women should not wail.' It is used only in general demands, in rules. We found it in a paragraph laying down that 'On the first days of the months, women are not wailing.' This is different from 'They must stop wailing now.'

Secondly, even in rules the participle is never employed where a basic, absolute, unquestionable principle is to be enunciated. The plain prohibition of murder could not be expressed by a participle, just as an English catechism would not say, 'One does not murder.' In these matters, the authoritative forms alone are adequate. It is when we come to a law such as that one may not kill a man who is about to profane the Sabbath (whereas one may kill one who is about to kill somebody else) that the participle becomes possible.[2] There is something secondary, derivative, debatable about this provision.

Thirdly, the participle is avoided where a teacher gives—or is represented as giving—personal advice to his disciples. Quite apart from the influence of Biblical models—mainly in the Wisdom Literature, in Proverbs, Ecclesiastes and so on—the participle, as it refers to the customary, is too impersonal, too cold, for this purpose. A teacher giving personal advice prefers the warmer 'Be friendly' to the distant 'One is friendly.' In the Mishnic tractate Aboth there is not a single participle of the correct practice.

---

[1] Mish. Shab. 1.3.   [2] Mish. San. 8.7.

This form of legislation is a result of the change from revelation to interpretation and stabilization of custom, from prophet to scholar and compiler. Its limitations are no less revealing than the fact of its sudden predominance in the earlier Rabbinic codes.

B. *Halakhah*

From early Tannaitic times, the principal term for a binding rule was *halakhah*, literally, 'the walking'. To be sure, even the Old Testament is rich in expressions like 'to walk in the ways of the Lord', 'to walk righteously' and so forth. But there is no noun from the verb in this sense; the laws given by God are called 'judgments', 'statutes', 'commandments' or the like.

The Rabbis did not feel entitled to lay down 'judgments', 'statutes' or 'commandments'. Leaving out of account the *taqqana* (in Aramaic *taqqanta'*), the 'putting straight', 'amendment', 'reform in an emergency', their main task was a subordinate one: to interpret, elaborate, protect by a 'fence' and order the traditional material—chiefly material contained in the Pentateuch, but also usages that had grown up without any such basis. In other words, they had carefully to work out the proper course to take in any set of circumstances, the *halakhah*, the walking expected of a man who desired to do the right thing. It is easy to see that this is exactly the milieu, the setting in life, which we postulated for the participles of the correct practice. They are the form of legislation corresponding to the notion of *halakhah*.

It is only natural that now and then attempts were made to put the *halakhah* on the same level as the laws of the Pentateuch. That does not alter its essential character—certainly not for the ancient Tannaitic period. Moreover it should be noted that the limitations of the participle-form which we outlined above apply also to the notion of *halakhah*, and apply to it up to this day. First, a *halakhah* invariably denotes a general rule, never an isolated order. A Rabbi might inform me that the *halakhah* is to recite the Eighteen Benedictions at a certain hour; but if, when the time comes, he tells me to recite them, this is not a *halakhah*. Secondly, a basic, absolute principle like the duty to honour father and mother or the prohibition of murder is never described as a *halakhah*. Indeed the term is rarely used of any law belonging to the written Torah. The commonest Rabbinic word to denote a written

H

law is *miṣwa*, 'commandment', from *ṣiwwa*, 'to command'. *Halakhah* signifies something less fundamental; not the directly revealed law but the correct practice. The gentiles, while bound by the seven Noachian 'commandments', are not bound by any *halakhah*. Thirdly, *halakhah* is different from personal advice. It is objective, meant for all members of the community.

There are quite a few terms related to *halakhah*. One playing a prominent part in New Testament times is *derekh* (*'oraḥ*), 'way'. To some extent it overlaps with the other: a *halakhah* indicates the proper *derekh* to go, or at least part of it. But there is this difference, that a *halakhah*, 'the correct walking', refers to a conscious human action. *Derekh*, 'the proper way', refers to an external phenomenon, something that exists irrespective of human action; it has a wider range.

In consequence *halakhah* became the term for a rule prescribing what a Jew should or should not do, a rule stating the correct walking under the Law. *Derekh* might signify not only the proper way for men but also the proper way of things: the natural growth of a tree, for instance, or the ordinary symptoms of life and death, the 'Two Ways'. With regard to men, it is not only the good ones who have their typical way, but also the bad ones. Again, while the proper way of a Jew would certainly imply observance of all the *halakhoth*, all the rules concerned with the Law, it would include much more than that—pure sentiments, good manners, prudent behaviour and so on. It might indeed vary according to rank and education. The way of a *talmidh ḥakham*, a scholar, must be different from that of a plain citizen. Of the two tractates on *derekh 'ereṣ*, 'the manner of the land', 'the conduct of a normal, cultured person', one (Derekh Eretz Zuta) is more specially composed for the use of scholars. Actually, in some respects, each person has his own, individual way, and similarly each thing. Gentiles, though not at all bound by the *halakhah*, might yet follow a proper way, i.e. live a decent, civilized life.[1] No doubt it is partly owing to the strongly universal and ethical character of *derekh* that, in the tractates on *derekh 'ereṣ* just mentioned, the dry, precise participles of the correct practice are far outnumbered by other forms of guidance.

A term of some interest is *serekh*, 'a clinging to something', 'imitation', 'habit', 'rule'. In the Zadokite Fragments it signifies 'the regula-

---

[1] For some further observations on the notion of *derekh* see the writer's article in *Festschrift Schulz*, 1951, I, pp. 140 ff.

tion' binding on the sect.[1] The secondary, derivative character, however, is far less pronounced than in the case of *halakhah*. True, like the Rabbis, the 'lawgiver' (*meḥoqeq*) of the sect only 'expounded' (*darash*) the existing Torah; he did not introduce a novel one as Moses had done. Nevertheless he was looked upon as a prophet, as a messenger of God, in a way in which the Rabbis were not. In the eyes of the Zadokites, that is, the era of revelation was not over. Hence the forms of legislation to be found in the Fragments in the main follow the Biblical pattern: 'And on the sabbath day, no man shall utter (imperfect) a word of folly or vanity'[2] and so on.

Another factor probably contributed to this result. The provisions enunciated by the 'lawgiver' seem to have been conceived of in much the same fashion as the Sadducees conceived of theirs, *scil.* as mere restatements of the written law: hence the phrases *serekh hattora*, 'the regulation of the Torah', and *serekh ha'areṣ 'asher miqqedhem*, 'the regulation of the land that prevailed of old'.[3] There were, in principle, neither elaborations nor inferences nor additions nor changes. This may well have favoured the retention of the old imperative style. In theory at least, the ordinances laid down by the 'lawgiver' were nothing but clearer repetitions of the Biblical ones.

Here may be the place to insert a remark—a very conjectural one—on the *sepher hahaghu* which occurs three times in the Zadokite Fragments.[4] Charles hesitatingly suggests that the words are corrupt and that the original may have spoken of a work circulating under Haggai's name, *sepher ḥaggay*. But perhaps we ought to translate the phrase as it stands: 'the Book of the Study', 'the Book of Meditation'. *Haghu* might be an Aramaic noun derived from *hagha'*, as *galu* and *galutha'*, 'exile', derive from *gela'*, *zenu* and *zenutha'*, 'unchastity', from *zena'*, *ḥezu* and *ḥazutha'*, 'vision', from *ḥaza'*, etc. The verb *hagha'*—or in Hebrew *hagha*—means 'to recite' or 'to meditate'.

In the history of Pharisaism it plays an important role. 'Meditating

---

[1] 9.1, 11.1, 15.1, 4, 16.1, 17.1; cp. also Aramaic and Greek Fragments of an Original Source of the Test. of Levi and Jub., vv. 29 f. [2] 13.2.
[3] The latter phrase seems to refer in particular to the Biblical rules (e.g. Num. 1.1 ff.) concerning the way the people should camp or, having reached Palestine, arrange their settlements. Among the Rabbis, too, we meet with the doctrine that the Pentateuchic regulation of this matter applies also to Jerusalem (Bab. Zeb. 116b): 'As was the camp in the wilderness, so should be the camp in Jerusalem; from Jerusalem to the mountain of the House should be the camp of the Israelites, from the mountain of the House to the gate of Nicanor should be the camp of the Levites, and from thenceforward should be the camp of the Divine Presence.' Cp. also Heb. 13.11. [4] 11.2, 15.5, 17.5.

on Scripture', for the Pharisees, became largely identical with 'deducing further laws from the written ones'; and, in coining the terms 'written Torah' and 'Torah by mouth', 'oral Torah', they probably had in mind a passage from Joshua:[1] 'This book of the Torah shall not depart out of thy mouth, but thou shalt meditate (hagha) therein day and night, that thou mayest do according to all that is written therein.' One of Job's friends mentions 'the sound (heghe) that goeth out of God's mouth'.[2] R. Judah b. Elai, a pupil of Akiba, explained[3] that heghe must mean Torah in the sense of rulings, halakhoth, made known by God in the heavenly court.

The sect responsible for the Zadokite Fragments certainly had a different attitude: the duty of their leaders was not to elaborate the written Torah, but on the contrary to preserve it absolutely intact. But 'meditating' on Scripture was no less necessary for this task than for that undertaken by the Pharisees. It is noteworthy that every time the sepher hahaghu is mentioned, the reference is to 'those who have insight into it' or 'are able to interpret it'. Actually a sentiment of the kind to be found in the first Psalm, 'Blessed is the man whose delight is in the Torah of the Lord and who meditates (hagha) in his Torah day and night', might well have been the slogan of this sect who called themselves 'the House of the Torah'.

It might perhaps be objected that the Aramaic form haghu is not consistent with the fairly (though not completely) pure Hebrew of the Zadokite Fragments. But the term may have been technical and therefore been taken over by the author without change. This would also account for the Hebrew article, hahaghu, 'the haghu', 'the Meditation', which does not really fit an Aramaic form of noun. The word, being technical and familiar, was treated as Hebrew.

Serekh recurs in the recently discovered Sectarian Manual of Discipline,[4] and here once more Biblical, imperative forms of legislation predominate: prophetic revelation was still possible. It is not accidental that, in the same circle, the form of the Psalm also continued to flourish. The hymns of this sect that have come to light are of great beauty. The Rabbis no longer ventured to compose fresh Psalms, and their legislative form was the participle.

However, the participle of the correct practice too appears in the

---

[1] 1.8. See the writer's article in *Hebrew Union College Annual*, 22, 1949, p. 258 f.
[2] Job 37.2.   [3] Gen. Rabba on 18.7.   [4] Col. 11.16.

Sectarian Manual. All I have seen so far of the document is a reproduction, smaller than the original, of column 1;[1] but, luckily, the second half contains a few instances. The reception of converts, we are told, is to be accompanied by the following ceremonies:[2] 'And the priests are narrating the exploits of God and are proclaiming his grace for Israel, and the Levites are narrating the iniquities of the children of Israel, and those who enter into the Covenant are confessing after them, We have been perverse, we have rebelled.'

Five points are worth mention. In the first place, the participles are used in a section which cannot possibly have been considered as going back to the Bible, a section dealing with the initiation of persons prepared to obey the *serekh hayyaḥadh*, 'the regulation of the community'.[3] Even if this 'regulation' itself was thought of as representing the true Biblical law, the initiation of those desiring to return to it was clearly on a different level, a less fundamental, newer custom, no part of the old revelation. As in Rabbinic codes, that is, the participle expresses the secondary character of a rule.

In the second place, the participles of the Sectarian Manual are still descriptive rather than fully legislative. They sound like an account of the ritual given by an enthusiastic spectator rather than injunctions in the strict sense. The author takes it for granted that the addressees will act upon his rules without being expressly told to do so.

In the third place, we evidently have before us the constitution of a very select body—comparable to the Associates referred to above. It is the conventions of a holy band which are formulated by means of the participle.

In the fourth place, just as in the Rabbinic codes, the participle-form alternates with other forms coming down from the Bible. In fact, as we have just seen, the Biblical forms are the rule in the Manual, while the participle is the exception. Thus the very first duty of priests and Levites on the occasion of a reception of converts is[4] that 'they shall be (imperfect) blessing the God of salvations'.

In the last place, there is preserved a Tannaitic summary of the procedure to be adopted for proselyte baptism.[5] The participle-form is used throughout, and its legislative quality is rather more in evidence than in the Sectarian Manual. None the less the two cases are essentially

---

[1] In Dupont-Sommer, *The Dead Sea Scrolls*, transl. by E. M. Rowley, 1952, p. 45.
[2] Ll. 21 ff.   [3] L. 16.   [4] Ll. 18 f.   [5] Bab. Yeb. 47a f.

parallel. In the Manual we read 'And the priests are narrating the exploits of God and the Levites are narrating the iniquities of Israel and those who enter are confessing after them'; similarly among the Rabbinic rules we find 'And two Scholars are standing by him and are telling him some of the lighter commandments and some of the weightier commandments.'

C. HAUSTAFELN

To turn to the New Testament, it has long been seen that in various epistles the unattached participle sometimes stands for an admonition. 'Abhorring that which is evil, in honour preferring one another', says Paul,[1] meaning by it, 'Christians should abhor the evil, should honour one another.' 'The servants subjecting themselves to their masters', says I Peter,[2] meaning by it, 'Christian servants should subject themselves.'

Moulton attempted to prove that this usage was common in the vernacular Greek of the time, but his evidence, taken from closing formulas of letters, is quite unconvincing. Not the remotest trace of the usage is discernible in any of the Hellenistic Haustafeln, such as Epictetus 2.10.

The most probable explanation of these strange participles in the epistles is that they are literally taken over from the Hebrew. 'Abhorring that which is evil, in honour preferring one another, the servants subjecting themselves to their masters'—all this would be perfectly regular in Rabbinic teaching. It may be recalled—as we have already pointed out—that the auxiliary verb 'to be' is always omitted in Hebrew in this connection. The Hebrew, that is, would always be 'Abhorring the evil', not 'They are abhorring', and 'The servants subjecting themselves', not 'The servants are subjecting themselves.' What strikes us as atrocious in the Greek was excellent in the underlying source.

In other respects also the participles are used exactly as they are used in Tannaitic codes. They appear, not in basic injunctions like the prohibition of murder, but in directions as to the proper behaviour of members of the new Christian society; they appeal to the pride of those addressed—'that ye walk worthy of the vocation wherewith ye are called;[3] they are meant for a small group only, for the elect; and they occur side by side with other forms of exhortation, such as im-

[1] Rom. 12.9 f.   [2] 2.18.   [3] Eph. 4.1.

peratives and infinitives. Everything points to the existence of early Christian codes of duties in Hebrew, from which the participles of the correct practice crept into the Greek of the epistles. Freedom in the spirit did not relieve the Church of the necessity of insisting on a definite moral order.

Once this is recognized, various difficulties disappear. A minor one, concerning a point from Romans, we shall have occasion to speak about when we discuss Missionary Maxims (in Part III). Here we may mention two of some importance. First, the unattached participles are to be met with only in certain epistles of the New Testament, and even there only in a single context, in the so-called Haustafeln, dealing with the conduct of Christians in their families, their communities and the state. If the form had been a genuine Hellenistic, vernacular development, why should its usage be restricted in this way? The view here advocated, however, gives a sufficient answer. The passages in question come from the Hebrew, and, in Rabbinic Hebrew, the participle was the normal form for such rules.

Again, it is the Haustafeln which I Peter is widely supposed to have borrowed from Paul. This would be curious in itself; and there is an additional problem, namely, that I Peter, with a Greek generally far better than Paul's, at least twice has the unattached participle where Paul has not.[1] It is now possible to assume that I Peter did not borrow from Paul, but that both of them drew on those Hebrew codes of the primitive Christian community. Incidentally, if this is right, one of the arguments against the authenticity of I Peter, its alleged Pauline character, loses much of its force.

We have still to ask what was the nature of the code or codes of which the writers of the New Testament epistles availed themselves. Several years ago I suggested that 'when we combine Demai (the constitution of the Associates in which their special obligations respecting Tithes and cleanness are laid down by means of the participle), Aboth (a collection of sayings concerning the right mode of living, where, however, the participle does not occur but only the more intimate forms of personal advice and the traditional forms of the Wisdom Literature) and Derekh Eretz (systems of social duties where the participle is occasionally used but, in the main, preference is given

[1] (1) I Pet. 3.1 against Eph. 5.22 and Col. 3.18; (2) I Pet. 2.18 against Eph. 6.5 and Col. 3.22.

to the same forms as in Aboth), we may be able to form some idea of what the codes behind Romans and so on looked like. It should be borne in mind that, if those codes said nothing of ritual obligations and barriers, in this respect more like the gentler Aboth and Derekh Eretz than Demai, the idea of chosenness, not being and acting like the others, must none the less have played a prominent part in them.' The Sectarian Manual of Discipline—if, as is likely, it dates from the period between the second century B.C. and the second century A.D.—comes fairly near the picture I tried to draw. Whether a little earlier or later than the epistles in question, it shows the kind of thing possible at that time in Judaism and, consequently, in primitive Christianity. It is a constitution like that of the Associates and definitely meant for a separatist group. But far greater emphasis than in Demai is laid on the social duties of the members towards one another, on missionary aims and on eschatological hope. And the participles of the correct practice are there.

D. A Passage from the Didache

Professor C. Moule most kindly draws my attention to chapter 5 of the Didache[1] which I ought to have considered when, in a note appended to Dr. E. G. Selwyn's commentary on I Peter, I investigated the unattached participles of the New Testament: 'But the Way of Death is this—it is evil, murders, adulteries, persecutors (διῶκται, noun denoting persons) of the good, hating (μισοῦντες, participle denoting persons) truth, loving (ἀγαπῶντες, participle denoting persons) lies' and so on.

Maybe the whole part from 'murders' should be construed as elliptic, exclamatory descriptions of what is to be seen on the Way of Death. On this basis, the nouns and participles denoting persons, though far from elegant, are not very extraordinary; and the structure is parallel, say, to the opening of Derekh Eretz Zuta, a guide for the use of Scholars: 'The ways of Scholars are—meek and humble in spirit, oppressed, beloved by every man, fearing sin' and so on.[2]

It is equally possible, however, that the section from 'persecutors' stands in the same line of descent as the participles of the correct prac-tice. To be sure, there is here no trace of an admonitory meaning: on the contrary, this is a list of doings to be avoided. But we may have

[1] Equals Ep. of Barnabas 20.   [2] Cp. Hippocrates, Decorum 3.

before us the kind of observation frequent in the Wisdom Literature and such tractates as Mishnah Aboth, i.e. that observation which, since it refers to a habit, easily assumes an admonitory meaning where the habit concerned is a desirable one. Above we quoted from Proverbs: 'A wise man (is) departing from evil, but a fool (is) raging.' As the ending shows, we cannot here substitute 'he should act thus' for 'he is acting thus'. But it is clear that, in a different context, the first half—'A wise man is departing from evil'—might come to signify 'he should depart'. The same is true of Aboth 5.7: 'There are seven marks of the clod and seven of the wise man; the wise man (is) not speaking before one greater in wisdom, and (is) not breaking in upon the speech of his fellow . . . and the opposites of these are the marks of the clod.' In an appropriate context, an observation like 'A wise man is not speaking before one greater in wisdom' would mean 'he should not speak'. The passage from the Didache, then, may be explained as going back to a Hebrew source which said: '(They are) persecuting the good, (they are) hating truth, (they are) loving lies.'

It is worth noting that the section discussed is reminiscent of, if not dependent on, a verse in Romans,[1] where we do find the unattached participle in an admonitory sense: 'Abhorring—one should abhor—that which is evil, cleaving—one should cleave—to that which is good.' The enumeration of vices in the Didache includes: 'Not cleaving to that which is good, being watchful not for that which is good but for that which is evil.'

The actual injunctions of the Didache, incidentally, are all given in the warmer, direct address, and several times to 'my child', e.g. 3.1 and 5.2: 'My child, flee from all that is evil', or 'May ye be preserved, children, from all these (vices).'

[1] 12.9.

V

A Baptismal Catechism

A. GENERAL

IN recent writings—notably those of Archbishop Carrington,[1] Dr. Selwyn[2] and Professor Davies[3]—much attention has been devoted to the pattern of the earliest Christian catechisms. It may be useful, therefore, to say something about the arrangement of that baptismal instruction which the Tannaites in the Talmud[4] recommend should be given to candidates for admission to Judaism.

The term 'baptismal instruction' may at first sight look strange, since it contains no reference to the other rites of entry into Judaism, circumcision and sacrifice. But, first, it has the advantage of brevity. Secondly, the instruction was in fact given by way of preparation for baptism. We shall see that its central part was repeated during the act of immersion. Thirdly, the sacrifice was never as essential as circumcision or baptism, and its cessation when the Temple was destroyed created no major problem. In all probability, it was widely understood to be the convert's first act of worship as a Jew. Fourthly, as for circumcision, it was of course required only in the case of a man. In that of a woman, even Judaism regarded baptism as the only indispensable rite of reception—a point not always given its due weight by those interested in the origins of the Christian ceremony. It is often claimed that Jewish baptism, in contradistinction to Christian, was crudely purificatory rather than moral, spiritual and sacramental; it had no higher significance—that was confined to circumcision. But if this were correct, we should be left with no actual rite of entry for female converts, no rite by which they were brought into the covenant. Yet they were more numerous than male converts.

We shall come back to this question of the nature of Jewish proselyte

---

[1] *The Primitive Christian Catechism*, 1940.   [2] *The First Epistle of St. Peter*, 1946.
[3] *Paul and Rabbinic Judaism*, 1948.   [4] Bab. Yeb. 47a f.; cp. Gerim 1.

baptism. But as it is not our main concern—we are primarily concerned with the pattern of instruction given to candidates for admission to Judaism—some preliminary remarks may be made in order to avoid repetition.

Those who think of Jewish proselyte baptism as levitical in the sense of quasi-physical rely almost exclusively on indirect, comparative, folkloristic evidence. But this has little bearing on the Judaism of New Testament times, an advanced religion. Even rites which were still largely purificatory had been sublimated to a greater or less degree.

Johanan ben Zaccai explained that neither did a person become really unclean by a corpse nor did he become really clean by the 'water of separation', but that the relevant provisions must be observed because it was the will of God.[1] A reader of the Mishnic tractate Mikwaoth ('Immersion-pools') might easily decide that the authors were dominated by notions of taboo. But the Mishnah is a code of laws and rarely indicates the ideas underlying them. As it happens, in another tractate[2] we learn that R. Akiba said: 'Blessed are ye, O Israel. Before whom are ye made clean and who makes you clean? Your Father in heaven. As it is written,[3] And I will sprinkle clean water upon you and ye shall be clean. And again it says,[4] O Lord, the hope, *miqwe* (which may also signify "immersion-pool"), of Israel: as the *miqwe* cleanses the unclean, so does the Holy One cleanse Israel.' This hymn concludes the tractate Yoma ('Day of Atonement')—which would be impossible if spiritual elements had not penetrated any kind of immersion, i.e. even immersion other than baptism of a proselyte. Proselyte baptism, however, was essentially quite outside the levitical sphere: pagans were not susceptible of levitical uncleannness, so in principle there was simply no room for purification.[5]

To be sure, a few Rabbinic passages apparently favour the opposite view. The one receiving most emphasis in modern treatises[6] occurs in Mishnah Pesahim,[7] where the problem from what moment a convert may share in the Passover is discussed side by side with that of unclean Israelites. But the connection is dictated by the strict Biblical prohibition of pagan participation in the Passover.[8] It was just as necessary to determine exactly who was excluded on this ground as who was

---

[1] Num. Rabba on 19.2, P. de-R.K. 40a f.   [2] Yoma 8.9.
[3] Ezek. 36.25.   [4] Jer. 17.13.   [5] Pal. Pes. 36b, Mish. Neg. 7.1.
[6] E.g. Strack-B., 1, 103 f., followed by Flemington, *The New Testament Doctrine of Baptism*, 1948, pp. 5 ff.   [7] 8.8.   [8] Exod. 12.43 ff.

excluded on the ground of uncleanness. The following chapter of the Mishnah deals with the second Passover,[1] to be celebrated four weeks after the first by those who missed the first—persons who were unclean at the time, persons who were away on a journey, persons who became converts too late. It is very rash to draw inferences as to the meaning of baptism from this treatment of the subject in the Mishnah. If modern— or ancient—election law refuses a vote to foreigners, absentees and lunatics, this does not mean that naturalization or return to one's domicile is deemed to be a step from insanity to sanity.

A significant fact, usually overlooked, is that the same problem—i.e. from what moment a convert may share in the Passover—recurs in Mishnah Eduyoth[2] in an entirely different context. Here it figures among the matters in regard to which the School of Hillel took a more stringent line than that of Shammai. In Pesahim, then, the association of conversion with cleanness is the result of the peculiar Scriptural regulations about the Passover meal. In Eduyoth, conversion is associated with certain subjects for a historical reason concerning the two Schools. Neither case justifies the conclusion that the topics put together had any fundamental affinity with one another.

The conflict between the two Schools is worth closer inspection. That of Shammai held that a pagan being converted on the eve of Passover might at once take part in the celebration; that of Hillel denied it, since 'he who separates himself from the uncircumcision is like one who separates himself from the grave'. In other words, according to the School of Hillel, he must wait for the second Passover, as one defiled by burial.

This dispute is attested in a number of sources. Moreover, the elder Eliezer ben Jacob (who survived the destruction of the Temple and, together with Hillelites of the type of Johanan ben Zaccai, helped to adapt Judaism to the new conditions) reports that on one occasion pagan soldiers fighting on the Jewish side became converts on the eve of Passover and were immediately admitted to the supper—in accordance with the Shammaite practice.[3] Hence there is direct proof that the conservative Shammaites at least did not look on the rites of entry as purificatory. It is the progressive Hillelites who brought a levitical concept into conversion. Indeed, of the elder Eliezer ben

---

[1] Cp. Num. 9.9 ff.
[2] 5.2.
[3] Pal. Pes. 36b, Tos. Pes. 7.13.

Jacob, just mentioned, we know that he attached much importance to its full and consistent application.[1] How is this to be explained?

In general, the Hillelites were more lenient than the Shammaites. Even in cases where they are said to have been stricter, we sometimes find that their strictness was superficial whereas, in reality, theirs was the more liberal attitude. For example, we are told that, though for the Shammaites the Book of Ecclesiastes did not render the hands unclean, the Hillelites insisted that it did.[2] The implication, however, is that the Shammaites refused to recognize this work as canonical, whereas the Hillelites recognized it.

It is, therefore, advisable to pay careful attention to the motives of the Hillelites wherever they advocated a more rigorous doctrine than the Shammaites; doubly advisable if they did so in a question respecting conversion. Hillel himself was famous—or notorious—for his readiness to facilitate conversion.[3] He admitted a pagan, for instance, who would acknowledge only a single ethical rule, 'What is hateful unto thee do not do unto a fellow-man.' (True, after the pagan had become a Jew, Hillel undertook to show him that the Law was binding since it was nothing but a logical elaboration of the golden rule.) One of Hillel's maxims was: 'Love mankind and bring them nigh unto the Law.'[4] Towards the end of the 1st cent. A.D., leading Hillelites—above all, Joshua ben Hananiah—claimed that baptism alone was sufficient to make even a male gentile Jewish.[5] They did not go quite so far as Paul: they did not deny that it was the duty of a male convert to be circumcised. But they did consider him fully Jewish as soon as he was baptized. It is interesting that their argument was that baptism was the decisive rite in the case of a woman, so it should be the same in that of a man.

Such, then, was the position of Hillel and his School as represented by the Talmud and Midrash; and we must consider that it is certainly toned down in these works, which were redacted much later than the Hillelite period. Judaism in the meantime had become more rigid and Hillel's universalism was now regarded as dangerous. Obviously, it would be a mistake to suppose that, in their conflict with the Shammaites, the Hillelites stood for a primitive view of conversion. On the contrary, their decision that 'he who separates himself from the un-

---

[1] Mish. Ker. 2.1, Bab. Ker. 8b. [2] Mish. Ed. 5.3.
[3] Bab. Shab. 31a. [4] Mish. Ab. 1.12. [5] Bab. Yeb. 46a.

circumcision is like him who separates himself from the grave' followed from the profound thought—doubtless earlier then Hillel[1]—that conversion meant a passage from death to life. We have before us an instructive example of the way in which, at a certain stage in religious evolution, the introduction of ritual may reflect, not a belief in taboo, but a highly spiritual attitude.

There are various points confirming our argument. For one thing, the parallelism in form between the two parts of the maxim—'he who separates himself from the uncircumcision is like him who separates himself from the grave'—is striking: it suggests a parallelism in substance, an actual comparing of him who rises above heathenism to one who rises from the dead. The language is remarkable in another respect. Had the Hillelites thought in crude levitical terms, the natural thing to say would have been that a convert was 'like one who has touched a corpse'.[2] The phrase 'like one who separates himself from the grave' indicates that their starting-point was the idea that, spiritually, heathenism equalled existence in a tomb. The levitical element was only used to give this idea clear and forceful expression.

It should be noted that the term 'uncircumcision' in the maxim discussed has the metaphorical sense of 'heathenism'. We are expressly told that the Hillelites applied the maxim to female converts as well as male ones:[3] the former also 'separated themselves from the uncircumcision' and, accordingly, were treated as 'separating themselves from the grave'.

The figurative use of the word 'dead' to denote an unenlightened person or a sinner is to be met with in most languages. It is adumbrated in the Old Testament[4] and existed in New Testament times: 'Let the dead bury their dead.'[5] But the Hillelite concept of conversion as resurrection was, of course, something far more specific.

Its influence may be seen in many utterances and incidents. There is, for example, an anonymous (and, therefore, undatable) comment on the verse from Ecclesiastes: 'So I saw the wicked ones buried, and they came.' This is interpreted by the Rabbis as referring to the proselytes:

---

[1] Below we shall quote Bab. Ta. 32a, giving a conversation between Alexander the Great and 'the Elders of the South'. Though legendary, it does reflect views current among Egyptian Jews in the two or three centuries preceding our era.

[2] Num. 19.16. Cf. e.g. Mish. Oho. 1.1: 'If a man touches a corpse, he contracts seven-day uncleanness.'

[3] Tos. Pes. 7.13.   [4] E.g. Ps. 106.28.   [5] Matt. 8.22, Luke 9.60.

proselytes are people who have risen from their graves.[1] Again, the Rabbis assumed that the Israelites with whom the Sinaitic covenant was concluded were circumcised. Two passages are quoted by way of evidence:[2] one from the Book of Joshua,[3] 'Now all that came out of Egypt were circumcized', and one from Ezekiel,[4] 'And when I passed by thee and saw thee polluted in thy blood, I said, In thy blood live, in thy blood live.' The repetition of the exclamation is found significant by the Rabbis: the first imperative is held to allude to the blood of circumcision, the second to that of the Passover lamb. The whole proof from Ezekiel, however, is distinctly more artificial than that from Joshua. No doubt it was added by the Hillelites, when they worked out the idea of conversion as a transition from death to life. At one time the passage from Ezekiel formed part of the Passover Haggadah, the narrative of God's redemption of Israel recited on Passover eve; presumably it was removed from fear of the blood accusation.

Very likely, some of the mocking questions which the opponents of the belief in bodily resurrection liked to put to the Pharisees were suggested by the Hillelite interpretation of conversion as a rising from the dead. The Alexandrians asked Joshua ben Hananiah (about A.D. 100) whether, on resurrection, the dead would need sprinkling, having been in contact with tombs: a clever way of ridiculing a Rabbi who taught that a convert, since he had risen from the grave, fell under the provisions respecting corpse-uncleanness.[5]

Enough of the conflict between the Schools. Let us remember that, for both of them, the decisive moment in proselyte baptism was the 'going up' or 'coming up'—no doubt because of its symbolical value. The relevant Tannaitic provision—which, we shall see presently, is alluded to in the New Testament—runs: 'When he has undergone baptism and come up, *tabhal we'ala*, he is like an Israelite in all respects.'[6] How easily such a detail is overlooked once its role is no longer appreciated may be seen from the fact that even scholars like Montefiore and Loewe, in translating the provision,[7] simply cut out *we'ala*. Their rendering is: 'When he has been baptized, he is regarded in all respects as an Israelite.' Yet it is a detail of the highest importance. The 'coming up' was the decisive moment because of its symbolic meaning,

[1] Eccles. Rabba on 8.10.   [2] Bab. Ker. 8a.   [3] 5.5.   [4] 16.6.
[5] Bab. Nid. 69b ff.   [6] Bab. Yeb. 47b.   [7] *Rabbinic Anthology*, 1938, p. 579.

and once such symbolism was established, it could always be used in new ways.

It is, for example, conceivable that among the reasons why the Baptist chose to baptize in the Jordan was that he saw in the 'coming up' a new entry into the Promised Land. The usual verb for 'to go up to Palestine from abroad' is 'ala. Moreover, it figures prominently in the scene where Joshua crosses the Jordan dry-shod:[1] 'On that day the Lord magnified Joshua. And he spake, saying, Command the priests that they come up out of Jordan. Joshua therefore commanded the priests, saying, Come ye up. And when the priests were come up, the waters of Jordan returned. And the people came up out of Jordan on the tenth day of the first month.' Josephus records[2] that Theudas, who claimed to be a prophet—he is mentioned in Acts[3] and no doubt claimed to be 'the prophet like unto Moses'[4]—declared he was capable of dividing the Jordan. As for Hillel's interpretation of proselyte baptism as a passage from death to life—'ala may denote 'to rise from the grave'.[5]

In fact, the 'coming up' is expressly noticed in the narrative of Jesus's baptism as told by Matthew and Mark;[6] conclusive evidence—if any were still needed—that Christian baptism originated in Jewish proselyte baptism. The notice makes sense only if we regard it as alluding to the provision quoted above. The 'coming up' is the decisive moment—it is at this moment that Jesus sees the heavens opened and the Spirit descending. Luke and John[7] omit the reference. Luke or his public no longer understood the Jewish ritual. John, unlike the Synoptics, does not purport to give a full account of the event; indeed, he does not speak of an actual baptism of Jesus at all. So we cannot expect him to mention the 'coming up'. But he was surely familiar with the Jewish law on the matter. In any case, that law was far from levitical in a primitive sense.

One more principle may be advanced which was generally recognized by the Rabbis of the New Testament period, and which would be quite incompatible with the notion of baptism as a merely purificatory act: a convert—and even a female one, received by baptism alone—had the status of a new-born child.[8] Had this doctrine been the basis

---

[1] Joshua 4.14 ff.   [2] Ant. 20.5.1.97 ff.   [3] 5.36.   [4] Deut. 18.15.
[5] E.g. Mish. San. 10.3: 'The company of Korah shall not rise up.'
[6] Matt. 3.16, Mark 1.10.   [7] Luke 3.21, John 1.32.
[8] Bab. Yeb. 48b, quoting Rabbis of the 1st and 2nd cents.

only for such teachings as that a proselyte's former sins are forgiven,[1] it might be argued that it was just an academic whim. But it influenced important legal decisions.

In principle, a proselyte, being newly born, could marry any of his relatives even if the relative, too, had become a Jew. It was only in order to prevent a convert from gaining the impression that he had passed 'from a weightier sanctity into a lighter sanctity' that the Rabbis enacted limitations to the principle. One group of Rabbis excluded those unions which were contrary even to gentile, Noachian morality.[2] (Paul adopted this standard when he condemned the marriage of a convert with his widowed stepmother as 'fornication that is not so much as named among the Gentiles'.[3]) There was no objection, however, to, say, a proselyte marrying his paternal half-sister or a proselytess marrying her paternal half-brother, even after both had become Jewish. No blemish of any kind attached to the off-spring of such a union—they might marry into priestly families. It is obvious that the notion of a new birth was taken seriously; more seriously (a strange thought) than it seems to be taken by modern Christianity. And we may note again that in the majority of conversions—namely, in conversions of women—the new birth was effected by baptism alone.

B. The Pattern of Instruction

1. The test

When we analyse the baptismal instruction recommended in the Talmud, five divisions emerge, of which the first is in the nature of a test. The person wishing to become a Jew 'at this time' should be asked whether he does not know that 'Israel at this time is broken down, pushed about, driven about and tossed about, and that sufferings befall them'. If he replies 'I know and am not worthy', no further tests are needed, but he should at once be admitted as a candidate and be taught.

---

[1] E.g. Eccles. Rabba on 1.8, quoting Joshua ben Hananiah. According to Pal. Bik. 65c f., R. Zeira, at the beginning of the 4th cent., hesitated to accept ordination but finally consented because, on ordination, his previous sins would be wiped out. This effect of ordination had, of course, been established long before his time. The proof for it was seen in the forgiveness of sins extended to proselytes. The belief that a proselyte's sins are forgiven must, therefore, be even older.   [2] Bab. Yeb. 22a, San. 58a ff., Qid. 77a ff.

[3] I Cor. 5.1. That some Rabbis considered marriage with a widowed stepmother as permissible under Noachian law is irrelevant. Paul sided with those like Akiba (Bab. San. 58b) who did not so consider it.

I

The first thing to be noticed is that, in strictness, the question and reply here envisaged do not form part of the prospective convert's preparation: they precede it. It is the gentile who approaches the Jews, not the Jews who approach the gentile; and the Rabbis lay down that, before his proper initiation can even begin, he must have grasped the fundamentals of the faith—he must recognize even that Israel's humiliation in this age means exaltation.

No doubt it would all be resumed and elaborated in the course of his instruction; and Israel's sufferings in particular might form not only the final subject of the preliminary negotiations, but also the introductory one of the lessons. But for the present it is important to realize that, in the Rabbinic system before us, the main place of the elements of the faith is prior to the actual catechism. The candidate must have familiarized himself with them beforehand. This accords with several reports regarding conversions in New Testament times. Three gentiles wanted to be received into the Jewish fold on special terms—terms rejected by Shammai but agreed to by Hillel.[1] One would recognize only the written Law but not the oral; another required that he should be taught the entire Law while he could stand on one foot; and a third demanded to be made High Priest. We need not here consider the exact significance of these stories. What is relevant is that by the time the preparation of these men began, they had already decided that Judaism was best.

The scheme reflects the normal attitude of the Tannaites to proselytizing. (In reality, on occasion, matters might take a very different course. There might even be compulsory conversion. Josephus tells us[2] how a mob proposed to place before two pagan noblemen who had deserted from Agrippa the alternative between undergoing circumcision and facing death or expulsion. But the circumstances were exceptional, and at any rate the plan of the mob was diametrically opposed to the prevalent Rabbinic teaching.) They did desire converts. But in general they refrained from persuasion, since a gentile complying with the seven Noachian commandments, the elementary principles of morality, was preferable to a Jew spurning any one of the numerous regulations of the Law.

Moreover, some of these regulations—the law of circumcision, for instance—were of such a nature as to render mass proselytizing impos-

---

[1] Bab. Shab. 31a.   [2] Life 23.113, 31.149 ff.

sible. Matthew,[1] where he speaks of the missionary zeal of the Pharisees, distinctly contemplates the proselytizing of individuals. It is against this background that we must see the provisions respecting baptismal teaching. They refer to the case of a gentile—a single gentile—asking to be received, and he is expected to know about the essence of Judaism even at this stage.

Nevertheless there were Rabbis who considered it all-important to win over fresh adherents and did not hesitate to make occasional concessions. Hillel belonged to this wing; while circles somewhat removed from Rabbinic orthodoxy went even further in relaxing the Law with a view to gaining converts or, indeed, half-converts. It is well known that in the Hellenistic era not a few pagans lived on the fringe of Judaism: without formally joining it, they had adopted some of its dogmas and customs. In this connection it should be recalled that two kinds of propaganda were favoured by all Jewish parties: they all wished to convince the gentiles of the validity of the Noachian commandments, the simplest demands of morality, and they all wished the heathen world at least to respect the Jewish religion. Evidently, where the latter aim was pursued, apologetic motives were at work as well as missionary ones.

It is not surprising, therefore, to find plans of instruction very different from that just described, namely, plans where the instruction starts practically 'from scratch'. Josephus in his defence of Judaism begins by demonstrating the antiquity of the nation, then he dwells on its contribution to civilization, then he goes on to explain its conception of God and his worship—Strabo too had learned about this[2]—and finally he discusses its laws. In works like this, the author would normally address himself to the gentile masses, not merely to one or two exceptional individuals.

There was indeed another kind of mass proselytizing which should not be overlooked: the inner mission, and above all, the attempts of certain sects to convince their fellow Jews of the superiority of their particular doctrines. The problem of circumcision did not here arise. A Jewish propagandist could not hope to cause large numbers of gentiles to submit to the Law. But, say, a good Essene preacher or writer might well attract large numbers of Pharisees. Of John the Baptist we hear that he had a considerable following.[3]

[1] 23.15.   [2] 16.2.35.   [3] Matt. 3.5, Mark 1.5, Luke 3.7, Josephus Ant. 18.5.2.118.

In such cases, naturally, the teaching would be more or less confined to features peculiar to the sect, items as to which it differed from the Judaism surrounding it. But the same sect might have several catechisms. For one thing, just as there were Jews and people half-converted to Judaism, so some of the sects consisted of an inner circle, the initiated, and several outer circles, those on the way to full membership. Three years were the minimum period between application for admission to the order of the Essenes and final reception.[1] The instruction of a candidate doubtless varied according to the state he had attained.

The presumption is that the different kinds of Jewish missionary teaching all had their counterparts in the early Christian Church, and that they all have left traces in the New Testament. Peter at Pentecost,[2] like the Baptist, appealed to his fellow Jews at large, of whom three thousand are said to have undergone baptism; and his sermon dealt exclusively with the Messiahship of Jesus, the great distinctive tenet of his group. As the conditions of reception were revised—first unofficially and later officially—mass proselytizing of gentiles also became feasible. Henceforth, however, missionaries frequently had to concentrate on matters which, in addressing Jews, they could take for granted. The belief in salvation through Jesus might take root among a set still approving of incestuous relations. A situation of this sort would necessitate something like the Tannaitic scheme of preparation: the teacher's task would be, not so much to convince his public of a fundamental dogma, as to impress on them its implications and the practical consequences to be drawn. Again, one plan might be suitable for a gathering of vague sympathizers and another for candidates already knowing a good deal and resolved to join the new religion.

It is widely held that not a few sections of the Epistles repeat, or allude to, baptismal teaching. If one looks at the pattern suggested by the authorities named at the beginning of this chapter, one receives the impression that, as a rule, early Christian catechists, like the Tannaites, expected their pupils to be acquainted with the essence of the creed.

The catechisms they used were in the main intended for such as had already heard—and accepted—the gospel. There is little sign of a complete exposition and argumentation such as would be required for inducing outsiders to come over. The emphasis lies on affirmation, clarification and rules of conduct. (The Haustafeln in particular, far

---

[1] Josephus, Bell. 2.8.7.137 ff.   [2] Acts 2.14 ff.

from placing at the head a description of the proper attitude to God, are silent on the subject: the addressees are supposed to know about it.) What remained to do once actual preparation for baptism began was, first, to make clear to candidates the deeper significance of the revelation they acknowledged, and secondly, to give them directions as to the life they ought to lead in future.

Let us now inspect more closely the nature of the test which the Tannaites impose on a candidate before instruction may commence. He must, we are told, show a proper understanding of the sufferings of Israel. This means that a mere declaration of willingness to live under the Law is not enough. It might be dictated by unworthy or inadequate motives: fear of enemies, desire for advancement, love of a Jewess or the like.[1] But, as Josephus puts it, only that proselyte is welcome who takes the step from προαίρεσις, and not ἐκ παρέργου, from deliberate choice and not incidentally, while in reality pursuing a different object.[2] So the purity of his intentions must be proved—by his attitude to Israel's fate.

There is reason to believe that early Christian catechisms usually opened by a reference to affliction and temptation.[3] Carrington rightly stresses its traditional character, adducing the beginning of the second chapter of Sirach. When he goes on to say, however,[4] that it was only Christianity which added the idea of rejoicing or boasting in adversity, we must dissent. According to the Tannaites, the prospective convert, on having his attention drawn to the sufferings of Israel, is supposed to reply: 'I know and am not worthy.' Whether we interpret the answer as meaning 'I am not worthy to share these sufferings' or 'I am not worthy to bend my neck under the yoke of him who spake and the world came into being',[5] it is more than a resigned acceptance of an evil. Israel's sufferings are here looked upon as resulting from a special relationship to God; and from this point of view, they are Israel's hidden glory.

The associations of the phrase 'sufferings befall them' are relevant. In the verse[6] 'As a man chasteneth (makes to suffer) his son, so the Lord thy God chasteneth (makes to suffer) thee', the Rabbis maintain[7] that

---

[1] Bab. Yeb. 24a.
[2] C.Ap. 2.28.209 f. Cp. 2.39.284, about the Law conquering mankind without the bait of pleasure.   [3] E.g. Rom. 5.3, I Thess. 1.6, I Pet. 1.6, Jas. 1.2.   [4] Pp. 22, 59.
[5] The former interpretation is given by Rashi on Yeb. 47a, the latter in Gerim 1.
[6] Deut. 8.5.   [7] Mekh. on Exod. 20.23.

the apposition 'thy God' is not superfluous: it means that the Lord is in a special sense the God of him who suffers—'the name of God rests upon him whom sufferings befall'. The expression 'sufferings are beloved, precious' occurs again and again, in the earliest and latest parts of the Talmud. Paul's word 'we glory in tribulations' is thoroughly Jewish.[1] Nor should we forget about a particular quality the Rabbis ascribe to sufferings: sufferings help a man to inherit the World to Come. R. Eleazar ben Zadok, who flourished about A.D. 100, declared this to be the reason why God 'let sufferings befall the pious'.[2]

In fact, the Syriac Apocalypse of Baruch contains the admonition:[3] 'Rejoice in the suffering which ye now suffer, and prepare your souls for the reward which is laid up for you.' There is no reason to assume that this passage was inspired by Christian models. It is Jewish.

Here is the place to remark on another suggestive feature of the Tannaitic plan: the eschatological undertone of the introductory point. The repetition of the words 'at this time' is striking: if a gentile asks to be received 'at this time', the Rabbis hold, Israel's sufferings 'at this time' should be emphasized. 'At this time' signifies 'while Israel is oppressed'—a state which roughly covers the entire period between the reigns of David and Solomon in the past and the Messianic reign in the future.[4] Certainly, even nowadays there may be occasional periods when Israel prospers and God betrays his preference for his people. But R. Nehemiah, about A.D. 150, says that persons who join Israel at one of these moments cannot be considered genuine until they give proof of their loyalty 'at this time', i.e. in the face of persecution; or at least, if they have no opportunity of documenting their faith in this way, their motives ought to be as sincere as if they were converts 'at this time', i.e. as if there were persecution.

We shall presently see that eschatology is the principal theme of the concluding part of the Tannaitic catechism; and the notion 'at this time' recurs there, being opposed to 'the World to Come'. Manifestly eschatology plays a role even at the opening stage. 'At this time' means an interlude evoking reminiscences of a happier past but also, and even primarily, the expectation of a glorious future.

The eschatological setting of John's baptism and early Christian baptism turns out to be inherited from Judaism. Certainly both John and the early Christians accorded greater prominence to this element.

---

[1] See Strack-B.   [2] Bab. Qid. 40b.   [3] 52.6.   [4] Bab. Yeb. 24a, A.Z. 3b.

But it was there before John. John, believing the kingdom of heaven imminent, preached the baptism of repentance. A Rabbi like Eliezer ben Hyrcanus, about A.D. 100, predicted[1] that at the approach of the Messiah the gentiles would come in flocks to be received. Eliezer would never have applied proselyte baptism to people already Jewish. It was because John did so[2] that he was called 'the Baptist'. Yet the eschatological character of his and early Christian baptism was Jewish. Some rebukes administered to Pharisees and Sadducees according to Matthew and Luke[3] closely correspond to an opinion, held by many Rabbis,[4] that people seeking admission in the days of the Messiah were not to be trusted.

As for Christian baptism, since, in a way, the kingdom had arrived, the rite, in a way, symbolized entry into the kingdom. Yet in this case also it is easy to exaggerate the difference from Jewish proselyte baptism. Flemington[5] deserves credit for stressing that, even for the early Church, all the eschatology was not 'realized'. There was still to be a future consummation, and this expectation affected baptismal teaching. At any rate, in the Tannaitic system, the gentile is asked whether he is not aware of Israel's humiliation 'at this time', and he replies: 'I know and am not worthy.' In I Peter we read: 'You who are kept through faith unto salvation in the last time, wherein ye rejoice though now for a season ye are in heaviness through manifold temptations, that the trials, being more precious than gold, might be found unto praise and glory at the appearing of Jesus Christ.' The Tannaitic influence is unmistakable.

2. The commandments

The actual preparation of the catechumen should begin by making known to him some of the lighter and some of the weightier commandments—at least if we follow the prevalent translation. It is certainly the most likely one. R. Judah the Prince gave the advice:[6] 'Be heedful of a light commandment as of a weighty one, for thou knowest not the reward for each.' The terms 'small' and 'great' may replace 'light' and 'weighty'.[7] Just so, we find Matthew speaking of judgment,

[1] Bab. A.Z. 24a.
[2] And not because of any distinctive form of his baptism—that would not account for the designation.
[3] E.g. Luke 13.25.
[4] Bab. A.Z. 3b.
[5] Op. cit., 74.
[6] Mish. Ab. 2.1.
[7] Deut. Rabba on 22.6.

mercy and faith as the 'weightiest' commandments;[1] we find Matthew and Mark speaking of the love of God and the love of one's neighbour as the 'greatest' commandments;[2] and we find Matthew condemning the abolition of even the 'smallest' commandment.[3]

However, a different rendering is just possible. The word *qal* may denote not only 'light' but also 'easy', and *hamur* not only 'weighty' but also 'burdensome'. Gamaliel and Simeon ben Azzai, about A.D. 100, considered[4] the prohibition of blood one of the 'easiest' (though definitely not one of the 'lightest') commandments, because man had no natural craving for the taste of blood. They taught that the special warning—'Only be steadfast'—prefixed by the Bible to this easy commandment must all the more be taken to heart in connection with burdensome ones. Josephus says[5] that even those practices which the Jews find 'the easiest'—working with one's own hands, observing restrictions as regards diet, sexual relations and extravagance, and resting on the Sabbaths—others would not put up with. Again, a Rabbi might *heqel* or *hehemir*, interpret a law (whether it was 'light' or 'weighty') in an 'easy', lenient, way, or in a 'burdensome', restrictive, way. According to Matthew, the scribes incline to do the latter, to 'bind heavy burdens'.[6] So the provision discussed conceivably means that a catechumen should be told about some of the easier and some of the more burdensome commandments.

Whichever translation we adopt—and maybe we ought to adopt both, since the authors of the plan may not have strictly distinguished between the various nuances of *qal* and *hamur*—the instruction appears to be, not simply in the chief duties, but in the general atmosphere of the new life. This part of the catechism, therefore, would be the most important.

The conclusion is confirmed by the fact that this part alone recurs at a subsequent stage of the procedure: during the act of baptism, during immersion, we learn, two Scholars are to stand by—in the case of a woman they are to stand outside but within hearing—in order again to communicate to the proselyte some lighter and some weightier com-

---

[1] 23.23. Luke 11.42 omits the technical description.
[2] Matt. 22.35 ff., Mark 12.28 ff. Luke 10.25 ff. again avoids the term and re-writes the question put to Jesus, with the result that it is of a type less technically Rabbinic and more adapted to the understanding of a non-Jewish public.   [3] 5.19.
[4] Siph. on Deut. 12.23 f., in conjunction with Bab. Mak. 23b.   [5] C.Ap. 2.32.334.
[6] 23.4. Cp. Luke 11.46, where, however, the technical term is not used.

mandments. We may regard this as another sign that, by the Tannaitic epoch at least, proselyte baptism was no purificatory rite but had a moral and spiritual significance: instruction in the commandments would not be a fitting accompaniment of a primitively levitical ceremony. It should also be observed that not one commandment dealing with levitical purity is singled out for mention.

Actually, we may go as far as to assert that, in listening to the commandments during baptism, the proselyte stood at mount Sinai. From the beginning of the 1st cent. A.D. down to our day the ceremonies of reception into Judaism have been based on the same principle:[1] they must be identical with those by which the Israelites were received into the Sinaitic covenant. According to the Rabbis—or most of them, at any rate—the Israelites were received through circumcision, baptism and sacrifice. The texts by which they support this assumption are, for circumcision, 'All the people that came out of Egypt were circumcised' and 'When I passed by thee, I said, In thy blood live, in thy blood live';[2] for baptism, 'Sanctify the people and let them wash their clothes' and 'Moses sprinkled the blood of the covenant on the people';[3] and for the sacrifice, 'Moses sent young men which offered burnt offerings.'[4] That to us some of these texts may seem inconclusive does not matter; we are concerned with the ideas current in New Testament times.

Like the Israelites, the proselyte must enter by circumcision, baptism and sacrifice. We have already mentioned that the sacrifice was less essential a requirement than the other two; and that circumcision was necessarily confined to male converts—the minority. In any case, the entire procedure, far from being levitical in a quasi-physical sense, was conceived of as a re-enactment of the exodus and the pilgrimage ensuing on it, with the gift of the Torah as the climax.

In a previous chapter—on 'Ye have heard, but I say unto you'—we referred to the formula 'I might hear, understand', used in the old Midrash to introduce interpretations of Scripture which, though conceivable, are not to be approved; and we pointed out that the bringing up and rejecting of such interpretations is frequently no academic game, but a very serious measure—those interpretations being actually believed in by some earlier or rival school. It is, then, of interest to note

---

[1] See Pal. Pes. 36b, Bab. Yeb. 46a, Bab. Ker. 9a, Siph. on Num. 15.14, citing the Schools of Hillel and Shammai, R. Eliezer ben Hyrcanus and R. Joshua ben Hananiah.
[2] Joshua 5.5, Ezek. 16.6. [3] Exod. 19.10, 24.8. [4] Exod. 24.5.

the Midrash on the provision: 'And when a stranger shall sojourn with thee and will keep the passover, let all his males be circumcised.' The Rabbis start by saying:[1] 'I might understand that as soon as a person has been converted he should celebrate the Passover.' (We must remember that the identification of 'stranger' with 'proselyte' and of 'to sojourn' with 'to be a convert' is common in Rabbinic exegesis.)

The special point of the interpretation here mentioned as conceivable is that, at a pinch, the Hebrew could be translated: 'And when a stranger—proselyte—shall sojourn—be a convert—with thee, then at once let him keep a Passover; and let his males be circumcised.' This interpretation is then refuted with the help of another verse. What emerges as likely, however, is that there was an ancient school according to which a gentile, on attaching himself to Judaism, had actually to bring a paschal offering to symbolize his conversion.

To return to baptismal teaching, it is designed to bring out the general atmosphere of Jewish life. Significantly, it is to deal with the 'commandments', miṣwoth; an exposition of the learned and subtle Rabbinic directions, the halakhoth, is not prescribed. (That an instructor might take for granted some familiarity with the fundamentals of the faith we pointed out above.) The candidate must hear about the kind of things God has told the Jews to do or not to do. He need not—as yet—concern himself with the exact manner in which the Rabbis hold that those precepts should be carried out.

To be sure, an instructor cannot help presenting the Law in the light of that Rabbinic interpretation to which he is used; besides, he will be neither able nor willing to refrain from enlarging on one point or the other and introducing some results of pious exegesis and moral reflection. But, if he is true to the plan, he will concentrate on basic obligations. He will, for instance, inculcate the duties of loving God with all one's heart, soul and might, and of commemorating the exodus every year, without necessarily going into the precise implications of each of the three terms, 'heart', 'soul' and 'might',[2] or into the proper order of the Passover-eve service.

The decision exactly which commandments may suit a given case is left to the teacher, whose choice would depend partly on his own bias

---

[1] Mekh. on Exod. 12.48.
[2] For conclusions drawn by the Rabbis from this accumulation, see the Targumim, Mish. Ber. 9.5 and Bab. Ber. 61b.

and partly on the needs of his audience. Presumably certain collections became traditional. As a Jewish catechist, however, would normally have to do, not with a large class, but with one person, and a rather extraordinary one at that, the greatest attention must have been paid to individual requirements.

What may an anthology of precepts have looked like? In the Song of Solomon there occurs the exclamation 'Thou art fair, my love.' For the Rabbis[1] it is addressed to Israel and means: 'Thou art fair through the commandments and loving deeds; through the commandments both positive and negative; through the commandments concerning the house, through heave-offerings and tithes; through the commandments concerning the field, through gleanings, the forgotten sheaf, the corner, the second tithe and property renounced; through mixed seeds, the show-fringes, the first-fruits, the fourth year of planting; through circumcision, the uncovering of the corona, prayer, the reading of the Shema (confession of the unity of God), the door-posts, the phylacteries, the Lulab and Ethrog (to be used on the Feast of Tabernacles); through repentance and good works; thou art fair in this world and in the World to Come.' This list would have been in order for baptismal instruction, though there is no saying whether it was ever put to such use.

Occasionally, however, we come across a selection indubitably reflecting catechetical teaching. For instance, we are told[2] that when the Israelites reached the desert, God began to announce 'some of the lighter and some of the weightier commandments, such as those concerning the Sabbath, incestuous unions, the show-fringes and the phylacteries'. We have just shown that, in New Testament times, a convert to Judaism was thought of as passing through the experience of Israel rescued from Egypt. In this legend, the Israelites, just rescued from heathen surroundings, are represented as converts. They are introduced to the general character of Jewish life as one would introduce a candidate for baptism. The phrase 'some of the lighter and some of the weightier commandments' is a direct reference to the rules respecting the instruction of proselytes.

Similarly, it is probable that remarks on passages from the Book of Ruth sometimes contain clues as to the way candidates were taught. Ruth, after all, was one of the outstanding converts of the Bible. One

[1] Cant. Rabba on 1.15.　　　　　　　[2] Siph. on Num. 15.41.

example may suffice.[1] When Ruth said to Naomi, 'Whither thou goest
I will go', that, the Rabbis claim, was in reply to Naomi's observation
that Jews were forbidden to move outside a limited area on the Sabbath. When she went on, 'And where thou lodgest I will lodge', it was
in reply to Naomi's pointing out to her that a Jewess was forbidden to
meet in private any man but her husband. 'Thy people shall be my
people' was in reply to the warning that there were 613 commandments; and 'Thy God shall be my God' in reply to the warning that no
idolatry was permitted. We must remember that Naomi gave these
illustrations of lighter and weightier laws after Ruth had begged for
permission to accompany her and share her poverty. The part on commandments, that is, follows the gentile's approach 'at this time',
while Israel is forsaken—the real test.

Levitical regulations are rarely, if ever, conspicuous in Tannaitic
comments of this kind. By contrast, prominence is often accorded to
the ethical aspect of the Law. Josephus maintains[2] that the Jewish laws
are calculated to instil the virtues of justice, love, liberality, industry,
courage and so on—all of them, he says, facets of piety, reverence for
God, εὐσέβεια.

Nor was he out of step with the practice of some Rabbis. Many no
doubt would have thought his emphasis wrong; even of those who did
not, many would have drawn up a different catalogue of virtues. But,
fundamentally, Hillel would have been on his side. To the gentile who
demanded to be taught the entire Law while he could stand on one
foot, he said 'What is hateful unto thee, do not to a fellow creature';
and he added that all the detailed provisions of the Law had no purpose
but to ensure the observance of this maxim. Let us also note that, where
Josephus enumerates as the essentials of Jewish religion justice, tem-
perance, fortitude and complete harmony between all members of the
community,[3] it is only the first three of these qualities which coincide
with the demands of the Platonic School. The fourth, harmony, replaces the Platonic wisdom—surely a most revealing change.

This is not to deny that the catechisms of some sects may have insisted more strongly on levitical rules: the community which has left us
the Zadokite Fragments probably tended this way. Again, the concept
of priesthood must have played a greater part than might appear from

---

[1] Bab. Yeb. 47b, Ruth Rabba on 1.16 f.
[2] C.Ap. 2.16.170, 2.14.146, 2.41.291 f.　　　　　　　　[3] C.Ap. 2.16.170.

our Talmudic sources—most of them dating from after the destruction of the Temple. The gentile who approached Hillel with the request to be made High Priest was attracted by the splendour of that office. That this was not an isolated occurrence is shown by a number of Rabbinic utterances to the effect[1] that the descendant of a proselyte may in fact become High Priest. Evidently, that was an important consideration for many a prospective convert.

The different lines a catechist might take come out in the different expositions of the Biblical verse 'The Lord loveth the stranger in giving him food and raiment.'[2] The Rabbis[3] identify the stranger with the proselyte; and whereas according to some 'food' means the Torah and 'raiment' the *tallith*, the resplendent coat of men distinguished by piety and scholarship (it is mentioned in Mark and Luke),[4] according to others 'food' means the showbread reserved for priests and 'raiment' the priestly robes. The latter interpretation obviously antedates the fall of the Temple, the former was adopted about A.D. 100 by Joshua ben Hananiah, on being questioned concerning the status of converts by the convert Aquila who translated the Bible into Greek. Doubtless in most cases an instructor tried somehow to do justice to all branches of the religion; but some measure of preference for one or the other would be unavoidable.

When we compare early Christian catechisms we see that they also appear to have attempted, not so much to give a systematic account of dogmas and duties, or even of the major dogmas and duties, as to convey an impression of the atmosphere of the new life. Lighter and weightier matters, easier and more burdensome duties, stand side by side. The candidate was very gradually led towards the goal, at first hearing only about 'some of the commandments': he was given milk before he could receive strong nourishment,[5] just like the Israelites in the desert or the converts to Judaism. Mass proselytizing enabled a greater degree of standardization than Judaism had known. But there are enough variations to show that no rigidly fixed syllabus was followed. Different teachers still emphasized different aspects. There never was a single *Ur*-catechism.

On the whole, then, the Jewish scheme was taken over. Support for

---

[1] Gen. Rabba on 28.20, Exod. Rabba on 12.43.
[2] Deut. 10.18.   [3] Gen. Rabba on 28.20.
[4] Mark 12.38, Luke 20.46.   [5] I Cor. 3.2, I Pet. 2.2, Heb. 5.12 f., also 6.1 f.

this view is furnished by parallels in detail. For example, in the Jewish scheme, part (2), the commandments, must have included large tracts in an impersonal form: 'One may pray only in a sober mood', 'One must maintain the poor non-Jews with the poor Jews', 'The proselyte should bring the first-fruits'.[1] Literally translated, these provisions run: 'Praying only in a sober mood', 'Maintaining the poor non-Jews with the poor Jews', 'The proselyte bringing the first-fruits'. This use of the participle, which we discussed above, under Haustafeln, was common in Tannaitic rules. But, as we shall see when we come to part (4), the catechumen was also directly addressed: 'Know that conversion involves such and such risks', and so on. Primitive Christian catechisms in Hebrew seem to have alternated in the same way. In I Peter[2] we find the clause 'The servants being subject to their masters.' It means 'They should be subject' and is clearly an over-literal rendering of a Hebrew rule which employed the participle. This impersonal rule, however, may well go back to the same code as its explanation, 'For even hereunto were ye called', or the admonitions 'Honour all men, fear God'[3]— all in the direct address.

Again, the Jewish character of much of the Christian catechetical vocabulary and imagery has long been realized. A careful search would reveal an even closer continuity than is commonly assumed. As we have seen, the exodus and the events that followed it were at the heart of pre-Christian baptismal teaching. One source of Paul's predilection for ἐνδύειν, 'to put on',[4] surely was the allegorical interpretation of the verse 'The Lord loveth the stranger—the proselyte—in giving him food and raiment.' Or when he says[5] that a covetous man is an idolater —not merely 'like an idolater' but 'an idolater'—we are reminded of the Rabbinic dictum that 'he who multiplieth his wealth by usury is Esau the wicked'.[6] Josephus[7] mentions wars for the satisfaction of covetousness among the evils against which the Jewish laws are directed. Nor should his remark be dismissed as purely Hellenistic. The list in which it occurs, while using terminology palatable to a gentile public, distinctly represents Jewish and early Christian ethics.

---

[1] Mish. Ber. 5.1, Bab. Git. 61a, Mish. Bik. 1.4.   [2] 2.18.   [3] 2.21, 17.
[4] Rom. 13.12, Eph. 4.24, Col. 3.10, I Thess. 5.8.   [5] Eph. 5.5.
[6] Exod. Rabba on 22.26. This is the reference which Schöttgen had in mind and which Strack-B., vol. 2, 1924, p. 607, confess themselves unable to find. True, Schöttgen put 'idolater' instead of 'Esau the wicked'. But there is little difference in sense. He may have committed a slip under the influence of Eph. 5.5, or he may have had before him an edition which did read 'idolater'.   [7] C.Ap. 2.41.291 f.

3. Charity

Next the candidate is to be told of the guilt incurred by a Jew who fails to give away the gleanings, the forgotten sheaf, the corner and the poor man's tithe.[1] These are imposts, not in favour of the Temple, but in favour of the poor. Evidently, it is not sufficient to advert to them in the course of part (3), the commandments in general. A separate section of the baptismal catechism must be devoted to them. It may be remarked that this insistence on charity can hardly depend on Christian models. If it did, one would expect references to less specific and more impressive demands, such as 'Thou shalt love thy neighbour as thyself.'[2]

In principle, the four duties applied only within the Jewish community. Admittedly, 'for the sake of the ways of peace', if a gentile came to reap the gleanings, the forgotten sheaf or the corner, he must not be prevented.[3] (The same rule was not necessary in the case of the poor man's tithe: this was not left in the open for anyone to take, but distributed on the threshing-floor or in the house.) The Rabbinic codes contain many concessions of this kind—i.e. 'for the sake of peace'—both with regard to relations between Jews and gentiles and with regard to relations among Jews; and Paul occasionally adopts the idea, for example, in discussing dietary questions (which bear on the relations among Christians) or the dissolution of a marriage by the non-believing partner (where the relations between a Christian and a non-Christian are affected).[4] Nevertheless, essentially, the gleanings, the forgotten sheaf, the corner and the poor man's tithe were intended to benefit fellow Jews.

Why are these examples of charity singled out? Certainly, a teacher might add others. But it is obvious that, in the eyes of the authors of the scheme, these are of particular relevance.

There are various reasons. First, the honest fulfilment of these commandments involved much self-abnegation. According to the Talmud, a poor man might live on gleanings: R. Johanan ben Nuri, at the beginning of the 2nd cent. A.D., did so.[5] That this is no exaggeration may be seen from ancient works on agriculture. Varro writes[6] that normally, the harvest being over, a landowner should sell the gleanings.

---

[1] Lev. 19.9 f., 23.22, Deut. 24.19 ff., 14.28 f. [2] Lev. 19.18.
[3] Mish. Git. 5.8. [4] Rom. 14.17 ff., I Cor. 7.15; see also Rom. 12.18.
[5] Pal. Peah 20d. [6] R.R. 1.53; cf. Digest 50.16.30.1, 18.1.40.3.

Secondly, the Bible, in prescribing these imposts, expressly mentions 'the stranger'—'the proselyte' according to Rabbinic interpretation—as entitled along with the poor. We have observed that the assurance that God gives the stranger 'food and raiment' is referred by the Rabbis to spiritual nourishment. But they do not, on this account, deny its implications in the material sphere: a proselyte in need has the same right to be looked after as a home-born.[1] This principle did not remain a dead letter: the expectation to become a recipient of alms is sometimes enumerated by the Rabbis among the unworthy motives for conversion.[2] In some of the Biblical provisions in question the stranger is actually named first, and once a reminder is added that the home-born himself was not always in his privileged position: the tax 'shall be for the stranger, the fatherless and the widow, and thou shalt remember that thou wast a bondman in Egypt'. When, in addition, we remember the way Boaz treated the proselytess Ruth as she came to glean in his field, we can understand the suitability of this and similar obligations for a baptismal catechism.

For wealthy gentiles, incidentally, the prospect of alms cannot have meant a great deal; and if poor ones were attracted by it too much, rich ones may have been attracted too little. A story about the proselyte Aquila—about A.D. 100—part of which we have already recounted, seems to reflect this problem. Aquila found the promise of 'food and raiment' far from grand. Joshua ben Hananiah, we saw, explained to him that the phrase signified 'Torah and *tallith*'. But R. Eliezer was less accommodating. He angrily pointed out that the patriarch Jacob himself had prayed for no more than that God 'will give me food to eat and raiment to put on'.[3] The story makes it probable that the warning against greed in I Timothy—'having food and raiment let us be therewith content'[4]—derives from Jewish catechetical teaching.

[1] Gen. Rabba on 28.20—quoting a retort of R. Eliezer to the proselyte Aquila which we shall consider in detail presently. There are many similar cases of the Rabbis insisting on the material aspect of an institution in addition to the spiritual. A section of the Haggadah composed in Babylonia before or shortly after the destruction of the Temple requests 'all that are hungry to come and eat, all that are needy to come and celebrate the Passover'. This is primarily a genuine invitation—or at least the formalized reflection of a genuine invitation—to the meal. It may be recalled that while the Temple stood the inhabitants of Jerusalem were under an obligation to give free hospitality to the pilgrims (Mish. Ab. 5.5, Ab. de-R.N. 35, Bab. Yoma 12a, Matt. 26.18, Mark 14.13 f., Luke 22.10 ff.). Certainly it is also an offer of the divine food of the religion; it is even a summons to outsiders to join the true faith (this may explain the odd form *weyiphsah*, 'and celebrate the Passover' or 'and leap over'). But the primary, material sense is not sacrificed to the spiritual one.   [2] Yal. 1.645 on Lev. 23.22.   [3] Gen. 28.20.   [4] 6.8.

It is interesting that a candidate should be reminded, not just of the importance of charity, but of the guilt incurred through neglect of it. From Josephus we know[1] that the practice of charity was one of the things sympathizers with Judaism imitated; and we are told in Acts[2] how the gentile Cornelius, even before he became a Christian, 'gave much alms to the people'. The task of a Jewish catechist was to impress on his pupil that, from his reception, charity was no longer voluntary, an 'extra', but a definite duty.

No doubt this is a further reason why the authors of the plan choose such specific, clear-cut orders as those concerning gleanings and so on rather than vaguer exhortations—'Thou shalt not shut thine hand from thy poor brother'[3] or the like. Charity, for a Jew, was a definite duty. It was to be exercised in honour of God,[4] and though ordinary, human tribunals could do nothing in such matters, God would punish him who was remiss. A few of the Biblical commandments end with the exclamation 'I am the Lord, your God', by which, in the view of the Rabbis,[5] God promised to reward those who did their share and threatened to take revenge on those who did not.

That in early Christian catechisms a section was set apart for charity within the community is strongly suggested by certain tracts in the Epistles, for instance, in Romans and I Peter.[6] It would be quite in keeping with Jewish precedents. Equally so is the concept of charity as practised for the sake of God, or Jesus, a concept permeating all Christian teaching on the topic. Again, when a series of exhortations is followed by an announcement of reward in case of obedience and divine punishment in case of disobedience—'The eyes of the Lord are over the righteous, but his face is against them that do evil'[7]—this plainly corresponds to Tannaitic proselyte instruction.

No special mention is made in the Tannaitic scheme of humility and subordination. This does not indeed mean that Jewish catechists were silent on these subjects. The treatise Derekh Eretz Zuta opens: 'The ways of Scholars are, Meek and humble in spirit.' We have just quoted a clause from I Peter, 'The servants being subject to their masters', which is certainly derived from a code in Hebrew and may well have originated in Judaism.

---

[1] C.Ap. 2.39.283. [2] 10.2. [3] Deut. 15.7.
[4] Pal. Peah 15d, Bab. B.B. 10a. [5] Siph. on Lev. 19.10, 23.22, also on 18.2.
[6] Rom. 12.1–13, I Pet. 3.8–12. [7] I Pet. 3.12.

K

Antigonos of Soko, in the 3rd cent. B.C., distinguished[1] between slaves ministering for the sake of reward and slaves ministering from no such motive. He demanded that one should be like the latter, urging his audience 'to let the fear of Heaven be upon you'. It looks as if the association in early Christian catechisms of the notion of 'fear' with the duty of subjection[2] were Jewish. For that pronouncement of Antigonos is not isolated. We have already adduced—in discussing some Lukan allusions to the young Samuel—a favourite saying of Abaye's (first third of the 4th cent. A.D.), extolling the value of humility. It may now be added that here also a reference to 'fear' is introduced: 'A man should always be wise in fear, a soft answer turneth away wrath (this is taken from Proverbs),[3] and he should increase peace with everybody, including gentiles, in order to be beloved by God and men.'[4] In the same connection we mentioned a passage from the Letter of Aristeas:[5] 'God accepts the humble, and the human race loves those willing to subject themselves.' Both the Letter, a piece of pre-Christian Jewish propaganda, and Abaye, much later, contain the idea—also frequent in early Christian catechetical material—that if you humble yourself before others you will be approved by God and men.

Again, an Essene neophyte had to take an oath:[6] 'To keep faith towards all, in particular the rulers, since there is no government but through God, and should he (the neophyte) himself come to govern, never to boast of his power or to outdo those subject to him by his garments or ornaments.' This coupling of the duty to respect your superiors with that to be considerate to inferiors recurs in several Epistles: 'The elders I exhort, Feed the flock not as being lords but being examples; likewise ye younger, submit yourselves unto the elder.'[7]

The fact remains that the particular Tannaitic plan under notice, while assigning a place of its own to charity, says nothing on humility and subordination. There is here some support for Dr. Selwyn's conclusion,[8] reached by an entirely different route, that early Christian catechists evolved one pattern with love or benevolence as the chief virtue and another or others where humility and subordination were equally prominent.

---

[1] Mish. Ab. 1.3.   [2] Eph. 5.21, 33, 6.5, Col. 3.22, I Pet. 2.18, 3.2, Didache 4.11.
[3] 15.1.   [4] Bab. Ber. 17a.   [5] 257.   [6] Josephus, Bell. 2.8.7.140.
[7] I Pet. 5.1 ff.; cp. 3.1 ff., Eph. 5.22 ff., Col. 3.18 ff.   [8] Pp. 374, 414 f., 460.

4. The penalties

Now the candidate is to be instructed in the penalties for transgressions; and the difference between his former state, when he could eat forbidden fat or violate the Sabbath without incurring extirpation or stoning, and his new state, when he cannot,[1] is to be impressed on him. The warning is in the direct address: 'Know that before thou camest unto this dispensation thou couldst eat suet', etc. This part provides further evidence of the antiquity of the scheme: the death penalty by stoning for desecration of the Sabbath is still in force—otherwise there would be little point in the warning.

The section deals not—or not primarily—with minor slips, but with serious crimes: the penalties of extirpation and stoning applied solely to sins committed with full intent or even in a spirit of defiance, apostasy. Once we realize this, the arrangement appears perfectly natural. Having been informed of the nature of the life he is about to enter, a candidate must be cautioned as to what will happen should he later repudiate his undertakings.

Persons joining the Essenes, the Zadokites or the band who composed the Sectarian Manual were also threatened with dire consequences should they fall away.[2] Possibly, in the catechisms of these sects, the warnings occupied the same place as in the Tannaitic system—after the duties.

At any rate, as pointed out above, certain Rabbinic comments on the first dialogue between Ruth and Naomi reflect catechetical practice. There we do find the sequence from 'some lighter and some weightier commandments' to 'penalties for transgressions'. Naomi (the Rabbis explain) told Ruth that, as a Jewess, she could not move beyond a fixed limit on the Sabbath, and Ruth replied 'Whither thou goest I will go.' Naomi told her that, as a Jewess, she must meet no man in private but her husband, and Ruth replied, 'Where thou lodgest I will lodge.' Naomi told her that there were as many as 613 commandments, and Ruth replied, 'Thy people shall be my people.' Naomi told her that idolatry was prohibited, and Ruth replied, 'Thy God shall be my God.' So far the commandments. Then Naomi asked Ruth to remember the various modes of capital punishment the courts might inflict, but Ruth

---

[1] Lev. 7.23 ff., Exod. 35.2, Num. 15.32 ff.

[2] Josephus, Bell. 2.8.8.143, Zadokite Fragments 9.28 ff., Sectarian Manual col. 2, according to Dupont-Somer, op. cit., p. 49.

replied, 'Where thou diest will I die'; and when Naomi mentioned the plots used for the burial of persons executed, Ruth replied, 'And there (where thou art buried) will I be buried.' Clearly, this agrees with the Tannaitic plan.

How skilfully the plan is drawn up may be seen from the way part (4) hangs together with (3). In the first place, even in part (3), on charity, reference is made to the culpability of whoever disregards the laws concerning gleanings and so on. Part (4) takes up this theme and works it out in a more general fashion, for all departments of the Law. In the second place, the punishment envisaged in part (3), for uncharitableness, is in the hands of God. So part (4) begins with extirpation, a penalty inflicted by the heavenly tribunal. Only then does it go on to stoning, carried out by man. In the third place, like part (3), part (4) starts from such provisions as were often followed by semi-converts. In the same chapter where Josephus remarks on the imitation by pagans of Jewish charity, he mentions their adoption of the dietary rules and the Sabbath. In Rabbinic writings,[1] among the inadequate motives for joining Judaism, we meet with the desire to exchange the nasty, unclean food of the heathen table for the decent Jewish food and to participate in the pleasant Sabbaths and festivals. So in this part, as in (3), emphasis is placed on the fact that observances which, before conversion, were voluntary and might be given up at will, would henceforth be compulsory and might never be shaken off.

In one respect, part (4) is meant as an antithesis to (3). Whereas part (3) is devoted to good deeds within the community, part (4) dwells on opposition to the outside world. It is hardly accidental that the two institutions singled out, the dietary laws and the Sabbath, are those which then as today most effectively separated the Jew from his non-Jewish neighbour. Tacitus describes the Jews as 'taking their meals apart', Rutilius Namatianus speaks of 'humanis animal dissociale cibis', and Juvenal ridicules the half-convert 'for whom every seventh day is removed from any contact with life'.[2] The proselyte enters into the congregation of the Lord, a holy brotherhood. But he must pay a price. He must renounce his former life and the unholy world around him; and he will look back at his peril.

It seems that early Christian catechisms normally contained a similar section or sections, where the previous or outside life, 'according to the

[1] T. de-Be El. 146.   [2] Hist. 5, De Reditu Suo 1.384, Sat. 14.105 f.

former lusts in your ignorance', was contrasted with life in the Christian Church, and where the wrath of God, 'who judgeth according to every man's work',[1] was called down upon whoever would relapse into sin. Moreover, there are indications that warnings of this kind often followed the proclamation of duties.[2] The penalties are as a rule such as God would carry out—which is natural, considering the circumstances of the Church about the middle and towards the end of the 1st cent. But, occasionally,[3] separation from or excommunication of the sinner is enjoined.

In respect of arrangement of matter, maybe even portions of Christian catechisms not dealing with penalties are indebted to parts (3) and (4) of the Tannaitic scheme. Chapter 12 of Romans is in point. Its first half is concerned with charity towards fellow-Christians, the second with the attitude of Christians to non-believers. This structure may well derive from Tannaitic baptismal teaching, with its transition from part (3), on gleanings and similar obligations, i.e. the duties of brotherhood, to part (4), on dietary rules and the Sabbath, i.e. isolation from the gentiles.

5. The reward and the World to Come

Finally, the catechist should draw attention to the reward of keeping the commandments. The World to Come is made only for the sake of the righteous. 'At this time' Israel can receive neither the greater part of the good nor the greater part of the retribution it deserves. But—the Tannaites add—a catechist should give no long or detailed exposition of these matters.

This part, then, contains the promise offered by the religion, taking up the theme of part (1) on a different level. At the opening stage, the applicant must humbly and half-blindly admit that Israel's sufferings are Israel's glory. Now he receives explicit assurance that it is so, and that those doing their duty in the face of present affliction—and only those—will be exalted when history comes to an end. 'According to the suffering, so is the reward' was the favourite saying of one of the pagans whom Hillel had converted.[4] The resumption of the concept 'at this time' is significant. It occurs twice in the introductory part, and it

---

[1] I Pet. 1.14 ff.
[2] Matt. 7.24 ff., Gal. 6.7 f., Eph. 5.5 ff., Philip. 3.18 ff., Col. 3.25, I Thess. 4.5 ff., Heb. 6.4 ff., 10.26 ff., 13.4, I Pet. 3.12.
[3] Matt. 18.15 ff., Rom. 16.17 ff., I Cor. 5.11 ff., Tit. 3.10 f.   [4] Mish. Ab. 5.23.

recurs here, in the concluding part—where 'the World to Come' is contrasted with it. The entire catechism is thus set in an eschatological framework. It is instruction as to man's purpose, task and hope in the passing phase that is this world.

A closer analysis, however, will show that the part under discussion is itself subdivided. It seems to begin, not with any eschatological prospects, but with rewards God may grant you on this earth. In other words, it starts—soberly enough—by counter-balancing the penalties announced in part (4). Just as he who spurns the commandments is liable to penalties—inflicted by God or by human courts—so he who fulfils them may be rewarded—by God alone, of course. As far as this antithesis is concerned, the rewards thought of are no doubt of this world: long life, children and the like.

The Bible lays down[1] that if you take the young of a bird you should let the dam escape, 'that it may be well with thee and thou mayest prolong thy days'. The Rabbis[2] declare that a promise given for the fulfilment of such a 'light commandment' must *a fortiori* be valid for the 'weighty commandments'. This comment may well have originated in baptismal teaching. Similarly, to the prohibition of blood[3] the Bible adds: 'that it may go well with thee and thy children after thee'. The Rabbis conclude[4] that if such a reward is bestowed on him who abstains from blood, which man does not crave for (so that the prohibition is light in the sense of 'easy to observe'), it must *a fortiori* be bestowed on him who abstains from dishonest gain and unchastity, towards which our evil instincts do draw us.

From this point onwards, however, eschatology is in the foreground. It is noteworthy that here again, as in the section warning the candidate of the risks he faces, the intimate form of the direct address appears: 'Know that the World to Come is made only for the sake of the righteous ones.' In a sense, this supplements the references to rewards in this age. It is a common experience that, in this age, just as a sin is not inevitably followed by failure, so piety does not always lead to success. The Tannaites held[5] that matters would be put right in a future aeon. God is just.

Now we reach the last phase of the teaching: Israel 'at this time' can receive only some of the favours and some of the retribution due to it.

---

[1] Deut. 22.7.   [2] Mish. Hul. 12.5.   [3] Deut. 12.25.   [4] Bab. Mak. 23b.
[5] E.g. Mish. Ab. 2.16, a saying of R. Tarphon, of the first half of the 2nd cent. A.D.

The catechism here proceeds from the question of individual fortunes to that of the corporate destiny. Part (1), it may be recalled, opens by a reference to the present status of Israel as a whole. Part (5) closes by one to its future status. The proselyte must know that, as a Jew, though he will have his personal task to perform and may expect punishment and reward according to his efforts, yet his fate is inextricably bound up with that of the people to whom he belongs. He shares their humiliation —and exaltation—now; he will also share what is in store for them in the World to Come.

It is in consequence of this transition from individual to corporate destiny that the motif of punishment is introduced once more. As far as the individual is concerned, the penalties are dealt with in part (4), so that part (5) may be devoted to rewards. But the mention of the corporate destiny entails a further allusion to punishment, or rather, since the word used is *pur'anuth*, to 'solution', 'payment', 'disaster'. For when this age comes to a close, Israel, though in a sense assured of salvation, will none the less be judged by a severe God.[1] The main idea of this section, incidentally, was incorporated in a prayer for rain by Honi the circle-drawer, a miracle worker of the last century B.C., who is mentioned by Josephus.[2] He wanted neither too much rain nor too little, since 'Israel can bear neither too much good nor too much retribution.'

The Tannaites direct that a catechist should not dwell unduly on these matters. Some commentators are of opinion that this mandate covers all parts of the catechism (which would mean that catechisms must be short), others that it forbids a catechist to exercise either over-much persuasion or overmuch dissuasion. But the natural sense of the clause is that the eschatological part should be kept down. At least in the 3rd cent. A.D., it appears to have been still understood in this way. Eleazar ben Pedath tried to find Scriptural support for it, and he adduced the verse from the Book of Ruth:[3] 'When Naomi saw that Ruth was steadfastly minded to go with her, she left speaking to her.' For the Rabbis, we saw, Naomi's decision to accept Ruth followed a proper baptismal instruction. On this basis, clearly, 'she left speaking', i.e. she became reticent, when she reached the concluding part of the catechism—eschatology.

---

[1] E.g. Test. of Benjamin 10.8: 'And the Lord shall judge Israel first, for their un-righteousness; and then shall he judge all the Gentiles.'
[2] Bab. Ta. 23a, Ant. 14.2.1.22 ff. [3] Bab. Yeb. 47b, Ruth 1.18.

Very possibly, this recommendation of brevity is later than the main body of the catechetical scheme. It may be anti-Christian; that is to say, it may have been appended at a time when speculation about eschatology was dangerous because it might lead to inquiry into or even acceptance of the Christian tenets. Still, one school of Rabbis always discouraged excessive occupation with problems of this sort, and certainly any discussion of them with, or in the presence of, immature or unlearned persons. Be this as it may, the warning shows that, left to their own devices, Jewish catechists were prone to enlarge on the subject.

To come back again to the Rabbinic elaboration of the scene between Ruth and Naomi, we found reflected in it the test, i.e. the eagerness of the candidate to share Israel's sufferings, the commandments—Naomi explained to Ruth some light and some weighty duties—and the penalties—Naomi told Ruth of the different kinds of capital punishment and the graves for criminals. The exposition has come down to us in two versions. It is significant that only in one of them[1] are any eschatological hints preserved, and even they seem to be mutilated. When Ruth said, 'The Lord do so to me and more also', Naomi admonished her to be tireless in the fulfilment of commandments and the doing of good deeds in this world, since as for the World to Come —'death will part thee and me'. This is enough to prove that part (5) was represented. But, manifestly, the tendency was to suppress or shorten utterances about this topic.

In the Zadokite Fragments, the promise of pardon for the faithful[2] succeeds the threats of punishment for the treacherous. In the Sectarian Manual of Discipline, to go by the brief description of Dupont-Somer,[3] the opposite sequence is to be found. We cannot, of course, be sure about the arrangement adopted by these groups in their catechisms. It is, however, interesting that the promises and threats of the Zadokites contain distinctly eschatological elements.

That early Christian catechisms finished by a section on eschatology is agreed. It must have differed in important respects from the corresponding Jewish section. Yet, fundamentally, there was no break. There was the promise of ultimate reward for the good, there was the warning that the godless would not share in it, there was the expectation that even the believers would be judged—'and if the righteous scarcely be

[1] Ruth Rabba on 1.16 f.   [2] 9.50 ff.   [3] P. 49.

saved, where shall the sinner appear?'[1]—and there was also the recognition of the corporate character of the Christian band, the common fate of those within as opposed to those without.

Dr. Selwyn[2] distinguishes between two patterns of Christian eschatological teaching: a primitive one, where eschatology was used as an incentive to conduct befitting the baptized, and a later one, where it served to inculcate the correct attitude to a persecution. The phrase 'at this time' which occurs in the final part of the Tannaitic plan, and which refers to this age in which 'Israel is broken down and sufferings befall it', suggests that, in Jewish proselyte instruction, the discussion of eschatology normally touched on the theme of persecution. But, naturally, the degree of emphasis accorded to it would vary with the times, and we are far from claiming that Dr. Selwyn's thesis is seriously affected.

The Christian eschatological vocabulary is to a large extent traditional. A word like καρτερία—the Hebrew equivalents are 'amaṣ and ḥazaq, the Aramaic ones ṭeqaph and 'alem—would be worth investigating. (It plays a prominent part in Josephus's Contra Apionem.[3]) Again, we have referred to the Rabbinic notions of conversion as a rising from death to life, a new birth and a liberation from former sins. It is safe to suppose that catechists discussed these notions partly in the introductory section, but chiefly in the final one, concerning the reward and the World to Come. The effect of these ideas on early Christianity can hardly be overrated. The believer is thought of as 'begotten again', 'a newborn babe', 'a new man', 'a new creation'.[4] 'He who separates himself from the uncircumcision is like one who separates himself from the grave' was a principle of the School of Hillel. Paul says:[5] 'And you, being dead in the uncircumcision of your flesh, hath he quickened.'

There is an old Talmudic legend[6] according to which Alexander the Great asked the Elders of Africa, 'What shall a man do that he may live?' They answered: 'Let him kill himself.' Then the King asked, 'And what shall a man do that he may die?', to which the Elders replied: 'Let him keep himself alive.' Some New Testament allusions to the true convert dying and rising with Jesus are very similar—for example, 'He that loveth his life shall lose it, and he that hateth his life in this world shall keep it unto life eternal.'[7] Even the doctrine that

---

[1] I Pet. 4.18.   [2] Pp. 375 ff., 439 ff.   [3] E.g. 2.16.170, 2.39.283.
[4] E.g. I Pet. 1.3, 2.2, Col. 3.10, II Cor. 5.17.   [5] Col. 2.13.
[6] Bab. Ta. 32a.   [7] John 12.24 f., Matt. 10.39, Luke 9.24, 17.33.

baptism, as it means a rising from the dead in a moral and spiritual sense, also means a dying to the sinful world,[1] has its root in Jewish teaching. Joshua ben Hananiah, towards the end of the 1st cent. A.D., received a gentile woman into Judaism though she confessed that her eldest son was the father of her youngest—that is to say, she had transgressed the most elementary Noachian laws. But the Rabbi justified his attitude by saying that 'as soon as she resolved to become a proselyte, she no longer lived to the world'.[2]

It would lead too far afield to give further illustrations of the Jewish influence in this domain. Perhaps we may say, in conclusion, that the frequency with which the phrases 'we know', 'ye know', 'know ye not', occur in the Epistles—and not only in eschatological pronouncements —will appear less strange if we assume that in the catechisms to which they often refer back, just as in the Tannaitic one, fresh paragraphs were occasionally opened by 'Know': 'Know that before thou camest unto this dispensation, thou couldst eat suet without incurring extirpation, but now' etc., or 'Know that the World to Come is made only for the righteous.'

C. Josephus

From the point of view of form, the Tannaitic catechism falls into five parts: (1) the test, (2) the commandments, (3) charity, (4) the penalties, (5) the reward and the World to Come. There is a lengthy section in Josephus's Contra Apionem[3] the structure of which is strikingly similar. The two main differences are these. One, there is no reference to a test. But this must be expected, since Josephus is not dealing with an actual applicant for admission to Judaism; his concern is to defend and explain his religion to the world at large. Two, instead of a special part on charity within the community, he has one on humanity to aliens, enemies and even beasts. Charity within the community is relegated to a subordinate place in the part on commandments. This deviation also is easily understandable. The work is directed against those many antisemites who accuse the Jews of being haters of all the rest of mankind. The sequence, then, is: commandments, humanity (instead of charity), penalties, reward.

It might perhaps be argued that the sequence is so inevitable that the

---

[1] E.g. Rom. 8.6 ff., Eph. 2.1 ff., Col. 2.11 ff.
[2] Eccles. Rabba on 1.8.   [3] 2.22.190 ff.

agreement—such as it is—with the Talmudic catechism means nothing. But this is hardly convincing. An exposition of Judaism would be conceivable with humanity coming first, for example, or penalties last, or with penalties not mentioned at all. Moreover, the fact that, though the Contra Apionem was composed a considerable time after the fall of the temple, Josephus writes as if it still stood and as if the cult still continued, suggests dependence on earlier models. The agreement does seem significant; and the points of difference only confirm, what we observed already, that even where several authors or teachers used more or less the same scheme of instruction, each would adapt it to his particular requirements.

Josephus begins by stating that he will say something about the commandments, positive and negative. (The reading ἀπαγορεύσεις is no doubt the right one: the distinction was current in Rabbinic Judaism.) He lists easy and difficult precepts, light and important ones. He speaks about the one God, whose form it would be sinful to conjecture, but who is manifest by his works and lovingkindness. He goes on to the one temple—one, like God—its priests, worship and sacrifices. Then he outlines the marriage laws, mentioning the prohibitions of unchastity, of paying any attention to dowry in taking a wife and of killing any offspring, born or not yet born. He makes reference to certain purificatory rites. He emphasizes the duties of properly educating one's children, of piously observing the traditional funeral ceremonies, of honouring one's parents, of showing respect to one's elders, and of being loyal to one's friends, incorruptible as judge, charitable to those in need and honest. Clearly, an attempt to convey a general impression—a favourable one, of course—of life under the Law.

Now follows the chapter concerning the attitude to non-Jews. Any of them who elects to become a Jew may be sure of a genuine welcome. Those who do not wish to join cannot be admitted to much intimacy, since that might lead to corruption of Jewish conduct. Nevertheless, all must be treated with friendliness, and even enemies and beasts are entitled to mercy.

The penalties for transgressions of the laws are declared by Josephus to be heavier than among other nations, and he gives illustrations. It is interesting that the Tannaitic catechism mentions only two very serious punishments: extirpation and stoning.

The last part deals with the reward of the pious. It is no crown of olive or such-like worldly distinction, but the gift of a better life in a new aeon. It is because of this conviction, Josephus adds, that Jews prefer to endure the most terrible sufferings rather than abjure their faith. As in the Tannaitic catechism, the promise of exaltation in the future is closely linked with the theme of persecution in the present. It is also linked, very naturally, as in many New Testament passages, with the idea of steadfastness in the face of dangers. And in accordance with the Rabbinic warning discussed above, Josephus refrains from giving any details about resurrection; in fact he is remarkably brief.

VI

Public Retort and Private Explanation

WE have already remarked that the way in which Mark describes the controversy about divorce represents a specific Rabbinic form—public retort and private explanation. Let us now consider this form, which is attested in Jewish sources from the 1st cent. A.D. onwards. One of our results will be that it may be advisable to adopt a somewhat more conservative estimate of certain pericopes of the gospels than is prevalent among the leading modern authorities.

To start from the Rabbinic side, a pagan asked R. Johanan ben Zaccai (middle and second half of the 1st cent.) whether it was not sheer sorcery to purify a person who had been in contact with a corpse by means of water containing the ashes of a red heifer.[1] The Rabbi, by his reply, induced his questioner to conclude that the 'water of separation' had the same efficacy as those roots which pagans were accustomed to burn in order to cast out an evil spirit that had entered into a man. After the pagan had left, however, the disciples remarked: 'Rabbi, him you pushed away with a fragile reed; what will you answer us?' Whereupon the real solution was propounded: neither—Johanan ben Zaccai said—was uncleanness caused by a corpse nor cleanness by the 'water of separation', but the statute of the red heifer was one of those which had to be accepted as the will of God though no rational basis could be discerned.

The episode may be divided into four parts: (1) the question put by an opponent; (2) the public retort, mysterious if not misleading, sufficient to silence the questioner but not stating the truth in plain language—actually, in this case, the pagan is led to think that the Rabbi believes in the virtue of magic; (3) when the opponent has gone, a demand by the followers for proper elucidation; and (4) the private explanation, the real answer clearly expressed—in this case, a rejection

[1] Num. Rabba on 19.2, P. de-R.K. 40a f.

of any magic and an interpretation of rites apparently magical as expressing submission to God's command.

In determining the setting in life of this form, we must pay particular attention to two points. In the first place, the form reflects a severe division, and indeed enmity, between the outside world, to be 'pushed away with a fragile reed', not deserving full enlightenment, and the elect, who are to be entrusted with it. In the second place, it is the outsiders who are attacking and the elect who are on the defensive: part (1), the hostile question, proceeds from the former.

It is worth observing that, from the 3rd cent., quite a few controversies between the Rabbis and Minim, i.e. Jews converted to Christianity, are clothed in this form by Talmud and Midrash. For example, R. Simlai (middle of the 3rd cent.), we are told,[1] was asked by the Minim how he accounted for the plural in the verse from Genesis: 'Let us make man in our image.' He replied that this was rectified by the singular in the verse immediately following: 'So God created man in his image.' The Minim having left, the disciples desired fuller information. Then the Rabbi explained that, by using the plural, God meant to indicate that while he alone would make Adam of earth and Eve of one of Adam's ribs, any further procreation would have to take place through husband, wife and the Divine Presence together. (Note that this interpretation, like the Christian interpretation to which it is opposed, sees in the plural a reference to three persons; only it is not the three persons of the Trinity.)

Once again, we find (1) a question by an outsider, (2) a retort good enough for him but not revealing the deeper truth, (3) the request of the disciples, and (4) the full explanation in private.

A close New Testament parallel to the anecdote of Johanan ben Zaccai is furnished by the discussion concerning the washing of hands preserved in Matthew and Mark.[2] (1) The Pharisees ask Jesus why his disciples omit to wash their hands before meals, thus defiling the food. The subject, that is, is opened by the outsiders putting a hostile question. (2) Jesus, after some general reflections on the behaviour of his opponents, declares: 'There is nothing from without a man that entering into him can defile him, but the things which come out of him, those are they that defile a man.' This is a correct statement of his position, but it is deliberately obscure. In fact, to the public at large, the

---

[1] Gen. Rabba on 1.26, Pal. Ber. 12d f.   [2] Matt. 15.1 ff., Mark 7.1 ff.

uninitiated, it must sound like an allusion to some strange piece of magic. (3) At home, the disciples ask to have the saying explained. (4) The explanation is given them. No relevance, Jesus tells them, attaches to food, which enters and leaves a man without affecting his heart; it is only his vicious leanings which can defile him. In other words, the notion of mechanical defilement is rejected, a person is clean or unclean according to his moral attitude.

Professor Dodd regards parts (3) and (4) as later accretions.[1] Even if they were, whoever added them might have followed the Rabbinic model. We have just pointed out that the form is fairly frequent in Jewish sources where controversies dating from the first few centuries A.D. are recorded.

But Dodd's criticism is hardly convincing. The pericope in question is so similar to the story about Johanan ben Zaccai which we have quoted—similar in structure, setting and substance—that it is difficult to doubt its essential unity. In all probability, parts (1) and (2) never stood by themselves, the four parts formed one whole from the outset—that is to say, from the moment that the incident was recounted in any literary form at all. This does not, of course, mean that none of the details now to be met with in this pericope may be secondary.

The Markan description of the dispute concerning divorce is another illustration of the same form. There are four parts: (1) The Pharisees, in whose opinion divorce is permissible, begin the dispute by putting a hostile question. (2) Jesus gives them a mysterious reply, alluding to the creation of the androgynous Adam ('male and female') and to marriage as the re-union of two halves that once belonged together ('they twain shall be one flesh'). The public may or may not guess at the myth referred to; certain it is that they are not supposed to grasp its full implications. (3) At home, the disciples ask for further information. (4) They receive a clear answer: there can be no valid divorce and, indeed, it is adultery even for a man to remarry after dismissing his first wife—such is the strength of a union making of husband and wife one composite being.

We may note that, as far as this pericope is concerned, Professor Dodd does not seem to claim a growth in two stages; and, in fact, it is clear that we have to do with a single whole. But if the unity of the entire pericope is granted in this case, there is no reason for denying it

[1] *The Parables of the Kingdom*, 1935, p. 61, n. 1.

in the case of the dispute about the true nature of defilement. From the point of view of form, the two cases are exactly the same.

A minor feature may be mentioned. Part (2), the reply in public, falls itself into two sections. In (2a), Jesus puts a counter-question: 'What did Moses command you?' This leads to an answer by which his antagonists become vulnerable: 'Moses suffered to write a bill of divorcement and put her away.' He only 'suffered' it (ἐπέτρεψεν), it was a concession. We need not decide why the Pharisees admit this. Either they proceed from the view—often expressed in the Talmud[1]— that divorce is morally undesirable. Or (less probably) they assume that divorce is in principle illegal and sanctioned only for the Israelites.[2] Or (more probably) they construe the law in Deuteronomy[3] not, as, say, Josephus,[4] 'When a man's wife find no favour, then let him write her a bill of divorcement' etc., but: 'When a man's wife find no favour and he write a bill of divorcement and she go and be another man's wife and the latter write her a bill of divorcement, then her former husband may not take her again.' That is to say, divorce is merely tolerated as an established custom, but no express approval is given. The main thing is that the Pharisees do speak of divorce as a concession. In (2b), Jesus uses their answer as the starting-point for his retort: 'For the hardness of your heart he wrote you this precept, but from the beginning' etc.

Very possibly, in the controversy about defilement also, (2a) at one time consisted of counter-question and inadequate answer. Matthew still has a counter-question:[5] 'Why do ye also transgress the tradition of the elders?'

At any rate, when we go into the Rabbinic examples of the form public retort—private explanation, we find quite a few where part (2) is composed in this peculiar mode.

To take, for instance, the story about Johanan ben Zaccai, part (1) gives the question of the heathen, who looks on the use of the 'water of separation' as mere witchcraft. In part (2a), Johanan ben Zaccai puts a counter-question: 'What does one do for a man possessed by an evil spirit?' And the heathen is forced to say: 'One burns roots' etc. This

---

[1] How Simeon ben Johai (about A.D. 150) prevented a divorce is told in Cant. Rabba on 1.4.

[2] From the 3rd cent. A.D. onwards this opinion occasionally appears; see Pal. Qid. 58c.

[3] 24.1 ff.   [4] Ant. 4.8.23.253.   [5] Matt. 15.3.

makes it possible for the Rabbi, in part (2b), to declare that the 'water of separation' has the same effect as those roots.

The same subdivision of part (2) occurs in an episode recorded of R. Joshua ben Karha, of the middle of the 2nd cent. A.D.[1] (1) A gentile asked him why the Jews did not join the more numerous pagans, seeing that, according to Rabbinic doctrine itself, decisions about religious observances were to be made by the majority. (2a) The Rabbi put a counter-question: 'What about your children?' And the heathen had to admit that each of them worshipped a different god from the other. (2b) It was now easy to tell him that, before attempting to get the Jews to join him, he ought to bring about unity in his own family. (3) After the gentile had left, the disciples asked for elucidation. (4) So R. Joshua pointed out to them that whereas the Bible used the plural 'souls' of Esau's small family, it used the singular 'soul' of Jacob's large one[2]—an indication that paganism, with its many conflicting deities, was not to be considered a united majority as compared with Israel, serving the one God.

Again, Hadrian is said[3] to have remarked to Joshua ben Hananiah (who was very old when Hadrian became emperor, but they seem to have met) that whereas in each of the first five of the Ten Commandments—according to the Jewish numbering—the name of God was mentioned, in order to threaten any transgressor with punishment,[4] it was never mentioned in the second half; since the second half alone applied also to the gentiles (no murder, adultery, theft, false witness, coveting), they had an advantage, they were not threatened with punishment. This is part (1), the attack. The Rabbi took Hadrian for a walk through the city, and images of the emperor were everywhere except in lavatories. Joshua asked why none were to be found there; to which no reply was possible but that it would be no honour for the ruler to be linked with such places. This is part (2a), the counter-question compelling the attacker to lay himself open to refutation. Now Joshua declared that it would be no honour for God to have his name linked with the crimes listed in the second half of the Decalogue, murder etc. This is part (2b), the retort. It sufficed to discomfit the attacker, though it was only on his level, implying some crude notions

---

[1] Lev. Rabba on 4.1 f.   [2] Gen. 36.6, Exod. 1.5.   [3] P.R. 21.
[4] Such is the Rabbinic interpretation of 'I am the Lord thy God', 'I the Lord thy God am a jealous God', 'for the Lord will not hold him guiltless', 'it is the sabbath day of the Lord thy God', 'the land which the Lord thy God giveth thee'.

L

both as regards the unclean character of lavatories and as regards the avoidance of any reference to God in connection with certain matters. At home, however, his disciples wanted from the Rabbi the real reason why the name of God appeared only in the first five commandments: part (3). So he explained that it was because the Law was first offered to the gentiles, but they refused it. Israel alone accepted it. Thus the responsibility Israel undertook beyond the universal obligations occurring in the second half meant a distinction, it brought Israel closer to God. This is part (4), the true solution on a high level.

What renders this case particularly interesting is that W. Bacher, some seventy years ago, suggested that parts (3) and (4) might be additions[1]—a remarkable anticipation of Dodd's attitude. Bacher, however, did not generalize. He had a special reason for considering just this one anecdote as expanded: the idea that the Torah was first offered to the gentiles, he noted, recurred independently of this story in other sources.

But surely, the more plausible conclusion is that Joshua made use of a popular idea to account for a feature of the Decalogue. That it was a popular idea prior to Joshua is practically certain,[2] and we know that other Rabbis used it to explain other Scriptural passages.[3] Even, however, if Joshua was the first to conceive the idea, he might have done so in tackling a particular problem of the Decalogue, and it might subsequently have gained currency in its own right.

Be this as it may, the Talmudic parallels strongly support the thesis here advocated. Obviously, the controversy about divorce as depicted in Mark shows a highly elaborate form, a form made up of four parts, of which the second again contains two sections. Such a structure cannot be the work of several hands; we cannot explain it by assuming an original, brief report, supplemented by haphazard additions. The unity of the pericope is in fact beyond question.

In Matthew's treatment of the controversy, the form is no longer intact. We have already observed that, in his account, part (2), the reply to the Pharisees, is no longer veiled but quite open. It includes, that is, the explanation—'Whosoever shall put away his wife' and so on—which, in Mark, comes in part (4), where the disciples alone are

---

[1] *Die Aggada der Tannaiten*, vol. 1, 1844, p. 180, n. 2.
[2] For numerous references see Strack-B., vol. 3, pp. 38 ff. Add, e.g., IV Ezra 7.72.
[3] E.g. Tanh. on Exod. 6.2.

addressed. All further changes are largely the result of this fundamental one.

It may suffice to deal with the most significant of them. In the first place, the private talk between Jesus and his disciples which follows the public discussion must now be about a subject other than divorce. On divorce, everything has been said in public. If the disciples are to receive a special teaching in private, it must concern a different question—according to Matthew, it is the question of marriage as such.

In the second place, the disciples open the private talk, not by a straightforward question, but by a comment—though possibly a comment in an inquiring tone: 'If this is so, it is not good to marry.' As the question of divorce has been completely cleared up in public, they cannot, as in Mark, 'ask him again of the same matter'. What they do is to widen the theme, to proceed to the problem of marriage as such. That at one time this problem also may have been considered in relation to the myth of the androgynous being, we have already seen; but Matthew hardly any longer recognizes the connection.

In the third place, in Matthew, whereas the Pharisees are given a clear answer, it is the disciples to whom Jesus speaks in riddles: 'For there are some eunuchs. . . . He that is able to receive it, let him receive it.' This is a similitude, presented as if the addressees were 'those outside', who are not meant easily to understand. Evidently, we have moved far away from the original form. Matthew still has four parts, but they are of a very different kind from the original ones and, above all, no longer constitute a purposeful, coherent structure. Instead of (1) question by enemies, (2) retort, (3) question by disciples, (4) explanation, Matthew gives (1) question by enemies, (2) explanation, (3) comment by disciples, (4) retort.

Lastly, as for the subdivision of part (2)—we found that in Mark, as in several Rabbinic stories of this type, (2a) consists of a counter-question, answered in a way that makes possible (2b), the actual retort. As Matthew includes in part (2) the full explanation which, according to Mark, is entrusted only to the disciples, he is forced to alter the arrangement. He puts first what, in Mark, forms the climax of the retort ('male and female' etc.); then he gives, in the shape of a further question on the part of the Pharisees, what, in Mark, appears as their answer to Jesus's counter-question ('why then did Moses command to write a bill of divorcement?'); and it is Jesus's reply to this further question which he makes to culminate in the full explanation, part (4) in Mark ('whosoever shall put away his wife' etc.).

One or two smaller modifications are to be accounted for in the same way: for example, in Matthew, the Pharisees do not refer to Moses 'suffering' divorce, but Jesus, in his final reply, introduces the notion of divorce having been a concession. Enough has been said to show that Matthew is secondary, and that his treatment of the material represents a disintegration of the form we are discussing.

It remains to add three reservations. First, even in those pericopes of the gospels where the Rabbinic form is preserved best—i.e. in the Matthean and Markan sections about defilement and the Markan one about divorce—there is one little detail in which the New Testament diverges from its model. In the Rabbinic stories, the opponent in part (1) visits the Rabbi to question him, and the disciples in part (3) put their request for further information after the opponent has left. In the gospels, Jesus in part (1) is thought of as being in a public place where it is easy to approach him, and the disciples in part (3) put their request after he and they have reached home. The Rabbi, that is, throughout sits with his disciples in the house of study; Jesus, as the scene opens, is among the people and only later withdraws. Apparently, some slight adaptation of the Rabbinic form was unavoidable if it was to fit the altered setting, i.e. the conditions of Jesus's ministry as opposed to those of the typical Rabbi's profession. The difference is small but highly revealing.

That we are not overrating it may be seen from a Midrash designed to illustrate the meticulous justice of God.[1] When Moses wished to hear God, he had to go to the tabernacle; whereas in the case of Samuel, God visited him.[2] Why this discrimination? Because—the Rabbis explain—'Moses sat to judge the people',[3] i.e. he made them come before him; whereas 'Samuel went in circuit to Beth-el and Gilgal and Mizpeh and judged Israel in all those places.'[4] So God made Moses come before him, while he sought out Samuel. Evidently, people in Talmudic times were only too conscious of the difference between a great man who lets himself be approached and a great man who makes an effort to meet you. This consciousness is reflected in the deviation of the Matthean and Markan form from its Rabbinic model.

Secondly, we do not deny the existence, in New Testament times,

[1] Exod. Rabba on 12.21.   [2] I Sam. 3.10.   [3] Exod. 18.13.   [4] I Sam. 7.16.

of simpler forms, such as (1) aggressive question, (2) retort, without a subsequent conversation with an inner circle, i.e. without (3) request by the inner circle for elucidation and (4) the higher truth; or (1) aggressive question, (2a) counter-question and reply which renders the refutation easy, (2b) the refutation—again without parts (3) and (4). Indeed, we shall say something about the latter type in the next chapter. The point, however, is that there was also a more elaborate form which included (3) and (4), and which should not be criticized away.

Thirdly, we have tried to demonstrate the unity of the discussion respecting defilement as depicted by Matthew and Mark, and of the discussion respecting divorce as depicted by the latter: the Rabbinic parallels militate decisively against the view that parts (3) and (4) are accretions. Our conclusion, however, does not apply to the parables of the Sower and the Tares.[1] Here Dodd is doubtless right in regarding the private interpretation of the public utterance as a later addition.[2]

It is, indeed, probable that the early theologian responsible for these additions was familiar with the form public retort—private explanation. For one thing, he arranges the private talk in exactly the same manner: first a request of the disciples for explanation, then the explanation. For another, the whole which he produces, i.e. the parable together with the private talk appended to it, involves the same division as the original form between the outside world, destined to grope in the dark, and the elect, alone worthy of enlightenment.

Actually, he makes Jesus dwell on this division in the harshest terms: the outside world, Jesus says, is spoken to in riddles 'in order that they may see and not perceive, and hear and not understand'.[3] There is no justification for mitigating this statement by declaring ἵνα due to a mistranslation from the Aramaic, as is done, for example, by T. W. Manson.[4] From the beginning, the form in question is anything but universalistic. The author who used it when he supplied the parables of the Sower and the Tares with interpretations may have over-emphasized the exclusion of 'those without' from knowledge and salvation; but, essentially, the idea had always been implicit in the form.

Nevertheless, that these parables, unlike the pericopes about defilement and divorce or the Rabbinic episodes adduced, did not from the

---

[1] Matt. 13.1 ff., Mark 4.1 ff.   [2] Op. cit., 13, 180 ff.
[3] Mark 4.12.   [4] The Teaching of Jesus, 1931, pp. 76 ff.

outset show this form is clear from a number of points. Above all, the form public retort—private explanation, we saw, consists of four parts: (1) hostile question by outsiders, (2) retort, (3) question by disciples, (4) explanation. But in the parables mentioned part (1) is not to be found. Jesus addresses the public not in reply to a question, by way of defence, but unasked, spontaneously. Furthermore, when we pass from the form of teaching to its substance, we notice a great change. In the pericopes concerning the washing of hands and divorce, as in the Rabbinic stories, the point is invariably the misunderstanding by the outsiders, and the true understanding by the master and his circle, of Scripture or the Law. In those concerning the Sower and the Tares, it is not Scripture or the Law, but the nature of the new community, the kingdom, insight into which is withheld from the public at large but vouchsafed to the disciples.

These differences alone would be enough to suggest that we have not before us, in these two parables, a genuine application of the form under notice. The proof, however, is completed by a definite incongruity in the present structure. Jesus begins by addressing the people spontaneously, on the theme of the kingdom; in other words, he calls them. Then comes the private talk, according to which he did not call them but, on the contrary, addressed them in order to reject them for ever. Evidently, this confirms Dodd's proposition that the private talk is the work of a later hand.

We are, of course, concerned solely with the literary growth of these chapters; the ultimate authorship of the interpretations—i.e. whether in some form or other they go back to Jesus—is a different question, not here to be decided.

VII

Socratic Interrogation

IN the last chapter we discussed the form public retort—private explanation. It has four essential parts: (1) hostile question by an outsider, (2) reply sufficient to defeat him, (3) request by the inner circle for the true reply and (4) the true reply. We saw, however, that in the New Testament as well as in Rabbinic writings part (2) is occasionally subdivided. It may consist, that is, of (2a), a counter-question by answering which the enemy becomes vulnerable, and (2b), the triumphant conclusion from the enemy's answer. We also mentioned that, besides this intricate form, there is, as one would expect, a simpler one which, though it contains (1) the attack, (2a) the counter-question compelling the inadequate answer, and (2b) the refutation, lacks parts (3) and (4), the subsequent conversation with an inner circle. We propose to make some comments on this simpler form; and we shall call the question by the enemy part (1), the counter-question part (2), the answer which the enemy is forced to make part (3), and the refutation which thereby becomes possible part (4).

First, for the Rabbis. Tineius Rufus, who was governor of Judaea when Bar Kokhba's revolt broke out in A.D. 132, mockingly asked R. Akiba what might be the difference between the seventh day and the others—part (1). Akiba put the counter-question what might be the difference between Rufus and other men—part (2). Rufus answered that his master, the Emperor, wanted the distinction—part (3). Just so, Akiba rejoined, his master, God, wanted the distinction with regard to the Sabbath—part (4).[1]

Now for the New Testament. All three Synoptics use this form in the report about the controversy between Jesus and the authorities regarding his credentials.[2] If we discount certain elaborations, the main scheme is as follows: (1) Whence do you derive your authority? Hostile

[1] Bab. San. 65b.　　　　[2] Matt. 21.23 ff., Mark 11.27 ff., Luke 20.1 ff.

question. (2) Whence was the baptism of John? Counter-question. (3) We do not know, an admission that they dare not challenge the claims of the Baptist. This answer enables Jesus to proceed to (4), the rejoinder: Neither shall I tell you. His opponents are refuted, the implication being that his authority is no less valid than the Baptist's claims.

In some commentaries[1] it is considered remarkable that no emphasis is laid on the officials making themselves ridiculous by pleading ignorance as to the nature of John's baptism. It is, however, remarkable only so long as the form of the story is not appreciated. Part (3), the enemy's answer, is merely a means to an end, and it is a means to a particular end: part (4), the repulse of the attack and the successful establishing of one's own proposition—in this case, that Jesus's authority is more securely founded than his opponents thought when they started questioning him.

Two more examples may be found in Luke. One is a narrative about Jesus healing a sick man on the Sabbath.[2] Jesus's antagonists watch whether he will heal him despite its being a Sabbath—a hostile question, though not an open one: part (1). Jesus asks whether one may do good or evil on the Sabbath: part (2). His adversaries keep silence (though this is merely implied in the description of Jesus as 'looking round about upon them all'), since they cannot reject his premise: part (3). Jesus—by performing the cure—points out the result, namely, that one should heal: part (4). The other instance is the scene where Jesus is anointed by a sinful woman.[3] His host objects, though again not openly: part (1). Jesus puts a counter-question, part (2): which of two debtors would love his creditor more, he who had a large debt remitted or he who had a small one remitted? Simon answers that it would be the former: part (3). Thereupon Jesus draws the conclusion, culminating in the words 'Her sins, which are many, are forgiven, for she loved much': part (4).

The pattern accords with a Greek rhetorical rule. Aristotle writes:[4] 'You may employ interrogation of your opponent when one point is self-evident, as following from another which he will grant you on being questioned. Yet, when you have obtained your first premise by asking him to admit it, you must not put what is self-evident in the form of a further question, but simply state the conclusion yourself.'

---

[1] E.g. E. Klostermann, *Das Markusevangelium*, 4th ed., 1950, p. 120.
[2] 6.6 ff.   [3] 7.36 ff.   [4] Rhet. 3.18.2.

In the cases just adduced, Akiba interrogates Rufus as to a point which the latter will grant—his rank being willed by the Emperor—and Jesus employs the same method—his opponents must admit that John's baptism cannot be dismissed as worthless, that one may do good but no evil on a Sabbath, that a debtor let off a large sum will love his creditor best. Further, from the narrator's point of view at least, the next, principal point is obvious once the first is settled: the seventh day, set apart by God, deserves no less respect than a Roman governor, Jesus's authority cannot be impugned if John's baptism is not, seeing that one may do only good on a Sabbath one ought to heal, a great sinner will be particularly faithful if accepted in mercy.

What is highly significant is that, in accordance with Aristotle's rule, no second question is put in any of the cases. Akiba does not ask Rufus whether the seventh day, set apart by God, is of less account than a governor appointed by the Emperor; he just states the conclusion. Jesus's procedure is analogous.

The chief reason for the advice that, when your premise is obtained, you should not ask concerning the result but yourself declare it is, of course, that your opponent might prove obstinate: he might refuse to see that the conclusion follows. Indeed, Aristotle warns the person interrogated to be on his guard from the outset, i.e. even when replying to the first question which apparently admits only of one answer:[1] 'You must meet ambiguous questions by drawing a distinction, and not too concisely; questions likely to make you contradict yourself you should solve immediately, before the interrogator has time to ask the next one or draw the conclusion, for it is not difficult to notice the drift of his argument.' Rufus, instead of referring to his master's decree, ought at once to have exclaimed that an imaginary God was not comparable to a powerful Emperor, the Pharisees ought at once to have asserted that, though one should do good on a Sabbath, healing—except where a man's life was in danger—was prohibited for special reasons, and so on.

There is abundant evidence that the rhetoricians of the 1st cent. A.D. had not forgotten about the pattern. It may suffice to quote from Quintilian:[2] 'The method of argument chiefly used by Socrates was this: when he had asked about a number of things to which his adversary could only agree, he finally drew the principal conclusion, as analogous to the points already conceded.' Like Aristotle, Quintilian

[1] 3.18.5.   [2] I.O. 5.11.3.

enjoins the greatest caution in answering these 'Socratic', paradigmatic questions.[1]

In general, Socrates cultivated this interrogation for the purpose, not of meeting an attack, but of working out a thesis. In other words, his scheme would not be (1) question by an ill-wisher, (2) counter-question, (3) answer and (4) the refutation made possible by the answer; but part (1) would normally be absent. He would start interrogating a person—part (2); that person would give an answer by which he became vulnerable—part (3); and Socrates would draw the inference—part (4). The inference might indeed take the form of a new interrogation, a new part (2), bringing about a new part (3), and so on. Quintilian primarily thinks of this dialectic, philosophical scheme, despite a reference to its usefulness for the examination of witnesses in court. He recommends not a dramatic single question but 'the asking about a number of things', and the examples he cites confirm the impression:[2] 'What is the finest fruit? The best. The finest horse? The best. Who, then, is the finest type of man?' or again, 'If the woman next door has finer ornaments than yours, which do you prefer? Hers. If she has a more valuable dress? Hers. What if she has a better husband?'

This is not to deny that, in a sense, even here there is a part (1), namely, the popular misconception which the philosopher sets out to put right. But it remains latent, unexpressed. Formally, part (1) is lacking. The setting in life of philosophical interrogation is spontaneous inquiry, it is study not provoked by aggression.

Aristotle, on the other hand, has in mind what we may term the forensic variety of the pattern. He seems to speak of the putting of one or two decisive questions only. Above all, part (1) is definitely present. The setting in life of the forensic pattern involves attack. You are attacked, part (1); you put a well-chosen question, part (2); you receive the desired answer, part (3); and from it you deduce the point that squashes the attack, part (4).

It is noteworthy that though Aristotle also connects the form with Socrates, the example he cites is from Socrates's defence.[3] Meletus accuses Socrates of not believing in gods—part (1). Socrates asks whether he, Socrates, never mentioned 'something divine'—part (2). Meletus admits he did mention it—part (3). Socrates asks again

---

[1] 5.11.27.
[2] 5.11.4, 5.11.27 f.; cp. Cicero, Inv. 1.31.51.   [3] Cp. Plato, Apol. 15.27A ff.

whether divine beings must not be children of gods—another counter-question, another part (2). Meletus admits they must—another part (3). Now Socrates states the conclusion that nobody could believe in children of gods without believing in gods—part (4).

Whether, in ancient Greece, the philosophical variety of the form preceded the forensic or the forensic preceded the philosophical, we need not here decide. What matters is that, in all probability, the Rabbis adopted the forensic variety from Hellenistic rhetoric. (Interestingly enough, they made little use of the philosophical variety.) It might perhaps be objected that the form is so natural that we need assume no borrowing. But, in the first place, it was precisely because Hellenistic rhetoric was 'natural', i.e. useful and sound, that it achieved its tremendous popularity. In the second place, it is plain that in the last few centuries B.C., the Rabbis drew on Hellenistic rhetoric in many fields.[1] In the third place, the form is not so natural that it would be successfully handled by anybody and anywhere—it does not occur in the Old Testament—or that it would be the only possible form in any given case.

The last-mentioned point is easily illustrated. The section in John which, in some ways, corresponds to the Synoptic report about the nature of Jesus's authority,[2] is quite dissimilar in form: (1) demand of the Jews for a sign, (2) offer by Jesus of an apparently impossible miracle (were the Temple destroyed, he could rebuild it in three days), (3) expression of disbelief on the part of the Jews, (4) narrator's explanation that the offer had not the meaning it appeared to have and that the miracle was performed (Jesus alluded to his body).

Luke's narrative about healing to which we have drawn attention is closely parallel to a Markan one.[3] But the latter does not comply with the form under notice to the same extent. We do not get 1) watching by the enemies, (2) question, (3) silence admitting the premise, (4) conclusion; but (1) watching by the enemies, (2) question, (3) silence (Mark indeed states in so many words that the Pharisees kept silent), (3a) Jesus 'grieving for the hardness of their hearts', (4) conclusion. The conclusion does not follow the silence as the victorious termination of the dispute. It is separated from it by the remark about Jesus's sorrow

---

[1] See my studies on 'Rabbinic Methods of Interpretation and Hellenistic Rhetoric', in *Hebrew Union College Annual*, vol. 22, 1949, 239 ff., and 'Alexandrian Methods of Interpretation and the Rabbis', in *Festschrift Hans Lewald*, 1953, pp. 27 ff.
[2] John 2.18 ff.   [3] 3.1 ff.

and thus appears as a more independent action. Mark may have expanded his source, or Luke may have made the narrative suit a stricter pattern. In either case Mark proves that the form in question is not inevitable.

As for the remaining stories about healing on a Sabbath, they are given in entirely different forms. In Matthew,[1] the Pharisees also begin the dispute and Jesus also counters by a paradigmatic question—whether they would not rescue one of their sheep out of a pit on the Sabbath. But then he simply proceeds to explain his meaning by an inference *a minori ad maius*—'how much then is a man better than a sheep'—draws the conclusion and cures the sick man. After their opening of the argument, the Pharisees take no more active part, as they do, by their silence, in the narratives investigated above. Their opening, that is, leads to a *halakhic* lecture by Jesus, which is crowned by the action, the cure; it does not lead to that dramatic interrogation convicting the opponent. Again, in Luke 13,[2] a form is employed which we shall go into below: revolutionary action—protest—silencing of the remonstrants. Jesus performs the cure before he asks the question justifying his conduct—whether one does not lead one's cattle to the watering place on a Sabbath. In Luke 14,[3] the controversy is opened by Jesus himself asking whether one may heal on a Sabbath. He receives no answer, performs the cure and then puts the question to be found in Matthew—whether any of his antagonists would hesitate to save one of his animals that had fallen into a pit on a Sabbath.

To go on to the anointing of Jesus by a woman, none of the versions we meet with in Matthew, Mark and John[4] shows Luke's form, (1) criticism, (2) counter-question, (3) answer, (4) refutation of the criticism by using the answer. In all of them, the form is (1) criticism, (2) explanation.

Manifestly, Socratic interrogation, however natural a form, is not so common as to render unlikely the Hellenistic descent of its applications in Rabbinic and New Testament writings.

It remains to guard against a misunderstanding. In contending that this form comes from Hellenistic rhetoric, we do not claim that a New Testament narrative told in it goes back to a Hellenistic rather than a Jewish milieu. In that period, much of Hellenistic rhetoric was the common property of the civilized Mediterranean world. Its effects

---

[1] 12.9 ff.   [2] vv. 10 ff.   [3] vv. 1 ff.   [4] Matt. 26.6 ff., Mark 14.3 ff., John 12.1 ff.

are hardly less noticeable in Rabbinic literature than in Greek or Roman. As regards the particular form here in question, we have given a good, Rabbinic example at the beginning of this chapter; and we may repeat that, in a previous chapter, we found this form embedded within a more complicated one, for instance, in a story about Johanan ben Zaccai, who lived at the time of the destruction of the Temple, and in a very similar one about Jesus—both stories dealing with the concept of defilement.

To be sure, the fact that Luke offers more instances of the form than the other evangelists is conceivably due to his stronger Greek contacts: he was perhaps more inclined to give traditional material this shape. But the material may well be Jewish even in these cases. Certainly, it would be quite wrong to doubt the Jewish background of the controversy between Jesus and the officials about his authority, a controversy appearing in all Synoptics. There is every reason to suppose not only that it is in the main historical, but also that it had its present form from the start.

VIII

Four Types of Question

W E may now go on to another case where Rabbinic categories like *halakha*, 'teaching about law', and *haggadha*, 'teaching about non-legal matters', have influenced the New Testament material.

A. A FOURFOLD SCHEME

In Matthew and Mark,[1] four questions are discussed in one section: (1) Is it lawful to give tribute unto Caesar? (2) If a man dies without issue and his brother, in fulfilment of the religious duty of the levirate, marries the widow, the second husband also dies and the next brother marries her, and so on until seven brothers have had her, whose wife will she be at the resurrection? (3) Which is the most important commandment? and (4) How can the Messiah be the son of David, seeing that David in one of his Psalms[2] calls him his Lord?

That the four questions in fact date from the same historical occasion is highly improbable. Matthew alone coincides with Mark in putting them together, whereas Luke puts together questions (1), (2) and (4) only, giving (3) in a different connection.[3] Moreover, both in Matthew and Mark—though admittedly not in Luke—question (4) begins by a fresh description of audience or place: 'while the Pharisees were gathered together' and 'while he taught in the temple'. Which suggests that this question was originally independent of the others.

If this is correct, we must ask ourselves how the questions came to be united. The answer is that whoever united them followed a fourfold scheme with which the first-century Rabbis were familiar. More precisely, he regarded these questions as representative of four different types of question distinguished by the early Rabbis.

The Talmud reports the Alexandrians to have put to R. Joshua ben

---

[1] Matt. 22.15 ff., Mark 12.13 ff.   [2] 110.1.   [3] Luke 20.21 ff., 10.25 ff.

Hananiah—a leading Rabbi in the half-century following the destruction of the Temple—twelve questions of four kinds, i.e. three of each kind.[1] They put three questions of *ḥokhma*, 'wisdom'. These are *halakhic* questions, concerning points of law. For example, is a priest, who ought to observe special marriage restrictions,[2] allowed to marry the daughter of a woman who, after being divorced, remarried and, divorced again, returned to her first husband despite the Biblical prohibition of such a return?[3] Evidently a legal problem.

Next they put three questions of *haggadha*, with no bearing on the law. These questions concern apparent contradictions between different verses from Scripture. For example, Ezekiel's 'I have no pleasure in the death of him that dieth'[4] seems to conflict with the notice in I Samuel,[5] 'It pleased the Lord to slay the sons of Eli.' Or the verse from Psalms,[6] 'The Lord hath chosen Zion', seems to conflict with Jeremiah's 'This city hath been to me as a provocation of mine anger that I should remove it from before my face.'[7]

Next they put three questions of *boruth*, 'vulgarity'. They are mocking questions, designed to ridicule a belief of the Rabbi. And they are all directed against the same belief, namely, belief in resurrection. For example, did the child brought back to life by Elisha convey uncleanness, as a corpse? Or on resurrection, will the dead need sprinkling, having been in contact with corpses?

Finally, the Alexandrians asked three questions of *derekh 'ereṣ*, 'principles of moral and successful life'. What shall a man do to become wise? To become rich? To obtain male children? R. Joshua explained that, ultimately, there was only one answer: Seek the mercy of him who alone can give wisdom (for this, he invoked a line from Proverbs[8]), wealth (for this he invoked Haggai[9]), and sons (this he proved by a Psalm[10]). The same path leads to all three goals.

The four questions in Matthew and Mark can easily be brought under the headings just listed. Question (1), about tribute to Caesar, falls under *ḥokhma*. It is *halakhic*, it has regard to a point of law. It should be noted that the motive of the questioners, which is to 'catch Jesus in his words', does not alter the character of the question itself,

---

[1] Bab. Nid. 69b ff. [2] Lev. 21.7. [3] Deut. 24.4. [4] 18.32.
[5] 2.25. [6] 132.13. [7] 32.31. [8] 2.6.
[9] 2.8. The Delphic oracle had given a different answer to the question how to get rich: 'If thou acquirest what lieth between Corinth and Sicyon' (Athenaeus, Deipn. 5.219a).
[10] 127.3.

i.e. it does not turn the question into one of 'vulgarity'. There are numerous examples in the Talmud of *halakhic* questions asked with a view to 'catching' an opponent. The question asked by Jesus about the nature of the Messiah, though calculated to embarrass his adversaries, is far from 'vulgar'. So is his question, in another chapter, about the baptism of John,[1] where the kind of dilemma in which his antagonists find themselves is very similar indeed to that in which they hoped to place him by the question about tribute to Caesar. But a question of 'vulgarity' is different. It is one which could not be put in any other spirit than that of rude mockery.

Question (2), about the seven husbands, is clearly of this sort. It falls under *boruth*. It is designed to ridicule a belief held by Jesus; and significantly, the particular belief attacked in this manner is that which forms the target also in the illustrations of 'vulgarity' quoted by the Talmud.

Question (3), about the most important commandment, falls under *derekh 'ereṣ*. It is concerned with the fundamental principles on which to base one's conduct, as opposed to detailed ritual.

Question (4) falls under *haggadha*. Unlike (1), it has no reference to any point of law. It draws attention to a verse from the Psalms in disagreement with the current teaching of the scribes respecting the Messiah—which teaching, of course, also rests on Scriptural evidence.[2] That is to say, the problem consists in a conflict between various passages from the Bible.

Certainly, there are differences between the Talmudic episode and the New Testament parallel. First, the Talmud has twelve questions, the New Testament only four. No doubt, in a sense, both numbers are artificial. It would, for instance, have been easy, both for the author of the Talmudic episode and that of the New Testament section under notice, to introduce additional questions regarding *derekh 'ereṣ*, 'principles'. The higher number in the Talmud suggests that the author either had more material at his disposal or permitted himself greater freedom in supplementing questions actually submitted to R. Joshua by others similar in nature but not in fact submitted to him.

Secondly, the Talmudic episode is considerably more stylized than the corresponding New Testament section. (We are disregarding the comments by Rabbis later than Joshua which are appended to the third

---

[1] Matt. 21.24 ff., Mark 11.29 ff., Luke 20.3 ff.   [2] Isa. 11.1, 10, Jer. 23.5.

question of *ḥokhma* and the first of *derekh 'ereṣ*.) There is not so much historical detail, individualization of the settings of the various questions. Once again, we must conclude that either the Alexandrians really arranged a formal test of Joshua and themselves grouped their questions for the occasion in a systematic fashion, or it is the Talmudic author who has sacrificed detail and variety to regularity of arrangement. Whichever may be true, it is interesting that the Talmud starts from the four categories of questions: the several questions are adduced to illustrate the categories. The New Testament starts from the several questions; the fourfold scheme is responsible for no more than their being placed side by side as forming one series.

Thirdly, the order in the Talmud is points of law (*ḥokhma*), contradictions between passages from Scripture (*haggadha*), vulgarity (*boruth*), principles of conduct (*derekh 'ereṣ*), the order in the New Testament is points of law, vulgarity, principles of conduct, contradictions between passages from Scripture. Maybe there was no fixed order. If there was one, it was probably that of the Talmud. The New Testament sequence is perhaps to be accounted for by the assumption that, at some stage of the tradition, questions (1) and (2) stood together without questions (3) and (4), or questions (1), (2) and (3) stood together without question (4); and that (3) and (4), or (4), were added precisely in order to complete the fourfold scheme. However, even if we suppose that the New Testament questions were all collected at the same time by an author acquainted with the fourfold scheme, the deviation from the Talmud is understandable. The question asked by Jesus himself would naturally be placed at the end, as the climax of the series. With that exception, the order is indeed that of the Talmud: law, vulgarity, principles.

This brings us to one more difference worth noting. In the Talmud, all questions are put by the Alexandrians to R. Joshua. In the New Testament, the first three are put by one side, the adversaries or admirers of Jesus, but the fourth by the other, Jesus himself. Let us postpone for the moment discussion of this divergency; we shall come back to it.

There are indications that the fourfold scheme of questions is of Greek origin. For one thing, in the Talmudic episode, it is the Alexandrians who are the questioners. This is significant no matter whether the report is historical or not—and considering that Joshua, in A.D. 130,

M

as an old man, followed Hadrian to Egypt, it would be rash to assert that it cannot be historical.

Further, the use of the word *ḥokhma*, 'wisdom', for what is ordinarily described as *halakha*, 'legal points', also suggests a Greek background. Much later, in the 3rd and 4th cents., Eleazar b. Pedath and Raba used *ḥokhma* in this sense;[1] the former was a fervent advocate of Jewish missionary efforts,[2] the latter lived at Mahuza on the Tigris, in a community rich in proselytes. The term *haggadha*, too, is employed in a special sense in the story of Joshua and the Alexandrians. Whereas, generally, it denotes any exegesis of no immediate bearing on the law, here it is confined to the problem of 'antinomy', the apparent conflict between two verses.

Again, the appearance of *derekh 'ereṣ*, 'principles of moral and successful life', as one of the four cardinal types of question, points in the direction of Hellenism, where this branch of philosophy was greatly cultivated. The questions which, according to the Letter of Aristeas, King Ptolemy put to the seventy-two Jewish sages all concern *derekh 'ereṣ*: Which is the highest good in life? How can one attain wealth? Wisdom? Justice?

Similarly, the scorn poured on the belief in resurrection reflects an attitude widespread among Hellenized Jews. Elsewhere in the Talmud,[3] Queen Cleopatra is represented as wondering whether the dead will rise clothed or naked. This was the sort of thing expected of Alexandrians; they are here represented by Queen Cleopatra because the ambiguous flavour of the question suits her character. As for the New Testament, the question concerning resurrection breathes the same spirit as those to be found in the Talmud; and Herodians and Sadducees figure among the questioners.

It might be worth while to search Hellenistic writings on rhetoric for a parallel to, or rather the model of, the fourfold scheme.

At any rate, whoever collected the New Testament questions acted on a definite, artistic plan. Was it Mark or a pre-Markan narrator? Nothing seems to speak against the former alternative. It might perhaps

[1] Bab. Shab. 113b, 31a. In the story of the end of Eliezer ben Hyrcanus, Pal. Shab. 5b, the word seems to signify, not (as is maintained by Strack-B., vol. 4, 1928, pt. 1, p. 316, n. 1) *halakha*, but 'wisdom', 'intelligence', as opposed to disorder of the mind from which a dying person may suffer.

[2] Bab. Pes. 87b: God scattered Israel in order that they should convert the Gentiles to Judaism.   [3] Bab. San. 90b.

be objected that, if the classification is Greek in origin, it must have been imposed on the New Testament material by a pre-Markan, Hellenistic editor. But this does not follow at all. By the age of Mark, the classification was surely known to the most Jewish of Palestinian Rabbis. It would be used by them wherever it appeared suitable. It was not the only form of Greek origin they used. There is no reason why Mark should not be the author of the grouping to be met with in his and Matthew's gospels.

It is, of course, doubtful to what extent we may rely on the Talmudic pattern for filling in details in Matthew and Mark. Still, it should be observed that, where the Alexandrians put questions of *haggadha*, about apparent contradictions between passages from Scripture, the answer is invariably a 'distinction'. Both passages, that is, are upheld, each being assigned its proper field of application. For example, Ezekiel says that God 'has no pleasure' in a sinner's death; yet according to I Samuel, 'it pleased him' to kill the sons of Eli. Both verses, R. Joshua explains, speak the truth. The antinomy is to be solved by referring that from Ezekiel to the death of such as repent, that from I Samuel to the death of the impenitent. Similarly, 'the Lord chose Zion' before Solomon married a daughter of the Pharaoh, i.e. so long as the people kept away from foreign idols, but 'the city provoked his fury' from that marriage onwards.

If the New Testament question of *haggadha*, concerning the contradictory notions of the Messiah contained in Scripture, is closely analogous—as it may well be at least in Mark and Matthew, where the fourfold scheme is introduced—then the answer implied is not that one notion is right and the other wrong, but that both are right in different contexts. Say, the Messiah is David's son up to a certain moment in history, but his Lord from then; or—this would mean that we have before us an adumbration of Paul's teaching in Romans[1]—he is David's son according to the flesh, but his Lord according to the spirit.

B. THE PASSOVER HAGGADAH

The results we have reached are fully confirmed by a section from the Passover Haggadah, the traditional Jewish service on Passover eve.

The Bible four times ordains that children should be taught the

---

[1] 1.3 f.

significance of the exodus from Egypt. In the Haggadah of the Seder, the service on Passover eve, these passages are taken to allude to four different types of sons. (1) The *ḥakham*, the wise son, puts a question showing that he wishes to know about all the various laws concerning Passover: 'And when thy son asketh thee, What mean the testimonies, and the statutes, and the judgments, which the Lord our God hath commanded us? Then thou shalt say' etc.[1] This is a question of *ḥokhma*, 'wisdom', in the sense of 'points of law', *halakha*. The latter term (*hilekhoth happesaḥ*, 'detailed laws respecting the Passover') actually occurs in the reply the Passover Haggadah declares suitable for the wise son's question.

(2) The *rasha*ʻ, the wicked son, puts a scoffing question by which he rudely dissociates himself from the worshipping community: 'And when your children shall say unto you, What mean ye by this service? Ye shall say' etc.[2] In Rabbinic interpretation, the contemptuous 'What mean ye?' instead of 'What mean we?' indicates a question of *boruth*, 'vulgarity'. It is noteworthy that though it is not specifically directed against resurrection—the Rabbis could not insert an express reference to it into the Biblical text—yet in Talmudic theology to dissociate oneself from the community and to deny resurrection are very similar sins, marks of the same vicious disposition, one of them almost necessarily involving the other. For example, among those consigned to eternal damnation are 'atheists who repudiate the Law and deny the resurrection and separate themselves from the ways of the congregation'.[3]

(3) The *tam*, the son of plain piety, puts a simple question about the meaning of the festival in general: 'And when thy son asketh thee, What is this? Thou shalt say' etc.[4] He is not interested in details, only in the essential significance of things: 'What is this?'—the nearest to a question concerning *derekh ʼereṣ*, 'principles of life', that the Rabbis were able to find in these Biblical injunctions as to instruction of children.

(4) The fourth type of son is he *she'eno yodheʻa lish'ol*, 'who does not know how to ask', and whose father, therefore, must take the initiative in opening the instruction: 'And thou shalt show thy son in that day,

---

[1] Deut. 6.20 f. On the reading 'commanded us', instead of the usual 'commanded you', we shall make a few remarks presently.   [2] Exod. 12.26 f.
[3] Thus the School of Hillel; see Bab. R.H. 16b f.   [4] Exod. 13.14.

saying' etc.[1] In this case the Bible does not say 'And when thy son asketh thee', but at once states the duty to teach, 'And thou shalt show thy son'. So the Rabbis conclude that the passage must speak about a son incapable of questioning.

Evidently, the author of this Midrash works on the basis of the four-fold scheme of questions we have been considering, his aim being to impose it on his Biblical material. He succeeds in identifying three questions occurring in the Pentateuch with three types occurring in the scheme: law, vulgarity and principles. One type only he is compelled to abandon—contradictions in Scripture—because the fourth Biblical passage mentions no question. He has to substitute the person who cannot ask: with such a one it is incumbent on you to take the first step. The sequence in which he gives the types, it may be observed, is the same as in the Talmud, except that, very naturally, the son who cannot ask comes at the end. Hence, while the Talmudic order is law, contradictions in Scripture, vulgarity, principles, that in the Passover Haggadah is law, vulgarity, principles, he who does not know how to ask.

This piece of liturgy, then, testifies to the popularity of the fourfold classification of questions with the early Rabbis. The Midrash of the four sons is very old. It is preserved not only in the Passover Haggadah, but also, with certain variations, in the Mekhilta and the Palestinian Talmud.[2]

It supports, too, our opinion that, if there was a fixed order in which the four types used to be listed, it was that followed in the anecdote of Joshua and the Alexandrians. The order in the Passover Haggadah is best accounted for as derived from this one.

Furthermore, there is here additional evidence for our suggestion that this classification is a Hellenistic growth. For, surely, the Midrash under notice is Alexandrian. Quite apart from the significant use of *ḥakham*, 'wise', in the sense of 'interested in points of law, *halakha*'—we have already called attention to the corresponding use of the noun *ḥokhma*, 'wisdom', in the story of R. Joshua—it is clear that the Midrash proceeds, not from the Massoretic text of the Pentateuch, but either from the LXX itself or from a Hebrew text underlying the LXX. We have seen that the wicked son dissociates himself from the congregation by asking 'What mean ye?' instead of 'What mean we?' However, in the Massoretic text, the question which the Midrash

[1] Exod. 13.8.   [2] Mekh. on Exod. 13.8, 14, Pal. Pes. 37d; also Yal. on Exod. 13.14.

assigns to the wise son is little different in this respect; Deuteronomy 6.20 runs, 'What mean the testimonies, and the statutes, and the judgments, which the Lord our God hath commanded you'—'ethkhem, 'commanded you', not, as we should expect, 'commanded us'. It is only the LXX which has the latter: ἐνετείλατο ἡμῖν. That, in Greek or Hebrew, is what the author of the Midrash must have had before him when he gave this question to the wise son.

Actually, the old editions of the Passover Haggadah as well as the versions of the Midrash extant in the Mekhilta and Palestinian Talmud do all read 'othanu, 'us'. That modern editions assimilate the question to the recognized Massoretic text and put 'ethkhem, 'you',[1] is not surprising. But the reading 'us' alone makes sense from the point of view of the Midrash, with its emphasis on the contrast between the wicked son who defies the community and the wise son who regards himself as a member of it. And this reading 'us' points to Egypt.

It would be quite wrong to infer that the Midrash did not form part of the Palestinian liturgy in the New Testament period. There is, on the contrary, every reason to think that it did, considering its occurrence in the various sources mentioned. As far as the Passover Haggadah is concerned, it ought to be added that it is found in all rites without exception. The most Jewish circles of Palestine were by that time open to Alexandrian influence.

C. THE HAGGADAH AND THE GOSPELS

In fact, it looks as if we might draw from this Midrash one or two far-reaching conclusions as to the exact treatment of the fourfold scheme by Mark or his authority. Matthew and Mark have the four types of question distinguished in the story of Joshua and the Alexandrians. But there is a difference which so far we have only noticed but not explained: in the story of Joshua, all questions are put by one side, in Matthew and Mark three are put by various people to Jesus, but the fourth by Jesus to the people. This division of the questions into three by the others and one by Jesus is not so natural that any narrator would try to compose a chapter on such a plan. Mark or his authority here followed the Midrash of the four sons, only three of them ask, whereas in the case of the fourth his father must make the beginning.

[1] The same is true of some editions of the Mekhilta.

The Markan introduction to the fourth question, that by Jesus, is:[1] 'And no man after that durst ask him; and Jesus answered and said while he taught in the temple.' This is an unmistakable reference to the Passover Haggadah, which says: 'And he who does not know how to ask, thou open (the instruction) for him.'

To be sure, most editions of the New Testament print 'And no man after that durst ask him', not as leading up to the fourth question, but as describing the effect produced by Jesus's answer to the third. However, for one thing it does not fit in this part. The third question is a genuine, reasonable one—'which is the first commandment?'—and the discussion following it ends with the assurance by Jesus: 'Thou art not far from the kingdom of God.' This should have had an encouraging rather than a deterrent effect. For another thing, there is excellent ancient authority—rightly accepted by Weiss—for connecting the clause with the fourth question.[2]

Of course, readers and copyists unaware of the model, i.e. the Midrash of the four sons, would be tempted to treat it as an appendix to the third, despite its not really fitting there. Already Matthew and Luke failed to see its real point. Matthew placed it right at the end of the entire section, after the fourth question put by Jesus.[3] That this version is secondary compared with Mark is proved, not only by the Passover liturgy, but also by Luke, where the clause still, as in Mark, precedes Jesus's question concerning the Messiah.[4] But even Luke misunderstood its original function. Instead of regarding it as the introduction to Jesus's question—'And no man after that durst ask him, and Jesus answered and said'—he regarded it as giving the reason ($\gamma \acute{\alpha} \rho$) for the praise extended to Jesus by the scribes after his refutation of the Sadducees: 'Then certain of the scribes said, Master, thou hast well said, for after that they durst not ask him anything.' These different attempts to rationalize the clause serve only to underline its peculiar role in Mark.

In Mark, it may be repeated, it belongs to the question put by Jesus. Mark—or an earlier narrator—in accordance with a current scheme collected four questions of ḥokhma, boruth, derekh 'ereṣ and haggadha. But his division of these into three put by the people and one put by Jesus to them who do not dare to ask can be explained only as directly

[1] 12.34 f.
[2] See the apparatus in Eberhard Nestle's *Novum Testamentum Graece*, 13th ed. by Erwin Nestle, 1927, 122, and J. Weiss, *Die drei älteren Evangelien*, 3rd ed., 1917, *ad loc.*
[3] 22.46.   [4] 20.40 f.

dependent on the Passover Haggadah. We are here in touch with an author—no reason why it should not be Mark—who still spent Passover eve with his family or friends reciting the Haggadah.

General considerations render it probable that portions of the gospels grew up in the form of additions to the traditional Passover liturgy made in Jewish-Christian circles. While in former times this liturgy had centred exclusively on the exodus from Egypt, now, where Christians assembled to observe Passover eve, the new redemption also was celebrated. The Markan section discussed furnishes definite proof that matters took this course. It betrays the immediate influence of the Passover-eve recital. Very likely, it first came into existence, or at any rate was published, on the occasion of a Jewish-Christian Seder.

If this is granted, we may be able to understand that passage in Mark, so puzzling at first sight, where the scribe expresses his full agreement with Jesus as to the love of God and man and is told, 'Thou art not far from the kingdom of God.' No corresponding passage is supplied by Matthew and Luke. Indeed, they regard even the question about *derekh* *'ereṣ* as designed to ensnare Jesus. For Mark, it is put in good faith, just like the question of the son who is *tam*, 'a man of plain piety', in the Passover Haggadah; and it is a characteristic of the *tam* readily to accept good advice—hence the emphatic assent of the scribe, which Matthew and Luke would no longer appreciate. In Solomon's Song, the woman is called *tammathi*, generally translated 'my undefiled'. The Rabbis[1] hold that the reference is to Israel, who at mount Sinai showed plain piety by the unreserved promise 'All that the Lord hath said will we do and be obedient.'[2]

A problem is created by the fact that, in Matthew, the vulgar, wicked questioners—the Sadducees—are 'put to silence', 'muzzled', whereas Mark and Luke use a milder expression: Jesus 'answers them well' or 'says well'. The Passover Haggadah declares that your reply to the wicked son's question should be such as 'to make his teeth blunt'. 'To muzzle a person'—*ḥasam*—is not quite the same as 'to blunt a person's teeth'—*hiqha shinnayim*—but it is clearly far closer to it than is 'to answer well' or 'to say well'. Unless we assume that Matthew introduced the stronger term for reasons of his own (and one could think of such reasons), it looks as if he had here drawn on a variant older than what we find in the present form of Mark or Luke.

[1] Cant. Rabba on 5.2.   [2] Exod. 24.7.

It remains to add that the Midrash of the four sons, in the course of its transmission, suffered no fewer alterations than its Markan counterpart. For example, in the Palestinian Talmud and Mekhilta, the son who asks a simple, general question is no longer labelled as *tam*, 'of plain piety', but as *ṭippesh*, 'stupid'. The significance of the former type —the Biblical basis for which had been Jacob, the 'plain man', *'ish tam*[1]—is forgotten; *derekh 'ereṣ* has dropped out.

This change brings with it another regarding the order of the types. The original order, preserved in the story of Joshua and the Alexandrians, is: (1) *ḥokhma* (in the sense of *halakha*), (2) *haggadha* (contradiction between verses with no bearing on law), (3) *boruth*, (4) *derekh 'ereṣ*. As we saw, the Passover Midrash, owing to the nature of the Scriptural passages it uses, must abandon *haggadha* and substitute spontaneous instruction, instruction without question. This instruction without question is put at the end, so that the order now is: (1) *ḥokhma* (*halakha*), (2) *boruth*, (3) *derekh 'ereṣ*, (4) instruction of one unable to ask. It is the same order as that in Matthew and Mark (except that in Matthew and Mark number 4 is instruction in *haggadha* of one unable to ask).

However, the Mekhilta, which turns *derekh 'ereṣ* into stupidity, finds the latter an effective contrast to *ḥokhma*, 'wisdom'. Accordingly, it has the following arrangement: (1) *ḥokhma*, (2) stupidity (previously *derekh 'ereṣ*), (3) *boruth*, (4) instruction of one unable to ask. The Palestinian Talmud, though also replacing the plain questioner by the stupid one, still adheres to the sequence of the Haggadah: (1) *ḥokhma*, (2) *boruth*, (3) stupidity, (4) instruction of one unable to ask.

On the whole, the version of the Midrash given by the Passover Haggadah proves the least corrupt. It is easier to introduce major changes into a work studied by scholars—Mekhilta or Palestinian Talmud—than into a piece of liturgy in universal use. Certainly, there are exceptions. One we have discussed at some length: modern editions of the Haggadah assimilate the quotation of Deuteronomy 6.20 to the Massoretic text, printing 'commanded you' in the place of the 'commanded us' of the ancient editions. But this is really no more than an adjustment of the Passover liturgy to an even more important branch of liturgy—the reading of the law.

[1] Gen. 25.27. Cp. also in Talmudic language the antithesis between *tam* and *mu'adh*, things normally harmless and things likely to cause injury: e.g. Mish. B.Q. 1.4 f.

IX

Two Tripartite Forms

A. Revolutionary Action—Protest—Silencing
of the Remonstrants

THE Synoptics record at least[1] seven incidents taking this course:
(1) Jesus or his disciples perform a revolutionary action, (2) the
Pharisees remonstrate with him—or, on occasion, merely 'marvel'—
and (3) he makes a pronouncement by which they are silenced.

The actions in question are: he forgives a sick person's sins[2] (the place
of the pronouncement, the verbal argument, is in this case taken by a
further action—the person is made to walk and carry his bed—but from
the point of view of the present discussion the difference is irrelevant),
he sits at table with publicans,[3] the disciples pluck corn on a sabbath,[4]
he restores a man previously blind and dumb,[5] he or his disciples do not
wash their hands before a meal,[6] he heals on a Sabbath,[7] and children
call out 'Hosanna to the son of David'.[8] There are quite a few other
pericopes more or less closely approaching this form—e.g. those about
the disciples not fasting,[9] Jesus preaching in his home town,[10] and Jesus
acting and teaching in the temple,[11] also, in Acts,[12] the episode of
Peter's preaching in defiance of the council's prohibition.

Stories told in this way are, of course, to be found in all literatures. A

---

[1] The following enumeration may well be incomplete.
[2] Matt. 9.1 ff., Mark 2.1 ff., Luke 5.17 ff.
[3] Matt. 9.9 ff., Mark 2.15 ff., Luke 5.27 ff.
[4] Matt. 12.1 ff., Mark 2.23 ff., Luke 6.1 ff.
[5] Matt. 12.22 ff., Luke 11.14 ff.; but Mark 3.22 ff. is different.
[6] Luke 11.37 ff.; in Mark 7.1 ff. part (1) is slightly weakened, in Matt. 15.1 ff. it is
entirely merged in part (2).
[7] Luke 13.10 ff.; but the form is not employed in Matt. 12.9 ff., Mark 3.1 ff., Luke
6.6 ff., 14.1 ff.
[8] Matt. 21.15 ff., with part (1) weakened just as in Mark 7.1 ff.
[9] Matt. 9.14 ff., Mark 2.19 ff., Luke 5.35 ff.
[10] Matt. 13.53 ff., Mark 6.1 ff., Luke 4.15 ff.
[11] Matt. 21.23 ff., Mark 11.27 ff., Luke 20.1 ff.   [12] 5.25 ff.

Rabbinic example is that of R. Judah the Prince,[1] who once reversed a
ruling on which his father, grandfather and so on—all of them leading
scholars—had insisted (revolutionary action). His family objected
(protest). But he replied that Asa and Jehosaphat, when they removed
the idols from the land,[2] spared the brazen serpent in order that
Hezekiah should have the merit of breaking it;[3] just so, his own ancestors had left him room to distinguish himself by a novel decision
(silencing of the remonstrants). Any newspaper may report: 'Mrs. X
refused to fill in the census-paper, an official went to see her, but she
told him that as she had kept her age a secret from her husband, she
was not going to divulge it to Mr. Attlee.'

Manifestly, the situation reflected in this structure constantly occurs
in everyday life. It is indeed a special case of what must be one of the
oldest, simplest and most frequent types of conversation: unusual
conduct—question—explanation. An employee comes home at 6 p.m.
instead of 6.30, his wife inquires 'You are early today?' and he replies
'Yes, the office closed sooner for cleaning.'

However, if we ask why this form—revolutionary action, protest,
silencing of the remonstrants—is so prominent in the Synoptics, to say
that it is a natural form would not be an adequate answer. It is precisely
this fact which needs to be investigated: what do we mean by declaring
it natural, what is the setting in life of which it appears the only fitting
expression, in what situation would it be so popular as to be used again
and again?

We must not forget that there were other forms at the disposal of the
evangelists (or their precursors). They might, for instance, have employed a more academic style. Regarding the association with publicans,
they might have written: Jesus believed that the Pharisees showed too
little consideration for sinners, who, sick men, badly needed the
physician, therefore he went into their houses, ate with them and
called them to repentance. But even if they stuck to immediate,
dramatic presentation, there was a large choice.

As a matter of fact, the Synoptics five times describe a cure performed by Jesus on a Sabbath, but only once in the form under discussion. (As for John, he mentions two healings on a Sabbath,[4] employing a style quite different from the Synoptic.) In Luke 13, we find

---

[1] Bab. Hul. 6b f.   [2] I Kings 15.12 f., 22.43.
[3] I Kings 15.14, 22.44, II Kings 18.4.   [4] 5.1 ff. and 9.1 ff.

Jesus healing a crippled woman, the ruler of the synagogue protesting, and Jesus retorting: 'Doth not each one of you on the sabbath day loose his ox and lead him away to the watering? And ought not this woman, being a daughter of Abraham, be loosed?' This sequence is revolutionary action—protest—silencing of the remonstrants. But in Matthew 12, Mark 3 and Luke 6, the Pharisees question or watch Jesus, then he explains his attitude, and the action, the cure, comes at the end; while Luke 14 seems a conflation of the two forms—the Pharisees watch Jesus, then he explains his attitude, then he performs the cure, and finally he makes a second pronouncement to refute the opponents.

Luke 14, as a conflation, may perhaps be disregarded. So may the particular structure of Luke 6, which we discussed above, under Socratic Interrogation: the Pharisees watch, Jesus puts a question, they cannot answer, and he draws the conclusion by performing the cure. This is a somewhat elaborate structure. There remains, however, a perfectly good and simple form—the enemies on the watch for a certain action, pronouncement, the action—which was known to the evangelists and which they could have used much more often than they did in the place of the form we are considering. Clearly, we are justified in inquiring into the special significance of the form they preferred.

The following points may be relevant. First, the direct, dramatic presentation of revolutionary action, protest and silencing of the remonstrants—as opposed, say, to a more detached, academic record of events—is no doubt meant for a public still in a state of active, lively controversy with the Pharisees, and strongly feeling the need of refuting the troublesome enemy.

Secondly, by placing the revolutionary action at the head, emphasis is laid on the novel, startling character of the kingdom. We have just mentioned an alternative form—used to describe a cure on a Sabbath in Matthew 12, Mark 3 and Luke 6—where Jesus first explains and then acts. Clearly, the action will here cause less surprise to his antagonists, or to the public for whom the narrative is composed. Needless to say, this form also has its distinctive purpose, but we are not here concerned with it.

We modern readers, when we come to an incident commencing 'At that time Jesus went on the sabbath day through the corn, and his disciples were an hungred and began to pluck and eat', are not particularly excited: we are too habituated to such practice. In New

Testament times, however, the effect must have been comparable to that a Lutheran author would intend by starting a life of his hero thus: 'On the 20th of December 1520, Martin Luther publicly consigned to the flames a Papal Bull condemning his errors.' The narrative opens with a shock. It is a special case of a very ancient device of story-tellers, namely, the device of putting the result at the beginning and the causes leading up to it second. (Gen. 12.10 ff. informs us first of Abraham's reasons for introducing Sarah as his sister, and then of what occurred when she was so introduced. But Gen. 20.1 ff. starts by recording his action—he introduced Sarah as his sister—and we are kept wondering why till nearly the end of the story, in v. 11. Kleist excelled in this art. In the first paragraph of *Michael Kohlhaas* we are told that this good man became a bandit and murderer, and in the first paragraph of *Die Marquise von O . . .* that this lady, a widow and mother of untainted reputation, put an advertisement in the papers saying that she had become pregnant without her knowledge, and would the man come forward in order that she might marry him.)

Thirdly, the action is invariably one performed on a single, definite occasion; not 'Jesus used to sit at meat in the houses of publicans', but 'on a certain day, Jesus ate in the house of a certain publican'.[1] This point is connected with that just considered. The kingdom—such is the idea behind the form—manifested itself, broke in, step by step as Jesus and those around him fulfilled their task.

Certainly, underlying these specific actions there were general ideas, and the believers are obliged to pay heed to them; we shall presently see that they are given full expression in the pronouncements ending the encounters. Nevertheless, in this form, things are set in motion by single, datable actions. Which means that the general ideas first became reality in, and will always derive their ultimate sanction from, deeds done by Jesus and his followers at particular moments of their activity.

Fourthly, yet another feature points the same way: the action is always an action in the narrow sense, i.e. never a statement. For example, it is easy to imagine the following structure: (1) Jesus declared, 'It is praiseworthy to eat with publicans and sinners', (2) protest by the

---

[1] Matt. 15.1 ff., unlike Luke 11.37 ff. and Mark 7.1 ff., does not refer to a specific occasion; the failure of the disciples to wash their hands before a meal is represented as a practice. But, then, as remarked above p. 170, n. 6, the tripartite form in question is here altogether abandoned. The incident falls into question and retort, there is no separate part for the action.

Pharisees, (3) repartee by Jesus. This, however, would be an ordinary disputation, such as might from beginning to end be conducted before a learned audience; and however convincing the final repartee might be, the form as such would not show whether the revolutionary view remained a theory or was once at least put into practice.

By contrast, the structure of which the first member is an action in the strict sense—Jesus ate with publicans and sinners—indicates that the revolutionary programme was carried out, that the kingdom had in fact arrived. To this, the forgiving of sins[1] is, of course, no exception. It is a proper action, indeed, a serious crime according to the Pharisees. A mere statement would be: 'Jesus said, I could forgive this man his sins.'

Fifthly, the middle part of the form, the protest, sometimes consists in a direct accusation—'He blasphemeth', 'He doth not cast out devils but by Beelzebub'—and sometimes in a challenge to justify the objectionable conduct—'Why eateth your Master with publicans and sinners?' for instance. In both cases the remonstrants assume that Jesus and his followers ought to behave as they themselves would behave. Jesus and his followers, that is, are judged as essentially belonging to the same camp as the remonstrants; it is precisely for this reason that their conduct appears as a revolution. Complete outsiders, however strange their actions, would not be called to account in this manner.

Sixthly, the third member of the form, the silencing of the remonstrants, confirms the observation just made. Jesus justifies the action impugned by adducing a piece of teaching which his opponents also recognize as valid: a wise saying ('they that are whole have no need of the physician'), a passage from Scripture ('David did eat the show-bread', 'Out of the mouth of babes thou hast perfected praise'), an established ordinance ('Doth not each one of you on the sabbath loose his ox?'). In other words, he starts from the same basis as his antagonists. If he did not, if he quoted doctrines not accepted by them, it would not put them to silence.

Where he differs from them is as to the interpretation of the teaching adduced. From the maxim that the sick ones only need the physician, he infers—whereas his opponents do not—that it is his duty to sit at table with publicans and sinners; from David's conduct he infers—whereas his opponents do not—that his hungry disciples have the right to pluck corn on the Sabbath; the verse 'Out of the mouth of babes' in

---

[1] Matt. 9.1 ff., Mark 2.1 ff., Luke 5.17 ff.

his view—but not in that of his opponents—is applicable to the Hosanna by which the children greet him; the law allowing that animals may be led to watering on the Sabbath in his view—but not in that of his opponents—shows that one may certainly heal a Jewish person on the Sabbath. The relationship between the two parties is not dissimilar to that expressed by 'Ye have heard—but I say unto you', except that 'Ye have heard—but I say' is concerned only with the proper understanding of Scripture, while the third member of the form under discussion may refer to any teaching the proper understanding of which is relevant to life in the kingdom.

Seventhly, the third member describes the defeat of the Pharisees on their own ground, by an argument resting on a basis they themselves acknowledge. Here we come back to point one, but we can now be a little more precise: the form dates from a time when it was vital to defend the ways of the new community—revolutionary actions—in a technical, scholarly, Pharisaic manner.

Comparison with a different form may make this clearer. As already mentioned, the gospels several times describe a cure on a Sabbath in the following way: (1) the Pharisees watch whether Jesus will heal the sick person, (2) Jesus explains his attitude, (3) he performs the cure. In this form, which culminates in the cure, the final emphasis is on fearlessness: despite the hostility surrounding him, Jesus acts as he thinks he ought to act. The setting in life must be sought in a milieu where it was dangerous openly to practise the new religion. Evidently, it is different where we are told (1) how Jesus performed the cure, (2) the Pharisees remonstrated, and (3) he refuted them. The final emphasis here lies on the successful vindication of the revolutionary conduct.

Finally, the tripartite form as a whole may owe something to the forensic scheme: action—charge—defence, or successful defence. After all, this scheme, which might be used by any author, must have appeared particularly appropriate to those who recounted Jesus's deeds after his death. They were resuming the trial, they were appealing against the original decision.

B. Odd Gesture—Question—Pronouncement

This form also is a special case of the elementary triad: unusual conduct (the husband comes home at 6 p.m.)—question (his wife asks him why he is so early)—explanation (the office is being cleaned). It is, however, of a rather sophisticated nature. Part (1), the gesture—which may be an action in the narrow sense or an utterance—is performed, not so much for its own sake, as in order to provoke part (2), the question, and thus to furnish an opportunity for what really matters, namely, part (3), the pronouncement.

1. *Odd gesture*

The fool in King Lear offers Kent his cap: part (1). This action is intended to astonish Lear and Kent, who ask him what he means: part (2). It is only now, in part (3), that he makes the statement to which (1) and (2) have been leading up: he points out, what he realizes even at this early stage, that Kent is entering the service of one who is doomed. Till Eulenspiegel used to laugh when faced by a steep ascent and to weep when the road was downhill: part (1). His companions asked him about his strange conduct: part (2). Whereupon he explained—part (3) —that, going uphill, he rejoiced at the prospect of the comfortable walk that would follow, whereas, going downhill, the thought of having to climb up again later made him sad.

He had a forerunner in R. Akiba. Once he and his friends heard the noise of a Roman festivity, and while the others wept, he laughed. The others asked him how he could feel happy at such a moment. To which he replied that if sinful Rome was so fortunate, how glorious must be the future of obedient Israel. Similarly, when they came to the desecrated ruins of the Temple, the others wept but he laughed. Asked again, he replied that as God had so strictly fulfilled the prophecies of destruction, one could be quite confident that he would equally fulfil the prophecies of restoration.[1] (In both stories of Akiba, the form is expanded. It is not, however, necessary here to pursue this point. The main, tripartite framework—which alone we are presenting—is clearly perceptible.)

Another Rabbinic example of this form is a story about R. Johanan ben Zaccai.[2] The dying Rabbi, on beholding his disciples who came to visit him, began to sob: part (1). They inquired why he, the lamp of Israel, should do so: part (2). His answer was that he would be frightened if he had to appear before a weak, earthly tribunal; should he not be frightened now that he must appear before a judge who might con-

[1] Bab. Mak. 24b.   [2] Bab. Ber. 28b.

demn him to everlasting death? And as a last blessing for his disciples he prayed that their fear of Heaven might always be as great as (it need not be greater than) their fear of flesh and blood: part (3).

It is not always easy to distinguish this form from other cases of unusual conduct—question—explanation, and as we shall see, there is much overlapping. Still, as a rule, we can notice where part (1) is merely, or chiefly, a means of bringing about parts (2) and (3). For instance, in the anecdote of Johanan ben Zaccai, it is significant that he sobbed 'on beholding his disciples'. They did not come and find him sobbing; he began to sob when they came. Manifestly, the action was addressed to them rather than God. Its main purpose was to elicit the question in reply to which an important teaching might be conveyed.

It is safe to assume that this procedure—i.e. the startling of one's prospective public by an odd gesture in order to be able to deliver the message in reply to a genuine question—is one of the oldest ways of securing attention. Its psychological genesis is clear. Experience shows that a man who behaves in an unusual fashion is likely to be questioned (unusual conduct—question—explanation): consequently, if you wish to be questioned, you behave in an unusual fashion. Eve may well have moped for a few days, waiting for Adam to ask her what was the matter, when she could tell him that she wanted a new apron. In Terence's Eunuch,[1] the sly maidservant Pythias pretends to be unaware of Parmeno's presence (thus preventing any doubts on his part as to the reality of her terror) but takes good care that he should hear her muttering: 'Oh horrible deed, oh that wicked Parmeno who has brought such misfortune on the young gentleman.' Parmeno anxiously inquires what has happened, whereupon Pythias relates the fearful story she wants him to believe. This scene is quite life-like.

There need be no inner connection between the gesture and the pronouncement; the former may consist in any action that will rouse the curiosity of the public. A friend of mine, son of a Prussian colonel, was about five years old when, on coming down to breakfast one morning in midwinter, he found himself seized by his father who, without any apparent reason, gave him a terrific thrashing. The boy shouted: 'Let go of me! What have I done?' At last the colonel released him and said: 'The time has come for you to be told that the 28th of January is *Kaisers Geburtstag*. I am sure you will never forget it.'

[1] 5.4.943 ff.

N

2. *Significant gesture*

However, normally, the introductory gesture does give a hint of the pronouncement to come. In all the cases mentioned above—that of the fool offering Kent his cap, that of Eulenspiegel or Akiba laughing when others weep and *vice versa*, that of Johanan ben Zaccai sobbing on his death-bed, that of Eve moping because of her frock and that of Pythias uttering horrified exclamations—the gesture is not merely odd so that any other oddity would do just as well. Any other oddity would have done just as well for my friend's father: he might, for example, have thrown the milk jug against the ceiling. In all the other cases, however, once the teaching is conveyed, the gesture turns out to have been perfectly logical on that basis.

In other words, the gesture appears odd only because and so long as the final message is not known. In reality, it has a definite though hidden meaning, which the pronouncement will bring out. Therefore, instead of speaking of odd gesture—question—pronouncement, we should rather describe the usual sequence as significant but mystifying conduct—question—interpretation of the conduct.

Let us confine ourselves to this commoner type. What is its setting in life? No doubt it will flourish primarily where there is a master surrounded by his circle. If a negligible person performed the gesture, people would pay no heed; whereas a master's circle assembles precisely in order to watch his every movement and be enlightened as to its import. This is not to deny that occasionally a negligible person may get into a position where an odd gesture of his will be effective: the scene from Terence, where a maidservant frightens a valet, may be recalled. But we are here concerned with the problem against what background the tripartite sequence discussed would become a customary narrative form. To this the answer is: a master and his circle. It is in this situation that gestures worth inquiring about, actions strange at first sight but on interpretation seen to be full of wisdom, will be the rule.

Moreover, it is in this situation that actions full of wisdom will be performed, not for their own sake, but for the purpose of instruction, as gestures. That peculiar feature, the showing off, the addressing of the action to a public, the sobbing 'on beholding his visitors', though it may occur anywhere, has its most natural place where guidance is habitually sought and given. Only it should be borne in mind that the term 'master' in this connection has a very wide sense. It may mean a sage or a jester (like Eulenspiegel or the fool in King Lear), a prophet or a madman (a certain kind of prophecy and a certain kind of madness were quite close); in short, anyone to whom some circle would look for the disclosing of deeper truths.

The analysis can be carried a little further. A master might, and often does, explain first and act afterwards. In the form we are inspecting, however, the action precedes the explanation: mystifying conduct—question—interpretation. This arrangement corresponds to an attitude to education widespread in antiquity; a man who wished to learn did not attend impersonal, set lectures, but attached himself to a superior mind, lived with or near him, observed his behaviour from day to day and listened to such expositions as might be vouchsafed.

In this scheme, the master's conduct comes first, is noted first, while the theory behind it is only gradually revealed. We had occasion before (in discussing Precept and Example) to advert to the contrast made in Greek literature between two modes of instruction—example and theory. That the example furnished by the master's behaviour forms the beginning of education, to be followed by theoretical exposition, is stated by a writer like Xenophon:[1] 'I see that all teachers show their pupils how they themselves practise what they teach, and lead them on by explanation.' Evidently, he is speaking from experience, this was how the sage ordinarily taught those around him. The form under notice, which is very much older than Xenophon, reflects this manner.

In Xenophon, incidentally, we come across some rather elaborate specimens of the form. He reports, for instance,[2] that though the indictment had been drawn, Socrates talked to a friend without once referring to his defence: part 1, mystifying conduct. His friend commented upon it: part 2, question. (To be quite accurate, his friend reminded him that he ought to think about his defence. But, essentially, this is nothing but a question concerning his unusual behaviour; we must allow for a little variety of expression when we come to such an advanced class of writing.) Socrates answered that he had prepared for his defence all his life: part 3, interpretation of the odd conduct. However, part 3 again puzzles the audience, the answer itself is difficult to understand. Accordingly, this same part 3 constitutes part 1 of a fresh tripartite

[1] Mem. 1.2.17. [2] Mem. 4.8.4 ff.

sequence; it is another mystifying action, or rather statement. Xenophon goes on to tell us how Socrates's friend inquired what he meant:
part 2, question. To which Socrates replied that he had prepared for his
defence by always doing right: part 3, interpretation. This, too,
sounds queer, since everybody knows that innocence alone, unsup-
ported by effective argument, is no guarantee against condemnation.
Therefore, this is a further part 1. We next learn that the friend expressed his doubts: part 2. Whereupon Socrates said that when he did
try to work out an argument, the deity resisted: part 3. But once more
part 3 is intended, not only to explain, but also to cause renewed
bewilderment; that is to say, once more it is at the same time part 3 of
one triad and part 1 of the next. His friend now exclaimed, 'You speak
strangely' (θαυμαστὰ λέγεις): part 2. Here part 1 is expressly described
as 'strange', 'something that causes one to wonder'. This time at last
Socrates gave a full and intelligible exposition of his attitude.

The way the successive groups of three are interlocked in this chapter
is presumably an application of the dialectic method favoured by
Socrates and his admirers. It is a curious adaptation of an old popular
form to the fashionable requirements of logic.

One reason why, in the opinion of Hellenistic thinkers, it is preferable
to learn from the practice of a master rather than from theoretical
discourses is that this is the quicker way, or in more philosophical
language, that an ordinary person finds it less difficult to assimilate
particulars than universals.[1] Needless to say, the ancient master—circle
relationship is earlier than any reasons given for it in literature. Still, it
is true that, as a rule, people's curiosity is roused more easily by an
unusual action than by a lecture or treatise. An unadorned dry pronouncement might fall on deaf ears where one introduced by a mystifying gesture will be received with eager attention. It is worth noting
that the first part of the form in question, the gesture, is often deliberately
provocative, its queerness is accentuated as much as possible. The master
tries to make his audience 'sit up and take notice'.

Conversely, it seems that if an audience were of the highest intellec-
tual and moral standard, alive to the problems that matter and ever
thirsting after knowledge, the mystifying gesture must be superfluous;
there would be no need for any special effort to gain a hearing. The
form mystifying gesture—question—interpretation, then, essentially

[1] Seneca, Ep. 6.5, Aristotle, Rhet. 1.2.8 ff., Anal. Pr. 2.24.

presupposes an audience that requires shaking, awakening. To rouse his disciples from lethargy of the spirit and direct their minds to unexpected things, to fields beyond those familiar to them, are the foremost tasks of a true master.

As remarked above, the mystifying gesture may be an action or an utterance. However, if it is correct to hold that the form owes something to the ancient mode of learning—to wit, by attaching oneself to a master—we may perhaps conclude that, originally, there must be an action in the narrow sense: the disciple watches his master's practice, and it is by acting in an unusual fashion that the latter induces the former to question him. When, in the chapter from Xenophon, the mystifying conduct several times[1] consists in a strange utterance, in the master's talking to his disciple in riddles, this may well represent a later development of the form. But there is, of course, no certainty.

3. John

Turning to the New Testament, one thing we have to remark is that the tripartite form we discussed first—revolutionary action, protest, silencing of the remonstrants—may occasionally show elements of that which we are now concerned with—mystifying gesture, question, interpretation. The mere fact of a revolutionary action being done in public though it could be done in private gives it a little of the nature of a mystifying gesture, a means to an end—the end being the justification of the action. We know that Jesus at one time did perform cures in secret.[2] When, then, we hear of the healing of a dumb person in public, followed by a charge and its refutation,[3] it is arguable that, as seen by the author of this pericope, one aim of the action was to provoke opposition in order that it might be demolished. Similar considerations apply, for example, to the healing of a crippled woman on a Sabbath—in the synagogue, where this must necessarily produce a clash.[4]

However, while so much may be admitted, the essential character of the form revolutionary action—protest—silencing of the remonstrants remains unaffected, and plainly different from mystifying gesture—question—interpretation. The principal purpose even of these public cures is, not the ensuing controversies, but the cures, the realization of

---

[1] Not always. Socrates's refraining from any mention of his defence is an action—or inaction—in the strict sense.

[2] Matt. 8.2 ff., 9.27 ff., Mark 1.40 ff., 7.32 ff., Luke 5.12 ff.

[3] Matt. 12.22 ff., Luke 11.14 ff. [4] Luke 13.10 ff.

the Kingdom 'where the blind receive their sight and the lame walk'. To put it differently, the cure is in the first place addressed to the sick, and only in the second (if at all) to the public. True, as the Kingdom is to be made manifest, the action must be open; and as there are enemies, there must be controversy. This does not imply that the primary object of the action is the controversy. We must beware of laying too much stress on the latter. To modern readers, the healing of a person on a Sabbath or the plucking of corn on a Sabbath seems a small affair; whereas they are still impressed by the argument that if one may take an animal to watering one may surely help a man, or 'that in this place is one greater than the temple'.[1] But at the time, those actions, far from irrelevant, were striking, unheard of, a new way of life.

There is a simple test. In all cases we have labelled as revolutionary action—protest—silencing of the remonstrants, the first member alone would make a complete story. It would be a complete story to record that Jesus forgave a sick person's sins (without any controversy following), that he ate with publicans, that he healed on a Sabbath and so on. The action can always stand on its own feet. In contradistinction, it would not do if the fool offered Kent his cap and nothing further were said about it, or if we were told that Eulenspiegel or Akiba laughed when others wept, or that Johanan ben Zaccai sobbed on beholding his visitors, but were not told why, and so forth. The action in these cases receives its *raison d'être* from the interpretation, it is nothing by itself.

In fact, there is in the New Testament only one pericope distinctly approaching the form mystifying gesture—question—interpretation, namely, John's account[2] of how Jesus washed the feet of his disciples, how they were perplexed and how he explained the teaching to be inferred from his conduct: 'If I then, your Lord, have washed your feet, ye also ought to wash one another's feet.'

Here the opening action is performed, less for its own sake, than as a gesture, like Johanan's sobbing on his death-bed, in order to bring about question and interpretation. From the outset it is the latter, the message, with a view to which everything is done—just as Johanan from the outset intended to admonish his disciples to fear Heaven. Though the narrative contains many complications—John is an accomplished writer—the tripartite framework and the setting we have ascribed to it are quite plain. A master is surrounded by his circle. The former

---

[1] Luke 13.10 ff., Matt. 12.1 ff., Mark 2.23 ff., Luke 6.1 ff.   [2] 13.2 ff.

deliberately acts in a way for the moment unintelligible to the latter, in a way that must seem paradoxical, though its significance will ultimately be made clear: 'What I do thou knowest not now; but thou shalt know hereafter.' And once the significance is revealed, the master's practice turns out to have been right and worth imitating: 'For I have given you an example, that ye should do as I have done to you.' Even the term 'example' ($\dot{v}\pi\acute{o}\delta\epsilon\iota\gamma\mu\alpha$) occurs.

That the form should be employed solely in the fourth gospel is no accident. There is nothing in the Synoptics equivalent to Jesus's farewell speeches to his disciples which we find in John, and the atmosphere of which is that of the traditional master—circle relationship. It is interesting that the washing of the disciples' feet by Jesus comes not long before those speeches.

4. Ceremonies

Nevertheless it would be wrong to think that the whole importance of this form for the New Testament lies in its having influenced one pericope in John. On the contrary, it may well be that the first coherent accounts of Jesus's deeds, the *Ur*-gospels, came into existence as the third parts of such tripartite sequences, as explanations given in answer to inquiries about significant gestures. To substantiate this, we must investigate some further applications of the form, and above all its role in the ancient Jewish service on Passover eve.

It may occur that an unusual action, though not originally meant as a gesture, as a mere basis for question and interpretation, yet by some literary device or as a result of a change in outlook comes to be represented as such. Let us compare a few cases.

The ending of the Book of Jonah is definitely an example of significant gesture—question—interpretation.[1] (Once again, as is to be expected in an elaborate literary work, the form is not preserved in its purity but affected by the requirements of the larger composition.) God prepares a gourd for Jonah and then takes it away again: a strange action and one, be it noted, that would make no complete story if left unexpounded. Jonah is bewildered and, indeed, wishes to die. And then the lesson is imparted: 'Thou hast pity on the gourd, and should not I spare Nineveh?'

But take David's behaviour when his child died. Having fasted

---

[1] 4.6 ff.

during the boy's illness, he now ate; and to the servants who wondered he explained that so long as the child was alive he fasted in the hope that God might be merciful, but now 'can I bring him back again?'[1] Here the position is more complicated. Probably the author thinks of David as having broken his fast without any didactic purpose. His conduct, that is, was no gesture. Only it happened to strike the servants, so he was asked about it and had to explain. From this point of view, therefore, we have to do with a simple case of unusual action—question—explanation. On the other hand, for the author himself, no doubt the episode is worth recording mainly because of the teaching in which it culminated—that death must be accepted as an irrevocable fact. On this basis, the action is little more than a means of causing us to wonder and thus preparing us for the interpretation, which alone matters.

Similar oscillations are frequent in plays. Suppose the hero of a drama, a statesman, burns the photograph of the woman he loves; a friend surprises him and asks for the reason; the statesman declares that no one in these times is justified in tying another person's fate to his own. Within the drama, the hero's action is anything but a gesture. He had no intention of conveying a teaching; he did not even expect to be watched. It is an ordinary instance of unusual conduct—question—explanation. But the playwright does want to convey a teaching. And we may regard him, or his hero, as the master; and the public in the theatre as the disciples, whose mouth-piece is the hero's friend when he inquires what the action may mean. Considered from this angle, the burning of the photograph is a mere gesture, the object of which is to bring about the question and, through it, the message. We have already referred to the tendency among modern readers to regard as merely 'significant' some of Jesus's actions which the evangelists depict as 'revolutionary': thus the omission to wash his hands before a meal[2] becomes a means of being able to preach about the respective importance of various duties.

Religious ceremonies and customs are of particular interest in this connection. Many of them are obviously free from didactic intentions. The scapegoat is sent into the wilderness, laden with the sins of the people;[3] according to some Rabbis, one ought to put on the right shoe before the left.[4] These practices are not designed to convey a teaching—

[1] II. Sam. 12.20 ff.
[3] Lev. 16.22.
[2] Luke 11.37 ff., Mark 7.1 ff.
[4] Bab. Shab. 61a, D.E. 10.

at least not at the outset. They may indeed be re-interpreted as implying a message. Modern orthodox writers who adopt the rule that one should begin with the right shoe ascribe to it the object of impressing upon you the pre-eminence of justice, the right side symbolizing this virtue.[1]

There are, however, observances inherently of a didactic nature. Where, for instance, prospective converts are to be attracted, symbolic rites may be performed which allude to holy secrets; their ultimate aim is instruction. (Of course, even a practice not essentially representing a message may be used for proselytizing and thereby acquire a didactic character. A flagellant who scourges himself in private is performing an act of contrition; one who does it in the streets may intend to warn people of the approaching judgment.) Feasts or ceremonies of commemoration are plainly didactic: their principal object is to put you in mind of an important person or event. According to one version of the Ten Commandments the Sabbath is to recall God's resting from his creation.[2] The Feast of Tabernacles must be observed 'that your generations may know that I made the children of Israel to dwell in booths'.[3] Frequently the commemorative purpose is superimposed on an earlier, different meaning. But we need not go into this complication. It is clear that, by the time of the New Testament, the Jews had for many centuries been accustomed to rites performed in memory of turning-points in their or the world's history.

The historical event most commemorated was the exodus from Egypt. Some passages in the Old Testament betray a tendency to consider the entire religion, 'the testimonies and the statutes and the judgments', as designed to commemorate the exodus;[4] and it would lead too far afield here to enumerate the particular ceremonies to which this purpose is attributed. The second version of the Ten Commandments makes the Sabbath a commemoration of the exodus.[5] Naturally, the rules concerning the first-born of man and beast are brought into connection with the slaying of the first-born in Egypt.[6] But, as is well known, the chief commemoration of the exodus takes place on Passover eve: the sacrificing of the lamb and its eating with unleavened bread and bitter herbs.[7]

[1] L. Jacobs, Chayenu 20, 1952, 2. The author very kindly points out to me that the rudiments of his explanation are already to be found in medieval and Renaissance commentaries. [2] Exod. 20.11. [3] Lev. 23.43. [4] E.g. Deut. 6.20 ff. [5] Deut. 5.15. [6] Exod. 13.14 ff. [7] E.g. Exod. 12.1 ff.

Now there is a strong affinity between ceremonies aiming at instruction and the form under discussion: significant action—question—interpretation. The setting of such ceremonies is very much like that which we postulated for this form. There is a master—the priest in possession of secrets which the prospective converts do not know, the elders of the people in possession of the tradition to be perpetuated—and a circle—the prospective converts, the younger or more ignorant among the people. The latter's interest must be roused by mystifying rites; and these will then be explained by reference to the great message.

Admittedly all didactic ceremonies need not take the form in question. There are so many factors which may cause a deflection. Above all, very few rites are exclusively didactic. The Passover lamb, though professedly sacrificed in memory of the exodus, yet is not a mere reminder: even scholars living in a closed community, where no one was likely to forget about that miracle, would have to offer it.

None the less we do come across adumbrations of the tripartite form in several Old Testament passages dealing with commemorative ceremonies. One text,[1] where all religious practice is interpreted as glorifying the God who led the nation out of Egypt, runs: 'And when thy son asketh thee, What mean the testimonies and the statutes and the judgments? Thou shalt say, We were Pharaoh's bondmen in Egypt and the Lord brought us out with a mighty hand.' Again, the rules concerning the first-born are followed by this injunction:[2] 'And when thy son asketh thee, What is this? Thou shalt say, When Pharaoh would hardly let us go, the Lord slew all the first-born in Egypt.' Finally, there is a passage[3] specifically referring to the Passover ritual in which the sequence ritual—question—message is assumed: 'And when your children shall say, What mean you by this service? Ye shall say, It is the Lord's passover, who passed over the houses of the children of Israel when he smote the Egyptians.'

5. The Passover-eve supper

At any rate, the Passover-eve service, the Seder, as it existed in the time of Jesus was arranged within this tripartite framework. We shall presently have to discuss a fundamental change it underwent in a later period. In New Testament times, this service—which has never been

---

[1] Deut. 6.20 f.   [2] Exod. 13.14.   [3] Exod. 12.26 f.

analysed from a form-critical point of view—took the following course: (1) There was the meal, distinguished by special features, the most important of them the roasted lamb, the unleavened bread and the bitter herbs. (2) The youngest member of the company—the son if it was a family—had to ask what the strange ceremonies meant. (3) The leader of the company—the father if it was a family—had in answer to recount God's mighty deeds for Israel, beginning with shame (the heathen past and the slavery in Egypt) and ending with praise (the exodus, Sinai, the holy land and the Messianic future).

Manifestly, in this service, the commemorative rites are treated as mystifying gestures, intended to provoke inquiries into their significance on the part of the young or less learned. The latter do put the expected questions, and in reply the master reveals the message implied in the ceremonies.

It may be observed that neither part (2), the questions, nor part (3), the recital of God's deeds, was fully stereotyped by the time of the New Testament. The question would normally refer at least to the three prominent dishes we mentioned, roasted lamb, unleavened bread, bitter herbs; so would the reply—a R. Gamaliel (probably I, before the destruction of the Temple, possibly II, about A.D. 90) indeed declared it a duty to speak of these three. We also know that the reply from early times contained an exegesis of some verses from Deuteronomy,[1] outlining the miraculous history of Israel, a short Credo.

But that in New Testament times, and for centuries after, there was room for variety in detail is evident, in the first place, from the fragments of ancient Passover-eve liturgies discovered in the Cairo Genizah; in the second place, from Talmudic passages which show that the traditional questions and the traditional answers were freely added to or altered;[2] and in the third place, from the Midrash of the four sons, already considered in another connection (under Four Types of Question), which presupposes the possibility of different types of children asking different questions and receiving different answers. To repeat: the form of the service was odd gestures—questions—interpretation of

[1] 26.5-9.

[2] E.g. Bab. Pes. 115b f. Josephus (Ant. 2.9.3.212 ff.), for the speech by which God comforts Amram, clearly draws on his Passover Haggadah. The wanderings of the patriarchs under divine guidance, the division of their inheritance, the rapid increase of the nation, the quotation of 'Thy fathers went down into Egypt with three score and ten persons' (Deut. 10.22)—all come in the same sequence in the Haggadah used today. But there are also numerous, significant differences.

the gestures. But the wording of the questions and interpretation was not strictly fixed.

In the Haggadah as we have it, incidentally, there comes first a comprehensive question, 'Wherein is this night different from all other nights?' and then references to the particular oddities: 'For in all other nights we eat leavened food and unleavened food, this night only unleavened food', etc. A very similar formula recurs in a Rabbinic comment[1] on the story of how God gave the Israelites twice the usual amount of manna on Friday, how they informed Moses and how they were told that this was so in order that they should do no work on the following day, the Sabbath. (The incident is supposed to have taken place before the Sinaitic legislation concerning the Sabbath, so the people could not yet know.) The Midrash says that they came to Moses asking, 'Our teacher Moses, wherein is this day different from all other days?' Maybe the formula was technical where a question was to be put about the meaning of days or nights set apart for special religious purposes; or again, the authors of the Midrash about the manna and Sabbath may deliberately imitate the old Passover question.

What is relevant is that here also the question forms part (2) of the tripartite sequence we are discussing. For the Midrash, the extra ration is a mystifying incident, calculated to arouse curiosity and ultimately lead to the first teaching about the Sabbath: (1) God gives the people double the ordinary amount of manna, a strange happening, (2) they inquire what special significance this day may have, and (3) their master ('our teacher Moses' they address him) tells them of the Sabbath.

No doubt the earliest gospels, the earliest coherent accounts of Jesus's activity, came into existence on the Passover eves following the crucifixion. We need not here decide whether or not the last supper was a Passover-eve meal. For whichever view one may take, the fact remains that, for several decades at least after Jesus's death, his followers, like all other Jews, assembled every year on Passover eve to celebrate the liturgy which culminated in the solemn recital of God's deeds for Israel. We have seen that this recital was not yet then stereotyped. Is it even conceivable that the Jewish Christian groups did not add to the traditional account one of the deliverance freshly achieved? Or that they did not do so from the very first Passover after the crucifixion?

In fact, the entire service, not only part (3), must have been affected.

---

[1] Mekh. on Exod. 12.22.

It is safe to assume that parts (1) and (2), the ceremonies and questions, also received striking modifications calculated to draw attention to the new redemption; while part (3), the interpretation of the ceremonies, the narrative, was crowned by an exposition of the recent great events. Herein lies the real relevance to an understanding of the New Testament of the form (1) significant gesture (2) question (3) message: the Ur-gospels originated as parts (3) of such sequences.

A few points may be worth mention. First, the Passion, on which narrators surely bestowed particular attention from the outset, would perfectly satisfy the requirement, adverted to above, that the account of God's guidance of his people must begin with shame and end with praise.

Secondly, we have already pointed out (in considering Four Types of Question) that at least one section in Matthew and Mark[1]—namely, where tribute unto Caesar, a woman who married seven brothers, the greatest commandment and the Messiah are discussed—was composed in direct dependence on, as a deliberate parallel to, the Midrash of the four sons which figures in the Passover-eve liturgy.

Thirdly, it is perhaps possible to detect further cases of this kind. For example, as already observed, the Midrashic exegesis of a certain portion from Deuteronomy, an ancient Credo, belongs to the oldest parts of the reply to be given to the questioning youth. This portion begins thus, with shame: 'An Aramaean ready to perish was my father and he went down into Egypt.' For the Midrash, this means: 'An Aramaean, namely, Laban, wished to destroy my father, namely, Jacob—and Laban was even worse than Pharaoh, since whereas Pharaoh wanted to kill only the males, Laban wanted to kill all—and my father Jacob went down into Egypt, compelled to do so by the word of God.' Exactly how Laban's hostility caused Jacob's emigration to Egypt the Passover Midrash does not say. Maybe the escape from Laban is simply considered as the first and therefore decisive move in a series ultimately leading to emigration. Or there may at one time have been a more elaborate tale—now lost—in which Laban continued the struggle even after they had parted.[2]

At any rate it is tempting to assume that the first story Matthew tells

---

[1] Matt. 22.15 ff., Mark 12.13 ff.

[2] A remnant may be seen, for instance, in the view transmitted by the medieval Sepher Hayyashar that, when Jacob had got free from Laban, the latter counselled Esau to take over the task of undoing the enemy.

us of Jesus, his escape from Herod, is intended as an analogy to this first story of the Passover Midrash. Herod, an Idumean, an Aramaean in a sense, in any case closely resembling Laban in being at the same time an alien and a relation, wishes to kill Jesus and does kill the children of Bethlehem; and Joseph takes Jesus to Egypt, warned to do so by an angel.

Certainly there are details in Matthew reminiscent of the narrative of the exodus rather than that of Jacob and Laban: after all the Passover Midrash itself connects the two narratives. Herod consults the high priests, scribes and magi concerning the Messiah, just as according to the Rabbis Pharaoh had consulted his astrologers.[1] And the command given to Joseph after Herod's death—'go into the land of Israel, for they are dead which sought the young child's life'—distinctly echoes the command to Moses in Midian—'return into Egypt, for all the men are dead which sought thy life'.[2]

However, the latter allusion hardly counts in this connection. It occurs in a pericope which there is good reason to regard as a separate story—namely, about the journey to Nazareth. That Jesus stayed in Egypt only till the death of Herod is recorded already in a previous passage,[3] so that this information is not required to complete the account of the escape.

Quite apart from this, the narrative of Jacob and Laban—or more precisely, that narrative in the dress in which it appears in the Passover recital—seems more relevant than any other. So far we have only mentioned the general similarity between it and the Matthean story. Let us note some additional points of contact.

(a) Laban resembled Herod not only in being a hated half-foreigner, but also in fearing and persecuting the future Messiah. In the view of the Rabbis, he was identical with Balaam, who, well aware that there would 'come a Star out of Jacob',[4] tried to 'swallow the people, the house of Israel' (bela' 'amma').[5]

(b) Laban's usual designation, 'the Aramaean', was regarded by the

---

[1] Josephus, Ant. 2.9.2.205, Exod. Rabba on 1.22. Exod. Rabba mentions no earlier scholar than Jose b. Hanina, of the second half of the 3rd cent. A.D. Were it not for Josephus, we should have no proof that the Rabbinic tradition goes back to New Testament times.

[2] Matt. 2.20, Exod. 4.19.   [3] Matt. 2.15.   [4] Num. 24.17.

[5] Jerus. Targ. translates Num. 22.5, 'he sent messengers unto Balaam', by 'unto Laban the Aramaean, called Balaam because he wanted to swallow the people, the house of Israel'. Joshua b. Levi, of the first half of the 3rd cent., also identified him with Kemuel (Gen. Rabba on 22.21) because 'he stood up against the people of God', qam keneghedh 'ummatho shel 'el.

Rabbis as referring not only to his origin but also to his character as 'the deceiver', *rammay*;[1] and there are numerous descriptions of him stressing the same characteristic. Herod was 'a fox'.[2]

(*c*) Moses, unlike Jesus, escaped to Midian and, his persecutors dead, returned to Egypt. It was Jacob who—if we follow the Passover legend—escaped to Egypt and, as a nation, returned to the holy land. In a sense he returned even in person, since his body was buried there.[3]

(*d*) Jacob received the advice to go to Egypt from God in a dream, a feature absent from the narrative of Moses's flight but recurring (with modifications) in Matthew.[4]

(*e*) The passage 'I will go down with thee into Egypt, and I will also surely bring thee up again' was interpreted by the Rabbis as foreshadowing not only the redemption from Egypt but also the final redemption—one of their proofs lying in the repeated use of the fuller form for 'I', *'anokhi*, instead of *'ani*.[5]

(*f*) Matthew applies to Jesus's return the words of Hosea: 'Out of Egypt have I called my son.'[6] It is relevant to note that 'my son' in this verse signifies not Moses but Israel; and that this is not only the natural meaning of the phrase in its original context but also that given it by the LXX, the Targum and the Rabbinic exegetes.[7] The calling of Israel out of Egypt was the fulfilment of the promise made to Jacob.

(*g*) The reference to 'Rachel weeping for her children'[8] may well be an original component of the Christian Seder Midrash here postulated. Rachel was Jacob's wife: she would therefore come in by an association of ideas.

(*h*) Matthew has 'her children', τέκνα, whereas Jeremiah has 'her sons', *baneha*, in the LXX υἱοί. The difference may be accidental. On the other hand, when we consider that, according to the Passover Midrash, Laban, more cruel than Pharaoh, was out to destroy all, not only the males, the reading τέκνα may be intended to bring out the affinity between the old Laban and his modern counterpart. In the body of the episode the word used is παῖς, also fairly general: Herod slaughtered πάντας τοὺς παῖδας—there is no clear restriction to male children.[9]

---

[1] Gen. Rabba on 25.20. [2] Luke 13.32. [3] Gen. 50.12 f.
[4] Gen. 46.2 ff., Matt. 2.13. [5] E.g. Exod. Rabba on 3.12. [6] Matt. 2.15, Hos. 11.1.
[7] E.g. Deut. Rabba on 16.18. [8] Matt. 2.18, Jer. 31.15, in LXX 38.15.
[9] Matt. 2.16. In Homer, Il. 2.289, παῖδες νεαροί means 'little children' of either sex; Plato, Philebus 65C, says that our pleasures are like children, παῖδες, in being devoid of any reasoning power.

We are not pronouncing on the historicity of the massacre of the Innocents. We are only suggesting that, as placed in the *Ur*-gospels of the first Passover eves after Jesus's death, the tale may well have corresponded to that of Laban, more wicked than Pharaoh, and Jacob, sent to Egypt by the divine word.

The way Jewish Christians dealt with the Passover-eve celebration may furnish the explanation of a most puzzling thing that Judaism did to this liturgy. In New Testament times, we saw, there was (1) the meal distinguished by strange rites, (2) the questions, (3) the interpretation of the rites in the form of an account of God's deeds for Israel. The Midrash still has this natural sequence. The Gemara, however, places (1) after (2) and (3). Ever since then, what happens on a Jewish Seder is that the questions are asked before the ceremonies to which they refer are performed; for example, the child asks 'Why do we eat only unleavened bread tonight?' before anything has been eaten at all, leavened or unleavened. The questions are followed by the reply, the narrative of God's mighty works. And then at last the decisive ceremonies are gone through, the eating of unleavened bread and bitter herbs (the sacrifice of the lamb having ceased with the destruction of the Temple).[1]

Strack-Billerbeck[2] transfer the arrangement of the Gemara and modern Jewish liturgy back into the Mishnah, with queer results. Three examples may suffice. (1) In the Mishnah[3] it is ordained that when unleavened bread and bitter herbs have been served (the lamb was eaten only while the Temple stood), and a second cup of wine has been mixed, the son should put his questions. Which clearly means that he should put them during the meal, expressing his astonishment at the curious dishes. But Strack-Billerbeck, misled by the later re-arrangement, remark[4]—without justifying their statement—that the meal did not start until after the questions and, indeed, the recital given in answer to them. (2) In one paragraph of the Mishnah[5] the problem is treated exactly how to divide the Hallel, the 'hymn', Psalms 113–18, in two parts; and the next paragraph[6] deals with grace after the meal, to be followed by the second part of the Hallel. Which clearly implies that its first part is to be sung before grace, towards the end of the meal.

---

[1] See E. D. Goldschmidt, *Die Pessach-Haggada*, 1936, pp. 8 ff., with references to literature.   [2] *Op. cit.*, vol. 4, 1928, pt. 1, pp. 63 ff.
[3] Pes. 10.3 f.   [4] P. 67 under 4a.   [5] Pes. 10.6.   [6] 10.7.

But Strack-Billerbeck remark[1]—without giving any reasons—that the first part belongs before the commencement of the meal. (3) From the Mishnah[2] we learn that according to R. Tarphon (about A.D. 100) the first part of the Hallel should be concluded with the following blessing: 'Blessed be thou who hast let us reach this night to eat in it unleavened bread and bitter herbs.' To this R. Akiba, who expected the early restoration of the temple service through Bar-Kochba, added: 'So, our Lord, let us reach other festivals that are coming towards us, when we may rejoice in the building of thy city and in thy cult; and there we shall eat again of the sacrifices and passover lambs.' All this is most appropriate at the close of a meal where unleavened bread and bitter herbs have been taken but from which the sacrificial lamb has been missing—Akiba looks forward to Passover meals of the ancient kind in the near future. Yet Strack-Billerbeck[3] place it before the washing of the hands for the meal.

In point of fact, the change round makes nonsense of the questions and indeed of the whole structure of the service. It seems to have taken place about the end of the 2nd or beginning of the 3rd century.

It is one of the most tantalizing riddles in the history of Jewish liturgy. A widely accepted solution is that an orderly putting of the questions and an orderly giving of the reply may have proved difficult after a meal which included wine; hence the meal with its ceremonies was placed at the end.[4]

But this is quite unconvincing. For one thing, had drunkenness constituted a problem, the simplest way to deal with it would have been to decree that no wine might be taken but what was required by the ritual itself. That would have made two cups (one for the blessing of the day and one to go with the meal) for the whole time from the beginning of the service to the completion of the reply: hardly an excessive amount. It is noteworthy that this method of restriction was actually adopted by the Rabbis for the part of the service coming after the meal.[5] For another thing, on the basis of the solution under notice it becomes inexplicable why the second part of the Hallel,[6] the 'hymn' as it is called in the gospels,[7] was not also placed before the meal. But it

---

[1] P. 69, in their translation of 10.6. [2] Pes. 10.6. [3] Pp. 69 f. under 6b.
[4] Goldschmidt, op. cit., p. 10, n. 1, with some hesitation adopts this view.
[5] Mish. Pes. 10.7, Pal. Pes. 37d. It is possible, however, that the prohibition of drinking between the third and fourth cups antedates the reason given for it—to prevent drunkenness; the original reason may have been quite different.
[6] Ps. 113–18; the second part 114–18 or 115–18. [7] Matt. 26.30, Mark 14.26.

was not; it is still sung afterwards, as it was in the period of the New Testament[1] and in that of the Mishnah.[2] Was it considered right to recite these psalms under the table? Above all, why, if it was drunkenness which rendered necessary the placing of (1) after (2) and (3), are our sources absolutely silent upon this change? It was an enormous change; we should expect plenty of discussion about it; but we hear nothing.

It is much more likely that the transposition was undertaken in defence against Jewish Christian abuses. In the original arrangement—(1) ceremonial meal, (2) questions, (3) interpretation of the ceremonies—the nature of (2) and (3), the questions and the interpretation, must be largely determined by that of (1), the ceremonial meal. It is part (1), the performance of the unusual gestures, that sets in motion and decides the direction of all that follows. (Here may be the place to refer to Luke's report[3] that the disciples knew the risen Jesus 'in the breaking of the bread'. Most probably Luke means that Jesus repeated the pronouncement he had made at the Last Supper, 'This is my body'—of course, without prefacing it by 'The Lord Jesus took bread and gave thanks and said' or other words to the same effect. It was the direct 'This is my body' which caused the disciples to recognize Jesus.) In Jewish Christian circles part (1), the meal, was certainly transformed in such a manner that the emphasis from the outset lay on the new deliverance; and parts (2) and (3), the questions and recital, would proceed along the lines thus laid down.

By relegating part (1), the meal, to the end, the Rabbis took the life, or at least any undue vitality, out of it. The service now opened with some formal, orthodox questions; so formal that they referred to rites which had not yet even taken place. To these questions, an orthodox narrative would be given as reply. And the meal with unleavened bread and bitter herbs came at the end, as the fulfilment of a Scriptural precept. The sequence mystifying gestures—questions—interpretation was replaced by the sequence formal questions—reply—fulfilment of prescribed ceremonies. The danger of the service being set on a wrong course was eliminated.

None of the objections we raised against the prevalent explanation applies to that just advanced. The change round was a very clever means of preventing any fundamentally new significance being attached

---

[1] See the passages quoted in the preceding footnote.   [2] Pes. 10.7.   [3] 24.31, 35.

to the meal—whereas it would have been unnecessary had the aim been to prevent drunkenness. Again, we can now understand why the Rabbis, when making the transposition, left the second part of the Hallel in its original place after the meal: these psalms were innocuous, there was no real risk of any revolutionary innovation here. But had the transposition been caused by fear of drunkenness, these psalms also would have had to come before the meal. Finally, the silence of our sources on the affair ceases to be unintelligible. For one reason or another, the Rabbis were frequently reticent about measures taken to check the influence of heretical sects or to stress the separation from them.

X

The Last Beatitude

A T first sight a consideration of form might lead to the conclusion that the last beatitude in Matthew and Luke[1] did not originally belong to the same series as the preceding ones, but was added to them by Q. It is strikingly different—broadly speaking, longer and more comprehensive. Moreover, in Matthew, all the preceding beatitudes are of the type 'Blessed are the poor', 'Blessed are the mourners', and the last only is of the type 'Blessed are ye when men shall revile you'. In Luke, it is true, the direct address is employed from the beginning.

It is very doubtful, however, whether the argument outlined would be tenable. If the last beatitude is inconsistent, from the formal point of view, with the preceding ones, why did Q add it? It might perhaps be replied that Q did not see the inconsistency. But, then, why should the original author have done so?

In fact, it appears that, in declaring the last beatitude inconsistent—formally—with the preceding ones, we should be prejudiced by a rather narrow, modern definition of sound form and paying too little attention to ancient views. For at the bottom of the argument lies the requirement that, in a series, each member must be of more or less the same length as the other. It is clear, however, that a series with the last member extended is frequent in ancient literature, and may well have struck writers at the period of the New Testament as a pleasant and effective pattern.

It occurs even in modern literature, especially in nursery rhymes. The black sheep's three bags are

> one for the master,
> one for the dame,
> and one for the little boy that lives down the lane.

[1] Matt. 5.11 f., Luke 6.22 f.

In the Old Testament the pattern is common. Take the last five of the ten commandments, for instance. Admittedly, the final, lengthy prohibition of the tenth may be later than the rest. But if so, at least he who added it seems to have had in mind an accepted form of series, the main feature of which is the comparative length of the last member.

Two examples from Jewish liturgy may be instructive. There is a primitive hymn:[1]

(1) None is like our God, none is like our Lord, none is like our King, none is like our Saviour.

(2) Who is like our God, who is like our Lord, who is like our King, who is like our Saviour?

(3) We thank our God, we thank our Lord, we thank our King, we thank our Saviour.

(4) Blessed is our God, blessed is our Lord, blessed is our King, blessed is our Saviour.

(5) Thou art our God, thou art our Lord, thou art our King, thou art our Saviour, thou art he unto whom our fathers burnt the incense of spices.

Here the last member is not only longer than all others but also the only one to introduce the direct address: while all others speak of God in the third person, in the last 'he' becomes 'thou'. To be sure, the additional length of the last member—from 'thou art he unto whom'—may be due to an interpolation.[2] But for one thing, this is far less certain than is ordinarily assumed. For though the reference to incense must be spurious, there is reason to believe that it takes the place of a promise of salvation for Zion which did belong to the original hymn. For another thing, there still remains the direct address, and this cannot be easily explained away. The hymn, as it stands at any rate, is an acrostic, the initial letters of the five members making *'mn b'*, 'Verily, he is coming' or 'Verily, he is come' or 'Verily, come'.[3] Obviously, that the last member should contain the direct address, *'atta*, 'thou art', thus opening with an *'aleph*, is essential. It has been maintained that the acrostic order is not the original, since there are sources in which the lines are arranged differently.[4] But even in these sources, our last member, with the direct address, always remains the last.[5] Moreover, the

[1] Singer's *Prayer-book*, 15th ed., p. 167.
[2] See *Jewish Encyclopedia*, vol. 5, 1903, p. 154, *s.v.* En Kelohenu.
[3] First seen by Schiller-Szinessy; see C. Taylor, *The Teaching of the Twelve Apostles*, pp. 78 f. [4] Schechter, *Jewish Quarterly Review*, 4, 1892, p. 253.
[5] See Frumkin, *Siddur Tefillah* and *Seder Rab Amram*, qnṭ and 334.

probability is that the non-acrostic order is the result of deliberate disarrangement, directed against the eschatological mood of the hymn —highly reminiscent of early Christian utterances: 'Maran-atha (our Lord is come); the grace of our Lord Jesus Christ be with you', 'Let grace come and this world pass away; Hosanna to the God of David; Maran-atha; Amen', or 'He which testifieth these things saith, Surely, I come quickly; Amen, come, Lord Jesus.'[1] After all the first traces, or rudiments, of the hymn are to be found in works of Essene origin.[2]

Here is another hymn that was in common use in the oldest Gaonic period and probably dates from Talmudic times:[3]

(1) Blessed be he who spake and the world existed, blessed be he.
(2) Blessed be he who was the maker of the world in the beginning.
(3) Blessed be he who speaketh and doeth.
(4) Blessed be he who decreeth and performeth.
(5) Blessed be he who hath mercy upon the earth.
(6) Blessed be he who hath mercy upon his creatures.
(7) Blessed be he who payeth a good reward to them that fear him.
(8) Blessed be he who liveth for ever and endureth to eternity.
(9) Blessed be he who redeemeth and delivereth, blessed be his name.
(10) Blessed art thou, O Lord our God, King of the universe, O God and merciful Father, praised by the mouth of people, lauded and glorified by the tongue of the loving ones and thy servants. We will praise thee, O Lord our God, with the songs of David thy servant. O King, praised and glorified be thy great name for ever and ever. Blessed art thou, O Lord, a King extolled with praises.

Once again the last member is longer than the others, and there is a switching over from referring to God in the third person to addressing him directly.

It would lead too far afield to go into the origin of this form. One may speculate whether, in early worship, long before the Rabbinic era, there were hymns at the end of which the singers, who had so far looked in another direction, turned to face the deity; or at the end of which the deity was supposed to appear. But the form need not be of liturgical origin at all, or at any rate not exclusively so. To give the last member of a series a strikingly different form from the others is a plausible

---

[1] I Cor. 16.22 f., Didache 10 at the end, Rev. 22.20.
[2] Jellinek, *Beth Ha-Midrash*, vol. 2, p. 47, vol. 3, p. 86.
[3] Singer's *Prayer-book*, pp. 16 f.; *Jewish Encyclopedia*, vol. 2, 1902, p. 564, *s.v.* Baruk She-Amar.

course to take wherever it is to contain a summary of the whole, or wherever it is meant as the climax. Greater length must be a usual feature of these cases. A change from the quieter third person to the more vivid direct address may be another device. Be this as it may, it can hardly be doubted that there existed in ancient literature—and there still exists in some branches of modern—a recognized pattern of a series which involves making the last member longer than, and/or otherwise different from, the preceding members.

Isaiah, incidentally, in a part where he recalls God's intimate guidance of Israel in the past and looks forward to a renewal of this relationship, and Sirach, in his chapters on Solomon and Elijah,[1] provide remarkable examples of a change from the third person to the direct address. The change, it is true, does not occur at the end (though, in Isaiah, it may at one time have introduced the close of a prophecy). But it is none the less significant as evidence that Hebrew writers of various periods were acquainted with this mode of expressing a heightening of fervour.

Isaiah begins by referring to God in the third person: 'I will mention the lovingkindness of the Lord.' He continues like this for some time. Then he switches over to the second person: 'So didst thou lead thy people. Look down from heaven. Where is thy zeal and thy strength?' This is conscious art.

In Sirach, the section about Solomon begins calmly: 'And there stood up after him a wise son, Solomon, and God gave him rest and he prepared a house for his name.' After this, the main part uses the direct address: 'How wise wast thou in thy youth' and so on.

Similarly, the section about Elijah opens: 'There arose a prophet like fire.' It goes on in this way for several lines. Then the author is carried away: 'How terrible wast thou, o Elijah' and so on. Actually, there is in this case yet a further underlining of the rise in pitch: the first verse to use 'thou' is also the first to introduce the name 'Elijah'. Up to this point, Sirach has spoken of 'the prophet' (at least according to the Hebrew text, preferable in this respect; in the Greek, which has 'And the prophet Elijah arose', 'Elijah' is manifestly a gloss). Now he both addresses him directly and calls him by his name: 'How terrible wast thou, o Elijah, who didst raise up a man from death.'

To return to the beatitudes, there is no reason why, so far as form is concerned, we should boggle at a series in which all members are of

[1] Isa. 63.7 ff., Ecclus. 47.12 ff., 48.1 ff.

fairly equal length, except the last, which is longer than the others. From the standpoint of form, the last beatitude may be regarded as having been connected with, and formed the conclusion of, the shorter preceding ones from the outset. How many there were of the shorter preceding ones in the original series is here of no relevance.

In fact, applying a somewhat expanded principle of the *lectio difficilior*, we may even say that Matthew's transition from the minor key of the third person to the major of the direct address looks more original than Luke's smoother version. In other words, the original series quite possibly consisted of a number of members of equal length and referring to the blessed in the third person—'Blessed are the poor'—followed by a final member of greater length and addressing the blessed directly— 'Blessed are ye'. On this view, Luke's aim in using the direct address throughout would have been greater evenness of style. We must not forget that passages like the beatitudes were not intended by their authors as dull, academic lists, but as inspiring programmes of a new faith. In those circumstances, to finish an enumeration of 'Blessed are the poor', 'Blessed are the mourners', by a flourish of trumpets, 'Blessed are ye', may well have appeared highly appropriate.

The pattern here postulated is by no means rare in the New Testament. A section from Luke may be adduced:[1]

Judge not and ye shall not be judged.
Condemn not and ye shall not be condemned.
Forgive and ye shall be forgiven.
Give and it shall be given unto you; good measure, pressed down, and shaken together, and running over, shall men give into your bosom. For with the same measure that ye mete withal it shall be measured to you again.

Certainly Matthew's version of this is very different. But the passage does show that the pattern in question was used in the period of the New Testament, and a great many other instances might be added.

Of particular interest is the song of Zacharias.[2] God is throughout spoken of in the third person. But the second part opens with a prophecy directly addressed to the child: 'And thou, child, shalt be called the prophet of the Highest.' Since Gunkel it is widely held that the second part is an addition, more precisely a Christian addition, to a Jewish psalm. That may be true. Only it is wrong to invoke the form in

---

[1] 6.37 ff.   [2] Luke 1.68 ff.

support of this opinion. As regards the form, the song of Zacharias could easily be one whole. The sudden turning to the child after a lengthy thanksgiving does not indicate a fresh hand. It is a deliberate, artistic device of the time.

To conclude, the problem of the last beatitude is similar to that of the song of Zacharias. A number of authorities think that the contents of the last beatitude are incompatible with those of the preceding ones. Whether this view is correct need not here be examined. It is, however, submitted that any assumption of interpolation should be based exclusively on the substance of these verses and that the argument from form should be renounced. The form of the last beatitude is quite in order.

PART III

CONCEPTS AND CONVENTIONS

I

Rabbinic Authority

It would be surprising if the question of Jesus's Rabbinic authority had played no part in the course of his activity. For, though not ordained, he certainly claimed the status of a Rabbi. As a matter of fact, the gospels record two incidents at least which must be understood against the background of this problem.

A. 'A New Teaching with Authority'

Mark tells us[1] how the first time Jesus appeared in public—in the synagogue of Capernaum—the people 'were astonished at his teaching, for he taught as one having authority and not as the scribes'. Moreover, on the same occasion he expelled a demon from one of the persons present, and they 'were amazed insomuch that they questioned among themselves, What thing is this? A new teaching with authority, and he commandeth the unclean spirits'.

What is the meaning of 'authority' in this pericope? Once Jesus was recognized as the Messiah, the term, when used to describe his standing, almost invariably denoted something like 'divine authority' or even 'almightiness'. It is quite possible that Mark here employs it in this sense. His intention may be to indicate that the absolute supremacy of Jesus was acknowledged from the outset. But if this were the original point of the episode, it would strike one as a legend rather than as history.

Yet there are indications that it is in the main historical, or at any rate deriving from a sober, oral report. In the first place, the popular reaction is depicted not only in the usual, detached fashion—'they were astonished', etc.—but also by quoting a comment of the people themselves—'they said, What thing', etc. This should not lightly be

[1] 1.21 ff.

treated as made up after the event. In the second place, the people 'questioned', 'disputed'. There was no enthusiastic agreement of the kind to be expected in a legend. In the third place, there are incongruities—or apparent incongruities—which an evangelist freely composing might have avoided. The contrast between 'to teach with authority' and 'to teach like the scribes' is a crux up to this day: the scribes—if we identify them with the leading Rabbis of the time— were held in the highest esteem. Again, the amazement at Jesus's teaching is mentioned twice, once after the notice that he taught and another time after the expulsion of the demon. The repetition smacks of a version prior to any written source. What is particularly remarkable is that the emphatic reference to 'a new teaching' follows the exorcism, not the notice that Jesus taught.

We shall see below that Matthew and Luke smooth out much of this. The fact, however, that they do so in different ways confirms the superiority of Mark. His account, then, ought to be capable of being explained as the product of a very early date.

If this is correct, 'authority' cannot always have signified 'almightiness'. The equivalent in Hebrew or Aramaic is *reshuth* or *reshutha*', denoting *inter alia* Rabbinic authority. We may assume that, originally, 'authority' had this meaning. The people were surprised that Jesus should teach like one ordained.

Two further re-interpretations now become necessary. First, the word 'scribes'—*sopherim* or *saphrayya*'—in this narrative signified not the learned Rabbis but, on the contrary, ordinary teachers without the right to proclaim decisions. It can be shown that the term was current in this sense in New Testament times. Jesus, the people noted, taught as if possessing Rabbinic authority and not like the ordinary teachers. Secondly, the expression 'a new teaching with authority' is far more specific than might at first sight be supposed. It refers to the privilege, enjoyed only by a proper Rabbi, of introducing novel doctrines.

The difficulties listed above can all be solved on this basis. The text distinguishes not between 'to teach with authority' and 'to teach like the venerable Rabbis', but between 'to teach with Rabbinic authority' and 'to teach like those not ordained'. Further, the association by the crowd of authoritative new teaching with power over demons becomes intelligible. A great Rabbi was expected to be prominent in both fields, or rather, the two fields were not kept strictly separate. Johanan ben

Zaccai (who died about A.D. 80), a pupil of Hillel, received praise distinctly reminiscent of the passage under discussion. He was familiar, his admirers remarked, with 'Scripture and Mishnah, Talmud, *halakhoth* and *haggadhoth*, the subtleties of the Torah and those of the old scholars, the inferences *a fortiori* and those from analogy (i.e. the methods by which fresh laws, new teaching, might be derived from Scripture), astronomy and geometry, the conversations of angels and those of evil spirits' and so on.[1] It should be observed that, according to Matthew and Mark,[2] when Jesus taught at Nazareth, his listeners were taken aback both by his 'wisdom' and by his 'powers'; and in this case too we are not simply informed that it was so—'they were taken aback'—but are given the comment they made—'they said' etc. In Acts[3] we learn that Paul brought 'the word of God' to a deputy of the country. A sorcerer, who tried to turn the deputy from his faith, was punished with blindness: 'then the deputy believed, being astonished at the teaching of the Lord'. 'The teaching of the Lord' includes both Paul's instruction and the miracle wrought or announced by him.

We can now also appreciate the 'questioning' or 'disputing'. That a person not ordained should preach and act in the manner of one ordained must have evoked misgivings. His appearance at Capernaum would be all the more bewildering as, in that period, the general standard of learning in Galilee was low.[4]

To substantiate our thesis we must say a few words (1) about the institution of *reshuth*, 'Rabbinic authority', in the time of Jesus; (2) about the designation of inferior teachers, as opposed to scholars, by the name of *sopherim*, 'scribes'; and (3) about such concepts as 'a new teaching with authority' in Tannaitic utterances.

1. *Reshuth*

First, then, for *reshuth*. While authorization apparently never required much ceremony in Babylonia, in Palestine a solemn rite used to be performed up to some date in the 3rd cent. A.D.[5] The Rabbi who conferred authority 'leaned'—*samakh*—his hands on the candidate's head. Palestinian ordination was therefore called *semikha*, 'a leaning on'. The master communicated his personality, his status, to the disciple, who thus became a Rabbi with *reshuth*, 'authority', himself: henceforth

---

[1] Bab. Suk. 28a.
[3] 13.6 ff.
[4] Cp. John 1.46, 7.41, 52.
[2] Matt. 13.54, Mark 6.2.
[5] Siph. on Num. 27.18 ff.

he shared in that wisdom and power which, as was believed, ultimately descended from Moses.

For the Tannaites, Joshua's installation by Moses was the prototype of ordination, and since then each generation of spiritual leaders had been linked to the preceding one by the same mode. We read in the Bible that Moses 'leaned' his hands on Joshua, in order to bestow on him part of his glory. The Midrash explains that Joshua was thereby permitted to enunciate teachings, deliver judgments and sit on a special chair like Moses—obviously the privileges resulting from ordination in New Testament times. References to 'sitting on Moses's chair' occur in the New Testament as well as in Rabbinic writings;[1] and the continuity of tradition from Moses down to the Tannaitic age is stressed in the opening paragraph of the Sayings of the Fathers, 'Moses received the Law from Sinai and committed it to Joshua, and Joshua to the Elders, and the Elders to the Prophets', etc.[2] Incidentally, so long as an uninterrupted transfer of authority was assumed, this in itself would imply the possibility of a Rabbi being not only an inspired interpreter of the Law, but also something of a prophet and miracle-worker. We have already pointed out that in the period of Jesus these components of Rabbinic authority were not yet quite suppressed.

Semikha was designed to communicate Rabbinic authority, *reshuth*, and in principle it was the only means of communicating it. Once the chain was allowed to break, there would never be authority in the full sense—unless God restored it in some exceptional way. Hence the enormous importance attributed in the Talmud to a step taken by Judah ben Baba (who died about A.D. 135).[3] He was the only Rabbi to survive the Hadrianic war, and Hadrian had prohibited any further ordinations. In defiance of this decree Judah ordained several pupils of Akiba: the latter was already dead. The Romans slew him for his offence, but traditional authority lived on—for a time.

In the New Testament epoch, any man who was authorized himself, and only a man who was authorized himself, could authorize others.[4] Johanan ben Zaccai, for instance, ordained Eliezer ben Hyrcanus and Joshua ben Hananiah. We have just adverted to the ordination by Judah ben Baba of some of Akiba's pupils. *Semikha* meant the pouring of one man's wisdom and powers into another man. In a way, the man

---

[1] Matt. 23.2, P. de-R.K. 7b (Pisqa 1 on Num. 7.2 f. and I Kings 10.19).
[2] Mish. Ab. 1.1. [3] Bab. San. 13b f. [4] Pal. San. 19a.

receiving authority became a new being: some Tannaites contend[1] that sins committed prior to ordination are forgiven, like sins committed prior to election as King or Patriarch, to marriage or to conversion to Judaism. Admittedly, there may be an element of hyperbole in such statements; nor is it certain that they were universally approved. Nevertheless they do shed light on the character of *semikha*.

In the latter half of the 2nd cent. A.D. the right to ordain became the exclusive right of the Patriarch and his court, largely for the sake of greater uniformity of doctrine. But the 'leaning on' now lost most of its original significance. Instead of being a conveyance of the master's personality to his disciple, it was no more than a formal appointment. Still, even in later times, when the 'leaning on' was entirely dispensed with, scholars valued their 'pedigree' and on occasion based far-reaching claims on it. Rabbah bar Rab Huna (at the beginning of the 4th cent. A.D.) maintained[2] that, though living in Babylonia, he was not compelled to accept the views of the Exilarch, his authority having originated in Palestine: 'I obtained *reshutha*' from my father, he from Rab, Rab from R. Hiyya and R. Hiyya from R. Judah the Prince.'

In the time of Jesus, if we disregard the sacrificial cult and the case of a criminal to be stoned on whose head witnesses and judges must 'lean' their hands, the rite of *semikha*, 'leaning on', was confined to the grant of complete Rabbinic authority. It was not used for appointing minor officials or representatives. It was too sacred for that, its supernatural effects too weighty. The early Church took over the Jewish application of *semikha*: a bishop might ordain his successor in this manner.[3] However, the first Christians, convinced of a renewal of immediate, divine guidance in all affairs pertaining to their community, boldly extended the scope of the ceremony. A 'leaning on' of hands, in order to transfer one's qualities, took place not only where a Rabbi— or bishop—ordained his disciple, but also where the religious leaders wished to consecrate some of their number as special missionaries, where a congregation chose a few men to be distributors of charity, or where an apostle imparted the Holy Ghost. We shall discuss these cases in the next chapter (on The Laying on of Hands). In Judaism, it was not till after A.D. 200 that *semikha* might serve to give limited, well-defined rights as distinct from full Rabbinic authority.[4] But the reason

---

[1] Pal. Bik. 65c.   [2] Bab. San. 5a.   [3] I Tim. 4.14, 5.22, II Tim. 1.6.
[4] For examples, see Strack-B., vol. 2, 1924, pp. 656 f.

P

for this development, far from being a religious revival, was the change in the nature of *semikha* mentioned above: it no longer signified one man's pouring his personality into another, it was simply a form of appointment.

How much authority, *reshuth*, meant in Jesus's time and for the next hundred years or so may be gathered from the existence of those numerous parties and schools—the Pharisees, the Sadducees, the Essenes, the Hillelites, the Shammaites, the Schools of Akiba, Ishmael, Tarphon and so forth. They would have been impossible but for an extraordinary degree of independence on the part of each Rabbi. In fact, the further back we go in Talmudic history, the freer we find the Rabbis in their approach to the Law. Uniformity came by very gradual steps. It is revealing that the earlier of the ordained Tannaites often dealt with major cases only, whilst minor ones were submitted to their disciples. But under Judah the Prince (about A.D. 200) it was laid down[1] that even minor cases might be settled by a person not yet authorized only if he had received special permission from his Rabbi. A master who refused to concern himself with petty questions was no longer tolerated; and teaching of any sort must be under central control. There is no doubt that the standing of a man with 'authority' in the New Testament era was incomparably higher than that of such a man three or four centuries later.

2. Scribes

We must now consider the term 'scribes'. It is true that in the New Testament it normally denotes 'the learned theologians', as it often does in Rabbinic sources. But there are other meanings. Let us remember, above all, that in general the application just mentioned is far commoner in the last five centuries B.C.—the best-known example being 'Ezra the Scribe'—than later, when appellations such as *ḥakham*, 'Sage', *zaqen*, 'Elder', *mumḥe*, 'Expert', are preferred.[2] From the 1st cent. A.D., in Talmudic literature, 'scribe', *sopher*, frequently distinguishes 'the Rabbi of the olden time' from contemporary Rabbis. We may recall the eulogy, quoted above, on Johanan ben Zaccai, who 'was familiar with the subtleties of the old scholars': the Hebrew for

---

[1] Bab. San. 5b.
[2] See J. Jeremias, γραμματεύς, in *Theologisches Wörterbuch zum Neuen Testament*, ed. by G. Kittel, vol. 1, pp. 740 ff.

'old scholars' is *sopherim*. Actually, the New Testament is the latest work extant in which 'scribe' regularly means 'a learned man'. Even here one passage is to be found[1] where it means 'a keeper of records', 'a town-clerk'. Philo and Josephus both employ it almost exclusively in the sense of 'copyist', 'keeper of records'. In the Mishnah also it may signify 'a writer of documents',[2] and a post-Talmudic tractate is entitled 'Tractate for *sopherim*', since it states the rules for 'copyists', *scil.* of the Scriptures.

It follows that, when translating γραμματεύς or *sopher*, we can arrive at the exact nuance only by an examination of the context. Now in addition to the meanings enumerated, *sopher* has yet another, namely, that of 'elementary teacher' or 'Bible teacher' in contradistinction to the superior Rabbi. It is this meaning which γραμματεύς must originally have had in the narrative discussed. The 'scribes' are here manifestly opposed, and considered inferior, to those having 'authority'. The teaching with 'authority' is something exceptional and exciting; it is, as the Galilean crowd remarks, quite unlike the everyday instruction of the 'scribes', the 'elementary teachers'—of whom there were certainly more than enough in any Palestinian village.

Examples of this use of 'scribe' in Tannaitic utterances abound, and not a few are very early. A *sopher*, 'Bible teacher', we learn,[3] may explain in his simple, ordinary way even those portions—as, for instance, the priestly blessing and the story of David and Bath-sheba[4]— which as a rule must be left untranslated. The pair *sopherim umashnim* is constantly to be met with: the *sopherim*, 'scribes', merely teach the Bible while the *mashnim* are expounders of the Mishnah. In a conversation in the house of R. Tarphon (about A.D. 100) the question was asked[5] to what kind of people the Psalmist referred in the verse,[6] 'Blessed is he that doeth righteousness at all times'; and the answer was that he referred not to 'the Bible teachers and Mishnah teachers' but to those adopting an orphan as Mordecai had done. An Amoraic dictum[7] brings out well the difference between *sopherim* and *mashnim*: R. Asi and R. Ammi (about A.D. 300) declare them to be the best watchmen of a town because they recite (the *sopherim*) and expound (the *mashnim*) and thus guard the Torah day and night.

A lament—in Aramaic—of Eliezer ben Hyrcanus (about A.D. 90)

---

[1] Acts 19.35. [2] Git. 8.8 [3] Tos. Meg. 4.41. [4] Num. 6.23 ff., II Sam. 11.
[5] Est. Rabba on 2.4. [6] Ps. 106.3. [7] Lam. Rabba, Introduction, p. 2.

contains precisely the antithesis which, if we are right, was the original point of Mark's narrative.[1] As stated above, a proper Rabbi is often described as *ḥakham*, 'a Sage'. In commenting on the election of seventy elders recorded in Numbers, the Midrash enumerates the qualities a man must have to be made a *ḥakham*, i.e. to be ordained;[2] similarly, *ḥakham* occurs in that passage which refers to atonement through ordination. With these *ḥakhamim*, 'the Sages', 'the proper Rabbis', we find the *sopherim*, 'the teachers of lower standing', contrasted on many occasions. It may suffice to quote Eliezer's saying that since the destruction of the Temple the *ḥakkimayya'*, 'the Sages', have become mere *saphrayya'*, 'scribes', 'inferior teachers'. The ordained Rabbis, that is, are now of the standard previously attained by the mass of ordinary teachers, 'scribes'. He concludes by asking, 'On whom can we now rely?'; which means that nobody now is really able to apply and develop the Law and do the great things that the scholars used to do in former times. Clearly, here lies the clue to an understanding of the assertion that 'Jesus taught as having authority, and not like the scribes.'

3. 'A new teaching with authority'

As regards a 'new teaching with authority', this may mean a new rule, *halakha ḥadhasha* or *halakha 'aḥereth*, which only an ordained Rabbi was entitled to lay down.

Rengstorf[3] says that διδαχή is always synonymous with *talmudh*. This is an over-simplification. No doubt it often does correspond to *talmudh*. It unquestionably does so in certain sayings[4] derived from Isaiah 29.13, 'taught (*melummadha*) by the precept of men'. It may do so even in the Markan pericope with which we are concerned, and we shall presently consider this possibility. But it is no more than a possibility; and there are many cases where διδαχή definitely reflects some other Hebrew or Aramaic term. In the LXX, διδάσκω stands not only for *limmedh* but also for *hora* and *'illeph*.

Jesus did deliver decisions classifiable as 'new rules', 'new *halakhoth*', as when he defended his disciples who had plucked corn on a Sabbath. Even the type of argument he used—from a precedent set by David— is by no means foreign to the Talmud (though we have tried to

---

[1] Mish. So. 9.15.   [2] Siph. on Num. 11.16.
[3] *S.v.* διδαχή, in *Theologisches Wörterbuch zum Neuen Testament*, ed. by G. Kittel, 2, 166.
[4] Matt. 15.9, Mark 7.7, Col. 2.22.

demonstrate, in Precept and Example, that just about that time it gradually ceased to be treated as conclusive). The concept 'a new rule' occurs in a legend concerning Ruth.[1] Ruth is here identified with a woman of the name of Hodesh who appears in I Chronicles.[2] Hodesh is connected with ḥadhash, 'new'. It was Ruth's cognomen, we are told, because by her marriage with Boaz she created a new rule, or, more literally, 'the halakha was renewed'. According to a law in Deuteronomy[3] no Moabite may be received as a member of the community. Ruth, however, realized that this excluded Moabite men only, but not Moabite women. In this legend, Ruth figures as endowed with prophetic and Rabbinic vision, whereas Boaz is 'dumb respecting the words of the Torah'.[4]

If the phrase 'a new teaching' refers to Jesus's halakhic activity, it may also stand for horaya ḥadhasha. Halakha and horaya are often synonymous. But the former is derived from halakh, 'to walk', and essentially means the proper way to take in life; it is therefore mostly used of a general rule covering a set of facts wherever and whenever they may present themselves, or even of the entire system of law worked out by the Rabbis. The latter is derived from hora, 'to guide', 'to instruct', and is mostly used of a decision regarding only a particular case. The difference comes out in a provision to the effect that the pronouncement of a disciple not yet ordained is not a true horaya, 'decision', 'teaching', even if in perfect agreement with the halakha, 'the recognized rule'.[5] Strictly, Jesus's opinion when his disciples had plucked corn was of the nature of a horaya, concerning a particular case, while his opinion in the matter of healing on a Sabbath was more like a halakha, a general rule. However, just as halakha sometimes denotes a decision about a specific case, so horaya sometimes denotes the Law as a whole. (The place where Abraham was tested is called 'Moriah', a commentator says,[6] because from there the horaya, 'the Law', took its rise.) At any rate, it is quite conceivable that the people in Mark wondered at Jesus's delivering 'a new horaya to all appearances founded on authority'.

On the whole, it seems more likely that 'a new teaching' in this narrative has a wider sense, comprising Jesus's views about faith, ethics, the right mode of living and so on as well as about halakhic, i.e.

---

[1] Pal. Yeb. 9c. [2] 8.9. [3] 23.4.
[4] A pun on 'almoni, 'such a one', in Ruth 4.1—'illem signifying 'dumb'.
[5] Pal. Sheb. 36c. [6] Gen. Rabba on 22.2.

legal or ritual, questions. Matthew, we shall see, places the reference to his teaching with authority after the sermon on the mount,[1] which is anything but restricted to *halakhoth* and *horayoth*. On this basis, the underlying Hebrew or Aramaic might be *tora ḥadhasha* (*'aḥereth*), *'ulephan ḥadhath* (*'aḥaraya'*), *'orayetha' ḥadhatta'* (*'aḥaritti*), *dath ḥadhasha* (*'aḥereth*) or *talmudh ḥadhash* (*'aḥer*). With the exception of *dath*, the nouns are all connected with roots signifying 'to teach'.

Tora ḥadhasha, 'a new Law'—equated by the Rabbis with *ḥiddush tora*, 'a renewal of the Law'—and *'ulephan ḥadhath*, meaning much the same, have come down to us only in references to the Messianic age. Isaiah's promise 'Ye shall draw water out of the wells of salvation' is rendered by the Targum as: 'Ye shall receive a new Law from those chosen in righteousness.'[2] The Leviathan, an Amoraic scholar affirms, will not need to be slaughtered in the ritual fashion for the Messianic feast, because 'a new Law' will reign.[3] One might perhaps incline to conclude that, before Jesus was acknowledged as the Messiah, 'a new Law' could not be ascribed to him. But it looks as if, in the Tannaitic era, the expressions under notice had been used far more loosely than the extant applications would suggest. We find the Tannaites complaining of the fact that owing to the arrogance of some followers of Hillel and Shammai, the original Torah has become *kishete toroth*, 'like two Torahs'.[4] Evidently, 'Torah' did not necessarily signify the unique ideal Law of God, it might signify the Law as understood by a particular group. Jesus's audience, then, may well have exclaimed that he was adding another Torah, propounding a new kind of understanding the Law.

Frequently, *'orayetha'* is indistinguishable from *tora*, 'the Law'. In the famous consultation of a Christian philosopher by the wife of Eliezer ben Hyrcanus (about A.D. 90), 'the Law of Moses' is opposed to the Gospel, *'orayetha' 'aḥaritti*, 'another Law'.[5] (There are, it is true, variant readings like *'awen gillayon*, 'falsehood of blank paper'—a pun on εὐαγγέλιον—which may be older.) That *'orayetha'* need not always denote the Law of Moses is clear also from the Aramaic translation of Psalm 144.[6] The clause 'Their right hand is a hand of falsehood' appears in the Targum as 'Their Law—*scil.* the Law of the gentile nations—it is a false Law.' Moreover, *'orayetha'* may mean a teaching

---

[1] 7.29. [2] 12.3: *'ulephan ḥadhath*. [3] Lev. Rabba on 11.1: *tora ḥadhasha*.
[4] Tos. So. 14.9. [5] Bab. Shab. 116b. [6] Vv. 8, 11.

in the sense of 'interpretation of the Law' or 'interpretation of a portion of the Law'; and a scholar may be expected to bring with him *'oraya' hadhatta'*, 'a novel interpretation'.[1] Accordingly, it may be *'orayetha' hadhatta'* or *'aharitti* which underlies 'a new teaching' in Mark.

Dath hadhasha or *'ahereth* is a remote possibility. The Rabbis distinguish between 'the Law of Moses', ordinances found in or inferred from Scripture, and 'the Jewish Law', customs observed because of the special decency and piety required of Jews—for example, that a woman should not have her head uncovered.[2] *Dath* may even approach the sense of 'religion': *hemir dath* means 'to change the religion', 'to become an apostate'.[3] *Dath hadhasha*, therefore, might be used of a new doctrine embracing not only legal matters but all conduct. So, finally, might *talmudh hadhash*. *Talmudh* may signify an opinion about a particular point, *halakhic* or other (we hear of 'a firm opinion expressed by R. Johanan'—who lived in the 3rd cent. A.D.);[4] or the entire teaching or knowledge of a man (Judah ben Elai, about A.D. 150, holds that you are the disciple of him from whom you have acquired 'the greater part of your knowledge');[5] or that branch of scholarship which consists in the deduction of rules—usually *halakhic* ones—from other rules already established (Johanan ben Zaccai, we saw, was famous for his mastery of 'Scripture, Mishnah, Talmud' and so on).[6]

While it would be rash to reconstruct the exact Hebrew or Aramaic behind the Greek, it is safe to say that the concept we find in Mark, 'a new teaching with authority', would naturally occur to a Jewish audience in Jesus's age.

When we turn to the other Synoptics, we find in Luke[7] a pericope parallel to Mark's. Of the differences, the following ones are here relevant. First, the contrast between 'to teach with authority' and 'to teach like the scribes' does not recur in Luke. The people 'were astonished at his teaching, for his word was with authority'. Mark's more difficult version is plainly older. It is interesting that Luke shows himself aware of the unsoundness of opposing a 'teaching with authority' to a 'teaching like the leading scholars'. We have submitted that 'scribes' in this narrative originally referred to unordained, lesser instructors. Secondly, the somewhat technical expression 'a new teaching with authority' is avoided. Thus a further trace of the original

---

[1] Pal. Sheq. 47c.   [2] Mish. Ket. 7.6; cp. I Cor. 11.5.   [3] Bab. Suk. 56b, Pes. 96a.
[4] Bab. Sheb. 40b.   [5] Tos. B.M. 2.30.   [6] Bab. Suk. 28a.   [7] 4.31 ff.

point of the incident has disappeared. In fact, if it were not for Mark, we might no longer guess that at one time it had to do with the problem of Jesus's Rabbinic authority. Thirdly, there is no 'questioning' or 'disputing'. The people 'spake among themselves'. Jesus, that is, earns nothing but applause: the problem of Rabbinic authority does not come in.

What Luke has not entirely abandoned is the mixing up of teaching and miracle-working. Having witnessed the expulsion of the demon, the people 'spake, What a word is this? for with authority and power he commandeth the unclean spirits'. This may be more ambiguous than Mark, where the people exclaim 'A new teaching, and he commandeth'. But the introduction of the term 'word', used a few verses before of Jesus's teaching, still links the two kinds of authoritative activity. (At Emmaus the disciples speak of Jesus as having been 'mighty in deed and word';[1] and the opening verse of Acts refers to 'the former treatise of all that Jesus began both to do and teach'.)

No analogous section occurs in Matthew. He does, however, find a place for the notice that the people 'were astonished at his teaching, for he taught as one having authority and not as the scribes'. Only he puts it after the sermon on the mount.[2] Teaching and exorcism are not combined, the teaching stands by itself; and, as in Luke, no mention is made either of 'a new teaching'—Matthew may have a special motive for omitting the phrase in a context where he draws attention to the upholding of the Law by Jesus—or of any 'questioning', 'disputing'. There are indeed other passages in Matthew, Luke and John where the people are represented as taken aback by Jesus's teaching alone.[3] But as far as his activity at Capernaum is concerned, the earliest version indubitably placed equal emphasis on teaching and power over demons.

This is not to claim that the whole of Mark's narrative must go back to a pre-literary stratum. The final remark—that Jesus's fame spread[4]— may well have been added when the story was given its definite shape within a larger work. There may, of course, be other modifications. Still, the upshot seems to be that, according to the oral tradition, Jesus's lack of Rabbinic authority became an issue from the moment he commenced his task.

[1] Luke 24.19.
[2] 7.28 f.
[3] Matt. 22.33, Luke 4.22, John 7.15.
[4] Mark 1.28, Luke 4.37; it is taken over also by Matthew, in 4.24.

B. 'By What Authority Doest Thou These Things?'

Presumably Jesus's disciples from the beginning considered his authority to be unique, not inferior but superior to that conferred by the usual ordination. Jesus himself also must have shared this feeling. But his antagonists would not. The clash between their view that, to do the things he did, he ought to have Rabbinic authority of the recognized type and the belief of Jesus and his circle that he possessed all the authority of a Rabbi and more is preserved in a report of his questioning by Jewish officials towards the end of his activity. This report, substantially the same in the three Synoptics,[1] is all the more interesting as we may see from it how easily, according to a person's assessment of Jesus's position, the notion of 'Rabbinic authority' might pass into that of 'divine authority' or 'almightiness'.

Jesus, we learn, was asked: 'By what authority doest thou these things? and who gave thee this authority?' Whatever incident may have been the immediate occasion of the attack—and we shall go into this problem below—the cause was that Jesus acted like a Rabbi without being ordained. In fact, if there should be any doubts, this pericope proves that neither Jesus nor the Baptist was ever technically ordained. In the passage just cited 'authority' can mean only *reshuth* in the sense of Rabbinic authority. Jesus is requested to produce his licence. In New Testament times any Rabbi was entitled to create other Rabbis. Hence the general and somewhat rhetorical question, 'By what authority doest thou these things?' is followed by the specific one: 'Who gave thee this authority?' He ought to name the Rabbi from whom he derives his status.

It is equally clear that in the proud answer, 'Neither tell I you by what authority I do these things', *reshuth*, 'authority', acquires a very different sense. Here it alludes to a supreme title far above the common Rabbinic one. We need only consider that, before ending the dispute in this way, Jesus embarrasses his adversaries by the mention of the Baptist, whom 'all counted that he was a prophet'—a prophet, not just a Rabbi. If, as is probable, the major part of the pericope comes from the oral tradition—indeed, there is no reason to doubt its historicity—then this may be the earliest instance of 'authority', *reshuth*, referring to Jesus's 'divine authority' or 'almightiness'. In the narrative concerning

---

[1] Matt. 21.23 ff., Mark 11.27 ff., Luke 20.1 ff.

his appearance at Capernaum, we saw, the term originally meant no more than 'Rabbinic authority'. In other words, it is possible that the entire use of it to denote something like 'almightiness' has its root in the reply given by Jesus to the officials.

To understand why *reshuth* might so readily shade off from one meaning into the other, we must bear in mind that the word often refers to the domain of God or even to God himself. When Elisha ben Abuya (about A.D. 100), the great heretic, saw the chief angel Metatron, he thought: 'Perhaps there are two *reshuyoth*, governments of the universe.'[1] R. Isaac (in the second half of the 3rd cent. A.D.) explains[2] that the apparent plural word *'elohim*, 'God', is construed with the singular—'God creates', not 'create'—in order to refute dualism and make it quite clear that the world is not due to 'two governments'. Sometimes the distinction is made between the fallible 'earthly government', *reshuth shel maṭṭan*, and the infallible 'heavenly government', *reshuth shel ma'alan*.[3]

After all, Rabbinic authority and divine right have an essential feature in common: legitimacy. The Greek in the narrative about the reception at Capernaum as well as in that about the interrogation by the officials has ἐξουσία. In Hellenistic literature, words like κράτος, ἰσχύς, δύναμις usually mean 'strength', 'control', 'ascendancy', 'power', irrespective of the legal or moral side of the matter, that is to say, whether the power in question is justifiable or not. It is the fact that ἐξουσία signifies power lawfully exercised within an organized community which made the term specially suitable for describing both Rabbinic authority and the superior mandate of Jesus. (Foerster[4] draws attention to another pericope,[5] where the enemies of Jesus exclaim: 'Who is capable, δύναται, of forgiving sins but God?' Jesus in his reply does not use the same term: he says that 'the Son of Man has authority, is entitled, ἐξουσίαν ἔχει, to forgive sins'.) Roughly, it may be said that the concept of Jesus's ἐξουσία always, or for a long time at least, remained in touch with *reshuth* as Rabbinic authority; only that through his mighty works and Messianic message it also implied a higher title, namely, *reshuth* as supreme government or sphere of God.

A further point is of importance. We have already adduced the

[1] Pal. Hag. 15a. [2] Gen. Rabba on 1.1. [3] Pal. San. 23d f.
[4] S.v. ἔξεστιν in *Theologisches Wörterbuch*, vol. 2, pp. 563 ff.
[5] Mark 2.7, 10, Luke 5.21, 24.

opening lines of the Sayings of the Fathers: 'Moses received the Law from Sinai and committed it to Joshua and Joshua to the Elders and the Elders to the Prophets' etc. This refers not only to the instruction but also to the authorization of each generation of leaders by the preceding one. The first ordination, in the eyes of the Tannaites, had been that of Joshua; and since then there had been no break in the passing on of authority. However, Moses himself had, of course, not been ordained. He had received the Law—and his authority—'from Sinai', a circumlocution meaning 'from God (at Sinai)'. When Jesus claimed, in scarcely veiled language, that his authority, like John's baptism, was 'from heaven', another circumlocution meaning 'from God (in heaven)', he was applying to himself a doctrine which all Jews admitted at least in the case of Moses, and many no doubt in the case of a few other prophets too, namely, that, in very exceptional circumstances, authority could originate even in the absence of ordination, directly from God.

It is obvious that the aim of Jesus's questioners was not, as is widely believed,[1] to convict him of being 'an Elder that rebels against the court'. That would have presupposed recognition of his Rabbinic authority, the very thing they were determined to refuse. The Mishnah provides that not even the disciple of an Elder is liable to this charge, since he is not yet ordained.[2] The aim of Jesus's questioners must have been to convict him of teaching without any justification or, possibly, of being a false prophet.

A strange opinion held by some modern authorities is that the form of the narrative as it stands is not Jewish-Rabbinic. The counter-question by Jesus, it is claimed, must originally have been the end, the rest being secondary.[3] But this is certainly not correct. In the chapter on Socratic Interrogation (in Part II) we observed that the Tannaites were perfectly familiar with the form (1) hostile question, (2) counter-question, (3) answer by which the enemy becomes vulnerable, (4) refutation stated by way of inference from the answer. The form is evidenced from the 1st cent. A.D. onwards. Nor is this the only pericope

---

[1] Strack-B., vol. 1, 1922, pp. 860 ff., E. Klostermann, *Das Markusevengelium*, 4th ed., 1950, p. 119. [2] San. 11.2.

[3] Bultmann seems to be responsible for this proposition. J. M. Creed, in *The Gospel according to St. Luke*, 1930, p. 244, accepts the premise (that the form is not Jewish-Rabbinic) though he is not convinced of the conclusion (that the counter-question was the original ending). E. Klostermann, *op. cit.*, p. 119, is equally undecided.

in the New Testament where it is used. Admittedly, the narrative before us may contain a few additions and modifications as compared with its oral predecessor. As far as form is concerned, for example, the 'reasoning among themselves' of the enemies is not an essential part. But the main structure must have constituted a unit from the outset.

The same critics maintain that the intervention of the officials could not, as Mark appears to assume, have been produced by the cleansing of the Temple: the latter, they think, was not an appropriate occasion for a debate concerning Jesus's authority. But it was. Its importance lay not in the breach of peace. If, for example, some ruffians had driven out the merchants and upset the tables, it would have been an ordinary row: nobody would have dreamt of asking them by what authority they had proceeded. It was the deeper meaning of the action that put it on a different level. Nor does it matter whether Jesus condemned a specific abuse of the Temple only (so that we might speak of a *halakha* in the narrower sense) or at the same time the whole mistaken attitude behind it (so that he would proclaim a *halakha* in the wider sense or even a *tora*). Mark informs us expressly not only that Jesus accompanied his action by teaching, but also that it was the teaching implied in and accompanying the action which astonished the crowd; it was not the external disturbance as such.

In fact, the succession of ideas is closely analogous to that in the narrative about his first appearance at Capernaum; there is even verbal similarity. At Capernaum, the people were amazed by Jesus's teaching and wondered on what authority it might rest. In Jerusalem, the people were amazed by his teaching and the administration inquired on what authority it rested. Moreover, we saw that at Capernaum also the teaching is intimately associated with an action, though of a slightly different kind—the expulsion of a demon.

That the controversy was brought about by something more than mere teaching is suggested by the question itself: 'By what authority doest ($\pi o\iota\epsilon\hat{\iota}s$) thou these things?' Certainly it is not impossible for a phrase like 'thou doest these things' to refer to teaching and nothing else; the scope of the verb 'to do' is almost unlimited. But in Hebrew and Aramaic as well as in Greek and English it would as a rule be used of undertakings not purely academic.

The question, it may be noted, recurs in Matthew and Luke, though both clearly consider it as having regard to teaching only and divorce it from the cleansing of the Temple. But in Matthew, this treatment strikes one as artificial. 'And when he was come into the temple, the chief priests came unto him, who was teaching, and said' etc. The word διδάσκοντι, 'who was teaching', looks as if deliberately inserted by the evangelist in order to represent this activity as the immediate reason of the interrogation. Luke is far smoother. 'And on one of those days, as he taught in the temple and preached the gospel, the chief priests spake unto him.' On the whole, Mark, with that mixing up of a purposeful action and teaching which would characterize a great Rabbi or a prophet, seems superior to Matthew and Luke.

Finally a word about John. There is no official inquiry into Jesus's Rabbinic authority, *reshuth*. Nevertheless we find an incident corresponding to it,[1] where the Jews—the ordinary people, not the authorities —ask: 'What sign shewest thou unto us, that thou doest these things?'

Various points are of interest. First, as in Mark, it is the cleansing of the Temple which leads to a demand for credentials. This strongly supports Mark over against Matthew and Luke. Secondly, the people want a sign, not any proof of ordination. Rabbinic authority of the normal type does not matter; the doubt is whether Jesus can give evidence of a special, divine call as a prophet or the Messiah. Thirdly, it is in consequence of this different approach that any express mention of teaching is dropped. Jesus through his action purports to bring about the Messianic era. Hence the question does not concern his teaching and his authorization to propound it, but his action and his mission to perform it.

However, we must not establish too sharp a contrast between John and the Synoptics. To begin with, in New Testament times, as pointed out above, Rabbinic authority still included a prophetic element; and the greater a Rabbi, the more boldly he would not only teach but also act. Even in the Synoptics the question put to Jesus has regard to 'doing': 'By what authority doest thou these things?' It is significant that there was no need for John to alter the part about 'doing these things'. In fact it would be quite feasible to uphold the historicity of both the Synoptics and John, by supposing that while the former concentrate on the reaction of the authorities (if you are not ordained, either your doctrines and actions are ridiculous or you may be a false prophet), John concentrates on that of a section of the common folk—

[1] 2.18 ff.

those half-convinced of the uniqueness of these events (if you show us a sign, we shall acknowledge you as a prophet or the Messiah). This is not to minimize the difference between the theological preoccupations of the Synoptics and of John; it is only to warn against exaggerating them.

Let us also note that distinct adumbrations of the Johannine standpoint may be found in the Synoptics. We have already seen that in all three the term 'authority', as used in Jesus's reply, means much more than a technical Rabbinic privilege. It means a higher mandate and indeed something like almightiness. Jesus invokes the precedent of the Baptist, whom 'they counted that he was a prophet'. Moreover, in Matthew and Luke—though not in Mark—the pronouncement by which Jesus accompanies the cleansing is not called 'a teaching'. This brings them nearer to John. The pronouncement becomes a more integral part of the cleansing, the emphasis lies on the prophetic action which consists in cleansing plus pronouncement. Again, in Matthew—though not in Mark and Luke—the cleansing is followed by miraculous cures and the shout of the children, 'Hosanna to the son of David'—a Messianic acclamation.

The cures referred to by Matthew in this chapter deserve special attention. According to John, the people after the cleansing of the Temple required a sign. Miraculous cures would be a sign. True, Matthew, at first sight, stands alone among the Synoptics. But, for one thing, at Capernaum, Mark and Luke connect what might be regarded as a sign—the expulsion of an evil spirit—with authoritative teaching. For another, the cleansing of the Temple and some sign go together not only in Matthew but also in Mark: both of them place the story of the blasting of a fig-tree next to that of the cleansing. Actually, in Mark, the cursing of the tree immediately precedes the cleansing and the effect of the curse immediately follows it. This combination of the two stories is so strange that we ought probably to attribute it to an early, oral version. (It is absent from Luke, who may well have found it intolerable.) The original idea seems to have been essentially similar to John's: Jesus must show a sign and does so.

To sum up, the story of how the authorities called Jesus to account because he was not ordained and how he and his circle relied on a higher title certainly belongs to a very early stratum; and it may well be right to assign to the same stratum the report that it was the cleansing of the Temple which occasioned the official inquiry as well as demands for a sign. We may add that these matters would be of practical interest precisely among the first Christians. It was not only Jesus (and the Baptist) who had not been ordained—that was a difficult enough problem—but the same was true of his immediate disciples. Jesus's followers did perform *semikha*, 'a leaning on', the apostles did, the bishops did. But, as far as we can judge, Jesus himself did not. His immediate disciples were called in a different way. Which made it all the more important for the early Church to be assured that full authority to teach and act might be conveyed without the traditional rite.

II

The Laying on of Hands

A. THE OLD TESTAMENT

THERE is a widespread confusion regarding this matter. Robertson Smith says[1] that only in the case of the scapegoat was the laying on of hands interpreted as a transfer of the sins of the people.[2] By contrast, in the case of ordinary burnt-offerings and sin-offerings, no such transfer was thought of. Here, he maintains, the idea was the same as in acts of blessing and consecration,[3] namely, a general identification, by means of physical contact, of the person imposing his hands with the person or animal on whose head he imposed them. Other writers[4] agree that, on the whole, there was no difference in respect of the imposition of hands between an offering, a blessing and a consecration.

The weakness of this view is that it throws together ceremonies described in Hebrew by different terms signifying different things. Where an offering or a consecration is concerned, the texts invariably employ *samakh*, 'to lean one's hands upon somebody or something'; but where a blessing is concerned, the verbs used are *śim* or *shith*, 'to place one's hands'. Unfortunately the LXX translates both *samakh* and *śim* by $\dot{\epsilon}\pi\iota\tau\dot{\iota}\theta\eta\mu\iota$ and *shith* by $\dot{\epsilon}\pi\iota\beta\dot{\alpha}\lambda\lambda\omega$; and in English we do not distinguish at all, speaking indiscriminately of a laying on, putting on or imposition of hands no matter which of the three Hebrew verbs is in question. No doubt the reason why the LXX did not render *samakh* literally, i.e. by $\dot{\epsilon}\rho\epsilon\dot{\iota}\delta\omega$, was that the rite of leaning one's hands upon a being would have struck a Hellenistic public as very outlandish. It is *au fond* the same reason which accounts for our refusal to translate the verb by 'to lean'. However, if we wish to establish the original nature

---

[1] *Religion of the Semites*, 1889, pp. 401 f., taken over without substantial changes by S. A. Cook, in the 3rd ed. of 1927, pp. 422 f.

[2] Lev. 16.21.   [3] Gen. 48.14, Num. 8.10, Deut. 34.9.

[4] E.g. M. Grunwald, art. 'Hand', in *Jewish Encyclopedia*, 6, 1904, pp. 211 f.

of the various ceremonies, we must surely pay attention to the technical vocabulary of the Hebrew sources.

Let us begin by a summary comparison of *samakh*, 'to lean', and *śim* or *shith*, 'to place'. The latter two verbs, incidentally, may be treated as synonymous in this connection. Jacob, on his death-bed,[1] 'laid his right hand upon Ephraim's head', *shith*, whereupon Joseph told him: 'This —Manasseh—is the firstborn; put thy right hand upon his head', *śim*. We have, then, *samakh* on the one side and *śim* and *shith* on the other.

Samakh signifies 'to lean'. A person who is exhausted, for example, may 'lean his hands upon the wall'.[2] The rite of 'leaning one's hands upon somebody or something' involves the exercise of some force, and the force is concentrated at the base of the hand, near the joint. The attitude is familiar to travellers trying to close trunks into which they have packed too much. (A similar analogy occurred to the Rabbis.[3]) It is not the typical attitude of one pronouncing a blessing. What may have been the import of the ceremony in Old Testament times? In all probability, by leaning your hands upon somebody or something, by pressing in this way upon a person or animal, you were pouring your personality into him or it (the simile of pouring also may be found in Rabbinic literature[4]); or in other words, you were making him or it into your substitute.

Śim or *shith*, on the other hand, signifies 'to place'. The verbs have a far wider range, are far less specific, than *samakh*. The rite of 'placing one's hands upon somebody' will as a rule be of a gentler character than the rite of *samakh*. Vigorous pressure is not essential. Possibly there are occasions when it is enough to use the fingers. The main element of the ceremony is the touch. The idea no doubt was that, by placing your hands on a person, some magic attaching to them took effect upon him. At a later stage, maybe your hands were conceived of as transmitting an influence from above, one might almost say, like conductors.

So far we have argued more or less in the abstract. We must now test the result by inspecting the several applications of the terms under discussion in the Old Testament.

Samakh occurs some twenty times in the sense of 'to lean one's hands on an animal to be sacrificed'. With regard to the scapegoat, the context[5] makes it obvious that the ceremony meant loading it with the sins

---

[1] Gen. 48.14 ff. [2] Amos 5.19. [3] See Siph. on Num. 27.23, to be discussed below.
[4] Num. Rabba on 27.20 will be quoted below. [5] Lev. 16.21.

of the people: 'And Aaron shall lean both his hands upon the head of the goat and confess over him all the iniquities of the children of Israel and put them upon the head of the goat.' This is quite consistent with the basic idea of the rite here postulated—pouring your personality into the animal.

We must remember that in any religion, but particularly in an ancient one, an idea of this kind is capable of a good deal of adaptation to varying circumstances. In the case of the scapegoat, the sins of the people, their undesirable attributes, were transferred; the people *qua* sinners were replaced by the animal. The same clearly happened, say, when King Hezekiah abolished the idolatrous institutions of his father and when he and the congregation pressed their hands on the seven goats brought as a sin-offering.[1] But this does not exclude the possibility that, in other cases, the positive, beneficial qualities of a person were passed on. This aspect would predominate, for instance, where men leaned their hands on a peace-offering which symbolized the solidarity between the participants among themselves and between the participants and God. No need to dwell on the numerous nuances possible. It may safely be affirmed that all the passages where *samakh* is used in connection with a sacrifice are explicable by reference to the same fundamental notion.

We may next consider the use of *samakh* in a pericope telling us about the formal consecration of the Levites, in the course of which 'the children of Israel shall lean their hands upon them'.[2] Once more the idea must have been that the rest of the people merged in the Levites, made the Levites into their representatives, into their other selves. The Bible explicitly states that the Levites are to stand for the firstborn of the people: 'For they are wholly given unto me from among the children of Israel; instead of the firstborn of all the children of Israel have I taken them unto me.' In a way the case is very close to sacrifice. Only the basic idea again assumes a form modified in accordance with the special occasion.

Samakh three times describes the act of Moses who, when ordaining his successor Joshua, 'leaned his hands' on him.[3] Nor are we left in any doubt as to the meaning. 'And thou shalt put of thine honour upon him,' God commands Moses: and in the chapter recording Moses's death we read that 'Joshua was full of the spirit of wisdom, for Moses

[1] II Chron. 29.23.   [2] Num. 8.10.   [3] Num. 27.18, 23, Deut. 34.9.

had leaned his hands upon him.' Joshua, that is, became a second Moses. (We must not expect pedantic consistency: for the authors of the Bible there was no irreconcilable conflict between the view that Moses had conveyed his personality to Joshua and the view that 'there arose not a prophet since like unto Moses'.) This has nothing to do with sacrifice, of course, yet the ceremony has the same effect: the creation of a substitute.

Finally, there is the narrative of a blasphemer, concerning whom God told Moses:[1] 'Let all that heard him press their hands upon his head and let all the congregation stone him.' It must be admitted that this episode is rather problematic. Maybe the rite served to assimilate the death penalty to a sacrifice. But it is equally possible that the witnesses were regarded as themselves tainted by the crime and needing to throw back on to the actual culprit the guilt he had brought upon them. Or the whole community was tainted and the witnesses acted on its behalf. Or, maybe, the witnesses by anticipation threw back on the criminal the blood-guiltiness which would rest on them as a result of his execution. On any hypothesis, however, the basic idea seems to have been the same as in all other instances.

It should be noted, incidentally, that if—as is practically certain— Susannah is translated from a Hebrew original, the latter must have contained samakh:[2] 'Then the two elders stood up and leaned their hands upon her head,' scil. testifying against her. The LXX as usual has ἐπιτίθημι, and Theodotion τίθημι.

This completes the list of applications of the rite of samakh in the Old Testament. Śim and shith we have already met in the story of Jacob's death. It was clearly an act of blessing that was accompanied by his 'placing his hand' on the head of the person concerned: 'And Israel placed his right hand upon Ephraim's head and his left hand upon Manasseh's, and he blessed Joseph and said, The angel bless the lads.' And again, after Joseph had asked him to 'place his right hand' on the head of Manasseh, the Bible tells us how 'his father refused and said, He also shall be great, but his younger brother shall be greater, and he blessed them that day.'

Evidently, the physical attitude in a case of śim or shith is quite unlike that in a case of samakh: the word samakh implies the exercise of pressure, but there is no question of this at the moment of blessing. For one

[1] Lev. 24.14.   [2] 34.

thing, Jacob was in bed and dying. For another, the very position of his grandsons at the moment 'of *śim* or *shith* would have made physical pressure extremely difficult. Joseph, it may be recalled, had led Manasseh towards Jacob's right hand and Ephraim towards his left. Jacob had to cross his hands in order to place his right one on the younger. Had the ceremony consisted in 'leaning the hand', in *samakh*, he could hardly have been satisfied with this arrangement.

In view of the striking external difference between *samakh*, 'a leaning of the hands', and *śim* or *shith*, 'a placing of the hands', it would be odd if the two rites had had the same meaning. There is in fact no sign in the narrative of Jacob and his grandsons of the rite of *śim* or *shith* involving a merging of one personality in another. We may conclude that, by such contact, some beneficial virtue inherent in the hand of the blessing party would produce its results in the party blessed. It may be worth remembering that, when Aaron blessed the people, he merely 'lifted up (*naśa'*) his hands towards them'.[1]

A few words may be added about healing. In this case, just as in that of blessing, the notion of conveying one's personality in the sense of creating a substitute would be completely out of place. Accordingly, the term *samakh* never appears in this field.

Two instances deserve mention, though they are resurrections rather than healings. First, a dead man was buried in Elisha's sepulchre and when he touched (*nagha'*) the bones of the prophet, he revived.[2] Manifestly, the essential thing was the contact. It should be observed that it was not the prophet who deliberately touched the dead man, but the latter who by accident touched the bones of the prophet. Secondly, while Elisha was still alive, he once raised a child from the dead by lying on and bending over him (*shakhabh* and *gahar*).[3] He was following the example of Elijah[4] who had 'stretched himself', 'measured himself' (*hithmodhedh*) over a dead child to restore him. But even here there was no *samakh*, no 'leaning'; and another important difference is that whereas in the rite of 'leaning' the hands were always leaned on the head, in the cases under consideration the whole body was dealt with. Elisha, we learn, 'placed (*śim*) his mouth upon the child's mouth, and his eyes upon his eyes and his palms upon his palms'. There certainly flowed a vital force from the prophet to the dead child. But the mean-

---

[1] Lev. 9.22, Ecclus. 50.20.
[2] II Kings 13.21.   [3] II Kings 4.34.   [4] I Kings 17.21.

ing was not, as it was where a man leaned his hands upon the head of another being, a transfer of spiritual and moral qualities.

The upshot is that we must keep apart two different kinds of laying on of hands: (1) that which is described by the word *samakh*, (2) that which is described by either of the words *śim* or *shith*. The first kind of imposition is applied to certain offerings, to Levites at their consecration (which was in the nature of an offering by the people), to Joshua at his ordination by Moses and to a criminal convicted of a capital offence. It indicates, we suggest, the pouring of one's personality into another being, the creation of a representative or substitute. It is for this kind of imposition of hands that we propose to use the term *samakh*. The second kind of imposition is applied in blessing and, to some extent, in healing. It indicates the transference of something other than, or less than, the personality; it means the employment of a special, supernatural faculty of one's hands. For this kind of imposition of hands we propose to use the words *śim* and *shith*.

As remarked above, the latter words are far less technical than *samakh*; their range is very wide, and we cannot here go into all applications. Perhaps we ought to advert to Job's complaint about the inequality between him and God:[1] 'Neither is there any daysman betwixt us that might lay (*shith*) his hand upon us both.' Very likely the reference is to an arbiter to whom both Job and God would owe obedience and who might 'lay his hands upon both', *scil.* as a sign of sovereignty.

B. RABBINIC LITERATURE

When we come to the Rabbinic position in New Testament times, there is one change: the occasions on which *samakh* is performed have become fewer. The rite itself, as we shall see, is not altered, but it is practically restricted to two uses—the sacrificial cult and the ordination of a Rabbi. This is remarkable.

We should have expected its range of application to have increased. There are in the Rabbinic era so many new kinds of representation: the *shaliaḥ*, the delegate, of a private person, of a congregation (the precentor), of the Court (of the Beth-Din), of a district that must be represented at the daily offering in the Temple, the 'Seven of a City' and so forth.[2] Moreover, the nature of representation is fully realized;

[1] 9.33.   [2] Mish. Git. 4.1. Ber. 5.5, Yoma 1.5, Ta. 4.2, Tos. Ta. 4.2 f., Pal. Meg. 74a

again and again the governing principle is repeated that 'the delegate of a man is as if he were the man himself' or 'the Seven of a City are as if they were the city itself'. Yet the appointment of these agents is never effected by means of a 'leaning on of hands'. One cannot help feeling that, in the eyes of the Rabbis, 'leaning on' is a ceremony which they are not entitled to extend. It must remain confined to those cases where it has direct Mosaic sanction. This in itself suggests that *samakh* is still of a significance which does not attach to a mere *śim* or *shith*.

Actually, as already indicated, its scope has contracted. We find nothing corresponding to the consecration of the Levites by the rest of the people, nor is there any *samakh* on the part of witnesses at the moment of accusation. It might perhaps be argued that there could be no parallel to the former event, which had taken place in unique circumstances. But the New Testament shows—we shall have to go into this—that a community experiencing another age of revelation was quite capable of reviving the ceremony for what they felt to be similar purposes.

As for the disappearance of *samakh* from accusation, this is indeed due to special reasons. Since the beginning of the last century B.C. the Pharisees had opposed the ceremonial, collective testifying of witnesses against an accused, so easily misused for throwing dust in the eyes of the judges, and they had advocated instead an informal, cool cross-examination of each witness in the absence of the other. It was one of the principal aims of the Book of Susannah to demonstrate the superiority of the rational, modern method: as we have just seen, but for Daniel's intervention, Susannah's innocence would not have helped her once the wicked elders, taking advantage of the old procedure, had solemnly 'leaned their hands' on her head and proclaimed her guilty.[1] By the time of the New Testament, the Pharisaic innovation is widely adopted. It is the new method through which, if we go by Mark,[2] the attempt to get Jesus convicted for his utterance concerning the destruction of the Temple breaks down. At any rate, in Rabbinic writings, *samakh* is ousted from this area.

In the case of stoning, to be sure, the witnesses—and the judges—still perform *samakh*.[3] But they do so after the verdict is given, when the execution commences. The act is designed to throw back on the

---

[1] See Daube, *Revue Internationale des Droits de l'Antiquité*, 2, 1949, pp. 200 f.
[2] 14.59.   [3] Siph. on Lev. 24.14.

person to be stoned the blood-guiltiness which his violent death will bring on witnesses and judges, for the Rabbis explain that those 'leaning their hands' on the criminal should speak: 'Thy blood be on thy head for thou has caused this.' *Samakh*, then, retains its original meaning: the pouring of one's personality—in this case, of one's personality weighed down by blood-guiltiness—into another man.

Apart from this application, the rite continues only in connection with sacrifice and ordination, and here too it is never described by any other term than *samakh*: *śim* or *shith* occurs not a single time. Philo, in his discussion of sacrifice,[1] in addition to ἐπιτίθημι, which goes back to the LXX, uses ἐπιφέρω. This is a stronger term, suggesting that he correctly thinks of a true 'leaning' of the hands on the animal. But there is direct evidence that this 'leaning' is still vastly different from a 'placing'. We know of a controversy which started in the 2nd cent. B.C. and went on even after the death of Hillel and Shammai, in their Schools, as to whether leaning one's hands on an animal to be slaughtered was permissible on a festival.[2] One party took the view that, as it is performed by a man 'with all his strength' (*bekhol koḥo*), he is causing the animal to bear his burden; and to use an animal on a festival is prohibited.[3]

It is inconceivable that such a controversy could ever have arisen with regard to blessings. Actually, up to this day it is precisely on Sabbaths and festivals that Rabbis and parents are accustomed to 'place' (*śim*) their hands on the children's heads and bless them; while the priestly blessing is still accompanied by a mere 'lifting' (*naśa'*) of the priest's hands.[4]

Similarly, in the case of ordination, it can be clearly shown that, at least up to the first half of the 2nd cent. A.D., the rite is executed in the original manner and with the original intent: it involves a real 'leaning on' as opposed to a gentle 'placing', and its object is the pouring of the ordaining scholar's personality into the scholar to be ordained. The Bible says that Moses 'leaned his hands on Joshua'.[5] This clause the Midrash Siphre, which goes back to the school of R. Ishmael, interprets as meaning: 'He pressed on him as one presses on a vessel already full to

---

[1] Leg. Spec. 1.37. 198 ff.   [2] Mish. Bet. 2.4, Hag. 2.2 f., Bab. Bet. 20a, Hag. 16b.
[3] J. Levy is of opinion (*Wörterbuch über die Talmudim und Midraschim*, 3, 2nd ed., 1924, p. 545) that the dispute originally was about a different point. Even if he is right, the Talmudic description of *samakh* as performed 'with a man's whole strength' remains—enough for our purpose.   [4] E.g. Mish. Tam. 7.2.   [5] Num. 27.23.

overflowing (Joshua having been endowed with the Spirit even before his ordination[1]) in order to stuff even more into it.' (Such is the sense of the Siphre's comment.[2] The prevalent rendering[3] is slightly incorrect, but it would furnish even stronger support for the thesis here advanced: 'Moses pressed on Joshua in order to make him like a vessel full to overflowing.') Since for the Siphre Joshua's appointment is simply the first Rabbinic ordination on which all further ones are modelled, it is plain that the rite of *samakh*, by this time, has lost nothing of its specific character.

It is significant that in the Tosephta[4] 'leaning' for the purpose of ordination and 'leaning' for the purpose of bringing a communal sacrifice[5] appear side by side. We may also mention two similes which the Rabbis introduce again and again: though Moses 'leaned his hands on Joshua', he did not lose his own faculties because he was 'like one kindling a light with a light'; and when he 'put of his honour upon him', he was 'like one pouring from vessel to vessel'.[6]

From the latter half of the 2nd cent. A.D., far-reaching reforms were introduced into the institution of Rabbinic ordination. Above all, whereas before that time any scholar himself authorized could confer authority on others, now the right to ordain became the exclusive right of the Patriarch and his court. About the middle of the 3rd cent. at the latest the ceremony of *samakh* itself was abandoned. The centralization of ordination at the Patriarch's court may have contributed to this result. For one thing, it was certainly a factor making for the ordination of absent candidates, in which case the rite was physically impossible; for another, once it was no longer the teacher who ordained his own disciple, the notion of the creation of a second self would naturally lose ground. Again, the practices of the Patriarch Judah II, who seems on occasion to have sold the Rabbinic authority for money, doubtless helped to diminish the importance of the ceremony: a *samakh* performed by such a man cannot have been regarded as a sacred act. Another reason for giving it up[7] probably was the increasing role played by the imposition of hands in the Christian religion.

---

[1] According to Num. 27.18: 'Take Joshua, a man in whom is the spirit, and lean thine hands upon him.'

[2] See Kuhn, *Rabbinische Texte*, 2nd ser., *Tannaitische Midraschim*, 2, p. 577, n. 12.

[3] Adopted e.g. by Strack-B., 2, 1924, 648.   [4] San. 1.1.

[5] As prescribed by Lev. 14.15.   [6] Num. Rabba on 27.18, 20.

[7] Suggested by Bacher and accepted, for example, by Strack-B., 2, 1924, 655 f.

Anyhow, henceforth ordination took place without any 'leaning of the hands' on the candidate's head. The Midrash Siphre Zuta is from the School of Akiba and generally represents a later stage of the tradition than the Midrash Siphre from which we quoted above. It explains that when God ordered Moses 'Lean thine hands upon Joshua',[1] he did so 'that thy disciple may be blessed through thee'. Here the ceremony of *samakh* is no longer strictly distinguished from that performed in a case of blessing, though even now the term would hardly be interchangeable with *śim* or *shith*. The comment must date from a period when the rite of *samakh* was in decline, if not obsolete.

As for healings, while some Rabbis are credited with the power of healing or even raising a person from the dead, there is never any imposition of the hands or touching. Mostly the result is achieved by fervent prayer. Thus Hanina ben Dosa, of the 1st cent. A.D., successfully invoked God's mercy for the sick children of Johanan ben Zaccai and Gamaliel II.[2] Sometimes we come across a sort of command. A pupil of Judah the Prince, of the second half of the 2nd cent., restored a dying servant of the Roman emperor by saying: 'Why doest thou lie and thy master standeth on his feet?'[3] The command 'Arise from thy flux' was commonly used—i.e. not only by Rabbis—when giving medicaments to a woman suffering from an issue of blood.[4] Also in common use was anointing with or without prayer or incantation.[5]

C. THE NEW TESTAMENT

From the foregoing considerations it follows that, in the earliest Jewish Christian community, the ceremonies in which the imposition of hands is described by the words $\dot{\epsilon}\pi\iota\tau\dot{\iota}\theta\eta\mu\iota$ or $\tau\dot{\iota}\theta\eta\mu\iota$ in the New Testament cannot all have had either the same form or the same import. Modern authorities speak of a single rite of 'the laying on of hands', though, to be sure, they admit that it served various purposes. Strack-Billerbeck, for instance,[6] after discussing blessings pronounced over children, go on to say: 'On the laying on of hands in connection with ordination, see below', etc. The implication is that there is no fundamental distinction. Foakes Jackson and Kirsopp Lake[7] are guilty of the same error. So is

---

[1] Num. 27.18.   [2] Bab. Ber. 34b, Pal. Ber. 9d.   [3] Lev. Rabba on 8.2.
[4] Bab. Shab. 110a; see Strack-B., I, 1922, 520, 2, 1924, 10.
[5] Pal. M.S. 53b; see Strack-B., I, 1922, 429.   [6] I, 1922, 807 f.
[7] *The Beginnings of Christianity*, pt. I, *The Acts of the Apostles*, 1933, p. 137.

Flemington[1] who puts together, as far as Jewish sources are concerned, blessings, sacrifices, the consecration of the Levites, the installation of Joshua and the ordination of Rabbis; and as far as the New Testament is concerned, blessings pronounced over children, healings and the giving of the Spirit. But it is evidently necessary to discriminate between *samakh* and *śim* or *shith*.

To take the easier part first, when Jesus blessed the children, we have to assume *śim* or *shith*, a gentle 'placing of the hands'.[2] The touch is the main element of the ceremony. It is noteworthy that, while according to Matthew he was asked to 'place his hands on them' and did so, according to Mark and Luke he was asked to 'touch them', *nagha'*, and, in compliance with the request, 'placed his hands on them'.[3] There are several examples in Rabbinic literature of the belief that the hands of a saintly person might be possessed of a beneficent virtue. In a previous lecture we mentioned a legend according to which Ruth ate her fill and left some of her food even though Boaz had given her only a little; and we found the Rabbis discussing the question whether a special blessing rested within her or on his fingers.

Towards the end of Luke,[4] incidentally, Jesus blesses his disciples by 'lifting up', *naśa'*, his hands. This, we have seen, was the gesture prescribed for the priestly blessing. Its introduction here may have something to do with the fact that Luke, at the close of the gospel, takes his readers back to the Temple where his story began. He may wish to indicate that, for the believers, the service from now had a new meaning.

Śim or *shith* would be the appropriate expression also where healings are concerned. (We leave out of account for the moment the restoration of Paul's sight by Ananias.) A 'laying on of hands' is mentioned in connection with the revival of a girl believed to be dying or dead (Jesus is asked to 'place his hands on her',[5] though what he actually does is to take her by the hand[6]); the curing of sick people in general;[7] the curing of a deaf-mute;[8] the curing of a blind man;[9] and the curing of a man suffering from fever and a flux of blood.[10]

[1] *The New Testament Doctrine of Baptism*, 1948, p. 44.

[2] Matt. 19.13 ff., Mark 10.13 ff., Luke 18.15 ff.

[3] Luke omits to mention the action.   [4] 24.50.

[5] Matt. 9.18, Mark 5.23. In Luke 8.41 he is simply asked to come.

[6] This mode of healing recurs in Matt. 8.15, Mark 1.30, Matt. 9.25, Mark 5.41, Luke 8.54 and Acts 3.7.

[7] Mark 6.5, 16.18, Luke 4.40, probably Acts 28.9 (in conjunction with the preceding verse), possibly Acts 5.12, 14.3, 19.11.

[8] Mark 7.32 f.   [9] Mark 8.22 ff.   [10] Acts 28.8.

That *samakh*, a 'leaning', is out of the question is obvious. One does not 'lean one's hands on a blind man's eyes', one only 'places them there'. Moreover, as in acts of blessing, it is the touch which is of primary relevance. In the case of the deaf-mute, Jesus is asked to 'place his hands on him'; what he does—clearly in accordance with what he is expected to do—is to 'put his fingers in his ears', to 'touch his tongue' and so on. (In addition he pronounces a command: 'Be opened.') Conversely, in the case of the blind man, he is asked to 'touch him'; and what he does is to 'place his hands on him', to 'place his hands on his eyes' and so on. As is well known, there are cures where we hear only of Jesus 'touching', *nagha'*, the sick and nothing of a 'laying on of hands': they concern a leper,[1] blind people[2] and the high priest's servant wounded in the course of Jesus's arrest,[3] and we may add the raising of a young man from the dead by touching his bier and a command 'Arise'.[4] Again, here and there we meet with the Old Testament notion, or more precisely, with extended applications of it, that a cure may take place even if—instead of the miracle-worker taking action—the person in need touches the miracle-worker or something belonging to him: the story of a woman with an issue of blood is recounted in detail,[5] and there are notices about many sick persons healed in this way.[6]

Incidentally, when cures were expected if 'the shadow of Peter would overshadow the sick',[7] this manner of healing may well have been a modified imitation of what Elijah and Elisha had done: the former had 'measured himself' over a dead boy, the latter 'lain and bent' over one. Peter was one of the apostles; according to the Rabbis[8] Elijah and Elisha, when restoring the children, acted as *sheliḥim*, delegates of God, literally, as 'envoys', 'apostles'.

It is interesting that the Epistles contain not a single reference to healing by a 'laying on of hands'. As it appears from Mark and Acts[9] that such healing was practised in the early Church, this may be accidental. But it is quite possible that some writers found themselves

---

[1] Matt. 8.2 ff., Mark 1.40 ff., Luke 5.12 ff.
[2] Matt. 9.29, 20.34. In Mark 10.52 and Luke 18.24 the word of Jesus alone suffices.
[3] Luke 22.51.   [4] Luke 7.14.
[5] Matt. 9.20 ff., Mark 5.27 ff., Luke 8.44 ff.
[6] Matt. 14.36, Mark 6.56, Luke 6.19, Acts 19.12.
[7] Acts 5.15.   [8] Mid. Ps. on 78.29, Bab. San. 113a.
[9] Mark 16.18, Acts 28.8 f., 9.10 ff. The question of the provenance of Mark 16.9 ff. is not here relevant.

in a situation in which, while far from opposing the practice, they did not want to encourage it.

As a matter of fact, the question of healing is brought up in only two Epistles, in I Corinthians and James.[1] In the former nothing is said about the procedure except that it must be 'in the one Spirit'. In the latter, a normal Jewish procedure is enjoined: prayer and unction. True, to go by the prevalent reading, the anointing is to be performed 'in the name of the Lord', and 'the Lord' certainly means not God in the Jewish sense, but Jesus. To this extent Christian influence is noticeable. But it is rather doubtful whether the words 'of the Lord' are genuine.[2] If we omit them, there remains anointing 'in the (divine) name', i.e. invoking or thinking of God, which would be perfectly in order in Jewish circles.[3]

So much for *śim* or *shith*, 'to place one's hands', an act suitable for blessing and healing. When we go on to ordination and suchlike matters, we enter the department of *samakh*, 'to lean one's hands', a rite quite unlike *śim* or *shith* in form as well as meaning. Before inspecting the texts alluding to it, we may put forward an argument which is none the less strong for being drawn from silence. Nowhere in the whole of the New Testament does Jesus commission a disciple by means of an imposition of hands. There is the call, 'Follow me'; there is the appointment to a task, 'And as ye go, preach, heal the sick, cast out devils'; there is the grant of powers, 'Whatsoever thou shalt bind on earth shall be bound in heaven', and so on. But none of these injunctions or promises is ever accompanied by a laying on of hands. Why not?

Hardly because under Rabbinic law Jesus, having no Rabbinic authority himself, had no right to confer it on others (though even if this were the reason, it would bring out the radical difference between *samakh* and *śim* or *shith*: no formal authorization was needed for a laying on of hands to bless or heal). His followers considered his authority fully equal to that of a Rabbi.[4] The point is that a laying on of hands for such a purpose would be not *śim* or *shith*, but *samakh*; and *samakh*, in contradistinction to *śim* and *shith*, implies the pouring of one's personality into another being. Joshua, on whom Moses had 'leaned' his hands, had thereby become a second, if in many respects

---

[1] I Cor. 12.9, 28 f., Jas. 5.14.   [2] See the apparatus.
[3] For an appeal for mercy 'in the name' (*bashshem*) see Mish. Yoma 6.2, Pal. Yoma 40d ff.
[4] Mark 1.22, 27, Luke 4.32, Matt. 21.23 ff., Mark 11.27 ff., Luke 20.1 ff.

inferior, Moses. In the view of the New Testament writers, there could be no second Jesus. A *śim* or *shith* on his part was possible; a *samakh* was not.

Among the first Christians, however, the ceremony enjoyed a striking revival. In Rabbinic Judaism, we saw, it was confined to the sacrificial cult, for which it was prescribed by the Bible, and the ordination of a Rabbi, the passing on by a master to his disciple of the wisdom and authority which he in turn had received from his master and which ultimately went back to Joshua, ordained by Moses. But 'the Seven of a City', for example, were installed without any *samakh*. It was customary for the Jewish inhabitants of a Palestinian city to choose seven worthies to look after the common affairs, and these administrators had full power of representation: 'the Seven of a City are as if they were the city itself'. Yet as it was not ordination in the sense outlined above, the rite of *samakh* was not performed.

When the Christians of Jerusalem decided to appoint seven distributors of charity[1]—no doubt on the model of 'the Seven of a City'—they did use the ceremony. *Samakh* was a sacred means of creating a substitute. In this case a few members of the community were to stand for all in a matter of great religious importance. So, when the people had elected them, they 'set them before the apostles and leaned their hands on them'. They 'set them before the apostles', thus formally demonstrating their confidence in these men and recommending them to the apostles, and they 'leaned their hands on them', thus making them into their representatives, their extended selves, *vis-à-vis* the apostles. The distribution of charity was now in the hands of the community—the community living in its deputies.

It is true that the verse just quoted is generally interpreted in a different way, namely, as meaning that, while it was the people who presented those elected to the apostles, it was the latter who imposed their hands. Even on this basis, *samakh* would involve the passing on of one's personality, only now the distributors of charity would become 'extensions' of the apostles and not of the people. Our main thesis, that is, would remain unaffected. But the interpretation is artificial. If we follow the natural sense of the Greek, the subject of the verb 'they set'—in the clause 'whom they set before the apostles'—is also the subject of the following verbs—in the clause 'and having prayed, they leaned

[1] Acts 6.1 ff.

their hands on them'. There is one subject: the people. It might perhaps be objected that, when first proposing the scheme, the apostles speak of men 'whom we may appoint over this business'. But 'we' here most probably includes those whom they address; it means 'we, the Christians of Jerusalem', not 'we, the apostles'; it says nothing about the mode of installation. The correct view seems to be that the appointment was made jointly by the apostles and the rest in the sense that the former suggested the new office; that the rest of the community elected the holders and accredited them to the apostles, i.e. presented them and, by 'leaning' their hands on them, made them into their representatives; and that the apostles agreed with the choice. It is relevant to note that Paul's companion appointed to help him administer the funds collected[1] appears as a delegate of the Macedonian churches at large, not of any apostles. Indeed his office would serve little purpose if he represented the leaders instead of the people.

Codex Bezae, to be sure, favours the orthodox opinion. It has a reading making it quite clear that the 'leaning on' was done by the apostles. But the reading is surely secondary. Its introduction is in fact evidence for rather than against the original meaning here advocated: it goes back to someone who no longer approved of the idea of the community participating to such a degree in the installation of officers. Whether he already desired to make of the incident the prototype of apostolic succession may be left undecided. The author of Acts certainly has no such thing in mind. For one thing, the office in question, the office of a deacon, though highly important, is inferior to that of an apostle; therefore, what is said about the appointment of deacons does not really bear on that of apostles or the successors of apostles. For another, taken as the prototype of apostolic succession, or even delegation in a wider sense, the incident would not show at all that a single apostle has power of ordaining. In any case we ought to reject not only the reading of Codex Bezae but also its meaning; and adhere strictly not only to the *lectio difficilior* of the other codices but also to their *sensus difficilior*.

How do we know that it was a 'leaning', *samakh*, and not a mere *śim* or *shith* that took place? Apart from general considerations, there are distinct allusions in this pericope to the appointment of Joshua. He had been fit for his office because he was already endowed with the spirit:

[1] II Cor. 8.19 f.

'Take thee Joshua, a man in whom is the spirit.'[1] So are the distributors of charity: 'Look ye out seven men of honest report, full of the Holy Ghost and wisdom, and they chose Stephen, a man full of faith and the Holy Ghost' and so on.[2] Again, in the case of Joshua, Moses had presented him to the people and publicly made him into his substitute: 'And Moses set him before Eleazar the priest and all the congregation, and he leaned his hands upon him.'[3] So, in the case of the distributors of charity, the community presents them to the apostles and publicly makes them into its substitutes: 'And the multitude chose Stephen and Philip etc., whom they set before the apostles, and having prayed they leaned their hands on them.'

This taking over of language from Joshua's appointment not only proves that there was *samakh*, but also underlines a feature referred to above: the self-confidence of the first Christians. The appointment of the distributors of charity was no Rabbinic ordination (not even if we accept the variants of Codex Bezae). Their task was more closely circumscribed than a Rabbi's, their authority narrower. None the less the first Christians regarded a major step in the development of their organization as of sufficient moment to be linked with that outstanding event in Old Testament history.

Let us proceed to the consecration of Paul and Barnabas as missionaries, when, at the bidding of the Holy Ghost, their fellow prophets and teachers at Antioch appointed them by 'leaning their hands' on them.[4]

It is hardly necessary to point out that this also was not Rabbinic ordination. We are expressly told that Paul and Barnabas belonged to that group of prophets and teachers. They were not students to be promoted. They were equals—indeed, leading figures—to be detailed for an exceptional task. Still, their installation took the form of *samakh*. The earliest Christians did not hesitate to apply this rite outside its traditional field where a man's personality was to be conveyed to another under divine guidance. Here, then, the idea was that the two should carry out their special duties on behalf of all. They were sent out as representatives of the whole group. The others made them into their extended selves.

---

[1] Num. 27.18.

[2] The addition of 'wisdom' in Acts may be due to Deut. 34.9: 'And Joshua was full of the spirit of wisdom, for Moses had leaned his hands on him.' But it need not be: the same addition is to be found in Luke 2.40, 52, as compared with I Sam. 2.26.

[3] Num. 27.22 f.

[4] Acts 13.1 ff.

This interpretation—that the rite took the form of *samakh* and that it meant making Paul and Barnabas into representatives of the group—is confirmed by the language used, which echoes that of the Old Testament in the chapter dealing with the consecration of the Levites. 'Take the Levites from among the children of Israel' and 'Thus shalt thou separate the Levites', God had commanded Moses.[1] 'Separate me Barnabas and Saul' is the bidding of the Holy Ghost. The LXX uses διαστέλλω for 'to separate', whereas in Acts we find ἀφορίζω; but the meaning is the same, the Hebrew *hibhdil*. The special work for which the separation is required is called ἔργον both in the LXX[2] and Acts. Clearly, the ceremony performed at Antioch is a 'leaning on' of hands, and it still serves to create a substitute. As the Israelites had delegated the Levites by this means, so the prophets and teachers of Antioch delegate Paul and Barnabas.

As observed above, the Levites had, in a sense, been an offering brought by the Israelites: God had accepted them in lieu of the first-born. This particular nuance, it seems, no longer plays any part in the New Testament episode. But the connection established with the consecration of the Levites is not purely formal. The two missionaries are thought of as entrusted with a service analogous to that of the Levites of old; and they are in a fuller sense than their fellows 'wholly given unto the Lord'.

We cannot here go into the implications of this concept; nor into its possible role in other passages; nor into the question how far its growth may have been stimulated by certain practices of the Levites in New Testament times. It may suffice to say that the notion of the 'separation' of the missionary which occurs in Acts is not a freak. As is well known, Paul twice refers to his being singled out, 'separated', for missionary work in addition to being an apostle, in Romans and Galatians;[3] and both times he uses ἀφορίζω.

Whether he is in exact agreement with Acts as to the nature of this separation is a different matter. In Galatians he emphasizes that it was God who separated him 'from my mother's womb' (drawing on similar utterances by Isaiah and Jeremiah,[4] but, significantly, neither of these has ἀφορίζω, *hibhdil*). This by itself would not conflict with the record of Acts; even according to Acts, Paul and Barnabas were 'sent

---

[1] Num. 8.6, 14.　　　　　　　　　[2] Num. 8.11, 15.
[3] Rom. 1.1, Gal. 1.15.　　　　　　　[4] Isa. 49.1, Jer. 1.5.

forth by the Holy Ghost'.[1] The further remark, however, that he passed many years as a missionary without having consulted any of the other leaders—except, on one occasion during that period, Peter and James—raises a serious problem. Possibly one of the factors responsible for his attitude—we are far from denying that there were others as well—was uneasiness about the increased use of *samakh* in the early Church, the extension of the rite to fresh cases; an uneasiness he need not always have felt; and one due not only to his Rabbinic background but also, and even primarily, to the fear lest this transfer of qualities might to some extent disguise the free and direct bestowal of gifts by God.

We must now say something on the communication of the Spirit. Still postponing the discussion of the case of Paul and Ananias, we have to consider the story of the Samaritans to whom, after they were baptized, the apostles sent Peter and John in order to impart the Spirit to them, which they did by a laying on of hands; the story of the Ephesians who, baptized unto John's baptism, were baptized once more by Paul in the name of Jesus and invested with the Spirit by a laying on of hands; and the enumeration of the laying on of hands, side by side with the doctrine of baptisms, among the Christian fundamentals in Hebrews.[2]

A negative statement can at once be made: the imparting of the Spirit was not Rabbinic ordination. In the first place, it was far more freely granted, it was granted to any converts, it was not reserved for a few as an exceptional privilege. In the second place, at the time of the New Testament, a Rabbi ordained himself was entitled to ordain others. But the story of the conferment of the Spirit at Samaria shows that not everybody who had received the Spirit could pass it on: Simon Magus asked the apostles to sell him their special faculty of being able to do so.

Unfortunately, as regards the question whether the laying on of hands consisted in *samakh* or a mere *śim* or *shith*, there is nothing in the texts pointing one way or the other. However, there can be no doubt that it consisted in the former, and that the idea, as in the other instances of *samakh*, was the pouring of one man's personality into another.

This is not to deny that, in certain circumstances or in certain circles or at certain times, this idea might be quite absent and the gift of the Spirit be looked upon as coming direct from heaven without any

[1] 13.4.   [2] Acts 8.14 ff., 19.1 ff., Heb. 6.2.

R

laying on of hands—whether spontaneously, as at Pentecost, or as the result of repentance and baptism, listening to the gospel or the like. All we mean to say is that, where there was imposition of hands, it was a *samakh*. The communication of the Spirit is too near those other cases to be connected with *śim* or *shith*. (Carrington's proposition[1] that the laying on of hands in the course of baptism 'would harmonize well with counsels to humble oneself and be subordinate' is, therefore, untenable for the New Testament period. A laying on of hands by way of symbolizing authority and subjection would be *śim* or *shith*. Above we cited a probable example from Job.[2]) That the basic idea of the ceremony—the creation of a second self—underwent modifications so as to suit the nature of each case we have mentioned already. Here a particular gift was conveyed, a gift, however, which affected the whole life of him who possessed it.

The account, in Acts,[3] of the restoration of Paul's sight by Ananias presents difficulties, but they are not insuperable. Paul, deprived of his sight, had a vision of Ananias laying his hands on him in order that he might see again. Ananias in turn had a vision in which he was informed of this and sent to Paul. He went and laid his hands on him in order that he might see again and—here comes the crux—be filled with the Spirit. Paul immediately did see again and received baptism.

The laying on of hands for the purpose of healing was a gentle act, a placing of the hands, *śim* or *shith*. It is this act which we must assume Ananias to have performed. Yet he was sure that it would not only cure Paul physically but also bring him the Spirit. How can this be reconciled with our view that the laying on of hands for the purpose of imparting the Spirit took the form of a leaning, *samakh*?

The answer seems to be that this was not a communication of the Spirit by one person to another at all. More precisely, Ananias did not confer the Spirit on Paul in the way Peter and John conferred it on the Samaritans or Paul himself on the Ephesians. What Ananias was ordered to do and did was to restore Paul's sight. As this marked the last phase of a change of heart, he knew it would be followed by the gift of the Spirit. The Spirit was not, however, thought of as transferred by Ananias but as falling upon Paul direct from heaven. In this respect, that is, the case is parallel to the descent of the Spirit at Pentecost, or as a result of baptism or listening to the word of God—with no human

---

[1] *The Primitive Christian Catechism*, 1940, p. 84.   [2] 9.33.   [3] 9.10 ff.

intervention, no laying on of hands. There was, in short, no *samakh* because it was not Ananias who bestowed the Spirit on Paul. After all, the triumph of faith, or baptism as its expression, is often enough described as a passing from darkness to light. In this case, a regaining of sight was considered a sign of a triumph of faith; and it was the latter which, as in the parallel instances just referred to, led to the gift of the Spirit.

In Paul's epistles no mention is made of imposition of hands on converts, whether before or after baptism. This silence need not be significant. On the other hand it may be. Flemington holds[1] that there was no need for him specially to refer to the rite since for those with a Jewish background it was such an obvious custom. But that is precisely what it was not. In Judaism, *samakh* was restricted to the sacrificial cult and Rabbinic ordination. There was no *samakh*—nor, for that matter, any *śim* or *shith*—in connection with the reception of proselytes. The widening of the scope of this ceremony is a distinctive and suggestive feature of early Christianity. Neither is there much force in the argument that, in one passage,[2] Paul appears to distinguish the grant of the Spirit from baptism. It is difficult to see why this should necessarily imply an imposition of hands.

In the narrative of Jesus's baptism the distinction is clearly made. First comes the actual baptism, completed as Jesus comes up. (On the significance of 'coming up' we remarked above, in Part II, in the chapter on A Baptismal Catechism.) Then the Spirit descends on him. These are two different things, however closely linked. But, manifestly, no laying on of hands takes place. In fact, as far as Mark is concerned, the word 'straightway' very likely qualifies 'he saw', not 'coming up' ('and straightway, coming up, he saw the heavens opened', not 'and straightway coming up, he saw the heavens opened'); and its sense may be less vague than usual; that is to say, it may be intended definitely to exclude any thought of John having imposed his hands on Jesus.

To repeat, Paul's silence need not be significant, but it may be. So once again the question arises—we first put it in discussing his 'separation' as a missionary—whether, from a certain moment at least, he may not have had scruples about the imparting of the Spirit by means of *samakh*. Quite apart from the austere Rabbinic attitude in this matter, he may have felt uneasy at the suggestion of human intervention im-

[1] *Op. cit.*, p. 44.   [2] II Cor. 1.21 f.

plicit in this passing on of the Spirit from one person to another, and have preferred the notion of a direct flow from heaven.

It remains to inspect three passages from the Epistles to Timothy.[1] In the first, the writer admonishes Timothy not to neglect 'the gift that is in thee, which was given thee by prophecy, with the laying on of hands of the presbytery'. The conclusion generally drawn is that Timothy was made bishop by an imposition of hands on the part of the presbytery. It may be correct, but it is difficult to reconcile with the second passage, where Timothy is warned to 'lay hands suddenly on no man'. This, at first sight at least, seems to assume that the imposition of hands is performed by the bishop, not by the presbytery; or in other words, that a bishop is appointed by a previous bishop. There are, of course, several ways of harmonizing the texts. We may, for example, regard the second passage as speaking not of the appointment of a further bishop, but of the bestowal of the Spirit on a convert.

The problem becomes almost insoluble, however, when we add the third passage, from II Timothy, where the writer admonishes Timothy to stir up 'the gift of God which is in thee by the laying on of my hands'. Here the only natural interpretation is that Timothy was installed by the writer and no one else. To say, as is usually said, that 'the laying on of my hands' means 'the laying on of my hands—together with the presbytery' is reading a great deal into the text; not to mention the fact that even so the conflict is not quite resolved, unless we take a further step and say that, in the first passage, 'the laying on of the hands of the presbytery' means 'the laying on of the hands of the presbytery —together with me'.

However, such is the prevalent view, and it may be right. If so, it is impossible to decide whether the ceremony still consisted in *samakh* and still involved the idea of creating a representative, an extended self, or whether it had lost its original form and meaning and become a *śim* or *shith*, with the touch as the principal element.

We incline to a different solution. The clue seems to lie in the first passage. The phrase ἐπίθεσις τῶν χειρῶν τοῦ πρεσβυτερίου looks like a rendering of the technical term *semikhath zeqenim*,[2] literally, 'the leaning on of elders'; its meaning being 'the leaning on of hands on persons in order to make elders, Rabbis, of them', or briefly, 'Rabbinic ordination'. In the only two other New Testament texts where

---

[1] I Tim. 4.14, 5.22, II Tim. 1.6.   [2] E.g. Bab. San. 13b.

πρεσβυτέριον occurs,[1] it stands for *zeqenim*, 'elders'; and the most likely reason why the collective noun is put instead of πρεσβύτεροι is that the reference is not to individual Rabbis, but to the Sanhedrin as a body. Surely, as *semikhath zeqenim* denotes not the ordination of specified individuals, not the appointment of certain men as elders, but the rite of ordination in general, πρεσβυτέριον is here the proper equivalent of *zeqenim*. On this basis we ought to translate: 'Neglect not the gift which was given thee by prophecy, with *semikhath zeqenim*, due ordination, ordination conferring full authority.'

The difficulties with which the current interpretation has to contend are now removed. Rabbinic ordination in the New Testament era took the form of *samakh*, 'a leaning on of hands': the master would lean his hands on his disciple's head, thus passing on the wisdom and authority which Moses had passed on to Joshua, Joshua to his successors and so on. In the passage under discussion, the installation of a bishop is likened to Rabbinic ordination, indeed, is supposed to be the corresponding Christian practice.

It follows that Timothy must have been ordained by his master alone, and that is exactly what is implied in the similar exhortation in the Second Epistle: 'Stir up the gift of God which is in thee by the laying on of my hands.' Again, at that time any Rabbi himself authorized was entitled to authorize others. But there are many stories in the Talmud showing that great care was exercised to ordain only such as deserved it; and as a rule a candidate must be forty years old.[2] It is, therefore, open to us to connect the rule 'Lay hands suddenly on no man' with ordination. It is a warning that might have been given by any Rabbi to a younger colleague.

The result is curious. The installation of the seven distributors of charity, normally treated as an adumbration, if not the prototype, of apostolic succession or delegation, was no such thing. Those officers were the delegates of the ordinary people who had leaned their hands on them. Conversely, the passage in I Timothy, commonly interpreted as speaking of a democratic installation of a bishop by the presbytery, turns out to be the earliest reference to apostolic succession, i.e. the creation of a bishop by a *samakh* on the part of one who is bishop already—on the model of Rabbinic ordination.

[1] Luke 22.66, Acts 22.5.
[2] See the comment of R. Judah ben Elai (middle of the 2nd cent. A.D.) in Exod. Rabba on 2.14; cf. also Mish. San. 4.4, reflecting the attitude of the Mishnic period.

So once again a question concerning the silence of our sources arises, the last one: why do we not hear of an equivalent of Rabbinic ordination—of a disciple being invested with full authority by a master leaning his hands on him—prior to the Epistles to Timothy? (If the translation of ἐπίθεσις τῶν χειρῶν τοῦ πρεσβυτερίου here suggested is rejected, then even these Epistles offer no certain instance of this kind of succession.) As nearly always, the silence may be accidental. But in all probability it is not. One can think of various reasons why some time should have elapsed before semikhath zeqenim was definitively taken over by the Church for the appointment of bishops.

First, Jesus himself had been without Rabbinic authority: he had, indeed, been attacked on this ground.[1] Secondly, the attitude expressed in the words 'The scribes and Pharisees sit in Moses' seat' may have delayed the adoption of the Rabbinic practice. (In the Rabbinic writings preserved, 'the seat of Moses', qathedhra' demoshe, does not occur before the 4th cent. A.D.:[2] a striking illustration of the fact that an institution or idea may be early even though mentioned only by the later Rabbis.) Thirdly, the working out of the principles of church government was an enormous task. Even when the principles were agreed on, such details as the way in which to ordain a bishop need not have been immediately obvious. Jesus, we have seen, had never used the rite of samakh, 'leaning on', for commissioning his disciples; they had been called and given power as Moses had been—by the word alone. When it came to the appointment of successors, the exact mode of installation may well have presented a problem.

This does not mean that Rabbinic ordination cannot have been applied to bishops before the Epistles of Timothy, even, perhaps, in the time of the apostles. The description of the installation of a bishop as semikhath zeqenim must in any case go back to a fairly early date, when Jewish Christians were still in close and living contact with the Synagogue. Only, from the silence of the earlier portions of the New Testament, as well as from general considerations, it does seem likely that a few decades at least were needed for Rabbinic ordination to find its lasting place in Christianity.

The later development, when 'leaning' became confused with 'placing', lies outside the scope of our inquiry.

[1] Matt. 21.23 ff., Mark 11.27 ff., Luke 20.1 ff.
[2] R. Aha of Lydda, in P. de-R.K. 7b.

III

Basic Commandments

A. THE CREDO

THE Synoptics tell us[1] how a Pharisee wanted to know from Jesus the fundamental principle of a good life. We saw above (in Part II, under Four Types of Question) that, in Mark, the question corresponds to one in the Passover Haggadah, put by the *tam*, the man of simple piety, who is interested in *derekh 'ereṣ*, general rules of decent conduct. In Matthew, the connection with the liturgy of Passover eve is less noticeable, in Luke it is completely absent. Luke has abandoned also another narrowly Jewish feature: whereas in Matthew and Mark the scribe asks which is the greatest commandment, in Luke he asks what to do to inherit eternal life.

Jesus's answer—which Luke puts into the mouth of the questioner—is that two things are essential: the love of God and the love of man. These were coupled as basic requirements already in pre-Christian Judaism. There is pre-Christian evidence.[2] But even without it, the conclusion would be unavoidable, in view of numerous passages from Philo and early 2nd cent. Tannaites.[3]

The first part of Jesus's reply, however, where the love of God is emphasized, creates a problem. In Matthew and Luke, Jesus quotes only the verse 'And thou shalt love the Lord', whereas in Mark he quotes also the preceding one: 'Hear, o Israel, the Lord is one.' Which quotation did Jesus give, or to put it differently, which was attributed to him by the earliest tradition: the shorter or the longer?

---

[1] Matt. 22.34 ff., Mark 12.28 ff., Luke 10.25 ff.

[2] Test. of XII Patriarchs, Issachar 5.2, 7.5, Dan 5.3—not to mention Micah 6.8.

[3] Philo, Sept. 6.63.282, Decal. 22.108 ff., Siph. on Lev. 19.18. The last-mentioned text records a difference between Akiba and Ben Azzai. Akiba ascribed cardinal importance to 'Thou shalt love thy neighbour as thyself.' Ben Azzai preferred Gen. 5.1, according to which passage every man is akin to God: for Ben Azzai, that is, the love of man rested, or should rest, on the love of God.

At first sight, one might perhaps argue in favour of the shorter. We have just referred to ancient Jewish sources where the duties to love God and to love man are combined. The actual credo, 'The Lord is one', occurs in none of them. This appears to support Matthew and Luke, without the credo; and on this basis we should have to assume that Mark added it. In fact, he must have thought the addition highly important, since the scribe, when expressing his agreement with Jesus, comes back to the unity of God.

However, while this view is tenable, we incline to assign priority to the longer quotation. Long before the New Testament period, the section from Deuteronomy beginning 'Hear, o Israel' had acquired a central position in Jewish life and worship. Nor was the opening verse any less prominent than the rest. On the contrary, it was because of this verse that the recital of the whole section was looked upon as an acknowledgment of the one God's rule, as 'a taking upon oneself of the kingdom of heaven'.[1] Akiba died a martyr's death with the word 'one' on his lips—the last word of the opening verse.[2] It is quite likely that the original version of Jesus's answer did include the verse.

Why is it omitted in Matthew and Luke? It probably suffices to inquire why it is omitted in Matthew. For it is hardly to be supposed that the two evangelists cut out the credo each independently of the other. It seems that the Lukan text has suffered assimilation to Matthew in one or two other points. For instance, in its present form, Luke, like Matthew, speaks of the Pharisee 'tempting' Jesus. That Luke has been assimilated to Matthew and not Matthew to Luke follows from the consideration that the 'tempting' does not really fit Luke's story, where the questioner—in answer to a counter-question—himself provides the correct reply, stressing the love of God and man. It may well have been assimilated in the matter of the credo too.

There is indeed a further possibility, however remote. The credo may have been given up by a stratum of the tradition common to Matthew and Luke. (It need not be what is ordinarily labelled as Q.) But it would make little difference to our discussion; only what we shall say of Matthew would apply, not to Matthew, but to that earlier stratum.

Let us ask, then: why did Matthew dispense with 'Hear, o Israel'? Surely not just for the sake of brevity. He did occasionally shorten a narrative or saying. But there must have been a better reason for

[1] Mish. Ber. 2.2, 5.   [2] Bab. Ber. 61b.

dropping a verse of such significance. Was it that the Jews found in the verse ammunition against the Christian concept of the nature of God? Considering the early date this is unlikely, and a different solution may be preferable.

In a previous chapter (Precept and Example, in Part II) we pointed out that Matthew was careful to base religious observances on Old Testament precepts, on imperative pronouncements—of course, we include in this class not only the imperative 'do', but also forms like 'thou shalt do'—in contradistinction to Old Testament examples. This suggests that his notion, or his opponents' notion, of what constituted a precept was rather technical. The Pharisee requests Jesus to name the greatest 'commandment', ἐντολή, miṣwa (though, as remarked above, Luke makes him seek the road to eternal life). Presumably Matthew felt that the actual credo, 'Hear, o Israel, the Lord is one', did not, in strictness, fall under this category. It might be called 'a comprehensive maxim', kelal, 'an essential part of the Torah', guph—but not 'a commandment'. It was only 'Thou shalt love the Lord' that was a precept in the full sense. This verse alone, in the view of Matthew or those he had to convince, ought to figure in a statement concerning the greatest 'commandment'.

As is well known, the exact division of the Decalogue may well have been controversial as early as in New Testament times; and it is possible that many experts even then considered the verse 'I am the Lord, which have brought thee out of the house of bondage' to be one of the ten portions forming the whole.[1] This does not, however, affect our thesis respecting Matthew's notion of 'a precept'. It should be remembered that the Rabbinic term for 'Decalogue' is 'the Ten Words', 'aśereth haddibberoth, not 'the Ten Commandments'. The Old Testament, to be sure, refers to 'the covenant which he commanded you to do, the ten words'.[2] But this does not mean that the Rabbis of the New Testament era did not distinguish between 'words' and 'commandments'. Again, it is true that, in course of time, even the subtlest Rabbinic teachers classed as 'commandments' some utterances showing no imperative form—chief among them 'I am the Lord which have brought thee out' and 'the Lord is one'. But this development is post-Tannaitic.

In the Letter of Aristeas,[3] one of the wise men remarks: 'God has

---

[1] See the Jerus. Targ., Mekh. on Exod. 20.16, Bab. Mak. 24a.
[2] Deut. 4.13.
[3] 228.

given us a very great commandment concerning the honouring of one's parents; in the next place he reckons the attitude between friends, speaking of a friend which is as thine own soul.' It may not be accidental that the term 'commandment' (and, as in the gospels, it is a question of 'a very great commandment') is applied only to a precept in the strict sense: 'Honour thy father and thy mother.' It is not applied to the passage from Deuteronomy[1] which, though it refers to a good friend, does not actually enjoin the honouring of one's friends.

The upshot seems to be that a quotation spontaneously and naïvely used by Jesus was curtailed by Matthew—or someone prior to him—so as to suit meticulous Rabbinic scholarship.

B. A JEWISH PRAYER

It is relevant to note that, in Matthew, the ending of Jesus's reply is couched in far more erudite terms than it is in either Mark or Luke: 'on these two commandments hang all the law and the prophets'. *Tala*, 'to hang', 'to depend on', 'to follow from', 'to be derivable or intelligible from', is a technical term of Rabbinic exegesis. In the Bible we read that the injunctions enumerated in Leviticus 19—of which 'Thou shalt love thy neighbour as thyself' is one—are to be proclaimed by Moses, not just 'to the children of Israel', but 'to all the congregation of the children of Israel'. According to the Tannaites[2] this means they had to be proclaimed in a solemn assembly, the reason being that 'the majority of the essentials of the Torah hang on them', i.e. are derivable from them. For Bar Kappara (beginning of the 3rd cent. A.D.), 'all essentials of the Torah hang on a tiny section', namely, on a verse from Proverbs:[3] 'In all thy ways acknowledge him.'

The idea of many conclusions following from one or two premises was applied by the Rabbis also to the way they elaborated their legal system. On the few Biblical laws concerning the Sabbath, they rested a host of detailed regulations: the latter were said (towards the end of the 1st cent. A.D.[4]) to be 'like mountains hanging on a hair'. In the province of *haggadha*, non-legal exposition, the Tannaites found that often 'a great matter was made by Scripture to hang on a smaller one'.[5] That is

---

[1] 13.6. The quotation is from LXX. [2] Siph. on Lev. 19.2.
[3] 3.6; see Bab. Ber. 63a. [4] Mish. Hag. 1.8, Tos. Hag. 1.9, Tos. Er. 11.23 f.
[5] The 14th rule of interpretation of Eliezer ben Jose Ha-gelili.

to say, a great matter might be compared to a smaller one—God's speech to the roar of a lion[1]—in order that it should become intelligible.

However, though by the time of Jesus most Rabbis held that the entire religion was implied in a small number of first principles, or even in a single one (Hillel received into the fold a pagan who recognized only the rule 'What is hateful to you, do not do to your fellow'),[2] yet they never ceased to insist on the absolute and independent validity of each particular commandment. That at least certain early Christian circles shared this view is obvious from such New Testament passages as 'one jot shall in no wise pass from the law'. As Christianity—and other sects—gradually concentrated on the principles, to the exclusion of minor regulations, Judaism reacted by various measures, for example, the abrogation of the daily recital of the Decalogue in synagogues.[3]

One development is interesting since it resulted in a prayer—still widely used—which contains a clause very reminiscent of the Matthean ending of Jesus's reply or Bar Kappara's proposition, yet expressive of the opposite approach.

The interdependence of all precepts, their fundamental equality, the importance of even the minor ones, or apparently minor ones, because of their association with the weightiest—these were common themes among the Tannaites. When Ben Azzai (first third of the 2nd cent. A.D.) taught that 'you should run to do the lightest duty, for one duty draws another after it, and the reward of a duty is a duty',[4] he was only summing up, and giving a deeper meaning to, the prevalent doctrine. Nevertheless, in the case of some minor commandments, the Rabbis deemed it either particularly needful or particularly easy to prove their connection with further commandments.

The Bible lays down[5] that a garment ought to be provided with fringes. The Rabbis maintained that whoever observed this commandment was considered by God as if he had observed all; and they pointed out that the numerical value of the letters of ṣiṣith, 'fringe', was 600, so that, if one added the eight threads and five knots of a correct fringe, one obtained 613—the total number (in their opinion) of Biblical precepts.[6] The Biblical basis for these reflections was, of course, the verse: 'It shall be unto you for a fringe, that ye may look upon it and

[1] Amos. 3.8.   [2] Bab. Shab. 31a, Ab. de-R.N. 15.
[3] Bab. Ber. 12a.   [4] Mish. Ab. 4.2.
[5] Num. 15.38 ff., Deut. 22.12.   [6] Siph. on Num. 15.39, Num. Rabba on 15.38.

remember all the commandments.' This verse does make the fringes into a sign of submission to the entire Torah. Moreover, the Rabbis argued that the word 'all', at first sight superfluous (the Bible might have said, 'that ye may remember the commandments', without 'all'), must be intended to equate the performance of this duty with that of all.

Several prayer-books under the Ashkenazi rite include the following meditation, to be recited on putting on an under-garment or prayer-cloak with the prescribed fringes at its four corners: 'May it be thy will, o Lord, that the observance of this commandment be accounted as though I had fulfilled it in all its details and particulars and intentions, and the 613 commandments that hang on it.' The same prayer is said on putting on the phylacteries, and the history is much the same as in the case of the fringes. Among the Biblical portions contained in the phylacteries is:[1] 'Hear, o Israel, the Lord is one: and thou shalt love him with all thine heart; and these words which I command thee shall be in thine heart; and thou shalt talk of them when thou sittest, and when thou walkest, and when thou liest down; and thou shalt bind them for a sign upon thine hand.' No wonder Eliezer ben Hyrcanus (towards the end of the 1st cent. A.D.) claimed[2] that whoever fulfilled the duty of wearing the phylacteries was considered by God as if he had occupied himself with the Torah day and night.

What is more remarkable is the extension of the prayer to the swinging of the Lulab on the Feast of Tabernacles. True, Abba bar Kahana (of the beginning of the 4th cent. A.D.) emphasized that the precept concerning the Lulab involved many others:[3] he may have thought of the rules that the Lulab must be used together with a citron, that it must be your own, not a borrowed one, and the like. Still, the prayer in question assumes, not that many commandments are involved, but that 'the 613 hang on this one'. The difference is far from negligible. It is indeed taken into account of in a similar meditation, also recited on the Feast of Tabernacles, on entering the Sukkah, the booth. Here the text runs: 'May it be thy will that the observance of this commandment be accounted as though I had fulfilled all the commandments that hang on it.' It is not claimed that the entire 613 commandments are implied in that concerning the booth.

The prayer under discussion is not ancient. In fact, it hardly antedates

[1] Deut. 6.4 ff.   [2] Mid. Ps. on 1.2.   [3] Lev. Rabba on 23.40.

the 16th or 17th century. The idea that the wearing of fringes or phylacteries in a way means the fulfilment of the whole Torah has, we saw, its
roots in early Rabbinic theology. The extension of the idea to the
swinging of the Lulab no doubt rests on the doctrine that any duty of
whatever kind is performed with a view to hallowing the name of the
one God and doing his unfathomable will in its entirety. Naturally,
this notion is given greater prominence in the case of a duty which looks
irrational—like the swinging of the Lulab—than in that of a duty con-
sonant with human reason—say, the giving of charity.[1]

In any case, the prayer uses the language of sayings like those of
Jesus (in Matthew) and Bar Kappara, in order to express the opposite,
almost a paradox: on a single precept of no obvious importance depend
all the others. We have already mentioned that the Christian tendency
to recognize first principles only may have contributed to the working
out by Judaism of the contrary approach. It remains to add that, in
Singer's English *Prayer-book* for Jews,[2] as in numerous others, the
clause in question is not to be met with at all. No doubt some authorities find it altogether too sophisticated or one-sided.

---

[1] Akiba once said that so long as a man observed one of the great duties—abstention
from oppression, honesty and so on—he would be saved; and a somewhat pedantic
interpreter added that such a man would count as having observed all great duties (Bab.
San. 81a, Mid. Ps. on 15.5). But the idea here is not that one duty implies, contains in
itself, all the rest.

[2] Pp. 14 f., 218, 232.

IV

Eye for Eye

MATTHEW tells us[1] that Jesus opposed to the old maxim 'An eye for an eye' the rule 'Resist not evil: but whosoever shall smite thee on the right cheek, turn to him the other also.'

The passage raises many problems. First, Luke indeed has the rule 'And to him that smiteth thee on the one cheek, offer also the other.'[2] But he has not the old maxim 'An eye for an eye' to which it is opposed in Matthew. Which, if either, of the two versions is original? Or is it too old-fashioned to suggest that possibly both are, going back to different sermons? (A minor item relevant in this connection is that while Matthew speaks of 'the right cheek' and the other, Luke speaks of 'the one cheek' and the other.) Secondly, is the rule 'Resist not evil' a natural product of the Jewish teaching of the time—or at any rate, of one school of Rabbinic theology—or is there anything new? Thirdly, how far does the passage allude back to the description of the suffering servant of the Lord in the Old Testament and forward to the treatment meted out to Jesus during the trial?

These and several more points cannot here be discussed; and we shall concentrate on two questions only. First, was the teaching of Jesus—or whoever the author of the passage may have been—directed against talion in the literal sense; or, in other words, was talion in the literal sense still practised or taught in the circle he addressed? Secondly, what is the significance, for the history of the Jewish law concerning insult, of the connection to be found in this passage between the maxim 'An eye for an eye' and the case of smiting a man's cheek? Our answer to the first question will be in the negative; and to the second, that the passage most probably reflects a pre-Talmudic state of the law.

[1] 5.38 f.   [2] 6.29.

A. Talion

First, then, we submit that the teaching under notice was not directed against talion in the literal sense. For one thing, there are various general considerations making it likely that, by the time of Jesus, retaliation in the case of damage to a person had been superseded by money penalties. Not a single instance of the practice of retaliation is mentioned in the sources. Both Mishnah and Mekhilta reject any literal interpretation of 'Eye for eye' and lay down that the wrongdoer has to pay damages.[1] It might perhaps be objected that these works, though containing old material, were not completed until the end of the 2nd cent. A.D. (Mishnah) or even later (Mekhilta). But this argument loses much of its weight when we remember that the system of damages of Mishnah and Mekhilta is of so elaborate and subtle a nature—we shall soon have to quote a few illustrations—that we must allow a long time for its growth. In other words, talion must have been ousted by a pecuniary settlement long before the detailed provisions concerning the latter which we find in Mishnah and Mekhilta were established. Consequently, even if we assume that these provisions do not belong to the older material—an unlikely assumption in this general form, though one instance of divergence from the law of the time of the New Testament will be given below—we still arrive at the conclusion that talion can no longer have formed part of the law in the age of Jesus. Had he attacked this principle, he would have been guilty of a strange anachronism.

There are, it is true, two points occasionally adduced for the opposite view.[2] A group of Sadducees, the Boethusaeans, seem to have been in favour of actual retaliation, and their attitude was shared by at least one Talmudic authority, R. Eliezer. It is, however, doubtful whether this doctrine represents a genuine survival of ancient legal ideas; it may well have been a revival due to the Sadducean theory that the Bible ought to be interpreted quite literally and not, as among the Pharisees, in a way that rendered it possible to introduce outside notions. What is more important: it is difficult to see why Jesus should have addressed the words here discussed precisely to the holders of that theory. There is no sign of his singling out Sadducean doctrines anywhere in the sermon on the mount.

[1] For references, see Strack-B., I, 1922, 341 ff.   [2] See Strack-B., I. c.

The other point sometimes advanced is a paragraph from Josephus,[1] where he says that a man who mutilates another should be mutilated in the same manner, unless the person wronged is satisfied with damages. Now this regulation is not referred to at all in other Jewish sources. It agrees neither with that of the Pharisees nor with that of the Sadducees nor with that of any dissentient authority. It very much looks as if Josephus, when he had to interpret the Biblical maxim 'Eye for eye', had gone to Roman law for guidance. The XII Tables do give a regulation somewhat like his.[2] Admittedly it was out of date by the time he wrote. But he was not a lawyer; he had to make the Biblical injunction palatable to his Roman readers; and a provision of the XII Tables known to Festus and Gellius, and obviously a favourite topic of debate, may have been known to him. *Si membrum rupit, ni cum eo pacit, talio esto*, says Festus,[3] *Si membrum rupit, ni cum e pacto, talio esto*, says Gellius.[4] In any case Josephus is so much out of touch with the main line, or lines, of Jewish law on this matter that his testimony must be ruled out.

So far we have appealed to external evidence only, and we grant that it might not be regarded as fully conclusive. Actually the principal reason why the question has remained controversial up to our day seems to be that nothing but external evidence has ever been considered. (A subsidiary reason is the desire on the part of Christian scholars to make the preaching of Jesus as original as possible and the desire on the part of Jewish ones to explain away any originality.) There is, however, a clue in the text itself.

Its author opposed to the maxim 'An eye for an eye' the rule 'Resist not evil', and he illustrated the rule by the case where a man has his ears boxed; in this case, he said, the other cheek should be offered. Supposing for a moment the maxim 'Eye for eye' had then meant actual talion for mutilation and Jesus had intended to attack this principle, would the case of a slap in the face not have been an excessively weak illustration of his new position? Would it not have been absolutely necessary to give a far more serious example? Would he not have said something to this effect: But whosoever tears out one of thine eyes, forgive him and do not require that one of his be torn out? Certainly, nowadays we can use the exhortation 'Turn the other cheek' even for the most serious cases. But we must not take our proverbial use back into the New

---

[1] Ant. 4.8.35.280.   [2] VIII 2.   [3] V.S. p. 363.   [4] A.N. 20.1.14.

Testament. The author of this passage cited the offence of smiting a man's cheek, not as a proverbial case covering all kinds of injury, even the gravest, but as the best example available of the situation to which the warning not to demand 'An eye for an eye' was to apply. Which shows that he was not combating talion in the case of mutilation.

In fact it shows that he was not thinking of the law concerning damage to a person at all. A slap in the face is a case, not of mutilation, but of insult—a very different thing. From the choice of this example it is evident that he meant to pronounce immoral not the law concerning mutilation but that concerning insult. A man should be meek under an insult, this was his teaching, and not insist on such redress as the maxim 'An eye for an eye' would give him—which was such a sum of money for this kind of insult and such a sum for another kind.[1] It follows that, in the eyes of the author of this passage, the maxim 'An eye for an eye' governed the law concerning insult, was the basis for the fines to be paid by him who had committed an insult to the person insulted. In the eyes of the author, that is, that maxim, far from enjoining literal talion for mutilation, simply stood for the idea of accurate reparation, the exaction of amends precisely corresponding to the wrong done. In the case of insult there had never been any talion—how could there be?—but always money penalties. Where the maxim 'An eye for an eye' is connected with this offence, its horrifying character must have gone; it can have reference only to fines.

All this is argument from purely internal evidence. And the result is that this utterance is the earliest positive testimony preserved to us of that stage of Jewish law where the principle 'Eye for eye' had only the refined meaning of restitution by means of money.

Once this is recognized, three points, otherwise incompatible with the verses analysed, become intelligible and indeed provide strong confirmation of the interpretation submitted. In the first place, in the Mishnah also—and in Roman law—the case of smiting a man's cheek serves to illustrate just that situation where there is only insult but no damage to a person. We shall come back to this point later on, but would lay much emphasis on it in the present connection.

In the second place, neither of the two further examples given in Matthew ('If any man will sue thee and take thy coat, let him have thy cloke also; and whosoever shall compel thee to go a mile, go with him

---

[1] A list of fines is quoted from the Mishnah by Strack-B., *loc. cit.*

S

twain') is a case of mutilation. We need not here inquire whether they come from the same hand as the first one, the case of smiting a man's cheek. It is sufficient to remark that whoever put them in their present place did not think of combating retaliation, but regarded the cry 'An eye for an eye' as characterizing him who stands on his rights and honour instead of humiliating himself before his fellow-man. He proceeded from the refined Rabbinic meaning of the maxim, from 'An eye for an eye' as signifying the claim to accurate, nicely calculated compensation.

In the third place, it is noteworthy that when Jesus quoted the old Biblical maxim, he omitted the first clause 'Life for life' and mentioned only 'Eye for eye, tooth for tooth'. This is highly significant. In the case of homicide, the Rabbis did not abolish retaliation, at least not in theory: a murderer was liable to capital punishment, and even he who killed a man unwittingly could save himself only by escaping into a city of refuge.[1] Accordingly the clause 'Life for life' was not divested by the Rabbis of its literal meaning in the way the other clauses 'Eye for eye, tooth for tooth' and so on were. The natural result was that the two parts of the maxim drifted apart, in law and in the minds of the people: the clause 'Life for life' belonged to criminal law, was connected with the death penalty, the other clauses 'Eye for eye' and so on belonged to private law, were connected with monetary compensation. Had this development not yet been completed by the time of the New Testament, had 'Eye for eye' still implied actual talion, the omission of 'Life for life' would be incomprehensible. It is readily accounted for, however, on the basis of the thesis here proposed. When the passage under notice was written, 'An eye for an eye' was no longer interpreted as demanding literal talion but was referred to damages. The separation of 'Eye for eye' and so on from 'Life for life' was complete, and it did not occur to the author, who was thinking of insult, a matter of private law, to bring in the criminal law clause, 'Life for life.'

Perhaps we may add that if this part of the sermon on the mount is properly understood, its religious implications come out the more clearly. It is not concerned—not even secondarily—with a certain historical system of punishment. It is concerned with something far more fundamental, namely, the urge to resent a wrong done to you as an affront to your pride, to forget that the wrongdoer is your brother

[1] A survey of the law is given by Strack-B., *op. cit.*, pp. 254 ff.

before God and to compel him to soothe your unworthy feelings; and it advocates, instead, a humility which cannot be wounded, a giving of yourself to your brother which will achieve more than can be achieved by narrow justice. Insult, because immediately aimed at the victim's dignity as a human being, and thereby at the image of God, was considered by the Rabbis as a terrible sin. For them, one striking his fellow, or even one putting his fellow to shame by a hurtful remark, was the typical *rasha'*, 'godless man'.[1] (The rendering 'Resist not the wicked man' or, for that matter, 'Do not prosecute the wicked man'[2] would be no less in agreement with the Rabbinic attitude than 'Resist not evil'.) It is precisely this most direct attack on your personality which the saying here discussed expects you to bear without resentment. It breathes the spirit of the Rabbinic teaching (Gamaliel II, towards the end of the 1st cent. A.D., Judah ben Elai, middle of the 2nd) that if you are struck you must forgive the offender even though he does not ask your forgiveness,[3] or of a prayer which the Jew says three times a day (if he says his prayers!), in the morning, in the afternoon and in the evening: 'My God, unto those that curse me may my soul be dumb, yea, may my soul be as dust unto all.'[4]

B. INSULT

At this juncture, however, a problem arises which seems completely to have escaped notice. In Rabbinic law as we know it from Mishnah and Mekhilta, the case of smiting a man's cheek does not fall under the provision 'An eye for an eye' at all, but under the provision, to be found in Deuteronomy,[5] 'Then thou shalt cut off her hand.' In other words, in Rabbinic law as we know it, the insulting party's duty to pay a fine to the party insulted is based on that injunction from Deuteronomy. Yet Jesus assumed that it was based on 'An eye for an eye': when he demanded that a man should reply to a slap in the face by offering the other cheek, he was illustrating an attitude that leaves behind the old principle 'An eye for an eye.'

This is a real conflict, which calls for an explanation. We thus come to the second question: Is there any significance for the history of the

[1] Bab. San. 58b, B.M. 59b.
[2] ἀνθίστημι means 'to go to law' or something like it, for instance, in Deut. 19.18, Isa. 59.12, Jer. 14.7 (the Hebrew in these cases has *'ana*) and Isa. 50.8 (*'amadh*).
[3] Tos. B.Q. 9.29 f.   [4] Singer's *Prayer Book*, 54, 119, 142, 166.   [5] 25.11 f.

Jewish law concerning insult in the connection occurring in Matthew between the maxim 'An eye for an eye' and the case of smiting a man's cheek, and, if so, what is it?

In order to answer this question, a closer inspection of the Rabbinic law on the matter and its evolution will be necessary. As pointed out already, smiting a man's cheek appears in Rabbinic argument as a typical case of insult, of insult unqualified, without actual damage to a person. The same is true of Roman law, where the praetor's edict gave as example of actionable insult the case that *Aulo Agerio pugno mala percussa est*.[1] Indeed already the first Roman codification, the XII Tables, laid down a penalty of twenty-five asses for *iniuria*, understanding by this such modes of insult as a box on the ears.[2] There is no reason to assume any influence of Roman on Jewish law (though it is impossible to disprove it). A slap in the face must have been so natural an example of insult in ancient times that the lawyers of various countries would think of it independently of one another. We find it mentioned as part of the humiliating treatment of the suffering servant of the Lord in the Old Testament, we find its insulting character considered in Germanic systems.[3] It should be remembered that mere insulting words were not enough to justify proceedings; that dangerous words such as hostile spells belonged to a different class of delicts altogether, at least for a long period; and that in the case of blows resulting in serious injury such as the loss of a limb, the element of actual damage to a person was very much more important than that of insult —which, be it noted, might be entirely absent, for instance, if there was an honest fight or a mishap. It is easy to see how the kind of insult expressed by a slap in the face became the prototype of insult in the legal sense.

The very term employed by the XII Tables, *iniuria*, reflects this development. The XII Tables declared punishable first *membrum ruptum*, secondly *os fractum*, and thirdly *iniuria*. Whereas the two former involved actual damage to a person (no need here to go into the exact difference—a hopeless task), *iniuria* signified harmless blows such as a slap in the face. Why was this word, the native meaning of which is 'an unlawful act' or 'illegality', used to denote a slap in the face? Were *membrum ruptum* and *os fractum* not also instances of *iniuria* in this wider,

---

[1] Lenel, *Das Edictum Perpetuum*, 3rd ed., 1927, p. 398.
[2] VIII 4.   [3] See His, *Das Strafrecht des deutschen Mittelalters*, 2, 1935, 97.

untechnical sense? They were, and no doubt the Romans knew it. But it was only in cases like a slap in the face that unlawfulness alone, so to speak, constituted the offence; that the rather abstract notion of 'violation of another person's rights' was in the foreground, not concealed behind any more concrete facts like a broken limb or a torn-out eye; that the plaintiff could show the judge no glaring damage but appealed for redress on the sole ground that 'a wrong', *iniuria*, had been done to him. Consequently it was cases like a slap in the face, cases of wrong pure and simple, that received the technical appellation of *iniuria*, 'unlawfulness proper'. It was they which made early lawyers aware of the existence of a thing like violation of another person's rights as such, independent of real damage. As we concluded above, the kind of attack expressed by a slap in the face became the prototype of that spiritual delict, insult.

Whether under Roman influence or no—and probably there was none—the Rabbis used the case of smiting a man's cheek as illustration of the delict of insult. When it came to making this delict actionable, however, they were in some difficulty. In Roman law the XII Tables mentioned the delict, and any reforms desirable were easily effected by the praetor. The Bible, however, had no obvious provision concerning insult. Yet—and this is a point of vital importance for a correct assessment of the evolution—in the view of the Rabbis, if there was to be a regulation, it must have its basis in the Bible. In one way or another, that is, any action that was to lie in the case of insult must be derived from Scripture. We have no details left of the various attempts—for there must have been more than one—that they made to solve the problem. We do know, however, the ingenious method by which it was finally mastered.

The final system as set forth in Mishnah and Mekhilta may be summarized thus.[1] If a man attacked another, there were five kinds of damages that had to be considered; according to the particular circumstances, sometimes it was only one of them, sometimes several or even all, to which the wrongdoer was liable. First, there was compensation for actual damage to a person; secondly, for the pain caused; thirdly, for loss of time, incapacity to work; fourthly, for the cost of healing, doctor's fees; and fifthly, for insult. The Biblical basis for the first four

[1] See, in the main, Mish. B.Q. 8 and Mekh. on the passages from Exodus to be quoted in the course of the following discussion.

the Rabbis found in the *Mishpatim*, the 'Judgments', the legal chapters in Exodus. Compensation for actual damage to a person was rested by them on 'Eye for eye, tooth for tooth, hand for hand, foot for foot.'[1] We have already observed that, for the Rabbis, this provision referred to a pecuniary settlement. Here it must be added that they confined it to the case where real damage has been inflicted on a person, where, for example, an eye or foot has been lost. The second kind of compensation, for pain, the Rabbis deemed to be indicated by the words 'Burning for burning, wound for wound, stripe for stripe.'[2] By this enumeration of several hardly distinguishable and apparently negligible modes of wounding, the Rabbis argued, the Bible intended to impose on the offender the obligation to make amends for pain even if no physical damage may have resulted, for instance, if he touched another man with a hot spit. For the third kind of compensation, compensation for loss of time, the Rabbis adduced the verse: 'Only he shall pay for the loss of his time' (literally, 'for his ceasing', or perhaps 'for his sitting down').[3] The same verse served as basis for the fourth kind, compensation for the cost of healing: 'And he shall cause him to be thoroughly healed.'

So far, so good. The linking of the first four kinds of compensation with the 'Judgments' in the fashion just described may appear artificial to a modern reader, but it is at least intelligible and not vastly different from Roman 'interpretations' of statutes and edicts, especially the logic of the Pontiffs, or even from certain feats of English jurisprudence. Of all these four kinds of compensation—or, more cautiously, of all except compensation for pain—even a modern historian has to admit that the beginnings at any rate were really there in the Bible. But what about the fifth kind, compensation for indignity inflicted? Where did the Rabbis get Scriptural authority for this? They got it from Deuteronomy: 'Then thou shalt cut off her hand.' This provision, if we read it without Rabbinic spectacles, ordains that a woman who commits a certain obscene and vicious crime shall have her hands cut off. According to the Rabbis it ordains that he who insults a man—for example, by smiting his cheek—shall pay damages.[4]

It must be chiefly two factors that account for this surprising

---

[1] Exod. 21.24.   [2] 21.25.   [3] 21.19.
[4] The Siphre, it is true, also mentions the somewhat less astounding interpretation that these verses refer to the duty to prevent a person from serious crime by incapacitating him.

Rabbinic use of the law in question. In the first place, the crime originally contemplated must have been exceedingly rare long before the Rabbinic era. But even if it did occur, it could be adequately dealt with under the general rules concerning attack on a person which we have outlined above and some other rules. We are safe, therefore, in assuming that the provision in its original sense had long been a dead letter. It follows that the Rabbis were free to use it for other purposes, or rather, since it was their doctrine that the Bible contained no superfluous provision, that they were compelled to use it for other purposes. They did so by declaring it the basis for compensation in the case of insult. In the second place, there was indeed a verbal link—or maybe it was just a little more than that—between the passage from Deuteronomy and the delict of insult. The woman of whom this provision speaks seizes a man by his *mebhushim*, 'shameful parts'. The Rabbinic technical term for insult suffered was *bosheth*, 'shame', coming from the same root. Surely, this also led the Rabbis to see here the Biblical regulation of the delict of insult.

Be this as it may, the fifth kind of damages, damages for insult, was derived by the Rabbis from this Deuteronomic law. It should be noted, however, that even when they had overcome their main difficulty in the matter of insult, and recognized the provision discussed as sufficient Scriptural authority for an action, they had yet to prove one more item, namely, that the words 'Then thou shalt cut off her hand' meant no more than monetary compensation. To prove this they made use of one of their traditional rules of hermeneutics, the inference *a minori ad maius*. They argued that, since the maxim 'Eye for eye', though referring to the serious case of actual damage to a person, prescribed money compensation only, *a fortiori* the injunction 'Thou shalt cut off her hand', which referred to mere insult, had to be considered as prescribing money compensation. We have here, incidentally, another piece of evidence showing that the interpretation of 'Eye for eye' as speaking of a pecuniary settlement goes back to a very early date. Clearly, it must have been firmly established by the time that it was employed for reading a pecuniary settlement into other laws such as that from Deuteronomy.

Such, then, is the system of Mishnah and Mekhilta, and it will be agreed that we did not say too much in the first part of this discussion when we maintained that we ought to allow a considerable time for its growth. We can now proceed to answer the question posed above. Jesus looked upon 'An eye for an eye' as the principle governing compensation in the case of insult. In Rabbinic law as we know it the principle governing compensation in the case of insult was 'Then thou shalt cut off her hand.' How is this divergence to be explained? To put if differently, it is plain that Jesus was ignorant of the technical Rabbinic analysis of the delict of insult as it appears in Mishnah and Mekhilta. What can be the reason?

There are two possibilities. One is that he had not penetrated into those details and took it for granted, as presumably anyone not belonging to the learned circles would, that any kind of damages had its basis in the old maxim 'Eye for eye.' In other words, he was not enough of a scholar to be aware of the distinction between compensation for actual damage to a person and compensation for indignity inflicted, and of the subtle derivation of the latter from the unlikely provision in Deuteronomy. If we take this line, Matthew represents a popular, unlearned view as distinct from academic teaching. From the standpoint of Jewish legal history, incidentally, the result remains much the same if we assume that the author himself was familiar with the Rabbinic technicalities but discarded them out of consideration for his unlearned audience.

We are, however, inclined to prefer the second possibility. This is that in the period when Jesus preached, or when the verses in question were composed, that highly technical treatment of the delict of insult did not yet exist. The Rabbis themselves, that is, in this period still regarded the maxim 'Eye for eye' as sufficiently comprehensive to include cases like smiting a man's cheek as well as cases like breaking a man's arm. It was not till later, say, the end of the 1st or beginning of the 2nd century, that they sought a separate basis in the Bible on which to rest compensation for insult, finally resorting to the law from Deuteronomy. Whether or not the several texts used with reference to damages for pain, loss of time and cost of healing were already fixed in the age of Jesus may be left undecided, though quite probably they were. They all, like 'Eye for eye', are from the 'Judgments', the legal chapters in Exodus, the principal source of ancient Hebrew private law and the source most relied on by the early Rabbis. 'Thou shalt cut off her hand' is the only provision in the system of damages reviewed that lies outside the 'Judgments', being taken from Deuteronomy. At any rate, the fact that this provision is introduced from outside furnishes strong support for the second alternative, for the view that when the author of the utterance we find in Matthew started from 'An eye for an eye' as demanding compensation in the case of insult, he was in agreement with the then prevailing Rabbinic law. This maxim was still interpreted at the time as prescribing compensation not only for actual damage to a person but also for insult. We may add that in Roman law also, in the XII Tables, *iniuria*, insult, was still placed together with *membrum ruptum* and *os fractum*, and that its separation from those grave cases was a result of gradual development.[1]

If this is true, then not only have we a satisfactory explanation of the problem created by the Matthean passage, but we also have some indication, vague though it be, as to its date of composition. It must have been a comparatively early date, before the delict of insult was severed from 'An eye for an eye' and assigned to 'Thou shalt cut off her hand.' Above all, however, we have here a plain instance—there cannot be many—where the New Testament has preserved to us a pre-Talmudic stage of Jewish private law, a stage far removed from the law of the Bible (monetary compensation instead of talion, and legal consideration of insult as well as of actual wounds) but less advanced than that of Mishnah and Mekhilta (no separate Scriptural texts as yet for compensation for actual damage and compensation for insult, but both resting on 'Eye for eye'). That stage might perhaps have been inferred even without this evidence from general considerations respecting the evolution of Rabbinic doctrines and with the help of comparative methods. To have chapter and verse for it, however, is a different matter, especially as we are here moving in a period of Jewish private law on which the light of the sources shines only dimly.

---

[1] That to some extent they ultimately met again—namely, when the edict on *iniuriae* was extended to serious wounds—is irrelevant to the present discussion. It may be noted, however, that even in its widest application this edict never included the unintentional causing of *membrum ruptum* or *os fractum*; i.e. at least half the field covered by the *membrum ruptum* and *os fractum* of the XII Tables remained outside the scope of the edict.

V

The Offices of a Disciple

ACCORDING to Matthew, the Baptist considered himself unworthy to carry the shoes (or sandals) of Jesus, according to Mark, Luke, John and Acts to take them off.[1] In Talmudic utterances, whenever a slave's services are illustrated, these two—carrying the master's things before him to the bath-house and taking off his shoes (when he comes home)—are listed together.[2] Let us note, however, that the Baptist was willing to do them for Jesus not as a slave, but as a disciple. It was a general rule that a son or disciple owed the duties of a slave.[3]

Why does Matthew mention one of the two services and Mark, Luke, John and Acts the other? Or supposing the original saying referred to both, why does Matthew omit one and Mark and so on the other? Of course it may be due to an accident of transmission, or we may have to invoke one of the modern theories concerning Q. On the other hand, there may be an altogether different explanation.

R. Joshua ben Levi held that a disciple should do for his teacher anything a slave would do—except take off his shoes.[4] It is true that this Rabbi flourished about A.D. 250. But his principle may be much older. (The earliest datable identification of the Suffering Servant with Israel in Jewish literature is as late as the 12th century. Yet we know from Origen that it was prevalent in certain Jewish circles in his time, some 900 years before.) If the principle had followers in the New Testament epoch, it may account for the difference. Matthew represents the Baptist as having adhered to the principle: he spoke only of carrying the shoes of Jesus, but not of taking them off. The latter is not a disciple's task. The other sources represent the Baptist as eager to perform for Jesus precisely that service which some Rabbis thought too low for one who was free, even if he was a great man's disciple.

[1] Matt. 3.11, Mark 1.7, Luke 3.16, John 1.27, Acts 13.25.
[2] Mekh. on Exod. 21.2, Siph. on Num. 15.41, Bab. Qid. 22b.
[3] Bab. Ket. 96a.   [4] Bab. Ket. 96a.

In the following chapter (on Redemption) we shall find that there were Rabbis who imposed heavier duties on a son or disciple than on a slave. Their object was to exempt a slave from degrading services; but they felt that no service was degrading if done by a son or disciple for his father or teacher. An idea like this may also have contributed to the non-Matthean version of the Baptist's saying.

VI

Redemption

In this chapter, as in most others, we can only call attention to a few points not always sufficiently considered.

A. General

The two most prominent Hebrew terms for 'to redeem' are *ga'al* and *padha*. The former primarily signifies 'to recover a man or thing that had once belonged to you or your family but had got lost', the latter 'to ransom a man or thing whose fate would otherwise be destruction, consecration or slavery'. Thus *ga'al* suggests the return of men or things into their old, legitimate place, *padha* the deliverance of men or things from their doom. Whereas men, animate things and inanimate things may be the object of *ga'al*, since any of these are capable of being 'recovered', there appears to be no case of an inanimate thing being the object of *padha*: only men and beasts can be 'ransomed from a doom'.

Admittedly, the two terms are often interchangeable. If the owner of a firstborn animal, which is God's, pays the priests its value instead, the transaction may be called a 'recovering' or a 'ransoming'; and a prophet may speak of God 'recovering' or 'ransoming' Israel. But the difference remains; and it accounts for the fact, surprising at first sight, that in Old Testament and Rabbinic utterances concerning deliverance through God, *ga'al*, 'to recover', occupies a more conspicuous place than *padha*, 'to ransom'. The point is that the notion of *ga'al* is central in the social legislation of Old Testament times—regarding the recovery of a relative enslaved, of family property alienated, of the blood of a murdered relative, of the childless widow of a relative—and that the social legislation has exercised an enormous influence on the religious concept of redemption.

The social legislation of Old Testament times was largely designed to safeguard the integrity of a family. Accordingly, if one of your relatives had had to sell himself into slavery, if you had had to sell part or all of your ancestral land, if one of your relatives had been murdered or if one of them died leaving a childless widow, it was your right and duty to 'recover', *ga'al*, the enslaved relative, your land, your murdered relative's blood (by slaying the murderer) or the widow (by marrying her—given certain conditions). In the Pentateuch, these and other social laws are founded on the exodus: 'And thou shalt remember that thou wast a bondman in Egypt and the Lord redeemed thee', or 'Unto me the children of Israel are servants, they are my servants whom I brought forth out of Egypt.'[1] But it is clear that the exodus itself is depicted in terms taken from social legislation—in fact from social laws which, though not completely identical with those preserved in the Pentateuch, yet must have been very similar.

In the exodus, God acts as a father demanding back his son from the tyrant who has enslaved him—'Israel is my son, let my son go'[2]—as a mighty person regaining an impoverished relative or his legitimate property from the hands of a stranger—'thy people which thou hast acquired, thou shalt plant them in the mountain of thy inheritance'[3]— or as the revenger of blood—'I have heard the groanings of the children of Israel, and I will bring you out from under the burdens of the Egyptians and I will redeem you with a stretched out arm and great judgments.'[4] Nor must we forget that the verb *yaṣa'*, 'to go out', so frequent in the story of the exodus, the 'going out'—'The selfsame day the hosts of the Lord went out from Egypt'[5]—is technically used of a slave 'going out free' under the social legislation.[6] The Hiphil of this verb, *hoṣi'*, 'to bring out', may connote a 'bringing out from slavery to freedom' in more passages than would appear at first sight. The connotation is plain in a verse like 'I am the Lord thy God which have brought thee out of Egypt, the house of bondage.' But it may also be present, say, in the clause 'for by strength of hand the Lord brought us forth out of Egypt'.[7]

We have before us, then, a development in three stages. There were social laws more primitive than, though similar to, those extant in the Pentateuch. These determined the whole way in which the exodus was

[1] Deut. 15.15, Lev. 25.55.   [2] Exod. 4.22 f.   [3] Exod. 15.16 f.   [4] Exod. 6.5 f.
[5] Exod. 12.41. The noun *yeṣi'a*, 'exodus', 'the going out', is post-Biblical; in Rabbinic literature the phrase *yeṣi'ath miṣrayim*, 'the going out from Egypt', is extremely common.
[6] E.g. Exod. 21.7, Lev. 25.54.   [7] Exod. 13.16.

thought of and described. And the narratives of the exodus in turn influenced, on the one hand, the further history of the social laws and, on the other, the direction which the ideas about God's intervention on behalf of his people or man in general were to take.

That the exodus was construed as an application, on a higher plane, of the social laws is hardly surprising, in view of the particular genius of Hebrew priests and prophets. The Israelites had actually been subjected in Egypt to the most oppressive slavery, and no human kinsmen or former owners with a stronger right had come to the rescue. Yet they were freed: it was, the religious leaders concluded, God who had stepped in and enforced the demands of social justice.

Once that deliverance was interpreted in this fashion, the significance of the social laws even as operating here on earth necessarily increased a thousandfold. Ought not the Israelite to be mindful of the example set by God in putting them into practice? Ought he not to be mindful of his wretched past and miraculous salvation, and ought not this memory to affect his ordinary, daily dealings with his fellow? And ought he not to see in each of his brethren a special protégé of God? Moreover, this tremendous fact at the beginning of the national history—the exodus thought of as an application of the social laws—inspired a firm expectation that, whenever Israel was in distress and no human aid was available, God would act as redeemer again and again. 'Then he remembered the days of old, Moses and his people, That led them by the right hand of Moses, dividing the water before them. Look down from heaven. Where is thy zeal and thy strength? are they restrained? Thou, O Lord, art our father, our redeemer.'[1]

It was not only the nation as a whole, but also the individual that would look to God for redress if none could be obtained elsewhere. As is natural, the social legislation of the Old Testament was not always strictly observed. The weak did not receive their due. Occasionally, no doubt, the hope was expressed that a great king would remedy this state of affairs: 'He shall redeem the needy people's soul from deceit and violence, and precious shall their blood be in his sight.'[2] But in general it was realized that the only one who would never desert the poor and who was incomparably stronger than any worldly power was God: 'Remove not the old landmark, and enter not into the fields of the fatherless; for their redeemer is mighty.'[3]

[1] Isa. 63.11 ff.   [2] Ps. 72.14.   [3] Prov. 23.10 f.

Let us note that, from the first, the liberation from Egypt meant much more than a liberation from physical sufferings. From the first, the exodus included mount Sinai. It meant, therefore, salvation both in the physical and the spiritual sense.

This element remains attached to divine redemption throughout. Whenever Hebrew priests or prophets represent God as redeemer—be it of his people or of an individual, be it that they speak of deeds he performed in the past or of deeds he will perform in the future—they have in mind redemption not only from material misfortunes but also, in a greater or lesser degree, from impurity, sin and error. Both aspects are clearly noticeable in passages like 'No lion shall be there, but the redeemed shall walk there, and the ransomed of the Lord shall come to Zion with songs, they shall obtain joy and gladness', or again, 'I know that my redeemer liveth, and that he shall stand up at the latter day upon the earth.'[1] But even where the spiritual side alone is referred to, there is no break with the original concept; the most refined notion of redemption by God is descended from the old construction of the exodus. The assurance 'I will ransom them from the power of the grave, I will redeem them from death' occurs in the same group of sayings as the verse 'Yet I am thy God from the land of Egypt.'[2]

So far we have considered certain nuances of redemption in the Old Testament. They all, however, live on in Rabbinism, as may be seen from the comments, Tannaitic and Amoraic, on the relevant Old Testament passages: and it is mainly the features outlined which distinguish the Jewish—and Christian—view of salvation from that of the surrounding Hellenistic and Oriental world. That world was full of hope and speculation as to final deliverance. Yet nowhere but in Judaism—and Christianity—was final deliverance guaranteed by having its ultimate basis in the social laws: God would, in fact, he must, 'recover' those who were his property, his children, friends or slaves. Nowhere but in these religions was final deliverance guaranteed by an undisputed historical precedent, the exodus, of which, in a sense, it would be a repetition, though an infinitely superior one and one that would end all history. It is evident that, with this setting, 'recovery', ge'ulla, by God must be widely different from, say, $\sigma\omega\tau\eta\rho\iota\alpha$, and that it could never for any length of time share the nebulous, vague and eccentric character pertaining to not a few elaborations of the Greek idea.

[1] Isa. 35.9 f., Job 19.25. [2] Hos. 13.14, 4.

Moreover, while the Jewish—and Christian—image of redemption, 'recovery', had its roots in the social laws and their miraculous application in the exodus, and indeed never ceased to be in rejuvenating contact with these sources—at the same time the social conscience of Judaism was constantly stimulated by the religious image. Nowhere but in Judaism—and Christianity—did divine salvation involve such emphasis on the establishment of social justice and (this is the point) lead to such an insistent appeal to man to assist, anticipate and emulate God by doing justice here and now. If Jesus dealt with the world in charity, and if both his deeds and his teaching impressed on his followers the need of taking the same course, this was only in line with the traditional nature and role of redemptive activity in Judaism.

It is sometimes contended that the aspect of the New Testament here contemplated is due to a revolutionary spirit that had got hold of the suppressed masses of the time. Should this be the case, the spokesmen of the revolution would none the less have moved within a framework coming down from the generation who had experienced the deliverance from Egypt as it is set down in the Pentateuch and thought of by priests, prophets and Rabbis.

B. A Change of Master

1. *The Old Testament*

In many parts of the Old Testament we come across the notion that it was through the liberation from Egypt that Israel became God's people: 'And I will take you to me for a people, and I will be to you a God, and ye shall know that I am the Lord your God, which bringeth you out from under the burdens of the Egyptians.'[1] Actually we are so accustomed to the notion that it seems quite natural to us. But it is not. It is unique, and it calls for an explanation. The explanation lies in the fact we tried to bring out above—that the exodus is construed as an application of the social laws, as a 'recovery' by God of an enslaved son, relation or friend or of property fallen into the hands of strangers.

Under the social regime of Old Testament times, an enslaved son, relative or friend who was redeemed, 'recovered', by the person nearest to him came into the power of the redeemer; and similarly, family land redeemed by a member of the family became the redeemer's property.[2]

[1] Exod. 6.7.   [2] E.g. Jer. 32.6 ff.

(We disregard the effects of the Seventh Year or the Jubilee. We also disregard modern interpretations[1] according to which a slave redeemed did not become the redeemer's subject but acquired full freedom, and family property redeemed went to the former owner or his heir even if another member of the family had redeemed it. These interpretations are in conflict with the texts. Even if they were right, it would still remain true that the actual redeemer of a slave or of family property must be the one to gain effective control, no matter where control might reside in theory: as he proved able to recover what had got lost, it is he who would continue being looked up to as the real protector.) Just so, in the view of the Old Testament writers, the Hebrews, as a result of their redemption from thraldom by God, became his subjects —as sons or slaves—or his property: 'They are my servants whom I brought forth (or we may translate: freed) out of the land of Egypt', 'Thy people pass over, O Lord, which thou hast purchased' and so on.[2]

This notion is extended from the exodus to any acts of deliverance God may perform for Israel in the course of history, and also to the final deliverance which will end all history: 'Fear not, I have redeemed thee, thou art mine.'[3] Liberation by God, in analogy to 'recovery' prescribed by the social laws, means, not liberation pure and simple, but a change of master. It means a passage from a distressing, foreign and arbitrary yoke to contentment and security under the rightful authority.

As is to be expected, usually no strict distinction is drawn between the different types of 'recovery'. In other words, it is not usually specified whether God redeemed, or will redeem, Israel as his son, relation, slave or property. The main idea is always the same: God exercises his right of 'recovery' and the Hebrews, previously under the rule of alien tyrants, return into the hands of their true sovereign.

Admittedly, in some passages one of the various nuances may definitely predominate. Admittedly, too, some Old Testament writers do see a tension—unresolved and maybe incapable of being resolved— between the various nuances, say, between Israel the son and Israel the slave. But in most cases God simply acts as the 'recoverer' in general; and occasionally we find several types of redemption put side by side in the most unsophisticated manner, as in the request 'Israel is my first-

---

[1] My rejection of them in *Studies in Biblical Law*, 1947, pp. 51 f., 73, was too half-hearted. [2] Lev. 25.55, Exod. 15.16. [3] Isa. 43.1.

T

born son, Let my son go that he may serve me.'[1] Here God appears as father and as master at the same time. It is true that, at a certain stage of civilization, the position of a son while his father lives and that of a slave would not be so very dissimilar. Again, the verb 'abhadh, 'to serve', means not only 'to serve as slave', but also 'to serve as labourer', 'to worship', 'to honour', 'to cultivate', 'to work'. In a text like that just quoted one or two of the milder senses may play a part. We must also remember that to be 'the slave of the Lord' may be a distinction as great as to be 'his son'.

Another tension often alluded to is that between God's being the father, friend or owner of the Hebrews for ever and his none the less ceding temporary power over them to their enemies. The reason for his doing so is generally found in the people's sinfulness: 'O that they were wise. How should one chase a thousand except their Rock had sold them?','And the anger of the Lord was hot, and he sold them into the hands of their enemies.'[2] But the oppressors are not on this ground justified: 'Ye have been sold for nought and ye shall be redeemed without money.'[3] This last passage again makes direct reference to the laws concerning 'recovery'.

Significantly, where it is a question of Israel abandoned and accepted again, we sometimes meet with the term *hikkir*, a term which, in technical usage, denotes the formal, binding 'acknowledgment' of a fact of legal relevance. In the story of Judah and Tamar, Judah 'acknowledged' the signet, bracelets and staff to be his.[4] The fact to be 'acknowledged' may, of course, be a personal status or relationship. There is a provision insisting that though a man's firstborn son was borne to him by the less beloved of two wives, yet he must 'acknowledge' his position and give him the larger share which is his due.[5] The Levites, when fighting the worshippers of the golden calf, 'did not acknowledge their brethren'.[6]

This usage of *hikkir* must be borne in mind in interpreting passages like 'Doubtless thou art our father though Jacob acknowledge us not: thy name from everlasting is our redeemer.'[7] God, who for a while has turned away from the nation, will one day 'acknowledge' the relationship which all others, even the patriarchs, might repudiate. However desperate the momentary situation, God is the reliable, eternal 're-

---

[1] Exod. 4.22 f.   [2] Deut. 32.29 f., Judges 2.14.   [3] Isa. 52.3.   [4] Gen. 38.25 f.
[5] Deut. 21.17.   [6] Deut. 33.9; cp. Exod. 32.27 ff.   [7] Isa. 63.16.

coverer' of his own, the redeemer 'from everlasting'. Thus we read: 'I will acknowledge them that are carried away captive of Judah, and they shall be my people and I will be their God.'[1] Once more, 'acknowledgment' and 'recovery' clearly imply not liberation in the crude sense, but a change of master: the redeemed ones become the subjects of the redeemer. The same confidence, incidentally, is expressed in the same terminology by the individual in distress: 'There was for me no one', says the Psalmist,[2] 'to acknowledge me, refuge failed me; I cried unto thee, O Lord, save me from my persecutors, bring my soul out of prison.'

2. Rabbinic sources

The Old Testament ideas and phrases are taken over by the Rabbis, though, inevitably, there is addition, elaboration and a greater awareness of the problems and conflicts involved.

As for the fundamental notion that the exodus was a 'recovery', by which the people automatically came under the rule of God, their father, master or owner—a glance at the Rabbinic comments of the relevant Biblical texts will show that it retains all its weight. (We shall find ample confirmation of this when we come to the Passover ritual as practised in the Tannaitic era.) As already remarked, in the Pentateuch the laws for the protection of bondmen are supported by the reminder: 'they are my servants whom I brought forth out of Egypt'. The Rabbis make God say: 'my bill is older (than any which could be drawn up now)'.[3] By freeing the nation from strange despots, God acquired it as one acquires a slave: the Mishnah lays down[4] that 'A Hebrew slave is acquired by money or by a bill.' The Rabbis are fully conscious of the meaning of the reminder. The emphasis they place on it, incidentally, is proof that, even at that time, this concept of the exodus as a divine model of 'recovery' still helped to stimulate the social sense in everyday dealings.

A few examples of somewhat different versions of the idea may be of interest.

The rules concerning clean and unclean animals in Leviticus end with the warning, 'For I am the Lord that hath brought you up out of Egypt to be your God; ye shall therefore be holy'; and a similar warning follows the prohibition of usury, 'I am the Lord which brought you

[1] Jer. 24.5 ff.   [2] 142.5 (4) ff.   [3] Siph. on Lev. 25.42, 55.   [4] Qid. 1.2.

forth out of Egypt to be your God.' In both cases the Rabbis explain
that God delivered the people on condition that they would receive the
yoke of his commandments; and that he who denies the commandments denies the deliverance.[1] Here, strictly speaking, there is no
automatic passage from service in Egypt to the service of God. The
service of God is voluntarily agreed to, accepted, by the people on
being liberated—and if they go back on this compact, they also give up
the privileges flowing from it. Possibly this construction is influenced
by a custom widespread in antiquity: a master about to manumit his
slave exacted from him an undertaking to perform certain offices once
he was freed. At any rate, despite the fresh nuance introduced, manifestly the exodus still means a change of master.

Again, the Rabbis raise the question[2] why the exodus is mentioned in
connection with so many commandments. The matter, they reply, may
be compared to the ransoming by a king—God—of the captive son of a
friend—Abraham. The king, however, ransoms the prisoner not to
treat him as free or as a son, but to make him his own slave. That is why
the commandments are accompanied by references to the ransoming
from Egypt: the Israelites, having become slaves of God, may not
protest against any burdens imposed on them. In this parable, too, the
passage from service in Egypt to the service of God is not regarded as
the only conceivable possibility: the king, God, had he wished so,
might have granted the people absolute freedom. Of course, in actual
life also, a 'recoverer' might, if he liked, refrain from asserting his right
over the person or property 'recovered'. But God did not do so; he
claimed the people as his own, as his slaves. We shall see below that, in
a deeper sense, to be God's slave, to be God's son and to be truly free
were held to mean the same thing by the Rabbis.

As in the Old Testament, in general, the Israelites are described as
'God's slaves' or 'God's sons' without much thought being given to
the precise choice of epithet. It is of course as great an honour to be 'the
slave (servant) of the Lord' in the way Isaiah understands this role as to
be 'God's son'. Frequently, however, the phrase 'slaves of God' implies
an emphasis on the duties owed. A saying of Antigonos of Soko (of the
3rd cent. B.C.) was:[3] 'Be not like slaves who minister to the master for
the sake of a reward.' At other times, the Rabbis do place slavery and
sonship into opposition. The clause 'Is not he thy father, thy owner

[1] Siph. on Lev. 11.45, 25.38.   [2] Siph. on Lev. 15.41.   [3] Mish. Ab. 1.3.

(purchaser, acquirer)?'[1] is interpreted as indicating that when the Israelites do God's will, he deals with them as with sons, but when they do not, he deals with them as with slaves.[2]

Ultimately, I suppose, while our world continues, the conflict between these two expressions of man's relationship with God is unavoidable, just like other conflicts in the region approaching the limits of our understanding—those between grace and merit, predestination and free will and so on. Let us note that, in evaluating particular texts, great care is required, since so many complicating factors must be taken into account. For instance, some Tannaites hold that a slave may be ordered to take off his master's outdoor shoes and put on his indoor ones or to carry his things to the bath-house; others that a slave need not perform these services, but that a son or disciple must—in the case of a son or disciple they cannot be degrading.[3] The Baptist certainly shares the view that a disciple may show his respect by doing them.[4]

The old tension between God's everlasting reign over Israel and his temporary desertion of them also recurs in Rabbinic theology and—what is important in this connection—is often illustrated by comparisons with affairs based on social laws or, more particularly, the laws respecting slavery. The Israelites are represented as arguing that they need not observe God's will: they have passed out of his power since he himself sold them to foreign nations. But the argument, the Rabbis declare (and prove by a passage from Ezekiel), is fallacious. God sold them only for a time. There is a proviso attached to the sale that after a while they will fall back into his ownership.[5] In the end, God will assert his superior claim.

One change, small in itself but relevant—as we shall see—to the correct exegesis of New Testament texts is that *hikkir*, 'to acknowledge', appears to be no longer employed by the Rabbis as a term of art to signify the acknowledgment of kinship by him who exercises the right of redemption. Already in the Old Testament it is sometimes paired off with *yadha'*, 'to know', which verb has a wider range and cannot be said to be in technical legal use. In the Rabbinic sources, *hikkir* and *yadha'*, when referring to God's attitude to his people or to the pious,

---

[1] Deut. 32.6.   [2] Exod. Rabba on 15.22.
[3] Siph. on Num. 15.41, Mekh. on Exod. 21.2.
[4] Matt. 3.11, Mark 1.7, Luke 3.16, John 1.27, Acts 13.25. See above, on The Offices of a Disciple.
[5] Siph. on Num. 15.41.

are quite synonymous and mean 'to know' in the sense of 'to choose', 'to care for', 'to be intimate with'.

It is almost superfluous to observe that the Rabbis are aware that subjection to God is identical with freedom in the highest sense. No doubt when Joshua ben Levi, about the middle of the 3rd cent. A.D., preaches that 'thou findest no freeman but him who occupies himself with the study of the Law',[1] this particular dictum may be directed against, and therefore dependent on, the Christian view of freedom, which implied an abandonment—a partial one at least—of the Law. But the principal insight inspiring the saying can be shown to be extremely ancient. We need only mention these points. One is the constant description of the passing into God's service as a ransoming, a redemption or the like; we have seen enough instances of this. The second is the effect of this notion on the social consciousness. This also we have sufficiently illustrated. But we may add that in the opinion of the Tannaites, when the Bible speaks of a Hebrew slave, it does so 'against its will'.[2] It tolerates slavery reluctantly: he who is a son or slave of God ought to be no man's property even in appearance. Thirdly, there is the testimony of the New Testament itself. John tells us[3] how the Jews answered Jesus: 'We be Abraham's seed and were never in bondage to anyone.' Abraham's selection by God and his acceptance of it spelled freedom. This is not the place to go into the misinterpretations, misunderstandings and controversies to which the idea necessarily gave rise wherever it took root.

3. *The Haggadah and the New Testament*

In the New Testament, the teaching that redemption through Jesus means a change of master is stressed on a number of occasions and implied far more commonly than is obvious at first sight. Even if we confine ourselves to the passages where it is distinctly set forth—principally in John, in the epistles of Paul and in I Peter—there will remain no doubt that it is fairly central. It is a teaching which in many respects separates Christianity from the pagan religions and philosophies surrounding it. Dr. Selwyn observes, apropos of Peter's remark that Christians are free not to do evil but to be slaves of God: 'The connection of freedom with virtue was well established in antiquity. But Christian freedom rests not on escape from service but on a change of

---

[1] Mish. Ab. 6.2.   [2] Mekh. on Exod. 21.2.   [3] 8.33.

master.'[1] This early Christian concept which, if we disregard Judaism, is unique, comes directly from Old Testament and Rabbinic theology.

Deliverance by God is 'recovery'. The notion goes back to ancient social legislation. It was transferred to the exodus, which in turn gave a new impetus to the social laws. It was applied to later deeds of God for his people. It was also applied to the rescue by God of the faithful individual and to his final salvation of his own at the end of days. In the New Testament it is applied to the redemption through Jesus.

It is worth pointing out that the notion occurs in the New Testament in many various nuances. God may be represented as the Christian's father or as his master; the Christian's release may be from enslavement to men[2] or from enslavement to sin;[3] and so forth.

For a proper appreciation of the New Testament texts we should remember, what I have hardly touched on so far, that both before and after the destruction of the Temple, the exodus, construed as a 'recovery', played a prominent part in the Passover celebration.

In the Haggadah, in the Passover-eve liturgy, the recital of the miracles performed by God opens: 'We were slaves unto Pharaoh in Egypt, and our God brought us out (freed us) from there.' This is a quotation from Deuteronomy.[4] In Deuteronomy, the following verses make it clear that the giving of the commandments formed the climax of the deliverance. The idea in the Haggadah is the same. God redeemed his people; from being slaves of men, they have become slaves of God.

Naturally, the tension between the external situation of the Jews, sinful and oppressed, and their real, internal freedom as belonging to God, finds full expression in the liturgy. An Aramaic portion of the Haggadah, which was composed in Babylonia before or shortly after the destruction of the Temple, contains this wish: 'This year here, the next year in the land of Israel: this year slaves, the next free men.' The emphasis lies on the external situation; and, as usual, the prayer is for spiritual as well as political restoration—the two cannot be kept strictly apart.

On the other hand, the real freedom of the Jews as God's people comes out, for instance, in the provision of the Mishnah[5] that for the Passover supper 'even the poorest in Israel must recline (on a couch)'; a

[1] *The First Epistle of St. Peter*, 1946, p. 174.
[2] E.g. I Cor. 7.21 ff.   [3] E.g. Rom. 6.18.   [4] 6.21.   [5] Pes. 10.1.

provision the significance of which becomes intelligible when we consider that in Hellenistic times free men took their meals in this fashion, while slaves ate sitting. In fact, one of the questions traditionally put on Passover eve in order to provoke in reply a recital of God's deeds for Israel is why, at this meal, all participants assume a recumbent position. To this day it is usual for the participants in the Seder, the Passover-eve ceremony, to lean on a cushion placed on one's left side, as did the free men in antiquity. (The right hand must be disengaged to handle food and drink.)

That this custom dates from the New Testament epoch would be plain from its nature, even if there were no allusion to it in Mark and Luke: 'He will show you a room furnished with cushions.'[1] The Passover supper is taken by those already free, since they are already 'recovered' by God: the first part of the Hallel, the 'hymn', concludes with a praisegiving for his salvation.[2]

On the whole, the true freedom of God's people, irrespective of the external situation, receives more prominence on Passover eve than usual—the ceremony is largely a re-enactment of the exodus and, so to speak, a 'pre-enactment' of the final deliverance. But we saw above that it was not only on Passover that the consciousness of never having been anyone's slaves since Abraham was strong among the Jews of the New Testament era.

Again, the Hallel, consisting of Psalms 113–18, forms part of the Passover-eve liturgy. We know that this was so in New Testament times. This group of psalms is sometimes called himnon, ὕμνος, by the Rabbis, and from Matthew and Mark we hear[3] that those taking part in the last supper 'sung an hymn'. Moreover, while the Temple stood, it was these psalms that were sung during the slaughtering of the Passover lambs.[4] Now the first of them begins: 'Praise ye the Lord, O servants of the Lord.' According to Raba[5] the antithesis implied is 'servants of the Lord—not servants of Pharaoh'. Admittedly, Raba lived in the first half of the 4th cent. A.D. But as he takes this interpretation for granted and, indeed, uses it to prove another point, it must be considerably older. Anyhow, once more we have before us the idea that through their liberation from Egypt the Hebrews, up to then slaves to men, turned into slaves to God.

---

[1] Mark 14.15, Luke 22.12. Cp. κλίνη ἐστρωμένη in Ezek. 23.41, LXX.
[2] Mish. Pes. 10.6.   [3] Matt. 26.30, Mark 14.26.   [4] Mish. Pes. 5.7.   [5] Bab. Meg. 14a.

There is, incidentally, a Midrash on 'I am thy God which have brought thee out of the house of bondage', which must be very old and which insists that the Hebrews in Egypt were slaves, not to slaves, but to kings.[1] It is difficult to decide what motive or motives may underlie it: to establish a contrast between Israel and Canaan who is condemned to be 'a slave to slaves',[2] to make the past less degrading, to suggest that God is strong enough to defeat the mightiest among humans, to bring the oppression in Egypt into line with what in fact often happened to the nation when it was laid under tribute by foreign rulers ('Behold, we are servants this day and the land that thou gavest unto our fathers yieldeth increase unto the kings whom thou hast set over us because of our sins'[3]). What is highly probable is that the exchange of earthly kingship for divine kingship, so conspicuous a theme in the Haggadah, is in the author's mind.

If divine 'recovery' may mean a liberation from human sovereigns to pass under the sovereignty of God, it may also mean a liberation from the service of false gods to pass into that of the true one. A section of the Haggadah—which, some Rabbis held, ought to open the recital rather than the opening mentioned above ('We were slaves unto Pharaoh and God freed us')—begins thus: 'Originally our fathers were slaves of strange slavery (or: worshippers of strange worship—the technical designation of idolaters), but now God hath brought us near to his slavery (worship).'

The context shows that here, where the antithesis is between slaves to false gods and slaves to the true God, the change of master is thought of as having commenced long before the actual exodus, namely, when God called Abraham. The whole process from that call to the deliverance from Egypt and relevation at mount Sinai is one: an undoing of the chains of idolatry by the rightful lord. It is interesting that the verb 'to bring near', occurring in the clause 'he hath brought us near to his worship', is technical in Tannaitic language of conversion. 'Hillel used to say: Be of the disciples of Aaron, loving mankind and bringing them near to the Law.'[4]

We have just quoted a Midrash according to which 'I am thy God which have brought thee out of the house of bondage' refers to God's liberation of the Hebrews from earthly kings. Earthly kingship was

---

[1] Mekh. on Exod. 20.2. [2] Gen. 9.25.
[3] Neh. 9.36 f. [4] Mish. Ab. 1.12; see also e.g. Pal. Qid. 65b.

exchanged for divine kingship. It should now be added that an alternative interpretation was that God liberated the Hebrews from enslavement to idols, or from life among slaves of idols, idolaters.[1] Enslavement to idols was exchanged for enslavement to God.

It is surely against the background of the Jewish concept of redemption, 'recovery', and in particular against that dominating the Passover-eve liturgy, that the New Testament references to a change of master acquire their full meaning: John's assertion[2] that the truth, or the Son, would cause to be free, or to be sons, those who are slaves to sin; Paul's discourse in Romans[3] on the way the slaves of sin, by becoming free of sin, turn into slaves of righteousness; his explanation in I Corinthians[4] that those bought to be slaves of Jesus are free from men (and that those free as regards their civil status are yet slaves of Jesus); his warning in Galatians[5] that release by Jesus from the Law and sin involves enslavement to one's fellow-men in love; and I Peter's teaching[6] that the Christians are free from men, whatever their worldly position may be, but that they are free only to be slaves of God.

Each of these passages represents some version or versions of the Jewish notion of deliverance. To none of them can we do justice without paying attention to the role the Jewish notion played both generally, and more specifically in regard to Passover. The traditional contrasts between subjection to men and freedom in the hands of God, and between subjection to idols and freedom in the hands of God; the basic connection between divine redemption and brotherly love on earth; the perennial tension and harmony between being God's sons and being his slaves; the different shades of the term 'to serve' ('to serve as a slave', 'to serve as a son', 'to serve as a free labourer', 'to worship', 'to cultivate')—they all have contributed to the New Testament texts in question.

Occasionally, salvation is equated with 'being known by God'.[7] To some extent we must reckon with the influence of Hellenistic mysticism. But it has long been seen that there is also a Hebrew root: as already remarked, when the Old Testament or a Rabbi speaks of God 'knowing' his people or the faithful, the meaning is that he has chosen and cares for them. A remarkable feature, however, is that Paul, in Galatians, uses γιγνώσκω, 'to know', *yadha'*, in much the way in which ἐπιγιγνώσκω, 'to acknowledge', *hikkir*, is used in the Old Testament—

---

[1] Mekh. on Exod. 20.2.   [2] 8.32 ff.   [3] 6.16 ff.   [4] 7.20 ff.
[5] 5.1, 13 ff.   [6] 2.13 ff.   [7] E.g. I Cor. 8.3, 14.38, Gal. 4.8 f.

but hardly in Rabbinic literature—of one who legally, effectively, recognizes a relative and redeems him from a strange master: 'When ye knew not God, ye were in bondage to them which are no gods; but now after that ye have known God, or rather are known of God, how turn ye to the weak elements whereunto ye desire again to be in bondage?'

Paul's discourse in Romans deserves special mention, since it has been somewhat harshly treated by modern commentators. He combats the view that those living under grace need not be afraid to sin, and he combats it by affirming that slavery to sin has been replaced by slavery to righteousness.

Dodd, who is highly critical of this section, begins by saying[1] that, as the misconception of grace is already dealt with in the previous section, there is no advance in principle. This may be correct. But even if there is no advance in principle, it is only here that Paul introduces the old notion of a change of master. In the previous section, he spoke of baptism, and of dying and rising with Jesus, as eliminating sin. Now he dwells on the passage from the service of sin to that of righteousness. For himself, and no doubt for a large part of the recipients of the letter, the historical and religious setting of that notion, and above all its association with Passover, would amply justify the place and importance he assigns to it at this stage.

Another objection preferred is that Paul contrasts with enslavement to sin, not sonship to God, but enslavement to God. The latter idea, Dodd remarks,[2] will later have to be corrected into the more adequate one of sonship. This also seems a little one-sided. As we saw above, though, from a certain point of view, there is a conflict between being God's sons and being his slaves, yet both relations (and several more) are necessary: they not only conflict with, but also supplement, one another, and it depends on the particular situation, on the experience and purpose at a given moment, which may be in the foreground. Here Paul is concerned with the need of obedience; hence it is natural to refer to service.

There is indeed a third criticism which is less easily met. Paul contrasts with enslavement to sin, not only enslavement to God, but also enslavement to righteousness. 'Ye were servants of sin, but ye have obeyed that doctrine which was delivered you; being then made free

---

[1] 'The Epistle of Paul to the Romans', in *The Moffat New Testament Commentary*, 1932, p. 96. [2] P. 99.

from sin, ye became the servants of righteousness.' And again, 'As ye have yielded your members slaves to iniquity, so now yield them slaves to righteousness.' This, Dodd says,[1] is rather sub-Christian: conversion is represented as simply the acceptance of the ethical teachings of a rule of faith.

What makes the matter really problematic, however, is that the expression is not only 'sub-Christian', but also 'sub-Jewish'. There is not a single Old Testament or Rabbinic text with the phrase 'slaves of righteousness' or anything like it—say, 'slaves of the Law' or 'slaves of good deeds'. The faithful are 'slaves of God'; they could be slaves to no one and nothing else.

Paul himself is aware that his language—only his language, not his thought—is bold in the extreme, bordering on the blasphemous, and he apologizes in words which he uses on other, similar occasions, and which were doubtless technical for this purpose in Jewish circles:[2] 'I speak after the manner of men.' He apologizes not, as Dodd thinks, because his illustration is 'sub-Christian' or because it is not going well in general, but because it is 'sub-Jewish'. The exhortation to be 'slaves to righteousness', unless qualified by this apology, i.e. unless declared to be a mere metaphor, would scandalize the good Jews.

The question, then, arises: Why does Paul use the term 'slaves to righteousness'? Why is he not satisfied with the orthodox 'slaves to God'?

The answer is that, as already stated, he is trying to refute the argument that, since grace is free and the Law has ceased to be valid, sin need not be shunned and holiness need not be sought, and that, indeed, it may be desirable to sin. His aim is to impress on the addressees of the letter that they must none the less do good. His very insistence on life under grace and without the Law, plus the misinterpretation put on it by radical antinomians, drives him to use a term which the Rabbis, who held fast to the Law, had no need to use.

The Rabbis had no need to require the people to be 'slaves to righteousness'. Everything they wanted was implied in the requirement to be 'slaves to God'. Paul, preaching life under grace and without the Law, but at the same time opposing antinomianism, feels compelled to demand that Christians should be 'slaves to righteousness'—though he does not fail to add an apology proving him loyal to the Jewish tenet that, fundamentally, what is demanded is to be 'slaves to God'.

[1] P. 98.   [2] Pace Strack-B., vol. 3, 1926, p. 136. For a full discussion see below.

VII

Violence to the Kingdom

MATTHEW and Luke[1] preserve a saying about the kingdom suffering violence and being taken by force, or its being preached and everybody pressing into it, the import of which is highly controversial. Let us concede at the outset that all interpretations to be found in modern literature, and quite a few not to be found, are reconcilable with a Jewish milieu. In fact the Rabbinic texts do not enable us to arbitrate. Nevertheless it may be useful to draw attention to a few points which, though relevant to the discussion, are generally neglected. While we cannot clear up the meaning of the saying, we can find out a little more than appears to be known about the possible ideas behind it and the material with which it was traditionally combined.

A. THE SAYING

1. *General*

First, a preliminary remark regarding its authenticity. We are not here concerned with this question. However, one argument occasionally advanced[2] is weak: that the saying cannot go back to Jesus because he survived John only for a short time and ἀπὸ τῶν ἡμερῶν or ἀπὸ τότε, 'since the days' or 'since then', presupposes a longish interval. It is difficult to see why the interval must be longish. Moreover, the argument seems to assume that 'since John' necessarily signifies 'since the death of John'. Yet ἀπό and—if we think of a Hebrew or Aramaic form of the saying—*min* may be inclusive. That is to say, 'since John' may signify 'since John began his activity'. In Thucydides[3] ἀπὸ παλαιοῦ, 'from the earliest times', means 'from the beginning'; it does not mean 'since the earliest times were passed'. 'I have walked before you from

---

[1] Matt. 11.12, Luke 16.16.
[2] E.g. by R. Knopf, *Einführung in das Neue Testament*, 2nd ed., 1923, p. 259.
[3] 1.2.6.

my youth unto this day', says the old Samuel;[1] 'O house of Jacob', we read in Isaiah,[2] 'which are carried by me from the womb'; and of David we are told that he had not displeased Adonijah 'at any time', literally, 'from his days'.[3] In all these cases *min* is clearly inclusive.[4] In Rabbinic writings, incidentally, we sometimes have the choice between the readings 'since the days of' (*mime-*) and 'in the days of' (*bime-*), the sense remaining the same whichever we prefer.

The saying under notice distinguishes between three periods: that up to John's activity or death, that from John till now, and a future one. There may be good reasons for making the period from John till now start at his death rather than at his first public appearance. There may also be good reasons for denying the authenticity of the saying. All that we maintain is that the clause 'since the days' or 'since then' does not prove what some critics think it does.

2. '*Βία*' and '*ἁρπάζω*' in Matthew

Now for Matthew. It is often said, rightly, that, as a rule, when *βία* and *ἁρπάζω*—or derivatives of these words—appear together, they denote some wrong. Josephus records[5] that two relatives of King Agrippa were 'violent (*βίαιοι*) and bent on plundering (*ἁρπάζω*) the goods of the weaker'. Unfortunately this statistical consideration gives little help: there is no evidence that the saying in question uses the words in their most frequent sense. We may recall the passage 'How can one spoil a strong man's goods except he first bind him?'[6] This refers to a legitimate plundering, *ἁρπάζω* or *διαρπάζω*. True, the term *βία* does not occur. But it would make no difference if it did, if mention were made of an overpowering of the strong by force.

3. *The kingdom breaks through*

Those who regard *βιάζομαι* as a middle and translate 'the kingdom forces its way', 'breaks through', may assume some form of *beza‘*, *baqa‘*, *barah*, *berah*, *giah*, *paraṣ* or *peraṣ* at the Hebrew or Aramaic stage. As for *paraṣ*, the LXX several times renders it by *βιάζομαι*. A verse from Micah[7]—where the LXX, it is true, has not *βιάζομαι*—runs: 'The breaker is come up before them, they have broken up, and their

[1] I Sam. 12.2.   [2] 46.3 f.   [3] I Kings 1.6.
[4] Strangely, in Gesenius' *Handwörterbuch*, 16th ed., by F. Buhl, 1915, p. 433, only the last-mentioned instance is classed under the inclusive usage.
[5] Ant. 20.9.4.214.   [6] Matt. 12.29, Mark 3.27.   [7] 2.13.

king shall pass before them and the Lord on the head of them.' This, an anonymous Midrash explains,[1] is a description of the way 'God will reveal his kingdom'. Ἁρπάζω, for the advocates of this interpretation, may correspond to *lakhadh* or *lekhadh*. The verb occurs in the clause 'So Saul took the kingdom over Israel',[2] and the LXX translates it by ἁρπάζω in Amos.[3] But many other verbs are equally suitable: *'aḥaz*, *'aḥadh*, *taphaś* and so on.

4. *Suppression of the message*

One possibility, however remote, is that the saying is concerned—or at one time was concerned—with suppression, misinterpretation or repudiation of the message of the kingdom. *Kabhash* or *kebhash* is a reasonable Jewish equivalent of βιάζομαι. It is used of a prophet who 'does violence to' his message, suppressing it as Jonah tried to do;[4] also of a Rabbi who 'does violence to' the *halakha*, misinterpreting or repudiating it. R. Jose (middle of the 2nd cent. A.D.), when a colleague was going to act contrary to a decision of his in his presence, quoted from the Book of Esther:[5] 'Wilt thou force (*kabhash*, βιάζομαι in the LXX) the queen before me in my house?' 'The queen' is made to stand for 'the law'. *Paraq* or *peraq* ought perhaps to be mentioned, because of the phrase 'to cast off, tear asunder, the yoke of the kingdom of heaven'. Nehunia ben Ha-kanah (about the time of the destruction of the Temple) said that 'he who throws off the yoke of the Law, on him shall be laid the yoke of the worldly kingdom and worldly affairs'; and judges who give preferential treatment to the great are described as 'throwing off the yoke of heaven and acknowledging a king of flesh and blood'.[6]

The suppression of a message may be justified or unjustified. In the case of Jonah it was the latter. When we are warned, 'Give not that which is holy unto the dogs',[7] or not to entrust the secrets of the Law to the young,[8] or when we hear that since the bold ones became numerous the Divine Name was confided only to the discreet in the priesthood and they let it be drowned in the chant of their colleagues[9]—the suppression is from the unworthy and commendable. By contrast, misinterpretation and repudiation of the kingdom are always blameful.

[1] P.R. 161a.   [2] I Sam. 14.47.   [3] 3.4.   [4] Mish. San. 11.15.
[5] 7.8; see Tos. Ber. 5.2.
[6] Mish. Ab. 3.5 (our modern problems in a nutshell), Tos. So. 14.1.
[7] Matt. 7.6.   [8] Cant. Rabba on 1.2.   [9] Bab. Qid. 71a.

If we proceed from legitimate suppression, the Hebrew or Aramaic behind ἁρπάζω must be a word which, besides 'to seize', 'snatch', may signify 'to hold fast', 'withhold': perhaps *taqaph*, *teqaph* or *ḥasan*. If we proceed from illegitimate suppression, misinterpretation or repudiation, a verb like *ḥaṭaph* deserves consideration. In the Targum, it often represents ἁρπάζω. But it also occurs in Ezekiel's charge:[1] 'Her priests have despoiled (Hebrew *ḥameṣu*, violated, LXX ἀθετέω) my law, neither have they showed difference between the unclean and the clean, and have hid their eyes from my sabbaths.'

5. *Persecution*

The view that the saying refers to persecution of the Christian sect is supported by many familiar Rabbinic utterances where the oppression of Israel or the pious counts among the signs heralding the end. Several Hebrew and Aramaic verbs—such as *'anas*, *shadhadh*—denote 'to do violence to', 'oppress', at the same time as 'to seize by force', 'rob'. (God will not arise, says R. Phinehas ben Hama,[2] till the poor are 'oppressed' or 'robbed'.) It is conceivable, therefore, that the same verb —perhaps in different conjugations, say, Qal and Piel—underlies βιάζομαι and ἁρπάζω. If so, the original version of the saying would have been somewhat poetic, of a style not uncommon in gnomic literature.[3] The Gospel according to the Nazarenes reads διαρπάζεται instead of βιάζεται, apparently employing the same verb in both halves of the saying.

An apostate may be guilty of persecution of his former brethren as well as misinterpretation and repudiation of the true faith. *Paraṣ* or *peraṣ*, which may have preceded βιάζομαι, is comprehensive enough to express both. In a 3rd-century exposition of the Psalmist's prayer 'that there be no breaking in', *pereṣ*,[4] Ahithophel, who took part in Absalom's revolt, is paired off with Jesus, who publicly[5] disgraced the teaching he had received.

Rabbinic terms corresponding to βιασταί would be *'aneshe zero'a* and *ba'ale zero'a*. Phinehas ben Jair, towards the end of the 2nd cent., complained that 'when the Temple was destroyed, men of violence and loud tongue prevailed'.[6]

---

[1] 22.26. [2] Gen. Rabba on 32.2, with reference to Ps. 12.6.
[3] Prov. 11.7, Ecclus. 11.10, 25. [4] 144.14, Bab. Ber. 17b.
[5] This is how the Rabbis interpret the last word of the verse: 'in our streets'.
[6] Mish. So. 9.15, Bab. B.M. 118a, San. 58b. Cp. Job 22.8.

6. Political hotheads

The use of ἁρπάζω by John[1] where he speaks of the popular attempt 'to seize' Jesus in order to make him king may be invoked by those who interpret the saying as dealing with political impetuosity. Most of the Hebrew and Aramaic verbs already mentioned as equivalents of βιάζομαι and ἁρπάζω would be reconcilable with this theory. The text from Micah quoted—'The breaker is come'—would also suit it. As it contains paraṣ, it is from early Tannaitic times brought into connection with the birth of Pharez, who overtook his twin and whom the midwife addressed, 'How hast thou broken forth.'[2] Actually, in the eyes of some Rabbis, it provides evidence that the Messiah will be a descendant of Pharez. One opinion seems to distinguish between (a) a number of people breaking in or through, (b) the king, i.e. the Messiah, and (c) the Lord, i.e. God. The coupling in the saying of paraṣ, 'to break in, through' with ἁρπάζω would be far from unique. There is a proverb:[3] 'A breach attracts the thief.' However, we may repeat that the original form of the saying possibly had the same root for βιάζομαι and ἁρπάζω: 'anas, shadhadh, baraḥ, beraḥ.

7. Forcing the end

There is nothing to show whether political impetuosity is approved or deplored. Nor can we decide whether the saying is intended to praise or condemn if it should allude to a forcing of the end—which might indeed overlap with political impetuosity.

In Rabbinic writings it is frequently stressed that God, who knew exactly beforehand when he would deliver the Hebrews from Egypt, also knows the exact date of the final redemption. (The idea is implied in the section of the Passover-eve Haggadah opening: 'Blessed is he who keeps his promise to Israel.') He alone knows. It is a mystery beyond the grasp of mortals, asserts R. Nathan (end of the 2nd cent. A.D.), on the basis of a passage from Habakkuk;[4] the same passage which, in the recently discovered ancient Commentary, is taken to mean that, though God revealed to the prophet the things to come about in the last generation, he did not reveal to him 'the consummation of time'.[5] We are told that not even Elijah knows about that moment. In fact it is sinful for a man to calculate the end. Nor may he do anything to

---

[1] 6.15.   [2] Gen. Rabba on 38.29, Jerus. Targ.   [3] Bab. Suk. 26a.
[4] 2.3, Bab. San. 97b.   [5] Dupont-Somer, op. cit., p. 41.

U

hasten it, or, for that matter, to delay it. He must do his duty and wait. 'All the times of God arrive in their due seasons,' says the Commentary on Habakkuk.[1] The general formulation, 'all the times', is deliberate. In the Talmud, too, we meet with the warning that you should refrain from forcing any event, not only the ultimate deliverance.[2] The Sectarian Manual enjoins 'not to take a single step outside any of the works of God in their times, not to anticipate their times and not to be late for any of their feasts'.[3]

But the opposite attitude is also represented. Indeed we ought not to think of it as strictly separate from that just outlined. The same Rabbi, for example, might on one occasion admonish his public to submit to God's eternal design and on another to move him by repentance and good deeds. In any case we hear of saints and sages who did obtain, or try to obtain, insight into the end; of a shortening or lengthening by God of the period of waiting originally fixed; of the desirability of man's influencing by his action both his individual fate and the fate of the world. Sin may delay redemption, holiness may hasten it—though God may hasten it also freely, from mercy. Again, from a certain moment the people—or some people, like Elijah—are entitled to press forward towards the goal.

As for prayer, some Rabbis favour short prayers, others long ones and others again short or long ones according to the need of the situation. (Eliezer ben Hyrcanus, about A.D. 100, said: 'There is a time to abbreviate and a time to prolong.'[4]) Here we are interested in the power widely attributed to insistent prayer. You may 'conquer' (naṣaḥ, neṣaḥ) God by it;[5] it is almost as if you 'seized hold' (taphas, tephas) of him and did not let him go till your request was granted;[6] 'impudence' (ḥuṣpa') prevails against heaven;[7] 'the impudent' (ḥaṣipha') conquers the wicked one, how much more the Good One of the World.[8] This last-mentioned adage, incidentally, which is cited by Simeon ben Halaphta (second half of 2nd cent. A.D.), is clearly used in Luke.[9] Still, such remarks about prayer rarely have a specific application to the arrival of the Messiah. They are of a general character, valid at all times.

---

[1] P. 42.   [2] Bab. Ber. 64a.   [3] Col. 1, Dupont-Somer, p. 47.
[4] Mekh. on Exod. 15.25.   [5] P. de-R.K. 161a.
[6] Bab. Ber. 32a.   [7] Bab. San. 105a.   [8] P. de-R.K. 161a.
[9] 18.6 f. It is debatable whether the fact that these two verses are an adaptation of a proverb speaks for or against Jülicher's thesis that they did not from the outset belong to the main body of the parable, 18.1–5. I am inclined to think that it speaks against him.

Certainly, a forcing of the end would as a rule involve more than prayer, however earnest and unceasing.

This is not the place to investigate the numerous traces of the notions just sketched throughout the New Testament. Confining ourselves to the saying under discussion, we may point out that, if it refers to a forcing of the end, then, in addition to some of the verbs already listed, two deserve closer attention: *gudh* and *daḥaq* or *deḥaq*.

The former is rare. It occurs, however, in Jacob's blessing: 'Gad, a troop shall overcome, harass, him (πειρατεύω in the LXX) but he shall overcome, harass, their heel', or 'at the last'. According to the Rabbis,[1] Jacob is thinking of Elijah, a descendant of Gad, 'who shall overcome, harass, the end', or 'at the end'; and in support they adduce Malachi's assurance,[2] 'Behold, I will send Elijah, before the day of the Lord.' If, as is not unlikely, *gudh* in this Midrash implies the use of violence, it is plainly violence of a legitimate kind. From a certain date, Elijah at least is entitled to force.

Daḥaq or *deḥaq* is more important. It is used in the general warning, referred to above, against 'pushing one's hour'.[3] It recurs in the suggestion by Helbo (middle of the 4th cent.) that 'I charge you, O daughters of Jerusalem, that you stir not up my love till he please' is an adjuration by God not to force the end;[4] and further, in Joshua ben Levi's exposition of the verse from Isaiah, 'Say to them that are of a fearful heart.'[5] Joshua ascribes to *nimhar* the sense 'impetuous', 'hasty', instead of 'fearful'.[6] He infers that those who are forcing the end are meant.

What is noteworthy is that this verse introduces the prophecy of the blind who shall see and so on which, in Matthew, is declared fulfilled a few verses before the saying about violence to the kingdom. In other words, the message sent by Jesus to John is the paragraph addressed, according to Joshua, to those who force the end—only that, for Isaiah and Joshua, the signs lie in the future whereas Jesus speaks of them as now come about. It is probable, though not certain, that Joshua's intention is to discourage a forcing of the end: he tells the impatient ones that God will indubitably act at the proper time. He lived in the first half of the 3rd cent.; but he often preserves traditions of his teacher Phinehas ben Jair, a Tannaite of Essene leanings. On the other hand,

---

[1] Gen. Rabba on 49.19.   [2] 3.23.   [3] Bab. Ber. 64a.
[4] Cant. Rabba on 2.7.
[5] 35.4, Lev. Rabba on 15.25.   [6] In Hab. 1.6 it does mean 'impetuous' or 'hasty'.

as he had discussions with Jewish converts to Christianity, we must reckon with the possibility of Christian influence.

Perhaps the Old Testament passage most likely to have been in the mind of the author of the saying is that where God, immediately before the revelation at mount Sinai, though allowing Moses to ascend, twice commands that the people may not 'break through'.[1] The Hebrew has *haras*, Onkelos *peghar* (Pael), the Jerusalemite Targum *kun* (Pael), and the LXX once ἐγγίζω and once βιάζομαι. The Mekhilta equates *haras* with *dahaq*, 'to force', 'to push'. It explains that even a single person might by his over-eagerness 'impair (*ma'aṭ* in Piel) the entire community' or, according to an alternative reading, 'prevent', 'delay' ('*akhabh* in Piel)—it is not said what, but deliverance is the object to be supplied. There are numerous texts in which the Piel of '*akhabh* signifies 'to delay the exodus, redemption, from Egypt'[2] or 'to delay the final redemption'.[3] Possibly *mi'eṭ*, too, means not just 'to impair' but 'to retard the deliverance for a short time'—on the strength of Haggai's vision,[4] 'Yet once, it is a little while (*me'aṭ*), and I will shake the heavens.'

Two further points should be observed. First, the Mekhilta dwells on the distinction between different groups with different rights as regards the approach to God: Moses is in a division by himself, the priests form another, less privileged division and the rest of the people a third. Such a precedent may have been of some effect on speculations in New Testament times. Secondly, a 'breaking through' or 'forcing' in connection with the Sinaitic revelation is obviously unlawful. Yet even if the New Testament saying here discussed is inspired by this section, it would be rash to deduce that it must equally frown on impetuosity. It may well do so. But it is quite conceivable that it intends to establish a contrast with the events at mount Sinai: then a 'forcing' had been condemned, now—at the close of history—it is commendable.

8. 'The kingdom is preached' in Luke

When we go on to Luke, it seems agreed that 'the kingdom is preached' is substituted for the more obscure Matthean 'it suffereth violence' or 'it forceth its way'. The word εὐαγγελίζομαι, however,

[1] Exod. 19.21, 24.
[2] E.g. Mekh. on Exod. 13.19, in Moses's address to the dead Joseph.   [3] Bab. San. 97b.
[4] 2.6 (7). Cp. on the one hand Heb. 12.26, following the LXX, and on the other Akiba's interpretation in Bab. San. 97b.

suggests that Luke, or whoever substituted it, found in Q a connection still extant in Matthew: namely, between the saying and the message to the Baptist that the time of glad tidings had arrived. In Matthew, this message comes almost directly before the saying,[1] though in Luke it is placed many chapters previously.[2]

9. 'To press into the kingdom'

Luke's 'to press into the kingdom', εἰς αὐτὴν βιάζεται, if we treat it as translated from the Hebrew or Aramaic, may—though it need not—go back to an original which meant the same as Matthew's 'to violate the kingdom' or 'to take it by force'. Of the Hebrew and Aramaic verbs denoting 'to violate' or 'to take by force', most (such as kabhash, kebhash) can be construed with the prepositions be, le or 'al just as well as with the mere accusative. In other words, εἰς, 'into', might be due to an over-literal rendering, perhaps a rendering intentionally over-literal, designed to alter the original meaning.

10. 'Every man presseth into it'

As has long been realized, the emphasis on 'everybody' pressing into the kingdom is consistent with Luke's universalistic tendency. All the same it may derive from a less personal, conventional stock of ideas.

For one thing, the two great qualities of the Law, permanence and attractiveness for all, are eulogized side by side in earlier literature, Philo, for instance.[3] In Luke the sequence is reversed: attractiveness of the kingdom for all and permanence of the Law. But this difference is not very serious.

For another thing, we may read in the Talmud that with the approach of the Messiah 'all (gentiles) will become proselytes dragged along', 'proselytes attaching themselves by foul means like the Gibeonites when Joshua proved victorious'.[4] Eliezer ben Hyrcanus (second half of the 1st cent. A.D.) detects confirmation in Zephaniah:[5] 'Then will I turn to the people a pure language, that they may all call upon the Lord.' Most Rabbis, to be sure, think little of these last-minute converts and predict that they will desert again before the ultimate consummation.[6] Still, at

---

[1] Εὐαγγελίζομαι occurs at the end of 11.5.   [2] 7.22.
[3] Moses 2.3.14 ff.   [4] Joshua 9.   [5] 3.9, Bab. A.Z. 24a.
[6] Maybe we ought to render A.Z. 24a not 'all (gentiles) will become proselytes attaching themselves by unfair means', but 'all (proselytes coming over as late as that) will be proselytes attaching themselves by unfair means', i.e. will belong to the worthless class of bandwagon proselytes.

some moment near the end people will come in flocks to accept Judaism. The term by which they are designated, *gerurim*, is closely analogous to ἑλκόμενοι.[1] But βιαζόμενοι, or even ἁρπαζόμενοι, might do as a translation.

B. THE CONTEXT

1. *General*

It is arguable that the Matthean version of the saying reflects an earlier stage than the Lukan. On the other hand, the original context would seem to have left stronger traces in Luke than in Matthew. It is the far greater obscurity of the Lukan sequence of ideas—the bringing together of violence with the retention of the Law, for example, or of the retention of the Law with the exclusion of divorce—which tempts one to assign it priority and, indeed, to seek its roots in an ancient layer of the development crystallized in our documents. If it is a sound rule to prefer the *lectio difficilior*, we ought to apply it also to the *connexio difficilior*.

2. *Inclusiveness and lastingness*

The first impression is confirmed by closer inspection.

We have already noted that the association in Luke between the notion of 'every man pressing into the kingdom' and that of 'its being easier for heaven and earth to pass away than the law' is not altogether new. Philo writes that the Mosaic institutions will remain 'so long as sun and moon and the heaven and universe exist', but that the true marvel is that 'they attract all, barbarians, Greeks, the whole inhabited world'.

3. *Preaching the gospel and violence*

We also suggested that somehow the preaching of the gospel and the exercise of violence must have been coupled in Q. In Matthew, Jesus's message to John that the time of glad tidings has come almost immediately precedes the saying concerning violence to the kingdom. In Luke, the message is recorded in a different chapter. But the preaching of the gospel figures in the saying about violence itself. Joshua ben Levi,

---

[1] Cf. Hab. 1.15. To the ordinary New Testament instances of ἕλκω should be added οἱ ἑλκοντες ἡμᾶς in the Gospel according to the Hebrews. Unfortunately none of the reconstructions of this paragraph is more than guesswork.

we may recall, holds that Isaiah's vision of the return to God, the opening of the eyes of the blind and the unstopping of the ears of the deaf is addressed to those who would speed up the end.

4. *The advent of John and violence*

There are other points of interest.

That the law and prophets contemplated the advent of John, and that his advent is followed by violence, must have been mentioned side by side in Q. Matthew puts the reference to violence first and Luke that to the law and prophets. Moreover, Matthew speaks of 'the prophets and law', Luke of 'the law and prophets'. But these are minor differences. By 'the law', incidentally, seems to be meant the prediction in Deuteronomy[1] of a leader the peer of Moses.

The Fourth Gospel[2] apparently looks on Jesus as the prophet predicted in Deuteronomy. It is remarkable that the attempt of the people to crown him by force is recorded immediately after the identification. It looks as if here also there were a connection between the advent of this prophet and violence.

In Acts[3] the passage from Deuteronomy is quoted as applying to Jesus, and we are told that Moses—i.e. the law—and the prophets contemplated these days. There is no allusion to violence. However, as in Matthew and Luke, the period ushered in by the advent of the promised leader is provisional: in Matthew and Luke it lies between John and the future, in Acts between Jesus's death and his return.

5. *The advent of John and the Law*

In Luke, the reference to John, the preaching of the gospel and violence leads to an emphatic declaration that the Law must stand. This combination is so strange that he must have found it in his source. It is easy to understand why Matthew transferred the declaration to the sermon on the mount, at the head of the re-interpretation of some fundamental Old Testament provisions.[4] Certain vestiges of the old context may still be noticed. In the sermon on the mount, as in Luke, the declaration follows an acknowledgment of 'the law and the prophets'—though the exact import of the acknowledgment is different in the two cases. Further, in the sermon on the mount the declaration is followed by a revaluation of the conditions for smallness and greatness

---

[1] 18.15.   [2] 6.14 f.   [3] 3.22 ff.   [4] 5.18.

in the kingdom (he who breaks a single law will be the smallest, he who observes all the greatest). In Luke, a revaluation—though with a different point—comes just before the acknowledgment of the law and prophets (what enjoys esteem among men is rejected by God); and similarly the Matthean remark on violence is preceded by a revaluation —again with a different point (the least in the kingdom is greater than John). Lastly, Luke deals with an intermediate period, between John and the definitive completion of God's plan. So in the sermon on the mount the Law must stand 'till all be fulfilled'.

How are we to explain the original combination? It may well be that the identification of John with Elijah, expressly made by Matthew in connection with the saying about violence, played a part from the beginning. More precisely, it may well go back to the common tradition underlying both Matthew and Luke. Now Elijah, according to a Rabbinic view, is the prophet promised in Deuteronomy, 'like unto me, unto him ye shall hearken'.[1] In any case, we saw that both Matthew and Luke probably regard John as the prophet of Deuteronomy. But this prophet has extraordinary powers. From the clause 'unto him ye shall hearken' the Rabbis infer that he must be obeyed even if he orders a transgression of a Scriptural commandment. The Bible relates that Elijah brought a sacrifice on mount Carmel, that is to say, outside the Temple, at an illicit place.[2] According to the doctrine under notice he was entitled to do so, and he will be entitled to act contrary to the Law again when he reappears in the future. Obviously, this is a very early comment. As time went on, and as Pauline Christianity became a factor to be reckoned with, the idea of a prophet having the right to abrogate an established law was more and more disliked by the Jews. In fact, the existence of this comment on the passage from Deuteronomy is surely the principal reason why the latter is so rarely quoted in Rabbinic literature: it was too embarrassing.

We may assume, then, that in the New Testament era the introduction of John as Elijah, or as the prophet promised in Deuteronomy, would evoke the thought of an abolition of the Law, or of part of it. Hence the importance of making it clear that, for the time being at least, the Law must be respected: although Elijah, or the prophet of Deuteronomy, has come and enormous changes are taking place in consequence, yet the Law is still valid.

[1] Siph. on Deut. 18.15.   [2] I Kings 18.30 ff.

6. The Law and divorce

What have the permanence of the Law and the rejection of divorce to do with one another? Their association must be pre-Lukan: it is so abrupt.

Three explanations are feasible. First, we may fill in any gaps in the argument by drawing on the sermon on the mount. The result would be as follows: the Law stands and, indeed, ought to be kept in a fuller way than so far; thus, whereas formerly divorce was recognized provided the wife was given a bill, from now it will have no legal effect at all.

No doubt this is the simplest answer, and modern scholars are perhaps rightly satisfied with it.[1] We confess to grave misgivings. Why is nothing said in Luke about a 'fulfilment', a greater perfection, of the Law? If the evangelist had reasons for suppressing this aspect, would he not have replaced it by something else to smooth the transition from the statement about the Law to that about divorce? Why, of all the examples of 'fulfilment' enumerated in the sermon on the mount, should Luke—or Q—contain just divorce? Is it methodically proper to transfer from the sermon on the mount to Luke an argument of a very peculiar nature?

Another tenable explanation is this. From long before New Testament times it was expected that Elijah, when returning to proclaim the Messianic age, would concern himself with the purity of the nation. He would make known who were descended from legitimate unions and who from illegitimate ones; and he would restore to the nation families removed by force, zero'a,[2] and remove from it families introduced by force.[3] The saying about violence may proceed from this tradition, its meaning being—or having once been—that, paradoxically, since the days of John, i.e. Elijah come back, the influx into Israel of such as use force is greater than ever. Yet (thus the argument may run) the Law will ultimately triumph. Above all, the purity of the nation will not be neglected. Therefore, it is essential to heed the prohibition of adultery, and especially the stricter prohibition imposed on the new sect.

---

[1] E.g. Creed, op. cit., p. 206.

[2] Above, under A5, we remarked that βιασταί might represent 'aneshe zero'a or ba'ale zero'a.

[3] Mish. Ed. 8.7, Bab. Qid. 70a f. From the Mishnah it is evident that by the time of Johanan ben Zaccai, who lived during the destruction of the Temple, this tradition was of long standing.

However, this line is too far-fetched to carry conviction. We incline to a different solution.

The sanctity of every jot of the Law and the condemnation of polygamy are intimately linked in the teaching of heterodox Jewish groups of the New Testament epoch, a teaching which, in a modified shape, was adopted by leading Tannaites.

Let us begin with Simeon ben Johai's story (about the middle of the 2nd cent. A.D.) of the Book of Deuteronomy, which went up to heaven to charge Solomon with annulling a *yodh* in the precepts respecting the king. Instead of *l' yrbh* (with vowels *lo' yarbe*), 'he shall not multiply wives to himself',[1] this ruler—the Book of Deuteronomy pleaded—read *l'rbh* (*le'arbe*), 'to a multitude of wives for himself'. Such a cancellation of a *yodh* in a way amounted to a cancellation of the entire Law. God, however, assured the complainant: 'Solomon and a thousand like him will perish, but a word of thee will not perish.'[2]

In addition to the obvious points of contact with Luke, there are quite a few which, while less obvious, are equally relevant. As regards formulation, the pronouncement 'Solomon and a thousand such' and so on is fairly close to 'It is easier for heaven and earth to pass' and so on. It is closer to it than to the Matthean 'Till heaven and earth shall pass, one jot or tittle shall in no wise pass from the law.' Matthew has a straightforward, temporal clause; he does not compare a higher and a lower degree of durability. Again, though it is the *yodh* which accuses Solomon, several versions represent God as replying that not 'a tittle', a *qoṣe*, will be dropped. Matthew mentions both 'jot' and 'tittle', Luke the latter only—no doubt because his public would be puzzled by the former.

As regards substance, it would be wrong to treat Simeon's story as an isolated, fanciful speculation about Solomon. This Rabbi was a strong opponent of divorce as well as polygamy. He could not, without cutting himself off from orthodox Judaism, declare the institutions illegal. But even in a case where a couple remained childless he was in favour neither of divorce nor of the husband's taking an additional wife.[3] Moreover, he accepted the view that the union between husband and wife made them into one being, and he actually contended that this mystery was hinted at in the Deuteronomic regulation of divorce—a very bold method of combating divorce. The opening words of that

---

[1] Deut. 17.17.   [2] Pal. San. 20c, Exod. Rabba on 6.2.   [3] Cant. Rabba on 1.4.

regulation, he claimed, 'When a man taketh a wife', referred to the man's seeking the portion of his body he had lost.[1] It should also be remembered that, while according to other Rabbis none but the children of kings might use rose-oil to anoint a wound on a Sabbath, Simeon permitted it generally, on the ground that 'all Israelites are children of kings'.[2] The same argument would lead him to consider as generally binding the law that 'the king shall not multiply wives to himself'.

In the Zadokite Fragments, in the section directed against polygamy, and almost certainly against remarriage after divorce,[3] the Scriptural texts adduced are 'Male and female created he them', 'There went in two and two into the ark' and—'He shall not multiply wives to himself.' Moreover, we learn that David did not consult the Book of the Law, hence his transgressions of this prohibition. But the latter is treated as obligatory on any pious person, not only the king—maybe from the consideration, which is propounded in another part of the Fragments, that 'the king' means 'the congregation'.[4]

At any rate, it is clear that the rule 'He shall not multiply wives to himself' was used in the struggle to ban polygamy and divorce before Simeon ben Johai. The idea that the rule had suffered neglect, and that this neglect in a sense affected the entire Law, also evidently antedates him: David, who was polygamous, is said to have been altogether ignorant of the Law. It would not be surprising if the emphasis on the role of the *yodh* in the field of divorce belonged to the same ancient stratum. Simeon ben Johai's achievement lay in giving the traditional material dramatic expression, in personifying the *yodh*, in representing it as an accuser, and so on.

Luke's statement about divorce implies a condemnation of polygamy; otherwise a second marriage by the husband could never be adultery. In fact it is based on the assumption of husband and wife becoming one indissoluble being. This statement is preceded by the declaration that the universe will cease to exist rather than a particle of the Law. Most probably we have before us a connection similar to that in the Zadokite Fragments and Simeon's story—between the sanctity of the precept 'He shall not multiply wives to himself', or rather, the *yodh* in it, and the rejection of polygamy and divorce.

May we go even further? The commandment 'He shall not multiply wives' is in strictness meant for the king only. Yet the Zadokites,

---

[1] Deut. 24.1, Bab. Qid. 2b.   [2] Mish. Shab 14.4.   [3] 7.1 ff.   [4] 9.7.

Simeon ben Johai and—if we are right—Q ascribe to it universal validity. As we saw, Simeon thought of all Israelites as children of kings; and the Zadokite reasoning may well have been identical. Possibly, in Q or prior to Q, the reference to the commandment in question was deliberately introduced after the proclamation of the approaching kingdom—it does not here matter whether the kingdom was represented as victorious or suffering. The new community are all children of a king and must conduct themselves as such.

7. Conclusion

To sum up, it must be admitted that, both in Matthew and Luke, the saying concerning violence to the kingdom with the area surrounding it is a *Trümmerfeld*, a heap of ruins; which indicates that there was here matter the Church preferred to omit. Any suggestion as to the original structure is bound to be conjectural. With all due reservation, something like the following line of thought appears likely:

John is Elijah and the prophet promised in Deuteronomy. Miracles are performed (by Jesus), the gospel is being preached, the age foretold in the Scriptures is dawning. The old values are changing; what was great will be small and the small will be great. At this transitional stage however, much violence is still done to the kingdom. Yet nothing has occurred that would cancel the duty to go on observing the Law, which attracts everybody and will endure longer than this world endures. John, whatever his powers may be, has not abrogated the Law. The faithful will not disregard even the *yodh* in the precept 'He shall not multiply wives to himself.' It is a precept for royalty, but the true members of the kingdom will cherish it the more on this account. Man and woman by sexual union return to, or re-approach, the ideal androgynous state. A husband remarrying after divorce, or a man marrying a divorced wife, commits adultery.

VIII

Disgrace

A. 'Niwwul'

THE term *niwwul* and other words from the same root are used in various interesting senses by the Tannaites. Like αἰσχύνη or ἀτιμία, they may signify 'disgrace' in general. Since the judges took to accepting bribes, the Rabbis complain, vulgar people were raised and exalted ones degraded, so that the government 'fell into contempt'.[1] Paul says: 'Ye are honourable, we are despised'; 'we minister by honour and dishonour'; 'hath not the potter power to make one vessel unto honour, and another unto dishonour?' And he contrasts 'less honourable' or 'shameful' parts of the body with others.[2] Again, an unchaste woman is called 'dishonoured' in the Talmud, and indeed considered as 'dishonouring' all her sex; idols are described as 'disgraceful'; and in figurative speech, 'the disgraceful one' may stand for the evil inclination, the tempter.[3] So Paul speaks of men's 'vile affections' by which they 'dishonour their bodies'.[4]

It is far from certain that Paul in these texts thinks of *niwwul*. There are other Hebrew and Aramaic words with a similar meaning, for example *bizzayon*. He may not be influenced by Hebrew or Aramaic at all. What is clear, however, is that αἰσχύνη, ἀτιμία, and *niwwul* are roughly synonymous.

Frequently *niwwul* refers to disgrace attaching to a person's appearance. A man letting the hair grow too long, or a woman shaving it off, is termed 'undignified'; while a woman who, suspected of adultery, must undergo the ordeal of the bitter water, 'is rendered despicable' by

---

[1] Bab. So. 47b.
[2] I Cor. 4.10, II Cor. 6.8, Rom. 9.21 (cp. II Tim. 2.20), I Cor. 12.23.
[3] Tos. So. 2.3, Siph. on Deut. 22.21 (with reference to the Scriptural *nebhala*, 'folly' or 'outrage'), Cant. Rabba on 1.9, Bab. Qid. 30b.
[4] Rom. 1.24 ff.

having her head uncovered, her hair loosened and so on.[1] In the latter case, needless to say, the disgrace is brought about not only by the appearance as such—the uncovered head, the dishevelment—but also by the circumstances, the fact that it had to come to a trial of this kind. Moral disgrace and physical disgrace are here not strictly distinguished. Paul says that 'every man praying, having his head covered, dishonoureth his head, but every woman that prayeth with her head covered honoureth her head', and again, 'if a man have long hair, it is a shame unto him, but if a woman have long hair, it is a glory to her'.[2] The passage quoted above, where he condemns those who, by giving in to 'vile affections dishonour their bodies', furnishes an example of moral disgrace involving physical disgrace.

The desecration of a corpse also constitutes *niwwul*. Under Rabbinic law, if the validity of transactions into which a person entered shortly before his death depends on whether or not he had attained maturity, it is none the less forbidden to exhume and strip the corpse and perform an autopsy: that would be *niwwul*. For the same reason, if a man is killed by another, you may not examine the body in order to see whether there might have been a fatal disease which would in any case have resulted in death at the moment of the murder.[3] Mark tells us that one of the servants sent out by the owner of a vineyard to receive the fruits from the lessees was 'dishonoured' by them. The meaning may be that they showed disrespect by beating him, or that they ill-treated him in a manner producing disfigurement, or that they stoned him to death and desecrated the body. It should be noted that according to Mark (here again Matthew and Luke differ) the owner's son was killed and his body thrown out of the vineyard. Evidently they left him unburied, a flagrant case of *niwwul*—whether or not the author of the pericope has in mind the actual term.[4]

Perhaps the gravest kind of *niwwul* is that disfigurement of a person, alive or dead, which may have an adverse affect on resurrection. In New Testament times it was widely—though by no means universally —held that the dead would rise in the shape in which they were buried. God might subsequently heal any wounds, abolish any flaws; but to

---

[1] Pal. M.Q. 81c, Num. Rabba on 16.6, Siph. on Deut. 21.12, Bab. Yeb. 48a, Bab. So. 8b (cp. Num. 5.18).
[2] I Cor. 11.4 ff.
[3] Bab. B.B. 154a f., Hul. 11b.
[4] Mark 12.4 ff., Matt. 21.35 ff., Luke 20.11 ff.

begin with, the original figures would reappear.[1] Moreover, in popular belief at least, the bones played a particular part: a person whose skeleton was damaged might not be able to rise at all. The curse 'may his bones be ground' must be understood on this basis,[2] maybe also the death of Judas according to Acts—by 'bursting asunder'.[3] Again, death by the sword 'disgraces', whereas death from hunger does not.[4]

Of course, most Rabbis stood above such superstitions. For them, God simply had the power to bring the dead back to life. In fact, a man, precisely by dying a 'disgraceful' death, by being tortured, beheaded, left unburied, might contribute to the wiping out of sins committed by himself or others; and if he suffered martyrdom for the sake of God, the reward would be all the greater.[5] Still, the problem was not easy. We come across compromise solutions, such as that by Joshua ben Hananiah—about A.D. 100—who held that a tiny part of the spine was indestructible and would be used by God for raising the dead.[6] Paul felt it necessary to explain to the Corinthian community how 'it is sown in dishonour, and raised in glory'.[7] The analogy of the grain has long been recognized as Rabbinic.[8] The allusion to the disfigurement of a decaying corpse suggests that the addressees were worried by some of the popular ideas just indicated.

B. Criminal Law

In criminal procedure, niwwul might on occasion be not only admissible but even enjoined. We have already mentioned the woman suspected of adultery who, in the course of the ordeal of the bitter water, suffers the disgrace of having her head uncovered by the priest and so forth. Another notable instance is the burial of executed criminals in a plot kept by the court, without the usual ceremonies—or as Josephus puts it, 'dishonourably, by night'.[9]

---

[1] Apoc. Bar. 50.1 ff., Gen. Rabba on 46.28. Cp. Constance's speech in *King John*, after her son's arrest: 'Oh father Cardinal, I have heard you say That we shall see and know our friends in heav'n. If that be, I shall see my boy again. But now will canker-sorrow eat my bud, And he will look as hollow as a ghost, And so he'll die; and rising so again, When I shall meet him in the court of heav'n, I shall not know him.' For a different view see e.g. Gen. Rabba on 2.7.

[2] Gen. Rabba on 32.26, Lev. Rabba on 19.23; cp. Dan. 6.25.
[3] 1.18.   [4] Bab. B.B. 8b.
[5] II Macc. 12.43 f., 7.10 f., Gen. Rabba on 2.7, Siph. on Num. 15.31, Bab. Ber. 61b.
[6] Lev. Rabba on 15.1.   [7] I Cor. 15.43.   [8] Strack-B., vol. 3, 1926, p. 475.
[9] Mish. San. 6.5 f., Ant. 4.8.6.202, 4.8.24.264, 5.1.14.44.

Certain forms of capital punishment dating from the pre-Christian era would involve a disfigurement serious enough to create difficulties for the early believers in resurrection. The Old Testament, when it imposes stoning, means the putting to death of a criminal by hurling stones at him. Yet if this is done, he is bound to suffer fractures, some of them very visible. Similarly, where the burning of a criminal is ordained, if the precept is really followed, the body will be turned into ashes.

Regarding a murderer, the Old Testament demands that he should be killed. No doubt for a long time, whoever was charged with carrying out the penalty—mostly the nearest relation of the person murdered —slew the offender as best he could. As the court undertook the task, maybe there were groups in favour of precise talion: the murderer ought, as far as possible, to be despatched in the fashion in which he had despatched the victim. But there is no proof that this system was ever advocated. Those scholars who think it was normally rely on passages from the Book of Jubilees, II Maccabees and Philo. But in Jubilees and II Maccabees it is God who inflicts retaliation.[1] (Charles[2] also adduces a passage[3] where we learn that Nicanor's head, and his hand 'which he had stretched out against the house of the Almighty', are shown to the people. This, however, is not talion at all. It is punishment of the member through which the sin was perpetrated, 'mirroring' punishment.) As for Philo, he observes[4] that a murderer must suffer the same as he whom he murdered. This need not refer to the manner of execution. It probably means nothing but that the murderer, having killed, is to be killed in his turn. Another custom is much better evidenced: it seems to have been usual at one time to execute a murderer by means of an axe, that is to say, exactly as, according to a section in Deuteronomy, if a murderer remains undetected, a heifer is to be slaughtered in expiation of the deed.[5] However, whether the murdered person's relation kills the culprit as best he can, whether exact talion is inflicted, or whether the axe is used—damage to the murderer's bones must almost invariably result.

Between about 100 B.C. and A.D. 100 a far-reaching reform of the

---

[1] Jubilees 4.32, II Macc. 5.10.
[2] In commenting on Jubilees 4.31 f. (*Apocrypha and Pseudepigrapha of the Old Testament*, vol. 2, 1913, p. 19).
[3] II Macc. 15.32.   [4] Leg. Spec. 3.15.84, 3.19.106.
[5] Mish. San. 7.3, Tos. San. 9.11, Mekh. on Exod. 21.12, Bab. San. 52b, cp. Deut. 21.1 ff.

modes of execution was effected by the Pharisees.[1] First, stoning, they decided, was to be performed, not by pelting the criminal to death, but by pushing him down from a moderate height; if this did not suffice, one stone was to be dropped on his heart; and only if he stayed alive even then, stoning proper was to take place. This reformed mode of stoning—which appears, for example, in the story of Susanna as given by the LXX[2]—is obviously designed to avoid a breaking of the skull, chest, legs and so on. Secondly, burning, in the Pharisaic opinion, was to be performed, not by burning the criminal at the stake, but by forcing material set on fire down his throat. This, too, will exclude any destruction of the skeleton. Thirdly, wherever the Bible did not specify the form of execution, the Pharisees insisted on strangling 'by a towel of coarse stuff within one of soft stuff':[3] in this case no mark whatever will be left on the body.

Decapitation of a murderer remained even in the reformed Pharisaic code. The axe was replaced by the sword; which entailed the further change that, whereas formerly the person condemned was stretched out face downwards, with his head resting on a block, and the blow fell from behind, now he knelt, with his head inclined backwards, and the blow came from the front. A few Rabbis took exception to the introduction of the sword, regarding it as a 'disgraceful' Roman method. But the majority considered the ancient procedure, where the murderer was treated like the heifer from Deuteronomy, to be 'the most disgraceful way of all'.[4]

We need not here inquire why, in the case of murder, the disfiguring punishment was retained. Let us note, however, that there are traces of attempts—unsuccessful attempts—to extend the reform even to this field. It looks as if certain Rabbis had suggested the substitution of strangulation for decapitation; and as if others had made use of the verse 'Whoso sheddeth man's blood, by man shall his blood be shed',[5] and argued that a murderer should not be beheaded but be bled to death—his skeleton thus remaining intact.[6] As they stand in the Midrash, these views sound purely academic. But, as pointed out above, in Part II, under 'Ye have heard but I say unto you', many points which, in the Rabbinic discussions preserved to us, appear to be made only for

---

[1] For references see A. Büchler, *Monatsschrift für Geschichte und Wissenschaft des Judentums*, vol. 50, pp. 550 ff., 683 ff., and 704 ff.   [2] 62.   [3] Mish. San. 7.3.
[4] Mish. San. 7.3.   [5] Gen. 9.6.   [6] Mekh. on Exod. 21.12.

x

argument's sake were once seriously maintained by one school or another.

Now we must not conceive of the reform of the Pharisees as a single effort, with no antecedents or vacillations and devoted to one purpose only. Two at least of the modes of execution which they favoured are very ancient indeed, though not figuring among those prescribed by the Old Testament: the pushing down of a criminal from a height, by which they replaced stoning, and strangulation, which they applied where no other mode was specified in the Bible.

Further, it seems that the original method of stoning—pelting a person to death—was on occasion resorted to even in New Testament times.[1] It would naturally happen where there was an element of lynching. Josephus tells us[2] how he feared being stoned by the mob. (As we know from Luke,[3] even lynching might take the form of hurling from a rock.) But it might also occur by way of an official execution—though perhaps only if the court was under the direction of Sadducees.[4]

Again, there were influential Pharisaic groups who considered it more important that a man sentenced to death should suffer as little as possible than that his skeleton should be preserved. From their standpoint, some of the changes we have outlined were far from commendable; and decapitation, for instance, would be a less severe mode of execution than strangulation.[5] ('O Ping Siang, select the most agreeable manner and weapon for your end—By your side this person perceives a sword, his only request is that the blow shall be a sufficiently well-directed one.'[6]) In other words, we must reckon with Sadducean opposition, with a good deal of wavering among the Pharisees, with local differences and so on.

Lastly, strangulation may have been given preference over other modes not only because it left the body intact, but also because it required little machinery and ceremony. It was, therefore, suitable even in periods when, in principle, the Romans alone exercised capital jurisdiction. Origen's remark[7] that Jewish courts inflict the death

---

[1] We need only refer to passages like John 8.1 ff., 8.59, 10.31 ff., Acts 7.56 ff., Josephus, Ant. 4.8.23.248, 20.9.1.199 f.
[2] Life 13.76.   [3] 4.29.   [4] Cp. Josephus, Ant., *loc. cit.*
[5] Mish. San. 7.1, Tos. San. 9.11. Cp. Tertullian, Apol. 9.7, 'ferro enim mori optaverit'.
[6] E. Bramah, 'The Vengeance of Tung Fel' (in *The Wallet of Kai Lung*).
[7] Ad Africanum 14.

penalty 'neither quite openly nor keeping it secret from the government' is significant. So is the fact that adultery, which according to the Old Testament as well as the early Tannaites was as a rule punishable by stoning ('He that is without sin, let him first cast a stone at her'),[1] from the 1st cent. A.D. gradually became punishable by strangulation. Origen tells us[2] that a Jewish court 'homicidam punire non potest nec adulteram lapidare, haec enim sibi vindicat Romanorum potentia'. In the case of murder, where the Pharisees retained beheading, the Roman intervention created no great problem: a murderer would be beheaded by the Romans, instead of by the Jews. In the case of adultery, however, the Romans in the first few centuries A.D. would only rarely inflict the death penalty; on the other hand, they did not allow the Jews to stone the guilty parties. This may well have been an additional motive for substituting strangulation, a punishment attracting less notice.

Nevertheless, when all necessary reservations are made, it remains true that between about 100 B.C. and A.D. 100 the Pharisees carried through a radical reform of the traditional modes of execution; a reform so radical that it would be inexplicable but against the background of a momentous religious movement. It was the movement which stressed the bodily resurrection of the dead.

We have already pointed out that, for most Rabbis, God's power to raise a man from the dead did not depend on the integrity of the skeleton. Even the opinion that the dead would in the first instance come to life in the form they had possessed when last on earth was never shared by all. Why, then, did the majority support the reform in question? Principally, we may assume, in order to strengthen the belief in physical resurrection among the masses: the masses would accept the dogma more readily if the religious leaders did everything to emphasize the importance of the body, everything to save the most durable parts, the bones, from destruction. This seems to be the object also of the warning against dissection in the Pseudo-Phocylidean poem: 'not to break up the structure of a human body, because we hope the

---

[1] John 8.7. Strack-B., vol. 2, 1924, p. 520, claim that the woman can have been engaged only, not married, since in the Rabbinic sources an adulterous married woman is liable to strangulation. But these sources reflect an innovation not yet universally recognized when the episode recorded in John took place or was written down. Ezek. 16.40 refers to stoning; and similarly, according to the LXX, Susanna, had she not been saved by Daniel, would have been stoned (v. 62)—though in the reformed, Pharisaic manner, i.e. she would have been pushed from a height.

[2] In his commentary on Romans, according to Rufinus's version, l.6. c.7.

remains of the departed will again come forth from the earth'.[1] The hostility to cremation shown up to our day by orthodox Judaism[2] and several branches of Christianity offers something of a parallel.

C. THE CRUCIFIXION

It has recently been argued that it was not the suffering of Jesus as such, but the abject form it took, which the Jewish antagonists found 'scandalous'.[3] Certainly, about A.D. 130, R. Ishmael, when facing martyrdom, is said to have exclaimed: 'Do I weep because we are to be slain? No, but because we are to be slain like murderers and desecrators of the Sabbath.'[4] The Jew Tryphon is represented by Justin as remarking on the 'disgraceful' death of Jesus.[5]

Be this as it may, John at least is concerned to deny that Jesus underwent a particular kind of *niwwul*, namely, that disfigurement which—in popular thought—might stand in the way of resurrection. He records that Jesus's legs were not broken.[6] He also informs us that it was the Jews who, since they wanted the bodies taken down before the Sabbath, proposed the breaking of the legs. This suggests that the anti-Christian party used the disfigurement as an argument against the resurrection of Jesus. John is warding off an attack, he asserts that things did not happen as his opponents imagine and wish them to have happened. That is also why he adds so emphatically that it is his version which gives the truth. It may indeed be one of his motives (though one can think of others which are perfectly adequate) for omitting the institution of the Eucharist: hostile readers might misinterpret the breaking of the bread as hinting at a breaking of Jesus's body. No direct mention of a breaking of bread is made in chapter 6, where there is a discourse about the significance of the Eucharist;[7] and though in chapter 2 the phrase 'to destroy the Temple' is explained as referring to the destruction of Jesus's body,[8] the expression λύω, 'to destroy', 'to undo', is too general to be suggestive of a breaking of bones.

It should be recalled that John insists more strongly than even Luke on the appearance of the risen Jesus in the precise form he had when last alive. In Luke, Jesus says: 'Behold my hands and feet, handle me and see.' Neither of the two other Synoptics mentions this. John, how-

---

[1] 101 ff.   [2] Tacitus was angry about it with the Judaism of his time: Hist. 5.5.
[3] I Cor. 1.23, Gal. 5.11; see W. D. Davies, *Paul and Rabbinic Judaism*, pp. 283 f.
[4] Sem. 8.   [5] Dial. 32, 89.   [6] 19.31 ff.   [7] V. 48 ff.   [8] V. 19 ff.

ever, in addition to an analogous passage, has the detailed narrative about Thomas.[1] Incidentally, ideas concerning resurrection may well play a similar part in the Martyrdom of Polycarp.[2] The Jews, we are told, were very keen on burning him, but as the fire refused to kill him, an executioner had to stab him to death. Thereupon the Jews interceded with the magistrate not to give up the corpse to the martyr's friends, and the corpse was burned. Yet even now the bones remained and were gathered by the faithful.

According to John, Jesus's body remained intact 'that the scripture should be fulfilled, A bone of him shall not be broken'. A number of modern critics hold that the reference to the Passover lamb came first, and the story of how a breaking of the legs was avoided second. John, they maintain, wrote the story in order to assimilate Jesus to the lamb. But surely, this purpose could have been achieved in a less complicated manner. From the foregoing discussion it is clear that priority belongs to the story: it was essential to rule out *niwwul* in the sense of destruction of the bones. The reference to the Passover lamb is added by way of interpretation. Nor was the quotation inappropriate. When we consider that a verse like 'The Lord keepeth all the bones of the righteous, not one of them is broken'[3] occurs in an ancient Jewish prayer for the dead, or that Ezekiel's vision of the revival of the dried up bones[4] forms the prophetic lesson on the mid-festival Sabbath of Passover, it appears probable that, even before John, the inviolability of the bones of the Passover lamb was widely regarded as symbolizing the individual's hope of resurrection as well as the nation's of a glorious future.

John's exclusion of a disfiguring *niwwul* is adumbrated in Matthew and Luke. Mark speaks of Jesus's dead body as πτῶμα, which, as has long been seen, is more primitive than σῶμα, employed by Matthew, Luke and John.[5] The usual explanation of the change is that σῶμα was found more respectful in a general way than πτῶμα. There may indeed be some truth in this. But the main factor must have been the consideration that πτῶμα was particularly suitable for describing a mutilated corpse, and thus a corpse mutilated in the course of an execution. (The word corresponds to *pegher* in Hebrew, *peghar* or *pigra'* in Aramaic.

[1] Luke 24.39, John 20.20 (cp. I John 1.1), 20.24 ff.
[2] 13 ff.   [3] Ps. 34.21.   [4] 37.1 ff.
[5] Mark 15.43, 45, Matt. 27.58, Luke 23.52, John 19.38, 40. Even in Mark 15.43 σῶμα has ousted πτῶμα in a number of MSS.

Isaiah says:[1] 'But thou art cast out of thy grave like an abominable branch, and as the raiment of them that are slain, thrust through with a sword, that go down to the pit, as a carcase trodden under feet.' 'Carcase' represents *pegher* in the Hebrew, *peghar* in the Targum.) In the New Testament itself πτῶμα occurs where the beheaded Baptist is buried.[2] As applied to Jesus, there was danger of the term suggesting that his legs were crushed. But it is John alone who expressly denies this *niwwul*, by giving a circumstantial account of how it was avoided.

D. JESUS'S GRAVE

As stated above, Rabbinic law contained provisions respecting the burial of a person who had been executed. While nothing was to be done that might impede resurrection, most of the customary ceremonies in honour of the deceased must be omitted. One rule which involved 'disgrace' was that executed persons might not at once be buried in the family grave. The court kept two plots for their provisional burial by relatives or officials. It was only after a year or so that the bones were gathered and transferred to the family burying place.

Quite possibly this was another—though less serious—allegation of *niwwul* made by the anti-Christian party: the burial of Jesus in one of the public plots. To be sure, even if he was buried there, his followers could have argued that it constituted part of his suffering for the sake of the Kingdom. They could have referred to as early a case as that of the true prophet whom Jehoiakim 'slew with the sword and cast his dead body into the graves of the common people', or to the prophecy about the servant of the Lord, whose 'grave was made with the wicked'.[3] But the enemies would have disagreed with this interpretation. At any rate, the gospels reveal an inclination in some Christian circles to deny the existence of this *niwwul*.

According to Mark, Jesus was buried in 'a sepulchre'—which may mean any grave, even a public one for criminals; it clearly does not mean the grave of Jesus's family. According to Luke, however, he was buried in 'a sepulchre wherein never man before was laid'. John concurs; indeed he adds the attribute 'new', it was 'a new sepulchre'.

---

[1] 14.19.
[2] Matt. 14.12, Mark 6.29. In Matthew the Koine reading is σῶμα, clearly secondary.
[3] Jer. 26.20 ff., Isa. 53.9.

Luke and John intend to rule out burial in a grave previously used for other executed persons. They do not say that the grave did not belong to the court—John's remark that it was near the place of crucifixion might be taken as an indication that it did—but they do say that it had never been desecrated by the corpse of a sinner. Matthew states that it was the family grave of Joseph of Arimathaea, newly built. That is to say, it was definitely not a public one, nor had it ever been used either for sinner or for saint.[1]

The accounts are not necessarily contradictory as far as historical events are concerned. It is possible that Mark, Luke and John no less than Matthew are thinking of Joseph's family grave; and there are other ways of reconciling the facts related by the evangelists. (Incidentally, as Jesus was executed by the Romans, it is doubtful whether, under the Jewish law of the time, he ought to have been buried in a plot for criminals. The question is complicated by his having been found guilty of blasphemy by the Sanhedrin.) For our purpose it suffices to bring out the concern of three at least of the four definitely to mitigate or exclude 'disgrace'.

In the Tosephta[2] it is laid down that 'even if the criminal were a king of kings, he may not be buried in the grave of his fathers, but only in that prepared by the court'. The term 'king of kings' designates the king of the Persians, the Roman emperor or the like. Its use here seems to be figurative, since a Jewish court was never likely to pronounce sentence of death on a foreign ruler of such rank. Probably the provision simply means that, however highly placed, a criminal executed must suffer the 'disgrace' of a criminal's burial. It is, however, conceivable that the rule contains an anti-Christian point. The hyperbole may have been introduced in order to show that Jesus could not have escaped being buried in a public grave. The paragraph under discussion ends by quoting a verse from Psalms: 'Gather not my soul with sinners.'[3] According to the Tosephta, David here implores God not to be buried as a criminal.

E. JESUS'S BURIAL CLOTHES

Normally, in New Testament times, funerals were conducted with great luxury, and even the poorest felt obliged to bury relatives or friends in valuable burial clothes. It was Gamaliel II, about A.D. 90, who,

---

[1] Mark 15.46, Luke 23.53, John 19.41, Matt. 27.60.   [2] San. 9.8.   [3] 26.9.

in order to relieve poor people of this burden, had himself buried in a plain linen cloth.[1] Before that reform, a plain cloth chosen without care would be used only for a criminal or at best a person despised by everyone. It would be a sign of shame.

It is interesting, then, that whereas according to Luke and John, Jesus was wrapped in 'a linen cloth', Matthew and Mark make it clear— in different ways—that it was a new cloth.[2] The historicity of the latter view need not be doubted. But the presumption is that Luke and John are closer to the original tradition. The emphasis on the freshness of the cloth which we find in Matthew and Mark springs from the desire to eliminate any suggestion of *niwwul* marking the burial.

The presumption is confirmed by the manner in which Matthew and Mark refer to the quality of Jesus's burial clothes, a manner which proves these references to be intrusions into the earlier account. Mark tells us that Joseph of Arimathaea, having obtained permission to bury Jesus, 'bought a linen cloth'—the implication being that he did not just use any cloth that was to hand. But this buying of cloth on the first day of Passover—and for Mark at least that was the date—constitutes an old crux. Jewish law forbade buying on a festival day. Some modern authorities indeed argue that the Greek of Mark may be due to a mistranslation of an Aramaic word which did not signify 'to buy'.[3] But we need not accept this counsel of despair. The most likely solution is that Mark, or his source, when introducing the point as to the quality of the burial clothes, went too far and, by some oversight, spoke of a purchase on the first day of Passover.

Matthew seems to have noticed the difficulty. He omits the purchase, and simply makes 'a clean linen cloth' of the 'linen cloth' to be found in the other evangelists. The effect as regards the problem of *niwwul* is the same as in Mark: there was no 'disgrace'. But the transgression of the rules about the observance of festival days is avoided.

F. The Anointing at Bethany

Preoccupation with the question of *niwwul* may well have been a major factor in the growth of the narrative of the anointing at Bethany. In

---

[1] Bab. Ket. 8b. Tacitus, Hist. 5.5, remarks on the care bestowed by the Jews on the bodies of the dead.
[2] Luke 23.53, John 19.40, Matt. 27.59, Mark 15.46.
[3] E.g. Strack-B., vol. 2, 1924, p. 833.

other words, the different versions[1] seem to reflect so many different explanations of the treatment of Jesus's body at the time of his burial.

1. *Mark and John: the main distinction*

The fundamental difference between Mark and John is that in Mark the woman anticipates, i.e. here and now performs, the burial rite of anointing, whereas in John she does not. In Mark, Jesus says of her that 'she is come aforehand to anoint my body to the burial'. The import of this ought not to be watered down: her act is boldly declared a valid, though proleptic, anointing of the body for burial. Jurists would call the statement a legal fiction, an authoritative interpretation of facts as something which, but for that interpretation, they would not be. On the basis of the interpretation in Mark, the burial rite of anointing has now taken place. The sources show that the Rabbis were quite familiar with acts of this sort—acts with immediate legal or religious effect though, in reality, an essential element is still to come. (The equivalent of προλαμβάνειν in the relevant texts is *qadham* or *hiqdim*. You can reward a service in advance; a *prosbul* made out in anticipation of a loan to be given is valid; if I send you a gift in order that you should make me a loan, this is interest paid in advance and therefore prohibited.[2])

In contradistinction, in John, if we accept—as we must[3]—the reading 'let her alone, that she may keep it against the day of my burial', no such fiction is established. No assertion is made that a burial ceremony has been performed, but the burial is thought of, quite naturally, as entirely belonging to the future. It is relevant to notice that Jesus speaks, not as in Mark of 'the burial', which may in a sense be celebrated now, but of 'the day of the burial'—a reference to a distinct point in time, a future date.

To understand the difference, it is necessary to consider the treatment which the two evangelists assume Jesus's body received after his death. According to Mark, who has a burial ceremony by way of anticipation, Joseph of Arimathaea did not anoint the body, and the women who intended to do so came too late. According to John, who has no burial ceremony by way of anticipation, Joseph and Nicodemus anointed the

---

[1] Matt. 26.6 ff., Mark 14.3 ff., Luke 7.36 ff., John 12.1 ff.
[2] Pal. So. 22d, Mish. Sheb. 10.5, B.M. 5.10.
[3] The Koine reading τετήρηκεν is an assimilation to Matthew and Mark.

body with a hundred pounds of spices.[1] The position cannot be the result of a series of coincidences. Both Mark and John take care to point out that the burial rite of anointing was performed. For Mark, it was performed at Bethany—by virtue of a fiction—and nothing was done after Jesus's death. For John, Jesus's body was actually anointed after his death, and the action at Bethany is not represented as performance of the rite.

Very probably, the earliest tradition was that Jesus had been buried unanointed, like a common criminal, 'dishonourably, by night'.[2] This tradition was unbearable to the believers. We have already remarked on the luxury practised in that period even by the poorest when it came to burying a relative or friend. Moreover, the Jewish unbelievers doubtless seized on this additional *niwwul*, as a confirmation of the 'scandal' of the crucifixion. If it was the form of Jesus's suffering rather than his suffering as such which constituted the 'scandal', the omission of anointing would be an integral part of the charge. Mark gives one reply: Jesus's body was anointed in advance. John gives another: his body was anointed by Joseph and Nicodemus.

This does not imply that John's report is historically worthless. John may have had access to information which Mark lacked. It would be far from surprising since, if his report is true, it is to be supposed that Joseph and Nicodemus did everything to avoid publicity. Nor would it be right to deny that the way Mark understood the incident at Bethany had some basis in historical reality. But these questions are beyond the scope of our investigation. We are concerned less with what happened than with the ideas that influenced the New Testament writers. It does look as if they had been exercised by the problem of the 'disgrace' that would be produced if Jesus's body was left unanointed. Mark found the solution in the episode at Bethany, John in the action of Joseph and Nicodemus.

It is noteworthy that John—and John alone of all evangelists—lays emphasis on an actual absence of *niwwul*, on a regular anointing after death. As we saw above, he alone expressly testifies to the intactness of Jesus's body, the failure of the soldiers to break his legs. Surely his attitude to the two matters is dictated by the same fundamental considerations.

[1] Mark 15.42 ff., John 19.39 f.
[2] Mish. San. 6.5 f., Josephus, Ant. 4.8.6.202, 4.8.24.264, 5.1.14.44.

2. *Mark and John: continuation*

Four details may be added.

First, in Mark's version of the anointing at Bethany, since a burial rite here and now is contemplated, the box is broken and the entire ointment poured over Jesus's head. No doubt we are meant to infer that the ointment covered him; this is borne out by his own words, 'to anoint my body'. In any case, it is not the way in which one would ordinarily anoint a guest or teacher. In John, as no present burial rite is contemplated, the box is not broken, and it is Jesus's feet that are anointed, presumably with the hand. No anointing of the body is implied in Jesus's words, 'let her alone' etc. The Talmud mentions superstitious scruples entertained by people about anointing themselves, not with the hand, but direct from a flask.[1] Very likely these fears had their root in the association of the latter method with funerals.

Secondly, in Mark, the argument is as follows. Some contend that the value of the ointment ought to have been spent on almsgiving. Jesus's reply is in three parts, forming an ascending line. He begins by saying that the woman has done 'a good work'. This is a technical term. It means almsgiving, putting up strangers, visiting the sick, burying the dead or the like.[2] (According to R. Simlai, of the second half of the 3rd cent. A.D., the Torah opens with 'a good work', God clothing the naked, and concludes with one, God burying Moses.[3]) So the first part of the reply is intended to mystify the audience: Jesus affirms that the woman's action is 'a good work' just as much as almsgiving. Exactly what kind of 'good work' he means he does not yet explain, and his hearers can hardly be expected to guess. Next he adds that 'ye have the poor always . . . but me ye have not always'. This is reminiscent of the Rabbinic doctrine[4] that almsgiving is less praiseworthy than the other 'good works', one reason being that the former can be done only for the living whereas the latter extend also to the dead. Here, then, he commences to specify the 'good work' he has in mind: it is superior to almsgiving, superior because done to one—and that one Jesus—whom 'ye have not always'. There follows the culmination, the revelation to

---

[1] Bab. San. 101a.
[2] For numerous references see Strack-B., vol. 4, 1928, pt. 1, pp. 536 ff. and 559 ff.
[3] Bab. So. 14a.
[4] Tos. Peah 4.19, Bab. Suk. 49b.

which the first two parts of the reply have been leading up: the woman has performed the burial rite of anointing.

Now in John, all this is different. The first part is completely missing. The woman's action is not called 'a good work'. It could not be: the anointing does not constitute a burial rite. The reply begins with 'let her alone' etc., corresponding to the third part in Mark, but, as pointed out above, quite unlike in substance. There is no assertion of a present burial ceremony, but a reference to the future day of burial. The clause 'for the poor always ye have with you' etc., coming second in Mark, to prepare the revelation that this is the anointing for burial, comes last in John. As no burial rite here and now is in question, this reflection on Jesus's death would make an unsuitable beginning. It must not precede the allusion to the future day of burial. If the impression of abruptness is to be avoided, it must be introduced as an afterthought to, a fuller explanation of, that allusion.

Thirdly, in Mark, the incident takes place after the entry into Jerusalem and very near Passover—as near the actual burial as possible. In John, it takes place before the entry and not quite so near.

Fourthly, John emphasizes that Joseph and Nicodemus dealt with the body 'as the manner of the Jews is to bury'. This does sound as if directed against disparaging talk on the part of Jewish opponents. John flatly denies any basis in fact for their charge. There is no mere re-interpreting of some other action as standing for the rite. The rite was really performed in the correct, indeed, in a particularly splendid, fashion. The presence of Nicodemus, which at first sight looks somewhat unmotivated, may well be stressed as guaranteeing the proper observance of the ritual: he was a respected Pharisee.[1]

As for dependence, it is obvious even at this stage that Mark was ignorant of an actual anointing after death. Otherwise he would not have dropped it in favour of anointing by anticipation. A fiction, however good a substitute for fact, is still a substitute. Unbelievers would not readily accept it, and even a believer, unless trained in such matters, might feel uneasy. (This is not to judge—let it be repeated—about the historical value of Mark's interpretation.) Neither, however, is it likely that John used Mark. There would have been no reason for replacing the anointing of the head by one of the feet. Certainly, John did not need an anointing of the head—and body—since, in his eyes, the woman

[1] John 3.1.

was not there and then performing the burial rite. But it is difficult to think of any objection he might have had against this mode of anointing had he been following Mark. (The breaking of the box is a different matter. That he might have rejected as peculiar to the anointing of a corpse.) Another change would be even more inexplicable: in John, the woman wipes the anointed feet with her hair. If John was following Mark, why should he have inserted this unnatural feature?[1]

We shall submit a conjecture as to the growth of the narrative at the end of our inquiry.

3. 'That she may keep it'

So far we have not gone into the precise meaning of this phrase which occurs in John. Our main thesis is indeed unaffected by the question; nevertheless it may be worth while to draw attention to a few points.

(1) The usual—and probably the correct—way in which it is understood is: 'that she may keep the ointment'. In John, it should be recalled, there is no breaking of the box and pouring out of the entire contents, as at burial. The woman anoints Jesus's feet. So some ointment may be left.

But what is the purpose of keeping it? It is to be kept 'against the day of my burial'. It is tempting to see here a trace of the tradition represented in Mark and Luke, though not in John (nor in Matthew), that after Jesus's death several women planned to anoint the dead body. The identification in John of the woman of Bethany with Mary—not to be found in the Synoptics—points in the same direction: according to Mark and Luke, Mary was among the women that hoped to anoint the body. If this is so, the phrase under discussion means that she ought to keep the ointment for that anointing. As John, however, does not report the attempt of the women to anoint the dead body, it would follow that he cannot be the original author of the phrase. He must have taken it over from a source which still did report, and attach great importance to, the women's plan. We should have before us, that is, a pre-Johannine nuance of Jesus's remark, which, in John, has lost its point.

Mary, then, is to keep it for that subsequent occasion. Her present gesture of reverence adumbrates what she will do, or attempt to do,

[1] Wagner, however, in his *Parsifal*, adopts it: Kundry, having washed the hero's feet, anoints them and only then dries them with her hair.

when Jesus is dead. Here we may come back to that very strange feature in John's version that, having anointed Jesus's feet, she dries the ointment with her hair. It will appear less strange if the version grew out of another, in fact out of one like that preserved in Luke, where a penitent woman washed his feet with her tears, dried them with her hair and then anointed them. In John, the washing is omitted, in order to achieve a closer foreshadowing of the anointing after death. Only the drying is still retained, illogically and with a disturbing result.

(2) However, there is a well-known difficulty about the interpretation 'that she may keep the ointment': one would expect the text to speak of 'the rest', τὸ περισσεῦον, or the like. So perhaps we should paraphrase 'that she may treasure up the act'.[1] It would be reading a great deal into the pronoun αὐτό, 'it' ('that she may keep it'), but it cannot be ruled out. The sense would be that Mary should treasure up the act for the day when she and others would wish, but be unable, to anoint the dead body. In other words, we should have to do, not yet with a definite proleptic burial rite as in Mark, but with something coming rather near it. Treasuring up an act for a future occasion is not quite the same as performing here and now an act strictly appropriate only to the future, but it contains the germ of the latter idea.

Once again, as John does not report the plan of the women to anoint the dead body, we must assume—if we accept this rendering—that he took the clause from his source. That the source had not yet, like Mark, fully reached the idea of a burial ceremony by anticipation is confirmed by various significant differences. In Mark, the head is anointed; in the version before John, it was still the feet. In Mark, there is no drying of the ointment with the hair; in the version before John, it still occurred. The version before John had not yet, like Mark, shed the vestiges of an earlier stage, when the narrative simply concerned a penitent woman paying homage to Jesus.

(3) The verb τηρέω, 'to keep', sometimes denotes 'to keep in one's memory', 'to remember'. The phrase in question could be translated: 'that she may remember it'—scil. the ointment she has used, or (but this again would probably be giving αὐτό too much weight) this incident, this act. We do not regard this meaning as likely. But it is just conceivable, and the difficulty attaching to the interpretation 'that

[1] This was very kindly suggested to me by Professor C. Moule of Cambridge, but I hasten to add that he does not subscribe to my conclusions.

she may keep the ointment that is left' does not arise. The woman is to remember the ointment with which she anointed Jesus's feet, or the entire incident; so no reference to 'the rest', τὸ περισσεῦον, is wanted.

Three other passages with derivatives of τηρέω come to mind: two from Luke—Mary 'kept in her heart' what the shepherds had said and how the young Jesus had taught in the Temple—and one from Genesis —Jacob 'retained in his memory' Joseph's dreams.[1] In all these cases, the event remembered adumbrates, provides the understanding one with a foretaste of, the real thing to come. Joseph's dreams point forward to his exaltation in Egypt, the testimony of the shepherds to the worship of the Church, the young Jesus's discourse amidst the doctors to the message of the mature Jesus. Presumably—if we take τηρέω in this sense—the ointment used at Bethany is to be remembered as foreshadowing the costlier one used by Joseph and Nicodemus in the most tragic and yet most glorious circumstances.

Should this be the meaning of John, there are three possibilities. Either John drew on a version of the narrative with no reference to Jesus's burial whatever—a version of the kind we find in Luke—and he himself turned the incident into one foreshadowing the final anointing by Joseph and Nicodemus. That is to say, he himself suppressed the woman's contrition and tears—with the awkward result that she dries the ointment with her hair—and introduced the clause 'Let her alone that she may remember ...' and 'For the poor always ...' This solution, however, is extremely improbable. Once it was established that Jesus's body was actually anointed after his death in the proper mode, there was no need for violent interference with an entirely different type of anointing during his life.

Or John drew on a version which, like Mark, saw in the anointing at Bethany a present, proleptic performance of the burial rite. As John taught that Jesus was in fact anointed after his death, he did not want this rite to be anticipated. Consequently, he eliminated the fiction of a present burial, he changed performance in advance into adumbration, he cut out the description of the woman's action as 'a good work' and toned down the expression 'she has come aforehand' into 'that she may remember it against the day when Joseph and Nicodemus will actually observe the ritual'.

Or, finally, the version before John used 'to keep' in the sense of 'to

[1] Luke 2.19, 51, Gen. 37.11.

treasure up an act', and regarded the anointing at Bethany as an adumbration of the women's later, unsuccessful plan to anoint the dead Jesus. John made no verbal alteration, but he regarded the action as adumbrating the real anointing by Joseph and Nicodemus, he used 'to keep' in the sense of 'to keep in memory an event apparently unimportant and incomplete, yet prefiguring a great fulfilment in the future'.

It may be repeated that the account John knew can at most have been like Mark's—namely, in insisting on a burial rite in advance, or in treating Mary's action as foreshadowing her subsequent attempt to anoint the dead body—but it cannot have been the Markan account itself. In the version before John, it was still the feet that were anointed, and the woman still dried the ointment with her hair. In other words, though that version may already have contained the fiction of a burial rite here and now, or something approaching this fiction, it had not yet drawn out all the consequences. It was a 'proto-Markan' version, and John gave up any allusion to the performance of a burial rite by Mary in favour of an adumbration—to be remembered—of the true anointing by Joseph and Nicodemus.

4. Matthew

Matthew is fairly close to Mark. As in Mark, the incident takes place after the entry into Jerusalem, very near Passover. True, the box is not broken. But the ointment is poured over Jesus's head and also, quite clearly, over his body: 'for in that she hath poured this ointment on my body', Jesus says. Further, as in Mark, Jesus's reply consists of three parts, and is designed to prove the superiority of the woman's action, as constituting a burial ceremony, over almsgiving—in accordance with Rabbinic doctrine. As for the statement 'she hath done it for my burying', it expresses performance of the burial rite here and now even more strongly than Mark's 'she is come aforehand to anoint'. Accordingly—the most significant fact from the point of view of the thesis here advocated—Matthew, like Mark, has no real anointing after death.

Where they differ, Matthew as a rule appears secondary. Let us take a few examples.

In the first place, 'she is come aforehand to anoint to the burial', in Mark, is the formulation of somebody still wrestling with the problem, somebody who must explain how an anointing of the living Jesus could stand for one after his death. Matthew has the much simpler declaration 'she hath done it to my burying'—which indicates that the Markan solution of the problem has been fully accepted. She has performed the burial rite: the fact that it is done by anticipation, the element of fiction, is no longer even hinted at.

The substitution by Matthew of the verb, 'to bury me', for Mark's noun, 'to the burial', also follows from this perfect assurance that the burying takes place at this moment. 'To the burial'—Mark—is still slightly more formal, less concrete, than 'to bury me'—Matthew.

Again, in Mark, that the ointment poured over Jesus's head covered his body is only indirectly conveyed, implied, in the interpretation of the action: 'she is come aforehand to anoint my body'. In Matthew also it comes in the interpretation, but quite explicitly: 'for in that she hath poured this ointment on my body'.

There is another sign that Mark is not yet comfortable: the clause 'she hath done what she could', which is absent from Matthew. Mark is still conscious that the burial rite at Bethany is a second best, an 'as if'. Matthew no longer shares this feeling.

How completely satisfied Matthew is may be inferred from his omitting the attempt of the women to anoint the dead Jesus, which is still extant in Mark. The omission is striking. Matthew doubtless held that such an attempt was not only superfluous after the performance of the rite at Bethany, but even apt to weaken the definitive 'she hath done it to my burying'.

5. Luke: the growth of the narrative

The clue to the different versions of the anointing at Bethany lies in the recognition that the development of the narrative was determined by the tendency to free Jesus's burial from any *niwwul*—a tendency understandable in itself, but in all probability intensified by the Jewish attitude to the 'scandal' of Jesus's end.

Surely we must start from Luke. He knows nothing of the anointing by Joseph and Nicodemus, and the women came too late. Neither, however, is there any allusion to Jesus's death in the chapter about the sinful woman who anoints him while he lives. We do not meet with the phrase 'good work', which could fit so well if it had the vague sense of any fine deed. Its absence confirms the technical interpretation we have put on it in Mark and Matthew; but in Luke there is no thought of the performance of a funeral rite. The incident—not yet

Y

located at Bethany—is right outside the passion cycle, and the woman does not pour ointment over Jesus's head, but washes with her tears, dries with her hair and anoints Jesus's feet. While there may be secondary elements, Luke on the whole stands nearest the original tradition. It is noteworthy that, in depicting the action of the woman, John is close to Luke, except for the omission of her tears in favour of an exclusive stress on the anointing of the feet. Of course, John has the complaint about the waste and the reply 'Let her alone' and so on—both foreign to Luke.

The following stages in the evolution of the tradition regarding Jesus's burial are suggested.

(1) A woman washed with her tears, dried with her hair and anointed Jesus's feet while he lived. After his death, nobody anointed or attempted to anoint his body. This stage is not preserved in any of our sources.

(2) The 'disgrace' was mitigated by introducing an attempt of some women to anoint the corpse (which may be perfectly historical). They could not carry out their plan because, in the meantime, Jesus had risen. This was a justification of their failure more than sufficient for the faithful. But why had they not come earlier? Because 'they rested on the sabbath day according to the commandment'. This ought to silence the Jewish questioners. They could say nothing against strict compliance with the Law, which prohibited any buying—and therefore the buying of spices—on a Sabbath. Curiously, Luke—though not Mark—assumes that the act of anointing itself was forbidden on a Sabbath, and not, or not only, the purchase of spices. It would be rash to deny that some Rabbis may have held this view in New Testament times. But the Mishnah allows the anointing of a corpse,[1] while buying would be a grave transgression of the rules. Mark agrees with the Mishnic doctrine; so it is possible that Luke misunderstood the matter.

However, apart from this detail, the stage of the tradition just outlined is preserved in Luke. Its distinctive mark is that the non-observance of the rite of anointing is still admitted. Only it is claimed that it resulted not from a treatment of the body as that of a criminal, but from keeping the Sabbath and the resurrection immediately afterwards. The non-observance of the rite is explained, but not yet explained away, still less flatly denied.

[1] Shab. 23.5.

(3*a*) One possibility is that the incident at Bethany was now made into an adumbration of the women's attempt to anoint the dead body—perhaps in order to endow that attempt with greater weight. It had, after all, failed. This might explain the account in John, if we paraphrase the clause 'that she may keep it' either by 'that she may keep the ointment' or by 'that she may treasure up the act'. The naming of Mary as well as the omission of the woman's tears, with the strange result that what she dries with her hair is the ointment, would fit: these features can be ascribed to a desire to effect a closer foreshadowing of the plan to anoint the dead Jesus.

However, the development, though it produced the account in John, would have to be pre-Johannine. For John himself discards the attempt of the women, asserting that there was successful anointing by Joseph and Nicodemus. So he himself would not have connected the anointing at Bethany with that attempt. He himself simply denies that there was any neglect at the time of Jesus's burial.

(3*b*) If we take 'that she may keep it' in the sense of 'that she may remember it against the day when Joseph and Nicodemus will anoint the body', there is a remote possibility that John himself turned a contrite washing and anointing of the feet into an adumbration of the final anointing by two faithful men. The omission of the tears, with its awkward consequence, and the formulation of the saying 'Let her alone' etc. would be due to himself.

(3*c*) However, should this interpretation of the clause be tenable at all, it is better to suppose that John proceeded from a more advanced stage than that represented by Luke; namely, from a stage where the anointing at Bethany was already thought of as anticipating the burial rite, as constituting an anointing for burial here and now, or at least as adumbrating Mary's later attempt to perform the rite. To be sure, in the version before John it is still the feet that are anointed, and there is still drying with the hair; we are midway, that is, between Luke and Mark. As John had the actual rite after death, he changed performance in advance ('she is come aforehand') or adumbration of Mary's unsuccessful attempt ('that she may treasure up the act') into adumbration of the actual rite ('that she may remember it against the day Joseph and Nicodemus will do it'); and, accordingly, he dropped the reference to Mary's 'good work on me'. For him, an event of apparent insignificance prophetically pointed towards a great fulfilment.

If John drew on a 'proto-Markan' account, incidentally, it may have included some eulogy similar to that occurring in Mark, 'wherever this gospel shall be preached, this also shall be spoken of'; and the corresponding passage in John may be the remark that 'the house was filled with the odour of the ointment'. Admittedly, it is perhaps fanciful to credit the latter clause with a deeper meaning. The ancients liked strong scent, and a description of this kind need contain no symbolism. 'Were Hera's perfume shaken in the palace of Zeus,' Homer says,[1] 'its savour would reach unto earth and heaven.' Still, it may be recalled that the Rabbis liken Abraham before he went out to preach to a flask of perfume stowed away so that its odour cannot spread; and that, in their view, 'precious ointment spreads from the bedchamber to the dining-room, but a good name spreads from one end of the world to the other'.[2]

(4) Mark, who does not know the anointing by Joseph and Nicodemus, far from giving up performance by anticipation—'she is come aforehand'—and the 'good work', follows out some further implications of the idea of a present burial rite. He puts the story after the entry into Jerusalem, immediately before the crucifixion; replaces the anointing of the feet by a breaking of the box and pouring of the ointment over Jesus's head—and body; and suppresses the drying. At the same time, he still retains the attempt of the women after Jesus's death; and there are other indications—such as 'she hath done what she could'—that he is aware that his account, au fond, constitutes an explaining away of such facts as have been handed down to him.

(5) Matthew, finally, takes over the Markan solution, but with far more confidence. Its problematic nature is no longer felt, as is shown, for instance, by the omission of 'she hath done what she could' and by the straightforward 'she did so' in the place of 'she is come aforehand to do so'. The most notable innovation in this respect is the abandonment of the attempt of the women to anoint the corpse as superfluous.

[1] Il. 14.173, commented on by Athenaeus, Deipn. 1.17b.
[2] Gen. Rabba on 12.1, Eccles. Rabba on 1.3, 7.1.

IX

The 'I Am' of the Messianic Presence

AT the foundation meeting of the *Studiorum Novi Testamenti Societas*, a few years ago, Professor T. W. Manson read a paper in which he discussed the New Testament use of ἐγώ εἰμι, literally 'I am', in the sense of 'The Messiah is present'. It is prominent in John. At the end of the conversation between Jesus and the Samaritan woman, for example, the woman says 'I know that Messias cometh, he will tell us all things', and Jesus replies 'I am'—meaning 'the Messiah is here'; or in the account of his arrest we are told that 'as soon then as he had said unto them, I am, they went backwards and fell to the ground'.[1] But in Mark and Luke also there occurs an utterance like 'Many shall come in my name, saying, I am',[2] where 'I am' must be an announcement of the second coming of the Messiah: 'he is here'. Matthew, who writes 'I am the Christ',[3] obviously no longer understands the exact, original sense of the expression.

It is submitted that the evangelists are following a Rabbinic model, though this has been preserved in one source only, the Passover Haggadah. As pointed out already, the nucleus of the Haggadah consists in the exposition of some verses from Deuteronomy, referring to Israel's deliverance from Egypt.[4] It is in the course of this exposition that the words 'I am' are used to denote the personal presence of the redeeming God on that occasion.

Before quoting the paragraph in question, let us recall that as early as in the Pentateuch we come across two conceptions of the exodus, one according to which God himself rescued the nation and another represented by statements such as that 'he sent an angel and hath brought us forth out of Egypt'.[5] The opposition between these different

---

[1] 4.25 f., 18.6. Other relevant texts are 8.24, 28, 58, 9.9, 13.19, 18.5, 8.
[2] Mark 13.6, Luke 21.8.　　　　　　　　　　　　　　　　　　　[3] 24.5.
[4] 26.5 ff.　　　　　　[5] Num. 20.16. See E. D. Goldschmidt, *op. cit.*, p. 54 n. 1.

schools of thought continues throughout Biblical and Rabbinic times. Isaiah says 'the angel of his face saved them', but the LXX translates 'neither a messenger nor an angel but he himself saved them';[1] and Exodus Rabba[2] observes that 'some say he smote the Egyptians through an angel, and some say the Holy one did it himself'. Considering the whole atmosphere of the Jewish Passover-eve service, it is only natural that the prevalent doctrine should here be that of God's direct intervention.

The Credo from Deuteronomy contains the declaration: 'And the Lord heard our voice, and the Lord brought us forth out of Egypt with a mighty hand and with an outstretched arm and with great terribleness and with signs and with wonders.' The authors of the Passover Haggadah see in the repetition of 'the Lord'—'the Lord heard our voice and the Lord brought us forth' instead of simply 'and he brought us forth' —an indication of God's personal activity; and, as usual, they support their contention by other texts from Scripture. This is what they say by way of comment: 'Not through an angel, and not through a seraph, and not through a messenger, but the Holy one in his glory and himself; as it is written (in Exodus[3]), For I will pass through the land of Egypt this night, and I will smite all the firstborn, and against all the gods of Egypt I will execute judgment, I the Lord.' Then they go on to explain that each of the four clauses of the supporting text is intended to announce the carrying out of these deeds by God himself:[4] 'For I will pass through Egypt—this means, I and not an angel; and I will smite all the firstborn—this means, I and not a seraph; and I will execute judgment—this means, I and not the messenger; I the Lord—this means, I am and no other.'

It will be noted that, whereas the first part of the Midrash has 'not through an angel, and not through a seraph, and not through a messenger', the second speaks of 'the messenger', not 'a messenger': 'I and not the messenger'. This way of putting the matter may well have arisen when Christianity had to be combated: 'the messenger' probably

---

[1] 63.9.   [2] On 12.23.
[3] 12.12.
[4] E. D. Goldschmidt, *op. cit.*, pp. 54 f., holds that this explanation does not belong to the original stratum of the Haggadah. But, for one thing, he may well be wrong. He says that it adds nothing of importance to the preceding part—an untenable view as soon as the particular force of *'ani hu'*, 'I am', is recognized. For another thing, even if he were right, it would not affect our principal argument. The passage would still show that the manner in which the New Testament employs 'I am' is Rabbinic.

is Jesus.[1] There are versions of the Midrash with more anti-Christian or anti-gnostic interpolations, such as the addition 'and not through the Word'.[2]

The point here to be made is that in the last few words of the Midrash, 'I am and no other', we have before us the model for that ἐγώ εἰμι. Usually these words are taken as meaning 'I am he, *scil.* the Lord who does all these things, and no other.' But such an interpretation suffers from two flaws. First, *'ani hu* can hardly signify 'I am this or that', referring back to some previous attribute. In the Old Testament it appears in the sense of 'I am the Absolute' or the like,[3] and this application certainly prepared the ground for the ἐγώ εἰμι of the Messianic Presence. But neither in the Old Testament nor in Rabbinic language is it used as denoting 'I am this or that'. To translate 'I am he who does it all' would be carrying modern usage into Rabbinic language.

Secondly—and this is decisive—the purpose of the Passover Midrash is to prove that, in the deliverance from Egypt, God acted himself. The Rabbis, that is, are compelled to explain 'I the Lord' as emphasizing God's personal intervention. Consequently, when they say it means *'ani hu' welo' 'aḥer*, we must translate 'I am and no other', in the sense of 'God's own person will be present and no other.' This is the ἐγώ εἰμι of that particular value: 'the Divine Presence, the Divine Redeemer, is here'. Any other rendering would miss the point of the Rabbinic argument. In fact the special force of the two words must have been firmly established by the time the Midrash was composed. The authors take it for granted that their paraphrase—'I am and no other'—will express the idea of God's personal appearance more clearly than the Scriptural 'I the Lord'.

It is interesting that the passage from the Haggadah discussed seems to be the only Rabbinic text extant where this application of *'ani hu'* is to be met with. Presumably there was a time when it was not so rare, but the Rabbis found it dangerous and were afraid of abuse. (The Mekhilta, among other things, says this about 'I the Lord' in Exodus: 'What flesh and blood cannot possibly say.' This is manifestly directed against Christianity.) They eliminated the expression as far as possible.

[1] This is following up a remark by Abrahams, *Jewish Quarterly Review*, 10, 1898, p. 49 n. 2. On the role of the article in Rabbinic exegesis, see below, under The Abomination of Desolation, A.

[2] Abrahams, *op. cit.*, pp. 41, 45 ff., 51.   [3] Deut. 32.39, Isa. 43.10, 13 etc.

But in liturgy, in the Passover-eve service, it withstood the pressure: liturgy is very difficult to expurgate. Even here, however, we know of attempts to suppress the 'I am'. Certain medieval authorities—Zedekiah ben Abraham, for instance[1]—forbade the recital of the portion containing the phrase. Obviously they were still familiar with its implications. To be sure, there do exist allied phrases, such as 'I and He'. But they are not quite the same, and even they have mainly survived in liturgy, for example, in the service of Hoshanna Rabba.

It should be added that the continuation of the exegesis of the Deuteronomic Credo to be found in the Haggadah fully bears out the view here advanced. For we learn there that in the course of the exodus there took place a *gilluy shekhina*, 'an uncovering, a baring, of the Divine Presence'. This is a technical term suggesting precisely that milieu where we should expect the curious use of 'I am'.

According to Deuteronomy, God delivered Israel 'with a mighty hand and with an outstretched arm and with great terribleness and with signs and with wonders'. The Haggadah—and it may be repeated that we are concerned with a very early section—specifies the meaning of each of these adverbial phrases, adducing other texts for confirmation. Thus 'a mighty hand' is claimed to signify pestilence; 'an outstretched arm' the sword; 'signs' the rod; 'wonders' the blood. The comment on 'great terribleness' runs as follows: 'This means the baring of the Divine Presence; as it is written (in another passage from Deuteronomy),[2] Or hath God assayed to come to take him a nation from the midst of another nation with great terrors.' The supporting text, it should be remarked, also speaks of 'great terrors' (the plural of 'great terribleness'); and, for the Rabbis, the proof that this implies the actual descent of God lies in the words saying that 'he came to take the people' —instead of merely 'he took the people'. Onkelos translates *le'ithgela'a lemiphraq*, 'to uncover himself to redeem', a distinct reference to the Divine Presence in the act of redemption or, we might now say, to 'I am'.

To conclude, it has long been seen that the association of terribleness or terrors with the manifestation of the Divine Presence must have been favoured by the similarity in sound between the Hebrew words *mora'*, 'terribleness', and *mar'e*, 'appearance'. The LXX, in the verses from Deuteronomy quoted,[3] renders 'with great terribleness (terrors)' by

---

[1] In his Shibbole ha-Leqet.   [2] 4.34.   [3] 26.8, 4.34.

ἐν ὁράμασι μεγάλοις, and Onkelos by *ubhehizwana' rabba'* (*ubhehiz-wanin rabhrebhin*), 'with great sights'. It may be worth bearing this in mind when dealing with passages like that mentioned at the beginning of this discussion, 'as soon then as he had said unto them, I am, they fell to the ground'; or even, perhaps, when inquiring into the report, towards the end of the Markan gospel,[1] that the women, on finding the grave empty and being informed that they would soon see the risen Jesus, fled and dared not speak about it for fear.

[1] 16.4 ff.

X

Two Incidents after the Last Supper

A. The Omission of the Fourth Cup

1. *The omission of the fourth cup*

Of the four cups of wine prescribed for the Passover-eve service, the third, over which grace is said, is to be taken immediately after the supper.[1] In technical language it appears as 'the cup of blessing', *kos shel berakha, kasa' debhirketha'*.[2] According to the Synoptics and Paul, this third cup is the cup of the New Covenant. Paul actually adopts its technical designation.[3]

There is, however, in Matthew and Mark a reference also to the fourth and last cup of the Passover liturgy. It is contained in the words:[4] 'I will not drink henceforth of this fruit of the vine until I drink it new in my father's kingdom' or 'in the kingdom of God'. The meaning is that the fourth cup will not be taken, as would be the normal thing, at a subsequent stage of this service; it will be postponed till the kingdom is fully established.

Four points may be mentioned in support of this interpretation.

First, from the phrase 'fruit of the vine' it is clear that Jesus, or whoever the author of the saying may be, has in mind a drinking after a further, formal benediction: 'Blessed art thou, O Lord, who createst the fruit of the vine.' Normally, on Passover eve, that would be the fourth cup.

Secondly, whereas under Jewish law additional, non-liturgical drinking is permissible between the first and second cups and between the second and third cups of the service, it is not permissible between the third and fourth.[5] Jesus's announcement, therefore, that he will drink no more from now, i.e. from after the third cup, till the next

---

[1] Mish. Pes. 10.7. [2] Bab. Ber. 51a. [3] I Cor. 10.16.
[4] Matt. 26.29, Mark 14.25. [5] Mish. Pes. 10.7.

formal, liturgical drinking is in accordance with the Rabbinic rules concerning the interval between the third cup of the Passover-eve service and the last.

Thirdly, we have seen that the third cup, the 'cup of blessing', is taken immediately after supper. Normally, on Passover eve, over the fourth cup (if we disregard accretions later than the New Testament era) there is completed a group of psalms called the Hallel or 'hymn' and there is recited 'the blessing of the song', *birkath hashshir*, consisting in an acknowledgment of the universal reign of God. It is doubtful whether the earliest 'blessing of the song' is the piece beginning with 'All thy works shall praise thee' (*yehalelukha*) or that beginning with 'The breath of every living being shall bless thy name' (*nishmath kol ḥay*). (The glorification of Jesus in Philippians 2.6 ff. shows striking affinities with the latter.) The question does not, however, affect our argument. In both of them we find the clause 'and they shall assign kingship to thy name, our King' (*weyamlikhu 'eth shimekha malkenu*), giving expression to the principal theme. The fourth and last cup of the Passover-eve service, then, is taken to celebrate God's kingdom. When Jesus says that he will drink no more till he can drink in the kingdom, he is only substituting the real, perfect, final kingdom for that which is still to a large extent a matter of belief and hope. But he is evidently referring to the fourth cup.

Fourthly, the notice that 'when they had sung a hymn they went out into the mount of Olives' now acquires a fuller sense. The implication is that they go out directly after the 'hymn', without drinking the fourth cup and probably also without reciting the 'blessing of the song'. This portion of the liturgy is postponed till the arrival of the actual, final kingdom.

We do not intend here to discuss the Lukan version, except to say that it is far less technically Rabbinic than Matthew and Mark.

2. 'Only one kid'

Perhaps a note may be added about 'Only one kid' which, in some regions, is the last of the poems recited after the fourth cup. It does not seem to antedate the 15th century. Yet it is not inconceivable that it replaces a far earlier piece—maybe a less poetic one—the main idea of which was the same. The lack of direct evidence to prove the existence of a predecessor may be due to the fact that, like 'Only one kid', it was of a somewhat esoteric character and, in consequence, never gained universal recognition but remained confined to one or two rites.

'Only one kid' is a story about a kid which was bought by 'my father' for two coins, and devoured by a cat. The cat was killed by a dog. The dog was slain by a stick. The stick was burnt by fire. The fire was extinguished by water. The water was drunk up by an ox. The ox was slaughtered by a slaughterer. The slaughterer was slaughtered by the angel of death. The angel of death was slaughtered by the Holy one, blessed be he.

This is strangely reminiscent of Paul's declaration in I Corinthians[1] that, in the end, Jesus will destroy 'all rule and authority and power'— which phrase clearly includes both human and non-human forces— and that the last enemy to be destroyed will be death. As is well known, I Corinthians is rich in references to Passover. (T. W. Manson thinks it was written shortly before that festival.[2]) The passage in question could be an allusion to a predecessor of 'Only one kid'. It is far from certain, but it would be rash to consider it as impossible.

B. The Sleeping Companions

According to Matthew and Mark, when Jesus and his disciples came to Gethsemane, they still formed a *ḥabhura*, a company united for the celebration of the Passover. To be sure, the Bible ordains that 'in one house shall the passover be eaten'. But for one thing, the phrase 'in one house' was from early times taken by the Rabbis to signify 'in one company'; under Rabbinic law, therefore, a company was perfectly entitled to commence the meal in one place and continue it in another.[3] For another thing, Jesus and his disciples may well have finished the actual meal indoors, yet gone on with the service—prayers, recounting the deeds of God for Israel, praise of God—on the Mount of Olives; that would be enough to leave the *ḥabhura* intact. The Jewish Passover Haggadah, the liturgy used on Passover eve, contains a story about some Rabbis of the early 2nd cent. A.D., who spent the whole Passover night discussing the exodus from Egypt, until their disciples reminded them that it was dawning and the time had come to recite the morning

---

[1] 15.23 ff.　　　　　　　　　　　　　[2] *Journal of Theological Studies*, 46, 1945, p. 8.
[3] Mekh. on Exod. 12.46, Targ. Onk. and Jerus. (both translating 'in one house' by 'in one *ḥabhura*').

prayer. We need not conclude that these scholars kept eating all the time: the ḥabhura remained in existence through the continued occupation with the great theme of the festival.

At Gethsemane, then, Jesus asked his disciples, the members of his company, to stay awake while he was saying a prayer by himself. He returned and discovered that they had not stayed awake. He admonished them, or Peter in particular, and prayed again. But again, when he returned, he found them asleep, and indeed, in a deeper slumber—it seems—than before. We are told that 'their eyes were heavy'; Mark even states that 'neither wist they what to answer him', which presumably means that, on being spoken to, they were able to reply at random only. Once more Jesus prayed, but now they fell into a proper sleep, as may be gathered from the emphatic καθεύδετε καὶ ἀναπαύεσθε, a reference to sleep as a complete rest (no matter whether we ascribe to the clause an imperative, an interrogative or any other sense). This time Jesus said, 'It is enough, the hour is come, the Son of Man is betrayed' and so on.

It is generally held that Jesus requested his disciples to stay awake because he wanted to feel that they shared in his struggle. They failed to do so, however, thus leaving him alone.

This explanation is no doubt correct, only it is not the full explanation. If it were, one could understand the view of those scholars who regard the scene as legendary, as artificially composed in order to illustrate a theological truth. For it would be difficult to refute the argument that, first, Jesus's request to his disciples lacked a sufficiently specific motivation, and secondly, that their very natural sleepiness was treated as more significant than would seem warranted—except in the province of legend.

For a proper understanding of the scene, it is necessary to consider a rule transmitted by Jose ben Halaphta,[1] to the effect that if some members of a Passover company doze, the meal may be resumed again, but if they fall into deep sleep, it may not be resumed again.

Five points may be noted. First of all, R. Jose, though he lived about the middle of the 2nd cent. A.D., frequently preserves earlier traditions. The presumption is that the rule quoted, or a similar one, goes back to the New Testament era. (A remark in the Mekhilta[2] suggests that the rule may originally have been rested on the verse from Exodus which

---

[1] Mish. Pes. 10.8.   [2] The concluding remark on Exod. 12.42.

refers to the Passover night as 'the night of watchfulness'. But we need not here settle this question.) Secondly, in the Mishnah, the rule occurs in a paragraph dealing with the stage of the celebration after the ceremonial eating of the prescribed portion of the Passover lamb. The case contemplated is that of members of the company getting tired during this later stage of the service. The rule, that is, applies to precisely that part of the celebration which Jesus and his disciples had reached when they came to Gethsemane. Thirdly, there are Talmudic precepts[1] designed to ensure that even children taking part in the service should stay awake at least until the completion of the essential ceremony —which, after the destruction of the Temple, was the eating of unleavened bread. (From the fall of the Temple, the lamb, like all sacrifices, ceased to be offered.) Modern writers are apt to miss the point of these warnings: they must have originated in circles where it would have been a grave matter if any members of the company had fallen asleep during the first part of the evening. Fourthly, R. Ashi, at the beginning of the 5th cent., defines the meaning of 'a doze', which does not bring about a dissolution of the *ḥabhura*, as opposed to 'a proper sleep', which does. A man, he says, merely dozes 'if, when addressed, he replies but does not know how to answer sensibly'.[2] This late comment is curiously reminiscent of Mark's description of the state in which the disciples were when Jesus returned the second time: 'neither wist they what to answer him'. There is, however, nothing surprising in the coincidence. As soon as any relevance is attached to the distinction between dozing and sleeping, some criterion like that recognized by Mark and R. Ashi is bound to be set up. Fifthly, in the Sectarian Manual of Discipline discovered a few years ago, falling asleep in the assembly is considered a major breach of discipline, punishable by exclusion from the assembly for thirty days.[3]

We may conclude that, though Jesus asked his disciples to stay awake because he wanted to feel they were with him in mind, yet his request had also a more specific meaning: they should not let the *ḥabhura* come to an early close. Similarly, while the giving in of the disciples to their natural desire for rest did leave him alone, it left him alone not only in a general sense but also in the sense that the Passover union was ended.

---

[1] Tos. Pes. 10.9, Bab. Pes. 109a. [2] Bab. Pes. 120b.
[3] See J. Hempel, *Die Funde in der Wüste, Almanach auf das Jahr des Herrn* 1954, p. 13. No such serious view, however, seems to be taken of the offence in Acts 20.9 ff.

Luke has abandoned all reference to the Rabbinic law concerning the Passover ḥabhura. Jesus does not ask his disciples to stay awake: he tells them to pray. The distinction between slumber and sleep plays no part. Jesus prays and returns only once. The disciples fall asleep, not from natural fatigue, but from sorrow. Jesus's final remark is not 'It is enough' and so on, implying that from now he must go forward without them, but a repetition of the command to pray.

Luke almost certainly depends on the longer account. We need not decide whether he did not understand the Rabbinic provisions or whether he thought his readers might not understand them. What is interesting is that he has not turned the narrative into a legend, but has left it its historical, factual character. If the scene is dissociated from the Rabbinic law concerning a ḥabhura, then a request to the disciples to stay awake, or the attribution of a profound significance to their sleep, assumes the colour of legend. Luke, however, when he dropped the allusions to Rabbinic law, also dropped both the request to stay awake and the interpretation of the sleep of the companions as placing Jesus apart.

The omission of the scene from John is part of a wider problem, into which it is not intended here to inquire.

XI

Missionary Maxims in Paul

THE purpose of the following remarks is to suggest that two striking ideas about missionary methods are taken over by Paul from Jewish teaching on the subject: the idea that you must adopt the customs and mood of the person you wish to win over, and the idea that, to be a successful maker of proselytes, you must become a servant of men and humble yourself.

A. ACCOMMODATION

1. *I Corinthians*

First, for the idea of accommodation. Let us start from a passage in I Corinthians:[1] 'Unto the Jews I became as a Jew, that I might gain the Jews; to them that are under the law, as under the law, that I might gain them that are under the law; to them that are without law, as without law, that I might gain them that are without law; to the weak became I as weak, that I might gain the weak; I am made all things to all men, that I might by all means save some.'

This attitude had formed part of Jewish missionary practice long before Paul. Two Talmudic illustrations of Hillel's work are relevant:[2] he accepted into the fold a gentile who refused to acknowledge the oral Law, and he accepted another who refused to acknowledge any Law beyond the most fundamental ethical principle. True, he admitted them in order subsequently to instruct them and get them to see the absurdity of adhering to the written Law only, and the importance of rendering ethics practicable by means of a detailed code. But the fact remains that, at the decisive moment of conversion, he fell in with the notions of the applicant and declared himself satisfied with recognition of the written Law or a single, basic moral precept.

It is worth noting that the incidents are preserved in two versions, of

[1] 9.20 ff.　　　　　　　　　　　　　　　[2] Bab. Shab. 31a, Ab. de-R.N. 15.

which one, manifestly secondary, normalizes Hillel's method by making the detailed instruction precede the initiation. Whereas according to the older version—in the tractate Shabbath—Hillel 'received the candidate into the faith' on the candidate's terms and then led him to a better understanding, according to the secondary version—in Aboth de-Rabbi Nathan—he merely invited the candidate 'to sit down' to study and then led him to a better understanding. According to the secondary version, that is, Hillel's generosity consisted only in not showing the unenlightened applicant the door; according to the original version, he immediately accepted him as a Jew. The medieval commentator Rashi, too, finds it necessary, and not a little difficult, to justify the procedure described in the tractate Shabbath. Evidently, its dangerous implications were fully realized by later authorities, who attempted to get rid of them. Hillel, we might put it, was made all things to all men, that he might by all means save some.

Did he, or other Rabbis, formulate any maxim to express this method? His saying 'Keep not aloof from the congregation'[1] clearly contemplates life within the community. But there is another, which may chiefly contemplate relations to outsiders:[2] 'Do not appear naked, do not appear dressed, do not appear laughing, do not appear weeping —as it is said,[3] A time to weep and a time to laugh, a time to embrace and a time to refrain from embracing.'

To be sure, the place of the saying in the Tosephta shows that those who incorporated it in that compilation regarded it as a rule of seemly conduct, enjoining polite compliance with the habits of your company. It is possible, however, that, when first enunciated by Hillel, it was meant as a piece of advice for intercourse with prospective proselytes. There was in those centuries a constant two-way traffic between principles of morality or courtesy represented as of absolute validity and principles represented as useful for the treatment of such as might be converted to one's faith or prevented from leaving it.

On the one hand, many rules belonging to the former class were taken over into the latter. Both Jewish and Christian circles which were desirous of proselytes, in approaching heathens, deliberately stressed the precepts concerning decency and good manners at the expense of levitical and theological ones. Hillel, we have just seen, admitted a man who undertook to observe a single injunction: 'What is hateful to you,

[1] Mish. Ab. 2.5. [2] Tos. Ber. 2.24. [3] Eccles. 3.4 f.

Z

do not do to your fellow man.' Naturally some precepts of this type proved more effective, from the missionary point of view, than others, and as a result acquired prominence. When Simeon ben Shatah (of the first half of the 1st cent. B.C.) gave as reason for dealing honestly with an Arab that 'he preferred hearing the Arab say, Blessed be the God of the Jews, to all gain of this world',[1] he was turning an absolute ethical rule into one useful in the missionary field. Exactly the same is done by I Peter,[2] admonishing the faithful to 'have your conversation honest among the Gentiles, that they may by your good works glorify God'. Honesty—and not only to Arabs or gentiles—was an established virtue before Simeon ben Shatah or I Peter. In the passages cited, it becomes a missionary instrument.

Quite generally, the favourable or unfavourable impression of good or bad deeds on onlookers, and in particular onlookers from a different camp, was considered of enormous importance. To impress them favourably meant a sanctification or magnification of God's name, to impress them unfavourably a profanation. 'If ye work that which is good', we read in the Testament of Naphtali,[3] 'God shall be glorified among the Gentiles through you, but through him that doeth not that which is good God shall be dishonoured.' We may compare the exhortation in the sermon on the mount:[4] 'Let your light so shine before men that they may see your good works and glorify your Father.'

On the other hand, it happened that rules originally having regard to missionary activities in course of time lost their specific character. In Judaism, this must have been almost the normal development. As missionary zeal gave way to exclusiveness and rigid insistence on every detail of the Law, written or oral, those sayings were no longer suitable in their proselytizing sense. Some were discarded as heretical, others were re-interpreted as innocuous principles of proper conduct in general.

The phenomenon, however, occurs in Christianity also. There also the missionary setting of an utterance was occasionally lost sight of or eliminated. In the Letter of Aristeas[5] we find the argument that, though most people are generous to their friends, it is more important to be generous to your opponents, in order to make them realize what is right. The sermon on the mount also emphasizes the importance of

[1] Pal. B.M. 8c.   [2] 2.12.   [3] 8.4 ff.   [4] Matt. 5.16.   [5] 227.

loving your enemies,[1] but the missionary motive is far less pronounced; while in Paul's Epistle to the Romans,[2] that motive does come in again.

Suppose (we cannot be certain) that Hillel's saying referred to proselytizing, it would not be surprising that the Tosephta, composed at least two hundred years later, when concessions of the kind made by him had ceased to be tolerated, should treat it as a mere demand of politeness. We pointed out above an analogous alteration suffered by the stories of how he received into the community gentiles who did not recognize the Torah as understood by the Rabbis. According to the revised text—in Aboth de-Rabbi Nathan—Hillel did not really yield to these candidates, not even temporarily; he did not receive them and then instruct them. He was merely patient with them; instead of sending them away, he instructed them and then received them.

It is, however, in any case likely that, behind Hillel's missionary maxim (if it was one), there had stood a general rule of etiquette; just as a general rule underlies Simeon ben Shatah's and I Peter's exhortation to honesty with a view to conversions. R. Meir (of the middle of the 2nd cent. A.D.) quotes the proverb:[3] 'If you come into a city, do according to their customs.' There is no sign that this proverb, similar in substance to Hillel's advice and, maybe, as old or older, originated in missionary circles. Hillel may have known it. If not, he knew others little different. The point is that he seems to have given the idea a new turn; he seems to have realized its value for the achievement of his great aim of 'bringing the creatures nigh to the Law'.[4]

In the treatises Derekh Eretz Rabba and Derekh Eretz Zuta,[5] we meet with descendants of Hillel's maxim. The former contains this paragraph: 'A man should not be joyful among the weeping, nor weep among the joyful, nor wake among the sleeping, nor sleep among the waking, nor stand among the sitting, nor sit among the standing—the principle of the matter is, A man should not make different his mind from that of his fellows and the sons of men.' The passage from Derekh Eretz Zuta is substantially the same, with two exceptions: there is a further pair of warnings, 'nor should he read Scripture among those reading Mishnah, nor Mishnah among those reading Scripture', while

---

[1] Matt. 5.43 ff., cf. Luke 6.32 ff.
[2] 12.14, 20 f.
[3] Gen. Rabba on 18.8, Exod. Rabba on 34.28.
[4] Mish. Ab. 1.12.
[5] D.E. Rabba 8.4, D.E. Zuta 5.5.

the summing up runs, 'A man should not differ from the usage of the creatures.'

These paragraphs are evidence that Hillel's idea was taken up by others and lived on. Moreover, the changes in Derekh Eretz Zuta may be regarded as illuminating the process already mentioned: missionary maxims showing some laxity are turned into general rules of seemly conduct in strict harmony with the legalistic attitude. The version of Derekh Eretz Rabba might still come down direct from a missionary setting, where it meant: 'Accommodate yourself to any type of people, in order to convert them.' Derekh Eretz Zuta, on the contrary, includes technical details of a definitely Jewish nature, the additional pair of warnings concerning Scripture and Mishnah; and its summing up makes it quite clear that you are expected to adapt yourself only in matters of 'usage', social habits. It can only mean: 'Good manners require a certain degree of accommodation.'

Like Hillel's counsel in the Tosephta, the paragraphs discussed are both placed side by side with principles of courtesy. No wonder seeing that the treatises in which they occur were put together even later than the Tosephta. It should, however, be remembered that a growing number of scholars incline to the view that much of the material of these treatises goes back to a section of Judaism of strongly proselyting tendencies.

Two further points may be noticed. For one thing, rules about courtesy to strangers were apt to interest missionaries and become part of their programme. To be with strangers—whether they come to you or you to them—frequently means to be with persons whose creed differs from yours: they should be won over. For the Rabbis, the first great maker of proselytes was Abraham, who was hospitable to strange visitors. A text like 'The stranger would not lodge in the street, I would open my door to the traveller'[1] was widely interpreted as meaning that any gentile is welcome to God as a proselyte.[2] According to Matthew,[3] scribes and Pharisees would go out to distant countries in order to convert people. When Jesus appointed the first missionaries,[4] he gave them precise instructions as to the proper conduct in strange cities. As for the particular virtue of accommodation, in Greek literature and proverbs, for example, it is recommended mainly to travellers;

[1] Job 31.32.
[2] Exod. Rabba on 12.43.
[3] 23.15.
[4] Matt. 10.1 ff., Mark 6.7 ff., Luke 9.1 ff.

and it is recommended not as an absolute virtue, but as a means to an end. By adapting themselves to their hosts, they will obtain what they want.[1] All this renders it rather probable that Hillel did intend his maxim, which refers to behaviour among strangers, for use in missionary activity.

For another thing, in establishing the Jewish antecedents of Paul's plan, we need not rely exclusively on Hillel and sayings derived from his. In the Letter of Aristeas,[2] the king asks how he might meet with acceptance when travelling abroad; and the answer opens, 'By becoming equal to all', $\pi \hat{a}\sigma \iota \nu$ $\check{\iota}\sigma o\varsigma$ $\gamma \iota \nu \acute{o}\mu \epsilon \nu o\varsigma$. As it stands, it is advice for a traveller—a traveller who wishes to find favour with his hosts. Moreover, the term 'equal' has a political sense: the traveller is a king, and he is advised to make light of his rank. None the less it may be assumed that, as early as the time the Letter was composed, this was also a slogan of proselyte-makers. The author of the Letter himself was a Jewish propagandist.

Paul, when he wrote the passage from I Corinthians quoted at the beginning, was drawing on a living element in Jewish religion.

2. Romans

We must now turn to Romans:[3] 'Rejoice with them that do rejoice, and weep with them that weep; be of the same mind one toward another.' At least that is how the verses are usually translated.

That they are reminiscent of the rules in Derekh Eretz Rabba and Derekh Eretz Zuta has long been recognized; though, curiously, the older saying by Hillel is never adduced in this connection. But it is universally held that Paul has here in mind, not the missionary problem, not relations between Christians and outsiders, but life within the Christian society. This interpretation is not intrinsically untenable. There is no reason why the same principle of morality or etiquette should not be employed once with regard to missionary work and another time with regard to conduct within the community or even as of absolute validity; no reason why Paul should not have recommended accommodation as useful for proselytizers in I Corinthians and as a virtue within his flock in Romans.

As a matter of fact, however, the probability is that in Romans, too, he is dealing with relations between Christians and outsiders. This could

[1] Athenaeus, Deipn. 7.317a, 12.513b ff.   [2] 257.   [3] 12.15 f.

not, of course, be realized so long as the missionary setting—or at least the potential use for missionary purposes—of Hillel's maxim and its descendants was unsuspected. Once it is realized, a troublesome difficulty about the passage disappears.

The difficulty concerns the position of the passage in the structure of chapter 12. A series of demands are addressed to the new community. Verses 1 to 13 speak of conduct within the community, ending with an exhortation to hospitality. In view of what we said above about rules respecting the treatment of strangers, it is significant that, immediately after this exhortation, Paul goes on to relations with those outside: verse 14 runs, 'Bless them which persecute you, bless and curse not.' It is at this juncture that confusion appears to set in. According to the current interpretation, the next two verses, i.e. 15 f., 'Rejoice with them that do rejoice' etc., return to conduct within the community. Verses 17 to 21 again speak of conduct to outsiders, beginning with: 'Recompense to no man evil for evil, provide things honest in the sight of all men.' (The latter half of this verse enjoins honesty as a means of attracting unbelievers, on the same lines as Simeon ben Shatah and I Peter.) The awkwardness of this arrangement has not escaped modern commentators.[1]

In reality, the arrangement is in order. Verses 1 to 13 are devoted to conduct within the community, and 14 to 21 to conduct to those outside, or more precisely, individuals outside. Chapter 13, on the attitude to the Roman state, forms a logical continuation. The theme of conduct to individuals outside is far from interrupted by 15 f., 'Rejoice' etc. In these two verses Paul takes up the concept of accommodation we meet with in the Letter of Aristeas and, in a more elaborate form, in Hillel and the treatises about Derekh Eretz.

His way of putting it is nearest Derekh Eretz Rabba, but there are two notable differences. First, he has only one antithesis, rejoicing and weeping, whereas the Talmudic treatise has three. Hillel, it may be recalled, has two.

Secondly, the maxim in Derekh Eretz Rabba is negative, but Paul's is positive. Instead of 'A man should not be joyful among the weeping nor weep among the joyful, a man should not make different his mind from that of his fellows', in Paul we find: 'Rejoice with them that do rejoice and weep with them that weep, be of the same mind one toward

[1] E.g. C. H. Dodd, *The Epistle to the Romans*, 1932, p. 198.

another.' That the deviation is due to Paul is not, however, likely. There were no doubt positive versions prior to him. The proverb cited above is positive: 'When you come into a city, do according to their customs.' It has no reference to proselytizing, but we saw that general rules of this sort often formed the basis for specifically missionary ones; and in the Letter of Aristeas there is the positive injunction 'to become equal to all'.

The question is similar to that concerning the Golden Rule. In that case also both negative and positive formulations were known in pre-Christian times. Aristeas[1] combines the negative, not to do to another what you would not have done to yourself, with the positive, to let others partake of all the good of which you would want to partake. Alexander the Great, we hear in the Talmud, asked the Elders of the South: 'What should a man do to find favour with the creatures?' To which they replied: 'Let him hate kingship and power.' But he retorted: 'My thought is better than yours; I say, Let him love kingship and power, and do good to the sons of men.'[2] Whether historical or not, the anecdote is certainly very old. The Psalmist demands:[3] 'Keep thy lips from speaking guile, depart from evil and do good.' I Peter[4] quotes the negative beginning and the positive conclusion, and a 3rd cent. Rabbi expressly draws attention to the importance of 'not indulging in sleep' after observing the negative.[5] Eliezer ben Hyrcanus (about A.D. 90) says:[6] 'Let the honour of thy fellow be dear to thee as thine own.'

When an author preferred a prohibition to a positive precept or vice versa is a problem calling for a careful, impartial study. The Old Testament warns us:[7] 'If thine enemy be hungry, give him bread to eat, and the Lord shall reward thee.' This remains an important rule for the Rabbis, who declare the final clause to signify 'and the Lord shall make him a friend to thee'.[8] No doubt Paul accepts this interpretation when he replaces[9] 'and the Lord shall reward thee' by 'be not overcome of evil but overcome evil with good'. In the sermon on the mount,[10] we are admonished to 'bless them that curse you, pray for them which despitefully use you'. R. Meir (middle of the 2nd cent. A.D.) did pray for his enemies and saw that this was always the right course to take.[11]

[1] 207. [2] Bab. Tam. 32a. [3] 34.14 f. [4] 3.10 f.
[5] R. Alexander, in Bab. A.Z. 19b. [6] Mish. Ab. 2.10.
[7] Prov. 25.21 f. [8] Targ.: *nashlimeh* instead of *neshallemhe*.
[9] Rom. 12.21. [10] Matt. 5.44, cp. Luke 6.28. [11] Bab. Ber. 10a.

A more passive attitude is reflected in a meditation composed by Mar bar Rabina (beginning of the 5th cent. A.D.).[1] It is still recited by Jews three times a day, after the Eighteen Benedictions: 'To such as curse me let my soul be dumb, yea, let my soul be unto all as the dust.' Paul in Romans combines the positive and the negative: 'Bless and curse not.'

Verse 16 deserves special mention. 'Be of the same mind one toward another' must be misleading, i.e. must appear as concerned with behaviour within the community, unless we take account of the fact that it simply corresponds to the ending of the Jewish maxim: 'A man should not make different his mind from that of his fellows.' The negative injunction is replaced by a positive one, of the kind occurring in the Letter of Aristeas: 'Become equal to all.' That is the only change, which, plainly, does not detract from the missionary point of the rule; if anything, it renders it more intense in this context.

Admittedly, 'to be of the same mind' refers to unanimity within the community in other Pauline utterances.[2] But this is to be expected since, as repeatedly observed, accommodation was a recognized virtue before being made into a missionary method; and, of course, it always continued to rank among the forces holding a society together. Just so, the exhortations to honest dealings with outsiders do not mean that honesty has ceased to be a virtue within the community. It goes on to appear in the latter role.[3] Hillel, who went to such lengths in meeting prospective proselytes half-way, attached no less value to tolerance within Judaism: 'Keep not aloof from the congregation.' Again, the phrase 'one band', normally denoting a united Israel,[4] in a prayer prescribed for the New Year and Day of Atonement[5] includes the gentile world: 'O Lord, impose thine awe upon all thy works, that all creatures may prostrate themselves before thee and may all form one band to do thy will with a perfect heart.' There is nothing strange in Paul applying the notion 'to be of the same mind' to different situations.

It may be worth comparing two passages in Josephus's Contra Apionem,[6] where he praises mutual agreement, using ἀλλήλων or ἀλλήλους, 'one another'. In one of them he definitely thinks of the

[1] Bab. Ber. 17a, Singer's *Prayer Book*, p. 54.
[2] Rom. 15.5, II Cor. 13.11, Philip. 2.2, 4.2.   [3] E.g. Jas. 3.13.
[4] Lev. Rabba on 23.40, Tanh. ed. Buber, Debharim 24b f., on Deut. 29.9.
[5] Singer's *Prayer Book*, p. 239.
[6] 2.27.208, 2.19.179; cp. 2.16.170, 2.38.281, 2.39.283, 2.41.294.

inner life of the nation alone. After listing a large number of laws, he explains that it is these which 'keep together our association with one another', τὴν πρὸς ἀλλήλους ἡμῶν συνέχει κοινωνίαν. The other observation is of a more general character, not essentially confined to relations between Jews. Identity of religious belief, he says, and 'to differ from one another in nothing regarding life and habits will bring about a wonderful harmony in the natures of men', τῷ βίῳ μηδὲν ἀλλήλων διαφέρειν καλλίστην ἐν ἤθεσιν ἀνθρώπων συμφωνίαν ἀποτελεῖ.

The principal cause of the prevalent misinterpretation of verses 15 f., 'Rejoice', as contemplating life within the community is undoubtedly the fact that, for many centuries, translators have done scant justice to the original. It is verse 16 which has suffered most. The maxim to be found in Derekh Eretz is impersonal: 'A man should not make different his mind from that of his fellows.' In Romans, modern versions of the Bible—such as the English—put an imperative, a direct command addressed to the recipients of the letter: 'Be of the same mind one toward another.' Thus the impression is conveyed that the rule, far from being universal, has regard to internal conditions only. That is to say, 'one toward another' becomes equivalent to 'one of you toward another of you'. Yet the Greek has τὸ αὐτὸ εἰς ἀλλήλους φρονοῦντες, 'being of the same mind one toward another'. In the chapter on Haustafeln, we suggested that this constitutes an over-literal rendering of a Hebrew rule using the participle. The meaning is impersonal, and a closer translation would be: 'One should be of the same mind one toward another.' The Vulgate, incidentally, still retains the participle, 'idipsum invicem sentientes'.

When we consider that verse 15, in the Greek, is also impersonal, with two infinitives—still kept in the Vulgate, 'gaudere cum gaudentibus, flere cum flentibus'—the true connection with verse 14 becomes apparent. We must interpret thus: 'Bless them which persecute you; bless, and curse not. It is proper to rejoice with them that rejoice and weep with them that weep. One should be of the same mind one toward another.' There is here no break in the argument—unless we disregard the formulation of the original. It all concerns the attitude to those outside. It all has a missionary flavour.

We may perhaps add that, in the history of Christian mission, accommodation has often proved highly effective. It seems agreed that, if the Jesuits achieved greater things in China than the Franciscans, they did so because they paid more attention to the method in question.

B. SERVICE AND HUMILITY

1. *Paul*

The second part of Romans 12.16, so far left out of consideration, reads: 'Mind not high things, but condescend to low ones; be not wise in your conceits.' (The translation 'condescend to low ones', in the sense of 'undertake humble service', is preferable to 'condescend to men of low estate'.) In I Corinthians[1] the author declares that he has faithfully kept to this course: 'For though I be free from all men, yet have I made myself servant unto all, that I might gain the more.' We submit that this idea also is adopted by Paul from traditional Jewish teaching.

In Romans, the injunction 'Mind not high things' immediately follows 'Rejoice with them that rejoice.' In I Corinthians, the verse 'I have made myself servant unto all' immediately precedes 'And to the Jews I became as a Jew.' The intimate association of the duty of humble service with that of accommodation is indeed obvious.

Roughly, the latter duty—discussed above—may be said to follow from the former, which is wider: service demands many things, among them accommodation. The men Hillel had converted by falling in with their views met, we are told, and agreed: 'The meekness of Hillel brought us under the wings of the Shekhina.' Here, we find meekness as a missionary method traced back to Hillel, and we find it as closely connected with acceptance of the candidate's mood and customs as in Paul—meekness manifesting itself in acceptance of the other party's standpoint.

Hillel, however, was always meek, not only when he was out to gain a proselyte; and, of course, the general moral demand of meekness existed long before him—and not in Judaism alone. Even the notion that humility rather than self-assertion leads to greatness, success and the acquisition of friends considerably antedates Hillel, and it, too, is fairly universal, to be found all over the world. That you may have to 'stoop to conquer' was explained by Goldsmith neither under the influence of Hillel nor under that of Paul. (The idea may assume many

[1] 9.19.

different nuances. For instance, references to the conquest of an enemy by doing him good, 'beneficiis vincere', are no less frequent in pagan literature than in Jewish.)[1] It follows that, when men like Hillel introduced that specifically missionary twist, 'Stoop to conquer unbelievers', they were doing what was shown above to have been a common thing: they recognized the particular value of an ethical principle as a help in proselytizing.

In the Talmud and Midrash we come across a number of sayings by Hillel which express the idea that self-abasement is the road to glory as a general rule of morality, wisdom or good manners. It is quite conceivable that some of them were originally applied by him to the more specific question of the enlisting of new members of the faith. Take the statement 'My humility is my exaltation, and my exaltation is my humility.' In one source,[2] it is brought into connection with David's and Moses's humility before God, for which David obtained his victories and Moses the privilege of divine revelation. In another,[3] it is introduced as concerning humility before men, taking the lower seats, which conduct can only bring honour; and illustrations are taken from Moses's humility before God. Hillel himself may well have offered success in winning over unbelievers as further confirmation; or to put it differently, his saying may well have been meant to cover this province.

How freely the idea under notice passed from the domain of proper behaviour in general to that of behaviour to heathens and back again, may be seen from an anecdote[4] about a banquet provided by Gamaliel II (end of the 1st cent. A.D.). The venerable Rabbi stood to wait on his fellow-scholars. So far, this is just an example of humility in general. Some of the guests thought it wrong to accept the honour, but R. Joshua observed that Abraham had done the same for the angels though he took them for idolatrous Arabs (the Scriptural basis being the words 'and he stood by them under the tree').[5] There can be little doubt that Abraham's standing to wait on the 'Arabs' at one time figured among the many illustrations of his proselytizing activity, implying the maxim 'Stoop to conquer unbelievers.' In the anecdote, however, the missionary element has become irrelevant: his conduct simply means lowliness in general. But this is not the end. R. Zadok,

---

[1] Sallust, Bell. Jug. 9.3, Apuleius, Apol. 99.557.   [2] Exod. Rabba on 33.12.
[3] Lev. Rabba on 1.1.   [4] Mekh. on Exod. 18.12.   [5] Gen. 18.8.

the story goes on, was able to cap Joshua's quotation. He reminded the company that God himself served the creatures, sustaining the good and the bad, and even the worshippers of idols. Here we seem again to approach the universalistic, missionary side of the argument.

Pseudo-Phocylides[1] recommends sober persuasion of the wicked; he does not, like Hillel or Paul, go as far as to recommend humility. In the Letter of Aristeas we find three passages which bear on the matter in hand. The first says that one should persuade one's opponent in an attitude of subjection.[2] In the second,[3] the king asks how he might meet with acceptance when travelling abroad; and he is told 'to become equal to all and to behave rather as inferior than as superior to his hosts'. In the third,[4] he asks how to avoid pride; and he is told to bear in mind the virtue of equality, since God puts down the proud and exalts the humble. It is interesting that the two last-mentioned passages associate accommodation and humility, just as we find them associated in Paul and the stories about Hillel. True, in Aristeas, as far as accommotion is concerned, it is of a political rather than a social and theological character. The sequence in the Letter of Aristeas is the same as in Romans and the Rabbinic stories: accommodation—humility. In I Corinthians, we saw, it is humility—accommodation.

A closer examination of the grammar and vocabulary of the Pauline texts corroborates our thesis that he is working on an established Jewish missionary pattern. The exhortation 'Mind not high things but condescend to low ones', in Romans, like the first part of the verse ('Be of the same mind'), is framed in that curious way—by means of absolute participles—which must be explained as an over-literal rendering from Hebrew codes: $\mu\grave{\eta}$ $\phi\rho\rho\nuο\hat{\nu}\nu\tau\epsilon\varsigma$ $\grave{\alpha}\lambda\lambda\grave{\alpha}$ $\sigma\upsilon\nu\alpha\pi\alpha\gamma\acute{ο}\mu\epsilon\nu\omicron\iota$, 'Not minding but condescending.'

As for I Corinthians, Paul here uses $\kappa\epsilon\rho\delta\alpha\acute{\iota}\nu\omega$ for 'to win over an unbeliever'. In the next chapter we shall try to demonstrate that this application of the verb must be accounted for by reference to the Hebrew root *śkr* or its Aramaic equivalent *'gr*, and more particularly by reference to the use of *hiśtakker*. This term, with the primary meaning 'to profit', is employed by the Rabbis in the sense of 'to win over unbelievers or sinners'. There is a series of texts in which *hiśtakker* is so employed, and in which we find precisely the idea of making oneself servant that one might gain the more. It is, in fact, God who pro-

[1] 76 f.   [2] 266.   [3] 257.   [4] 262 f.

ceeds in this manner, who lets himself be conquered—i.e. induced to forgive—in order to gain the masses. So Paul, free from all men, serves all that he might gain the more. The similarity in thought and expression is too specific to make coincidence an acceptable solution.

The problem of date might perhaps be raised. In the Rabbinic texts, the earliest authority named is Ishmael ben Jose, who flourished towards the end of the 3rd cent. A.D. But, for one thing, various authorities base the idea on various sections in Scripture. This indicates that the idea as such is older than these authorities, who apply it each in his own way. For another thing, it is impossible to assume that the Rabbis drew on Paul's epistles in this matter. Quite apart from other arguments, the passage from I Corinthians was far too remote from and unimportant for them. Paul drew on a Rabbinic tradition. His background must be reconstructed by means of the texts containing *hištakker*—and, of course, those referring to Hillel and Abraham and the passages we have quoted from Aristeas and Pseudo-Phocylides. In all these latter cases, the question of date creates no difficulty at all; some are pre-Pauline and some roughly contemporary with Paul.

A further point deserves attention. When we go through the New Testament texts where $\kappa\epsilon\rho\delta\alpha\acute{\iota}\nu\omega$ is used as denoting 'to win over', a remarkable result emerges: they all represent humility as an instrument of conversion, however different may be the particular situations contemplated and the degrees of intensity with which the notion is set forth.

Enough has been said about I Corinthians, where $\kappa\epsilon\rho\delta\alpha\acute{\iota}\nu\omega$ appears five times in four successive verses. The first of them refers to the wider duty of serving in order to attract, the others to the duty of accommodation following from it.

I Peter[1] urges wives to 'be in subjection to your husbands, that if any obey not the word, they may be won by the conversation of the wives'. There is the absolute participle, $\alpha\acute{\iota}$ $\gamma\upsilon\nu\alpha\hat{\iota}\kappa\epsilon\varsigma$ $\acute{\upsilon}\pi\sigma\tau\alpha\sigma\sigma\acute{\sigma}\mu\epsilon\nu\alpha\iota$, 'the wives being in subjection to their husbands'. And there are good reasons for supposing that already in the source on which the author of the epistle drew, the demand of subordination was followed by a final clause giving conversion as the aim to be achieved in this way.[2]

Lastly, Matthew[3] contains an exhortation to self-restraint when you are wronged, in order to win over the offender: 'If thy brother shall

---

[1] 3.1.   [2] E. G. Selwyn, *The First Epistle of St. Peter*, 1946, p. 434.   [3] 18.15.

trespass against thee, tell him his fault between thee and him alone, and if he shall hear thee, thou hast gained thy brother.'

The most satisfactory mode of explaining this position is to postulate a missionary maxim—serve and be humble to gain those far from you—earlier than the codes underlying Paul, earlier than the source of I Peter and earlier than Matthew. This maxim in course of time was put to use in the most various domains. (Its absence from a section of Luke corresponding to that of Matthew here considered[1] may be due to Luke's unfamiliarity with the traditional way in which this maxim was expressed.) With this inference from internal evidence of the New Testament, the conclusion reached above on a comparative basis is in fullest harmony: that maxim was of Jewish origin.

2. *The Gospels*

We have just seen that one rule of conduct in Matthew at least is affected by our result. When we consider the range of application of the maxim in question in the Jewish sources—a king who travels should assume an attitude of lowliness if he wishes to find favour, an opponent will be more readily led to understanding if treated with deference, God lets himself be conquered in order to gain the masses, Abraham waits at table when dealing with prospective proselytes, Hillel remains submissive in the face of stupidity and arrogance on the part of candidates—it would not be surprising if it had influenced not only Paul and one exhortation in Matthew, but also some other pericopes in the gospels, both such as concern the activity of Jesus himself and such as concern the activity required of his followers. Furthermore, one would expect that difficulties of interpretation might occasionally be removed once we take due account of the fact that this and similar maxims had their roots in morality or wisdom in general, and that even after attaining particular, missionary significance, they were apt at any moment to become quite general again.

Mark offers one possible example.[2] The disciples wondered which of them was the greatest, whereupon Jesus exclaimed: 'If any man desire to be the first, the same shall be the last of all, and servant of all.' The text goes on: 'And he took a child and set him in the midst of them; and when he had taken him in his arms, he said, Whosoever shall receive one of such children in my name, receiveth me.'

[1] Luke 17.3.   [2] 9.33 ff. Cp. Matt. 18.1 ff., Luke 9.46 ff.

Of the latter verses Klostermann remarks:[1] 'They take over the motive of the blessing of children in 10.13–16, though it does not fit here. Where does the child of verse 36 come from? Why is it one only, against several in verse 37? Why is it being embraced?'

This criticism may be justified as far as it goes. None the less the association of the verses with what precedes appears less arbitrary if we suppose that it was effected by one for whom—rightly or wrongly, as far as the original sense of the saying is concerned—the phrase 'servant of all' was a missionary slogan, and the embracing of children symbolized the welcoming of converts. On this basis, the present place of the following verses, 38–40, which Klostermann finds even queerer, also becomes intelligible. For this section too, culminating as it does in Jesus's exhortation to tolerance towards those only loosely and unofficially bound to the new religion, contains an important principle as to the proper treatment of outsiders. Actually, the principle is similar in spirit to that discussed above, the principle of accommodation. Whoever made this arrangement would have looked on verse 41 as a suitable continuation: anyone showing kindness to Christians will be saved, even though he may not be a full member of the community. And verse 42 also was capable of being regarded as dealing with the same theme, namely, as a warning not to offend newcomers to the faith.

It is worth noting that the parallel section in Matthew is directly followed by the precept of reproving in private and thus winning over —κερδαίνω—one who has wronged you.

[1] *Das Markusevangelium*, 2nd ed., 1926, p. 105.

XII

A Missionary Term

Iт is generally held[1] that κερδαίνω in the sense of 'to win over an unbeliever to your faith'[2] or 'to win back a sinner to the way of life required by his and your faith'[3] is an 'echter terminus technicus der Missionssprache', with no precedent in either Hellenistic or Rabbinic language. This view is not correct. Admittedly, the sense is un-Greek. In Greek, κερδαίνω denotes 'to profit', 'to derive advantage', 'to traffic', but not 'to win over somebody'. The latter meaning would be more naturally expressed, say, by μετάγω or λαμβάνω, both occurring in the Letter of Aristeas,[4] or by (συν)αναπείθω, used by Josephus.[5] We may also grant that no Rabbinic parallels have so far been adduced. The most familiar Rabbinic words for 'to proselytize' are not to the point. *Qibbel* signifies 'to receive', not 'to gain', and there is no missionary fervour about it; while *hiqribh* is more fervent, but its proper meaning is 'to bring near', very different from κερδαίνω. Nevertheless the usage in question, though it may reflect a specifically Christian trend, is in the main determined by the Rabbinic vocabulary.

Three terms deserve consideration.

A. 'Kanas' (or 'kenas', 'kenash'), 'to gather'

In the Old Testament, this verb means 'to gather wealth': 'I gathered me silver and gold', or 'a time to cast away stones and a time to gather stones'.[6] It also means 'to gather men', and some of the passages are suggestive, speaking as they do of the bringing back of the diaspora: 'I caused them to be led into captivity but I have gathered them again', or 'The Lord gathereth together the outcasts of Israel.'[7]

---

[1] J. Weiss, *Der erste Korintherbrief,* 9th ed., 10th impr., 1925, p. 243, A. Schlier, *s.v.* κέρδος, κερδαίνω, in *Theologisches Wörterbuch zum Neuen Testament,* ed. by G. Kittel, vol. 3, 1938, p. 672. [2] I Cor. 9.19 ff., I Pet. 3.1. [3] Matt. 18.15.
[4] 227, 266. [5] Ant. 20.2.3.35. [6] Eccles. 2.8, 3.5. In both texts the Qal is used.
[7] Ezek. 39.28, Ps. 147.2. Piel in both texts.

In Rabbinic literature the verb continues to signify both 'to gather goods'—the Targum uses *kenash* in the text just cited, 'I gathered silver'—and 'to gather men'. There are the derivatives *kenesiyya*, 'a gathering of people', *beth hakkeneseth*, meaning on the one hand 'a storehouse for goods' (such as wood), on the other 'a synagogue', *keneseth yiśra'el*, 'the congregation of Israel', 'Ecclesia', *keneseth haggedhola*, 'the Great Synagogue'.[1] (The Aramaic forms are *kenisha'*, *kenishta'*.) It is noteworthy that the verb also retains the sense of 'to gather the diaspora'. The Targum employs it in the verse from Psalms, 'He will gather the dispersed of Israel';[2] and the Midrash explains that this line refers to the restoration of the diaspora, of the Ten Tribes, or of those excommunicated—people like Korah and his followers.[3] We are told that 'the diaspora will be gathered only as a reward of faith',[4] and that 'when he gathers them again, he will gather them only by means of clouds'.[5]

The term is used of 'the receiving, gathering in, of travellers'. The Jerusalemite Targum[6] makes Abraham say, 'I shall receive the passersby.' *Hakhnasath 'oreḥim*, 'the reception of travellers', 'hospitality', is a frequent expression.[7]

'To gather the diaspora', 'the excommunicated ones', 'the travellers' —to these uses must be added the blessing which a father had, and still has, to recite at his son's circumcision: 'Blessed art thou who hast commanded us to gather him into the covenant of Abraham.' The bystanders take up just this word and respond: 'As he has been gathered into the covenant, so may he be gathered to the Torah, nuptial canopy and good deeds.'[8]

But the verb is even directly used of 'the winning of proselytes'. For one thing, the well-known phrase 'to bring under the wings of the Shekhina', though as a rule a rendering of *hiqribh* or *qerebh*, 'to bring near', occasionally stands for a form of *kanas*, 'to gather'.[9] In Genesis[10] it is recorded that 'Abraham took all the souls that they had gotten.' The Hebrew is *'aśu*, the souls they had 'made'. The Midrash[11] accounts for the curious expression by asserting that Abraham took the souls 'they had gathered under the wings of the Shekhina'. The verb recurs in the famous utterance of Eleazar ben Pedath (of the second half of the

---

[1] Mish. Ab. 4.11, Pal. B.B. 14c, Mish. Meg. 3.1, Cant. Rabba on 1.4, Mish. Ab. 1.1.
[2] Ps. 147.2; Qal or Piel. [3] Cp. Mid. Ps. on 70.1 f.; Piel and Pual.
[4] Mekh. on Exod. 14.21; Hithpael. [5] Mekh. on Exod. 14.24; Piel.
[6] Gen. 18.3; Qal. [7] Bab. Shab. 127a. [8] Bab. Shab. 137b; Hiphil and Niphal.
[9] Qal, Piel or Hiphil. [10] 12.5. [11] Siph. on Deut. 6.5; cp. Lev. Rabba on 1.2.

2A

3rd cent. A.D. The text names Eliezer ben Hyrcanus, about A.D. 100, but this is universally considered to be a corruption. I am not entirely convinced. Eliezer's hostile remarks on proselytes as they are in reality do not prove that he may not have taken up a fundamentally positive attitude): 'God scattered Israel only in order that proselytes should be added; for Hosea says,[1] And I will sow her in the earth; does any man sow a small measure unless in order to gather many big ones?' This is a good illustration of the scope of the verb, which, in the phrase 'to gather big measures', denotes 'to win riches', yet alludes to 'the winning of converts' at the same time.

Finally, there is in the New Testament a close association between κερδανίω in the sense of 'to win over' or 'to win back' and σώζω , 'to save'.[2] This is to be expected. But it is interesting that in Rabbinic language, too, *kanas*, 'to gather', may be synonymous with *hiṣṣil*, 'to save':[3] 'Isaiah says,[4] Then Hezekiah (desperately ill) turned to the wall and prayed; according to Joshua ben Levi (first half of the 3rd cent. A.D.) he turned to the wall of Rahab, saying, Lord of the universe, Rahab saved only two souls for thee, *hiṣṣil* (the spies she helped to escape), and how many souls hast thou saved for her, *hiṣṣil* (all her family were spared);[5] my fathers gathered for thee all the proselytes, *kanas*, how much the more shouldest thou spare me!'

B. 'QANA' (OR 'QENE')

This is the usual verb, both in the Old Testament and in Rabbinic writings, for 'to buy', 'to acquire', though when God is the subject, it may also mean 'to found', 'to create'. It refers to 'the winning of men', for instance, in Sirach,[6] 'If thou gainest a friend, gain him by trial', and in the Mishnah,[7] 'Joshua ben Perahyah (second half of the 2nd cent. B.C.) says, Gain thee a fellow-disciple.'

It occurs in a maxim somewhat similar to that which we find in the Synoptics,[8] emphasizing the disappointment of a man 'if he shall gain, κερδαίνω, the whole world and lose his soul'. We are informed:[9] 'In Palestine they say, If a man has gained knowledge, what does he lack? If he has not gained that, what has he gained?'

---

[1] 2.25.
[2] I Cor. 9.22, I Cor. 7.16 in conjunction with I Pet. 3.1, Jas. 5.20 with Matt. 18.15.
[3] Eccles. Rabba on 5.6.   [4] 38.2.   [5] Joshua 2, 6.25.   [6] 6.7.
[7] Ab. 1.6; cp. 4.11.   [8] Matt. 16.26, Mark 8.36, Luke 9.25.   [9] Bab. Ned. 41a.

It is doubtful, however, whether the verb ever has the sense of 'to proselytize'. Perhaps we ought to mention a Rabbinic comment[1] on Melchizedek's greeting of Abraham: 'Blessed be thou of the most high God, creator—possessor, acquirer, *qone*—of heaven and earth.' R. Isaac (of the second half of the 3rd cent. A.D.) takes 'creator' as an attribute of Abraham: as he converted people to monotheism, God regarded him as his partner in the creation. *Qone*, then, is here interpreted as 'creator', but there may be a pun on the sense of 'gainer', 'converter'. The same pun may underlie a remark to the effect that Abraham, in Melchizedek's greeting, appears as a special possession of God: God 'possesses', or, if this pun is intended, 'converts', Abraham. That Abraham was the first proselyte is a favourite idea of the Rabbis.[2] Possibly, an allusion to proselytizing is contained also in the words addressed by God to Gabriel, *qene lekha 'edha*, 'found—or, gain—thee a congregation'.[3] But if so, it is remote, and in any case the passage is obscure. On the other hand, there are texts which certainly do not belong here, since it is the proselyte who 'gains God', not God or the faithful who gains the proselyte. For example, Jethro, the Midrash affirms,[4] is called a Kenite 'because he gained, *qana*, heaven and earth'. We have already quoted a maxim about the importance of 'gaining knowledge'—a similar usage of the verb; and we may add Hillel's saying (of the last cent. B.C.):[5] 'If a man has gained words of the Law, he has gained life in the world to come.'

C. 'Śakhar'

So far we have seen that the verbs *kanas* and *qana* signified both 'to acquire wealth' and 'to gain men'; and *kanas* at least was definitely a missionary term. Yet they do not fully account for the use of κερδαίνω in the manner indicated. Had they alone influenced the writers in Greek, surely the choice would have fallen on a Greek verb with the same basic sense as *kanas*, namely, 'to gather', or with the same basic sense as *qana*, 'to buy', 'to acquire'. Therefore, while *kanas* and *qana* no doubt helped to prepare the ground, we consider a third verb as the one of which κερδαίνω is an immediate translation: *śakhar* or, in the forms more common in the relevant texts, *niśkar* and *hiśtakker*. We may admit

---

[1] Gen. Rabba on 14.19.   [2] Bab. Suk. 49b.
[3] Bab. Pes. 118b.   [4] Siph. on Num. 10.29.   [5] Mish. Ab. 2.7.

at the outset that there is a slight gap in our evidence, which we shall point out. At any rate, here are the principal arguments.

First, the general range of the Rabbinic term, and the way in which it can be applied, are highly reminiscent of κερδαίνω. The noun *śakhar* denotes 'wages', 'profit', 'advantage', '*lucrum*'; it can be used exactly like κέρδος. The Mishnah lays down[1] that 'none may set up a shop-keeper on the condition of receiving half the profit'. In the spiritual sphere the Torah, Wisdom, Life to come, fulfilment of a commandment or martyrdom may be the *śakhar* of the pious.[2] So the Christian's κέρδος is Christ.[3] The Mishnah distinguishes various characters.[4] Of one, easy to provoke and easy to appease, it is said that 'his loss is cancelled by his gain'. The regular opposite of *śakhar*, 'profit', is *hephsedh*, 'loss'. It occurs in this saying, and it corresponds to ζημία, the regular opposite of κέρδος. Just so, the regular opposite of the verb *niśkar* or *hiśtakker*, 'to profit', is *hiphsidh* or *niphsadh*, 'to suffer loss', corresponding to ζημιοῦμαι, the opposite of κερδαίνω. 'But what things were gains, κέρδος, to me', Paul writes,[5] 'I counted loss, ζημία; I count all things loss, ζημία, for Christ, for whom I have lost all things, ζημιοῦμαι, that I may win Christ, κερδαίνω.' Philo[6] gives as a reason for the Seventh Year: 'Do not be entirely under the power of lucre, κέρδος, but submit to some loss, ζημία.' To quote a few more examples from the Rabbis—Judah the Prince says:[7] 'Reckon the loss (material loss) resulting from a precept against its reward (from God), and the reward (material) from a transgression against its loss (from God).' Another epigram is:[8] 'Some are industrious and gain— namely, those working all the week but not on the eve of the Sabbath— and some are industrious and lose—those working also on the eve of the Sabbath.' According to Admon (of the 1st cent. A.D.), a son who gets no inheritance because his father leaves just enough to maintain the daughters may complain: 'Must I suffer loss because I am a male?' Ben Nanos (of the first half of the 2nd cent. A.D.) disagrees with the view that, if a man is survived by several wives, only the one he married last may receive her jointure without taking an oath: 'Should she profit because she is the last?'[9] Instead of *śakhar*, sometimes its Aramaic equivalent, *'aghar*, *'aghra'*, is contrasted with *hephsedh*: 'A bond was

---

[1] B.M. 5.4.　　[2] E.g. Gen. Rabba on 6.3, Mish. Ab. 4.2, Bab. Men. 29b.
[3] Philip. 3.7 f.　　[4] Ab. 5.11.　　[5] Philip. 3.7 f., just adduced.
[6] Leg. Spec. 2.19.87.　[7] Mish. Ab. 2.1.　[8] Bab. Pes. 50b.　[9] Mish. Ket. 13.3, 10.5.

issued against the children of R. Ilish, stipulating half profits and half loss.'[1]

Secondly, as for the verb, *niśkar* or *hiśtakker*, quite apart from its relation to *hiphisidh*, *niphsadh*, $\zeta\eta\mu\iota\omega\tilde{\upsilon}\mu\alpha\iota$, just discussed, it might be rendered by $\kappa\epsilon\rho\delta\alpha\iota\nu\omega$ in a great many cases. It means 'to be at an advantage' in a decision by R. Meir (middle of the 2nd cent. A.D.)[2] that if an ox gores several oxen, the claim of the owner of the last takes precedence: the owner of the last 'is at an advantage'. A principle frequently operating is that the law must be formulated in such a way that a sinner or dishonest person should not 'profit', 'be at an advantage'. If dough becomes unclean, only a very small proportion need be given up as dough-offering; but should a woman intentionally render the dough unclean, the normal proportion is due, in order that the sinner 'shall not profit'.[3] Here also, the opposite *hiphsidh* occurs: R. Jose (middle of the 2nd cent. A.D.) rejects certain opinions because, if they were law, 'what loss would the deceiver suffer?'[4] This reasoning is clearly allied with that according to which a sinner 'must make no profit'. Again, the verb means 'to benefit by a thing'. Jacob, the Midrash says,[5] 'benefited by', 'derived advantage from', his flock, getting the milk and wool. The Talmud states[6] that 'no man knows by which enterprise he will profit'. It may even signify, like $\kappa\epsilon\rho\delta\alpha\iota\nu\omega$, 'to deal in', 'to traffic'. R. Ishmael (of the first half of the 2nd cent. A.D.) held that with the surplus of the Shekel-chamber wine and the like should be bought, that it should be resold to those wishing to bring a private offering, and that 'the profit', *śakhar*, should go to the Temple: while Akiba (his contemporary) was of opinion that 'one should not traffic' with what belongs to the Temple.[7] In popular, modern dictionaries,[8] *niśkar* and *hiśtakker* are listed as denoting 'to earn', 'to profit', or, in German, '*verdienen*', '*profitieren*'—values precisely equivalent to $\kappa\epsilon\rho\delta\alpha\iota\nu\omega$.

Thirdly, we have already adduced a Rabbinic saying comparable to the Synoptic one about him who 'gains the whole world and loses his soul'; in that saying *qana* is used. But we also find one where *hiśtakker*

---

[1] Bab. B.M. 68b.   [2] Mish. B.K. 4.1.
[3] Mish. Hal. 2.7. Cp. Mish. Sheb. 9.9, Bab. Yeb. 92b.
[4] Mish. B.M. 3.4 f.   [5] Tanh. Wayyeshebh 13 on Gen. 38.1.
[6] Bab. Pes. 54b. Cp. also Mish. Er. 3.6.   [7] Mish. Sheq. 4.3. Cp. Bab. B.B. 91a.
[8] E.g. I. Raffalovitch, *Anglo-Hebrew Modern Dictionary*, *s.vv.* 'earn' and 'profit', I. Elfros, J. Ibn-Shmuel Kaufman and B. Silk, *English-Hebrew Dictionary*, *s.vv.* 'earn' and 'profit', M. D. Gross, *Hammillon Hashshalem*, part I (Hebrew-German), *s.v. śakhar*.

takes the place of κερδαίνω. Simeon II ben Gamaliel II, Judah and Jose (all of the middle of the 2nd cent. A.D.) reproached a man who did not pay his tithes properly:[1] 'Thou hast gained money but destroyed—or lost, 'ibbedh—souls.' It is easy to see why, in this connection, 'ibbedh, 'to destroy', 'to lose', may be opposed to hiśtakker: its meaning is here no different from that of the normal opposite of hiśtakker, i.e. hiphsidh. However, hiphsidh itself occurs in an older version of the saying. Eleazar ben Azariah (of the first third of the 2nd cent. A.D.), combating the exemption of certain groups from certain tithes, exclaimed to his antagonist: 'Lo, thou wouldest make them enjoy worldly riches (mamon, our 'mammon'), yet thou wouldest but lose souls.'[2] (That this is the older version follows not only from the date of Eleazar but also from the fact that the plural, 'souls', fits his statement better than that of Simeon II, Judah and Jose: Eleazar contemplates whole sections failing to pay their tithes, the other Rabbis address one individual only.) It is also worth noting that just as hiphsidh is replaceable by 'ibbedh, so is ζημιοῦμαι by ἀπόλλυμι. In the Testament of Judah we read that a fornicator 'suffers loss', ζημιοῦμαι, in that of Reuben that fornication 'destroys', ἀπόλλυμι.[3]

Fourthly, Symmachus has κέρδος for śakhar in the verse:[4] 'Two are better than one, because they have a good reward for their labour.' The LXX, it may be observed, does not use κερδαίνω and κέρδος at all: it normally renders śakhar by μισθός. The reason is not far to seek. In the Old Testament, śakhar and its derivatives have not yet attained the range of κερδαίνω; μισθός and μισθοῦμαι more or less cover the ground; nor is there any other synonym of κερδαίνω. How far the development had gone by the time of the LXX, it is impossible to say. When Symmachus wrote, it was undoubtedly completed: śakhar had all the meanings to which we have referred. Its translation by κέρδος, in a verse where it plainly does not signify μισθός in the narrow sense, must now have appeared quite natural.

Fifthly and lastly, there is a series of texts of particular interest where hiśtakker denotes 'to win men'. The Psalmist says, 'He will not always chide.'[5] The Hebrew for 'always', laneṣaḥ, is interpreted by the Rabbis as meaning 'for conquest', so that they obtain: 'He will not chide for conquest.' God, the Midrash explains, reflects thus: 'Did I not conquer

---

[1] Tos. M.S. 3.18.   [2] Mish. Yad. 4.3.
[3] Judah 15.1, Reuben 4.7.   [4] Eccles. 4.9.   [5] 103.9.

the generation of the Flood and I suffered loss (*hiphsidh*, $\zeta\eta\mu\iota o\hat{v}\mu\alpha\iota$)? But when Moses conquered me (obtaining forgiveness for the people after they had made the Golden Calf) I profited (*hiśtakker*, $\kappa\epsilon\rho\delta\alpha\acute{\iota}\nu\omega$) in my world. Hence, He will not chide for conquest.' Resh Lakish (of the middle of the 3rd cent. A.D.) gives the main idea in a more general form:[1] 'God says, When I conquer I suffer loss (*hiphsidh*), but when I am conquered I gain (*hiśtakker*). I conquered dealing with the generation of the Flood, but I lost (*hiphsidh*), for I destroyed all those masses ('*okhloza*', the Greek $\check{o}\chi\lambda os$). But when the Golden Calf was made, Moses conquered me and I gained (*hiśtakker*) all those masses.' In another passage the idea is propounded in connection with the verse from Isaiah:[2] 'For he will not be wroth for conquest'—*laneṣaḥ* being taken in this sense instead of its real meaning 'always'. In support, the Midrash adduces the opening of a Psalm,[3] 'To the chief musician', *lamenaṣṣeaḥ*, which phrase is declared to mean: 'To him that rejoices when they conquer him.' Traces of this exegesis may be found in a remark attributed to Ishmael ben Jose, a contemporary of Judah the Prince.[4]

We submit that *niśkar* or *hiśtakker*, used of 'the making of a profit' and of 'the gaining by God of men whom he had cast away', accounts for the role of $\kappa\epsilon\rho\delta\alpha\acute{\iota}\nu\omega$ as a missionary term in the New Testament. Admittedly, we have come across no texts where the Rabbinic term denotes 'to convert'; and this particular nuance, therefore, may still be Christian, though we do not think so. This is the gap in our argument, which we announced at the beginning. The masses which God 'gains' in the series of texts just examined are Israelites condemned and reprieved, 'won back', not gentiles 'won over'. But it is not a serious gap, as three considerations will show.

In the first place, in Matthew at least,[5] $\kappa\epsilon\rho\delta\alpha\acute{\iota}\nu\omega$ signifies, not 'to win over proselytes', but 'to win back a sinner', just like the Rabbinic term. For this application, then, the evidence leaves nothing to be desired.

In the second place, in one ancient saying, the Aramaic equivalent of *śakhar*, to which we referred before, namely, '*aghar*, is employed in a manner all but positive proof that proselytes proper, won over from another faith, might be described by this word. Simeon ben Shatah (of the first half of the 1st cent. B.C.) refused to regard as his own a pearl

[1] P. R. 166b.
[2] 57.16; see P.R. 32b–33a.
[3] 4.1.
[4] Bab. Pes. 119a.
[5] 18.15.

found on an ass which had been bought for him from an Arab, declaring[1] that he was no *barbari*, barbarian, and that he preferred hearing the Arab say 'Blessed be the God of the Jews'—*scil.* whose followers are so honest—to all *'aghar*, 'gain', of this world. Surely, where such an expression was possible, it was also possible to 'gain a proselyte'. In an age when one might be recognized as belonging to a faith though very loosely attached to it, causing a gentile to praise God did constitute a kind of proselytizing. The New Testament contains suggestive passages like 'Let your light so shine before men that they may see your good works and glorify your Father.'[2] In chapter 2 of I Peter there is the admonition, 'Having your conversation honest among gentiles, that they may by your good works, which they shall behold, glorify God', in chapter 3, 'Ye wives, be in subjection to your husbands that if any obey not the word, they may be won while they behold your chaste conversation.'[3] The latter verse has κερδαίνω.

This leads to the third consideration. Nowadays we distinguish rather sharply between mission proper, the 'winning over' of un-believers, and *innere Mission*, the 'winning back' of lax and sinning members of the faith. Certainly the difference existed, was seen and had practical consequences even in the earliest Rabbinic period. But when we recall, what we just adverted to, that there were various degrees of membership of a faith, some in closer, some in vaguer contact with the centre; further, that there must have been a constant fluctuation be-tween them; and that the organization of a faith was quite generally not too rigid, we shall hardly expect two separate vocabularies for the two types of mission. Even nowadays we speak of 'the conversion of a sinner' as well as 'the conversion of a pagan'.

In other words, it is most unlikely that a writer using κερδαίνω of the 'winning back of a sinner', as it is used in Matthew, would have hesitated to use it, as it is used in Paul and I Peter, of actual 'proselyti-zing'. Nor can we think of any reason why the Rabbis, who used *niśkar* and *hiśtakker* of the 'winning back of sinning and doomed Israelites', should have avoided the term in speaking of 'missionizing' proper. However, even if we proceed from the former, narrower application, it is clear that when κερδαίνω became a missionary term in early Christianity, it was far from unsuitable. As a rendering of *niśkar* or *hiśtakker*, it was a good choice.

[1] Pal. B.M. 8c.   [2] Matt. 5.16.   [3] 2.12, 3.1 f.

In the last chapter (Missionary Maxims) we saw that the passages in the Epistles where κερδαίνω occurs in the sense of 'to win over to one's faith' are altogether modelled on Jewish missionary schemes— which corroborates our thesis regarding the origin of the usage of this verb.

XIII

Terms for Divorce

A. PAUL

LET us begin with Paul, whose terminology distinctly reflects the Rabbinic attitude. In his remarks on divorce he uses χωρίζεσθαι and ἀφιέναι. Both are good technical terms. Yet it is clear, on the one hand, that ἀφιέναι is a much better rendering of what a Jewish husband does when he 'expels', 'dismisses' or 'lets go away' his wife, namely, of *gerash*, *shillah* or *hoṣi'* (or, in Aramaic, *tarekh* or *peṭar*); and, on the other hand, that a Jewish wife under Jewish law cannot ἀφιέναι her husband but only 'go away' or 'separate' from him, *halakh*, *yaṣa'*, *parash* (*nephaq*, *perash*). 'To separate', incidentally, may denote the same as 'to go away', i.e. actual departure from the common domicile, or merely avoidance of intercourse. Strictly, only the husband can dissolve the marriage. The woman may run away or refuse compliance, which has no legal effect whatever. As Josephus puts it,[1] though she may 'separate by her own decision', διαχωρίζεσθαι καθ' αὑτήν, yet she cannot marry another man unless her husband first 'concedes' her, ἐφιέναι, or, to go by the less likely reading, 'dismisses' her, ἀφιέναι. It is true that given certain conditions—for example, if the husband practises the craft of a coppersmith or tanner, or is afflicted with boils—she may institute proceedings culminating in his being compelled to divorce her. But even then it is the husband who dissolves the bond, though against his will. Of her, it would still be said that she 'separates', 'goes away' or 'is let go away'.[2]

Accordingly, in the first two verses,[3] with reference to a marriage where both parts are believers, Paul uses the intransitive χωρίζεσθαι of the wife who 'separates', but the transitive ἀφιέναι of the husband who 'dismisses' his wife. This is in perfect agreement with the Jewish

---

[1] Ant. 15.7.10.259. [2] E.g. Mish. Ned. 11.12. [3] I Cor. 7.10 f.

ideas on the subject. In the next two verses,[1] with reference to a marriage where only one party is a believer, he uses the transitive ἀφιέναι both of the dissolution of the marriage by the husband and of its dissolution by the wife. The latter application of ἀφιέναι is justified since the procedure he has in mind is a non-Jewish one, Roman or Greek. Again, a little further on[2] he uses χωρίζεσθαι of the dissolution of the marriage by an unbelieving partner, husband or wife. No special justification is here needed, the verb being a proper term for divorce. We ought perhaps to add the noun λύσις, 'release', a somewhat untechnical word for divorce by the husband—Jewish or gentile—in the admonition:[3] 'Art thou bound unto a wife? seek not release.'

In confirmation of this analysis it may be pointed out that, in Rabbinic literature, the transitive *gerash*, 'to expel', is used once and once only of the wife divorcing her husband, and that it is in a discussion of gentile divorce. The Rabbis observe[4] that in some gentile nations the wife may 'expel' her husband. This is a close parallel to the way in which Paul uses ἀφιέναι of the action of the wife under gentile law. To be sure, divorce by mutual agreement—common throughout the Hellenistic world—may be described as 'expelling one another' whether the couple is gentile or Jewish.[5] As far as Jewish divorce is concerned, this expression is somewhat loose, seeing that the technical dismissal even here is the doing of the husband alone. But it is easy to understand how the phrase came into existence. Moreover, the earlier Rabbis may well have preferred the more exact 'leaving one another', 'being left by one another' or 'separate from one another':[6] *'azabh* and *parash* (*shabheq* and *perash* in Aramaic), 'to leave', are terms no less correct for a Jewish wife's part in divorce than for a husband's.

As regards Paul's 'Aryan' followers at Corinth, presumably most of them were either under Roman or Greek law. In the Roman law of the time, that kind of marriage by which the wife came into the *manus* of her husband (that is to say, passed out of her father's family and came under her husband's rule, *filiae loco*) could be dissolved only by the husband; while the other kind, without *manus*, could be dissolved by either party. The latter kind, without *manus*, was no doubt the more frequent by the 1st cent. A.D. As for Greek law, under the old

---

[1] 7.12 f.   [2] 7.15.   [3] 7.27.   [4] Gen. Rabba on 2.24, Pal. Qid. 58c.
[5] Gen. Rabba on 2.24, Pal. Qid. 58c (gentile divorce), Gen. Rabba on 2.21 (Jewish divorce).   [6] Cant. Rabba on 1.4.

Attic law a husband could divorce his wife, but a wife could dissolve the marriage only with the help of the Archon—a system not unlike the Jewish. She had to produce valid reasons, and the later writers of comedies were fond of this situation.[1] When we consider the Talmudic discussions of the question on what grounds a woman may claim release from marriage—a few of the recognized grounds have been mentioned above—we can well believe that here was material for the comedists. Nevertheless in some Greek states the women from early times seem to have enjoyed the same rights in regard to divorce as the men.[2] At any rate in the Greek law of the papyri, of particular importance in this connection, as a rule either party might dissolve the union.

It is, however, noteworthy that if a husband divorces his wife, the Roman sources regularly speak of *expellere, dimittere, exigere* and the papyri of ἐκβάλλειν, ἀποπέμπειν and the like, whereas if a wife divorces her husband, they speak of *abire, discedere,* ἀπαλλάττεσθαι, ἀποζεύγνυσθαι, ἀπολείπειν, ἐξέρχεσθαι, χωρίζεσθαι, and so on.[3] Diodorus Siculus, about the middle of the 1st cent. B.C., employs ἀπολύειν with reference to a wife divorcing her husband,[4] but for several centuries he appears to have had little following among non-Jewish writers. Two factors may account for this usage. For one thing, ordinarily, the husband would be the owner of the conjugal residence. Therefore, irrespective of any equality of rights in respect of divorce as such, dissolution of the marriage by him would involve eviction of his wife, while dissolution of the marriage by her would not involve eviction of her husband; it is still she who would have to depart. For another thing, even in the systems under notice, quite likely there was a stage when a wife either had not, or very rarely exercised, the legal power to end the marriage. Language is always conservative. It continued reflecting that stage even when it was a matter of the remote past. It was left to Paul and the Rabbis, who looked at the gentile practice from without, analysing it and comparing it with their own, to call it by its proper name. They saw, and said, that a gentile wife could 'expel'—αφιέναι, *gerash*—her husband.

---

[1] Lipsius, *Das Attische Recht*, vol. 2, pt. 2, pp. 485 ff.
[2] To this extent, Diodorus Siculus 12.18 probably deserves credit.
[3] See, besides the dictionaries, Mitteis and Wilcken, *Grundzüge der Papyruskunde*, vol. 2, 1912, pt. 1, pp. 216 f., and E. Levy, *Der Hergang der römischen Ehescheidung*, 1925, pp. 4 ff., 106 ff.
[4] 12.18.1.

It may be added that *gara'* (*mena'*), ἀποστερέω, 'to withhold', 'to reduce', does not mean a definite refusal of marital companionship, a separation like *parash*, still less a termination of marriage, but rather a grudging of intercourse. An ancient law in Exodus[1] provides that if a man buys another's daughter, lives with her and later takes a second wife, he may not 'diminish' the first one's due. Paul no doubt uses the verb in the same sense when he admonishes married couples[2] to fulfil their mutual obligations and not to 'defraud' one another.

B. 'And if a Woman shall put away her Husband'

Of all the synoptic passages concerning divorce, Mark 10.12 is the only one to contemplate an ending of the companionship by the wife. This in itself would constitute no serious difficulty. Even a Jewish wife could run away from her husband. Actually, in Paul, the warning that she ought not to do so precedes the warning that a husband must not divorce his wife.[3] The problem is that whereas Paul, in the rules referring to Jewish couples, speaks of the wife 'departing', 'separating', from her husband, Mark 10.12 uses the transitive ἀπολύειν, 'to dismiss'. This sounds quite un-Rabbinic.

There are two possible solutions: the un-Rabbinic formulation may or may not go back to Mark. It may go back to Mark because, though Jewish law did not allow a woman to divorce her husband, there were circles in which this occurred. Salome, we learn from Josephus,[4] did send her husband a bill of divorce, 'dissolving the marriage contrary to the laws of the Jews'; and the verb is ἀπολύεσθαι (middle)— ἀπολυομένη τὸν γάμον—though admittedly 'to dissolve the marriage' is not quite so strong as the Markan 'to dismiss the husband'. Again, there was Herodias. Formally, she went less far. She did not, that is, write her husband a bill of divorce but simply 'separated'—διαστᾶσα.[5] Yet she married again while he was still alive. Moreover, such criticism as has come down to us seems directed against her marrying her husband's brother rather than against her remarrying as such. It is, of course, possible that the crime of incest was considered so monstrous that little mention was made of other weak points about her second

---

[1] 21.10.
[3] I Cor. 7.10 f.
[4] Ant. 15.7.10.259.

[2] I Cor. 7.3 ff.

[5] Josephus, Ant. 18.5.4.136.

marriage; or again, her first husband may have divorced her when she left him. But it remains a remarkable affair.[1]

It should also be noted that from two papyri of the 5th cent. B.C. it looks as if at Elephantine at least a Jewish wife could legally terminate the union by 'disliking and leaving' (*śene' unephaq*) her husband or by a public declaration of 'dislike' (*śene'*).[2] The association of the term 'dislike' with divorce is old.[3] It has been maintained[4] that these texts refer, not to the wife's divorcing her husband, but to her compelling him to divorce her. But considering that one of them describes dissolution of the marriage by the husband in exactly the same words as its dissolution by the wife—'standing up in the congregation and saying, I dislike my partner'—the probability is that there were regions where the women had gained a stronger position than the Bible or Talmud accords them.

Despite these considerations, there is much to be said for the other alternative, namely, that ἀπολύειν in Mark 10.12 is not genuine. The point is that in Codex Bezae (D), the Koridethianus (Θ) and some *codices* of the Itala there may be found a variant reading, fully compatible with Jewish law and Paul's way of looking at the matter: not 'and if a woman shall put away her husband', ἀπολύειν, but 'and if a woman shall depart from her husband', ἐξέρχομαι, *exire*, *discedere*. According to Nestle's apparatus, the *codices* of the Itala supporting D and Θ are only few.[5] Strictly speaking this is correct. But in addition to those having *exire* or *discedere*, there are others (MSS. Bob., Colb. and Holm.) giving *relinquere*. From the legal point of view, there is no difference between 'departing from the husband' and 'leaving him'. Either was open to a Jewish wife under Jewish law. It is only *dimittere* which she could not do.

In fact the existence of the *codices* with *relinquere* should preclude any attempt that might be made to declare all the part of the Itala which is consistent with Jewish law as descended from the Greek represented by D, and then to declare D as for some reason or other irrelevant.

---

[1] F. C. Burkitt, indeed, in his *The Gospel History and Its Transmission*, pp. 100 f., takes the saying in Mark as directly referring to the action of Herodias.

[2] Cowley, *Aramaic Papyri*, 1923, pp. 26 ff., 45 ff.

[3] See the dictionaries and, on the technical meaning of the excuse given by Samson's father-in-law (Judges 15.2: 'I thought that thou hadst hated her'), Daube, *Revue Internationale des Droits de l' Antiquité*, 1949, pp. 193 f.

[4] L. M. Epstein, *Jewish Marriage Contract*, p. 202.

[5] E. Nestle, *Novum Testamentum Graece*, 13th ed., 1923, p. 113: '*pc* it'.

Relinquere presupposes ἀπολείπειν or the like. We must reckon, that is, with at least two Greek forms of the saying possible in a Rabbinic environment: one using ἐξέρχομαι (*exire, discedere*) and one using ἀπολείπειν (*relinquere*).

It would not be difficult to explain why, if Mark wrote ἐξέρχομαι or ἀπολείπειν, this was almost completely ousted by ἀπολύειν, and at an early date too. For one thing, the sentence immediately preceding is directed against a husband 'dismissing' (ἀπολύειν) his wife. So indeed are all remaining synoptic passages dealing with the subject.[1] Mark 10.12 may have been assimilated to them; it may have been made to refer, like them, to divorcing one's partner instead of to running away from him. For another thing, in the Graeco-Roman world divorce of the husband by his wife was permissible and frequent. We have seen that the practice even spread to certain Jewish groups. Consequently as soon as Mark 10.12 fell into Hellenistic hands, it would be natural to substitute 'to dismiss' for 'to walk out'.

If we regard ἀπολύειν as original, we shall have to assume that D, Θ and the versions of the Itala avoiding *dimittere* got their text from a source—or rather, from sources—in which the saying had been Judaised. This is by no means unthinkable. On the whole, however, the opposite evolution, the Hellenizing of an expression of a Rabbinic character, is more likely.

Brief mention only need be made of two further ways of dealing with Mark 10.12. One is to say that an original 'to depart' was replaced by 'to dismiss', or an original 'to dismiss' by 'to depart', through carelessness, and not under the influence of any Rabbinic or Hellenistic ideas. This seems incredible. The other is to attribute the un-Rabbinic 'to dismiss' to a mistranslation from a hypothetical Aramaic, which latter did agree with the orthodox Jewish attitude to divorce.[2] But quite apart from the more general objections to such an explanation, it makes the development unnecessarily complicated. The original Aramaic saying would have been based on sound Rabbinic doctrine; then it was mistranslated; finally it was re-Judaised again, in some versions by the introduction of 'to depart', in others by that of 'to leave'. Surely if the saying originally accorded with the Rabbinic view,

---

[1] Matt. 5.32, 19.9, Luke 16.18.
[2] This is the view taken by C. C. Torrey, *The Four Gospels*, 91, 302, *Our Translated Gospels*, 93 ff.

it is much more plausible to conclude that the *codices* reading or pre-supposing 'to depart' or 'to leave' have preserved it intact; and that the substitution of 'to dismiss' took place, not in the course of translation, but during its life in Greek.

C. 'WHAT THEREFORE GOD HATH JOINED TOGETHER, LET NOT MAN PUT ASUNDER'

We have already considered in a previous lecture (under Precept and Example) the import of this saying[1] against the background of Rabbinic speculations concerning an androgynous Adam. Here it is sufficient to recall that the verbs seem to be used each in two senses, a general, untechnical one and a more specific, technical one. More precisely, the primary meaning of the saying is doubtless that brought out by the current translation, with $\sigma\upsilon\nu\zeta\epsilon\upsilon\gamma\nu\acute{\upsilon}\epsilon\iota\nu$ denoting 'to join together' and $\chi\omega\rho\acute{\iota}\zeta\epsilon\iota\nu$ 'to put asunder' in a general way. But it is hardly a mere coincidence that the former verb is reminiscent of $\zeta\epsilon\acute{\upsilon}\gamma\nu\upsilon\sigma\theta\alpha\iota$, 'to marry', and the latter of $\chi\omega\rho\acute{\iota}\zeta\epsilon\sigma\theta\alpha\iota$, 'to separate from husband or wife'. In other words, the saying is intended to convey a narrower meaning as well: 'What therefore God hath married into one, let not man divorce.'

Significantly, the Rabbinic *ziwwegh* or *zawwegh*, which goes back to the Greek $\zeta\epsilon\hat{\upsilon}\gamma\sigma\varsigma$, while it may mean 'to join together two things' in any way, is often used of God's 'joining together husband and wife'[2] and, in the form *'izdawwagh*, means 'to marry'. A good Rabbinic equivalent of $\chi\omega\rho\acute{\iota}\zeta\epsilon\iota\nu$ is *parash* (*perash*), which may signify 'to put asunder' or 'to separate' (transitive) in a general sense and 'to separate' (intransitive) in the sense of 'to depart from husband or wife' or 'to avoid intercourse'. The Greek word, applied in a general sense, occurs in an admonition not so dissimilar to that here discussed, in the Testament of Zebulun:[3] 'Be not ye, therefore, divided—$\mu\grave{\eta}$ $o\mathring{\upsilon}\nu$ $\chi\omega\rho\iota\sigma\theta\hat{\eta}\tau\epsilon$ —into two heads, for everything which the Lord made hath but one head.' It is true that the particular division against which Zebulun warns his children is not that between husband and wife but political conflict.

Incidentally, the Shekhinah's presence throughout married life is

---

[1] Matt. 19.6, Mark 10.9.
[2] Deut. 34.6 in Jerus. Targ., Gen. Rabba on 28.10, Bab. So. 2a.   [3] 9.4.

assumed by many Rabbis. Akiba points out[1] that if husband and wife are worthy (or fortunate—the Hebrew may mean either), God is included in their union: the words for 'man' and 'woman', combined, contain the letters *yodh* and *he*, signifying 'Lord'. But if they are unworthy (or unfortunate), fire consumes them: without *yodh* and *he*, there remains the word *'esh*, 'fire'. Akiba held that a husband might divorce his wife even in order to marry another fairer than she.[2] Maybe he thought divorce preferable to burning—and the way Paul expresses his view regarding celibacy and marriage[3] may derive from a Rabbinic argument.

D. LXX, Philo and Josephus

The LXX renders 'to divorce a wife' by ἐκβάλλειν where the Hebrew is *gerash*, by ἐξαποστέλλειν or ἀποστέλλειν where it is *shillaḥ*. Perhaps we ought to add ἀφιστάναι and ἀφιέναι, since βίβλιον ἀποστασίου stands for *sepher kerithuth*, 'bill of divorce', and ἄφεσις for *shilluḥim*, 'dismissal', in the story of Jethro who 'took Zipporah, Moses's wife, after his dismissal of her (to lead her back to him)'.[4] It is far from certain, however, that the authors of the LXX thought of Moses's action as a divorce.

Be this as it may, it is curious that the Synoptics as well as Paul avoid both ἐκβάλλειν and (ἐξ)αποστέλλειν. The Synoptics keep βίβλιον ἀποστασίου for 'bill of divorce'; and they introduce χωρίζειν for 'to put asunder' with the connotation of 'to divorce'. But the two commonest verbs of the LXX are not used even where the Old Testament is quoted.[5] Invariably ἀπολύειν is preferred.[6] It is all the more striking as D and Θ, where they speak of a wife who 'departs' from her husband, do use a term applied by the LXX to the wife who is put away, ἐξέρχομαι.[7] As for Paul, he, as we have seen, employs ἀφιέναι and χωρίζεσθαι.

The explanation seems to be this. The LXX renders *gerash*, 'to expel', by ἐκβάλλειν. This is a good, literal translation. But it appears that, in

---

[1] Bab. So. 17a. For the departure of the Shekhinah from uncleanness, cp. e.g. Siph. on Deut. 23.15 (14). The Hebrew for 'unclean thing' in this verse is the same as in 24.1, about the ground of divorce.
[2] Mish. Git. 9.10.　　　　　　　　[3] I Cor. 7.9.　　　　　　　　[4] Exod. 18.2.
[5] As in Matt. 19.7, Mark 10.4, cp. Deut. 24.1.
[6] Matt. 1.19 is of course also an example of this usage.
[7] Exod. 21.11; elsewhere in the LXX usually ἀπέρχομαι.

general, the Greek verb was used only where the husband proceeded with some vehemence or particular inconsiderateness. (The Hebrew verb was not so restricted.) It is frequent, for example, in the speech against Neaera, the author of which affirms that Neaera was a slave and prostitute, that nevertheless she twice gave her daughter Phano in marriage to Athenian citizens—a serious crime—and that both husbands, on realizing the truth, did what the law demanded, i.e. 'expelled', 'threw out', Phano.[1] Josephus uses the word in describing that article of the compact between Herodias and her brother-in-law which provided that the latter, on marrying her (incestuously), would 'throw out' his present wife, the daughter of King Aretas of Petraea.[2] Obviously, such a term was not suitable for the detached, general discussions of divorce in the New Testament. Neither, however, was $(\dot{\epsilon}\xi)\alpha\pi o\sigma\tau\dot{\epsilon}\lambda\lambda\epsilon\iota\nu$. This is a good, literal translation of *shillah*, 'to send away'. But in ordinary Greek it was not used with reference to divorce. The New Testament writers, then, had to find other verbs. It is a clear case of a deliberate rejection of the terminology of the LXX in order to avoid misunderstandings and bring the language up to date.

Philo also has neither $\dot{\epsilon}\kappa\beta\dot{\alpha}\lambda\lambda\epsilon\iota\nu$ nor $(\dot{\epsilon}\xi)\alpha\pi o\sigma\tau\dot{\epsilon}\lambda\lambda\epsilon\iota\nu$. He uses $\dot{\alpha}\pi\alpha\lambda\lambda\dot{\alpha}\tau\tau\epsilon\sigma\theta\alpha\iota$ of the wife who 'leaves' her husband—be it because he dismisses her or be it because they have agreed to part company—as also of the wife who, falsely accused by her husband of not having come to him as virgin, may 'leave' him whether he wishes her to or not.[3] This liberty of the falsely accused, incidentally, is neither Biblical nor Rabbinic. Philo may have been influenced by ethical considerations, by gentile practice and by the analogous right of a seduced maiden to marry or refuse the ravisher.[4] In the latter case, there is Rabbinic support for his view.[5] Probably $\pi\alpha\rho\alpha\iota\tau\epsilon\hat{\iota}\sigma\theta\alpha\iota$ in one passage[6] means 'to divorce a wife'; and another verb to be noted is $\delta\iota\alpha\zeta\epsilon\upsilon\gamma\nu\dot{\upsilon}\epsilon\iota\nu$, occurring in his exposition of the law[7] that a man who has illicit intercourse with a virgin must marry her and can never divorce her—nothing but death 'will dissolve ($\delta\iota\alpha\zeta\epsilon\dot{\upsilon}\xi\epsilon\iota$) the marriage'.

His nouns are $\delta\iota\dot{\alpha}\zeta\epsilon\upsilon\xi\iota\varsigma$ and $\dot{\alpha}\pi\alpha\lambda\lambda\alpha\gamma\dot{\eta}$, both referring to divorce effected by the husband.[8]

As we have seen, Josephus once does employ $\dot{\epsilon}\kappa\beta\dot{\alpha}\lambda\lambda\epsilon\iota\nu$, where he

---

[1] See Lipsius, *op. cit.*, p. 487 n. 55.   [2] Ant. 18 .5.1.110.
[3] Spec. Leg. 1.9.105, 3.5.30, 3.14.82.   [4] Spec. Leg. 3.11.71.   [5] Bab. Ket. 39b.
[6] Spec. Leg. 3.11.70.   [7] Spec. Leg. 3.11.70.   [8] Spec. Leg. 3.14.80.

mentions Herod's intention of 'expelling' his wife, the daughter of Aretas.

Of his own first wife, Josephus tells us[1] that 'she did not remain long with me but left me', ἀπηλλάγη. It is clear that it was she who wanted and effected the separation; in fact she stayed behind in Palestine when he followed Vespasian to Egypt. Whether he put a formal end to the marriage by giving her a bill of divorce remains uncertain, but no doubt he did.

Elsewhere he speaks of a husband 'dismissing' his wife, ἀποπέμπεσθαι (middle), once indeed in recounting his second divorce.[2] His remark that he was 'dissatisfied with her behaviour' confirms what might be inferred from his exposition of the rules respecting divorce[3]—that he adhered to the liberal, Hillelite interpretation of the Old Testament reference to divorce 'because a man hath found some uncleanness in his wife'.[4]

Again, he puts the case of one who wishes to 'part from his wife', διαζεύγνυσθαι, and who must 'affirm in writing that he will no longer live together with her', γράμμασι περὶ τοῦ μηδέποτε συνελθεῖν ἰσχυρίζεσθαι;[5] and he emphasizes the requirement of a husband's 'conceding', 'permitting', his wife, ἐφιέναι[6], for a full, legal divorce.

The latter term is interesting, being a rendering of the Hebrew *hittir*. (He is in this paragraph explaining the Jewish practice to his readers.) The essential words in a bill of divorce were: 'Behold, thou art permitted, conceded (*muttereth*), to any man.'[7] We find here a clear expression of the idea that the divorcing husband renders possible a remarriage of his wife. In Matthew,[8] where the marriage bond is regarded as indissoluble, this leads to the warning that 'whosoever shall put away his wife causeth her to commit adultery'.

To return to Josephus, what Herodias did when she left her husband was διαστῆναι (aorist 2 of διαστάναι), 'to separate from him'.[9] Salome[10] went as far as πέμπειν γραμμάτιον ἀπολυομένη τὸν γάμον, 'to send a document, by which she dissolved the marriage', and προαπαγορεύειν τὴν συμβίωσιν, 'to renounce the union'. Such a measure, Josephus remarks, would be recognized only if taken by the husband. From the point of view of the law, her action was no more than

---

[1] Life 75.415.   [2] Ant. 4.8.23.247, 16.7.3.198, Life 76.426.   [3] Ant. 4.8.23.253.
[4] Deut. 24.1.   [5] Ant. 4.8.23.253.   [6] Ant. 15.7.10.259.
[7] Mish. Git. 9.3.   [8] 5.32.   [9] Ant. 18.5.4.136.   [10] Ant. 15.7.10.259 f.

a διαχωρίζεσθαι (passive) καθ' αὑτήν, a 'separating by her own decision', a walking out. It is noteworthy that, according to Josephus, when she explained her step to Herod, she used the expression ἀποστῆναι (aorist 2 of ἀφιστάναι), 'to part from the husband'. Maybe Josephus thought it unlikely that she herself would draw attention to the gross illegality of her procedure. 'To part from a husband', being intransitive, does not necessarily imply a dissolution of marriage by a bill of divorce; it may just signify a wife's running away.

XIV

Samaritan Women

A. THE DECREE OF A.D. 65/6

WHEN Jesus asked the Samaritan woman to give him to drink, John tells us,[1] she was surprised by his kindness. Why? Surely, for an unsophisticated mind, as a rule, it is the offer of a drink, not the request for one, which expresses love.

To appreciate the story, it is necessary to assume a technical Rabbinic background. A regulation of A.D. 65 or 66 laid down that, from the point of view of the laws of purity, 'the daughters of the Samaritans are menstruants from their cradle'.[2] This decree was much talked about in the first decades of its existence. For it was enacted in highly dramatic circumstances, on the eve of the revolt against Rome, by that famous synod of Hillelites and Shammaites where the extreme zealots among the latter were in the majority and, overawing the opposition, passed a large number of chauvinistic measures.[3] As late as the end of the century, bitter words could be exchanged between followers of the various parties about this episode and its consequences; and as the moderates gained the upper hand, the day when the synod had met came to be regarded as a day of calamity for the nation.[4]

The formal justification of the decree was, of course, that according to strict Pharisaic principles, as the Samaritan provisions concerning purity differed in some respects from the Pharisaic, there was always at least the possibility of a Samaritan woman being in a state of uncleanness. It is indeed very likely that, in the more rigid circles, this view had been prevalent, and acted upon, long before it was given full legal force. The point is of importance for the question of the historicity of the incident under notice. There is no reason to doubt that it may have

---

[1] 4.7 ff.   [2] Mish. Nid. 4.1.   [3] Bab. Shab. 16b.   [4] Pal. Shab. 3c.

occurred when John says it did, though, obviously, the interest in it must have been much intensified by the events of 65/6.

The woman Jesus met was deemed unclean, like a menstruant, and her uncleanness was conveyed to the vessel she held.[1] (We need not consider special cases where contamination might be avoidable.) If it was a vessel from which she used to drink, the case was particularly serious: the spittle of a menstruant was contaminating in a very high degree. In any case, a 2nd-century Rabbi praises the good old times when it was a matter of course for one in a state of purity not to eat together with a menstruant.[2] By asking the woman to give him to drink, Jesus showed himself ready to disregard that hostile presumption respecting Samaritan women for the sake of a more inclusive fellowship.

Maybe he already acted on the same principle when he let his disciples purchase food in the city near-by. Presumably they bought from Samaritans. But as certain dry food-stuffs were not regarded as susceptible to uncleanness, the question must be left open. The disciples may have confined themselves to these. Among the decrees of the synod referred to were some prohibiting the use of several important kinds of food obtained from pagans. Apparently, however, the Samaritans were not here mentioned.

We are told that the woman, when she went back into the city in order to call her friends, 'left her waterpot'. Bauer remarks[3] that he is unable to discover the significance of this detail. But for one thing, it helps to round off the story. Jesus had asked the woman for a drink, he himself having 'nothing to draw with, and the well was deep'. A conversation ensued, and now she placed the vessel at his disposal, to use it for getting water and drinking. This is indeed how the words have always been understood. (Towards the end of the Second Part of Goethe's *Faust*, the Mulier Samaritana invokes the Mater gloriosa's mercy 'bei dem Eimer, der dem Heiland kühl die Lippe durft berühren'.) What has not been seen is that his drinking from that pitcher was an act comparable to, and indeed more serious than, dealings involving contact with an Am-Haaretz, a Jew careless about the rules of cleanness. Clearly, for bringing out this aspect of the matter, a note like that in question is indispensable.

[1] Mish. Kel. 1.1 ff.
[2] Tos. Shab. 1.14.
[3] *Das Johannesevangelium*, 2nd ed., 1925, pp. 68 f.

B. The Meaning of συγχράομαι

So far, to be sure, the argument might appear somewhat conjectural. But there is support in the clause οὐ γὰρ συγχρῶνται Ἰουδαῖοι Σαμαρίταις.[1] Literally, of course, συγχράομαι means 'to use together', though sometimes it is employed in the more general sense of 'to use'. The natural interpretation is: Jews do not use—*scil.* vessels—together with Samaritans. This would confirm the thesis advanced; and in all probability, had the point of the incident been recognized, nobody would ever have thought of any other rendering.

That Samaritans in general are named, not only Samaritan women, may be explained in various ways. The author may have thought that the restriction to women was sufficiently implied by the context. ('Thou askest drink of me, which am a woman of Samaria?') Or he may have committed a slight mistranslation from the Semitic. Or—perhaps the most plausible solution—he did refer to a group of Pharisees that avoided contact of the kind contemplated not only with Samaritan women but also with the men. Logically, once the women were presumed to be menstruants, their husbands must be presumed to be defiled by them. Sadducean women received treatment not dissimilar to that of Samaritan women; and the Talmud records[2] that 'it happened that a (male) Sadducee was talking to a high priest in the market and spittle issued from his mouth and fell upon the clothes of the high priest; whereupon the face of the high priest turned pale and he went to see the other's wife (to inquire whether she had practised the proper, Pharisaic precepts)'.

However, the point of the story has not hitherto been recognized, and it is now universally believed that, in the passage quoted, συγχράομαι means 'to associate on friendly terms', 'to be familiar': Jews do not associate on friendly terms with Samaritans. Certainly, this translation is just possible. The simple verb χράομαι, besides 'to use', can signify 'to be intimate'; συγχράομαι, besides 'to use together', can signify 'to use'; since it may have one of the meanings of the simple verb, namely, 'to use', there is no *a priori* reason why it should not have another, namely, 'to be intimate'. Nevertheless there is one objection, not conclusive, but quite serious enough: the absence of any evidence, apart from the present text, of συγχράομαι in the sense of 'to be intimate'. Some

[1] 4.9.   [2] Tos. Nid. 5.3, Bab. Nid. 33b.

dictionaries say such evidence exists, but on closer examination the ultimate authority invariably turns out to be—the present text itself. (It should be observed that the allied meaning 'to have commercial dealings with' also is more than doubtful.)

Preisigke does not note the unusual sense at all. In former editions of Liddell and Scott, only this text was adduced for it. The latest edition adds a passage from Diogenes Oenoandensis,[1] following Moulton and Milligan; but we shall see that there is no justification for doing so. Moulton and Milligan, it is true, refer to three passages as analogous: one from Epictetus,[2] one from the Epistle of Ignatius to the Magnesians[3] and one from Diogenes Oenoandensis. But there is little doubt that, had it not been for the current interpretation of the clause from the Fourth Gospel, none of them would ever have been considered as containing the extraordinary usage.

In Epictetus, it is a question of 'using' certain criteria for deciding a problem: ταῖς τῶν ἐκτὸς ἀξίαις συγχρώμεθα. Oldfather translates:[4] 'But for determining the rational and the irrational, we employ not only our estimates of the value of external things, but also the criterion of that which is in keeping with one's own character.' There is no trace here of the meaning required for the orthodox explanation of the passage from John, 'to associate on friendly terms', 'to be familiar'.

According to the view here combated, Epictetus is speaking of a criterion commonly employed. Then the equation is made: 'commonly employed' equals 'familiarly employed', which equals 'to be familiar', which equals 'to associate on friendly terms'. Evidently, all this is twisting an innocent word for the purpose of obtaining a parallel to John. For Epictetus, the word means 'to employ' or, perhaps, 'commonly to employ'; but definitely no more. Moulton and Milligan, in adducing this text, rely on J. B. Lightfoot, on whose position we shall presently have to say a few words.

Let us go on to the Epistle of Ignatius to the Magnesians. He exhorts the recipients μὴ συγχρᾶσθαι τῇ ἡλικίᾳ τοῦ ἐπισκόπου ἀλλὰ πᾶσαν ἐντροπὴν αὐτῷ ἀπονέμειν, 'not to take advantage of the youth of the bishop, but to show him all respect'. Or if we credit συγχράομαι with its full force, we may translate 'not to take advantage together', 'not to combine to take advantage'. The Anglo-Latin version of the 13th

---

[1] 64.   [2] 1.2.7.
[3] 3.   [4] *Epictetus* (in the *Loeb Classical Library*), 1926, pp. 1, 17.

century has *couti*, though, admittedly, as it is always punctiliously literal, this is of little significance.

It might perhaps be argued that the author means to discourage undue familiarity. Even if that were granted, συγχράομαι would still denote 'to use' or 'to use together', not 'to be familiar'. Ignatius does not write μὴ συγχρᾶσθαι τῷ ἐπισκόπῳ which might justify the rendering 'not to be familiar with the bishop'; he writes μη συγχρᾶσθαι τῇ ἡλικίᾳ τοῦ ἐπισκόπου, which can only be rendered by 'not to exploit (together) the age of the bishop'—whether the exploitation consisted in undue familiarity or not. As a matter of fact the continuation of the letter shows that the danger lay, not in undue familiarity, but in insubordination.[1] Ignatius goes on to cite the praiseworthy example of the presbyters, whom he describes as 'not making use (προσειληφότας) of his manifest youth but yielding to him'; and he adds that it is necessary 'to obey without any hypocrisy'. Thus there is no conceivable basis for the rendering 'to be familiar'.

It was J. B. Lightfoot[2] who first thought that here was a parallel to John—to John misunderstood, we should say—and suggested that συγχράομαι ought to be translated by 'to presume upon', 'to treat lightly' (which, even if correct, would still not be quite the same as 'to be familiar' or 'to be friendly'). He, too, cited Epictetus as another illustration of the usage; we have already dealt with this passage. Lake's translation,[3] 'Now it becomes you not to presume on the youth of the bishop', and Srawley's translation,[4] 'You too should not treat lightly the youth of your bishop', are obviously based on Lightfoot. Others are more accurate, such as Bauer,[5] 'Für euch aber schickt es sich, euch das jugendliche Alter des Bischofs nicht zu nutze zu machen' ('to exploit'), and Hennecke,[6] 'Es ziemt euch aber, das jugendliche Alter eures Bischofs nicht zu missbrauchen' ('to abuse'). At any rate, this is decidely no case of συγχράομαι in any special sense.

There remains a fragment of Diogenes Oenoandensis, which now figures in Liddell and Scott. Towards the end, we find the passage οὐκοῦν ἑκάτερον ὑμῶν ἰδίᾳ δεῖ βαρεῖσθαι δι' ἡμᾶς, συγχρῆσθαι δὲ

---

[1] I Tim. 4.12, 'let no man despise thy youth', and Tit. 2.15, 'let no man despise thee', may refer to the same danger. In the latter text, the words immediately preceding are: 'rebuke with all authority'. [2] *The Apostolic Fathers*, 2nd ed., pt. 2, 1889, p. 112.
[3] *The Apostolic Fathers* (in *The Loeb Classical Library*), 1945, pp. 1, 199.
[4] *The Epistles of St. Ignatius*, 2nd ed., 1919, p. 54.
[5] *Die Apostolischen Väter*, 1923, p. 221.
[6] *Neutestamentliche Apokryphen*, 2nd ed., 1924, p. 524.

τῷ ἑτέρῳ τὸν . . . The rest of the text is lost, and though it is safe to assume that the word ἕτερον followed,[1] we do not know how the sentence ended. Consequently it would be rash indeed to pronounce on the exact meaning of συγχράομαι in this context. How, then, do Moulton and Milligan—the source of Liddell and Scott—come to take it as denoting 'to be familiar'?

This interpretation goes back to J. William. He, in the Preface to his edition of Diogenes Oenoandensis,[2] contended that the fragment could not, as had been suggested by previous commentators, be part of a letter written by Epicurus himself. The authorship of Epicurus, he maintained, was ruled out by the language, which must date from a subsequent period. And among the points proving the language late, he mentioned the use of συγχράομαι in the sense of 'to be familiar'. Here is the source of Moulton and Milligan.

Three things are to be said on this. First, William quite naturally was rather eager to detect late nuances in the fragment. Secondly, the sole evidence in view of which he felt it possible to attribute to συγχράομαι in Diogenes Oenoandensis the sense of 'to be familiar' is—the clause from the Fourth Gospel here under discussion. Thirdly, if, despite the fact that the sentence breaks off in the middle, we venture guesses as to its meaning, the most satisfactory results are obtained by proceeding from the properly established values of the verb, 'to use together' or 'to use'. In the passage immediately preceding, the author of the letter has referred to money sent him by his father and other friends. Now he says: 'It is not right that each of you should be burdened with his own share in my support,[3] but each should use together with the other'— and we may suppose that there came something like 'such extra sums as he is able to spend', 'such resources as are available'. The dative ἑτέρῳ, that is, if we translate 'to use together', would be connected, not with the main body of the verb, χράομαι, but with the prefix συν: 'to use together one with the other', not 'to use one another'. Again, if we translate 'to use', we get: 'It is not right that each of you should be burdened with his own share in my support, but each should make use of the other'. He means that they should ask one another to assist. This also makes much better sense than 'each should be familiar with the other'. No doubt other guesses are possible. But it is idle to speculate

[1] See J. William, *Diogenes Oenoandensis*, 1907, p. 60.
[2] XXVIII.   [3] The author constantly refers to himself as ἡμεῖς.

further. We do not know what the lost portion contained. What emerges is that there is no good reason why we should translate συγχράομαι here by 'to be familiar', 'to associate on friendly terms'.

The conclusion is obvious. Unless John applies the verb in a way recurring nowhere else—and it may be repeated that this is just possible —it must signify either 'to use something together with another person', or 'to use two things together' (this sense is less frequent than the others, but Preisigke is surely right, against Moulton and Milligan, in finding it in a papyrus[1] with the phrase συγχράομαι βίᾳ καὶ αὐθαδίᾳ, 'to use both force and stubbornness', and we may compare Polybius[2] where he speaks of Hannibal ἅμα δὲ συγχρησαμένου συναγωνιστῇ τῷ ποταμῷ καὶ τοῖς θηρίοις, 'using as fellow-combatants at the same time both the river and the elephants'), or simply 'to use something'. The meaning 'to use two things together', rare in any case, does not fit. Neither does the simple 'to use something'. A statement to the effect that Jews do not make use of Samaritans would be neither true nor—and this is decisive—to the purpose in this particular context: the woman must be referring to some plain unkindness on the part of the Jews. It should be observed, incidentally, that even if this argument is not accepted, we arrive only at 'to use', not at 'to associate on friendly terms'. The result is that, in all probability, the prefix is stressed, the verb denoting 'to use something together with another person': Jews do not use vessels together with Samaritans, most definitely not with Samaritan women. True, there is no clear case where the dative after συγχράομαι depends on the συν. Diogenes Oenoandensis is too problematic. But that is doubtless accidental. The possibility of this construction must have existed.

It may be worth adding that the Hebrew verb *hishtammesh*, 'to use', naturally occurs in Rabbinic discussions about clean and unclean vessels. According to the School of Shammai,[3] for example, 'it is forbidden to use—*lehishtammesh*—a vessel the outside of which has been rendered unclean by a liquid'.

C. The Syriac Version

The clause here analysed, οὐ γὰρ συγχρῶνται and so on, is missing in the Sinaiticus, the Codex Bezae and some representatives of the Itala

[1] BGU IV, 1187.22. [2] 3.14.5. [3] Bab. Ber. 52b.

(א D *a b d e*). The question therefore arises whether it goes back to the evangelist. If not, we must assume that the Gospel, after being completed, fell into the hands of an expert in Rabbinic lore. This is perhaps not inconceivable. Yet the easier explanation seems to be that we have before us a comment by John himself. As remarked above, that anti-Samaritan decree of A.D. 65 or 66 formed part of a famous, or rather notorious, legislation. The reason for the absence of the clause from the manuscripts named probably is that it was no longer understood when they were written. We ought to remember that, if the thesis submitted is correct, the interpretation of συγχράομαι as meaning 'to associate on friendly terms' was not known to ancient editors and scribes. So the passage must have sounded very queer to them.

Or did this interpretation spring up already at an early date? The Vulgate certainly is not acquainted with it: non enim coutuntur Judaei Samaritanis. (*Couti*, we saw, stands for συγχράομαι also in the Anglo-Latin version of Ignatius to the Magnesians.) But, to judge by modern translations, the Syriac version has it. A. L. Smith,[1] for instance, renders the Syriac of the passage from John thus: 'For the Jews have no dealings with the Samaritans.' Modern dictionaries agree, alleging that the relevant Syriac verb is here employed in the sense of 'to have dealings or intercourse with'.[2]

In point of fact, however, the Syriac version is as free from this error (error—on the basis of the view here advocated) as the Vulgate. This is not saying that the story was still properly understood at that time; it only means that it was not yet rewritten. The modern treatment of the Syriac version is due to the same lack of insight into the Rabbinic background which has already led to, first, the assignment of an exceptional sense to συγχράομαι in the Greek text and, secondly, the 'discovery' of this sense in Epictetus, Ignatius and Diogenes Oenoandensis. As there is now, thirdly, an unwarranted rendering of a Syriac verb, one wonders whether this avalanche will ever come to a halt.

The Syriac verb appearing in the passage concerned is the Ethpaʻal of *ḥashaḥ*. It occurs in five other passages.

(1) Acts 27.3. The Greek has φιλανθρώπως τε ὁ Ἰούλιος τῷ Παύλῳ

---

[1] *A Translation of the Four Gospels from the Syriac*, 1894, p. 169, and *Some Pages retranscribed from the Sinaitic Palimpsest with a Translation of the whole Text*, 1896, p. 88.

[2] J. Payne Smith, *Syriac Dictionary*, 1903, p. 162, R. Payne Smith, *Thesaurus Syriacus*, I, 1879, p. 1399 ('nullo commercio utuntur cum'), and W. Jennings, *Lexicon to the Syriac of the New Testament*, revised by U. Gautillon, 1925, p. 83.

χρησάμενος, 'Julius used Paul kindly.' In the Syriac version, what Julius used was, not Paul, but kindness: 'The centurion used mercy (*bimeraḥamenutha*') towards (*lewath*) Paul.' The verb means 'to use'. Accordingly, the lexicographers are wrong in singling out this passage for the sense 'tractare' or 'to behave self toward. to treat'.[1] Presumably their attitude is yet another indirect effect of the current interpretation of John. The next step would be to assert that Acts 27.3 provides a second example of the Syriac verb denoting 'to associate on friendly terms'. It is worth noting that there is a passage in Bar-Hebraeus[2] closely analogous to Acts 27.3—except that '*im*, 'with', is put instead of *lewath*, 'towards'—which is apparently destined to become the next victim. R. Payne Smith still gave the unprejudiced translation 'misericordia usus est erga incolas'. In J. Payne Smith, this has become 'he behaved mercifully towards the inhabitants', and the text is placed next to that from the Fourth Gospel. That is to say, we are given to understand that the meaning here approaches 'to associate on friendly terms'. But the verb unambiguously signifies 'to use'.

(2) I Corinthians 7.31, 'And they that use this world', χρώμενοι. Again, clearly 'to use'.

(3) I Corinthians 9.12, 'We have not used this power', ἐχρησάμεθα. The same.

(4) I Corinthians 9.15, 'But I have used none of these things', κέχρημαι. The same.

(5) I Thessalonians 2.5. The Greek has οὐ γάρ ποτε ἐν λόγῳ κολακείας ἐγενήθημεν. The English version gives 'For neither at any time used we flattering words', and this is exactly what we find in the Syriac. Again, 'to use'.

It follows that the Ethpaʿal of ḥashaḥ must be rendered by 'to use' and nothing else. (The Old Testament application of the root is consistent with this result. The root occurs—though never in the Ethpaʿal —three times[3] and always refers to what is needful.) It must be so rendered also in John. And it is desirable that this text should be deprived of its separate position in Greek and Syriac dictionaries, though as to Greek a slight doubt may remain. *A fortiori* all those passages pressed into service with a view to justifying that special position should be given back their original, innocent meaning.

[1] R. Payne Smith, *loc. cit.*, Jennings, *loc. cit.*
[2] Chronicon Syriacum 80.347.　　　　　　　[3] Dan. 3.16, Ezek. 6.9, 7.20.

We do not propose here to inquire exactly when the traditional misinterpretation of the clause under discussion came into being. By Luther's time it was established—'Denn die Juden haben keine Gemeinschaft mit den Samaritanern'—but it is no doubt much older. We have already mentioned that the original point of the narrative of Jesus and the Samaritan woman must soon have become unintelligible to Christian readers. Once that had happened, it was easy to assimilate it to passages like that in Acts:[1] 'Ye know how that it is an unlawful thing for a Jew to keep company (κολλᾶσθαι) or to come unto (προσέρχεσθαι) one of another nation; but God hath shewed me that I should not call any man common or unclean.'

[1] 10.28.

XV

Two Aramaisms

A. 'Multitude' and 'Width'

MARK and Luke,[1] as commonly understood, tell us that Jesus preached in a house at Capernaum; that a paralytic was to be brought to him in order to be healed; that the people who carried him could not enter the house διὰ τὸν ὄχλον, 'because of the crowd' besieging it; and that in consequence they uncovered the roof and let the bed down that way.

This interpretation is not quite satisfactory. For one thing, would the crowd not willingly have made room if a miracle was expected? For another, once the way to the door was barred, how did the people who carried the sick man succeed in taking the more difficult route across the roof? It has been suggested that, on beholding the crowd, they turned and ascended the roof from behind the house. Apart from the complete lack of textual evidence, however, if this was what happened, most members of the crowd would not have seen the paralytic. Their astonishment, therefore, when he was cured, would be hard to understand. In the second Philippic,[2] Cicero accuses Antonius of having had immoral relations with Curio. The latter's father, he says, set watchmen in order that Antonius might not cross his threshold; but Antonius at night was let down through the tiles. This certainly must have happened from a side of the house other than the front, which was guarded. But, then, the object of Antonius in entering via the roof was precisely to remain unnoticed by the watchmen. By contrast, the paralytic ought to have been discerned by all, or as many as possible.

We may admit that the problems here raised about the clause 'because of the crowd' are not very serious. Perhaps we should be content with noting them. Yet it is tempting to get rid of them by assuming a slight mistranslation of a Hebrew or Aramaic word. It is

---

[1] Mark 2.1 ff., Luke.5.17 ff.   [2] 18.45.

true that this particular mode of solving the difficulties involves us in a further drawback: we are conscious that to maintain a mistranslation in the New Testament is nearly always wrong and never clearly right.

One of the Hebrew equivalents of 'multitude' is *shiph'a*. The Bible uses it of a multitude of camels, horses or warriors.[1] In the last-cited case, 'he spied the crowd of Jehu' is rendered thus by the Complutensian Polyglot: εἶδεν τὸν ὄχλον Εἰού. In Rabbinic literature, however, the nouns *shiph'a* and *shippua'* (Aramaic *shiph'a'* and *shippu'a'*) as well as the verb *shapha'* (Aramaic *shepha'*) refer not only to the numerical size of a collective but also to the extent in space of a particular object. In other words, they signify not only 'multitude' or 'to be numerous', but also 'great length or breadth' or 'to be wide'. The primary meaning of the root seems to be 'to flow abundantly', 'to overflow':[2] it is easy to see how its range might have been enlarged in various directions.

He who has a *qora shopha'ath*, a 'strong, huge joist', we hear,[3] will place it in the centre of the room. Again, the Biblical provision 'and any overhanging part (of the curtains) thou shalt make to hang over (the backside of the tabernacle)' in the Jerusalemite Targum reads *weshippua' tashpa'*; and in the following verse 'it shall hang over' appears as *yehe' meshuppa'*.[4] Finally, the Mishnah deals with tents smaller at the bottom than at the top. As regards uncleanness, it is laid down[5] that everything lying under the upper, wider part of such a tent, even though actually outside the tent itself, shares the fate of the objects which are inside, and vice versa. The text runs as follows: 'All protruding parts of a tent, *shippu'e 'oholin*, count as the tent itself. In the case of a tent that protrudes, *shehu' shophea'*, at the top, slopes down and is but one finger-breadth at the bottom, if there is uncleanness inside the tent, vessels under the protruding part, *hashshippua'*, are also unclean. If there is uncleanness under the protruding part, *hashshippua'*, vessels inside the tent are also unclean.'

These examples could be multiplied. It is noteworthy that in the Jerusalemite Targum and the Mishnic rule *shippua'* does not simply denote 'hugeness'. It denotes, in a more specific sense, that portion of a thing by which it is bigger than another: the remaining part of longer curtains as compared with shorter curtains in the Targum, the wider part of a tent as compared with the smaller in the Mishnah.

[1] Isa. 60.6, Exod. 26.10, II Kings 9.17.
[2] Cp. the application of the nouns *shepha'* in Deut. 33.19 and *shiph'a* in Job 22.11, 38.34.
[3] Gen. Rabba on 2.7.   [4] Exod. 26.12 f.   [5] Mish. Oho. 7.2.

Supposing, then, that ὄχλος in the narrative under discussion stands for *shiph'a* or *shippua'* (*shiph'a'*, *shippu'a'*), the reason, in the original version, why the paralytic could not be brought through the door may well have been that the bed was too large, the door too small. This would at least avoid the weaknesses of the reason that is given in the present version. According to Mark, it was four men who carried the bed—a fact very possibly mentioned in order to indicate how big the bed was. The vernacular behind διὰ τὸν ὄχλον would have meant 'for the hugeness', *scil.* of the bed, or even, if *shiph'a* was employed in its more technical signification, 'for the protruding' of the bed.

How *shiph'a* came to be represented by ὄχλος may be left undecided. Seeing that the Rabbinic word does frequently denote 'a multitude', it was, perhaps, just a slip, committed when the Aramaic form of the story was turned into Greek. Whoever first told it in Greek may have been influenced by the mention, towards the beginning, of a great many people come to listen to Jesus.[1] On the other hand, this remark towards the beginning is quite possibly editorial, itself the result of ὄχλος occurring further on. However, there are so many other pericopes introducing a crowd that it would not be surprising if some narrator had taken *shiph'a* in this sense even where, for once, it meant something different.

If the theory suggested is correct, a Talmudic anecdote provides a much closer parallel than hitherto supposed. When Rab Huna died, his bed was too large to be brought out through the door. His disciples therefore began to remove the roof. Rab Hisda, however, pointed out to them that this procedure would be incompatible with the respect due to a deceased Rabbi. The disciples then proposed laying him on another, smaller bed. Again Rab Hisda intervened and observed that a great man like Rab Huna must be carried on his own bed. In the end they resorted to a rather rigorous course: they widened the entrance by destroying parts of the wall itself.[2]

It might perhaps be asked how the Rabbi's bed, if it was so broad, had originally been conveyed into the house. But, of course, no difficulty exists when there is no one lying on a bed, since one can then turn it round. This accounts also for the ending of the narrative of the paralytic,[3]

---

[1] Mark 2.2, Luke 5.17 (somewhat divergent).
[2] Bab. M.Q. 25a. Mid. Ps. on 24.7 also seems to suggest that the case of a door being too small for any big furniture to be brought in or out was not infrequent.
[3] Mark 2.12, Luke 5.25, also Matt. 9.7.

2C

where we read that, after being cured, he took up his bed and walked home. Actually, it is not improbable that the miracle partly consisted in the very fact that he was able to carry without assistance a bed of large dimensions.

B. 'To Beguile' and 'To Shake'

Paul writes to the Thessalonians[1] that he sent them Timothy, 'to establish you and comfort you concerning your faith, that no man should be moved in these afflictions'. The Greek for 'to move' is here σαίνω. In general, it may be used of a dog 'wagging' his tail, of an animal or person 'fawning' on somebody, and of a person 'beguiling' another person. The last-mentioned sense is no doubt in Paul's mind. A little further on he says that he was afraid 'the tempter might have tempted' his flock. The words 'that no man should be moved', we may suppose, refer to the importance of no one being 'beguiled', 'deceived', by Satan and his instruments.

Nevertheless, while admitting that the primary meaning of σαίνω in this passage is 'to beguile', we should expect it to have the connotation of 'to shake'. Timothy's task was to steady such as might have been caused to waver. The trouble is that no Greek author employs σαίνω in the sense of 'to shake'. It has been maintained[2] that Diogenes Laertius offers an example. But this claim is of the kind we came across in the previous chapter (on Samaritan Women, where we discussed συγχράομαι): in order to parallel a New Testament usage, real or imaginary, a word in some non-Christian, Greek source is interpreted in an artificial manner. Diogenes Laertius tells us[3] how Pythagoras lived in a cave and his mother secretly kept sending him notes of all that went on in the world; at last he reappeared again, looking like a skeleton, declared that he had visited Hades and read out to the people —of course, from his mother's notes—what had occurred in his absence. His hearers were σαινόμενοι, wept and looked on him as divine. Clearly, σαινόμενοι signifies 'beguiled', 'deceived'. If it were not for Paul's use of the verb, nobody would ever have thought of suggesting the translation 'shaken'.

Either, then, σαίνω in Paul has not the connotation of 'to shake',

---

[1] I Thess. 3.3.

[2] M. Dibelius, 'An die Thessalonicher', in *Handbuch zum Neuen Testament*, vol. 11, 3rd ed., 1937, p. 17.

[3] 8.1.41.

however much we may expect it. Or—the better view, we think—it has this connotation, in which case the likeliest explanation is that Paul is under the influence of the corresponding Hebrew or Aramaic, *kishkesh* or *kashkesh*. This verb is used of an animal 'wagging' its tail, of an animal 'striking about' with its tail (so as to do damage, for example), of a person 'patting', 'soothing', another person or an animal, and of a person 'shaking' an object (nuts, for instance, for a child's entertainment, or jars, in the course of washing up).

Of particular interest is a Rabbinic utterance to the effect that the evil impulse *mekhashkesh* the creatures, i.e. 'pats' or 'shakes' them in order to turn them from the proper path.[1] Salomon Buber[2] was of opinion that we ought to emend the text and substitute *mesakhsekh* or *mesakhsekh*: the evil impulse 'ensnares'. But apart from the fact that no emendation is necessary, there is not even convincing evidence that either of the two verbs recommended might signify 'to ensnare'. However, Jastrow in his dictionary carried the idea further. He postulated a verb, attested nowhere else, *kaskes*, which he regarded as a transposition of *sakhsekh*, and to which he attributed the meanings 'to entangle', 'to catch', 'to confound'. In Levy's dictionary, these conjectures are not adopted; they are in fact unwarranted. Paul uses σαίνω in the sense of 'to beguile'—as we saw above, a remark on the tempter follows—yet the nuance 'to shake' is also there. The Rabbis use *kishkesh* or *kashkesh* as denoting something between 'to soothe in order to seduce' and 'to shake in order to seduce'. It may be said that the passage from I Thessalonians and the Midrash throw light on, and support, one another.

[1] Eccles. Rabba on 4.14, Mid. Ps. on 9.2.
[2] *Midrasch Tehillim*, Wilna 1891, p. 82, par. 37.

XVI

Amen

IN the sermon on the mount[1] we come across for the first time that curious use of 'Amen' in the sense of 'verily'; i.e. as a particle, not confirming a previous statement, but opening a statement and emphasizing its truth and importance. It is universally held that 'Amen' was not so used before Jesus, and that there is no Rabbinic analogy.[2] The explanation most widely accepted seems to be that of Dalman:[3] Jesus was opposed to swearing, consequently he put 'Amen' in the place of an oath.

The difficulty is that if, in Jesus's view, 'whatever is more than Yea, yea or Nay, nay cometh of evil', it is hardly credible that he sought a device to evade this teaching. It is chiefly dodges, be it remembered, such as swearing by heaven instead of by God himself, which he is represented as attacking. 'Amen' surely would be a dodge of just this kind.

However, we do not intend here to pursue this problem, but a different, more pedestrian one. Whoever introduced the 'Amen' under discussion, be it in order to have an oath that was not an oath, or be it for other reasons, must have relied on some support in contemporary speech or in a special tradition. He could not have brought in the new use of 'Amen', as it were, *ex nihilo*. If he had, it would have produced no effect.

One tradition which may have been of influence is that going back to Isaiah who, where he speaks of the creation of a new heaven and earth, says that in those days 'he that sweareth shall swear by the God of Amen'.[4] That many modern critics think the original text had *'omen*, 'faith', instead of the present *'amen*, is irrelevant: in the New Testament

---

[1] Matt. 5.18
[2] Strack-B., I, 1922, pp. 243 f., *Jewish Encyclopedia*, vol. I, *s.v.* Amen.
[3] *Die Worte Jesu*, p. 186. [4] 65.16.

epoch, we may assume, 'amen was already established. The 'Amen' of the New Testament may be intended as a fulfilment of this prophecy. It is used only by Jesus himself and mostly, if not exclusively, where the advent of the true kingdom is concerned.

There may, however, be also a few roots in actual Hebrew speech. It is worth mention that in the Old Testament the particle 'omnam, 'verily', which is etymologically connected with 'amen, does occur at the beginning of a statement, like the New Testament 'Amen'; for instance, 'Verily, the kings of Assyria have destroyed the nations.'[1] But it is rare even in the Old Testament, non-existent in Rabbinic language, and in any case not identical with 'amen, however closely allied. So no great importance can be attached to it.

Yet some points suggest that, if there is no complete parallel of the New Testament 'Amen' in Jewish works preserved to us, it may none the less have been current at that time in certain circles.

For one thing, it is easy to imagine how the use in question might have come into existence. The 'Amen' confirming a previous statement is often expanded. This happened as early as in the period of the Old Testament. Jeremiah replied to a rival who contradicted his terrible forecasts and maintained that Judah would flourish: 'Amen, the Lord do so.'[2] In Jewish liturgy combinations like 'Amen, praise the Lord', 'Amen, let his great name be blessed for ever' or 'Amen, my help is from the Lord' are frequent.[3] In all these cases, it is true, the 'Amen' signifies acceptance of a preceding wish or prayer. Still one has only to think of it in connection with its appendix to come fairly near the meaning of 'verily'. In other words, as soon as the expanded 'Amen' is thought of as a more or less independent phrase, a translation would have to be: 'Verily, the Lord will do so' or 'Verily, my help is from the Lord.'

How easily the particle confirming a previous statement may become a particle opening and emphasizing a fresh one is illustrated by a repartee in Longfellow's *John Endicott*.[4] Norton, the Calvinist minister, exclaims: 'Anathema maranatha! The Lord cometh!' To which Edith, a Quaker, retorts: 'Yea, verily he cometh, and shall judge the shepherds of Israel.' This in Hebrew might well be 'amen ba' weshaphaṭ 'eth ro'e yiśra'el.

---

[1] II Kings 19.17, Isa. 37.18.   [2] 28.6.
[3] Num. Rabba on 4.16, Singer's *Prayer Book*, pp. 75 f.   [4] Act 1, Scene 1.

However this may be, there are at least two examples in Jewish literature of an 'Amen' almost corresponding to that of the New Testament. According to the Ashkenazi rite, if a man recites by himself the Credo, the *Shema*', the confession of the unity of God followed by some Scriptural portions, he ought to prefix the words *'el melekh ne'eman*, 'God, faithful King'.[1] This is an acrostic, the initial letters making 'Amen'. Indeed, the acrostic is particularly clever, seeing that the last letters of the last word also make 'Amen'. (Manifestly, the clause derives from the Eighteen Benedictions,[2] where, however, no acrostic is formed of it.)

It may be noted, first, that according to a Talmudic explanation 'Amen' itself is a Notarikon, i.e. an abbreviation standing for 'God, faithful King';[3] and secondly, that in the old prayer-books of Saadia and Amram and in the Mahzor Vitry, there is still left the proper 'Amen' before the Credo instead of the acrostic.[4] Here, then, we find 'Amen' introducing the solemn acknowledgment of the unity of God.

Another case is more interesting. Some seventy years ago a primitive hymn, 'None is like our God', still popular in Jewish liturgy,[5] was shown by Schiller-Szinessy to be an acrostic giving *'amen b'*. As far as the consonants are concerned, *b'* may mean either 'he is coming', 'he is come' or 'come!' Schiller-Szinessy indeed discovered a manuscript in which the initials of the lines are written in the place of the hymn and the two words thus formed are provided with vowels: *'amen ba'*.[6] On the basis of this pointing we should have to render 'Verily, he is coming' or 'Verily, he is come', while the imperative 'come' would be excluded. But the pointing need not, of course, represent the original one, which may have been *'amen bo'*, 'Amen, come'.

In any case, the hymn takes us to the mood of passages like 'Our Lord is come. The grace of our Lord be with you' (though Paul also may think of the imperative, 'Our Lord, come'—if we divide *marana tha* instead of *maran atha*), 'Let grace come and this world pass away. Hosanna to the God of David. Our Lord is come. Amen' (here again we could divide so as to obtain 'Our Lord, come'), and 'He which testifieth these things saith, Surely I come quickly. Amen, come, Lord

---

[1] Singer's *Prayer Book*, p. 40.   [2] Singer's *Prayer Book*, p. 47.
[3] Bab. Shab. 119b, San. 111a.   [4] *Encyclopaedia Judaica, s.v.* Amen.
[5] Singer's *Prayer Book*, p. 167.
[6] C. Taylor, *The Teaching of the Twelve Apostles*, pp. 78 f.

Jesus.'[1] It may be remarked that the hymn seems to have been designed as the final hymn of certain services; and most rites still place it at the end of those services for which it is used.[2]

Here a reservation must be made. It is possible that, originally, both these 'Amens' had the character of normal, concluding 'Amens'. The 'Amen' before the *Shema'*, the Credo, may have been meant, not to open the Credo, but to confirm the benedictions preceding it. This is strongly suggested by the fact that medieval scholars like Rashi and Hananel declare the benediction immediately preceding to be one of the few to which even a person praying by himself may add an 'Amen'. As a rule you may say 'Amen' only after a benediction recited by the precentor. The words 'God, faithful King', with which an Ashkenazi, when he prays alone, now begins the Credo, may simply derive from that 'Amen' referring to a previous benediction.[3] Similarly, the author of 'None is like our God' may have had in mind the preceding service, to which his 'Amen' should constitute the conclusion. In fact if we point *bo*', so as to get the imperative 'come', no other explanation is possible. We must have before us the ordinary, if expanded, 'Amen'; we cannot translate 'Verily, come!' but we must—on this pointing—assume that the author had the same intention that is found at the close of Revelation (and, if we divide *marana tha*, also in I Corinthians and the Didache). There the addressees receive the promise 'Surely, I come quickly', to which they reply, 'Amen, come, Lord Jesus'—the ordinary, though expanded, 'Amen'.[4] Just so, the author of 'None is like our God' would have composed his hymn for a service leading up to an assurance of salvation and the reply, in the form of an acrostic, 'Amen, come'.

The case of the hymn is complicated by two further points. First, it is not absolutely certain (though I have no doubt) that the hymn was an acrostic from the outset. There are sources in which the lines are arranged differently.[5] Secondly, Rashi—whom we have already mentioned in connection with the 'Amen' before the *Shema'*—deciphers the acrostic not as '*amen ba*', but as '*amen barukh 'atta*, 'Verily, blessed be

[1] I Cor. 16.22 f., Didache 10.6, Rev. 22.20.
[2] *Jewish Encyclopedia*, vol. 5, 1903, p. 154, *s.v.* En Kelohenu.
[3] *Encyclopaedia Judaica*, *s.v.* Amen.
[4] Curiously, one Armenian version presupposes ἦλθε instead of ἔρχου (Hoskier, *The Text of the Apocalypse*, vol. 2, p. 646), i.e. it has 'Verily, he is come'. The version is worthless, it seems. Nevertheless it shows with what freedom 'Amen' was treated.
[5] See Schechter, *Jewish Quarterly Review*, 4, p. 253.

thou'. This is a conceivable, though extremely artificial solution. It means that while we have to take the initial letters of the first three lines of the hymn, we have to take the entire initial words of the following two lines.

I do not think the significance of the two examples is essentially diminished by these difficulties. At the most cautious estimate, we may see from the instances adduced how what were at first ordinary 'Amens' in the course of time became 'Amens' closely resembling the introductory 'Amens' of the New Testament. For whatever its origin, the 'Amen' before the Credo is now connected, not with the benedictions that it follows, but with the Credo itself—though, admittedly, in the dress of *'el melekh ne'eman*, 'God, faithful King'. Whatever its history, the hymn 'None is like our God' now makes *'amen b'* with no reference to any previous prayer; and, as observed already, in one manuscript at least, it is represented by the pointed words *'amen ba'*, which can be rendered only by 'Verily, he is coming' or 'Verily, he is come'. At the most cautious estimate, therefore, the cases discussed are evidence that the development from the normal 'Amen' to something very much like the 'Amen' in the sense of 'verily' is feasible, and has taken place, in Hebrew, outside the New Testament. Whoever introduced the New Testament 'Amen', that is, did not go beyond the natural possibilities of actual Hebrew speech.

In fact, it may well be that the very difficulties outlined contain the key to a full understanding of the position. It looks as if the introductory 'Amen' had been disliked by the Rabbis. Supposing the 'Amen' in the sense of 'verily' was mainly employed in, roughly speaking, eschatological utterances. That would explain its frequency in the New Testament and its almost complete suppression in Jewish literature.

We might then argue that the 'Amen' before the Credo did start as an opening; and that, if the Sephardim dropped it entirely, the Ashkenazim disguised it as 'God, faithful King' and some Rabbis—Rashi among them—made it the ending of the benedictions preceding the Credo, thus turning it into an ordinary 'Amen', these were all different attempts to eliminate the dangerous 'verily'. Similarly, as for the hymn 'None is like our God', the acrostic order would have come first and a deliberate disarrangement would have followed later. Indeed, the acrostic form itself may have been chosen as a less open version of

'Verily, he is coming' or 'Verily, he is come'. Rashi's deciphering of the acrostic as *'amen barukh 'atta* would be an ingenious method of replacing 'Verily, he is coming' or 'Verily, he is come' by 'Amen, blessed be thou'; which latter clause, for synagogue-goers, would be merely one of the expanded 'Amens' described above—such as 'Amen, let his great name be blessed for ever.' Maybe it is no coincidence that the first traces, or rudiments, of this hymn are to be found in works of at least partly Essene origin.[1]

[1] Jellinek, *Beth Ha-Midrash*, vol. 2, p. 47, vol. 3, p. 86.

XVII

'I Speak After the Manner of Men'

A. PAUL

PAUL uses this phrase, or one very like it, four times. Strack-Billerbeck[1] maintain that it has a different meaning each time, and that it is not of a technical character. However, though there are slight differences—naturally, since no phrase has exactly the same meaning twice—the essential import is invariably the same, and the phrase must be regarded as technical. One suspects that it may have been the difficulty of linking it up with any technical phrase in Rabbinic literature which was a sub-conscious factor contributing to Strack-Billerbeck's conclusion: it drove them to deny its technical nature in Paul and to exaggerate the differences between the four passages where it occurs.

The phrase is an apology for a bold statement which, without such an apology, might be considered near-blasphemous—be it because it is too anthropomorphic or be it because it sounds otherwise lacking in reverence for God or an established religious idea.

Let us look at the four texts. In Romans 3.5 Paul apologizes for framing the hypothesis that God may be unrighteous. Of course he refutes the hypothesis. But the mere fact that he puts it, unless accompanied by this apology, might be judged blasphemous by a Jewish public.

In Romans 6.19 he apologizes for admonishing the recipients of the letter to become 'slaves to righteousness'. In a previous chapter (on Redemption) we pointed out that the Old Testament and the Rabbis never describe the faithful as slaves of anyone or anything but God. Paul's term is not only, as Dodd remarks, 'sub-Christian', it is above all 'sub-Jewish'. He has recourse to it in order to impress on antinomian doctrinaires that, just as formerly they were eager to sin, so now they

---

[1] Vol. 3, 1926, p. 136.

should be eager to do good, to live saintly lives. Nevertheless the apology is needed since, without it, in the eyes of good Jews, his exhortation would be objectionable.

In Galatians 3.15 he compares a disposition made by God with one made by a man, and besides he considers the question whether it is subject to repeal or change. However vigorously he denies this possibility, the mere hypothesis requires an apology. The case is very similar to Romans 3.5.

I have left I Corinthians 9.8 to the last, the matter being a little more complicated. But even here there is no doubt as to the meaning of the phrase.

Paul contends that an apostle is entitled to support from his congregations, as a shepherd takes milk from his flock; and he adds that he does not intend to apologize, i.e. he is not 'speaking after the manner of men'. Obviously he assumes that some of the recipients of the letter will expect this apology here. They will expect him to indicate that his words are not to be taken literally, that they are a bold metaphor which, without the apology, might be deemed wanting in reverence for God or an accepted religious custom.

Now in New Testament times the Rabbis were agreed that the word of God must be taught gratuitously. Hillel (about 30 B.C.) said, 'He who makes use of the crown (the Torah) will perish', and Zadok (about A.D. 50), 'Make not the words of the Torah a spade wherewith to dig.'[1] A few concessions were made in the case of elementary instruction of children; but even they seem to have been introduced at a later date. It is, then, the Jewish traditionalists among his addressees to whom Paul declares that there is to be no apology to mitigate his assertion. This assertion, that apostles are entitled to support, must be taken literally, and if it causes offence it cannot be helped.

That he anticipates opposition of the kind we have outlined is confirmed by the manner he argues. Having made his assertion, he does not simply refer to the pronouncement by which Jesus authorized his messengers to live by their office. On the contrary, he begins by adducing a passage from the Law, from Deuteronomy—'Thou shalt not muzzle the mouth of the ox that treadeth out the corn'—and this he interprets most freely with a view to extracting from it the proof he needs. But even when he goes on to Jesus's pronouncement, he

[1] Mish. Ab. 1.13, 4.5.

represents it as a mere extension by analogy of Old Testament regulations: 'They which minister about holy things live of the temple—
even so hath the Lord ordained that they which preach the gospel
should live of it.' Neither in Matthew nor in Luke[1] is Jesus's pronouncement rested on Old Testament authority (though, significantly, in
Matthew it appears in a far more restrained version than in Luke:
Matthew mentions a right to meat only, Luke one to hire). I Timothy
also,[2] though like I Corinthians it quotes first the Deuteronomic law
—'Thou shalt not muzzle' and so on—and only then Jesus's pronouncement, does not connect the latter with Old Testament rules.

Paul in I Corinthians has to deal with the charge that the right he
claims for apostles is contrary to a hallowed religious principle. Despite
the charge he insists on the right, explaining that he does not here 'speak
after the manner of men'.

The evidence bears out what we said at the beginning. The phrase 'I
speak after the manner of men' has one definite meaning. It constitutes
an apology for a statement which, but for the apology, would be too
bold, almost blasphemous. The author by this phrase emphasizes that
he is speaking with all due reserve. He is using the words apologized for
only because he sees no other way of bringing out his point. But his
words ought not to be pressed, no irreverence is intended.

The phrase occurs four times in Paul. This alone is sufficient to prove
it technical. In what circles was it technical? Clearly in Rabbinic ones—
no matter whether or not we can discover it in Jewish sources. For one
thing, the attitude reflected in it is Rabbinic. It is an attitude of humility
towards God and religious institutions: man's language is not always
capable of doing justice to them. (This distinguishes the phrase from,
say, 'sit venia verbo', which has no such background; in Pliny[3] 'venia
sit dicto' corresponds to our 'touch wood'.) For another thing, every
time Paul employs—or expressly refuses to employ—the phrase, he
does so in defence against what strict Jews might have to say. Which
shows that he regards them as familiar with it.

B. JEWISH SOURCES

The Jewish sources, however, pose a neat riddle. In Tannaitic
literature the technical apology for an overbold statement is *kibheyakhol*,

---

[1] Matt. 10.10, Luke 10.7.   [2] 5.18.   [3] Ep. 5.6.46.

'as if one could (say so)'.[1] Johanan ben Zaccai (who lived at the time of the destruction of the Temple) tries to explain why a thief, who steals in secret, must pay double, whereas an open robber need only repay the principal. He claims that the thief—in contradistinction to the robber—fears man more than God: 'as if one could say so, he thinks the Eye above will not see'.[2] The mere hypothesis that God might not see, even though the Rabbi ascribes it to a criminal, must be accompanied by this excuse. Another example is the saying that 'whenever Israel is enslaved, the Shekinah—as if one could say so—is enslaved with them'.[3] Without the apology, the statement would be too anthropomorphic.

Kibheyakhol, then, as far as sense is concerned, is very near Paul's 'I speak after the manner of men.' But it is manifestly another expression. Paul's phrase is not a rendering of it.

Yet from the late 9th century, we find anthropomorphisms occurring in the Bible justified by the maxim: 'the Torah speaks after the language of the sons of men'.[4] According to Judah ibn Koreish, Tobia ben Eliezer, Maimonides and so on, whenever the Bible refers to God sitting, standing, talking or the like, it is a concession to the human mind. We could not understand God's perfection were it not that 'the Torah speaks after the language of men'.

This phrase is highly reminiscent of Paul's; it is almost identical with it. There is only one material difference which, it is true, is of such importance that it greatly affects sense and application. Whereas Paul's phrase is an apology for a daring statement made by a human person, 'I speak so and so', the medieval phrase serves as an explanation and mitigation of an anthropomorphism to be found in Scripture itself, 'the Torah speaks so and so'.

The problem is complicated, but perhaps ultimately brought nearer a solution, by a further factor. The maxim 'the Torah speaks after the language of the sons of men' occurs already in Tannaitic literature; it is advocated by R. Ishmael, of the first half of the 2nd cent. A.D. Only its meaning is not the same as in the Middle Ages. It is of a far narrower scope, concerned with the philology of the Bible.

More precisely, Akiba and Ishmael disagree as to the proper method of interpreting the Bible. The former and his School hold that the Bible

[1] Bacher, *Die älteste Terminologie der Jüdischen Schriftauslegung*, 1899, pp. 72 f.
[2] Mekh. on Exod. 22.6 (5).   [3] Mekh. on Exod. 12.41.   [4] Bacher, *op. cit.*, p. 98.

chooses its expressions with incomparably greater care than would be applied to any human document. Hence *haggadhic* and *halakhic* conclusions may be derived from pleonasms, from an infinitive preceding the finite verb and the like. The latter and his School maintain that these phenomena, as they are common in daily speech, should not be made the basis for special deductions.

For instance, the Bible lays down that whoever despises the word of the Lord 'shall utterly be cut off'. The Hebrew text does not contain the word 'utterly'. Instead there is an infinitive before the finite verb: 'to be cut off, he shall be cut off'. Akiba sees in the twofold mention of 'to be cut off' evidence that the sinner in question is to be cut off from this world and from the next. (His view goes back to New Testament times, in whatever way it may then have been supported; this may be gathered from Matthew:[1] 'Whoever speaketh against the Holy Ghost, it shall not be forgiven him, neither in this world, neither in the world to come.') Ishmael refuses to accept Akiba's evidence. (He inclines to leniency in any case.) An infinitive preceding the finite verb is a feature of ordinary speech. It is used for emphasis, and Ishmael denies that it has any other purpose in Scripture. Consequently, in his opinion, the person is to be cut off only from this world: 'the Torah speaks after the manner of men'.[2]

C. PAUL AND THE JEWISH SOURCES

We now have the following data.

First, Paul avails himself of a phrase, which must have been technical in the Rabbinic Judaism of his epoch, to explain that an expression of his, though it might at first sight appear irreverent, is not to be pressed; he uses it in order to be understood by the ordinary public. No analogous phrase, however, is to be met with in extant contemporary Jewish utterances.

Secondly, Ishmael, in the first half of the 2nd cent. A.D., avails himself of a similar phrase to explain that an expression occurring in the Pentateuch, though some exegetes will draw far-reaching conclusions from it, should not be pressed; it is used in the way an ordinary author would use it.

Thirdly, from the 9th century, Jewish writers avail themselves of

[1] 12.32.   [2] Siph. on Num. 15.31.

Ishmael's phrase to explain that an expression occurring in the Bible, though it may at first sight appear anthropomorphic, should not be pressed; it is used in order that the ordinary public may understand.

The most plausible inference is that when Paul wrote, it was quite usual for a strict Jew to excuse an overbold statement by adding 'I speak after the language of men.' Ishmael transferred the phrase to Biblical philology; i.e. he and his followers took the view—against Akiba and his followers—that, on the whole, the Bible should be read like a human document, and syntactic and stylistic features which would pass as normal in daily speech should not be pressed merely because they occurred in the Bible. So he declared that 'the Torah speaks after the language of men'. It was this application of the phrase which, I believe, drove out the original one, 'I speak after the language of men.' At least it drove it out from official literature. As soon as there was a principle that 'the Torah speaks after the language of men', it would have sounded presumptuous if a person said of himself 'I speak after the language of men.' This is the reason why in Jewish sources only the term *kibheyakhol*, 'as if one could say so', remained to express what, before Ishmael, could also be expressed by 'I speak after the manner of men.' In other words, this is the reason why Paul's phrase, though a technical Rabbinic phrase, cannot be paralleled from Rabbinic writings.

When in the 9th century the scope of Ishmael's maxim expanded so as to cover Biblical anthropomorphisms, this may have been just a natural process: originally it had been directed against undue insistence on certain philological points, now it was also directed against undue insistence on certain statements about God. It is, however, possible that the phrase 'I speak after the language of men', in the sense of *kibheyakhol*, 'as if one could say so', though Ishmael's maxim had caused its disappearance from official sources, had lived on all the time in unrecorded usage. It would not be the only instance of an expression being eliminated from orthodox literature and yet continuing to be employed where people talk off their guard. If so, this phrase, 'I speak after the language of men', in the sense of 'as if one could say so', may well have helped to bring about the new application of Ishmael's maxim in the 9th century. That is to say, this new application to Biblical anthropomorphisms would have two roots: not only Ishmael's maxim respecting the philology of the Bible, but also the old Rabbinic phrase which we come across in Paul, which lived on in unofficial speech among Jews even after Ishmael and which was an apology for daring statements. It would be from these two roots that sprang the medieval principle 'the Torah speaks after the language of men' as an explanation of those passages where God is represented as sitting, standing or the like.

One might perhaps think of a third influence on the medieval role of this maxim: Paul's epistles themselves, or more precisely, those verses where he professes to 'speak after the manner of men' (or declares that he does not do so). However, that they should have directly contributed to the 9th-century extension of Ishmael's maxim seems to me unlikely in the extreme.

XVIII

Two Symbols

A. A SYMBOL OF EZEKIEL IN REVELATION

IN a vision Ezekiel sees his people punished.[1] But—in accordance with his doctrine that the just must not suffer with the wicked—those who are innocent have their foreheads marked at God's express command, and the destroyers are told not to come near them.

The procedure is of a kind common in antiquity when a fugitive, a ἱκέτης, was granted asylum. He might be marked as the property of his protector. If the protector was credited with superhuman power, the mark presumably had the additional purpose of exercising an apotropaeic effect, of averting evil.

The Hebrew word for 'mark' in the passage under discussion is *taw*, that for 'to mark' *tawa*. Probably *taw* acquired the meaning of 'mark', 'signature',[2] because, for one thing, it was the last letter of the Hebrew alphabet and, for another, in ancient script it looked more or less like an oblique cross, like x. But that Ezekiel represents it as the signature conferring protection may well have a further reason. In Egypt a fugitive to a sanctuary was marked with two crosses on the forehead, like the priests.[3] Ezekiel, of priestly stock himself, must have been familiar with such rites.

It is indeed possible that the *taw*, the cross, was employed in a similar fashion long before him. We are told how David fled from Saul to Achish, the king of Gath. As he feared the latter's jealousy, he acted the madman—the inviolable madman:[4] 'And he feigned himself mad in their hands and made *taws* on the doors of the gate and let his spittle fall down upon his beard.'

Versions and commentaries invariably try to explain away *wayethaw*, here translated by 'and he made *taws*'. Yet there is good evidence, on the

---

[1] 9.2 ff.
[2] Cp. Job 31.35.
[3] K. Latte, *Heiliges Recht*, 1920, pp. 107 f.
[4] I Sam. 21.14 (13).

one hand, that at least by the time of Ahab Israelite prophets bore marks on the forehead;[1] and, on the other, that the custom of protecting a house by signing the door-posts is very ancient—we need only recall the narrative of the exodus.[2] Here again, incidentally, Egyptian influence may play a part. When we remember in addition the sign of Cain and the frontlets, the *totaphoth*, also first mentioned in connection with the rescue from Egypt,[3] and later called *tephillin*, 'prayer-capsules', or phylacteries, it seems unnecessary to boggle at the appearance of *tawa* in the story about David.

The mark survives throughout the centuries. There is a figure of a priest of Isis dating from the Rome of the 1st cent. A.D., with the two crosses on his forehead.[4] To go by a Tannaitic report, the priests of the Temple were anointed in the form of the letter x.[5] Whether or not this is correct does not matter. Even if it is not, the fact remains that the Rabbis were acquainted with the use of this sign for consecration.

In Ezekiel, however, it is highly doubtful whether they still associated the *taw* with the cross. The old script, where *taw* was written in that form, had long gone out of fashion. Even the LXX renders the word simply by σημεῖον, 'sign', without specifying the shape. To be sure, some circles may have preserved a tradition giving the original form. But it is not probable.

Yet in Revelation, at the approach of the end, before the earth and sea are hurt, those of the children of Israel who are slaves of God are sealed on their foreheads with 'the seal of the living God'[6]—a scene unquestionably inspired by the Old Testament model: as in Ezekiel, some who are to escape the general ruin are to be visibly marked. The author of Revelation no doubt alludes to baptism. We may assume that by his time, when a person was baptized, he was signed on the forehead with a cross. It follows that the form of the saving mark is the same as that to which Ezekiel referred.

The problem is whether there is a direct line from Ezekiel to Revelation. In all likelihood there is not. The author of Revelation arrived at this form solely by proceeding from the Christian cross. His agreement with Ezekiel is just an odd coincidence.

We know, however, that he inclined to provide established symbols

---

[1] I Kings 20.38, 41. [2] E.g. Exod. 12.7 ff. [3] Exod. 13.16.
[4] Wolters, K. Glyptothek und Skulpturensammlung des Staates, Archäologischer Anzeiger 1910, cols. 470 ff. [5] Bab. Hor. 12a. [6] 7.2 ff.

with a new significance. Accordingly, we cannot rule out the possibility of his having in mind also the prevalent mark used for granting asylum (note that those to be signed are called 'the slaves of God', i.e. God's property); the Rabbinic theory concerning the anointing of Jewish priests (God and the Lamb, according to Revelation,[1] are the true Temple); and even the identification, which may still have lingered on in certain sects, of Ezekiel's *taw* with a cross. In other words, he may have interpreted one or two or all of these old symbols as the cross figuring at baptism. He may have seen in them the cross of Christ, 'the Father's name', 'the name of my God and the new Jerusalem', 'the name of God and the Lamb'.[2] His thought, of course, is focused on the Christian cross. But it is conceivable that he knew of the pre-Christian uses of this sign—his interests in general speak rather in favour of this assumption—and that his knowledge had some influence on the chapter here in question.

Naturally, in later times, Christian exegetes all ascribed to the mark occurring in Ezekiel the form of a cross: they looked on the Old Testament vision in the light of the scene from Revelation. What is more remarkable is[3] that the Christian view influenced not a few Cabbalists; and that in several medieval Jewish mystic works Ezekiel's *taw* is declared to be the cruciform Tree of Life, the source of all salvation.

B. 'Arepo' in the Sator Square

Since its discovery at Pompeii, the magic square, which can be read in different directions, is once again the object of much interest. Its better-known form is: 'The Sower Arepo holds with care the wheels.' Probably the other form is older: 'The wheels with care holds Arepo the Sower.' Here are both:

(1) SATOR	(2) ROTAS
AREPO	OPERA
TENET	TENET
OPERA	AREPO
ROTAS	SATOR

The difference is irrelevant for our purpose. Either version, as is widely accepted, is made up of PATERNOSTER twice over, and

---

[1] 21.22.   [2] 14.1, 3.12, 22.4.
[3] Zöckler, *Das Kreuz Christi*, 1875, pp. 31 f., 475 ff.

necessarily arranged as a cross (since the middle letter, N, appears only once in the square), plus the symbolic characters A and O twice over. That is to say, either version is a cryptogram of:

```
                A
                P
                A
                T
                E
                R
A  P  A  T  E  R  N  O  S  T  E  R  O
                O
                S
                T
                E
                R
                O
```

One word in the square is still unexplained: 'Arepo'. Many derivations have been attempted—the most recent from Celtic—but none is at all convincing. There is, however, a simple solution: it is a Hebrew or Aramaic rendering of ἄλφα ὦ, the epithet of God we find in Revelation;[1] and be it noted that wherever it occurs in Revelation, it occurs as ἄλφα ὦ, not say, as ἀ ὦ—hence something like 'Arepo' may be expected.

As just remarked, the square consists of the symbolic characters A and O twice over in addition to PATERNOSTER twice over. The author, that is, knew the epithet in question. Indeed he treated it as of fundamental importance—though, for obvious reasons, in choosing the letters with which to build the square, he proceeded from the shorter form, A O or ἀ ὦ. Clearly, if it can be shown that he intended ἄλφα ὦ as the name of the 'Sower', his square will make fairly good sense and sense in harmony with the constituent letters: 'The Sower Alpha O holds with care the wheels.'

Normally, ἄλφα ὦ, in Hebrew or Aramaic, would give 'alep o'. Here it is 'arep o'. Why? In both these languages, l and r are very close indeed. That writers from early times were conscious of the fact may be gathered from a pun by Micah:[2] rekhesh—lakhish ('horses'—'Lachish').

---

[1] 1.8, 21.6, 22.13.   [2] 1.13.

In other languages also, such as Greek, *l* sometimes becomes *r*. The author manifestly put 'arepo' as the nearest thing to 'alepo' he was able to attain. 'Arepo' followed from PATERNOSTER and, read backwards, supplied a suitable word, 'opera'; 'alepo' did neither; so 'arepo' it had to be. ('His name was not Bun but Wood, but Wood would not rhyme with gun but Bun would.') Considering the enormous difficulty of constructing such a square, he did not do too badly.

However, it is possible that a slight twist of this kind was even desired. The modified forms of the tetragrammaton in use among Jews, or the spelling 'Eloqim' for 'Elohim', may be recalled. 'Alep o' certainly enjoyed some degree of sanctity. We must reckon with a good deal of reverence, and no doubt also with a little superstition.

The view that 'Arepo' means 'alep o', standing for ἄλφα ὤ, has a bearing on the provenance of the square. We do not propose here to go into it, beyond observing, first, that a Jewish-Christian origin might account for several features which have puzzled scholars; and secondly, that it is unintelligible to me why so many historians, in investigating the Sator Square, proceed from the premise that no Christians, or Jewish Christians, can have lived at Pompeii prior to A.D. 79. I think some may have lived there from the middle of the century—whether they professed their faith or kept it to themselves. The Sator Square, incidentally, if affixed to a house, might serve as a secret mark of recognition among the initiated.

XIX

Chronology

A. The Problem

ACCORDING to Matthew[1] the devil tempts Jesus first by asking him whether he can turn stone into bread, next by leading him to Jerusalem and asking him whether he can cast himself down from the temple unhurt, and finally by taking him up to a mountain and offering him all kingdoms of the world. In Luke,[2] the first temptation is the same. But Matthew's third comes second—and there is no mention of a mountain—while Matthew's second comes third.

Creed[3] thinks Matthew has the original sequence: Luke altered it in order to avoid a second change of scene. In Luke, the temptations to turn stone into bread and to accept worldly rule take place in the same locality, and only that to leap from the temple takes place at Jerusalem; in Matthew, the temptation to turn stone into bread takes place in the desert, that to leap from the temple at Jerusalem and that to accept worldly dominion on a mountain. T. W. Manson, on the other hand, prefers the Lukan sequence.[4] Matthew's narrative, he argues, works up to an exciting climax: the devil tells Jesus to perform a sign, he tells him to perform a greater sign, he promises to make him ruler of the earth. Had Luke had this sequence before him, he would not have interfered with it. It is Matthew who rendered the original story more dramatic.

The writer inclines to Manson's view. But no matter how we account for the difference between the two versions, few modern scholars would maintain that an evangelist was incapable of regrouping incidents or sayings with a view to a more pleasing or stronger effect. The wider aims of an author—to retain the attention of his public, to impress certain points on them or to elaborate an important thesis—on

[1] 4.1 ff.   [2] 4.1 ff.   [3] *The Gospel according to St. Luke*, 1930, p. 63.
[4] Major, Manson and Wright, *The Mission and Message of Jesus*, pp. 334 ff.

occasion took precedence over adherence to strict chronology. In the Fourth Gospel, in particular, the order in which some matters are presented becomes intelligible only if we suppose that to exercise considerable freedom as to dates, to abandon a traditional sequence, to repeat the same thing twice or three times and so on, were not reckoned unforgivable sins.

How is this attitude to be explained? We are not concerned with changes resulting from carelessness; nor with those introduced because an evangelist—rightly or wrongly—believes that the order by which he replaces that handed down to him is the true, historical one, that he is restoring the original order. Certainly such cases are frequent. But here we are interested in those alterations which an author deliberately makes although he has no reason to doubt the accuracy of his source. Whether Luke rearranged the temptations in order to avoid a second change of scene, or whether Matthew rearranged them in order to render them more dramatic—there was a deviation from the traditional chronology for a reason other than that the chronology was deemed wrong. In the Synoptics, the temple is cleansed towards the end of Jesus's activity, in John near its commencement. The incident was redated—no matter by whom—in order to enhance its significance. Nowadays we constantly assume alterations of this sort, but we do not ever seem to inquire where an evangelist (or his precursor) might find his justification for them.

Perhaps, before attempting an answer, we ought to make a distinction. I may narrate events in a non-chronological order and yet convey the exact order in which they occurred. I may say, for example, that Churchill became First Lord of the Admiralty in 1911 and had been Home Secretary in 1910. This would be only a formal deviation from the historical sequence. The latter would not be materially upset unless I said that Churchill first served at the Admiralty and then became Home Secretary. It should, however, be borne in mind that if events are narrated in a non-chronological order, the chance of a listener or reader receiving a wrong impression of their actual relation is usually rather strong. If I say that Churchill, in the course of his career, was First Lord of the Admiralty and Home Secretary, giving no dates, my public may easily conclude that he started by being First Lord and was Home Secretary later. We shall come back to this question. For the moment it suffices to observe that, in general, where an evangelist arranges incidents or sayings in a non-chronological way without dating them, we may treat the case as a material deviation from the historical order.

B. 'There is no before and after in Scripture'

Among the factors which contributed to the attitude of the evangelists the most important may well have been a principle of interpretation we know to have been applied by R. Ishmael's school in dealing with *haggadhic*, non-legal, points of the Old Testament: 'There is no before and after in Scripture.' The Bible, that is, frequently puts a later event before an earlier; the order of events in reality is not always reflected in the order of events in the Bible.

The Mekhilta sees an illustration in a verse from the Song of Moses:[1] 'The enemy said, I will pursue.' This verse refers to something—the decision of the Egyptians to destroy the Israelites[2]—that happened before what is referred to in the opening lines of the Song[3]—the drowning of the Egyptians.[4] It would be more exact, chronologically, the Mekhilta holds, if the verse in question formed the beginning of the chapter and all mention of drowning came after it. However, the Biblical arrangement is accounted for by the rule 'There is no before and after in Scripture.' Another Midrash, Siphre on Numbers, makes use of the rule in commenting on the provisions, relating to Passover, which were made known to Moses 'in the first month of the second year after they were come out of Egypt'.[5] Nine chapters before, the Midrash notes, we are told about an event that must have occurred a month or so later, namely, God's request to Moses to take the sum of the children of Israel, a request made 'on the first day of the second month, in the second year after they were come out of Egypt'.[6]

It might be argued that in both these cases the Bible deviates from the historical order in a formal sense only, not in a material one. Every reader will know that the drowning of the Egyptians was later than their wicked scheming, and the incidents recorded in Numbers are provided with full dates. So let us add two more examples, one again from the Mekhilta. The first chapter of Ezekiel depicts a strange vision, the second his call. According to the Mekhilta, historically, the call

---

[1] Exod. 15.9.   [2] Exod. 14.5 ff.   [3] 15.1–8.
[4] Exod. 14.23 ff.   [5] Num. 9.1.   [6] Num. 1.1.

preceded the vision. Now this is a proposition far from self-evident, and at any rate the text as it stands does convey the impression that the vision preceded the call. Yet the Rabbis felt entitled to postulate the opposite sequence, since 'There is no before and after in Scripture.' The prophet, from theological motives, redated the actual events.

Similarly, R. Ishmael (first third of the 2nd cent. A.D.) and R. Joshua ben Levi (middle of 3rd cent.) contended that only the first two of the Ten Commandments ('I am the Lord' and 'Thou shalt have no other gods') were given to the Israelites directly by God. Their thesis was attacked on the ground that, according to the plain sense of the Biblical account, it was not till all Ten Commandments had been promulgated that the people asked Moses: 'Speak thou with us, but let not God speak with us, lest we die.'[1] But Joshua ben Levi made light of the objection, invoking the maxim 'There is no before and after': the people's request was made immediately after the Second Commandment.[2]

In a slightly modified form, the rule is to be found among the 32 Middoth, principles of interpretation, compiled by Eliezer ben Jose Ha-gelili for *haggadhic* exposition. It is the last Middah, and it runs: 'The before that comes after in the Biblical sections', or 'The after comes before in the Biblical sections.' Earlier and later periods in history are not necessarily dealt with in earlier and later sections of Scripture; many a section refers to an earlier period than a section preceding it.

Two illustrations are given in Eliezer's compilation. The seventh chapter of Numbers describes the ceremonies accompanying the setting up of the tabernacle. In reality, these took place—the Rabbis say—before the events recounted in the preceding chapters; they took place, that is, immediately after the events recounted towards the end of Exodus,[3] where it is stated that 'Moses reared up the tabernacle and fastened its sockets.' The other illustration may be more interesting in this connection since it concerns a chronological problem of a kind well known from the Fourth Gospel. In Genesis 12,[4] when Abraham leaves Haran for Canaan, he is said to be seventy-five years old. In Genesis 15,[5] when God announces to him what will befall his descendants, his age is not mentioned; but he cannot be older than seventy if the various

---

[1] Exod. 20.19.
[2] Bab. Hor. 8a, Cant. Rabba on 1.2.
[3] 40.17 ff.   [4] V. 4.   [5] 7-21.

dates referring to him in the Pentateuch are to be harmonized.[1] There is no difficulty in this for the Rabbis: the announcement recorded in chapter 15 was made to him before his immigration into Canaan recorded in 12. It is simply a case of 'The before that comes after in the Biblical sections.'

As for the age of this mode of interpretation, the instances adduced are most of them from the earliest Tannaitic Midrashim preserved to us. This in itself would not, perhaps, take us back farther than, say, A.D. 150. But there are two reasons at least for assuming a far earlier origin. First, the principle under notice appears in those Midrashim as firmly established. Even if none of the particular cases where we find it applied were older than R. Ishmael—an unlikely hypothesis—the rule as such must have grown up before. Of course, its exact formulation may have differed from that with which we are familiar. Secondly, an exegesis of the Old Testament stories and sayings on the supposition that there is minute historical arrangement, with no anticipation, no turning back, no repetition, is a glaring impossibility. It strikes any cursory reader. It must have struck the Rabbis, who spent their lives studying the Scriptures, from the outset. Nowadays discrepancies are eliminated by the methods of modern criticism, postulating different sources, ascribing mistakes to the writers of the Bible, and so on. None of these solutions was open to the Rabbis. The principle 'There is no before and after in Scripture', in one form or another, was the only and the obvious solution for them to adopt.

C. 'SERES'

It may be worth calling attention to another method of interpretation, also favoured by Ishmael's school, seres: a verse or section at first sight illogical might be made logical by turning round its several components.

---

[1] The calculation is as follows (S.O. 3). In Gen. 15.13, God says that the Israelites will be enslaved during 400 years. According to the Rabbis, this covers not only the time in Egypt (which, on the basis of other Biblical dates, must have been far briefer) but the whole period from Isaac's birth to the exodus. But in Exod. 12.40 we are told that the Israelites were slaves for 430 years. How is Exod. 12.40 to be reconciled with Gen. 15.13? The answer is that, while Gen. 15.13 takes as the beginning of the slavery Isaac's birth—400 years between then and the exodus—Exod. 12.40 takes the time when God announced to Abraham the future of his descendants, the very incident, that is, recounted in Gen. 15.7-21—430 years between then and the exodus. It follows that this incident, the announcement of what would befall the Israelites, occurred thirty years before Isaac's birth. As Abraham was 100 years old when Isaac was born, he was seventy when God made with him the covenant of Gen. 15.7-21.

This method was not only used to establish a plausible chronology. For example, the assurance 'In any place where I allow my name to be mentioned I will come unto thee'[1] was considered by some expounders as reversing what was really meant. The real meaning, they asserted, was: 'In any place where I come unto thee (scil. in the tabernacle and temple) I will allow my name to be mentioned.'[2] This has nothing to do with dates.

Still, as a rule, seres was resorted to where the Biblical chronology could not be accepted at its face value. The Bible tells us[3] that a number of men brought a problem 'before Moses and before Aaron', that Moses transmitted it to God and that God informed him of the solution. Rabbinic commentators claimed that the men must have approached Aaron first, and when he did not know they went on to Moses who had access to God. The real meaning, then, was that the problem was brought 'before Aaron and before Moses'. The Bible, for special reasons, deviated from strict chronology.[4] Similarly, from the text as it stands we learn that Jacob in a dream saw a ladder reaching to heaven and received a promise of divine help; then, on waking up, he vowed an altar if God should help him.[5] Some Rabbis argued that, had he already received that promise, he would no longer have used the conditional 'If God will be with me, this stone shall be his house.' They concluded that the vow in reality preceded the vision. The Biblical narrative, for a theological purpose, rejected the historical order, placing the vision first and the vow second.[6]

Interpretation by transposition, seres, was founded on the belief that the Bible, and in particular the Pentateuch, was inspired by God. Any passage might therefore contain various layers of meaning, one beneath the other (the words 'Then sang Moses', in the opinion of the Rabbis, referred to what happened in the past, after the destruction of the Egyptians, but also to what would happen in the future, after the resurrection of the dead, when a similar song would be recited),[7] or it might even convey theological or moral instruction if read as it stood and a historical point if read in a different order.

The verb haphakh sometimes figures as synonymous with seres.[8]

---

[1] Exod. 20.24.   [2] Bab. So 38a.   [3] Num. 9.6 ff.
[4] Siph. on Num. 9.6.   [5] Gen. 28.12 ff.   [6] Gen. Rabba on 28.20.
[7] Mekh. on Exod. 15.1, stressing the fact that the Hebrew for 'sang' is not the perfect shar but the imperfect yashir.
[8] Tanh. on Gen. 49.4.

Haphakh is the term which, in a saying by Hillel or one of his proselytes,[1] of the last half-century B.C., denotes the constant 'turning round' of each Scriptural passage, with a view to discovering ever deeper revelations. It is here not, indeed, confined to the method of *seres*, but embraces all methods by which a fuller understanding of God's word may be gained—or, as we moderns should put it, by which the text may be made to yield fresh insights. 'Turn it round and turn it round, for everything is in it'. Clearly, for scholars who proceeded from this conception of the nature of Scripture, *seres* was no more absurd a method than a division into sources is for us today.

D. THE EVANGELISTS

It is not improbable, we suggest, that the writers of the gospels, or some of them, were influenced by a rule of the type 'There is no before and after in Scripture.' At least it will be granted that, if this is so, many puzzles of long standing should prove less disquieting. (Needless to say, the explanation here advocated does not supply a panacea, and it will always remain necessary to take careful note of the special circumstances of each single case of rearrangement.) Those writers played the game when they disregarded dates, arranged and repeated incidents or pronouncements as they deemed best, combined several narratives or divided one. The readers were not supposed to look for a meticulous chronological order in their works.

A possible objection might be that the adage 'There is no before and after in Scripture' is a rule of interpretation, not one of writing. There is a difference, it might be argued, between recognizing that 'there is no before and after in Scripture' and writing oneself with little respect to the actual sequence of events; and the evangelists, though acquainted with deviations from the historical order in the Old Testament, would not, on that account, have dared to deviate from the historical order in presenting their own material.

There is, however, a reply to this. We may admit that the rule discussed was introduced by interpreters of a holy text, who were forced to reconcile conflicting dates. At the same time it is easy to imagine that it was gradually taken advantage of by authors as well, in particular by such of them as took the holy text as their model. These would not

---

[1] Mish. Ab. 5.22, Ab. de-R.N. 12.

necessarily think of themselves as replacing or supplementing the Mosaic revelation. As we have seen, the principle 'There is no before and after in Scripture' was applied by the Rabbis not only to the Pentateuch but also to other books of the Old Testament, the prophets, the psalms and so forth. It is unlikely that an exactitude which was considered to be absent from the Old Testament, and to be slighted, for example, by Ezekiel for the sake of a higher message he had to convey, was eagerly striven after by the religious story-tellers of the Talmudic era. The evangelists must have wished for much freedom in the matter of chronological arrangement, in order to emphasize ideas of greater importance in their eyes; and their licence was warranted by tradition. Elsewhere[1] I have tried to show that the Alexandrian model of *seres*, namely, ἀναστροφή, developed from a method of interpretation into a famous type of writing—the cento.

Here may be the place to refer to the Jewish liturgy of Passover eve. For hundreds of years before the New Testament it had included, as it still includes, an account of the redemption from Egypt. Certain portions of the gospels no doubt came into existence when the early followers of Jesus inserted into, or paralleled, this account by one of the new, greater redemption. It is, therefore, relevant to note that the traditional Jewish narrative does not list events in a rigidly chronological manner.

True, we do not know the precise age of the structure as we have it before us (even leaving on one side obviously medieval additions). But there is evidence that the 3rd- or 4th-century Rabbis at least, in fixing the arrangement, were not bent on accurate progress, step by step, from one period to the next. The Mishnah, in a provision certainly going back to New Testament times, lays down[2] that the recital 'should begin with the disgrace and end with the glory'. This in itself is not a historical plan in the narrow sense, for it means at least the omission of the ideal world before Adam's fall—the recital must open with 'disgrace'—and of any lapses after the acceptance of the Law at mount Sinai—the recital must end with 'glory'. It is, however, a controversy recorded in the Gemara about the precise import of the Mishnah which sheds more light on the Rabbinic attitude to chronology.[3]

In the opinion of Rab (first half of the 3rd cent. A.D.), we should begin with the paragraph 'Originally our ancestors were idolators';

---

[1] *Festschrift Hans Lewald*, 1953, pp. 27 ff.   [2] Pes. 10.4.   [3] Bab. Pes. 116a.

whereas according to Raba (middle of the 4th cent.),[1] we should begin with the paragraph 'We were slaves to Pharaoh', and recite the other section later. (It is widely held that the two parties each rejected the other's recital entirely—an improbable assumption.) There is no need to examine which of the two, if either, gives the right interpretation of the Mishnah. The point is that the question of chronological arrangement does not arise at all. The Rabbis are interested only in the problem when was that shameful past of the nation from which the Mishnah says we should start: was it when we were pagans or was it when we were slaves? In fact, Raba's view has prevailed in Judaism, because supported by R. Nahman (apparently bar Isaac, second half of the 4th cent.). The recital in use up to this day opens with the paragraph 'We were slaves to Pharaoh' and then only turns back to the earlier period, 'Originally our ancestors were idolators.' Admittedly, a company celebrating the Passover is expected to know the actual sequence of events despite any rearrangement—or at least the adult members are expected to know. The case accordingly falls under the category of formal rather than material deviation from the true dates. The fact remains that the order is here determined not by 'the before and after' in history, but by theological considerations.

A very ancient part of the Passover-eve narrative expounds the verse from Deuteronomy:[2] 'The Lord looked on our affliction and our trouble and our oppression.' We are told that 'our affliction' means the abstention of the Israelite husbands from intercourse with their wives, 'our trouble' Pharaoh's threat to their male babies, and 'our oppression' the toil imposed on the Israelites by their masters. Clearly, the verse is not credited with any chronological order; otherwise we should expect (1) the toil imposed on the Israelites, (2) the threat to their male offspring and (3) their abstention in order to have no offspring for Pharaoh to kill. In this case, an ordinary, unlearned participant in the Passover-eve ceremony might not immediately be able to substitute the historical order. There is a certain degree of material deviation from the actual sequence of events. The latter was of secondary importance for the authors of the narrative.

In a previous chapter (in Part II, on Four Types of Question) we

---

[1] An alternative reading is Samuel (a contemporary of Rab) instead of Raba. If this is accepted, the R. Nahman mentioned would be bar Jacob (firs thalf of the 4th cent.).
[2] 26.7.

tried to show that the four questions posed in Matthew 22 and Mark 12
—is it lawful to give tribute unto Caesar? etc.—were put together by
the evangelists as corresponding to the questions which are quoted in
the Passover-eve liturgy as suitable for different kinds of children.
Matthew and Mark, as they stand, both convey the impression that the
four questions were posed one after the other on the same day. We may
confidently assume that they were not. But we should also realize
that, when the evangelists dated them in the way they did, they were
only adopting a Rabbinic convention: there were claims overriding
those of chronology.

E. HELLENISTIC INFLUENCE

So far we have considered the Rabbinic evidence in isolation. It is
necessary, however, to remember that the Rabbinic principles of interpretation and story-telling are not a little indebted to Hellenistic
thought. This is not to deny that the early students of the Old Testament noticed discrepancies, and were driven to postulate deviations
from the historical order of events, independently of outside aid; nor
that Jewish religious story-tellers—like others—might make up their
own, unhistorical arrangement long before coming into contact with
Greek theories. Nevertheless the latter, when they did make their way
to the East, must have played a major part in causing what had been
done in a more or less haphazard, unconscious fashion to become a
proper art.

In an article referred to above[1] I have submitted that the method of
seres, interpretation by transposition, was taken over by the Rabbis
from Alexandria, and that the term *seres* itself is nothing but a rendering of ἀναστροφή. The formulation of a principle like 'There is no
before and after in Scripture', though the fact it expresses had probably
been realized for centuries, may also be a result of Hellenistic teaching.
It follows that, indirectly at any rate, the attitude of the evangelists is
connected with contemporary Hellenistic practice. We do not mean to
rule out direct Hellenistic influence on one or the other of them or their
precursors, but this is a question which we may leave undecided.

That the Iliad opens in the middle of the war against Troy instead of
at the beginning was a feature much commented on by the ancient

---

[1] *Festschrift für H. Lewald*, pp. 27 ff.

scholars.[1] Thucydides considered it important to bring out the exact historical sequence of events not only in matter but also in form: a historian must not only give the right dates—he reproached a predecessor for not doing so[2]—but also present the facts in the order in which they occurred.[3]

There were, however, others who considered this procedure as dull. Dionysius of Halicarnassus blamed Thucydides on this ground.[4] The notion—common in Hellenistic times—that primitive historians composed bare annals may also originally have implied some disparagement of a mechanical, chronological scheme.[5] Certainly, as regards non-historical literature—eulogies, forensic speeches and so forth—the general view was that chronological arrangement was only one of many possibilities. It might make for clarity, but not necessarily; and an author might legitimately prefer to proceed from the less weighty to the weightier (or vice versa), or from the simple to the complex (or vice versa), or indeed to divide up his narrative into sections and treat a separate topic from beginning to end in each of them.[6]

The question arises: were there Hellenistic doctrines allowing a historian to redate events in order to impress a certain moral on his public? There were. History was often classed as belonging to epideictic writing, i.e. writing designed to please the reader, to exhort the reader, to praise a person or the like.[7] In epideictic writing, it was permissible to twist the facts. (This liberty, of course, extended beyond chronology, to facts of any kind.) Quite a few authorities disagreed with this assessment of history and insisted on truthfulness. In one of his works[8] Cicero puts this point of view and, significantly, requires chronological arrangement. Frequently we come across what may be regarded as a compromise, a sensible one, though rarely worked out with any thoroughness: on the one hand, a historian should keep to the truth, on the other, he need not tell the whole truth—uninteresting or useless details might be omitted—and his work should be a vehicle for imparting philosophical ideas, ethical teaching, good advice.[9] Much of the discussion on the subject shows traces of Aristotle's distinction[10] between

---

[1] E.g. Quintilian, I.O. 7.10.11.
[2] 1.97.2.   [3] 2.1, 5.26.1.   [4] Thuc. 9, pp. 335 ff.
[5] Cicero, Or. 2.15.51 ff. But Cicero thinks very highly of Thucydides.
[6] Aristotle, Rhet. 3.16.1 f., Cicero, Part. Or. 4.12 ff., Inv. 1.20.29, 1.21.30, Quintilian, I.O. 7.10.11.   [7] E.g. Cicero, Or. 11.37.
[8] Or. 2.15.62 f.   [9] E.g. Lucian, Q.H.S.S.   [10] Poet. 9.

the poet, concerned with universal truths, i.e. what might or ought to be the facts, and the historian, concerned with particular truths, i.e. the facts as they are.

Speculations of this kind undoubtedly reached the Rabbis, who tried to find in the Scriptures both 'universal truths' and 'particular truths'.

As for the evangelists, let us add a reservation. To be sure, they only followed a convention in regrouping scenes and pronouncements with a view to a theological or literary effect. But we must not forget that there were limits to their freedom. They did want to put down what had actually happened as well as what it signified. They did want to report facts as well as to proclaim a religious message and glorify the person of Jesus. It is not, however, within the scope of this lecture to inquire just what were the restrictions on a New Testament writer's liberty to alter his sources and, in particular, their chronology.

F. Papias

Papias declares[1] that the Hebrew gospel of Matthew—whatever may be meant by this work—consisted of an ordered collection of the sayings of Jesus ($\sigma\upsilon\nu\epsilon\tau\acute{\alpha}\xi\alpha\tau o$). It is probable, though not certain, that the order he has in mind is chronological: Matthew, according to Papias, arranged the sayings in the order in which they were uttered. By contrast, of Mark we are told[2] that 'he wrote accurately, though not in any order ($o\dot{\upsilon}\ \tau\acute{\alpha}\xi\epsilon\iota$), what he remembered of the sayings and deeds of the Lord'. Again the order referred to—and referred to as absent—seems to be of a chronological character.

Mark's excuse, in the view of Papias, is that he was not a direct disciple of Jesus. He only followed Peter; but Peter had never composed an ordered collection ($\sigma\acute{\upsilon}\nu\tau\alpha\xi\iota s$) of the sayings of Jesus, he had simply taught as the moment demanded it. So the best Mark could do was to write down the single points ($\ddot{\epsilon}\nu\iota\alpha$) as he had heard them.

Two things are clear. First, Papias recognizes that the Markan order cannot always be regarded as reflecting the historical order—especially if Matthew should be treated as reflecting it. Secondly, this would be to Mark's discredit but for the defence just outlined. That is to say, Papias for one does not accord an evangelist any liberty in the matter of chronology; he demands strict adherence to the actual dates.

[1] Eusebius 3.39.16. [2] 3.39.15.

2E

XX

The Abomination of Desolation

A. A CONSTRUCTION 'AD SENSUM'

IN his oracle concerning 'the abomination of desolation standing where it ought not', Mark[1] defines the neuter noun, $\beta\delta\acute{\epsilon}\lambda\upsilon\gamma\mu\alpha$, 'abomination', by a masculine participle, $\acute{\epsilon}\sigma\tau\eta\kappa\acute{o}\tau\alpha$, 'who will stand'— no doubt with a view to conveying information as to the actual nature of the abomination. Famous as the text is, the question has never been raised what was the technical background of this exploitation of a grammatical irregularity. Yet the point is not without interest. For one thing, it is not enough to say, as is always said, that we have before us a construction *ad sensum*. Normally Mark, like every other writer, follows the rules of grammar, not of sense. If he deliberately deviates from them in one passage, there must have been some literary convention enabling him to do so. Otherwise, he would not have been understood. For another thing, as we shall see, there are grounds for suspecting that his device may have had its root in a pre-Greek phase of speculations about the 'abomination of desolation'. In fact he seems to follow as closely as possible an old Rabbinic analysis of the Hebrew term behind the Greek one.

The Rabbinic expounders of Scripture were ever ready to draw conclusions from any peculiarity of grammar therein. One example is their mode of dealing with irregularities concerning the singular or plural number of words. In the account of man's creation[2] there is a wavering between singular and plural. 'God created man in his image, in the image of God created he him (singular), male and female created he them (plural)', and so on. That was taken as basis for the view that the first man was androgynous.[3] We have seen that this interpretation of the verse contributed to its use in the New Testament

---

[1] 13.14.   [2] Gen. 1.27, 5.1 f.   [3] Gen. Rabba on 1.27.

as an argument against divorce: husband and wife are near the ideal state as it was at the beginning—they must not undo it by separation. Or take the passage where God says to Cain:[1] 'The voice of thy brother's blood which is shed crieth unto me.' Literally translated, the Hebrew gives: 'The voice of thy brother's bloods cry unto me.' The Samaritan Pentateuch substitutes the singular: 'crieth unto me.' The Rabbis, to explain the emphasized plural, say[2] some that Cain had destroyed not only Abel but also his potential offspring, others that Abel's blood was cast over trees and stones. The point is that they noted and found significance in the grammatical incongruity.

The Hebrew for 'abomination of desolation' occurs three times in Daniel, but only once[3] in a form which is grammatically correct: *shiqquṣ shomem*, 'the abomination which devastates' or 'the abomination of a devastator'. It has long been seen that the expression was intended to suggest *shiqquṣ shamayim*, 'the abomination of heaven'—Zeus Ouranios.

In the other two passages, however, there are grammatical difficulties. In one[4] we find the phrase *shiqquṣim meshomem*. However we may nowadays construe it, or emend it (both Kittel's *Biblia Hebraica*[5] and the latest edition of Gesenius's *Handwörterbuch*[6] make the somewhat facile proposal to turn the plural into a singular, *shiqquṣ*), to a Rabbi it must have seemed a noun in the plural, accompanied by a participle in the singular: something like 'abominations which renders desolate'. It ought to be noted that, if there is corruption, it is old enough for our purposes: the LXX read a plural, βδέλυγμα τῶν ἐρημώσεων. There can be little doubt that this passage gave rise to much ingenious interpretation. In fact a specimen is preserved in the Talmud.[7]

But the remaining passage[8] appears even more pertinent in the present connection. It has *hashshiqquṣ meshomem*, the article in 'the abomination' striking one as very odd. If the meaning intended by the author is 'the abomination of a devastator', we should expect the so-called construct state, 'abomination' without 'the'. In this case also emendations have been attempted (Kittel restores the syntax by reading *hashshiqquṣ hashshomem*). But whether they are justified or not, it looks as if Theodotion at any rate had read the strange article. For that may well be the reason why he translates here, not βδέλυγμα ἐρημώσεως, but

---

[1] Gen. 4.10. [2] Mish. San. 4.5. [3] 12.11. [4] 9.27.
[5] 2nd ed., 1925. [6] 16th ed. by Buhl, 1915. [7] Bab. Ta. 28b. [8] 11.31

βδέλυγμα ἠφανισμένον: he, or some precursor, found it impossible to regard the Hebrew as a construct state.

Now it was an established method of Rabbinic exegesis to read some meaning into any article, and in particular, of course, into any article that looked superfluous. Frequently such an article was interpreted as drawing attention to a specific, prominent person, thing or event. There is a law in Deuteronomy:[1] 'When ye come nigh unto the battle, the priest shall approach.' 'The priest', according to the Rabbis,[2] means, not any priest, but the priest anointed for the battle. The Psalmist exclaims:[3] 'The ungodly shall not stand in the judgment.' According to the Rabbis,[4] 'the judgment', with the article, means 'the Last Judgment'. It is hardly too rash to suggest that hashshiqquṣ meshomem, with its extraordinary article, must very early have been taken as a deliberate reference to something or somebody special. Quite possibly successive generations used the phrase in different ways. What emerges as probable is that behind Mark's Greek stands this passage from Daniel, with the article in Midrashic fashion interpreted as singling out a particular individual—the Antichrist, a heathen god, the Emperor or his statue, or whoever else it might be. In Greek, the implication could best be rendered by making the attribute of βδέλυγμα masculine instead of neuter.

Mark could be sure that the erudite part of his public would grasp the meaning: the Rabbis were used to attributing special significance not only any strange article or any discrepancy between singular and plural, but also to any discrepancy in gender. It would be a worth-while task to collect all these deductions from grammatical irregularities, with a view to bringing out the Rabbinic notions of regular grammar.[5] It is clear, for instance, that the Rabbis were fully conscious of the main principles concerning agreement in gender. In God's warning to Cain,[6] 'the sin crouches at the door', 'sin' is feminine (ḥaṭṭa'th), 'crouches' masculine (robheṣ). The prevalent modern solution is that originally there was a reference to a demon, 'the croucher is at the door'; later the word 'sin' was clumsily interpolated. The Rabbis assumed that the discrepancy was deliberate. There is a catena of explanations,[7] the first

---

[1] 20.2. [2] Mish. So. 8.1. [3] 1.5.
[4] Mish. San. 10.3. Above, pp. 326-7, we drew attention to a Passover Midrash where 'the messenger', instead of 'a messenger', signifies Jesus.
[5] A beginning has been made, and further monographs have been promised, by S. Rosenblatt, The Interpretation of the Bible in the Mishnah, 1935. See also the present writer's observations on the history of the hermeneutic rules of Ribbui and Mi'ut, in Bulletin of the John Rylands Library, 29, 1945, pp. 23 f. [6] Gen. 4.7. [7] Gen. Rabba ad loc.

apparently being that evil inclination begins by being weak as a woman and ends by being strong as a man.

As is well known, the LXX had little difficulty in copying in Greek a pun occurring in the Hebrew original.[1] What is more important: in the Aramaic Targum we may find many cases of renderings carefully chosen so as to guide readers familiar with Rabbinic methods towards certain conclusions.[2] According to the Hebrew text, Abraham said of Sarah:[3] 'And also, indeed, she is my sister, the daughter of my father.' Most Rabbis found this utterance inconvenient and tried to prove that 'sister' was here used in the sense of 'niece' only. Onkelos shares this view, and conveys it to his readers by a subtle modification. He translates 'and also' (wegham) by 'and yet' (ubheram). The particle 'yet' (Hebrew 'akh, Aramaic beram), according to a recognized hermeneutic rule, was looked upon as restricting a statement. Onkelos, by putting it, indicates that Abraham's declaration must not be taken at its face value.

A very relevant parallel to Mark is Onkelos's treatment of the verse[4] in which we are told how a certain proposal of Jacob concerning his wages was accepted by Laban: 'Behold, I would it might be according to thy words.' For here, as in Mark, an interpretation gained by the Rabbis with the help of one method seems to be brought out by the translation with the help of another, better suited to the language of the translation. To go by the plain meaning of the Biblical narrative, Jacob, while observing the letter of the agreement (to keep the brown goats separate from the spotted ones), quite disregarded its spirit (he placed coloured rods before the brown goats). In fact he cheated Laban. The Rabbis, loath to admit this, detected in the verse just quoted evidence that Laban was the first to tear up the treaty. They equated the Hebrew hen, 'behold', with the Aramaic hen, 'yes'; and they read lu, 'I would', as lo, 'no'. They maintained, that is, that what Laban had said was: 'It might be (yes)—it might not be (no) according to thy words.' Onkelos accepts the Rabbinic teaching; and he introduces it into his translation by taking advantage of precisely that rule concerning the restricting force of beram, 'yet', which we mentioned already. He translates: 'Yet (beram) I would it might be according to thy words'—apparently a smooth sentence. But any reader familiar with Rabbinic exegesis would

[1] E.g. Judges 10.4; see Kay's note on Susanna 54-9 in Charles's edition.
[2] See the writer's remarks op. cit., pp. 27 ff.   [3] Gen. 20.12.   [4] Gen. 30.34.

see the implication of 'yet': Laban withdrew his consent even while giving it. It was he who started the double-dealing.

It looks, then, as if Mark, when writing τὸ βδέλυγμα ἑστηκότα, was imitating as best he could *hashshiqquṣ meshomem* in Daniel, a Hebrew phrase for 'abomination of desolation' with a grammatical flaw—the article—which was traditionally explained as designed to suggest a certain person or his image. Even if it should be held, however, that this part of our thesis is going too far, even if it should be held that, in this particular case, Mark was following no model but that it was his own idea to enlighten us as to the nature of the βδέλυγμα by supplying it with a masculine attribute, the fact remains that the technique he employed was good Rabbinic technique. In other words, this much may be considered as certain, that the kind of construction *ad sensum* to be met with in this passage sprang from, and was intended for, a milieu thinking in Rabbinic terms and reading through Rabbinic spectacles.

B. 'Let him that readeth understand'

1. *A problem of punctuation*

It is universally assumed that, in Mark and Matthew,[1] 'let him that readeth understand' is a parenthesis advising us to find out exactly who or what is meant by the 'abomination of desolation'. Accordingly the sentence in which it occurs is supposed to consist of the following three parts: (1) protasis, 'When ye shall see the abomination of desolation', (2) apodosis, 'then let them that be in Judaea flee', and between these (3) parenthesis, 'let him that readeth understand'. On this basis, the passage differs widely from the Lukan parallel, both in form and substance. This parallel runs:[2] (1) protasis, 'When ye shall see Jerusalem compassed with armies', (2) apodosis, 'then know that the desolation thereof is nigh', and (3) a further admonition, 'then let them which be in Judaea flee'. Dodd has recently mentioned the point among his proofs[3] that Luke in this section was not merely re-editing Mark, but drew on an independent tradition as well.

Very likely the prevalent view is correct. It should be borne in mind, however, that there is another possibility. We could construe Mark and

---

[1] Mark 13.14, Matt. 24.15.   [2] Luke 21.20 f.
[3] 'The Fall of Jerusalem and the "Abomination of Desolation" ', *Journal of Roman Studies*, 37, 1947, p. 48.

Matthew thus: (1) protasis, 'When ye shall see the abomination of desolation', (2) apodosis, 'let him that readeth understand'—in the sense of 'let him pay heed to it and take the necessary steps', and (3) a further admonition, 'then let them which be in Judaea flee'. Taken in this way, the general pattern at least would be much the same as in Luke. The main difference in form would be that where Mark and Matthew have 'let the reader pay heed to it', Luke has the direct address, 'know that the desolation is nigh'. This might be due to Luke's bringing the clause into closer agreement with the protasis, 'when ye shall see'.

Several points may be noted. First, ever since Homer, the two verbs ἰδεῖν, 'to see', and νοεῖν, 'to understand' in the sense of 'to mark what one sees', form a pair—a fact unquestionably speaking in favour of the interpretation 'when ye shall see the abomination, let the reader mark it'. The antithesis 'to see'—'to mark' gets lost if we cut off 'let the reader understand' from the rest and treat it as a parenthesis.

Secondly, it might perhaps be objected that Mark and Matthew simply write 'let the reader understand', not 'let the reader understand it'; and that the addition of 'it' would be necessary if the meaning were to be 'let the reader mark it—i.e. the abomination—and take the requisite steps'. But again, as early as in Homer, we come across a sentence like this:[1] 'To the daughter of Zeus alone he brought no offerings, whether he forgot or whether he paid no heed'—without any pronoun specifying the exact object of his neglect.

Thirdly, according to the present division of the gospels into verses, in Mark, 'when ye shall see the abomination—let the reader understand —then let them in Judaea flee' forms one verse; which supports the view that 'let the reader understand' is a parenthesis. In Matthew, there is a full stop after 'understand'. We are given two verses, that is, one 'when ye shall see the abomination—let the reader understand', and the next 'then let them in Judaea flee'; which supports the treatment of 'let the reader understand' as the apodosis to 'when ye shall see the abomination'. Of particular interest, however, is the fact that, as the apparatus shows, there is ancient authority for a full stop after 'understand' even in Mark.

Nevertheless, as stated above, the prevalent construction of 'let the reader understand' as a parenthesis is probably justified. For one thing,

[1] Il. 9.536 f.

whereas Luke has 'then (τότε) know', so that the character of the clause as apodosis is unmistakable, Mark and Matthew have 'let the reader understand' without 'then'; it is only the following part which opens with 'then'—'then let them flee'. That in Matthew, and at one time also in Mark, the scholars who fixed the verses made a whole verse of 'when ye shall see the abomination, let the reader understand' may well be owing to their having been influenced by the Lukan parallel: they assimilated the other gospels to Luke. It may not be without interest to note that the Rabbis were familiar with the nature of a parenthesis. Indeed they had a technical term: 'the before which, as regards subject-matter, should come after'.[1] One of their illustrations was this passage:[2] 'And the lamp of God had not yet gone out—Samuel being asleep—in the temple of the Lord.'

We shall take it, then, that 'let him that readeth understand' is a parenthesis, intended to call attention to the cryptic βδέλυγμα ἐρημώσεως ἑστηκότα.

2. *The reader*

If the parenthesis goes back to Jesus, or anyone else who preached but did not write, then 'he who readeth' cannot mean the reader of this oracle: a preacher referring to his public would have spoken of 'him who heareth'. Consequently, if the parenthesis dates from the oral stage of the transmission, 'he who readeth' must be interpreted as 'he who habitually reads the Scriptures', 'the student of Scripture'. It must be the Biblical scholar who is exhorted to look carefully into the cryptic expression—so as to discover its connection with Daniel and, presumably, the traditional interpretations of Daniel.

However, to translate ὁ ἀναγινώσκων by 'the student of Scripture' is to credit the Greek verb with a sense not to be found in any other text. Nor does the Hebrew equivalent, *qore*', standing by itself, signify 'Biblical scholar'. There is indeed a Hebrew and Aramaic noun from the same root, and having exactly the same consonants, *qara*', which does mean 'Biblical scholar'. It is possible to argue that the parenthesis was originally in Aramaic; that *qara*' was used; and that it was somewhat clumsily rendered as 'he that readeth'.

On the whole it is more plausible to ascribe the parenthesis to Mark or whoever wrote down the oracle before him. That is to say, 'the

---

[1] The 31st of Eliezer ben Jose Ha-gelili's 32 rules of hermeneutics.   [2] I Sam. 3.3.

reader' means the reader of this—written—apocalypse.[1] He is asked to interest himself in the deeper meaning of the passage. Codex Bezae, supported by a small group of the Itala, contains an addition which, if it were genuine, would put the matter beyond doubt: the clause here is worded 'let the reader understand what he reads'. In this form, the request can only be addressed to the reader of the present oracle. Unfortunately the additional phrase—'what he reads'—is almost certainly spurious. Still, it seems to be consistent with the original meaning of the exhortation.

3. 'Let him that readeth understand'

When Spinoza rejected the authenticity of certain portions of the Old Testament, he was indebted to Ibn Ezra, the Spanish Jewish scholar of the first half of the 12th century. (Attempts on the part of hyper-fundamentalists to exonerate Ibn Ezra from the charge of critical insight into the sources[2] have proved complete failures, one is glad to think.) Ibn Ezra, however, had only hinted in veiled language at what Spinoza openly proclaimed. It is noteworthy that while Spinoza was excommunicated by his Amsterdam congregation, Ibn Ezra is still honoured and studied by the very strictest Jews. As Spinoza put it:[3] 'Aben Hezra . . . qui primus omnium quos legi hoc praeiudicium animadvertit non ausus est mentem suam aperte explicare, sed rem obscurioribus verbis tantum indicare.'

Perhaps Ibn Ezra's favourite method of conveying his opinion without too boldly expressing it was to remark that the text in hand contained a mystery, and to add: 'and let him that discerneth keep silence', 'and let him that understandeth keep silence', or 'and let him that discerneth understand'. Among the passages he calls attention to in this way are one from Genesis,[4] 'And the Canaanite was then in the land', and one from Isaiah,[5] 'Kings shall see and arise'. The former, he implies, can hardly go back to Moses, in whose time the population was still Canaanite: he would not have written that it was Canaanite 'then', i.e. in the time of Abraham. Similarly, the latter, Ibn Ezra holds, refers to

---

[1] Dodd, op. cit., p. 54, appears to hold, on the one hand, that the note is due to Mark, and on the other, that it means 'let the student of Scripture understand'. But ὁ ἀναγινώσκων, in ordinary Greek, signifies 'the reader', not 'the student of Scripture'.

[2] E.g. M. Friedlaender, in Publications of the Society of Hebrew Literature, ser. 2, vol. 4, 1877, pp. 60 ff.

[3] Tractatus Theologico-Politicus 8.   [4] 12.6.   [5] 49.7.

the termination of the Babylonian exile under Cyrus: how could it be the work of Isaiah, who lived some 150 years before?

One of the phrases quoted at least, 'let him that discerneth understand', is strongly reminiscent of 'let him that readeth understand'. It is most unlikely that Ibn Ezra was the first exegete to use it, and the others, in the fashion described, *scil.* as indicating the presence of a secret better not talked about (though, before him, the secret hardly ever consisted in higher criticism). For one thing, the phrases occur so often that one has the impression of a well-established method. However, it would lead too far afield to trace them back through early medieval literature; nor is it even certain that we should find them in such material as is preserved. Nevertheless it seems possible to arrive at the position in the age of the New Testament by a short cut. Let it be said at once that the precise words 'let him that readeth understand' are not extant in Talmudic writings. There are, however, a sufficient number of significant phenomena to show that the clause, if it was not current among the Rabbis, at least is in perfect harmony with their mode of thinking. In other words, it would be natural for a Rabbi to call attention in this way to a cryptogram, and particularly, it appears, to one of the nature of Mark's.

The general idea may, indeed, be met with in any civilized language. In Terence's Phormio,[1] the following dialogue takes place:

ANTIPHO: You must find the necessary money.
GETA (slave of Antipho's father): I should love to: but tell me where?
ANTIPHO: My father is back in town.
GETA: I know; but what follows?
ANTIPHO: Ah, a word is enough for the wise (verbum sapienti sat est).

Quintilian[2] discusses a class of figure 'whereby we excite suspicion that there is another, hidden meaning which the hearer may discover'; and he adds that it is used 'where it is not quite safe to speak openly'. Plutarch's explanation of the obscurity of the Delphic oracle may be compared.[3]

To establish the Rabbinic background of 'let him that readeth understand', we want more specific evidence than evidence of this kind. We propose to demonstrate, first, that the words are adumbrated in the Old Testament; secondly, that some Rabbinic contrasts between the out-

---

[1] 3.3.8; cp. already Plautus, Persa 4.7.19.   [2] 9.2.65 f.   [3] P.O. 26, in Mor. 407E.

ward aspect and deeper meaning of a text come fairly close to them; thirdly, that the root *bin*, 'to understand', which may be taken to underlie Mark's $\nu o\epsilon\acute{\iota}\tau\omega$,[1] is employed by the Rabbis preferably where the deeper meaning in question is of a secret, dangerous character; and fourthly, that the Rabbinic terminology accounting for 'let him that readeth understand' has influenced other passages in the New Testament as well.

(1) The clause under consideration is foreshadowed in the Old Testament. Two of Ibn Ezra's phrases come straight from there: one from Amos,[2] 'Therefore let him that discerneth keep silence, for it is an evil time', the other—the more important one for us—from Daniel,[3] 'The words are closed up, but the discerning shall understand', or 'but let them that discern understand'. It is worth pointing out that the next verse goes on to the 'abomination of desolation'.

In the story of Belshazzar's feast, the antithesis 'reading—explaining' (*qera'—peshar*) is repeatedly put; for instance, 'But they could not read the writing nor make known the explanation thereof'.[4]

There are frequent exhortations throughout the Old Testament to 'understand', *bin*, i.e. see the real significance of, historical events, 'Would they were wise, that they discerned this, that they understood their latter end';[5] or the nature of God, 'Have ye not known? have ye not heard? have ye not understood from the foundations of the earth?';[6] or the prophet's preaching or a wise man's utterance, 'Who is wise that he understand these things? understanding that he knows them?',[7] 'Hear ye indeed but understand not; make their ears heavy, lest they hear with their ears and their heart understand',[8] and 'My words are plain to him that understandeth';[9] or a vision or revelation, 'I am come to inform thee, therefore, be understanding in the vision.'[10]

The root *bin* appears as meaning 'to understand,' 'to be able to interpret', a foreign language:[11] 'Thou (the righteous) shalt not see a people of deeper speech than thou canst hear, of a stammering tongue of which thou hast no understanding.' (Of David we are told[12] that when

---

[1] *Hiśkil* is also conceivable, though less likely. Some of the following arguments would apply to this term as well; see below, pp. 428 n. 2, 431 n. 2 and 432 n. 3.
[2] 5.13; cp. also the less relevant texts Prov. 11.12 and 10.19.   [3] 12.9 f.
[4] Dan. 5.8; also 5.7, 15–17.   [5] Deut. 32.29; cp. Jer. 9.11, Ps. 107.43.
[6] Isa. 40.21; cp. 1.2 f., 43.10, 44.18.
[7] Hos. 14.10—the concluding sentence of the Book.
[8] Isa. 6.9 f.—applied in the New Testament to the parables of Jesus.
[9] Prov. 8.9; cp. 4.1, 5.1, 8.1 ff., 20.5, Job 34.16.
[10] Dan. 9.23; cp. 8.15, 17, 10.1.   [11] Isa. 33.19.   [12] II Sam. 12.19.

he saw his servants whispering, he 'understood', 'interpreted this as indicating', that his child had died.) More immediately interesting are two other passages. One says[1] that Daniel 'understood in the books the number of years whereof the word of the Lord had come to Jeremiah': *bin* here denotes 'to get to the bottom of allusions made in the sacred books'. In the other, which depicts the first ceremonial reading of the Law by Ezra, a distinction is made between 'reading' Scripture and 'understanding' or 'discerning' it: 'So they read in the Book in the Law of God distinctly, and applying discernment, and they showed understanding in the reading. And on the second day were gathered the chief of the fathers unto Ezra the scribe, even to discern the words of the Law.'[2] It is not enough to 'read'; you must perceive the import of a text.

(2) Here are some suggestive Rabbinic distinctions between the outward aspect of a text and its deeper meaning. What the text 'says', *'amar*, or what is 'written' in it, *kathubh*, is constantly opposed to what it 'tells' you, *higgidh*. 'Thou citest (*'atta 'omer*), In the beginning God created the heaven and earth (first chapter of Genesis). I might take it that the heaven came first. But there is a teaching in the words, In the day that the Lord God made the earth and heaven (second chapter). This tells you (*maggidh*) that both came simultaneously.'[3] The term 'Haggadah', from *higgidh*, signifies these implied pieces of information.

Frequently the contrast is between what the text 'says' or what is 'written' in it and what it 'teaches', *limmedh*, or what you may 'learn', *lamadh*. The words 'Then sang Moses'[4] are translatable also by 'Then Moses will sing'. R. Judah the Prince commented:[5] 'It is not written (*kethibh*) sang but will sing: thus we may learn, infer (*lemedhin*), the resurrection of the dead from the Torah.' The term *talmudh lomar*, 'there is a teaching in what the text says', is old and common. It may be found, for example, in the discussion of the creation quoted above: 'there is a teaching in what the text says, In the day that the Lord God

---

[1] Dan. 9.2.

[2] Neh. 8.8, 13; cp. Ps. 119.27, 34, 73, 95, 100, 104, 125, 130, 144, 169 (*bin*), 99 (*hiśkil*), 45, 155, Ezek. 7.10, I Chron. 28.8 (*darash*). It should be observed, in connection with the remark made above, p. 427 n. 1, that *hiśkil*, or some word from this root, is paired off with *bin* in several of the texts quoted: Dan. 12.9 f., Deut. 32.29, Isa. 44.18, Neh. 8.8, 13. Cp. also Dan. 9.22, 25, with 9.23, and Ps. 119.99 with the verses using *bin*. In Prov. 10.19 *hiśkil* alone appears. One of the qualities ascribed to Daniel in the story of Belshazzar's feast is *śakhlethanu*, Dan. 5.11 f., 14.

[3] Mekh. on Exod. 12.1.   [4] Exod. 15.1.   [5] Mekh. *ad loc.*

made the earth and heaven'. Equally usual is *ba' hakkathubh lelammedh*, 'what is written comes to teach'. The provision 'Thou shalt take him (the murderer) from mine altar that he may die' is said 'to come to teach that the Temple service (in contradistinction to the Sabbath) may not be set aside to save a human life'.[1] On the other hand, when a text must be taken literally, the Rabbis declare that there is 'no teaching in what it says', but 'matters are according to their writing', *debharim kikhethabham*.[2]

Similarly, what is 'written' may be contrasted with what you 'derive by interpretation', *darash*. Eliezer ben Hyrkanos (about A.D. 100) was reproached for going too far: 'Thou sayest to what is written, Be quiet while I interpret.'[3]

The 'distinct', *mephorash*, is opposed to the 'concealed', *sathum*. 'Thou shalt not steal' is a 'concealed' commandment, since it does not specify whether it refers to theft of persons, a capital crime,[4] or theft of property, less serious; whereas the two commandments allied with it, prohibiting murder and adultery, are 'distinct'.[5] (Bacher[6] is wrong, an extremely rare occurrence with him. The two 'distinct' commandments must be Exodus 20.13 and 14, since it is only from them that the Rabbis could deduce—what they wanted to deduce—that 20.15 also was concerned with a capital offence, theft of a person. Of the two passages given as 'distinct' by Bacher, one, Leviticus 19.11, in the opinion of the Rabbis, referred to a monetary, private delict only.)

There are several further pairs of this kind. It may suffice to present three more, in all of which one of the opposites is 'reading' Scripture, *qara'*. The first two are 'reading' Scripture and 'interpreting' it, *darash*, and 'reading' Scripture and 'making it distinct', *peresh*. The Ecclesiast says:[7] 'The dead know not anything.' R. Jonathan (at the beginning of the 3rd cent.) took this literally. R. Hiyya, however, told him: 'Thou knowest to read, but thou doest not know to interpret', and he adduced a verse from Deuteronomy:[8] 'This is the land which I sware unto Abraham, saying'. Here the Rabbis found 'a teaching in what the text says', to the effect that God speaks of the dead patriarchs as living.[9] Of a passage in Leviticus,[10] R. Johanan ben Zaccai claimed[11] that 'the

---

[1] Mekh. on Exod. 21.14.   [2] Bab. Qid. 17b, Eleazar ben Azariah, about A.D. 100.
[3] Siph. on Lev. 13.49.   [4] Exod. 21.16, Deut. 24.7.   [5] Mekh. on Exod. 20.15.
[6] *Die älteste Terminologie der Jüdischen Schriftauslegung*, 1889, p. 137.
[7] 9.5.   [8] 34.4.   [9] Pal. Ber. 4d; cp. Matt. 22.32, Mark 12.26, Luke 20.37.
[10] 6.16.   [11] Mish. Sheq. 1.4.

priests interpretated this text—or, this reading, *miqra' ze*—to their advantage'. Sometimes, if two Rabbis disagreed about the meaning of a text, one would upbraid the other: 'If thou hast read it, thou hast not done it twice, and if twice, not three times, and if three times, they have not made it distinct to thee.'[1]

The remaining pair is the most significant. Not only is here 'reading', *qara'*, distinguished from 'understanding', *bin*, as in Mark, but also, as in Mark, 'understanding' means penetrating beneath the surface by seeing through a grammatical irregularity—in fact, an ambiguity regarding the grammatical connection of a word with the rest of the sentence. A word, that is, may be explained as attached to what precedes it or to what follows it. We have already quoted the report about Ezra's reading of the Law: 'So they read in the Book and showed understanding in the reading.' One Rabbinic view is[2] that 'they showed understanding in the reading' means: they understood the passages lacking a 'weighing down of the scale', a 'turning of the scales', an 'adjudication', *hekhrea'*. This is a happy term to designate syntactic accuracy in the sense of clarity as to the relative place of a word, clarity as to whether a word is attached to what precedes it or what follows it. I have suggested elsewhere that the working out of the concept may owe something to the Hellenistic grammarians, for whom the case of a sentence which might be divided in several ways came under the heading of σύνθεσις and διαίρεσις.[3]

R. Isi ben Judah held[4] that there were five such ambiguous passages in the Pentateuch. Let us mention two. In God's warning to Cain,[5] the Rabbi said, the word *śe'eth*, 'pardon', might be construed as belonging to the portion preceding it or to that following it; so that we might interpret, in the natural way, 'Why is thy countenance fallen? Shall there not, if thou doest well, be pardon?', but might also get a deeper sense, a reference to Cain's ultimate reprieve, 'Why is thy countenance fallen? Surely it will not be if thou doest well. But pardon shall take place even if thou doest not well.'[6]

---

[1] Bab. M.Q. 16b, Ber. 18a.   [2] Gen. Rabba on 9.26.
[3] *Festschrift Hans Lewald*, pp. 34 ff. For an instructive example, see Athenaeus, Deipn. 1.12a f., about Il. 24.476.
[4] Mekh. on Exod. 17.9.   [5] Gen. 4.6 f.
[6] The point of this alternative, deeper (and highly artificial) interpretation seems never to have been appreciated. Strack-B., vol. 3, 1926, p. 26, do not see it. L. Blau, 'Massoretische Studien', *Jewish Quarterly Review*, vol. 9, 1896–7, p. 139 n. 2, remarks: 'I must confess I cannot understand how a Tanna could have had any doubt whether in Genesis

Another example given by Isi ben Judah was a verse from Deuteronomy,[1] where he declared *weqam*, 'and arise', to be connectible with what follows it, as a perfect, or with what precedes it, as a participle. If the former construction, the natural one, be adopted, we should translate: 'Behold, thou shalt sleep with thy fathers; and this people will rise up and go after the gods of the strangers.' If the latter, the text would provide proof of resurrection: 'Thou shalt sleep with thy fathers and rise up; as for this people, it will go after the gods of the strangers.' The latter construction, it may be recalled, was relied on by Gamaliel of Jabneh, about A.D. 90, in a controversy with the Sadducees.[2]

Obviously, where 'they showed understanding in the reading' might denote the gaining of insight into the deeper meaning of a text by taking note of a deliberate ambiguity in syntax—and we must never forget that, for the Rabbis, when a sentence in Scripture lacked a 'weighing down of the scale', when the relative position of a word was undecided, that was necessarily deliberate, a subtle hint on the part of the author—we are very near the precise use of 'let him that readeth understand' in Mark.

(3) The term *bin*, 'to understand', is favoured by the Rabbis where the message behind a text is of a particularly secret, dangerous nature.[3] The Mishnah lays down[4] that 'no one may interpret the Chariot[5] except a Sage who understands of his own knowledge', *mebhin midda'to*. Johanan ben Zaccai praised Eleazar ben Arak for 'showing understanding in, searching into and interpreting' this section, *lehabhin welahqor welidrosh*.[6]

The root is prominent in this sense as early as in the Old Testament. Some of the passages from Daniel quoted above come to mind,[7] and we may compare others: only the prophet 'understands' the manner in

---

4.7 *śe'eth we'im lo' theṭibh* was to be read. The matter is very obscure.' Yet a glance at Onkelos will show what Isi ben Judah was driving at. Onkelos gives an unusually long paraphrase in order to convey both the natural meaning, forgiveness if Cain does well, and the deeper one, forgiveness even if he does not: 'If thou doest well, thou shalt be pardoned; but if thou doest not well, for the day of judgment the sin is laid up if thou dost not repent; but if thou repentest, thou shalt be pardoned.'

[1] 31.16.

[2] Bab. San. 19b. As regards *hiśkil* (see above, p. 427 n. 1), the words 'and applying discernment' in Nehemiah 8.8 are taken in Genesis Rabba on 9.26 as indicating that, when the Law was read on that occasion, the divisions within the verses, the *ṭe'amim*, were properly observed.

[3] See Bacher, *Die Agada der Tannaiten*, I, 2nd ed., 1903, p. 70 n. 42.

[4] Hag. 2.1.　　　　　　　　　　　　　　　　　　　　[5] Ezek. 1 and 10.

[6] Bab. Hag. 14b.　　　　　　　　　　　[7] 9.2, 10.1, 12.9 f.; see also 12.8, 8.27.

which God reveals himself;[1] few 'understand' the tremendous powers of God;[2] God 'understands' all secrets.[3]

(4) It remains to point out that the Rabbinic terminology here held to account for 'let him that readeth understand' is reflected in other places. To begin with, a verse in Revelation[4] bids the reader ponder on a number supplied by the text: 'Here is wisdom. Let him that hath understanding, ὁ ἔχων νοῦν, count the number of the beast, for it is the number of a man.' He that 'understands' is not expressly opposed to him that merely 'reads', but the contrast seems implied.[5] (This is not to deny that the possession of νοῦς in Revelation may involve being a *Pneumatiker.*) It is interesting that the standard illustration which the Rabbis give of exegesis on the basis of the numerical value of letters[6] is the reference to Abraham's household in Genesis,[7] with 318 taken as the number of a man, namely, Eliezer, Abraham's trusted servant. According to the Epistle of Barnabas,[8] the figure represents IH = 18 = Jesus, plus T = 300 = Cross.

Possibly exhortations like 'Who hath ears to hear, let him hear'[9] are also intended to draw attention to a hidden meaning, though they might simply mean 'This is important, so listen.' Old Testament and Rabbinic usage would warrant either interpretation. The former one, however, was adopted by at least those versions of Mark which add 'and let him that hath understanding understand', ὁ συνίων συνιέτω. We may further note the remark that 'the Pharisees knew that he had spoken the parables against them'.[10]

One section from an early Christian tract outside the New Testament, the Epistle of Barnabas,[11] deserves consideration. Its close affinity to the Markan 'let him that readeth understand' is manifest. The author quotes Daniel's vision of 'the fourth beast, dreadful and terrible'.[12] He has in mind the Roman emperor. But, too prudent to state the application openly, he tells his readers to look for the true meaning behind the text: 'Now you must understand.'

So far we have dealt with passages speaking of 'understanding' in a way that suggests a contrast with mere 'reading'. There is also a group

---

[1] I Sam. 3.8, II Chron. 26.5.   [2] Job 13.1, 26.14.
[3] Prov. 24.12, Ecclus. 42.18. Of these texts, only Dan. 12.10 contains *hiśkil* as well: see above, p. 427 n. 1.   [4] 13.18.
[5] Cp. Dan. 9.2 quoted above: 'I understood in the books the number of years.'
[6] *Gemaṭreya*', the 29th of Eliezer ben Jose Ha-gelili's hermeneutic rules.
[7] 14.14.   [8] 9.8.   [9] Matt. 13.9, Mark 4.9, Luke 8.8.
[10] Matt. 21.45, Mark 12.12, Luke 20.19.   [11] 4.5 f.   [12] Dan. 7.7 f.

speaking of 'reading' in a way that suggests a contrast with 'understanding', namely, the rhetorical questions put into Jesus's mouth: 'Have ye not read this or that text?' It is conceivable that these should be paraphrased: 'Surely you have read this or that text, so you ought to understand its import', or 'but you do not seem to understand its import'. They occur in (a) Matthew 12.3, 5, Mark 2.25, Luke 6.3; (b) Matthew 19.4; (c) Matthew 21.16; (d) Matthew 21.42, Mark 12.10; (e) Matthew 22.31, Mark 12.26; and (f) Luke 10.26, with some slight modification.

In favour of this paraphrase speaks the fact that in each case Jesus does propound, or indicate, an interpretation going beyond the literal meaning. Moreover, as for (a), in Matthew at least[1] it is plainly stated that 'knowing' a text is what matters: 'But if ye had known what this is, I will have mercy.' In another chapter of Matthew we find the formulation:[2] 'But go ye and learn what this is, I will have mercy.' We have already discussed *lamadh* in the sense of 'to learn', 'to infer', something from Scripture; and the phrase *ṣe' ulemadh*, 'go out and learn', *scil.* this or that from the text, is technical in Rabbinic debate.[3] Regarding (e), the Sadducees who deny resurrection are described as 'erring', to which Matthew adds that they do not 'know', 'grasp', the Scriptures. One is reminded of the antithesis in Isaiah:[4] 'They that erred in spirit shall know understanding.' According to Matthew,[5] the multitude was struck by Jesus's διδαχή, here presumably corresponding to *talmudh* or *midrash*, 'teaching' or 'exposition'.[6] Luke in this controversy with the Sadducees makes Jesus use the highly technical term *remez*, signifying 'a hint', 'a slight covert indication', contained in a text:[7] 'That the dead are raised Moses hinted (ἐμήνυσεν or ἐδήλωσεν) when he calleth the Lord the God of Abraham, Isaac and Jacob.' We saw above that a Rabbi not aware of the 'teaching' of Deuteronomy 34.4, 'This is the land which I sware unto Abraham, saying', was considered as 'able to read but not to interpret'.[8] But we even meet with *remez* in this connection. Another verse from Deuteronomy,[9] 'I kill and I make alive', is claimed to be one of four Biblical passages in which 'a hint at the resurrection of the dead was given to the Israelites'. (The

---

[1] 12.7.   [2] 9.13.
[3] See Bacher, *Die älteste Terminologie der Jüdischen Schriftauslegung*, 1899, p. 75.
[4] 29.24.   [5] 22.33.
[6] On various possible translations of the word, see above, under Rabbinic Authority.
[7] See Bacher, p. 182 f.   [8] Pal. Ber. 4d.   [9] 32.39; see Siph. on 32.34.

same term, incidentally, underlies the Epistle of Barnabas where, as already mentioned, it is concerned with the 318 members of Abraham's household:[1] the Lord, we are told, $\delta\eta\lambda o\hat{\iota}$, 'hints at', 'gives a *remez* for', Jesus and the Cross.) Lastly, with (f) we might perhaps connect Mark 12.34. A man properly appreciating the most important commandments[2] is here praised as talking $\nu o\nu\nu\epsilon\chi\hat{\omega}s$, 'with understanding'.[3]

The author of Revelation begins by an admonition[4] to heed the prophecies; and very possibly, when he says that 'hearing' and 'keeping' or 'guarding' them is necessary in addition to 'reading', he may include careful interpretation. We have seen that an exclamation like 'Who hath ears to hear let him hear'[5] may signify something between 'This is important' and 'This calls for further inquiry if the deeper significance is to be grasped.'

However, a number of passages in Acts and Paul's epistles provide illustrations of an express opposition of 'reading' and 'understanding' Scripture. The Queen of Ethiopia's treasurer was asked by Philip[6] whether he 'knew', 'grasped', what he was 'reading'. That we have to give the distinction its full Rabbinic force is plain from the continuation: 'Then Philip opened his mouth and, beginning at the same text (from Isaiah), preached unto him Jesus.' In Rabbinic language, 'to open one's mouth', *pathaḥ piw*, as a rule shortened into 'to open', frequently denotes 'to open a lecture on Scripture' or even 'to lecture on Scripture'. (The history of the phrase postulated by Bacher is not convincing.[7] This is not the place to discuss the question, especially as it does not affect our main argument. It may suffice to point out that the section under consideration alone, Acts 8.30 ff., which he entirely overlooks, seems to disprove his theory.) R. Johanan ben Zaccai asked Eliezer ben Hyrcanus:[8] 'Open and expound', *pathaḥ udherosh*. Again, 'to begin at a certain text' sounds quite genuine. The Mishnah ordains[9] that, when commemorating the exodus on Passover eve, 'one should begin with the disgrace and end with the glory, and expound from the verse in Deuteronomy,[10] A Syrian ready to perish was my father.'

According to a report in Acts,[11] Paul accused the Jews of 'not knowing him (Jesus or, just conceivably, the Baptist) and the voices of the

---

[1] 9.8.   [2] Deut. 6.5, Lev. 19.18.   [3] Cp. Rev. 13.18, cited above, $\acute{o}$ $\check{\epsilon}\chi\omega\nu$ $\nu o\hat{\nu}\nu$.
[4] 1.3.   [5] Matt. 13.9, Mark 4.9, Luke 8.8.   [6] Acts 8.30.
[7] *Die Exegetische Terminologie der Jüdischen Traditionsliteratur*, 2, 1905, 174 ff., and *Die Pröomien der Alten Jüdischen Homilie*, 1913, 27 f.
[8] Ab. de-R.N. 8.   [9] Pes. 10.5.   [10] 26.5.   [11] 13.27.

prophets' (or of 'not understanding the writings of the prophets') 'which are read every sabbath day'. They 'read' Scripture, he complained, but did not 'know', 'grasp', it. Whatever one may think of the origin of this speech, it is certain that Paul did formulate charges like this. In II Corinthians[1] he writes: 'But their understanding, νοήματα, was blinded, for until this day remaineth the veil untaken away in the reading, ἀναγνώσει, of the Old Testament.'[2]

It is remarkable that Paul appears to transfer this terminology from Scripture to his own writings. In Ephesians[3] he says that those 'reading' his letter will be able to 'understand' the mystery it is his task to communicate. The idea seems to be that his message contains no secrets accessible only to the most learned. The recipients, if they will only trouble to peruse it, may be sure of acquiring the full substance.

That there is no discrepancy between the outward aspect of his words and their real significance when he speaks about his own person and plans, he feels compelled to emphasize in II Corinthians:[4] 'For we write none other things than what ye read and also acknowledge, ἀναγινώσκετε ἢ καὶ ἐπιγινώσκετε; and I trust ye shall acknowledge even to the end, as ye have already acknowledged us in part.' He continues his defence against the imputation of ambiguity in the following sentences, alluding to Jesus's saying concerning 'Yea, yea' and 'Nay, nay'.

In the next chapter,[5] the pair γινωσκομένη καὶ ἀναγινωσκομένη at first sight looks like an empty, stereotyped jingle, the 'knowing' preceding the 'reading'. For one thing, however, this part of the epistle reflects great strain and excitement, and there are several illogicalities. For another, conceivably, we are here moving in a completely different province from that considered above. Paul may not be thinking of a surface meaning and a deeper meaning at all. His point may be that his followers are recognized as such and, being recognized, are read as such—i.e. read as letters of commendation and letters of Christ.

It is evident that a large proportion of the New Testament passages making, or proceeding from, a distinction between 'reading' and 'understanding' Scripture refer to 'understanding' in the sense mentioned above, as often expressed by *bin*, namely, in the sense of understanding a particularly secret or dangerous meaning beneath the text.

[1] 3.14.   [2] Cp. also the following verse, 3.15.   [3] 3.4.   [4] 1.13 f.   [5] 3.2.

Revelation 13.18, Barnabas 4.5 f., Matthew 21.42, Mark 12.10, Matthew 22.31, Mark 12.26, Acts 8.30, II Corinthians 3.14, all tend in this direction.

Another detail is in harmony with the proper Rabbinic character of the whole complex. From the Rabbinic illustrations submitted it is clear that 'reading' might be opposed to 'understanding' whether it was private reading or reading the Sabbatic lesson. When a Rabbi told his colleague, 'Thou knowest to read but not to interpret', obviously, he was referring to private reading. On the other hand, a verse from Nehemiah[1] was declared to show that the people listening to Ezra's recital of the Law comprehended the passages lacking a 'turning of the scales'. Just so, in the story of the Ethiopian treasurer, the 'reading' is private, whereas in the charges preferred by Paul against the Jews it is liturgical.

C. A PARALLEL FROM PHILO

Dr. Wilfred Knox, of ever-cherished memory, pointed out to me that a section from Philo[2] furnished support of the view here taken of the manner in which Mark deals with the 'abomination of desolation'. Philo comments on the notice in Genesis[3] that 'all flesh had corrupted its way'—in Greek: κατέφθειρε πᾶσα σὰρξ τὴν ὁδὸν αὐτοῦ. He observes that the masculine αὐτοῦ, 'his way', is used with reference to the feminine σάρξ, 'flesh'; and he explains that this need be no grammatical blunder but may be put on purpose to indicate a second meaning. The first, apparent meaning is that the flesh corrupted its own way. But the deeper meaning, he says, may be that it sought to mar the way of God—and for this, we do want the masculine, 'his way'. Then Philo adds the remark:'Know that this is wisdom, for through it the understanding (ὁ νοῦς) reaches the goal.'

Dr. Knox suggested that the words 'Know that this is wisdom' might here signify, not so much 'Know that this way to God which the people of the flood marred is wisdom', as 'Pay attention to this piece of wisdom conveyed by the grammatical irregularity in the Biblical verse.' In Revelation,[4] we saw, the information conveyed by a number is described as 'wisdom', accessible to 'him that hath understanding'. However, quite apart from this clause, we clearly have before us a case of a disagreement in gender being used as basis for a teaching. And it is a

[1] 8.8.　　　[2] Q.D.I.S. 30.141 ff.　　　[3] 6.12.　　　[4] 13.8.

disagreement to be found only in the Greek version, not in the Hebrew original. In Hebrew, *baśar*, 'flesh', is masculine, so that there is no discrepancy between it and *darko*, 'his way'. (Of course, it is quite possible that even before Philo, and on the basis of the Hebrew text, some Rabbis had interpreted 'his way' as 'the way of God'.) If Philo was capable of adopting this kind of method, undoubtedly Mark and the circles from which he sprang were.

One may wonder whether R. Johanan (of the generation after Judah the Prince) also had in mind the incongruity in the Greek text when he inferred from this passage that the flood came because tame beasts cohabited with wild ones, men with animals, males with males and females with females.[1] The 'wrong' gender in grammar might have suggested to him the wrong sex in reality. True, there are other elements in the verse which would sufficiently account for his exegesis, especially the associations of *hishḥith*, 'to ruin', 'to pervert', and *derekh*, 'way', 'sexual intercourse'. Nor can we be even certain that he was the first to propose it. Still, his is the earliest name we come across in this connection. Besides, was it not he who gave permission to instruct girls in Greek[2] because a knowledge of that language would be an adornment to them? Surely, he must have been well acquainted with the LXX.

[1] Bab. San. 108a.
[2] See Bacher, *Die Agada der Palästinensischen Amoräer*, I, 1892, 257.

XXI

The Interpretation of a Generic Singular

P A U L's Rabbinic scholarship sometimes manifests itself more clearly in the manner of his argument than in the matter. In Galatians[1] he cites a verse where the holy land is promised 'to Abraham and to his seed'. He identifies 'the seed' with Jesus, taking the generic singular 'and to thy seed' as a proper, specific singular: 'He saith not, And to thy seeds, as of many, but as of one, And to thy seed, which is Christ.'

Before adducing any Rabbinic models he may have in mind, we ought perhaps to justify the assertion that he is dealing with a verse where the land is promised and not, as some authorities seem to hold,[2] with one saying that Abraham's offspring will be a blessing for the world. First, in the latter case, the Old Testament simply does not contain the clause commented on by Paul. The expression used is 'in thy seed', not 'to thy seed'; the Hebrew as well as the LXX read 'there shall be blessed in thy seed all the nations'.[3] It is only in promises of the land that 'and to thy seed' may be found—twice in the Hebrew,[4] three times in the LXX:[5] 'to thee will I give it (have I given it) and to thy seed'. This is the phrase Paul quotes. Secondly, we shall see below that it was in connection with a promise of the land that the Rabbis resorted to an interpretation of 'seed' with which Paul's has much in common. Thirdly, Paul in Galatians counts 430 years from the event of which he thinks to the giving of the Law. The Rabbis[6] counted this number of years from the covenant 'between the pieces' in Genesis 15, where the land is promised, to the giving of the Law. To be sure, in this chapter, the land is promised not 'to thee and to thy seed', but merely 'to thy seed'.[7] But for one thing, this chapter, with its mention of an affliction

---

[1] 3.16.
[2] Even Strack.-B., 3, 1926, p. 553, refer not only to Gen. 13.15 and 17.8, but also to 22.18. On the other hand, they omit 15.18 which, as will presently be shown, is undoubtedly of some relevance.   [3] Gen. 22.18.
[4] Gen. 13.15, 17.8.   [5] Gen. 13.15, 17.8, 24.7.   [6] S.O. 3.   [7] 15.18.

for 400 years and a return after four generations, formed the general basis for chronological speculations as to the interval between Abraham and Moses. For another, from the LXX[1] and Josephus[2] it appears that, in New Testament times, no strict distinction was made between the promise of the land Abraham received 'between the pieces' and promises of the land he received on other occasions. For the LXX and Josephus, 430 years elapsed between Abraham's arrival in Canaan—when there was a promise of the land 'to thee and to thy seed'[3]—and the exodus. Clearly, Paul takes the same line.

This is not to deny that, in the eyes of both Paul and the Rabbis, the promise of the land and that of becoming a blessing to all the earth are frequently one and the same thing. They are obviously one and the same thing in Galatians. Still, the actual verse Paul invokes is one where the land is promised.

To go on to the background of his argument, it is correctly observed by Strack-Billerbeck[4] that 'the interpretation of the number in which a word appears plays a certain part even in *halakhic* exegesis'. But Paul is not here concerned with *halakha*. No wonder that the Talmudic example supplied by Strack-Billerbeck, though it does show that the Rabbis paid attention to the number of a word, and though it has to do with the word 'seed', yet is without particular bearing on Paul's thesis. 'Whence do we know'—the example runs[5]—'that despite the prohibition of mingling diverse seeds,[6] five kinds of seed may be sown in a bed six handbreadths square, four on the sides and one in the middle? Because it is written,[7] As the garden causeth its seeds to spring forth. It is not written, its seed, but its seeds.' Nobody would maintain a direct connection between this piece of teaching and that in Galatians. One might even object that the word 'seed' is here employed in a generic sense throughout. The singular is not, as in Paul, treated as specific. Even if the garden brought forth 'its seed', not 'its seeds', one might object, it would still be one sort of seed; it would still not be, as it ought to be if the reasoning were really parallel to Paul's, a single plant. A further criticism might be made: the word for 'seed' decisive in this Talmudic provision, *zerua'*, is slightly different from that to be met with in God's promise to Abraham, *zera'*.

---

[1] Exod. 12.40. [2] Ant. 2.15.2.318. We need not go into other datings he gives.
[3] Gen. 13.15. [4] 3, 1926, 553.
[5] Mish. Shab. 9.2. [6] Lev. 19.19, Deut. 22.9. [7] Isa. 61.11.

As a matter of fact, there are two early *haggadhic* teachings the direct influence of one of which on Paul is certain, and the direct influence of the other not improbable.

When God concluded with Abraham the covenant 'between the pieces', he foretold: 'Thy seed shall be a stranger in a land not theirs, and they shall serve them and they shall afflict them four hundred years.'[1] The 400 years created a problem for the Rabbis, since according to the story of the exodus 'the sojourning in Egypt was four hundred and thirty years'.[2] Their solution—adopted by the LXX and Josephus— was (if we disregard the more subtle datings) that, on the one hand, the time between the covenant with Abraham and the exodus was 430 years: 'the sojourning in Egypt' included the wanderings of the patriarchs in Canaan. On the other hand, the covenant with Abraham was made thirty years before Isaac's birth—hence God predicted only 400 years of trouble for Abraham's descendants.[3]

It is the Rabbinic analysis of this prediction which Paul unquestionably follows. The Rabbis argued that 'thy seed shall be a stranger' signified 'Isaac shall be a stranger', i.e. Canaan would not yet definitively belong to him; 'in a land not theirs' signified the wanderings of Isaac and Jacob; 'and they shall serve them and they shall afflict them' signified the stay of the Israelites in Egypt; 'four hundred years' covered the whole period from Isaac's birth to the exodus. The point is that 'thy seed' was understood by the Rabbis to be a specific singular. It alluded to one person: Isaac. In support, they referred to the prophecy, 'For in Isaac shall thy seed be called.'[4] It is relevant to note, however, that though they felt it necessary to establish a scrupulously accurate chronology of the pre-Sinaitic era, yet they were convinced that the promise of salvation after sufferings which God gave to Abraham 'between the pieces' was valid not only up to the exodus but for the entire future history of Israel. This extension is demonstrably old: it occupies a prominent place in an early section of the Jewish liturgy for Passover eve ('And this is the promise that has held good for our ancestors and ourselves' etc.). Some Rabbis rested it on the expression 'and also' in God's assurance: 'And also that nation whom they shall serve will I judge, and afterwards shall they come out with great substance.'[5] God said 'and also', instead of just 'also', in order to include later oppressors of his people.

[1] Gen. 15.13.   [2] Exod. 12.40.   [3] S.O. 3.   [4] Gen. 21.12.   [5] Gen. Rabba on 15.14.

When we consider that Paul is proceeding from a verse in which Abraham receives a promise of the land, that he expressly introduces the Rabbinic chronology, that like the Rabbis he emphasizes the eternal validity of the promise, that the generic singular he makes into a specific one is 'seed', and that Isaac was regarded by the early Christians as prefiguring the Messiah in more than one way, we may confidently assume that the Midrash outlined is a source of Paul's argument. In fact, it is quite possible that he believes some at least of the recipients of his letter to be acquainted with it, and that he deliberately furnishes them with a deeper application.

In a *haggadha* about the creation of man, too, the Rabbis turned a generic singular into a specific one. The interpretation was famous in the Talmudic era, and quite conceivably Paul is drawing on it also.

The Bible tells us[1] that 'God created man in his image, in the image of God created he him, male and female created he them', and again, 'In the day that God created man, in the likeness of God made he him, male and female created he them and called their name Adam.' An ordinary reader would ascribe a generic sense to 'man' and 'he', the sense of 'a man and a woman', or maybe even that of 'mankind'. The Rabbis could not have admitted this, since if they had there would have been a conflict with the story of Eve's formation from a rib of Adam. In consequence they emphasized the curious wavering in the verses quoted between the singular and the plural: God created 'man' and 'him', yet at the same time he created 'them' male and female and called 'their' name Adam. This wavering was declared to prove—what was traditionally assumed anyhow—that the first, ideal man was androgynous. That is to say, the plural, it was held, indicated not several beings, but one composite being; and the singular was not of a generic character, it did not denote mankind, but it was a specific singular, it denoted one human being only, the first bisexual one, out of whom Eve was subsequently taken.

That this explanation is ancient would be probable, even if there were no other evidence, from the consideration that the two accounts of man's creation in chapters 1 and 2 of Genesis must have called for a harmonization from the moment the canon was treated as a faultless whole. (Indeed, a tendency to harmonize is perhaps noticeable in the

[1] Gen. 1.27, 5.1 f.

Biblical accounts themselves, but those early efforts would mean a rewriting, not a re-interpretation.) Fortunately, evidence is not lacking. According to a tradition preserved in numerous sources—among them the Mekhilta[1]—the clause 'male and female created he them' was one of the passages altered by the authors of the LXX in order to prevent misunderstanding on the part of King Ptolemy: they translated 'a male with his female parts created he them', or 'male and female (i.e. bi-sexual) created he him (singular, and plainly specific singular)'. Whether or not the tradition is historical—and it is difficult to believe that no Greek renderings of the kind described were in circulation—it could not have arisen unless the teaching which it presupposes, the androgynous Adam, had been of considerable age. Actually, as we tried to show above (under Precept and Example), the interpretation of 'male and female created he them' as alluding to the ideal, androgynous man occurs in the gospels as well as in Philo; and Paul himself in I Corinthians and Ephesians not only adopts the doctrine that sexual intercourse restores man and woman to an androgynous state, but even uses a verse from Genesis 2 in support.

The Rabbis, then, contended that the Bible, when speaking of 'man', did not mean 'man and woman', still less 'mankind', but the original, ideal Adam alone. A generic singular was given the force of a specific one. It is very possible that this *haggadha* as well as that about Isaac is in Paul's mind where he, in Galatians, avails himself of this method of exegesis. Needless to say, he does not think of an androgynous Jesus. Yet the sentence 'There is neither Jew nor Greek, neither bond nor free, neither male nor female'[2] may contain a trace of the myth respecting the first man. Again, it must be admitted that the Rabbinic Midrash concerning Adam and Paul's Midrash concerning Jesus are due to very different circumstances. The Rabbis wished to prove that all human beings, including Eve, were descended from the first man—in accordance with chapter 2 of Genesis—and they had to explain away in-convenient texts—like those referring to a creation of 'male and female'. Paul wishes to prove that what was promised to Abraham's offspring was promised to Jesus only, and he has to read an indication of this into the text itself. But there are elements common to the two cases, above all, the insistence on the ultimate unity of mankind. As the Rabbis laid stress on the oneness of Adam, father of all, so Paul lays

[1] On Exod. 12.40; cp. Gen. Rabba on 1.27.   [2] 3.28.

stress on the oneness of Jesus who, on the strength of the old promise, gathers up in himself all those redeemed.

We must not forget that Paul sees in Jesus the last Adam, and in the original Adam 'the figure of him that was to come'.[1] The absence from Galatians of any explicit reference to this notion does not necessarily mean that it plays no part. After all, Paul in this epistle does describe him who is in Jesus as 'a new creature',[2] which suggests a contrast with the first creation.

Three remarks in conclusion. First, Paul is given to emphasizing the oneness of Jesus, of the community, of Jesus with the community, of the events connected with Jesus and so on. One wonders whether quite a few passages containing this idea[3] may not reflect *haggadhoth* involving the method here discussed—the pressing of a singular. Of course, the *haggadhoth* need not have regard to Isaac or Adam, they may relate to entirely different figures or events. Philo[4] says that 'since God is one, there may be only one temple'. Similarly, in his Antiquities,[5] Josephus explains that 'there may be only one temple since God is one and the Hebrew race is one'. In his Contra Apionem[6] he mitigates the argument from the singularity of the nation and speaks of 'one temple for the one God, since like is ever the friend of like, and (here comes the part replacing the outspoken reference to the Jewish race) the temple must be common to all, belonging to God who is common to all'. Now these statements show distinct traces of popular philosophy. That 'like is the friend of like' was proverbial long before Aristotle.[7] Nevertheless even here, we cannot rule out the influence of certain traditional interpretations of Scripture. We know, for example, that many Rabbis saw an apparent contradiction between the promise that God would choose his dwelling-place 'out of all your tribes' (which in the opinion of these Rabbis, must mean that somehow all tribes would have a share in it) and the promise that he would choose it 'in one of thy tribes'.[8] There may well have been solutions of the difficulty accounting for Philo's and Josephus's views.

Secondly, we come across Rabbinic comments on the unity of God or mankind or both which, though they contain no explicit reference to an important singular in Scripture, yet are unquestionably based on

---

[1] Rom. 5.14.
[2] 6.15, cp. II Cor. 5.17.
[3] Such as Gal. 3.20, Eph. 2.14 ff.
[4] Leg. Spec. 1.12.67.
[5] 4.8.5.200 f.
[6] 2.23.193.
[7] Nic.E. 9.3.3; cp. 8.1.6, Ecclus. 13.15, 27.9.
[8] Siph. on Deut. 12.5, 14.

such a singular. For example, the question is raised[1] why man was created as one, and among the answers are these: in order that the *Minim*, the Christians, might have no ground for maintaining that there are several powers in heaven, or in order that the pious people might not claim a different ancestry from the wicked. Behind these affirmations there clearly stands the exegesis discussed above, according to which 'man' in the story of the creation is a specific singular.

Thirdly, it should be noted that, in Hebrew as in English, the word 'seed', 'issue', now and then refers to an individual even apart from any artificial interpretation. To be sure, the generic meaning is invariably present by way of connotation: if you call your son 'your seed', 'your offspring', the idea of the family, the line, as a whole is somehow brought in. Nevertheless, that 'seed' may be used in this way, of an individual, renders the Rabbinic and Pauline arguments less inappropriate. (Similarly, the Rabbis would not have taken 'man' as a specific singular in those passages from the story of the creation had the word not been capable of this meaning in ordinary language.) An example of 'seed' denoting an individual occurs in the remark by which Eve greeted Seth:[2] 'God hath appointed me another seed instead of Abel, whom Cain slew.' The passage is of some interest in this connection since at least from the 3rd cent. A.D., but probably long before, the Rabbis claimed that 'another seed' here alluded to the King Messiah who, Eve foresaw, would come 'from another place', from a strange place, namely, from Ruth, a Moabite woman, or even directly from God.[3] (That the striking phrase from Ruth, 'the seed which the Lord shall give thee', may have played a part in this legend was pointed out in a previous chapter.[4]) If Paul is familiar with this or a similar Midrash, his choice of argument in Galatians becomes even more understandable.

---

[1] Bab. San. 38a.   [2] Gen. 4.25.   [3] Gen. Rabba on 4.25.
[4] Part I, Ruth and Boaz, A3; see Ruth 4.12.

Index of References

I. OLD TESTAMENT

II. NEW TESTAMENT

III. RABBINIC SOURCES

IV. CLASSICAL SOURCES

THE JEWISH PEOPLE

HISTORY • RELIGION • LITERATURE

AN ARNO PRESS COLLECTION

Agus, Jacob B. **The Evolution of Jewish Thought:** From Biblical Times to the Opening of the Modern Era. 1959

Ber of Bolechow. **The Memoirs of Ber of Bolechow (1723-1805).** Translated from the Original Hebrew MS. with an Introduction, Notes and a Map by M[ark] Vishnitzer. 1922

Berachya. **The Ethical Treatises of Berachya, Son of Rabbi Natronai Ha-Nakdan:** Being the Compendium and the Masref. Now edited for the First Time from MSS. at Parma and Munich with an English Translation, Introduction, Notes, etc. by Hermann Gollancz. 1902

Bloch, Joseph S. **My Reminiscences.** 1923

Bokser, Ben Zion, **Pharisaic Judaism in Transition:** R. Eliezer the Great and Jewish Reconstruction After the War with Rome. 1935

Dalman, Gustaf. **Jesus Christ in the Talmud, Midrash, Zohar, and the Liturgy of the Synagogue.** Together with an Introductory Essay by Heinrich Laible. Translated and Edited by A. W. Streane. 1893

Daube, David. **The New Testament and Rabbinic Judaism.** 1956

Davies, W. D. **Christian Origins and Judaism.** 1962

Engelman, Uriah Zevi. **The Rise of the Jew in the Western World:** A Social and Economic History of the Jewish People of Europe. Foreword by Niles Carpenter. 1944

Epstein, Louis M. **The Jewish Marriage Contract:** A Study in the Status of the Woman in Jewish Law. 1927

Facets of Medieval Judaism. 1973. New Introduction by Seymour Siegel

The Foundations of Jewish Life: Three Studies. 1973

Franck, Adolph. **The Kabbalah, or, The Religious Philosophy of the Hebrews.** Revised and Enlarged Translation [from the French] by Dr. I. Sossnitz. 1926

Goldman, Solomon. **The Jew and The Universe.** 1936

Gordon, A. D. **Selected Essays.** Translated by Frances Burnce from the Hebrew Edition by N. Teradyon and A. Shohat, with a Biographical Sketch by E. Silberschlag. 1938

Ha-Am, Achad (Asher Ginzberg). **Ten Essays on Zionism and Judaism.** Translated from the Hebrew by Leon Simon. 1922. New Introduction by Louis Jacobs

Halevi, Jehudah. **Selected Poems of Jehudah Halevi.** Translated into English by Nina Salaman, Chiefly from the Critical Text Edited by Heinrich Brody. 1924

Heine, Heinrich. **Heinrich Heine's Memoir:** From His Works, Letters, and Conversations. Edited by Gustav Karpeles; English Translation by Gilbert Cannan. 1910. Two volumes in one

Heine, Heinrich. **The Prose Writings of Heinrich Heine.**
Edited, with an Introduction, by Havelock Ellis. 1887

Hirsch, Emil G[ustav]. **My Religion.** Compilation and
Biographical Introduction by Gerson B. Levi. **Including
The Crucifixion Viewed from a Jewish Standpoint:** A Lecture
Delivered by Invitation Before the "Chicago Institute for
Morals, Religion and Letters." 1925/1908

Hirsch, W. **Rabbinic Psychology:** Beliefs about the Soul
in Rabbinic Literature of the Talmudic Period. 1947

Historical Views of Judaism: Four Selections. 1973

Ibn Gabirol, Solomon. **Selected Religious Poems of Solomon Ibn
Gabirol.** Translated into English Verse by Israel Zangwill
from a Critical Text Edited by Israel Davidson. 1923

Jacobs, Joseph. **Jesus as Others Saw Him:** A Retrospect
A. D. 54. Preface by Israel Abrahams; Introductory Essay by
Harry A. Wolfson. 1925

Judaism and Christianity: Selected Accounts, 1892-1962.
1973. New Preface and Introduction by Jacob B. Agus

Kohler, Kaufmann. **The Origins of the Synagogue and
The Church.** Edited, with a Biographical Essay by H. G. Enelow.
1929

Maimonides Octocentennial Series, Numbers I-IV. 1935

Mann, Jacob. **The Responsa of the Babylonian Geonim as a
Source of Jewish History.** 1917-1921

Maritain, Jacques. **A Christian Looks at the Jewish Question.** 1939

Marx, Alexander. **Essays in Jewish Biography.** 1947

Mendelssohn, Moses. **Phaedon; or, The Death of Socrates.**
Translated from the German [by Charles Cullen]. 1789

Modern Jewish Thought: Selected Issues, 1889-1966. 1973.
New Introduction by Louis Jacobs

Montefiore, C[laude] G. **Judaism and St. Paul:** Two Essays. 1914

Montefiore, C[laude] G. **Some Elements of the Religious
Teaching of Jesus According to the Synoptic Gospels.** Being
the Jowett Lectures for 1910. 1910

Radin, Max. **The Jews Amongs the Greeks and Romans.** 1915

Ruppin, Arthur. **The Jews in the Modern World.** With an
Introduction by L. B. Namier. 1934

Smith, Henry Preserved. **The Bible and Islam;** or, The Influence
of the Old and New Testaments on the Religion of Mohammed.
Being the Ely Lectures for 1897. 1897

Stern, Nathan. **The Jewish Historico-Critical School of the
Nineteenth Century.** 1901

Walker, Thomas [T.] **Jewish Views of Jesus:** An Introduction
and an Appreciation. 1931. New Introduction by Seymour Siegel

Walter, H. **Moses Mendelssohn:** Critic and Philosopher. 1930

Wiener, Leo. **The History of Yiddish Literature in the
Nineteenth Century.** 1899

Wise, Isaac M. **Reminiscences.** Translated from the German and
Edited, with an Introduction by David Philipson. 1901